International Human Rights
Text and Materials

D1031198

AUSTRALIA
LBC Information Services
Sydney

CANADA and USA
Carswell
Toronto, Ontario

NEW ZEALAND
Brooker's
Auckland

SINGAPORE and MALAYSIA
Sweet & Maxwell Asia
Singapore and Kuala Lumpur

International Human Rights Text and Materials

By

Professor Rebecca Wallace M.A., LL.B., Ph.D.
Head of School of Law,
Napier University, Edinburgh

with

Kenneth Dale-Risk LL.B.(Hons), DIP. L.P.
School of Law,
Napier University, Edinburgh

London
Sweet & Maxwell
2001

Published in 2001 by
Sweet & Maxwell Ltd
100 Avenue Road
London NW3 3PF
Typeset by LBJ Typesetting Ltd of Kingsclere
Printed in England by MPG Books Ltd, Bodmin, Cornwall

No natural forests were destroyed to make this product;
only natural timber was used and re-planted

ISBN 0421 710 306

A CIP catalogue record for this book is available from the British Library

All rights reserved. U.K. statutory material is acknowledged as being Crown copyright.

No part of this publication may be reproduced or transmitted in any form or by any means, or stored in any retrieval system of any nature without prior written permission, except for permitted fair dealing under the Copyright, Designs and Patents Act 1988, or in accordance with the terms of a licence issued by the Copyright Licensing Agency in respect of photocopying and/or reprographic reproduction. Application for permission for other use of copyright material including permission to reproduce extracts in other published works shall be made to the publishers. Full acknowledgement of author, publisher and source must be given

©
R.M.M. Wallace
2001

FOREWORD TO THE SECOND EDITION

The purpose of this second edition remains as it was in the first—raising awareness of "man's inhumanity to man" and to the need for effective mechanisms to combat and prevent human rights violations. Instances of human rights violations are legion and they do not paint a picture of a world in which human rights are respected.

Children for instance are identified as a vulnerable group. Why is all too evident.

Some 300,000 children under the age of 18 years are thought to be fighting in conflicts round the world, 14 million children are refugees or internally displaced within their own countries as a result of conflicts — UNICEF estimates that some 12 million children under the age of five die every year from preventable diseases; some 10.3 million young people between the age of 15 and 24 years have have AIDS or are HIV infected, there are 500,000 to 800,000 orphans in South Africa alone through AIDS and its is estimated that that figure will rise to 1.5 million by 2005. One hundred and thirty million children still do not receive education, some 900 million people, that is one sixth of the world's population over the age of 15 are illiterate, 60 million girl children are not alive today because they are of the female gender. Some 90 per cent of girl children in certain communities in Asia are sold into prostitution and the number for boys is increasing, children are deliberately maimed because a cripple child beggar is more appealing.

Unpalatable these facts are certainly. Equally certain is how overwhelming the immensity of the task to eradicate the evils perpetrated against children and other groups often appear. However nothwithstanding this it is necessary to continue to aspire for change albeit change which evolves slowly. Why? Because, our humanity is what separates us from other species. Man's inhumanity to man apparently knows no bounds but neither does the resilience of the human spirit. It is because we are human that we seek to transcend the notion of the survival of the fittest. Human rights involves caring for the more vulnerable, disadvantaged members of society. We do so because we have a shared humanity. We have to work together in the international community to develop a human rights culture in which respect for all individuals is the norm. That is the task confronting the international community as it steps in to the twenty first century. If this text goes some way to developing such a culture then it will achieve its principle goal.

Thanks is due to Jo Kenny for her research assistance.

This text remains dedicated to Dr. Srini Chary but now also to Patrick Chary, born December, 1999—indeed a child of the new millennium—in the hope that his generation will live in a world in which "every yesterday is a happy memory and every tomorrow is a vision of hope".

Professor Rebecca M.M. Wallace.
Kenneth Dale-Risk
Edinburgh, April 2001.

INTRODUCTION

"Human rights and fundamental freedoms are the birthright of all human beings."[1]

Since 1948 the foregoing has generally been accepted and expressed in a plethora of international instruments. This has contributed to the development of substantive international human rights law and undoubtedly raised public awareness and extended protection to individuals. General human rights instruments apply to all individuals or certain groups of individuals because of their particular vulnerability and have been identified as meriting additional protection. Nevertheless in practice both individuals and groups remain the victims of human rights violations. The annual report of any human rights organisation such as Amnesty International, makes disturbing reading. A cursory glance is sufficient to highlight the abuses sustained by for example women, children, refugees and prisoners. The problem confronting the international community as it enters the twenty first century is that of effective enforcement of human rights protection. Lip service to human rights principles by governments is not sufficient and leads only to cynicism and derision of international human rights.

Steps to Vienna

The General Assembly adopted the Universal Declaration of Human Rights[2] on December 10, 1948.[3] The Declaration was heralded as "a common standard of achievement for all peoples and all nations, to the end that every individual and every organ of society, keeping this declaration constantly in mind, shall strive by teaching and education to promote respect for these rights and freedoms and by progressive measures, national and international, to secure their universal and effective recognition and observance, both among the peoples of Member States themselves and among the peoples of territories under their jurisdiction".[4]

The Declaration provides that the rights and freedoms set forth in the Declaration should be enjoyed by all without distinction of any kind, such as race, colour, sex, language, religion, political or other opinion, national or social origin, property birth or other

---

[1] Vienna Declaration, 1993, para 1. For complete text see Annex I.
[2] G.A. Res, 217A (III), GAOR, 3rd Session, Part I, Resolutions p.71.
[3] International Human Rights Day is celebrated annually on December 10.
[4] The text of the Universal Declaration is reproduced on Annex 1.

status. The rights and freedoms contained in the Universal Declaration were subsequently spelt out in greater detail in two United Nations Covenants, *viz* the Covenant on Civil and Political Rights[5] and the Covenant on Economic, Social and Cultural Rights.[6] These Covenants entered into force in March 1976 and January 1976 respectively. Parties to the Covenants are under an obligation to guarantee that the rights enunciated therein "will be exercised without discrimination of any kind as to race, colour, sex, language, religion, political or other opinion, national or social origin, property birth or other status."[7] The basic tenets of the Declaration were subsequently endorsed in The Teheran Proclamation[8] of 1968. The Proclamation being adopted at the conclusion of a gathering held to mark the twentieth anniversary of the Universal Declaration.

In the summer of 1993 a conference was convened in Vienna[9] for the purpose of considering the promotion and protection of human rights in the international community. The Conference was seen as affording a "unique opportunity" for conducting a comprehensive analysis of the international human rights system and of the machinery employed to afford protection. The Conference also supported the view that human rights are "universal, indivisible and interdependent and interrelated."[10]

The Conference concluded by adopting an Action Programme[11] identifying especially vulnerable individuals and highlighted the need for continual review and assessment of the consequently specific measures taken to ensure adequate protection of the rights of these groups. The Secretary-General of the United Nations in a report to the General Assembly on a follow up to Vienna heralded The Vienna Declaration and Programme of Action as undoubtedly "one of the major events in the United Nations history of human rights. If implemented, it will be a milestone in this history."[12]

---

[5] 999 UNTS 171; UKTS 6(1977), 61 AJIL 870 (1967).

[6] 993 UNTS 3; UKTS 6(1977); 6 ILM 360 (1967).

[7] Article 2.1 Covenant on Civil and Political Rights; Article 2.2. Covenant on Economic, Social and Cultural Rights.

[8] See Annex I.

[9] The Conference met from June 14-25, 1993 and was attended by representatives of 171 States.

[10] Part I, para 5. The opposing view is the relativist theory whereby human rights can differ from state to state depending on a state's values and cultural and religious tradition. China and a number of Islamic countries support cultural relativism. The issue of the universality or otherwise of human rights will continue to be divisive for the foreseeable future. The depth of the issue is such that it falls beyond the scope of this work. However it is an important area in contemporary international human rights debate and is an emerging area of research and study—see Bibliography.

[11] The text of the Action Programme was adopted by the Conference at its 22nd plenary meeting on June 25, 1993 and is reproduced in Annex A.

[12] Report of the Secretary-General to the General Assembly at as 49th session A/49/668.

The groups identified as being particularly vulnerable were women, minorities, indigenous people, children, persons with disabilities, refugees, migrant workers and prisoners. It is the current international protection afforded to these groups which remains the substance of this text. These groups although dealt with individually are not mutually exclusive and membership can straddle more than one group. Women for instance are not only women but may be refugees, migrant workers and a person with a disability. Likewise, children are vulnerable as children but also as refugees. Since 1993 there has not been a significant increase in the number of international human rights instruments and the developments that there have been have focused rather on the monitoring mechanisms for the implementation of the rights protected.

Women, minorities, indigenous people, children, persons with disabilities, refugees, migrant workers and prisoners were identified as particularly vulnerable and it is the current international protection afforded to these groups which forms the substance of this text.

A chapter has been devoted to each group. This text is not nor does it profess to be a substantive critique of international human rights law. It is a tool designed to facilitate an initial study of human rights law at the international level. Its primary aim is to guide the reader through the ever expanding documentation in this field. Each chapter sets out the relevant international instruments pertaining to the group in question. Some additional commentary is provided and where applicable reference is made to relevant jurisprudence, both international and on occasion national. This is done by extracting the principle instruments[13] from an ever increasing plethora of materials and setting them out in such a way as to be "user friendly". Suggestions for further reading on each topic can be found in the bibliography. The law presented is as of March 31, 2001, although some later amendments have been made where possible.

---

[13] Both hard and soft law. Soft law refers to those international documents which are not legally binding on states but which they nevertheless reflect contemporary thinking by interested bodies on particular issues of international concern. Soft law may subsequently become hard law.

CONTENTS

TABLE OF INTERNATIONAL CONVENTIONS

TABLE OF RESOLUTIONS

TABLE OF CASES

(All references to paragraph numbers in the outside margin)

Australia

Canada

Committee for the Elimination of Racial Discrimination

Committee for the Elimination of Torture

European Court of Human Rights

Table of Cases

France

Human Rights Committee

International Court of Justice

New Zealand

United Kingdom

United States of America

TABLE OF INTERNATIONAL COVENANTS

TABLE OF PROTOCOLS

TABLE OF STATUTES

TABLE OF UNITED NATIONS DECLARATIONS

CHAPTER 1

RIGHT TO DEVELOPMENT[1]

INTRODUCTION

The right to development, although recognised as a right is more **1–001** difficult to define as a human right. It tends to suggest the presence of certain conditions conducive to the realisation of human rights. It is also difficult to identify the duty incumbent on the State concerned. The four years since the first edition of this text have witnessed the emergence of social accountability in the vocabulary of corporations. Many companies now openly acknowledge the connection between international trade, poverty and the ability of States to achieve development for citizens. Most notably at the international level is the UN Secretary-General's Global Compact launched in 1999 which sets out an overall values framework for co-operation with the business community. The principles of the compact are based on intergovernmental agreements while also being deemed appropriate for business. The Global Compact's nine principles embrace the areas of human rights, labour standards and the environment. This relationship with business is reflected in the following pages.

WORLD CONFERENCE ON HUMAN RIGHTS
(JUNE 1993) VIENNA DECLARATION

10. The World Conference on Human Rights reaffirms the right **1–002** to development, as established in the Declaration on the Right to Development, as a universal and inalienable right and an integral part of fundamental human rights.

As stated in the Declaration on the Right to Development, the human person is the central subject of development.

While development facilitates the enjoyment of all human rights, the lack of development may not be invoked to justify the abridgement of internationally recognised human rights.

States should co-operate with each other in ensuring development and eliminating obstacles to development. The international

---

[1] In the classification of human rights under contemporary international law the right to development would be a "third generation right" and a group right. The right to development has moved to the forefront of the international agenda in recent years not least because of the current Secretary-General's "strong personal commitment to development", *An Agenda for Development*, Preamble, para. 4 (A/48/935, May 1994) see below. The international law of development is a burgeoning subject of a multidimensial character— for the apparent five major dimensions of development see *Agenda for Development*, below.

community should promote an effective international co-operation for the realisation of the right to development and the elimination of obstacles to development.

Lasting progress towards the implementation of the right to development requires effective development policies at the national level, as well as equitable economic relations and a favourable economic environment at the international level.

1–003   **11.** The right to development should be fulfilled so as to meet equitably the developmental and environmental needs of present and future generations. The World Conference on Human Rights recognises that illicit dumping of toxic and dangerous substances and waste potentially constitutes a serious threat to the human rights to life and health of everyone.

Consequently, the World Conference on Human Rights calls on all States to adopt and vigorously implement existing conventions relating to the dumping of toxic and dangerous products and waste and to co-operate in the prevention of illicit dumping.

Everyone has the right to enjoy the benefits of scientific progress and its applications. The World Conference on Human Rights notes that certain advances, notably in the biomedical and life sciences as well as in information technology, may have potentially adverse consequences for the integrity, dignity and human rights of the individual, and calls for international co-operation to ensure that human rights and dignity are fully respected in this area of universal concern

DECLARATION ON THE RIGHT TO DEVELOPMENT[2]

The General Assembly
Proclaims the following Declaration on the Right to Development:

Article 1

1–004   **1.** The right to development is an inalienable human right by virtue of which every human person and all peoples are entitled to participate in, contribute to, and enjoy economic, social, cultural and political development, in which all human rights and fundamental freedoms can be fully realised.

2. The human right to development also implies the full realisation of the right of peoples to self-determination, which includes, subject to the relevant provisions of both International Covenants on Human Rights, the exercise of their inalienable right to full sovereignty over all their natural wealth and resources.

[2] G.A. Res. 41/128, annex, G.A.O.R., 41st Session, Supp. (53), p. 186, UN Doc. A/41/53 (1986).

Article 2

1. The human person is the central subject of development and 1–005
should be the active participant and beneficiary of the right to
development.
2. All human beings have a responsibility for development,
individually and collectively, taking into account the need for full
respect for their human rights and fundamental freedoms as well
as their duties to the community, which alone can ensure the free
and complete fulfilment of the human being, and they should
therefore promote and protect an appropriate political, social and
economic order for development.
3. States have the right and the duty to formulate appropriate
national development policies that aim at the constant improvement of the well-being of the entire population and of all
individuals, on the basis of their active, free and meaningful
participation in development and in the fair distribution of the
benefits resulting therefrom.

Article 3

1. States have the primary responsibility for the creation of 1–006
national and international conditions favourable to the realisation
of the right to development.
2. The realisation of the right to development requires full
respect for the principles of international law concerning friendly
relations and co-operation among States in accordance with the
Charter of the United Nations.
3. States have the duty to co-operate with each other in
ensuring development and eliminating obstacles to development.
States should realise their rights and fulfil their duties in such a
manner as to promote a new international economic order based
on sovereign equality, interdependence, mutual interest and co-
operation among all States, as well as to encourage the observance and realisation of human rights.

Article 4

1. States have the duty to take steps, individually and collec- 1–007
tively, to formulate international development policies with a
view to facilitating the full realisation of the right to development.
2. Sustained action is required to promote more rapid development of developing countries. As a complement to the efforts of
developing countries, effective international co-operation is essential in providing these countries with appropriate means and
facilities to foster their comprehensive development.

Article 6

1–008 **1.** All States should co-operate with a view to promoting, encouraging and strengthening universal respect for and observance of all human rights and fundamental freedoms for all without any distinction as to race, sex, language or religion.

2. All human rights and fundamental freedoms are indivisible and interdependent; equal attention and urgent consideration should be given to the implementation, promotion and protection of civil, political, economic, social and cultural rights.

3. States should take steps to eliminate obstacles to development resulting from failure to observe civil and political rights, as well as economic, social and cultural rights.

Article 7

1–009 All States should promote the establishment, maintenance and strengthening of international peace and security and, to that end, should do their utmost to achieve general and complete disarmament under effective international control, as well as to ensure that the resources released by effective disarmament measures are used for comprehensive development, in particular that of the developing countries.

Article 8

1–010 **1.** States should undertake, at the national level, all necessary measures for the realisation of the right to development and shall ensure, *inter alia*, equality of opportunity for all in their access to basic resources, education, health services, food, housing, employment and the fair distribution of income. Effective measures should be undertaken to ensure that women have an active role in the development process. Appropriate economic and social reforms should be carried out with a view to eradicating all social injustices.

2. States should encourage popular participation in all spheres as an important factor in development and in the full realisation of all human rights.

Article 9

1–011 **1.** All the aspects of the right to development set forth in the present Declaration are indivisible and interdependent and each of them should be considered in the context of the whole.

2. Nothing in the present Declaration shall be construed as being contrary to the purposes and principles of the United Nations, or as implying that any State, group or person has a right to engage in any activity or to perform any act aimed at the violation of the rights set forth in the Universal Declaration of Human Rights and in the International Covenants on Human Rights.

Article 10

Steps should be taken to ensure the full exercise and progressive 1–012 enhancement of the right to development, including the formulation, adoption and implementation of policy, legislative and other measures at the national and international levels.

Note: In June 1992 delegates from more than 170 countries met in Rio de Janiero for the UN Conference on Environment and Development. Sustainable development was the focus of the Conference and the link between environment and development was reflected in the Conference's name; for the documents emanating from Rio see 31 ILM 814 *et seq.* (1992). In particular with respect to women and development see Report of the UN Conference on Environment and Development (Rio de Janeiro 3–14 June, 1992), chapter 24, see *Women* at para. 2–050.

AN AGENDA FOR DEVELOPMENT[3]

I. Preface

1. The General Assembly, in its resolution 47/181 of December 1–013 22, 1992, requested me to submit, in consultation with Member States, a report on an agenda for development.
  2. . . .

I. INTRODUCTION: WHY AN AGENDA FOR DEVELOPMENT?

3. Development is a fundamental human right. Development is 1–014 the most secure basis for peace.
  4. Taking stock of these principles, and in keeping with my strong personal commitment to development and the recognised needs of the United Nations at this point in history, the idea of an agenda for development took shape.
  5. The concept of development, and decades of effort to reduce poverty, illiteracy, disease and mortality rates, are great achievements of this century. But development as a common cause is in danger of fading from the forefront of our agenda. The competition for influence during the cold war stimulated interest in

[3] Report of the Secretary-General A/48/935, May 6, 1994.

development. The motives were not always altruistic, but countries seeking to develop could benefit from that interest. Today, the competition to bring development to the poorest countries has ended. Many donors have grown weary of the task. Many of the poor are dispirited. Development is in crisis.

1–015   6. The poorest nations fall farther behind. Nations in transition from command to open economies face immense hardships. Nations that have achieved prosperity see their success accompanied by a new array of problems, social, environmental, cultural and economic, and many are consequently reluctant even to pursue their assistance policies at former levels.

7. The current situation calls for wider intellectual understanding, deeper moral commitment and more effective policy measures. Without them, a half century of considerable progress could be undermined. Worse, all peoples of the world will live on a deteriorating planet, and will increasingly lose the ability to shape their destiny in a coherent way.

8. Specific suggestions and detailed proposals for development have been produced in great quantity and are deserving of serious study. The United Nations system has produced a wealth of studies and reports on various aspects of development; they are an invaluable resource.

9. Building upon these efforts, the present report seeks to revitalise the vision of development and to stimulate an intensified discussion of all its aspects.

1–016   10. The Charter of the United Nations makes possible a maturing elaboration of the crucial idea of development, but it has been left to us in the last decades of the twentieth century to try to bring the concept of development to fulfilment.

11. Concerns have been expressed that the United Nations puts greater emphasis on peace-keeping than on issues of development. These fears are not borne out by the regular budgets or the numbers of staff members engaged in peace and in development. Yet with growing requests for funds for peace-keeping, some Member States find it difficult to increase their contributions to the developmental activities of the United Nations. Without development, however, there is no prospect for lasting peace.

12. While national governments bear the major responsibility for development, the United Nations has been entrusted with important mandates for assisting in this task. The involvement of the United Nations in development spans five development decades and encompasses the full range of global problems of an economic, social, cultural and humanitarian character. It operates in all categories and at every level of development.

13. This agenda, therefore, is grounded in unique United 1–017
Nations experience. Section II sets forth the five major and
interlinked dimensions of development.[4]

14. In the light of the new vision of development that is
emerging, an alternative to the United Nations in development
simply does not exist. The United Nations is a forum where the
voices of all States, great and small, can be heard with equal
clarity, and where non-State actors can make their views known
to the widest audience. There is still time to move forward
together, but greater urgency is necessary. With each passing
day's delay, the work grows more costly and difficult.

15. While there is war, no State is securely at peace. While there
is want, no people can achieve lasting development.

IV. CONCLUSION
THE PROMISE OF DEVELOPMENT

231. A culture of development, in which every major dimension 1–018
of life is considered as an aspect of development, is emerging as a
result of immense and agonising effort. The possibilities for
common understanding and co-operative, co-ordinated action are
available as never before.

232. In the past few years near-universal recognition has been
achieved of the need for fresh consideration of ways in which the
goals of peace, freedom, justice and progress may be pursued in a
dramatically transformed global context. A culture of development can encompass these goals in a single, comprehensive vision
and framework for action. At the basis of this culture, there is the
fundamental commitment of the Charter to "the dignity and
worth of the human person". The institution of the United
Nations is irreplaceable.

233. Development has to be oriented towards each person in
the world. Beyond this must arise a recognition that this human
community includes the generations yet to come. The record of
this century has demonstrated the disastrous consequences when
the living are asked to suffer on behalf of a utopian future, or
when the present generation is heedless of the welfare of those
yet to be born. If one extreme characterised earlier decades of this
century, the other has more recently obstructed our vision.

234. Signs of a global era of development can be observed. They 1–019
offer a paradox. The agricultural and industrial revolutions are
now being succeeded by an age of information, communication

---

[4] The five major dimensions of development which were identified as being closely
linked were peace, the economy, the environment, society and democracy. "These
dimensions are not arbitrary, but emerge from a half-century of practical work by the
United Nations and others with Governments, organisations and people." See an *Agenda
for Development*, para. 138.

and advanced technology. This presents the potential for freeing
humanity from limits of time, place and resources that in the past
were regarded as given. At the same time, however, these
changes are accompanied by old forces that test the human
condition in new ways; natural and human disasters, demogra-
phy, disease, political confrontation, cultural and religious animosity, unemployment and ecological decay. These scourges are
as old as humanity itself, but they have taken on freshly virulent
forms and combinations.

235. From an understanding of development as limited to
transferring funds and expertise from the haves to the have-nots,
the perspective has shifted towards a broader concept encompassing the full range of human endeavour. The welfare of future
generations must not be compromised by incurring debts that
cannot be repaid, whether financial, social, demographic or
environmental. Equally important is the recognition of the
responsibility of the earth's present inhabitants to make the best
use of the hard-won ideas, ideals and institutions handed down
to us by our predecessors. Progress is not inherent in the human
condition; retrogression is not inconceivable.

236. If the human community is to continue to advance, it is
necessary to build respectfully upon what we have been given, to
recognise that current achievements must be accessible to all, and
to ensure that the work we leave behind stands not as a structure
in need of repair but as a platform for future progress. This must
be more than a matter for rhetoric.

1–020　　**237.** Whether this vision is fulfilled or not will be measured by
what this living generation of the world's peoples and their
leaders make or fail to make of the United Nations. Created at a
unique moment of unanimity, dedicated to purposes even more
expansive than its founders understood, embodying the best and
most comprehensive purpose of the world's peoples, and provided with the mechanisms required to bring practical results, the
Organisation stands at the meeting point of past, present and
future.

238. The intricate nature of the present world crisis must be
grasped in its entirety before effective action to resolve it will be
possible. The concepts of collective security, fundamental human
rights, international law and social progress for all are being
corroded by ethnocentrism, isolationism, cultural animosity and
economic and social debilitation. Even the concept of the State as
the foundation-stone of international co-operation is being
damaged by those who define it in exclusionary terms and others
who question its contemporary relevance and efficacy.

239. These concerns are felt in a context of unprecedented
global change. Ecological, technological, demographical and
social movements seem beyond the capacity of traditional forms

of international management. Faced with such a challenge, some even suggest that the modern project of international co-operation be abandoned for a return to power politics, spheres of influence and other discredited and dangerous techniques of the past.

240. This must not be allowed to happen. The United Nations, **1–021** as a key mechanism for international co-operation by Member States, possesses flexibility, legitimacy and a universal range of action. If employed prudently, efficiently and confidently, the United Nations is the best available instrument for managing the world situation with a reasonable expectation of success.

241. At present this mechanism is caught in a confining cycle. There is a resistance to multilateralism from those who fear a loss of national control. There is a reluctance to provide financial means to achieve agreed ends from those who lack conviction that assessments will benefit their own interests. And there is an unwillingness to engage in difficult operations by those who seek guarantees of perfect clarity and limited duration.

242. Without a new and compelling collective vision, the international community will be unable to break out of this cycle. The present report is, therefore, intended as a first contribution to the search for a revitalised vision of development.

243. . . ., I have described both the nature and scope of **1–022** development efforts. I have set out both the dimensions of the development process and the actors involved in it, in the hope that a new vision and culture of development will emerge. Such a vision must, however, be firmly anchored in agreed objectives and commitments on development adopted by the international community, and on a record of demonstrated results, if it is to command sustained support. The United Nations can offer such a record. In addition, the United Nations can bring to bear not only the unparalleled broadness of its scope, but its unique potential to integrate the many actors and dimensions of development.

244. If this promise is to be fulfilled, all organs and entities must perform fully the roles assigned to them by the Charter; roles clearly described but which have yet to be performed entirely as intended.

245. Inspired by the purposes and fundamental principles of the Charter, and mindful of the commitments and objectives adopted by the General Assembly, the international community can now proceed to outline a new vision of development. With the practical commitment of all peoples to the advancement of a new culture of development, the coming celebration of the United Nations first half-century will be marked as a turning-point in the story of all humanity.

Note: the foregoing Agenda was circulated to Member States, various UN agencies and public and private bodies. In the light of responses received and views expressed in general debate at the

General Assembly the Secretary-General submitted a number of
key recommendations to the General Assembly on November 11,
1994.

AGENDA FOR DEVELOPMENT[5]

An agenda for development: recommendations

I. INTRODUCTION

1–023   **4.** The general recommendations that have emerged can be
simply stated, but they are fundamentally important. Firstly,
development should be recognised as the foremost and most far-
reaching task of our time. Recognition of this imperative, commitment to achieving development, and continual, co-operative and
effective action towards it are crucial for humanity's common
future. It is urgent for governments, intergovernmental institutions and the United Nations to review their priorities with the
goal of elevating dramatically the attention and support given to
development.

5. Secondly, development must be seen in its many dimensions.
My report on an agenda for development of May 6, 1994
identified five dimensions of development: peace, the economy,
environmental protection, social justice and democracy. The
importance of these dimensions has been understood and supported by Member States. For most people and most countries,
economic growth is the *sine qua non* of development. Economic
growth is not an option; it is an imperative. But it is a means to an
end. New development approaches should not only generate
economic growth, they should make its benefits equitably available. They should enable people to participate in decisions
affecting their lives. They should provide job-led growth. They
must replenish the natural heritage on which all life depends.
They must be based upon a comprehensive vision of
development.

6. At its core, development must be about improvement of
human well-being; removal of hunger, disease and ignorance;
and productive employment for all. Its first goal must be to end
poverty and satisfy the priority needs of all people in a way that
can be productively sustained over future generations.

1–024   **7.** Thirdly, the emerging consensus on the priority and dimensions of development should find expression in a new framework
for international co-operation. The enterprise we call international
co-operation for development is needed now more than ever, but

[5] Report of the Secretary-General, A/49/665, November 11, 1994.

it must be revitalised in order to escape fully its cold war past and contribute fully to the realisation of development goals.

8. Fourthly, within this new framework for development co-operation, the United Nations must play a major role in both policy leadership and operations. Comments on the May 1994 report on an agenda for development have not only strengthened understanding of the dimensions of development. They have also revealed strong support for a revitalised role of the Organisation and for measures to enhance the coherence and relevance of the United Nations system in development.

9. The development mission and responsibilities of the United Nations stem directly from the Charter of the United Nations and the fundamental nature of the United Nations as an international political entity and moral force; from the inseparability of peace-keeping, humanitarian and development objectives; from the contribution of development to the universal goals of peace, freedom, social justice and environmental quality—goals for which the United Nations stands and for which it works daily around the world; and from the strengths of the programmes that have developed over its 50-year life. The United Nations cannot be a strong force for peace unless it is also a strong force for development.

10. It is time for the United Nations to realise its original 1–025 mandate in the social and economic fields, to make the comprehensive pursuit of development the centre of its action, and, in this new context, to assist Member States in their efforts to realise their diverse development goals.

11. The United Nations system—the United Nations itself, the specialised agencies, and the Bretton Woods institutions—has much to bring to the development process. But the system will realise its potential only if its intergovernmental processes are strengthened and made more coherent and if the various development assistance components integrate their complementary mandates into coherent and co-ordinated support for countries' aspirations. There is also great room for improvement in the Organisation's operations, including the linkages among peace-keeping, humanitarian assistance and development.

12. The general recommendations that have emerged from the 1–026 process of forging an agenda for development have brought to the fore three key objectives: to strengthen and revitalise international development co-operation generally; to build a stronger, more effective and coherent multilateral system in support of development; and to enhance the effectiveness of the development work of the Organisation itself—its departments, regional commissions, funds and programmes—in partnership with the United Nations system as a whole.

13. The recommendations presented in the following paragraphs are addressed and organised according to these three objectives, with a special focus in each case on what the United Nations can and should do. No real improvements will be possible unless the Member States are convinced of the need for, and unless nations and peoples everywhere share the fruits of, the proposed changes. Member States are challenged to grasp this opportunity and make the United Nations system a far more effective instrument of multilateralism.

V. CONCLUSION

1–027   **92.** The battle for people-centred and sustainable development will be won or lost not in the corridors of governments, but in every hamlet and home, in every village and town, in the daily enterprise of every member of the global community and every institution of civil society. The Charter of the United Nations begins with a pledge by "We, the Peoples . . .". It is the people, on whose behalf we all act, who are the true custodians of the emerging new vision of development. It is for them that we must work to achieve a new framework for development co-operation and the revitalization of the United Nations system.

An agenda for development: key recommendations[6]

1–028 Development must be driven by national priorities. Through a partnership involving government, civil society and strong private enterprise sectors, national capacities to plan, manage and implement development programmes must be built.

External macroeconomic forces must support development objectives. Developing countries must be provided equitable access to expanding global opportunities in trade, technology, investment and information. Development assistance must be brought closer to the agreed targets. New agreements should be reached on plausible interim goals for steady increases in official development assistance and a larger share should be allocated to the development work of the United Nations.

An adequate and permanent reduction in the stock of debt for countries in debt crisis undertaking economic reforms should be made. The debts of the least developed and poorest countries should be cancelled outright. Countries in transition to market economies should be supported by additional resources from the international community.

1–029   Further progress must be made on reducing military expenditures. Hearings by the President of the General Assembly on the connection between disarmament and development may be considered.

---

[6] The recommendations were presented in an Annex.

A common framework should be developed to implement goals established in United Nations conferences. Goals and targets should be synthesised, costed, prioritised and placed in a reasonable time perspective for implementation. The 50th session of the General Assembly should focus the attention of the international community on forging a new framework for development co-operation. In that context, the desirability of an international conference on the financing of development should also be considered. An effective multilateral development system requires that the unique role of the United Nations be recognised and supported: its universality, unmatched network, and capacity to build consensus, inform policy, and help rationalise public and private development efforts.

The General Assembly should identify critical issues and serve as a forum for emerging problems that fall between the purviews of more narrowly focused institutions in development, trade and finance. It should focus on requirements for a more effective management of global interdependence and the promotion of an integrated approach to economic and social development.

The early part of General Assembly sessions, with high-level representatives present, could focus dialogue on development issues in the plenary sessions. Special sessions on major aspects of international co-operation for development should be considered.

The Economic and Social Council must be revitalised to fulfil **1–030** the role envisaged in the Charter. A revitalised Council should:

— bring specialised agencies into a closer working relationship with the United Nations; serve as an international development assistance review committee, and function as a unifying governing entity to which the governing bodies of the United Nations funds and programmes would relate; and identify impending humanitarian emergencies and provide policy guidelines for co-ordinated initiatives.

Consideration should be given to an expanded bureau of the Council, meeting intersessionally, to facilitate agreement on issues for endorsement by the Council.

Greater co-operation between the United Nations and the Bretton Woods institutions should be pursued through joint initiatives, such as:

— poverty reduction strategies, sustainable energy development, post-conflict peace-building, capacity-building and improved public sector management.

The Organisation and the Bretton Woods institutions should **1–031** work together with concerned countries on the components of the policy dialogue and other initiatives that must accompany struc-

tural adjustment programmes. Governments' capacities to lead
the dialogue process must be reinforced, with the support of the
Resident Co-ordinator. Greater complementarity of country documents should be pursued.

The contributions of technical and sectoral agencies should be
integrated more fully in development strategies, in support of
comprehensive, sustainable development.

The integrity and comprehensive nature of the United Nations
system must be maintained. Bringing new organisations such as
the World Trade Organisation into relationship with the United
Nations deserves priority attention.

Members of the Administrative Committee on Co-ordination,
under the chairmanship of the Secretary-General, will pursue
further measures to strengthen the coherence and impact of the
work of the United Nations system. Further measures to improve
governance, management, funding, and allocation of responsibilities, co-ordination and staffing, must build upon reform
initiatives undertaken to date, . . . as well as other restructuring
and revitalisation efforts.

1–032   The empowerment of women, poverty eradication, preventive
and curative development, and special initiatives to support
African development, are crucial areas in which the United
Nations should provide leadership and focus action. Other key
goals which can unify the development work of the United
Nations include food, security, full employment, education for all,
and protecting and regenerating the natural resource base for
sustained production.

Efforts to enhance operational co-ordination should endeavour
to achieve the benefits of a unified system, while preserving the
strength of the current approach. Among the objectives should be:

— a more integrated, efficient, and effective structure for
   United Nations development assistance; strengthening
   United Nations capabilities in the co-ordination and delivery of humanitarian assistance; mobilising the analytical
   role of the Organisation in interrelated areas such as trade
   and access to technology in support of operations; integrating the regional commissions with the development work
   of the Organisation; strengthening the Resident Co-
   ordinator and country-driven approaches for a more integrated United Nations response to country priorities.

1–033   To these ends, the Secretary-General will convene frequent
meetings of all senior officials for the economic and social sectors
with the support of the Administrator of UNDP.

In peace-keeping operations, all elements of the United Nations
system at all levels undertaking development activities as part of

the mission must come under the command and direction of the Special Representative in command of that mission.

United Nations development efforts must be supported by adequate financial resources. Reliance on voluntary contributions alone, in light of the expanded development mandate of the Organisation, is no longer feasible. **Three principles are fundamental**[7]: more resources are needed; mandates and the resources provided for them must be in a sound relationship; and predictability in funding is essential so that operations are not undermined in the midst of performance.

NOTE: In December, 1994, the General Assembly adopted a Resolution[8] establishing an ad hoc open-ended working group to "elaborate further an action-oriented comprehensive agenda for development."[9]

Also, Mr Jose Ayala-Lasso in his statement to the 52nd Commission on Human Rights (April 9, 1996) stated the mandate of the Human Rights Commissioner extended to the right of development and that accordingly he had "endeavoured to respond to this duty giving the implementation of the right to development practical and tangible substance" and that the "emerging consensus—on the right to development is an important example of how to build on the spirit of Vienna and create a truly universal approach to human rights without perceived cleavages between North, South, East or West."

---

[7] Emphasis added.

[8] A/RES/49/126, January 20, 1995.

[9] For the Revised Synthesis of Chapters I and II of the Secretary-General's Report see WG/AGD/CRP.3/Rev. 1 (January 5, 1996; and A/AC:250 CRP 1 March 14, 1996); for Revised Synthesis on Chapter III see A/AC.250/CRP 1/ADD 1 (May 17, 1996)—available on the internet by UN Department for Policy Co-ordination and Sustainable Development (DPCSD).

CHAPTER 2

WOMEN

2–001   Although constituting more than half the global population women are still regarded as a vulnerable group. However, there is cause for some optimism in that increasingly measures are being taken to raise awareness of the plight of women. This is witnessed in the adoption of the Optional Protocol to the Convention on the Elimination of All Forms of Discrimination against Women (CEDAW) and the recognition of gender specific persecution in asylum claims. The rescinding of reservations to CEDAW is evidence of an increasing recognition of women's rights at national level. However, notwithstanding this admitted progress, women remain disproportionately disadvantaged to men in access to education, health and resources generally.

    The Optional Protocol to CEDAW provides a mechanism for reporting of alleged violations of women's rights to the Committee. This must be seen as a step forward on the road to realising the gender equality goal of Vienna. Access to the procedures for realising human rights has historically been denied to women and has indeed been a significant obstacle in the granting of rights to them both at an international and domestic level. Granting rights is only one means of enhancing a woman's quality of life. Another means is by way of preventive measures which rely primarily on education. Education that is of women and the girl child on the one hand, and those who perpetrate human rights violations against women on the other.

    A knowledge of the international instruments examined in the following pages and dissemination of their contents to as wide an audience as possible will help the evolution of a human rights culture in which women's rights are recognised as human rights.

"... the full and complete development of a country, the welfare of the world and the cause of peace require the maximum participation of women on equal terms with men in all fields."[1]

2–002   The human rights of women and of the girl-child are an inalienable, integral and indivisible part of universal human rights. The full and equal participation of women in political, civil, economic, social and cultural life, at the national, regional

---

[1] Preamble to the Convention on the Elimination of All Forms of Discrimination Against Women, 1979, UN G.A. Res. 34/180, G.A.O.R., 34th Session, Supp. 46, p. 193; Misc. 1 (1982), Cmnd. 8444.

and international levels, and eradication of all forms of discrimination on grounds of sex are priority objectives of the international community.[2]

"the progress achieved in reaching this goal (was) less than satisfactory. Although the ratification process has accelerated significantly, particularly since the Fourth World Conference on Women, held in Beijing in 1995, the number of 161 State parties merits concern. Additional efforts are necessary to achieve the goal of universal ratification by the year 2000".[3]

WORLD CONFERENCE ON HUMAN RIGHTS (JUNE 1993) VIENNA DECLARATION.[4]

18. Gender based violence and all forms of sexual harassment 2–003 and exploitation, including those resulting from cultural prejudice and international trafficking, are incompatible with the dignity and worth of the human person and must be eliminated. This can be achieved by legal measures and through national action and international co-operation in such fields as economic and social development, education, safe maternity and health care, and social support.

The human rights of women should form an integral part of the United Nations activities, including the promotion of all the human rights instruments relating to women.

The World Congress on Human Rights urges governments, institutions, intergovernmental and non-governmental organisations to intensify their efforts for the protection and promotion of human rights of women and the girl-child.

Part II(B) 3. The equal status and human rights of women

36. The World Conference on Human Rights urges the full and 2–004 equal enjoyment by women of all human rights and that this be a priority for governments and for the United Nations. The World Conference on Human Rights also underlines the importance of the integration and full participation of women as both agents and beneficiaries in the development process, and reiterates the objectives established on global action for women towards sustainable and equitable development set forth in the Rio Declaration on Environment and Development and Chapter of Agenda 21,. . .[5]

---

[2] Part I, para. 18, Vienna Declaration and Programme of Action, adopted following "United Nations World Conference on Human Rights", Vienna, June 1993.
[3] Five Year Review by UNHCR of the Vienna Declaration and Platform for Action, 1998.
[4] For full text of Action Programme see, 14 H.R.L.J. 353.
[5] (1992) 31 I.L.M. 814.

37. The equal status of women and the human rights of women should be integrated into the mainstream of United Nations system-wide activity. These issues should be regularly and systematically addressed throughout relevant United Nations bodies and mechanisms. In particular, steps should be taken to increase co-operation and promote further integration of objectives and goals between the Commission on the Status of Women, the Commission on Human Rights, the Committee on the Elimination of Discrimination Against Women, the United Nations Development Fund for Women, the United Nations Development Programme and other United Nations Agencies. In this context, co-operation and co-ordination should be strengthened between the Centre for Human Rights and the Division for the Advancement of Women.

2–005 **38.** In particular, the World Conference on Human Rights stresses the importance of working towards the elimination of violence against women in public and private life, the elimination of all forms of sexual harassment, exploitation and trafficking in women, the elimination of gender bias in the administration of justice and the eradication of any conflicts which may arise between the rights of women and the harmful effects of certain traditional or customary practices, cultural prejudices and religious extremism. The World Conference on Human Rights calls upon the General Assembly to adopt the draft Declaration on Violence against Women[6] and urges States to combat violence against women in accordance with its provisions. Violations of the human rights of women in situations of armed conflict are violations of the fundamental principles of human rights and humanitarian law. All violations of this kind, including in particular murder, systematic rape, sexual slavery and forced pregnancy, require a particularly effective response.[7]

39. The World Conference on Human Rights urges the eradication of all forms of discrimination against women, both hidden and overt. The United Nations should encourage the goal of universal ratification by all States of the Convention on the Elimination of All Forms of Discrimination Against Women by the year 2000.[7] Ways and means of addressing the particularly large number of reservations to the Convention should be encouraged. *Inter alia*, the Committee on the Elimination of Discrimination Against Women should continue its review of reservations to the Convention. States are urged to withdraw reservations that

---

[6] The Declaration was adopted by the General Assembly on February 23, 1994 (G.A.Res 48/104). See para. 2–029 *et seq.* below, 33 I.L.M. 1049 (1994).

[7] See also Article 4(b) Declaration on the Elimination of Violence Against Women, 1993, see below para. 2–032. CEDAW entered into force on September 3, 1981. Currently there are 166 contracting parties representing two-thirds of United Nations membership. Universal ratification, however, has not been achieved.

are contrary to the object and purpose of the Convention or which are otherwise incompatible with international treaty law.

40. Treaty monitoring bodies should disseminate necessary **2–006** information to enable women to make more effective use of existing implementation procedures in their pursuits of full and equal enjoyment of human rights and non-discrimination. New procedures should also be adopted to strengthen implementation of the commitment to women's equality and the human rights of women. The Commission on the Status of Women and the Committee on the Elimination of Discrimination Against Women should quickly examine the possibility of introducing the right of petition through the preparation of an optional protocol[8] to the Convention on the Elimination of All Forms of Discrimination Against Women. The World Conference on Human Rights welcomes the decision of the Commission on Human Rights to consider the appointment of a special rapporteur on violence against women at its 50th session.[9]

41. The World Conference on Human Rights recognises the importance of the enjoyment of women of the highest standard of physical and mental health throughout their life span. In the context of the World Conference on Women and the Convention on the Elimination of All Forms of Discrimination Against Women as well as the Proclamation Teheran of 1968,[10] the World Conference on Human Rights reaffirms, on the basis of equality between women and men, a woman's right to accessible and adequate health care and the widest range of family planning services, as well as equal access to education at all levels.

42. Treaty monitoring bodies should include the status of women and the human rights of women in their deliberations and findings, making use of gender specific data. States should be encouraged to supply information on the situation of women *de jure* and *de facto* in their reports to treaty monitoring bodies. The World Conference on Human Rights notes with satisfaction that the Commission on Human Rights adopted at its 49th session Resolution 1993/46 of March 8, 1993, stating that rapporteurs and working groups in the fields of human rights should also be encouraged to do so. Steps should also be taken by the Division for the Advancement of Women in co-operation with other United Nations bodies, specifically the Centre for Human Rights, to ensure that the human rights activities of the United Nations regularly address violations of women's human rights, including gender specific abuses. Training for United Nations human rights

[8] See below para. 2–025 *et seq.*

[9] The following States have withdrawn reservations: Belarus, Bulgaria, Canada, Czech Republic, France, Hungary, Ireland, Malawi, Mongolia, New Zealand, Republic of Korea, Russian Federation, Thailand, Ukraine.

[10] Para. 15.

and humanitarian relief personnel to assist them to recognise and deal with human rights abuses particular to women and to carry out their work without gender bias should be encouraged.

2–007   **43.** The World Conference on Human Rights urges governments and regional and international organisations to facilitate the access of women to decision-making posts and their greater participation in the decision-making process. It encourages further steps within the United Nations Secretariat to appoint and promote women staff members in accordance with the Charter of the United Nations, and encourages other principal and subsidiary organs of the United Nations to guarantee the participation of women under conditions of equality.

44. The World Conference on Human Rights welcomes the World Conference on Women to be held in Beijing in 1995 and urges that human rights of women should play an important role in its deliberations, in accordance with the priority themes of the World Conference on Women of equality, development and peace.

Human rights education

81. . . . the World Conference on Human Rights recommends that states develop specific programmes and strategies for ensuring the widest human rights education and the dissemination of public information, taking particular account of the human rights of women.[11]

CONVENTION ON THE ELIMINATION OF ALL FORMS OF DISCRIMINATION AGAINST WOMEN, 1979

2–008 The Convention which was adopted unanimously by the United Nations on December 18, 1979 entered into force on September 3, 1981, following receipt of the 20th ratification. Currently 168 countries are Contracting Parties to the Convention.[12]

Purpose of Convention

To eliminate discriminatory behaviour which is adverse to women.

Definition of Discrimination

The term "discrimination against women" is defined in Article 1 for the purposes of the Convention as meaning:

[11] See the section on education below, para. 2–019.
[12] As of July 2001.

"any distinction, exclusion or restriction made on the basis of sex which has the effect or purpose of impairing or nullifying the recognition, enjoyment or exercise by women irrespective of their marital status, on a basis of equality of men and women, of human rights and fundamental freedoms in the political, economic, social, cultural, civil or any other field."[13]

However it may be argued that the Convention is an improvement with respect to women's rights in that it focuses on discrimination against women specifically.

Obligation on Contracting Parties

Article 2

States Parties condemn discrimination against women in all its 2–009 forms, agree to pursue by all appropriate means and without delay a policy of eliminating discrimination against women and, to this end, undertake:

(a) To embody the principle of the equality of men and women in their national constitutions or other appropriate legislation if not yet incorporated therein and to ensure, through law and other appropriate means, the practical realization of this principle;

(b) To adopt appropriate legislative and other measures, including sanctions where appropriate, prohibiting all discrimination against women;

(c) To establish legal protection of the rights of women on an equal basis with men and to ensure through competent national tribunals and other public institutions the effective protection of women against any act of discrimination;

(d) To refrain from engaging in any act or practice of discrimination against women and to ensure that public authorities and institutions shall act in conformity with this obligation;

(e) To take all appropriate measures to eliminate discrimination against women by any person, organisation or enterprise;

---

[13] The above definition reflects the terminology employed in Article 1 of the 1966 Convention on the Elimination of Racial Discrimination although the latter excludes any reference to discrimination within the civil sphere. Article 1 has been criticised on the grounds that it is more limited in scope than, for instance, Article 2 of the 1948 Universal Declaration on Human Rights which provides that "Everyone is entitled to all the rights and freedoms set forth in this Declaration, without distinction of any kind, such as . . . sex". See also Article 2 of the International Covenant on Civil and Political Rights 1966 and Article 2 of the International Covenant on Economic, Social and Cultural Rights 1966. For general discussion see N. Burrows, "The 1979 Convention on the Elimination of All Forms of Discrimination Against Women" [1985] N.I.L.R. 419.

(f) To take all appropriate measures, including legislation, to modify or abolish existing laws, regulations, customs and practices which constitute discrimination against women;

(g) To repeal all national penal provisions which constitute discrimination against women.

Article 2 articulates a twofold obligation on Contracting Parties not only involving a mere condemnation of discrimination but necessitating the taking of appropriate measures to eliminate discrimination. This obligation incumbent on Contracting Parties is reinforced by Article 24 which provides that: "States Parties undertake to adopt all necessary measures at the national level aimed at achieving the full realisation of the rights recognised in the present Convention." Article 2 is central to the Convention's effectiveness being concerned with both *de facto* and *de jure* equality. Article 24 on the other hand is a more general statement. Nevertheless Article 2 does not provide a time framework for implementation and accordingly responsibility lies with the individual Contracting Parties.

The general obligation incumbent on Contracting Parties is further spelt out in Article 3 which is sufficiently vague to cover any deficiency in the definition contained in Article 1.

Article 3

2–010 States Parties shall take in all fields, in particular in the political, social, economic and cultural fields, all appropriate measures, including legislation, to ensure the full development and advancement of women, for the purpose of guaranteeing them the exercise and enjoyment of human rights and fundamental freedoms on a basis of equality with men.

Article 4

2–011   **1.** Adoption by States Parties of temporary special measures aimed at accelerating *de facto* equality between men and women shall not be considered discrimination as defined in the present Convention, but shall in no way entail as a consequence the maintenance of unequal or separate standards; these measures shall be discontinued when the objectives of equality of opportunity and treatment have been achieved.

2. Adoption by States Parties of special measures, including those measures contained in the present Convention, aimed at protecting maternity shall not be considered discriminatory.

Article 4 acknowledges the possibility of positive discrimination and provides for the introduction of temporary special measures designed to accelerate *de facto* equality between men and women. Article 4(2) constitutes a legitimate exception to the principle of non-discrimination as found in Article 1. Measures aimed at protecting maternity are however included in Article 11 within the context of employment law. At its 25th session the Committee on the Elimination of All Forms of Discrimination against Women began work on a general recommendation on temporary measures designed to encourage legal and policy initiatives to accelerate *de facto* equality.

Article 5

States Parties shall take all appropriate measures: 2–012

(a) To modify the social and cultural patterns of conduct of men and women, with a view to achieving the elimination of prejudices and customary and all other practices which are based on the idea of the inferiority or the superiority of either of the sexes or on stereotyped roles for men and women;

(b) To ensure that family education includes a proper understanding of maternity as a social function and the recognition of the common responsibility of men and women in the upbringing and development of their children, it being understood that the interest of the children is the primordial consideration in all cases.

Article 5 makes a limited contribution to the overall goal of improving the position of women. The obligation on Contracting Parties is undefined. Does Article 5 require the banning of women's magazines? Are media programmes promoting the rights of women obligatory? Article 5 is essentially concerned with policy rather than substantive measures benefitting individuals. For instance if maternity is regarded as a social function this may have serious and far reaching implications with respect to a woman's freedom of choice and rights as an individual. Article 5(b) may thus be in conflict with Article 16.1(e) which ensures the right of men and women equally to decide on the number and spacing of their children. Article 5 leaves interpretation of "a proper understanding of maternity" to each state's discretion. No mention is made of paternity as a social function. "Paternity leave", however, is becoming more common in European States though, see *Petrovic v. Austria*. Should states be the sole arbitrators and entrusted with exclusive responsibility in this sphere? Nor does Article 5 make any allowance for cultural diversity between contracting parties.

Article 6

States Parties shall take all appropriate measures, including 2–013 legislation, to suppress all forms of traffic in women and exploitation of prostitution of women.

Article 6 does not define the term "traffic" nor does it specify whether states are required to suppress exploitation of the prostitution of women or suppress prostitution itself. The distinction between the two lies in who profits financially. International law traditionally has dealt with exploitation of prostitution as opposed to prostitution itself.[14] A Belgian proposal which would have included the words "and attacks on the physical integrity of women" was rejected. Its acceptance would have ensured that states would have been required to take measures to counter sexual crimes such as rape and female circumcision. Resolution E/CN/RES/1999/40 Article 4 urges governments "to take appropriate measures—so as to eliminate trafficking in women" while Article 6 calls upon governments "to criminalise trafficking in women and girls".

Articles 7,8, 9, 15 and 16—civil and political rights

Article 7

2–014 States Parties shall take all appropriate measures to eliminate discrimination against women in the political and public life of the country and, in particular, shall ensure to women, on equal terms with men, the right:

(a) To vote in all elections and public referenda and to be eligible for election to all publicly elected bodies;

(b) To participate in the formulation of government policy and the implementation thereof and to hold public office and perform all public functions at all levels of government;

(c) To participate in non-governmental organisations and associations concerned with the public and political life of the country.

Article 8

2–015 States Parties shall take all appropriate measures to ensure to women, on equal terms with men and without any discrimination, the opportunity to represent their governments at the international level and to participate in the work of international organisations.

Article 9

2–016   1. States Parties shall grant women equal rights with men to acquire, change or retain their nationality. They shall ensure in particular that neither marriage to an alien nor change of

[14] See, *e.g.* 1949 Convention for the Suppression of the Traffic in Persons and the Exploitation of Prostitution of Others.

nationality by the husband during marriage shall automatically change the nationality of the wife, render her stateless or force upon her the nationality of the husband.

2. States Parties shall grant women equal rights with men with respect to the nationality of their children.

Articles 7–9 inclusive are concerned with the civil and political rights of women which have already been the focus of international attention particularly in the Convention on the Political Rights of Women, 1952[15] and the 1957 Convention on the Nationality of Married Women.[16] The 1979 Convention expands and elaborates the rights articulated in the earlier instruments and reinforces the guarantees contained therein. For instance, Article 9(2) was novel in that it sought to accord equality between men and women in respect of the nationality of children. However this represented a general principle which imposed no time scale on states for its realisation. Article 9 highlighted the derivative legal status of many women and Article 15 provides that women should not have their legal rights and responsibilities defined in a male context.

Article 15

1. States Parties shall accord to women equality with men **2–017** before the law.

2. States Parties shall accord to women, in civil matters, a legal capacity identical to that of men and the same opportunities to exercise that capacity. In particular, they shall give women equal rights to conclude contracts and to administer property and shall treat them equally in all stages of procedure in courts and tribunals.

3. States Parties agree that all contracts and all other private instruments of any kind with a legal effect which is directed at restricting the legal capacity of women shall be deemed null and void.

4. States Parties shall accord to men and women the same rights with regard to the law relating to the movement of persons and the freedom to choose their residence and domicile.

Although *prima facie* Article 15 would appear to raise and advance the status of women Article 15 does not provide a right to conclude contracts and administer property *per se* but rather where a State already has in place legislation concerning such, then these rights must be afforded equally between women and men. Article 15(4) was criticised on the grounds that it made no concessions for example to Islamic law.

[15] 193 U.N.T.S. 135.
[16] 309 U.N.T.S. 65.

Article 16

2–018   **1.** States Parties shall take all appropriate measures to eliminate discrimination against women in all matters relating to marriage and family relations and in particular shall ensure, on a basis of equality of men and women:

> (a) The same right to enter into marriage;
>
> (b) The same right freely to choose a spouse and to enter into marriage only with their free and full consent;
>
> (c) The same rights and responsibilities during marriage and at its dissolution;
>
> (d) The same rights and responsibilities as parents, irrespective of their marital status, in matters relating to their children; in all cases the interests of the children shall be paramount;
>
> (e) The same rights to decide freely and responsibly on the number and spacing of their children and to have access to the information, education and means to enable them to exercise these rights;
>
> (f) The same rights and responsibilities with regard to guardianship, wardship, trusteeship and adoption of children, or similar institutions where these concepts exist in national legislation; in all cases the interests of the children shall be paramount;
>
> (g) The same personal rights as husband and wife, including the right to choose a family name, a profession and an occupation;
>
> (h) The same rights for both spouses in respect of the ownership, acquisition, management, administration, enjoyment and disposition of property, whether free of charge or for a valuable consideration.

2. The betrothal and the marriage of a child shall have no legal effect, and all necessary action, including legislation, shall be taken to specify a minimum age for marriage and to make the registration of marriages in an official registry compulsory.

> Article 16 returns to the issue of marriage and family relations and deals with spousal equality in all aspects of family life. Not surprisingly Article 16 has given rise to the most controversy as is reflected in the number of reservations lodged to that Article.

Articles 10,11, 12, 13 and 14—social and economic rights

Articles 10 and 12—education and health care

Article 10

States Parties shall take all appropriate measures to eliminate 2–019
discrimination against women in order to ensure to them equal
rights with men in the field of education and in particular to
ensure, on a basis of equality of men and women:

(a) The same conditions for career and vocational guidance, for
access to studies and for the achievement of diplomas in
educational establishments of all categories in rural as well
as in urban areas; this equality shall be ensured in pre-
school, general, technical, professional and higher technical
education, as well as in all types of vocational training;

(b) Access to the same curricula, the same examinations, teaching staff with qualifications of the same standard and
school premises and equipment of the same quality;

(c) The elimination of any stereotyped concept of the roles of
men and women at all levels and in all forms of education
by encouraging coeducation and other types of education
which will help to achieve this aim and, in particular, by
the revision of textbooks and school programmes and the
adaptation of teaching methods;

(d) The same opportunities to benefit from scholarships and
other study grants;

(e) The same opportunities for access to programmes of continuing education including adult and functional literacy
programmes, particularly those aimed at reducing, at the
earliest possible time, any gap in education existing
between men and women;

(f) The reduction of female student drop-out rates and the
organisation of programmes for girls and women who have
left school prematurely;

(g) The same opportunities to participate actively in sports and
physical education;

(h) Access to specific educational information to help to ensure
the health and well-being of families, including information
and advice on family planning.

Article 10 focuses on non-discrimination in education. Article 10
requires contracting Parties to grant both sexes equal access to the

same educational processes but also requires the introduction of progressive policies designed to promote socio cultural changes. Article 10 has a negative aspect in that it denies discrimination and a positive aspect in the sense of encouraging an improvement in the status of women through forward planning and policy making in the sphere of education. Article 10 is undoubtedly one of the most important articles because without education women cannot effectively access rights in other areas of life. One hundred and thirty million children still do not receive education, some 900 million people, that is one-sixth of the world's population over the age of 15 are illiterate. Women make up two-thirds of this figure. World Education Forum, Dakar, 2000 Programme for Action sets as a goal "eliminating gender disparities in primary and secondary education by 2005 and achieving gender equality by 2015". Education is recognised as a tool for the implementation of Article 5(a)— it is only through education that attitudes will be changed and traditional "male"/"female" stereotypes abandoned. Education is the key to the realisation of the goals expressed in Article 12.

Article 12

2–020   **1.** States Parties shall take all appropriate measures to eliminate discrimination against women in the field of health care in order to ensure, on a basis of equality of men and women, access to health care services, including those related to family planning.

2. Notwithstanding the provisions of paragraph 1 of this article, States Parties shall ensure to women appropriate services in connection with pregnancy, confinement and the post-natal period, granting free services where necessary, as well as adequate nutrition during pregnancy and lactation.

Articles 11 and 13 employment and economic and social benefits.

Article 11

2–021   **1.** States Parties shall take all appropriate measures to eliminate discrimination against women in the field of employment in order to ensure, on a basis of equality of men and women, the same rights, in particular:

(a) The right to work as an inalienable right of all human beings;

(b) The right to the same employment opportunities, including the application of the same criteria for selection in matters of employment;

(c) The right to free choice of profession and employment, the right to promotion, job security and all benefits and conditions of service and the right to receive vocational training and retraining, including apprenticeships, advanced vocational training and recurrent training;

(d) The right to equal remuneration, including benefits, and to equal treatment in respect of work of equal value, as well as equality of treatment in the evaluation of the quality of work;

(e) The right to social security, particularly in cases of retirement, unemployment, sickness, invalidity and old age and other incapacity to work, as well as the right to paid leave;

(f) The right to protection of health and to safety in working conditions, including the safeguarding of the function of reproduction.

2. In order to prevent discrimination against women on the 2–022 grounds of marriage or maternity and to ensure their effective right to work, States Parties shall take appropriate measures:

(a) To prohibit, subject to the imposition of sanctions, dismissal on the grounds of pregnancy or of maternity leave and discrimination in dismissals on the basis of marital status;

(b) To introduce maternity leave with pay or with comparable social benefits without loss of former employment, seniority or social allowances;

(c) To encourage the provision of the necessary supporting social services to enable parents to combine family obligations with work responsibilities and participation in public life, in particular through promoting the establishment and development of a network of child-care facilities;

(d) To provide special protection to women during pregnancy in types of work proved to be harmful to them.

3. Protective legislation relating to matters covered in this article shall be reviewed periodically in the light of scientific and technological knowledge and shall be revised, repealed or extended as necessary.

Article 13

States Parties shall take all appropriate measures to eliminate 2–023 discrimination against women in other areas of economic and social life in order to ensure, on a basis of equality of men and women, the same rights, in particular:

(a) The right to family benefits;

(b) The right to bank loans, mortgages and other forms of financial credit;

(c) The right to participate in recreational activities, sports and all aspects of cultural life.

Articles 11 and 13 deal with non-discrimination in employment and economic and social activities respectively and set out goals to which contracting parties are to ascribe but the attainment of such goals will be dependent upon a state's economic development. In other words it is impossible to prescribe a rigorous time scale applicable to all contracting parties.

Article 14—rural women

Article 14

2–024   1. States Parties shall take into account the particular problems faced by rural women and the significant roles which rural women play in the economic survival of their families, including their work in the non-monetised sectors of the economy, and shall take all appropriate measures to ensure the application of the provisions of this Convention to women in rural areas.

2. States Parties shall take all appropriate measures to eliminate discrimination against women in rural areas in order to ensure, on a basis of equality of men and women, that they participate in and benefit from rural development and, in particular, shall ensure to such women the right:

(a) To participate in the elaboration and implementation of development planning at all levels;

(b) To have access to adequate health care facilities, including information, counselling and services in family planning;

(c) To benefit directly from social security programmes;

(d) To obtain all types of training and education, formal and non- formal, including that relating to functional literacy, as well as, *inter alia*, the benefit of all community and extension services, in order to increase their technical proficiency;

(e) To organise self-help groups and co-operatives in order to obtain equal access to economic opportunities through employment or self-employment;

(f) To participate in all community activities;

(g) To have access to agricultural credit and loans, marketing facilities, appropriate technology and equal treatment in land and agrarian reform as well as in land resettlement schemes;

(h) To enjoy adequate living conditions, particularly in relation to housing, sanitation, electricity and water supply, transport and communications.

Article 14 is unique in that it was the first international recognition of the special needs of women in rural communities. Two-thirds of the world's women inhabit rural areas and their position warranting special attention has been a recurring theme in a number of recent international instruments see, in particular, Rio Declaration.[17]

Enforcement of the Convention

The task of monitoring implementation of the Convention has been entrusted to a Committee set up in 1982 and was designated the Committee on the Elimination of Discrimination Against Women (CEDAW). **2–025**

Article 17

1. For the purpose of considering the progress made in the implementation of the present Convention, there shall be established a Committee on the Elimination of Discrimination against Women (hereinafter referred to as the Committee) consisting, . . ., of 23 experts of high moral standing and competence in the field covered by the Convention. The experts shall be elected by States Parties from among their nationals and shall serve in their personal capacity, consideration being given to equitable geographical distribution and to the representation of the different forms of civilization as well as the principal legal systems.
2. The members of the Committee shall be elected by secret ballot from a list of persons nominated by States Parties. Each State Party may nominate one person from among its own nationals.
Members who are elected for a term of four years (and may be re-elected) serve in their individual capacity and not as representatives of their government.

Article 18

1. States Parties undertake to submit to the Secretary-General of the United Nations, for consideration by the Committee, a report on the legislative, judicial, administrative or other measures which they have adopted to give effect to he provisions of the present Convention and on the progress made in this respect: **2–026**

(a) Within one year after the entry into force for the State concerned; and

(b) Thereafter at least every four years and further whenever the Committee so requests.[18]

---

[17] See *supra* n. 4.
[18] As of June 2001 the Committee has considered 111 initial, 77 second, 56 third, 22 fourth and 3 fifth Reports.

2. Reports may indicate factors and difficulties affecting the degree of fulfilment of obligations under the present Convention.

2–027   A major problem confronting the Committee has been the non submission of reports. As the number of State Parties increases so does the backlog of reports pending consideration by the Committee. Furthermore, if an effort is made to encourage states with overdue reports to submit them, the backlog will be inevitable. Currently there is now on average a lapse of three years from submission of report until its consideration by the Committee.[19] This leads to demands for updates regarding developments in the interim period and thereby results in an increase in the volume of documentation presented to the Committee. The Committee has been considering on average 14–16 reports during a three week session. The delay constitutes a disincentive to report. At the conclusion of the 24th session of the CEDAW Committee it was noted that some States have submitted more than one report in order to report their reporting schedule. Such submissions had increased the Committee's workload but had reduced the backlog. The Committee in an attempt to reduce the backlog further has recommended an amendment to Article 20 which limits the meetings of the Committee to "not more than two weeks annually" and pending such amendment has recommended that the General Assembly authorise the Committee to meet "exceptionally for two sessions of three weeks duration each year."[20] The Committee has been assisted by ad hoc working groups which were initially used by the Committee in its second session. The first working group in 1983 considered the guidelines for the preparation of States Parties' reports and since then the use of working groups has become a regular tool of the Committee. When a report of a state is being considered a representative of the State concerned is present and may participate in the discussion and answer questions regarding the report.[21] The World Conference on Human Rights suggested the introduction of a right of petition by means of an Optional Protocol to the Convention and thus in 1994 a draft optional protocol was submitted by an independent expert group.[22]

Article 21

2–028   **1.** The Committee shall, through the Economic and Social Council, report annually to the General Assembly of the United Nations on its activities and may make suggestions and general

---

[19] In 1985 the time lapse between receipt and consideration was 18 months.

[20] No such amendment has yet been introduced although Article 20 frequently appears on the agenda and most recently at a seminar for Pacific Region State in Auckland, February 2001.

[21] Rule 49, Committee's Rules of Procedure—the Rules of Procedure were adopted in accordance with Article 19 and were originally introduced in 1981. Since then the Committee has adopted by consensus a number of new procedures that could be interpreted as inconsistent with the published rules. Draft revised rules of procedure based on the Committee's current practices are scheduled to be considered at a future session.

[22] Meeting held in Maastricht, September 29—October 1, 1994.

recommendations based on the examination of reports and information received from the States Parties. Such suggestions and general recommendations shall be included in the report of the Committee together with comments, if any, from States Parties.

2. The Secretary-General shall transmit the reports of the Committee to the Commission on the Status of Women for its information.

In accordance with Article 21 the Committee can only make observations and has no power to declare a State Party to be in violation of the Convention. The Committee contributes to the interpretation of the Convention by way of General Recommendations of which there are to date 24.[23] These can be on procedural matters such General Recommendation No. 2,[24] substantive matters such as General Recommendation No. 14,[25] General Recommendation Nos 12, 19 23 and 24. CEDA has to date adopted 24 General Recommendations. Since 1997 the Committee has adopted a three-stage process for the formulation of General Recommendation:

1. Open dialogue between the Committee, NGOs and other interested parties regarding the subject matter of the proposed General Recommendation;

2. Drafting the General Recommendation in a form to be discussed within a working group at the next session of the Committee;

3. Adoption by the Committee of the revised draft.[26]

Impact of the Convention

The Convention is *the* major international instrument dealing   2–029
exclusively with the human rights of women. It goes further than previous Conventions and Declarations in recognising the importance of culture and tradition in shaping the thinking and behaviour of men and women and the significant part they play in restricting the exercise of basic rights by women. It has been suggested that international law is an inappropriate means of effecting change in long standing and deep rooted societal institutions and practices. However, this cannot be used as a justification for apathy and inaction in such a vital area. The Convention plays a crucial role in outlining "a clear human rights agenda for women" marking "an enormous step" forward.

The Optional Protocol has been introduced to address the historical weakness of the Convention *viz.* that reporting

---

[23] 13th Session, 1994.

[24] Concerning Initial Reports as Submitted by State Parties UN Doc. A/42/38, 6th Session 1987.

[25] Female Circumcision UN Doc. A/45/38, 9th Session, 1990.

[26] Violence Against Women, UN Doc. A/43/38, 8th Session, 1989; and UN Doc. A/47/38, 11th Session, 1992.

procedures alone do not effectively encourage compliance with international requirements. While the Convention is silent with respect to a time scale for the realisation of the goals within it the Optional Protocol introduces a potentially more effective redress mechanism for ensuring compliance. However, even by laying down objectives to be aspired to the Convention serves as a catalyst for the continued progress on the issues particularly relevant to the female sex. This is especially true with respect to violence against women. The Convention failed to deal comprehensively with violence against women although certain articles made reference to certain practices—*e.g.* Article 6. Traditionally gender-related violence, such as female genital mutilation and rape have not been regarded as being within the domain of international law whereas domestic violence has been regarded as "private" rather than a public matter. However such entrenched attitudes are being undermined.[27]

DECLARATION ON THE ELIMINATION OF VIOLENCE AGAINST WOMEN 1993[28]

Article 1

2–030 For the purposes of this Declaration the term "violence against women" means any act of gender-based violence that results in, or is likely to result in, physical or psychological harm or suffering to women, including threats of such act coercion or arbitrary, deprivation of liberty, whether occurring in public or private life.

Article 2

2–031 Violence against women shall be understood to encompass, but not be limited to, the following:

(a) physical, sexual and psychological violence occurring in the family, including battering, sexual abuse of female children in the household, dowry-related violence, marital rape, female genital mutilation and other traditional practices harmful to women, non-spousal violence and violence related to exploitation;

(b) physical, sexual and psychological violence occurring within the general community, including rape, sexual abuse, sexual harassment and intimidation at work, in

---

[27] See Vienna Declaration para. 38 *supra* para. 2–005. See also decision of ICTY in case of Kunavac, Kovac and Vukovic Juagnur, February 2001.
[28] Adopted by G.A.Res. 48/104, February 23, 1994.

educational institutions and elsewhere, trafficking in women and forced prostitution;

(c) physical, sexual and psychological violence perpetrated or condoned by the state, wherever it occurs.

The foregoing is an acknowledgment that women suffer violence specifically because of their gender and the Declaration's definition encompasses acts previously designated "private". The Declaration thus seeks to end the public/private dichotomy which has characterised human rights thinking.

Article 3 enumerates the rights which are afforded to women by other international instruments including the right to life, the right to the highest standard attainable of physical and mental health, and the right not to be subjected to torture, or other cruel, inhuman or degrading treatment or punishment. Article 3 does not acknowledge that violence may impede the exercise of such rights.

Under the Declaration certain tasks are incumbent on states. Although these tasks may be perceived as being morally strict they are not legally binding given that the Declaration has been adopted by way of a General Assembly is not a legally binding Convention Resolution.

Article 4

States should condemn violence against women and should not **2–032** invoke any custom, tradition or religious consideration to avoid their obligations with respect to its elimination. States should pursue by all appropriate means and without delay a policy of eliminating violence against women and, to this end, should:

(a) consider, where they have not yet done so, ratifying or acceding to the Convention on the Elimination of All Forms of Discrimination Against Women or withdrawing reservation to that Convention;

(b) refrain from engaging in violence against women;

(c) exercise due diligence to prevent, investigate and, in accordance with national legislation, punish acts of violence against women, whether these acts are perpetrated by the state or by private persons;

(d) develop penal, civil, labour and administrative sanctions in domestic legislation to punish and redress the wrongs caused to women who are subjected to violence; women who are subjected violence should be provided with access to the mechanisms of justice and, as provided for by national legislation to just and effective remedies for the harm that they have suffered; states should also inform women of their rights in seeking redress through such mechanisms;

(e) consider the possibility of developing national plans of action to promote the protection of women against any form of violence or to include provisions for that purpose in plans already existing, taking into account, as appropriate, such co-operation as can be provided by non-governmental organisations, particularly those concerned with the issue of violence against women;

(f) develop, in a comprehensive way, preventive approaches, and all those measures of a legal, political, administrative and cultural nature that promote the protection of women against any form of violence, and ensure that re-victimisation of women does not occur because of laws insensitive to gender considerations, enforcement practices or other interventions;

(g) work to ensure, as to the maximum extent feasible in the light of their available resources and, where needed, within the framework of international co-operation that women subjected to violence, where appropriate, their children have specialised assistance, such as rehabilitation, assistance in child care and maintenance, treatment, counselling, and health and social services, facilities and programmes, as well as support structures, and should take all other appropriate measures to promote their safety and physical and psychological rehabilitation;

(h) include in government budgets adequate resources for their activities related to the elimination of violence against women;

(i) take measures to ensure that law enforcement officers and public officials responsible for implementing policies to prevent, investigate and punish violence against women receive training to sensitise them to the needs of women;

(j) adopt all appropriate measures, especially in the field of education to modify the social and cultural patterns of conduct of men and women and to eliminate prejudices, customary practices and all other practices based on the idea of the inferiority or superiority of either of the sexes and on stereotyped roles for men and women;

(k) promote research, collect data and compile statistics, especially concerning domestic violence, relating to the prevalence of different forms of violence against women and encourage research on the causes, nature, seriousness and consequences of violence against women and on the effectiveness of measures implemented to prevent and redress violence against women; those statistics and findings of the research will be made public;

(l) adopt measures directed towards the elimination of violence against women who are specially vulnerable to violence against women;

(m) include, in submitting reports as required under relevant human rights instruments of the United Nations information pertaining to violence against women and measures taken to implement the present declaration;

(n) encourage the development of appropriate guidelines to assist in the implementation of the principle set forth in the present declaration;

(o) recognise the important role of the women's movement and non-governmental organisations worldwide in raising awareness and alleviating the problem of violence against women;

(p) facilitate and enhance the work of the women's movement and non-governmental organisation and co-operate with them at local, national and regional levels;

(q) encourage intergovernmental regional organisations of which they are members to include the elimination of violence against women in their programmes as appropriate.

Article 5

The organs and specialised agencies of the United Nations system 2–033 should, within their respective fields of competence, contribute to the recognition and realisation of the rights and the principles set forth in the present declaration and, to this end, should, *inter alia*:

(a) foster international and regional co-operation with a view to defining regional strategies for combatting violence exchanging experiences and financing programmes relating to the elimination of violence against women;

(b) promote meetings and seminars with the aim of creating and raising awareness among all persons of the issue of the elimination of violence against women;

(c) foster co-ordination and exchange within the United Nations system between human rights treaty bodies to address the issue of violence against women effectively;

(d) include in analyses prepared by organisations and bodies of the United Nations system of social trends and problems, such as the periodic reports on the world social situation, examination of trends in violence against women;

(e) encourage co-ordination between organisations and bodies of the United Nations system to incorporate the issue of violence against women into on going programmes especially with reference to groups of women particularly vulnerable to women;

(f) promote the formulation of violence or manuals relating to violence against women taking into account the measures referred to in the present declaration;

(g) consider the issue of the elimination of violence against women as appropriate in the fulfilling their mandates with respect to the implementation of human rights instruments;

(h) co-operate with non-governmental organisations in addressing the issue of violence against women.

Article 6

2–034 Nothing in the present declaration shall affect any provision that is more conducive to the elimination of violence against women that may be contained in the legislation of a state or in any international convention, treaty or other instrument in force in a state.

The Declaration is the culmination of an initiative of the Commission on the Status of Women recommending that the issue of violence against women should be addressed in an international instrument.[29] The Declaration is a step forward but nevertheless the fulfilment of the objectives contained therein remain the responsibility of all states.[30] Although the Declaration provides that states may not invoke custom and culture as a justification for discrimination against women, no time scale is prescribed to which states have to comply and the extent of a state's "obligation" is limited to "the maximum extent feasible in the light of their available resources."

Some women's rights advocates and analysts believe that the UN definition on gender-related violence does not go far enough and that it leaves in doubt whether issues not mentioned would constitute violence—*viz.* female foeticide or restrictive abortion policies.

Any definition of violence must have at its centre the core concepts of force and coercion, which distinguish between violent and

---

[29] This was proposed by the Commission in 1991 and recommended to the Economic and Social Council. The proposal contained the recommendation that the instrument be prepared in conjunction with the "Committee on the Elimination of Discrimination Against Women" and the "United Nations Committee on Crime Prevention and Control".

[30] The Declaration applies to all states and not only to contracting parties as in the case of the Convention on the Elimination of Discrimination Against Women.

merely oppressive behaviour such as perpetrated by an individual or the State and excludes laws, policies or structural inequalities that could be considered as violent.[31]

Ms. Heise and her associates would define violence as:

Any act of verbal or physical force, coercion, or life-threatening deprivation, directed at an individual woman or girl, that causes physical or psychological harm, humiliation or arbitrary deprivation of liberty and that perpetuates female subordination.

SPECIAL RAPPORTEUR ON VIOLENCE AGAINST WOMEN

The appointment of a Special Rapporteur was advocated in the Vienna Declaration (para. 4) and Radhika Coomaraswamy of Sri Lanka was appointed by the UN Commission on Human Rights. The task of the special rapporteur is the investigation of and reporting on "thematic" human rights issues. The Special Rapporteur has for instance addressed the issue of international trafficking for the purposes of the sex trade.[32]   2–035/6

Prior to the Declaration the Committee on the Elimination of All Forms of Discrimination Against Women produced General Recommendations on the issue of violence against women, *viz.* Recommendations Nos 12 and 19.   2–037

Recommendation No. 12

This recommended to Contracting States (*i.e.* to the Convention) "that they should include in their periodic reports to the Committee information about"   2–038

1. the legislation in force to protect women against the incidence of all kinds of violence in every day life (including sexual violence, abuses in the family, sexual harassment at the work place etc.);

2. other measures to eradicate this violence;

3. the existence of support services for women who are the victims of aggression or abuses;

4. statistical data on the incidence of violence of all kinds against women and on women who are the victims of violence.

---

[31] Lori Heise, a Director at the Pacific Insitute for Women's Health, in Washington D.C. Statement reproduced from "Violence Against Women", United Nations Department of Public Information, DPI/1595/Wom. 95–01657, January 1995.

[32] E/CN.4/RES/1999/40 on traffic in women and girls.

Recommendation No. 19

Background

2–039   1. Gender-based violence is a form of discrimination that seriously inhibits women's ability to enjoy rights and freedoms on the basis of equality with men.

Comments on specific articles of the Convention:

Article 11

17. Equality in employment can be seriously impaired when women are subjected to gender-specific violence, such as sexual harassment in the workplace.

Article 12

19. States parties are required . . . to take measures to ensure equal access to health care. Violence against women puts their health and lives at risk.

Article 16 (and article 15)

22. Compulsory sterilisation or abortion adversely affects women's physical and mental health, and infringes the right of women to decide on the number and spacing of their children.

23. Family violence is one of the most insidious forms of violence against women. It is prevalent in all societies. Within family relationships women of all ages are subjected to violence, including battering, rape, other forms of sexual assault, mental and other forms of violence . . .

Specific Recommendations

The Committee, in the light of the comments, made a number of specific recommendations (a)–(t) designed to combat gender-related violence. Many of these recommendations are contained in the 1993 Declaration, *e.g.* States parties should take appropriate and effective measures to overcome all forms of gender-based violence, whether by public or private act.

Female circumcision (female genital mutilation)

Recommendation No. 14[33]

2–040 Concerned about the continuation of the practice of female circumcision and other traditional practices harmful to the health of women,

---

[33] *ibid* p. 21.

That States parties

(a) . . . take appropriate and effective measures with a view to eradicating the practice of female circumcision. Such measures should include:

   (i) The collection and dissemination by universities, medical or nursing associations, national women's organisations or other bodies of basic data about such traditional practices;

   (ii) The support of women's organisations at the national and local levels working for the elimination of female circumcision and other practices harmful to women;

   (iii) The encouragement of politicians, professionals, religious and community leaders at all levels including the media and the arts to co-operate in influencing attitudes towards the eradication of female circumcision;

   (iv) The introduction of appropriate educational and training programmes and seminars based on research findings about the problems arising from female circumcision;

(b) . . .include in their national health policies appropriate strategies aimed at eradicating female circumcision in public health care. Such strategies could include the special responsibility of health personnel including traditional birth attendant to explain the harmful effects of female circumcision;

(c) . . . invite assistance, information and advice from the appropriate organisation of the United Nations system to support and assist efforts being deployed to eliminate harmful traditional practices;

(d) . . . include in their reports to the Committee . . . information about measures taken to eliminate female circumcision.

Recent United Nations reports inform that genital mutilation, a traditional practice affecting women's health, is practised in parts of Africa and Asia, and among immigrants in the U.S. and Europe. Globally, at least two million girls a year experience genital mutilation, approximately 6,000 new cases every day and five girls every minute.[34]

---

[34] Note Canadian decision T93–12197/12198/12199-Ramirez McCaffrey July 13, 1994 in which female genital mutilation (f.g.m.) was recognised as "persecution" for the purpose of granting refugee status. The applicant was a woman from Somalia and her two children, one of whom was a girl. This was the first occasion of the actual granting of refugee status because of f.g.m. However f.g.m. was recognised as "persecution" for the purposes of the Refugee Convention by the French Refugee Appeal Board (*Commission de recours des refugies*) in 1991 but in that particular case the applicant was unsuccessful as she failed to produce convincing supporting evidence—*Case of Mademoiselle X*, September 18, 1991, 164.078.

RAPE

GENEVA CONVENTION RELATIVE TO THE PROTECTION TO CIVILIAN PERSONS IN TIME OF WAR (1949)

Article 27

2–041 . . ., women shall be specially protected against any attack on their honour, in particular against rape, enforced prostitution, or any form of indecent assault.[35]

Crimes against humanity

Article 5(g) of the Statute of the International Tribunal for Prosecution of Persons Responsible for Serious Violations of International Humanitarian Law Committed in the Territory of The Former Yugoslavia[36]:

The International Tribunal shall have the power to prosecute persons responsible for the following crimes when committed in armed conflict, whether international or internal in character, and directed against any civilian population:

(a) . . .

(g) rape

Note: In February 2001 Dragoljub Kunarac, a Bosnian Serb was convicted of sexual enslavement and sentenced by the Tribunal to 28 years imprisonment. This was the first occassion "sexual enslavement" was held to be a war crime. Two other Bosnian Serbs were convicted at the same time of "war crimes and crimes against humanity by rape". They were sentenced to 20 years imprisonment.

See also Article 3 Statute of the International Tribunal for Rwanda[37] which also provides that the Tribunal shall have the power to prosecute persons responsible for the following crimes when committed as part of a widespread or systematic attack against any civilian population on national, political, ethnic, racial or religious grounds:

(a) . . .

(g) rape

---

[35] Endorsed in Article 76 Protocol 1 (1977).
[36] Established by Security Council 827 (1993) 32 I.L.M. 1159 (1993).
[37] Established by Security Council Resolution 955 (1994) 33 I.L.M. 1598 (1994).

The Statute of the International Criminal Court[38] reflects the terminology employed in the Statute of both Tribunals.

Article 7(g) of the ICC Statute provides that rape, sexual slavery, enforced prostitution, forced pregnancy, forced sterilisation (and other such crimes) constitute crimes against humanity, "when committed as part of a widespread or systematic attack directed against any civilian population, with knowledge of the attact".

DOMESTIC VIOLENCE

"Imagine a world in which three to four million people are suddenly struck by a serious, recurring illness. There is chronic pain, trauma and injury. Authorities fail to draw any connection between individual bouts with the disease and the greater public threat. Many suffer in silence."[39]

Sexual abuse is not only common but widespread in most countries. Women are at greater risk of violence and resulting injury in their homes and from men they know. At a police station in Sao Paulo, Brazil, 70 per cent of all reported cases of violence against women took place in the home. In Santiago, Chile, almost three-quarters of all assault-related injuries to women were found to be caused by family members. In Canada, 62 per cent of women murdered in 1987 died at the hands of their spouses. In the U.S., one woman is physically abused every eight seconds and one is raped every six minutes.

2–042/3

Spouse abuse is more common in the U.S. than automobile accidents, mugging and cancer deaths combined, notes a 1992 U.S. Senate Judiciary Committee report. In Canada, a 1993 study based on 420 randomly selected women found that more than 54 per cent of them had experienced some form of unwanted or intrusive sexual experience before reaching the age of 16; 51 per cent reported being victims of rape or attempted rape. In 25 per cent of the cases, women who were physically assaulted reported that their partners explicitly threatened to kill them. Based on the popular view that a wife is the property of her husband and that therefore he may do with her whatever he thinks fit, legal systems in some countries have recognised a husband's right to chastise or even kill his wife if she is considered disobedient or is thought to have committed adultery. A parliamentarian in Papua New Guinea, taking part in a debate on wife battering, went as far as to say, "Wife beating is an accepted custom. We are wasting our time debating this issue."[40] These statistics are still valid as is endorsed in a 2000 report from UNICEF which highlights that some 50 per

---

[38] Adopted at Rome, June 1998.

[39] Joseph R. Biden, former chairman of the U.S. Senate Judiciary Committee, cited in *Violence Against Women*, *supra* n. 33.

[40] Reproduced from United Nations Public Information Document, *supra* n. 33.

cent of all women and girls experience physical violence at the hands of either an intimate partner or family member. The Report also highlights that only 44 countries have enacted legislation dealing specifically with domestic violence.

REFUGEE WOMEN[41]

THE COMMISSION ON THE STATUS OF WOMEN

2–044   The Commission on the Status of Women was set up in 1946 by the UN Economic and Social Council and deals with policy decisions on women's status as well as preparing recommendations for the United Nations and monitoring the situation of women. The Commission is an intergovernmental body with a membership of 45 representing an equitable geographical distribution.[42] Each member is elected for a term of four years. The Commission meets once a year for at least eight days.

UNITED NATIONS DEVELOPMENT FUND FOR WOMEN (UNIFEM)

2–045   The Development Fund was established after the 1975 Inter-national Conference on Women held in Mexico City. It was originally a voluntary fund but has now evolved into an auto-nomous organisation within the United Nations. It funds pro-grammes to assist women within development regions and high on it list of priorities are agriculture and food security, trade and industry as well as policy making. The Fund also targets critical issues on the global agenda to ensure that such women's issues as

[41] See, for example, UNHCR Guidelines On The Protection of Refugee Women, Geneva July 1991, and UNHCR Executive Committee No. 73 (XLIV), 1993 Refugee Protection and Sexual Violence and in particular para. (e) which recommends the development by States of appropriate guidelines on women asylum-seekers, in recognition of the fact that women refugees often experience persecution differently from men. See also EXCOM No. 39 (XXXV1)—1985—Refugee Women and International Protection; No. 54 (XXX1X)—1988 Refugee Women; No. 60 (XL)—1989 Refugee Women; and No. 64 (XL1)—1990—Refugee Women and International Protection. See also Canada's Women Refugee Claimants; Fearing Gender-Related Persecution, Guidelines Issued by the Chairperson Pursuant to Section 65(3) of the Immigration Act (Ottawa, Canada, March 9, 1993) and U.S. Guidelines *viz* "Considerations for Asylum Officers Adjudicating Asylum Claims From Women" issued May 26, 1995. See also C.R.D.D. No. U92–08714, *Maraj and Shuter*, June 4, 1993 where the particular social group was held to be "unprotected Ecuadoran women subject to wife abuse". Note also U.S. decision of Immigration Judge Paul A. Najelski who granted refugee status to a Jordanian woman whose government "had failed to protect her from over three decades of physical and mental abuse by her husband." Reported in *Washington Post*, June 3, 1995. U.S. Board of Immigration Appeals (BIA) in May 1995 designated as binding precedent a 1993 case recognising rape as persecution *Case of Re Krome* (BIA, May 25, 1993). For further discussion see Chapter Seven on Refugees.

[42] Currently 13 states from Africa, 11 from Asia, four from eastern Europe, nine from Latin America and the Caribbean, eight from western Europe and other states.

refugees and displaced persons, human rights, global governance and the environment are integrated into international policies. The Fund operates at local, national, regional and international levels. UNIFEM, UNDP and ITU signed an agreement on July 6, 2000, guaranteeing that the impact of ICTS (information and communications technology) on women be incorporated in policy dialogue and decision-making. Governments and telecommunication industries are encouraged to recruit, train and employ women so as "to put new opportunities and knowledge at the disposal of those excluded from the revolution, particularly women."

UNITED NATIONS INTERNATIONAL RESEARCH AND TRAINING INSTITUTE FOR THE ADVANCEMENT OF WOMEN (INSTRAW)

INSTRAW was established in 1975 by the General Assembly on the recommendation of the Conference held in Mexico City. INSTRAW as an autonomous body within the United Nations has a mandate to carry out research, training and information activities throughout the world in order to promote women as key agents for sustainable development. One of the principal functions of INSTRAW is to collect statistics, for instance, in the area of migration of women, women, water and sanitation and women and environmental management as well as the image and participation of women in alternative and mass media. It has also created a New Gender Awareness and Information and Networking System (GAINS) and innovative electronic system which serves as a virtual workshop.

2–046

UN CONFERENCES ON WOMEN

A number of United Nations world conferences have dealt specifically with women's issues. The first conference, held during International Women's Year in Mexico City, 1975, adopted a plan of action that led to the declaration, by the United Nations General Assembly, of the United Nations Decade for Women. In 1979 the UN General Assembly adopted the Convention on the Elimination of All Forms of Discrimination Against Women, which to date has 168 States Parties. A committee of independent experts reviews the implementation of the Convention, discusses reports submitted and makes recommendations to governments for further improvement. These activities demonstrate the commitment of governments to bring about positive change.

2–047

At the second conference, held in Copenhagen, Denmark, in 1980, a programme of action for the second half of the decade for women was adopted, with emphasis on education, employment and health. The third world conference took place in Nairobi, Kenya, in 1985, to review and appraise achievements made and obstacles encountered during the decade for women. The Nairobi

Forward-looking Strategies for the Advancement of Women to the Year 2000 were adopted by consensus. The Strategies provided a framework for action at the national, regional and international level to promote empowerment of women and their enjoyment of human rights.

A 1990 evaluation of the Forward-looking Strategies by the United Nations Commission on the Status of Women revealed that the world community had become more conscious and sensitive to issues affecting women. However, there seemed to be some loss of momentum in implementation. More recently, the issue of violence against women has been placed on the global agenda, including the issue of sexual harassment. In 1993, the General Assembly adopted a landmark declaration on the Elimination of Violence Against Women. The impact of HIV/AIDS on women is has been an emerging issue of major concern during the last decade.

The theme of the Beijing Conference held in 1995 was:

"Action for equality, development and peace".

GOALS OF THE CONFERENCE

The objectives of the Conference were:

2–048
- To review and appraise the advancement of women since 1985 in terms of the objectives of the Nairobi Forward-looking Strategies for the Advancement of Women to the Year 2000.

- To mobilise women and men at both the policy-making and grass-roots levels to achieve those objectives.

- To adopt a "Platform for Action", concentrating on key issues—the "critical areas of concern"—identified as obstacles to the advancement of women in the world. This document will propose and suggest corresponding strategic objectives and action to be taken by governments, the international community, non-governmental organisations, the private sector and individuals for the removal of the remaining obstacles to women's full and equal participation in development in all spheres of life. It will include actions to eradicate poverty; eliminate inequality in education; ensure access to relevant health care, employment and economic participation; further protection and preservation of the environment; end inequality in sharing of power and decision-making; improve images of women in the mass media; promote women's human rights and eliminate violence against women.

- To determine the priority actions to be taken between 1996–2001 for implementation of the Nairobi Forward-looking

Strategies for the Advancement of Women to the Year 2000 by the international community, including the United Nations system.

BEIJING DECLARATION — PLATFORM FOR ACTION
BEIJING + 5

In a special session in June 2000 the UN General Assembly reaffirmed by consensus that governments have a responsibility to implement the Beijing Platform for Action and that the Platform remains a reference point for governmental commitment to women's rights in the 12 critical areas identified as meriting for concern.

The Session sought to strengthen the Platform in certain areas by making the action more focused and encompassing additional issues which had assumed a greater relevance in the last five years, *e.g.* AIDS and health generally. In respect of violence against women the Session called for legislative amendments designed to remove discriminatory provisions by 2005. Measures were also proposed to combat trafficking in women and girls. In sharp contrast to the optimism of the Special Session Amnesty International has expressed strong reservations on the progress made in respect of the human rights of women.[43]

INTERNATIONAL WOMEN'S DAY, MARCH 8

The idea of an International Women's Day first arose at the turn of the century, which in the industrialised world was a period of expansion and turbulence, booming population growth and radical ideologies. In 1909, in accordance with the Declaration by the Socialist Party of America, the first national Women's Day was observed across the United States on February 28, The following year the Socialist International meeting in Copenhagen established a Women's Day, international in character, to honour the movement for women's rights and freedom and to assist in achieving universal suffrage for women. In 1911 as a result of the Copenhagen decision, International Women's Day was marked for the first time in Austria, Denmark, Germany and Switzerland. The day was marked in Russia for the first time in 1913 and in 1914 on March 8, it was also observed elsewhere in Europe. International Women's Day has usually been marked on March 8, since and has become a rallying point for co-ordinated efforts to demand women's rights.

2–049

What does it say about the position of women in modern society that one day is still designated Women's Day?

---

[43] *Amnesty Magazine*, July/August 2000, p. 20.

2–050   A Conference held at the UN headquarters on March 14, 1995
addressed the issue of women and the United Nations.[44] Secretary-
General Boutros Boutros-Ghali in a speech to the Conference
acknowledged that the recruitment and promotion of women at
the United Nations had failed to live up to the promise of the
Charter and lagged dismally behind what it should be while the
record of Member States was no better. Of 185 missions only six
were headed by women and very few women were diplomats or
foreign ministers. The Secretary-General maintained that the
United Nations must lead by example.[45] The Secretary-General's
Strategic Plan of Action for the Improvement of the Status of
Women, 1995–2000 has three objectives:

1. an overall level of 35 per cent of women by 1995.
2. 25 per cent women at the senior level by 1997;
3. an overall level of 50 per cent—complete gender equality—
   by the year 2000.

For discussion as to the extent to which these objectives have
been achieved See—Charlesworth and Chinkin: The Boundaries
of International Law: a feminist analysis, pp. 177–179.

WOMEN IN DEVELOPMENT

REPORT OF THE UNITED NATIONS CONFERENCE ON ENVIRONMENT AND DEVELOPMENT[46] (RIO DE JANEIRO, JUNE 3–14, 1992)

CHAPTER 24

GLOBAL ACTION FOR WOMEN TOWARDS SUSTAINABLE AND EQUITABLE DEVELOPMENT PROGRAMME AREA

Basis for action

2–051   **24.1.** The international community has endorsed several plans
of action and conventions for the full, equal and beneficial
integration of women in all development activities, in particular
the Nairobi Forward-looking Strategies for the Advancement of

---

[44] The Conference was dedicated to the memory of Eleanor Roosevelt, former U.S. First
Lady and a delegate to the United Nations and whose photo appears on the cover of this
text.

[45] In March 1995 15 per cent of UN Director-level posts and above were held by women.

[46] A/CONF.151/26 (Vol. III) August 14, 1992.

Women,[47] which emphasise women's participation in national and international ecosystem management and control of environment degradation. Several conventions, including the Convention on the Elimination of All Forms of Discrimination against Women (General Assembly resolution 34/180, annex) and conventions of ILO and UNESCO have also been adopted to end gender-based discrimination and ensure women access to land and other resources, education and safe and equal employment. Also relevant are the 1990 World Declaration on the Survival, Protection and Development of Children and the Plan of Action for implementing the Declaration (A/45/625, annex). Effective implementation of these programmes will depend on the active involvement of women in economic and political decision-making and will be critical to the successful implementation of Agenda 21.

Objectives

24.2 The following objectives are proposed for national 2–052 Governments:

(a) To implement the Nairobi Forward-looking Strategies for the Advancement of Women, particularly with regard to women's participation in national ecosystem management and control of environment degradation;

(b) To increase the proportion of women decision makers, planners, technical advisers, managers and extension workers in environment and development fields;

(c) To consider developing and issuing by the year 2000 a strategy of changes necessary to eliminate constitutional legal, administrative, cultural, behaviourial social and economic obstacles to women's full participation in sustainable development and in public life;

(d) To establish by the year 1995 mechanisms at the national regional and international levels to assess the implementation and impact of development and environment policies and programmes on women and to ensure their contributions and benefits;

(e) To assess, review, revise and implement, where appropriate, curricula and other educational material, with a view to promoting the dissemination to both men and women of

---

[47] Report of the World Conference to Review and Appraise the Achievements of the United Nations Decade for Women: Equality, Development and Peace, Nairobi, July 15–26, 1985 (United Nations publication, Sales No. E.85.IV.10), Chap. I, Section A.

gender-relevant knowledge and valuation of women's roles through formal and non-formal education, as well as through training institutions, in collaboration with non-governmental organisations;

(f) To formulate and implement governmental policies and national guidelines, strategies and plans for the achievement of equality in all aspects of society, including the promotion of women's literacy, education, training, nutrition and health and their participation in key decision-making positions and in management of the environment, particularly as it pertains to their access to resources, by facilitating better access to all forms of credit, particularly in the informal sector, taking measures towards ensuring women's access to property rights as well as agricultural inputs and implements;

(g) To implement, as a matter of urgency, in accordance with country-specific conditions, measures to ensure that women and men have the same right to decide freely and responsibly the number and spacing of their children and have access to information, education and means, as appropriate, to enable them to exercise this right in keeping with their freedom, dignity and personally held values;

(h) To consider adopting, strengthening and enforcing legislation prohibiting violence against women and to take all necessary administrative, social and educational measures to eliminate violence against women in all its forms.

Activities

2–053　　24.3 Governments should take active steps to implement the following:

(a) Measures to review policies and establish plans to increase the proportion of women involved as decision makers, planners, managers, scientists and technical advisers in the design, development and implementation of policies and programmes for sustainable development;

(b) Measures to strengthen and empower women's bureaux, women's non-governmental organisations and women's groups in enhancing capacity-building for sustainable development;

(c) Measures to eliminate illiteracy among females and to expand the enrolment of women and girls in educational institutions, to promote the goal of universal access to primary and secondary education for girl children and for women, and to increase educational and training opportunities for women and girls in sciences and technology, particularly at the post-secondary level;

(d) Programmes to promote the reduction of the heavy workload of women and girl children at home and outside through the establishment of more and affordable nurseries and kindergartens by Governments, local authorities, employers and other relevant organisations and the sharing of household tasks by men and women on an equal basis, and to promote the provision of environmentally sound technologies which have been designed, developed and improved in consultation with women, accessible and clean water, an efficient fuel supply and adequate sanitation facilities;

(e) Programmes to establish and strengthen preventive and curative health facilities, which include women-centred, women-managed, safe and effective reproductive health care and affordable, accessible, responsible planning of family size and services, as appropriate, in keeping with freedom, dignity and personally held values. Programmes should focus on providing comprehensive health care, including pre-natal care, education and information on health and responsible parenthood, and should provide the opportunity for all women to fully breastfeed at least during the first four months post-partum. Programmes should fully support women's productive and reproductive roles and well-being and should pay special attention to the need to provide equal and improved health care for all children and to reduce the risk of maternal and child mortality and sickness;

(f) Programmes to support and strengthen equal employment opportunities and equitable remuneration for women in the formal and informal sectors with adequate economic political and social support systems and services, including child care, particularly day-care facilities and parental leave, and equal access to credit-land and other natural resources;

(g) Programmes to establish rural banking systems with a view to facilitating and increasing rural women's access to credit and to agricultural inputs and implements;

(h) Programmes to develop consumer awareness and the active participation of women, emphasising their crucial role in achieving changes necessary to reduce or eliminate unsustainable patterns of consumption and production, particularly in industrialised countries, in order to encourage investment in environmentally sound productive activities and induce environmentally and socially friendly industrial development;

(i) Programmes to eliminate persistent negative images, stereotypes, attitudes and prejudices against women through changes in socialisation patterns, the media, advertising, and formal and non-formal education;

(j) Measures to review progress made in these areas, including the preparation of a review and appraisal report which includes recommendations to be submitted to the 1995 world conference on women.

24.4 Governments are urged to ratify all relevant conventions pertaining to women if they have not already done so. Those that have ratified conventions should enforce and establish legal, constitutional and administrative procedures to transform agreed rights into domestic legislation and should adopt measures to implement them in order to strengthen the legal capacity of women for full and equal participation in issues and decisions on sustainable development.

24.5. States Parties to the Convention on the Elimination of All Forms of Discrimination against Women should review and suggest amendments to it by the year 2000, with a view to strengthening those elements of the Convention related to environment and development, giving special attention to the issue of access and entitlements to natural resources, technology, creative banking facilities and low-cost housing, and the control of pollution and toxicity in the home and workplace. States Parties should also clarify the extent of the Convention 5 scope with respect to the issues of environment and development and request the Committee on the Elimination of Discrimination against Women to develop guidelines regarding the nature of reporting such issues, required under particular articles of the Convention. CEDAW General Recommendation 24 (1999) links access to clean water supply with health.

(a) Areas requiring urgent action

2–054   **24.6.** Countries should take urgent measures to avert the ongoing rapid environmental and economic degradation in developing countries that generally affects the lives of women and children in rural areas suffering drought, desertification and deforestation, armed hostilities, natural disasters, toxic waste and the aftermath of the use of unsuitable agro-chemical products.

24.7. In order to reach these goals, women should be fully involved in decision-making and in the implementation of sustainable development activities.

(b) Research, data collection and dissemination of information

24.8. Countries should develop gender-sensitive databases, information systems and participatory action-oriented research and policy analyses with the collaboration of academic institutions and local women researchers on the following:

(a) Knowledge and experience on the part of women of the management and conservation of natural resources for incorporation in the databases and information systems for sustainable development;

(b) The impact of structural adjustment programmes on women. In research done on structural adjustment programmes, special attention should be given to the differential impact of those programmes on women, especially in terms of cut-backs in social services, education and health and in the removal of subsidies on food and fuel;

(c) The impact on women of environmental degradation, particularly drought, desertification, toxic chemicals and armed hostilities;

(d) Analysis of the structural linkages between gender relations, environment and development;

(e) The integration of the value of unpaid work, including work that is currently designated "domestic," in resource accounting mechanisms in order better to represent the true value of the contribution of women to the economy, using revised guidelines for the United Nations System of National Accounts, to be issued in 1993;

(f) Measures to develop and include environmental, social and gender impact analyses as an essential step in the development and monitoring of programmes and policies;

(g) Programmes to create rural and urban training, research and resource centres in developing and developed countries that will serve to disseminate environmentally sound technologies to women.

(c) International and regional co-operation and co-ordination

24.9. The Secretary-General of the United Nations should 2–055 review the adequacy of all United Nations institutions, including those with a special focus on the role of women, in meeting development and environment objectives, and make recommendations for strengthening their capacities. Institutions that require special attention in this area include the Division for the Advancement of Women (Centre for Social Development and Humanitarian Affairs, United Nations Office at Vienna), the United Nations Development Fund for Women (UNIFEM), the International Research and Training Institute for the Advancement of Women (INSTRAW). For example, INSTRAW conducted a national training seminar on "women, environmental management and sustainable development" in the Solomon Islands in 1988, and the women's programmes of regional commissions. The review should consider how the environment and development programmes of each body of the United Nations system could be strengthened to implement Agenda 21 and how to incorporate the role of women in programmes and decisions related to sustainable development.

24.10. Each body of the United Nations system should review the number of women in senior policy level and decision-making posts and, where appropriate, adopt programmes to increase that number, in accordance with Economic and Social Council resolution 1991/17 on the improvement of the status of women in the Secretariat.

24.11. UNIFEM should establish regular consultations with donors in collaboration with UNICEF, with a view to promoting operational programmes and projects on sustainable development that will strengthen the participation of women, especially low-income women, in sustainable development and in decision-making. UNDP should establish a women's focal point on development and environment in each of its resident representative offices to provide information and promote exchange of experience and information in these fields. Bodies of the United Nations system, governments and non-governmental organisations involved in the follow-up to the Conference and the implementation of Agenda 21 should ensure that gender considerations are fully integrated into all the policies, programmes and activities.

Means of implementation

Financing and cost evaluation

2–056   **24.12.** The Conference secretariat has estimated the average total annual cost (1993–2000) of implementing the activities of this chapter to be about $40 million from the international community on grant or concessional terms. These are indicative and order-of-magnitude estimates only and have not been reviewed by Governments. Actual costs and financial terms, including any that are non-concessional, will depend upon, *inter alia*, the specific strategies and programmes Governments decide upon for implementation.

CHAPTER 3

MINORITIES

INTRODUCTION

3–001   The third decade to combat racism and racial discrimination is nearing its conclusion. Plans are well advanced for the World Conference Against Racism and Racial Discrimination, Xenophobia and Related Intolerance to be held in Durban, South Africa in September 2001. The venue is appropriate in view of the collapse of apartheid, one of the clearest examples of racial discrimination in recent years. However, there are many instances of racial discrimination throughout the world and it is a sad indictment that such intolerance is still so prevalent. It also highlights that although there is a role for international human rights instruments they in themselves will not rid the world of human rights violations. It is to be hoped that the World Conference will provide a focus for future concerted efforts to promote the Convention and ensure that its aims and objectives are articulated at every level of society. It is all too apparent that eradication of such discrimination is somewhat in the future and does depend upon changing attitudes and prejudices. That should not deter concerted efforts being made to remove racial intolerance from future generations.

WORLD CONFERENCE ON HUMAN RIGHTS (JUNE 1993) VIENNA DECLARATION

3–002   **19.** Considering the importance of the promotion and protection of the rights of persons belonging to minorities and the contribution of such promotion and protection to the political and social stability of the States in which such persons live.

The World Conference on Human Rights reaffirms the obligation of States to ensure that persons belonging to minorities may exercise fully and effectively all human rights and fundamental freedoms without any discrimination and in full equality before the law in accordance with the Declaration on the Rights of Persons Belonging to National or Ethnic, Religious and Linguistic Minorities.

The persons belonging to minorities have the right to enjoy their own culture, to profess and practise their own religion and to use their own language in private and in public, freely and without interference or any form of discrimination.

Part II (B) Equality, dignity and tolerance

1. Racism, racial discrimination, xenophobia and other forms of intolerance

19. The World Conference on Human Rights considers the 3–003 elimination of racism and racial discrimination, in particular in their institutionalised forms such as apartheid or resulting from doctrines of racial superiority or exclusivity or contemporary forms and manifestations of racism, as a primary objective for the international community and a worldwide promotion programme in the field of human rights. United Nations organs and agencies should strengthen their efforts to implement such a programme of action related to the third decade to combat racism and racial discrimination as well as subsequent mandates to the same end. The World Conference on Human Rights strongly appeals to the international community to contribute generously to the Trust Fund for the Programme for the Decade for Action to Combat Racism and Racial Discrimination.

20. The World Conference on Human Rights urges all governments to take immediate measures and to develop strong policies to prevent and combat all forms and manifestations of racism, xenophobia or related intolerance, where necessary by enactment of appropriate legislation, including penal measures, and by the establishment of national institutions to combat such phenomena.

21. The World Conference on Human Rights welcomes the 3–004 decision of the Commission on Human Rights to appoint a Special Rapporteur on contemporary forms of racism, racial discrimination, xenophobia and related intolerance.[1] The World Conference on Human Rights also appeals to all States parties to the International Convention on the Elimination of All Forms of Racial Discrimination to consider making the declaration under Article 14 of the Convention.

22. The World Conference on Human Rights calls upon all governments to take all appropriate measures in compliance with their international obligations and with due regard to their respective legal systems to counter intolerance and related violence based on religion or belief, including practices of discrimination against women and including the desecration of religious sites, recognising that every individual has the right to freedom of thought, conscience, expression and religion. The Conference also invites all States to put into practice the provisions of the Declaration on the Elimination of All Forms of Intolerance and of Discrimination Based on Religion or Belief.

---

[1] The UN Commission on Human Rights at its 49th session adopted resolution 1993/20 of February 26, 1993, whereby Mr Dossou was appointed Special Rapporteur. See 14 H.R.L.J. 132 (1993).

23. The World Conference on Human Rights stresses that all persons who perpetrate or authorise criminal acts associated with ethnic cleansing are individually responsible and accountable for such human rights violations, and that the international community should exert every effort to bring those legally responsible for such violations to justice.

24. The World Conference on Human Rights calls on all States to take immediate measures, individually and collectively, to combat the practice of ethnic cleansing to bring it quickly to an end. Victims of the abhorrent practice of ethnic cleansing are entitled to appropriate and effective remedies.

2. Persons belonging to national or ethnic, religious linguistic minorities

3–005   **25.** The World Conference on Human Rights calls on the Commission on Human Rights to examine ways and means to promote and protect effectively the rights of persons belonging to minorities as set out in the Declaration on the Rights of Persons belonging to National or Ethnic, Religious and Linguistic Minorities. In this context, the World Conference on Human Rights calls upon the Centre for Human Rights to provide, at the request of governments concerned and as part of its programme of advisory services and technical assistance, qualified expertise on minority issues and human rights, as well as on the prevention and resolution of disputes, to assist in existing or potential situations involving minorities.

26. The World Conference on Human Rights urges States and the international community to promote and protect the rights of persons belonging to national or ethnic, religious and linguistic minorities in accordance with the Declaration on the Rights of Persons belonging to National or Ethnic, Religious and Linguistic Minorities.

27. Measures to be taken, where appropriate, should include facilitation of their full participation in all aspects of the political, economic, social, religious and cultural life of society and in the economic progress and development in their country.

UNIVERSAL DECLARATION OF HUMAN RIGHTS[2]

Article 1

3–006 All human beings are born free and equal in dignity and rights. They are endowed with reason and conscience and should act towards one another in a spirit of brotherhood.

---

[2] UN Doc. A/811, December 10, 1948.

Article 2

Everyone is entitled to all the rights and freedoms set forth in this Declaration, without distinction of any kind, such as race, colour, sex, language, religion, political or other opinion, national or social origin, property, birth or other status . . .[3]

UN COVENANT ON CIVIL AND POLITICAL RIGHTS 1966

Article 18

1. Everyone shall have the right to freedom of thought, cons- **3–007** cience and religion. This right shall include freedom to have or adopt a religion or belief of his choice, and freedom, either individually or in community with others and in public or private, to manifest his religion or belief or belief in worship, observance, practice and teaching.

2. No one shall be subject to coercion which would impair his freedom to have or to adopt a religion or belief of his choice.

3. Freedom to manifest one's own religion or beliefs may be subject only to such limitations as are prescribed by law and are necessary to protect public safety, order, health, or morals or the fundamental rights and freedoms of others.

4. The State Parties to the present Covenant undertake to have respect for the liberty of parents and, when applicable, legal guidelines to ensure the religious and moral education of their children in conformity with their own convictions.

NOTE: See the case of *Bhinder v. Canada* (Communication No. 208/19)[4] in which Article 18 was held not to have been breached. The author of the Communication—a Seikh and a nationalised Canadian citizen—claimed that his dismissal from employment because of his refusal to wear safety head gear at work, was a violation of Article 18. The Committee held that there had been no violation of Article 18, because even if the requirement that the hard hat be worn were regarded as raising issues under Article 18, the limitation in question was justified by reference to the grounds laid down in Article 18(3). The Committee also concluded that there had been no violation of Article 26[5] because the legislation requiring that workers be protected from injury and electric by the wearing of hard hats were to be regarded as reasonable and

---

[3] Note also Advisory Opinion in *Legal Consequences for States of the Continued Presence of South West Africa in Namibia (South West Africa) Notwithstanding Security Council Resolution 276 (1970), Order No. 1 of January 26, 1971, I.C.J. Rep. 1971,* p. 3.

[4] Decision of the Human Rights Committee, November 9, 1989.

[5] See below para. 3–012.

directed towards objective purposes and were compatible with the Covenant.[6]

General Comment No. 22(48) on Article 18/Freedom of Thought and Religion[7]

3–008   **1.** The right to freedom of thought, conscience and religion (which includes the freedom to hold beliefs) in Article 18(1) is far-reaching and profound; it encompasses freedom of thoughts on all matters, personal conviction and the commitment to religion or belief, whether manifested individually or in community with others. The Committee draws the attention of States parties to the fact that the freedom of thought and the freedom of conscience are protected equally with the freedom of religion or belief. The fundamental character of these freedoms is also reflected in the fact that this provision cannot be derogated from, even in time of public emergency, as stated in Article 4(2) of the Covenant.

2. Article 18 protects theistic, non-theistic and atheistic beliefs, as well as the right not to profess any religion or belief. The terms belief and religion are to be broadly construed. Article 18 is not limited in its application to traditional religions or to religions and beliefs with institutional characteristics or practices analogous to those of traditional religions. The Committee therefore views with concern any tendency to discriminate against any religion or belief for any reason, including the fact that they are newly established, or represent religious minorities that may be the subject of hostility by a predominant religious community.

3. Article 18 distinguishes the freedom of thought, conscience, religion or belief from the freedom to manifest religion or belief. It does not permit any limitations whatsoever on the freedom of thought and conscience or on the freedom to have or adopt a religion or belief of one's choice. These freedoms are protected unconditionally as is the right of everyone to hold opinions without interference in Article 19(1). In accordance with Articles 18(2) and 17, no one can be compelled to reveal his thoughts or adherence to a religion or belief.

3–009   **4.** The freedom to manifest religion or belief may be exercised "either individually or in community with others and in public or private". The freedom to manifest religion or belief in worship, observance, practice and teaching encompasses a broad range of

---

[6] In addition to *Bhinder v. Canada (supra)* other communications which have argued an alleged violation of Article 26 include, *inter alia*, *Aumeeruddy-Cziffra v. Mauritius*, Selected Decisions H.R.C. 67 (1981), see Chapter on Women; *Broeks v. The Netherlands*, 2 Selected Decision H.R.C. 196 (1987) see Chapter on Women; For a recent consideration of a breach of Article 26 see *Simunek et al v. Czech Republic* (Communication No 516/1992) Decision of July 19, 1995, 17 H.R.L.I. 13 (1996).

[7] UN Doc. A/48/40, Part I, p. 208.

acts. The concept of worship extends to ritual and ceremonial acts giving direct expression to belief as well as various practices integral to such acts, including the building of places of worship, the use of ritual formulae and objects, the display of symbols and the observance of holidays and days of rest. The observance and practice of religion or belief may include not only ceremonial acts but also such customs as the observance of dietary regulations the wearing of distinctive clothing or headcoverings, participations in rituals associated with certain stages of life, and the use of a particular language customarily spoken by a group. In addition, the practice and teaching of religion or belief includes acts integral to the conduct by religious groups of their basic affairs such as, *inter alia*, the freedom to choose their religious leaders, priests and teachers, the freedom to establish seminaries or religious schools and the freedom to prepare and distribute religious texts or publications.

5. The Committee observes that the freedom to "have or to adopt" religion or belief necessarily entails the freedom to chose a religion or belief, including, *inter alia*, the right to replace one's religion or belief with another or to adopt atheistic views, as well as the right to retain one's religion or belief. Article 18(2) bars coercions that would impair the right to have or to adopt a religion or belief, including the use of threat of physical force or penal sanctions to compel believers or non-believers to adhere to their religious beliefs and congregations, to recant their religion or belief or to convert. Policies or practices having the same effect, such as, for example, those restricting access to education, medical care, employment or the rights guaranteed by Article 25 and other provisions of the Covenant are similarly inconsistent with Article 18(2). The same protection is enjoyed by holders of all beliefs of a non-religious nature.

6. The Committee is of the view that Article 18(4) permits public school instruction such as the general history of religions and ethics if it is given in a neutral and objective way. The liberty of parents or legal guardians to ensure that their children receive a religious and moral education in conformity with their own convictions, set forth in Article 18(4), is related to the guarantees of the freedom to teach a religion or belief stated in Article 18(1). The Committee notes that public education that includes instruction in a particular religion or belief is inconsistent with Article 18(4) unless provision is made for non discriminatory exemptions or alternatives that would accommodate the wishes of parents and guardians.

7. According to Article 20, no manifestations of religions or **3–010** beliefs may amount to propaganda for war or advocacy of national, racial or religious hatred that constitutes incitement to discrimination, hostility or violence . . . State parties are under the obligation to enact laws to prohibit such acts.

8. Article 18(3) permits restrictions on the freedom to manifest religion or belief only if limitations are prescribed by law and are necessary to public safety, order, health or morals, or the fundamental rights and freedoms. The freedom from coercion to have or adopt a religion or belief and the liberty of the parents and guardians to ensure religious and moral education cannot be restricted. In interpreting the scope of permissible limitation clauses States parties should proceed from the need to protect the rights guaranteed under the Covenant including the right to equality and non-discrimination on all grounds specified in Articles 2, 3 and 26. Limitations imposed must be established by law and must not be applied in a manner that would vitiate the rights guaranteed in Article 18. The Committee observes that paragraph 3 of Article 18 is to be strictly interpreted: restrictions are not allowed on grounds not specified there, even if they would be allowed as restrictions to their rights protected in the Covenant, such as national security. Limitations may be applied only for those purposes for which they were prescribed and must be directly related and proportionate to the specific need on which they are predicated. Restrictions may not be imposed for discriminatory purposes or applied in a discriminatory manner. The Committee observes that the concept of morals derives from many social, philosophical and religious traditions; consequently, limitations on the freedom to manifest a religion or belief for the purpose of protecting morals must be based on principles not deriving exclusively from a single tradition. Persons already subject to certain legitimate constraint such as prisoners continue to enjoy their rights to manifest their religion or belief to the fullest extent compatible with the specific nature of the constraint. States parties' reports should provide information on the full scope and effects of limitations under Article 18(3), both as a matter of law and of their application in specific circumstances.

9. The fact that a religion is recognised as a state religion or that it is established as official or traditional or that its followers comprise the majority of the population shall not result in any impairment of the enjoyment of any of the rights under the Covenant, including Articles 18 and 27, nor in any discrimination against adherents of other religions or non-believers. In particular, certain measures discriminating against the latter, such as measures restricting eligibility for government service to members of the dominant religion or giving economic privileges to them or imposing special restrictions on the practice of other faiths, are not in accordance with the prohibition of discrimination based on religion or belief and the guarantee of equal protection under Article 26. The measures contemplated by Article 20, paragraph 2, of the Covenant constitute important safeguards against infringements of the rights of religious minorities and of other religious groups to exercise the rights guaranteed by Articles 18 and 27, and against acts of violence or persecution directed toward those groups. The Committee wishes to be informed of measures taken by States parties concerned to protect the practices of all religions or beliefs from infringement and to protect their followers from discrimination. Similarly, information as to respect for the rights of religious minorities under Article 27 is necessary for the Committee to assess the extent to which the freedom of thought, conscience, religion and belief has been implemented by States parties. States parties should also include in their reports information relating to practices considered by their laws and jurisprudence to be punishable as blasphemous.

10. If a set of beliefs as official ideology in constitutions, **3–011** statutes, proclamations of the ruling party, etc., or in actual practice, this shall not result in any impairment of the freedoms under Article 18 or any other rights recognised under the Covenant nor in any discrimination against persons who do not accept the official ideology or who oppose it.

11. Many individuals have claimed the right to refuse to perform (conscientious objection) on the basis that such right derives from their freedoms under Article 18. In response to such claims, a growing number of States exempted from compulsory military citizens who genuinely hold religious or other beliefs that forbid the performance of military service and replaced it with alternative service. The Covenant does not explicitly refer to a right of conscientious objection but the Committee believes that such a right can be derived from Article 18, in as much as the obligation to use lethal force may seriously conflict with the freedom of conscience and the right to manifest one's religion or belief. When this right is recognised by law or practice, there shall be no differentiation among conscientious objectors of the basis of the nature of their particular beliefs, likewise, there shall be no discrimination against conscientious objectors because they have failed to perform military service. The Committee invites States parties to report on the conditions under which persons can be exempted from military service on the basis of their rights under Article 19 and on the nature and length of alternative national service.

Article 26

All persons are equal before the law and are entitled without any **3–012** discrimination to the equal protection of the law. In this respect, the law shall prohibit any discrimination and guarantee to all persons equal and effective protection against discrimination on any ground such as race, colour, six, language, religion, political or other opinion, national or social origin, property, birth or other status.

Article 27

In those States in which ethnic, religious or linguistic minorities exist, persons belonging to such minorities shall not be denied the right, in community with the other members of their group, to enjoy their own culture, to profess and practise their own religion, or to use their own language.[8]

General Comment No. 23(50) on Article 27/Minority Rights[9]

3–013   1. Article 27 of the Covenant provides that, in those States in which ethnic, religious or linguistic minorities exist, persons belonging to those minorities shall not be denied the right, in community with other members of their group, to enjoy their own culture to profess and practice their own religion, or to use their own language. The Committee observes that this article establishes and recognises a right which is conferred on individuals belonging to minority groups and which is distinct from, and additional, to all the other rights which, as individuals in common with everyone else, they are entitled to enjoy under the Covenant.

2. In some communications submitted to the Committee under the Optional Protocol, the right protected under Article 27 has been confused with the right of peoples to self-determination proclaimed in Article 1 of the Covenant. Further in reports

---

[8] Article 27 has been the basis for a number of cases which have been brought before the UN Human Rights Committee, see, *e.g. Lovelace v. Canada*, 2 Selected Decisions 28 (1981), a well known case in which the Human Rights Committee concluded in the affirmative that there had been a violation of Article 27. Sandra Lovelace, a Maliseet Indian on marriage to a non-Indian, lost her status as an Indian pursuant to the Canadian Indian Act. As a consequence on the dissolution of her marriage the author was unable to return to the Tobique Indian Reserve. The Committee expressed the view that Sandra Lovelace belonged to a minority within Article 27 and was entitled to claim the benefits of that Article and although the right to live on a reserve as such was not guaranteed by Article 27—the right of Sandra Lovelace to access her native culture and language in community with the other members of her group had been infringed because there was "no place outside the Tobique Reserve where such a Community exists" (para. 15) and that regardless of "[W]hatever may be the merits of the Indian Act in other respects, it does not seem to the Committee that to deny Sandra Lovelace the right to reside on the reserve is reasonable, or necessary to preserve the identity of the tribe." Canada subsequently amended the offending legislation.

In *Kitok v. Sweden*, H.R.C. Report, G.A.O.R., 44th Session, Supp. 271 in which no violation of Article 27 was found, the Committee expressed the view that any restriction upon the right of an individual must be shown to have a reasonable and objective justification and to be necessary for the continued viability and welfare of the minority as a whole, (para. 9.8). See also *Lubicon Lake Band v. Canada*, decision of March 26, 1990, 11 H.R.L.J. [1990] 305; and *McIntyre et al v. Canada*, 14 H.R.L.J. 171 [1993].

[9] UN Doc. A/48/40, Part I 208. Text also reproduced in 15 H.R.L.J. 233 (1994). See also M. Nowak, "The Activities of the UN Human Rights Committee: Developments from August 1, 1992 to July 31, 1995" 16 H.R.L.J. 377 at 379–340 (1995).

submitted by States parties under Article 40 of the Covenant, the obligations placed upon States parties under Article 27 have sometimes been confused with their duty under Article 2(1) to ensure the enjoyment of the rights guaranteed under the Covenant without discrimination and also equality before the law and equal protection of the law under Article 26.

3.1. The Covenant draws a distinction between the right to self-determination and the rights protected under Article 27. The former is expressed to be a right belonging to peoples and is dealt with in a separate part (Part I) of the Covenant. Self-determination is not a right cognisable under the Optional Protocol. Article 27, on the other hand, relates to rights conferred on individuals as such and is included like the articles relating to other personal rights conferred on individuals, in Part III of the Covenant and is cognisable under the Optional Protocol.

3.2. The enjoyment of the rights to which Article 27 relates does not prejudice the sovereignty and territorial integrity of a State party. At the same time, one or other aspect of the rights of individuals protected under that Article—for example to enjoy a particular culture—may consist in such a way of life which is closely associated with territory and use of its resources. This may particularly be true of members of indigenous communities constituting a minority.

4. The Covenant also distinguishes the rights protected under **3–014** Article 27 from the guarantees under Articles 2(1) and 26. The entitlement, under Article 2(1), to enjoy the rights under the Covenant without discrimination applies to all individuals within the territory or under the jurisdiction of the State whether or not those persons belong to a minority. In addition there is a distinct right provided under Article 26 for equality before the law, equal protection of the law and non-discrimination in respect of rights granted and obligations imposed by the States. It governs the exercise of all rights whether protected under the Covenant or not, which the State party confers by law on individuals within its territory or under its jurisdiction, irrespective of whether they belong to the minorities specified in Article 27 or not. Some States parties who claim that they do not discriminate on grounds of ethnicity, language or religion, wrongly contend, on that basis alone, that they have no minorities.

5.1. The terms used in Article 27 indicate that the persons designed to be protected are those who belong to a group and who share in common a culture, a religion and/or a language. Those terms also indicate that the individuals designed to be protected need not be citizens of the State party. In this regard, the obligations deriving from Article 2(1) are also relevant, since a State party is required under that article to ensure that the rights protected under the Covenant are available to all individuals within its territory and subject to its jurisdiction except rights which are expressly made to apply to citizens, for example, political rights under Article 25. A State party may not, therefore, restrict the rights under Article 27 to its citizens alone.

5.2. Article 27 confers rights on persons belonging to minorities which "exist" in a State party. Given the nature and scope of the rights envisaged under that Article it is not relevant to determine the degree of permanence that the term "exist" connotes. Those rights simply are that individuals belonging to those minorities should not be denied the right, in community with members of their group, to enjoy their own culture, to practice their religion and to speak their language. Just as they need not be nationals or citizens, they need not be permanent residents. Thus, migrant workers or even visitors in a State party constituting such minorities are entitled not to be denied the exercise of those rights. As any other individual in the territory of the State party, they would also for this purpose, have the general rights, for example, to freedom of association of assembly, and of expression. The existence of an ethnic, religious or linguistic minority in a given State party does not depend upon a decision by that State party but requires to be establish by objective criteria.

5.3. The right of individuals belonging to a linguistic minority to use their language among themselves in private, or in public, is distinct from other language rights protected under the Covenant. In particular, it should be distinguished from the general right to freedom of expression protected under Article 19. The latter right is available to all persons, irrespective of whether they belong to minorities or not. Further, the right protected under Article 27 should be distinguished from the particular right which Article 14(3)(f) of the Covenant confers on accused persons to interpretation where they cannot understand or speak the language used in the courts. Article 14(3)(f) does not, in any circumstances, confer on accused persons the right to use or speak the language of their choice in court proceedings.

3–015   **6.1.** Although Article 27 is expressed in negative terms, that article, nevertheless, does recognise the existence of a "right" and requires that it shall not be denied. Consequently, a State party is under an obligation to ensure that the existence and the exercise of this right are protected against their denial or violation. Positive measures of protection are common therefore, required not only against the acts of the State party itself, whether through its legislative, judicial or administrative authorities, but also against the acts of other persons within the State party.

6.2. Although the rights protected under Article 27 are individual rights, they depend in turn on the ability of the minority group to maintain its culture, language or religion. Accordingly, the positive measures by States may also be necessary to protect the identity of a minority and the rights of its members to enjoy and develop their culture and language and to practise their religion, in community with the other members of the group. In this connection, it has to be observed that such positive measures must respect the provisions of Articles 2(1) and 26 of the Covenant both as regards the treatment between different minorities and the treatment between the persons belonging to them and the remaining part of the population. However, as long as those measures are aimed at correcting conditions which prevent or impair the enjoyment of the rights guaranteed under Article 27 they may constitute a legitimate differentiation under the Covenant, provided that they are based on reasonable and objective criteria.

7. With regard to the exercise of the cultural rights protected **3–016** under Article 27 the Committee observes that culture manifests itself in many forms, including a particular way of life associated with the use of land resources specially in the case of indigenous peoples. That right may include such traditional activities as fishing or hunting and the right to live reserves protected by law. The enjoyment of those rights may require positive legal measures of protection and measures to ensure the effective participation of members of minority communities in decisions which affect them.

8. The Committee observes that none of the rights protected under Article 27 of the Covenant may be legitimately exercised in a manner or to an extent inconsistent with the other provisions of the Covenant.

9. The Committee concludes that Article 27 relates to rights whose protection imposes specific obligations on States parties. The protection of these rights is directed to ensure the survival and continued development of the cultural, religious and social identity of the minorities concerned, thus enriching the fabric of society as a whole. Accordingly, the Committee observes that these rights must be protected as such and should not be confused with other personal rights conferred on one and all under the Covenant. States parties, therefore, have an obligation to ensure that the exercise of these rights is fully protected and they should indicate in their reports the measures they have adopted to this end.

The 1966 Convention on the Elimination of All Forms of Racial Discrimination heralded a new generation in human rights instruments. The Convention was designed to meet a specific purpose; *viz* it was a response to counter the resurgence of anti-semitism in the Convention entered into force within three years of having been opened for signature.

INTERNATIONAL CONVENTION ON THE ELIMINATION OF ALL FORMS OF RACIAL DISCRIMINATION 1966[10]

3–017 . . . Convinced that any doctrine of superiority based on racial differentiation is scientifically false, morally condemnable, socially unjust and dangerous, and that there is no justification for racial discrimination, in theory or in practice, anywhere,

. . . that discrimination between human beings on the grounds of race, colour or ethnic origin is an obstacle to friendly and peaceful relations among nations and is capable of disturbing peace and security among peoples and the harmony of persons living side by side even within one and the same State,

. . . that the existence of racial barriers is repugnant to the ideals of any human society,

Alarmed by manifestations of racial discrimination still in evidence in some areas of the world . . .

Resolved to adopt all necessary measures for speedily eliminating racial discrimination in all its forms and manifestations, and to prevent and combat racist doctrines and practices in order to promote understanding between races and to build an international community free from all forms of racial segregation and racial discrimination,

. . .

Have agreed as follows:

PART I

Article 1

3–018   **1.** In this Convention, the term "racial discrimination" shall mean any distinction, exclusion, restriction or preference based on race, colour, descent, or national or ethnic origin which has the purpose or effect of nullifying or impairing the recognition, enjoyment or exercise, on an equal footing, of human rights and fundamental freedoms in the political, economic, social, cultural or any other field of public life.

2. This Convention shall not apply to distinctions, exclusions, restrictions or preferences made by a State Party to this Convention between citizens and non-citizens.

3. Nothing in this Convention may be interpreted as affecting in any way the legal provisions of States Parties concerning nationality, citizenship or naturalisation, provided that such provisions do not discriminate against any particular nationality.

[10] U.N.T.S. No. 195; U.K.T.S. 77 (1969), Cmnd 4108; 60 A.S.I.L. 650 (1966); 5 I.L.M. 352. The Convention entered into force 1969 and as of December 31, 1995 there were 150 Contracting Parties. The Convention was preceded by the United Nations Declaration on the Elimination of All Forms of Racial Discrimination of November 20, 1963 (G.A. Res. 1904 (XVIII)).

4. Special measures taken for the sole purpose of securing adequate advancement of certain racial or ethnic groups or individuals requiring such protection as may be necessary in order to ensure such groups or individuals equal enjoyment or exercise of human rights and fundamental freedoms shall not be deemed racial discrimination, provided, however, that such measures do not, as a consequence, lead to the maintenance of separate rights for different racial groups and that they shall not be continued after the objectives for which they were taken have been achieved.[11]

"Racial discrimination" is broadly defined but does not include discrimination on grounds of religion or nationality. Note for the activity to be characterised as discriminatory under the Convention it must have the *purpose or effect* (emphasis added) of impairing the individual's human rights.

Committee on the Elimination of Racial Discrimination (CERD) General Recommendation VIII (38th session) 1990[12]

The Committee on the Elimination of Racial Discrimination, 3–019 having considered the reports from States parties concerning information the ways in which individuals are identified has as being members of a particular racial or ethnic group or groups, is of the opinion that such identification shall, if no justification exists to the contrary be based upon self-identification of the individual concerned.

(CERD) General Recommendation XIV (42nd session) 1994 Article 1, Paragraph 1 of the Convention

. . .

2. The Committee observes that a differentiation of treatment 3–020 will not constitute the discrimination for such differentiation judged against the objectives and purposes of the Convention are legitimate or fall within the scope of Article 1, paragraph 4, of the Convention. In considering the criteria that may have been employed the Committee will acknowledge that particular actions may have varied purposes. In seeking to determine whether an action has an effect contrary to the Convention, it will look to see whether that action has an unjustifiable disparate impact upon a group distinguished by race, colour, descent, or national or ethnic origin . . .

---

[11] *i.e.* affirmative action.
[12] UN Doc. A/45/18.

Article 2[13]

3–021   **1.** States Parties condemn racial discrimination and undertake to pursue by all appropriate means and without delay a policy of eliminating racial discrimination in all its forms and promoting understanding among all races, and, to this end:

(a) Each State Party undertakes to engage in no act or practice of racial discrimination against persons, groups of persons or institutions and to ensure that all public authorities and public institutions, national and local, shall act in conformity with this obligation;

(b) Each State Party undertakes not to sponsor, defend or support racial discrimination by any persons or organisations;

(c) Each State Party shall take effective measures to review governmental, national and local policies, and to amend, rescind or nullify any laws and regulations which have the effect of creating or perpetuating racial discrimination wherever it exists;

(d) Each State Party shall prohibit and bring to an end, by all appropriate means, including legislation as required by circumstances, racial discrimination by any persons, group or organisation;

(e) Each State Party undertakes to encourage, where appropriate, integrationist multi-racial organisations and movements and other means of eliminating barriers between races, and to discourage anything which tends to strengthen racial division.

3–022   **2.** States Parties shall, when the circumstances so warrant, take, in the social, economic, cultural and other fields, special and concrete measures to ensure the adequate development and protection of certain racial groups or individuals belonging to them, for the purpose of guaranteeing them the full and equal enjoyment of human rights and fundamental freedoms. These measures shall in no case entail as a consequence the maintenance of unequal or separate rights for different racial groups after the objectives for which they were taken have been achieved.

Article 3

States Parties particularly condemn racial segregation and apartheid and undertake to prevent, prohibit and eradicate all practices of this nature in territories under their jurisdiction.

---

[13] Obligation on Contracting parties. Essentially the obligation incumbent on States party to the Convention is to neither practise nor encourage discrimination.

Article 4

States Parties condemn all propaganda and all organisations 3–023 which are based on ideas or theories of superiority of one race or group of persons of one colour or ethnic origin, or which attempt to justify or promote racial hatred and discrimination in any form, and undertake to adopt immediate and positive measures designed to eradicate all incitement to, or acts of, such discrimination and, to this end, with due regard to the principles embodied in the Universal Declaration of Human Rights and the rights expressly set forth in Article 5 of this Convention, *inter alia*:

(a) Shall declare an offence punishable by law all dissemination of ideas based on racial superiority or hatred, incitement to racial discrimination, as well as all acts of violence or incitement to such acts against any race or group of persons of another colour or ethnic origin, and also the provision of any assistance to racist activities, including the financing thereof;

(b) Shall declare illegal and prohibit organisations, and also organised and all other propaganda activities, which promote and incite racial discrimination, and shall recognise participation in such organisations or activities as an offence punishable by law;

(c) Shall not permit public authorities or public institutions, national or local, to promote or incite racial discrimination.

(CERD) General Recommendation XV (42nd session) Article 4 of the Convention

1. When the International Convention on all Forms of Racial 3–024 Discrimination was being adopted Article 4 was regarded as central to the struggle against racial discrimination. At that time, there was a widespread of the revival of authoritarian ideologies. The proscription of the dissemination of ideas of racial superiority, and of organised activity likely to incite persons to racial violence, was properly regarded as crucial. Since that time, the Committee has received evidence of organised violence based on ethnic origin and the political exploitation of ethnic difference. As a result, implementation of Article 4 is of increased importance . . .

4. In the opinion of the Committee, the prohibition of the dissemination of all ideas based upon racial superiority or hatred is compatible with the right to freedom of opinion and expression. This right is embodied in Article 19 of the Universal Declaration of Human Rights and is recalled in Article 5(d)(viii)

of the International Convention on the Elimination of All Forms
of Racial Discrimination. Its relevance to Article 4 is noted in the
Article itself. The citizen's exercise of this right carries special
duties and responsibilities, specified in Article 29, paragraph 2, of
the Universal Declaration, among which the obligation not to
disseminate racist ideas is of particular importance. The Committee wishes, furthermore, to draw to the attention to States
parties Article 20 of the International Covenant on Civil and
Political Rights, according to which any advocacy of national,
racial, or religious hatred that constitutes incitement to discrimination, hostility or violence shall be prohibited by law . . .

Article 5

3–025 In compliance with the fundamental obligations laid down in
Article 2 of this Convention, States Parties undertake to prohibit
and to eliminate racial discrimination in all its forms and to
guarantee the right of everyone, without distinction as to race,
colour, or national or ethnic origin, to equality before the law,
notably in the enjoyment of the following rights:

(a) The right to equal treatment before the tribunals and all
other organs administering justice;

(b) The right to security of person and protection by the State
against violence or bodily harm, whether inflicted by government officials or by any individual, group or institution;

(c) Political rights, in particular the rights to participate in
elections—to vote and to stand for election—on the basis of
universal and equal suffrage, to take part in the government as well as in the conduct of public affairs at any level
and to have equal access to public service;

(d) Other civil rights, in particular:

(i) The right to freedom of movement and residence
within the border of the State;

(ii) The right to leave any country, including one's own,
and to return to one's country;

(iii) The right to nationality;

(iv) The right to marriage and choice of spouse;

(v) The right to own property alone as well as in
association with others;

(vi) The right to inherit;

(vii) The right to freedom of thought, conscience and
religion;

(viii) The right to freedom of opinion and expression;

(ix) The right to freedom of peaceful assembly and
association;

(e) Economic, social and cultural rights, in particular:

    (i) The rights to work, to free choice of employment, to just and favourable conditions of work, to protection against unemployment, to equal pay for equal work, to just and favourable remuneration;

    (ii) The right to form and join trade unions;

    (iii) The right to housing;

    (iv) The right to public health, medical care, social security and social services;

    (v) The right to education and training;

    (vi) The right to equal participation in cultural activities;

(f) The right of access to any place or service intended for use by the general public, such as transport, hotels, restaurants, cafes, theatres and parks.

(CERD) General Recommendation XX (48th Session) 1996 on Article 5[14]

1. Article 5 of the Convention contains the obligation of States 3–026 parties to guarantee the enjoyment of civil, political, economic, social and cultural rights and freedoms without racial discrimination. Note should be taken that the rights and freedoms mentioned in Article 5 do not constitute an exhaustive list. At the head of these rights and freedoms are those deriving from the Charter of the United Nations and the Universal Declaration of Human Rights, as recalled in the preamble to the Convention. Most of these rights have been elaborated in the Covenants. All States parties are therefore obliged to acknowledge and protect the enjoyment of human rights, but the manner in which these obligations are translated into the legal orders of States parties may differ. Article 5 of the Convention, apart from requiring a guarantee that the exercise of human rights shall be free from racial discrimination, does not of itself create civil, political, economic, social or cultural rights, but assumes the existence and recognition of these rights. The Convention obliges States to prohibit and eliminate racial discrimination in the enjoyment of such human rights.

2. Whenever a State imposes a restriction upon one of the rights listed in Article 5 of the Convention which applies ostensibly to all within its jurisdiction, it must ensure that the restriction, neither in purpose nor effect, is incompatible with Article 1 of the Convention as an integral part of international human rights standards. To ascertain whether this is the case, the Committee is obliged to inquire further to make sure that any such restriction does not entail racial discrimination.

[14] UN Doc. CERD/48/Misc. 6/Rev. 2.

3. Many of the rights and freedoms mentioned in Article 5 are to be enjoyed by all persons living in a given State, such as the right to equal treatment before tribunals; some others are the rights of citizens, such as the rights to participate in elections, to vote, and to stand for election.

4. The States parties are recommended to report about the non-discriminatory implementation of each of the rights and freedoms referred to in Article 5 of the Convention one by one.

5. The rights and freedoms referred to in Article 5 of the Convention and any similar rights shall be protected by a State party. Such protection may be achieved in different ways, be it by the use of public institutions or through the activities of private institutions. In any case it is the obligation of the State party concerned to ensure the effective implementation of the Convention and to report thereon under Article 9 of the Convention. To the extent that private institutions influence the exercise of rights or the availability of opportunities, the State party must ensure that the result has neither the purpose nor the effect of creating or perpetuating racial discrimination.

(CERD) General Recommendation XIII (42nd Session) 1993—the training of law enforcement officials in the protection of human rights

. . .

3–027   **2.** The fulfilment of these obligations very much depends upon national law enforcement officials who exercise police powers especially the powers of detention or arrest, and upon whether they are properly informed about the obligations their State has entered into under the Convention. Law enforcement officials should receive intensive training to ensure that in the performance of their duties they respect as well as protect human dignity and maintain and uphold the human rights of all persons without distinction as to race, colour or national or ethnic origin . . .

3. In the implementation of Article 7 of the Convention, the Committee calls upon State parties to review and improve the training of law enforcement officials . . .

(CERD) General Recommendation XVII[15]

The Establishment of national institutions to facilitate the implementation of the Convention

3–028 The Committee on the elimination of Racial Discrimination,

Considering the practice of States parties concerning the implementation of the International Convention on the Elimination of All Forms of Racial Discrimination,

---

[15] 42nd Session, 1993.

Convinced of the necessity to encourage further the establishment of national institutions to facilitate the implementation of the Convention,

Emphasising the need to strengthen further the implementation of the Convention,

1. Recommends that States parties establish national commissions of other appropriate bodies,

(a) To promote respect for the enjoyment of human rights without any discrimination as expressly set out in Article 5 of the International Convention on the Elimination of All Forms of Discrimination;

(b) To review government policy towards protection against discrimination;

(c) To monitor legislative compliance with the provisions of the Convention;

(d) To educate the public about the obligations of States parties under the Convention;

(e) To assist the Government in the preparation of reports submitted to the Committee on the Elimination of Racial Discrimination.

2. Also recommends that, where such commissions have been established, they should be associated with the preparation of reports and possibly included in government delegations in order to intensify the dialogue between the Committee and the State party concerned.

Article 6

States Parties shall assure to everyone within their jurisdiction 3–029 effective protection and remedies, through the competent national tribunals and other State institutions, against any acts of racial discrimination which violate his human rights and fundamental freedoms contrary to this Convention, as well as the right to seek from such tribunals just and adequate reparation or satisfaction for any damage suffered as a result of such discrimination.

Article 7

States Parties undertake to adopt immediate and effective measures, particularly in the fields of teaching, education, culture and information, with a view to combating prejudices which lead to racial discrimination and to promoting understanding, tolerance and friendship among nations and racial or ethnical groups, as well as to propagating the purposes and principles of the Charter of the United Nations, the Universal Declaration of Human Rights, the United Nations Declaration on the Elimination of All Forms of Racial Discrimination, and this Convention.

Minorities and self-determination. The following recommendation was adopted by the Committee for the Elimination of Racial Discrimination in March 1996.

(CERD) General Recommendation XXI (1996) on Self-Determination[16]

3–030   **1.** The Committee notes that ethnic or religious groups or minorities frequently refer to the right of self-determination as a basis for an alleged right to secession. In this connection the Committee wishes to express the following views:

2. The right to self-determination of peoples is a fundamental principle of international law. It is enshrined in Article 1 of the Charter of the United Nations, in Article 1 of the International Covenant on Economic, Social, and Cultural Rights and Article 1 of the International Covenant on Civil and Political Rights, as well as in other international human rights instruments. The International Covenant on Civil and Political Rights provides for the rights of peoples to self-determination besides the right of ethnic, religious, or linguistic minorities to enjoy their own culture, to profess and practice their own religion or to use their own language.

3. The Committee emphasises that in accordance with the Declaration of the United Nations General Assembly 2625 (XXV) of October 24, 1970 on Principles of International Law Concerning Friendly Relations and Co-operation among States in accordance with the Charter of the United Nations it is the duty of States to promote the right to self-determination of peoples. But the implementation of the principle of self-determination requires every State to promote, through joint and separate action, universal respect for and observance of human rights and fundamental freedoms in accordance with the Charter of the United Nations. In this context the Committee draws the attention of governments to the General Assembly Declaration on the Rights of Persons Belonging to National or Ethnic, Religious, and Linguistic Minorities.

3–031   **4.** In respect of the self-determination of peoples two aspects have to be distinguished. The right to self-determination of peoples has an internal aspect, *i.e.* the rights of all peoples to pursue freely their economic, social and cultural development without outside interference. In that respect there exists a link with the right of every citizen to take part in the conduct of public

---

[16] UN Doc. CERD/48/Misc. 7/Rev. 3 (48th Session, 1996) adopted on March 8, 1996.

affairs at any level as referred to in Article 5(c) of the International Convention on the Elimination of All Forms of Racial Discrimination. In consequence, governments are to represent the whole population without distinction as to race, colour, descent, national, or ethnic origins. The external aspect of self-determination implies that all peoples have the right to determine freely their political status and their place in the international community based upon the principle of equal rights and exemplified by the liberation of peoples from colonialism and by the prohibition to subject peoples to alien subjugation, domination, and exploitation.

5. In order to respect fully the rights of all peoples within a state, governments are again called upon to adhere to and implement fully the international human rights instruments and in particular the International Convention on the Elimination of All Forms of Racial Discrimination. Concern for the protection of individual rights without discrimination on racial, ethnic, tribal, religious, or other grounds must guide the policies of governments. In accordance with Article 2 of the International Convention on the Elimination of All Forms of Racial Discrimination and other relevant international documents, governments should be sensitive towards the rights of persons of ethnic groups, particularly their right to lead lives of dignity, to preserve their culture, to share equitably in the fruits of national growth, and to play their part in the government of the country of which its members are citizens. Also, governments should consider, within their respective constitutional frameworks, vesting persons of ethnic or linguistic groups comprised of their citizens, where appropriate, with the right to engage in such activities which are particularly relevant to the preservation of the identity of such persons or groups.

6. The Committee emphasises that, in accordance with the Declaration of the General Assembly on Friendly Relations, none of Committee's actions shall be construed as authorising or encouraging any action which would dismember or impair, totally or in part, the territorial integrity or political unity of sovereign and independent states conducting themselves in compliance with the principle of equal rights and self-determination of peoples and possessing a government representing the whole people belonging to the territory without distinction as to race, creed or colour. In view of the Committee international law has not recognised a general right of peoples to unilaterally declare secession from a state. In this respect, the Committee follows the views expressed in the Agenda for Peace (paras 17 *et seq.*), namely that a fragmentation of States may be detrimental to the protection of human rights as well as to the preservation of peace and security. This does not, however, exclude the possibility of

arrangements reached by free agreements of all parties
concerned.

PART II

Article 8

3–032   **1.** There shall be established a Committee on the Elimination of
Racial Discrimination (hereinafter referred to as the Committee)
consisting of 18 experts of high moral standing and acknowledged impartiality elected by States Parties from among their
nationals, who shall serve in their personal capacity, consideration being given to equitable geographical distribution and to the
representation of the different forms of civilisation as well as of
the principal legal systems.

2. The members of the Committee shall be elected by secret
ballot from a list of persons nominated by the States Parties. Each
State Party may nominate one person from among its own
nationals.

3. The initial election shall be held six months after the date of
the entry into force of this Convention. At least three months
before the date of each election the Secretary-General of the
United Nations shall address a letter to the States Parties inviting
them to submit their nominations within two months. The
Secretary-General shall prepare a list in alphabetical order of all
persons thus nominated, indicating the States Parties which have
nominated them, and shall submit it to the States Parties.

3–033   **4.** Elections of the members of the Committee shall be held at a
meeting of States Parties convened by the Secretary-General at
United Nations Headquarters. At that meeting, for which two-
thirds of the States Parties shall constitute a quorum, the persons
elected to the Committee shall be those nominees who obtain the
largest number of votes and an absolute majority of the votes of
the representatives of States Parties present and voting.

5. (a) The members of the Committee shall be elected for a term
of four years. However, the terms of nine of the members
elected at the first election shall expire at the end of two
years; immediately after the first election the names of these
nine members shall be chosen by lot by the Chairman of the
Committee.

(b) For the filling of casual vacancies, the State Party whose
expert has ceased to function as a member of the Committee shall appoint another expert from among its
nationals, subject to the approval of the Committee.

6. States Parties shall be responsible for the expenses of the
members of the Committee while they are in performance of
Committee duties.

NOTE: This has resulted in considerable financial problems for the CRED as Contracting Parties have fallen behind in their contributions.

Article 9

1. States Parties undertake to submit to the Secretary-General of the United Nations, for consideration by the Committee, a report on the legislative, judicial, administrative or other measures which they have adopted and which give effect to the provisions of this Convention: (a) within one year after the entry into force of the Convention for the State concerned; and (b) thereafter every two years and whenever the Committee so requests. The Committee may request further information from the States Parties. *NOTE*: The Committee subsequently decided that "comprehensive reports" require to be submitted by contracting Parties every four years and that "brief updating reports" are adequate on each "intervening period"[17]].

2. The Committee shall report annually, through the Secretary-General, to the General Assembly of the United Nations on its activities and may make suggestions and general recommendations based on the examination of the reports and information received from the States Parties. Such suggestions and general recommendations[18] shall be reported to the General Assembly together with comments, if any, from States Parties.

(CERD) General Recommendation XVI[19] application of Article 9 of the Convention

1. Under Article 9 . . ., States Parties have undertaken to submit, through the Secretary-General of the United Nations, for consideration by the Committee, reports on measures taken by them to give effect tot he provisions of the Convention.

2. With respect to this obligation of the States Parties, the Committee has noted that, on some occasions, reports have made references to situations existing in other States.

3. For this reason, the Committee wishes to remind States Parties of the provisions of Article 9 . . . concerning the contents of their reports, while bearing in mind Article 11, which is the only procedure available to States for drawing to the attention of the Committee situations in which they consider that some other State is not giving effect to the provisions of the Convention.

Article 10

1. The Committee shall adopt its own rules of procedure.

3–034

3–035

3–036

---

[17] CERD Report, G.A.O.R. 43rd Session, Supp. 18.
[18] To date the Committee has issued 27 General Recommendations.
[19] 42nd Session, 1993.

2. The Committee shall elect its officers for a term of two years.

3. The Secretariat of the Committee shall be provided by the Secretary-General of the United Nations.

4. The meetings of the Committee shall normally be held at United Nations Headquarters.

Article 11[20]

3–037　1. If a State Party considers that another State Party is not giving effect to the provisions of this Convention, it may bring the matter to the attention of the Committee. The Committee shall then transmit the communication to the State Party concerned. Within three months, the receiving State shall submit to the Committee written explanations or statements clarifying the matter and the remedy, if any, that may have been taken by that State.

2. If the matter is not adjusted to the satisfaction of both parties, either by bilateral negotiations or by any other procedure open to them, within six months after the receipt by the receiving State of the initial communication, either State shall have the right to refer the matter again to the Committee by notifying the Committee and also the other State.

3. The Committee shall deal with a matter referred to it in accordance with paragraph 2 of this article after it has ascertained that all available domestic remedies have been invoked and exhausted in the case, in conformity with the generally recognised principles of international law. This shall not be the rule where the application of the remedies is unreasonably prolonged.

4. In any matter referred to it, the Committee may call upon the States Parties concerned to supply any other relevant information.

5. When any matter arising out of this article is being considered by the Committee, the States Parties concerned shall be entitled to send a representative to take part in the proceedings of the Committee, without voting rights, while the matter is under consideration.

Article 12

3–038　1.(a) After the Committee has obtained and collated all the information it deems necessary, the Chairman shall appoint an ad hoc Conciliation Commission (hereinafter referred to as the Commission) comprising five persons who may or may not be members of the Committee. The members of the Commission shall be appointed with the unanimous

---

[20] Article 11 creates a system of interstate application. To date there have been no such applications.

consent of the parties to the dispute, and its good offices shall be made available to the States concerned with a view to an amicable solution of the matter on the basis of respect for this Convention.

(b) If the States Parties to the dispute fail to reach agreement within three months on all or part of the composition of the Commission, the members of the Commission not agreed upon by the States Parties to the dispute shall be elected by secret ballot by a two-thirds majority vote of the Committee from among its own members.

2. The members of the Commission shall serve in their personal capacity. They shall not be nationals of the States Parties to the dispute or of a State not Party to this Convention.

3. The Commission shall elect its own Chairman and adopt its own rules of procedure.

4. The meetings of the Commission shall normally be held at United Nations Headquarters or at any other convenient place as determined by the Commission.

5. The secretariat provided in accordance with Article 10, 3–039 paragraph 3, of this Convention shall also service the Commission whenever a dispute among States Parties brings the Commission into being.

6. The States Parties to the dispute shall share equally all the expenses of the members of the Commission in accordance with estimates to be provided by the Secretary-General of the United Nations.

7. The Secretary-General shall be empowered to pay the expenses of the members of the Commission, if necessary, before reimbursement by the States Parties to the dispute in accordance with paragraph 6 of this article.

8. The information obtained and collated by the Committee shall be made available to the Commission, and the Commission may call upon the States concerned to supply any other relevant information.

Article 13

1. When the Commission has fully considered the matter, it 3–040 shall prepare and submit to the Chairman of the Committee a report embodying its findings on all questions of fact relevant to the issue between the parties and containing such recommendations as it may think proper for the amicable solution of the dispute.

2. The Chairman of the Committee shall communicate the report of the Commission to each of the States Parties to the dispute. These States shall, within three months, inform the

Chairman of the Committee whether or not they accept the recommendations contained in the report of the Commission.

3. After the period provided for in paragraph 2 of this article, the Chairman of the Committee shall communicate the report of the Commission and the declarations of the States Parties concerned to the other States Parties to this Convention.[21]

Article 14[22]

3–041 **1.** A State Party may at any time declare that it recognises the competence of the Committee to receive and consider communications from individuals or groups of individuals within its jurisdiction claiming to be victims of a violation by that State Party of any of the rights set forth in this Convention. No communication shall be received by the Committee if it concerns a State Party which has not made such a declaration.

2. Any State Party which makes a declaration as provided for in paragraph 1 of this article may establish or indicate a body within its national legal order which shall be competent to receive and consider petitions from individuals and groups of individuals within its jurisdiction who claim to be victims of a violation of any of the rights set forth in this Convention and who have exhausted other available local remedies.

3. A declaration made in accordance with paragraph 1 of this article and the name of any body established or indicated in accordance with paragraph 2 of this article shall be deposited by the State Party concerned with the Secretary-General of the United Nations, who shall transmit copies thereof to the other States Parties. A declaration may be withdrawn at any time by notification to the Secretary-General, but such a withdrawal shall not affect communications pending before the Committee.

3–042 **4.** A register of petitions shall be kept by the body established or indicated in accordance with paragraph 2 of this article, and

---

[21] [The findings and any recommendations made are not binding upon the States involved].

[22] *i.e.* Article 14 creates an optional system of individual communication. Currently 34 States have made a declaration under Article 14. Article 14(7) demands that domestic remedies must be fully exhausted. The first individual communication which successfully invoked the Article 14 procedure was *Yilmaz-Dogan v. Netherlands*, decision of August 10, 1988, CERD Report, G.A.O.R., 43rd Session, Supp. 18, p. 59 (1988). In its decision the CERD held that the petitioner had not been afforded protection in respect of her right to work as provided for in Article 5(e) of the Convention. The Committee's opinion is not binding. The suggestion put to the Netherlands by the Committee was that if Ms Yilmaz Dogan was found not to be gainfully employed that "it (*i.e.* the Netherlands) uses its good offices to secure alternative employment for her, and/or to provide her such other relief as may be considered equitable". Ms Yilmaz Dogan received £3,000 compensation. Other individual communications which have come before the Committee are: *D.T. Diop v. France*, Opinion of March 18, 1991, 12 H.R.L.J. 301 (1991); *LK v. The Netherlands*, Opinion of March 16, 1993, 14 H.R.L.J. 249 (1993); *Narrainen v. Norway*, Communication No. 3/1991, Opinion of March 15, 1994, UN Doc. A/49/18.

certified copies of the register shall be filed annually through appropriate channels with the Secretary-General on the under-standing that the contents shall not be publicly disclosed.

5. In the event of failure to obtain satisfaction from the body established or indicated in accordance with paragraph 2 of this article, the petitioner shall have the right to communicate the matter to the Committee within six months.

6. (a) The Committee shall confidentially bring any communica-tion referred to it to the attention of the State Party alleged to be violating any provision of this Convention, but the identity of the individual or groups of individuals con-cerned shall not be revealed without his or their express consent. The Committee shall not receive anonymous communications.

   (b) Within three months, the receiving State shall submit to the Committee written explanations or statements clarifying the matter and the remedy, if any, that may have been taken by that State.

7. (a) The Committee shall consider communications in the light of all information made available to it by the State Party concerned and by the petitioner. The Committee shall not consider any communication from a petitioner unless it has ascertained that the petitioner has exhausted all available domestic remedies. However, this shall not be the rule where the application of the remedies is unreasonably prolonged.

   (b) The Committee shall forward its suggestions and recom-mendations, if any, to the State Party concerned and to the petitioner.

8. The Committee shall include in its annual report a summary of such communications and, where appropriate, a summary of the explanations and statements of the States Parties concerned and of its own suggestions and recommendations.

9. The Committee shall be competent to exercise the functions provided for in this article only when at least ten States Parties to this Convention are bound by declarations in accordance with paragraph I of this article.

Article 15

1. Pending the achievement of the objectives of the Declaration 3–043 on the Granting of Independence to Colonial Countries and Peoples, contained in General Assembly Resolution 1514 (XV) of December 14, 1960,[23] the provisions of this Convention shall in no

[23] G.A. Res. 15/1514, G.A.O.R. 15th Session, Supp. 16, p. 66 (1960).

way limit the right of petition granted to these peoples by other international instruments or by the United Nations and its specialised agencies.

2. (a) The Committee established under Article 8, paragraph 1, of this Convention shall receive copies of the petitions from, and submit expressions of opinion and recommendations on these petitions to, the bodies of the United Nations which deal with matters directly related to the principles and objectives of this Convention in their consideration of petitions from the inhabitants of Trust and Non-Self-Governing Territories and all other territories to which General Assembly Resolution 1514 (XV) applies, relating to matters covered by this Convention which are before these bodies.

(b) The Committee shall receive from the competent bodies of the United Nations copies of the reports concerning the legislative, judicial, administrative or other measures directly related to the principles and objectives of this Convention applied by the administering Powers within the Territories mentioned in sub-paragraph (a) of this paragraph, and shall express opinions and make recommendations to these bodies.

3. The Committee shall include in its report to the General Assembly a summary of the petitions and reports it has received from United Nations bodies, and the expressions of opinion and recommendations of the Committee relating to the said petitions and reports.

4. The Committee shall request from the Secretary-General of the United Nations all information relevant to the objectives of this Convention and available to him regarding the Territories mentioned in paragraph 2 (a) of this article.

Article 16

3–044 The provisions of this Convention concerning the settlement of disputes or complaints shall be applied without prejudice to other procedures for settling disputes or complaints in the field of discrimination laid down in the constituent instruments of, or in conventions adopted by, the United Nations and its specialised agencies, and shall not prevent the States Parties from having recourse to other procedures for settling a dispute in accordance with general or special international agreements in force between them.

Article 22

Any dispute between two or more States Parties with respect to the interpretation or application of this Convention, which is not settled by negotiation or by the procedures expressly provided for in this Convention, shall, at the request of any of the parties to the dispute, be referred to the International Court of Justice for decision, unless the disputants agree to another mode of settlement.

NOTE: A number of States, over 20, have made reservations to Article 22.[24]

DECLARATION ON THE ELIMINATION OF ALL FORMS OF RELIGIOUS INTOLERANCE[25]

The General Assembly,   **3–045**

Recalling that all States have pledged themselves, under the Charter of the United Nations, to promote and encourage universal respect for and observance of human rights and fundamental freedoms for all without distinction as to race, sex, language or religion,

Recognising that those rights derive from the inherent dignity of the human person,

Reaffirming that discrimination against human beings on the grounds of religion or belief constitutes an affront to human dignity and a disavowal of the principles of the Charter,

. . .

Reaffirming the call of the World Conference on Human Rights for all governments to take all appropriate measures in compliance with their international obligations and with due regard to their respective legal systems to counter intolerance and related violence based on religion or belief, including practices of discrimination against women and the desecration of religious sites, recognising that every individual has the right to freedom of thought, conscience, expression and religion,

. . .

---

[24] *Article 20* (1). The Secretary-General of the United Nations shall receive and circulate to all States which are or may become Parties to this Convention reservations made by States at the time of ratification or acession. Any State which objects to the reservation shall, within a period of ninety days from the date from the date of the said communication, notify the Secretary-General that it does not accept it.

2. A reservation incompatible with the object and purpose of this Convention shall not be permitted, nor shall a reservation the effect of which would inhibit the operation of any of the bodies established by this Convention be allowed. A reservation shall be considered incompatible or inhibitive if at least two-thirds of the States Parties to this Convention object to it.

3. Reservations may be withdrawn at any time by notification to this effect addressed to the Secretary-General. Such notification shall take effect on the date on which it is received.

[25] A/RES/48/128, December, 20 1993. This Resolution reaffirmed an earlier resolution 36/55 November, 1981, G.A.O.R. 36 Session, Supp. 51, p. 171 (1981) which called for the elimination of intolerance and of discrimination on religion or belief.

Reaffirming the dismay and condemnation expressed by the World Conference on Human Rights at the continued occurrence of gross and systematic violations and situations that constitute serious obstacles to the full enjoyment of all human rights, including religious intolerance,

Believing that further efforts are therefore required to promote and protect the right to freedom of thought, conscience, religion and belief and to eliminate all forms of hatred, intolerance and discrimination based on religion or belief,

3–046   1. Reaffirms that freedom of thought, conscience, religion and belief is a human right derived from the inherent dignity of the human person and guaranteed to all without discrimination;

2. Urges States to ensure that their constitutional and legal systems provide full guarantees of freedom of thought, conscience, religion and belief, including the provision of effective remedies where there is intolerance or discrimination based on religion or belief;

3. Recognises that legislation alone is not enough to prevent violations of human rights, including the right to freedom of religion or belief;

4. Urges all States therefore to take all appropriate measures to combat hatred, intolerance and acts of violence, including those motivated by religious extremism, and to encourage understanding, tolerance and respect in matters relating to freedom of religion or belief;

3–047   5. Urges States to ensure that, in the course of their official duties, members of law enforcement bodies, civil servants, educators and other public officials respect different religions and beliefs and do not discriminate against persons professing other religions or beliefs;

6. Calls upon all States to recognise, as provided in the Declaration on the Elimination of All Forms of Intolerance and of Discrimination Based on Religion or Belief, the right of all persons to worship or assemble in connection with a religion or belief, and to establish and maintain places for those purposes;

7. Also calls upon all States in accordance with their national legislation to exert utmost efforts to ensure that religious places and shrines are fully respected and protected;

8. Considers it desirable to enhance the promotional and public information activities of the United Nations in matters relating to freedom of religion or belief and to ensure that appropriate measures are taken to this end in the World Public Information Campaign for Human Rights;

3–048   9. Invites the Secretary-General to continue to give high priority to the dissemination of the text of the Declaration, in all the official languages of the United Nations, and to take all appropriate measures to make the text available for use by the United Nations information centres, as well as by other interested bodies;

10. Encourages the continuing efforts on the part of the Special Rapporteur appointed to examine incidents and governmental actions in all parts of the world that are incompatible with the provisions of the Declaration and to recommend remedial measures as appropriate;

11. Encourages governments to give serious consideration to inviting the Special Rapporteur to visit their countries so as to enable him to fulfil his mandate even more effectively;

12. Recommends that the promotion and protection of the right to freedom of thought, conscience and religion be given appropriate priority in the work of the United Nations programme of advisory services in the field of human rights, including work on the drafting of basic legal texts in conformity with international instruments on human rights and taking into account the provisions of the Declaration;

13. Notes with interest the adoption by the Human Rights 3–049 Committee of a general comment on Article 18 of the International Covenant on Civil and Political Rights, dealing with freedom of thought, conscience and religion[26];

14. Welcomes the efforts of non-governmental organisations to promote the implementation of the Declaration;

15. Requests the Secretary-General to invite interested non-governmental organisations to consider what further role they could envisage playing in the implementation of the Declaration and in its dissemination in national and local languages;

16. Urges all States to consider disseminating the text of the Declaration in their respective national languages and to facilitate its dissemination in national and local languages;

17. Requests the Commission on Human Rights to continue its consideration of measures to implement the Declaration;

18. Decides to consider the question of the elimination of all forms of religious intolerance at its 49th session under the item entitled Human Rights Questions.

DECLARATION ON THE ELIMINATION OF ALL FORMS OF INTOLERANCE AND OF DISCRIMINATION BASED ON RELIGION OR BELIEF 1981[27]

Article 1

1. Everyone shall have the right to freedom of thought, cons- 3–050 cience and religion. This right shall include freedom to have a religion or whatever belief of his choice, and freedom, either

---

[26] See *supra* n. 5.
[27] G.A. Res. 36/55, G.A.O.R., 36th Session, Supp. 51, p. 171 (1981).

individually or in community with others and in public or private,to manifest his religion or belief in worship, observance, practice and teaching.

2. No one shall be subject to coercion which would impair his freedom to have a religion or belief of his choice.

3. Freedom to manifest one's religion or beliefs may be subject only to such limitations as are prescribed by law and are necessary to protect public safety, order, health or morals or the fundamental rights and freedoms of others.

Article 2

1. No one shall be subject to discrimination by any State, institution, group of persons, or person on grounds of religion or other beliefs.

2. For the purposes of the present Declaration, the expression "intolerance and discrimination based on religion or belief" means any distinction, exclusion, restriction or preference based on religion or belief and having as its purpose or as its effect nullification or impairment of the recognition, enjoyment or exercise of human rights and fundamental freedoms on an equal basis.

Article 3

3–051 Discrimination between human beings on grounds of religion or belief constitutes an affront to human dignity and a disavowal of the principles of the Charter of the United Nations, and shall be condemned as a violation of the human rights and fundamental freedoms proclaimed in the Universal Declaration of Human Rights and enunciated in detail in the International Covenants on Human Rights, and as an obstacle to friendly and peaceful relations between nations.

Article 4

1. All States shall take effective measures to prevent and eliminate discrimination on the grounds of religion or belief in the recognition, exercise and enjoyment of human rights and fundamental freedoms in all fields of civil, economic, political, social and cultural life.

2. All States shall make all efforts to enact or rescind legislation where necessary to prohibit any such discrimination, and to take all appropriate measures to combat intolerance on the grounds of religion or other beliefs in this matter.

Article 5

3–052 **1.** The parents or, as the case may be, the legal guardians of the child have the right to organise the life within the family in accordance with their religion or belief and bearing in mind the moral education in which they believe the child should be brought up.

2. Every child shall enjoy the right to have access to education in the matter of religion or belief in accordance with the wishes of his parents or, as the case may be, legal guardians, and shall not be compelled to receive teaching on religion or belief against the wishes of his parents or legal guardians, the best interests of the child being the guiding principle.

3. The child shall be protected from any form of discrimination on the ground of religion or belief. He shall be brought up in a spirit of understanding, tolerance, friendship among peoples, peace and universal brotherhood, respect for freedom of religion or belief of others, and in full consciousness that his energy and talents should be devoted to the service of his fellow men.

4. In the case of a child who is not under the care either of his parents or of legal guardians, due account shall be taken of their expressed wishes or of any other proof of their wishes in the matter of religion or belief, the best interests of the child being the guiding principle.

5. Practices of a religion or beliefs in which a child is brought up must not be injurious to his physical or mental health or to his full development, taking into account Article 1, paragraph 3, of the present Declaration.

Article 6

In accordance with Article 1 of the present Declaration, and **3–053** subject to the provisions of Article 1, paragraph 3, the right to freedom of thought, conscience, religion or belief shall include, *inter alia*, the following freedoms:

   (a) To worship or assemble in connection with a religion or belief, and to establish and maintain places for these purposes;

   (b) To establish and maintain appropriate charitable or humanitarian institutions;

   (c) To make, acquire and use to an adequate extent the necessary articles and materials related to the rites or customs of a religion or belief;

   (d) To write, issue and disseminate relevant publications in these areas;

   (e) To teach a religion or belief in places suitable for these purposes;

   (f) To solicit and receive voluntary financial and other contributions from individuals and institutions;

(g) To train, appoint, elect or designate by succession appropriate leaders called for by the requirements and standards of any religion or belief;

(h) To observe days of rest and to celebrate holidays and ceremonies in accordance with the precepts of one's religion or belief;

(i) To establish and maintain communications with individuals and communities in matters of religion and belief at the national and international levels.

Article 7

3–054 The rights and freedoms set forth in the present Declaration shall be accorded in national legislation in such a manner that everyone shall be able to avail himself of such rights and freedoms in practice.

Article 8

Nothing in the present Declaration shall be construed as restricting or derogating from any right defined in the Universal Declaration of Human Rights and the International Covenants on Human Rights.

DECLARATION ON THE RIGHTS OF PERSONS BELONGING TO NATIONAL OR ETHNIC, RELIGIOUS AND LINGUISTIC MINORITIES[28]

3–055 Noting the importance of the even more effective implementation of international human rights instruments with regard to the rights of persons belonging to national or ethnic, religious and linguistic minorities,

Welcoming the increased attention given by human rights treaty bodies to the non-discrimination and protection of minorities,

Aware of the provisions of Article 27 of the International Covenant on Civil and Political Rights concerning the rights of persons belonging to ethnic, religious or linguistic minorities,

Considering that the United Nations has an increasingly important role to play regarding the protection of minorities,

. . .,

. . .,

Stressing the need to ensure for all, without discrimination of any kind, full enjoyment and exercise of human rights and fundamental freedoms,

[28] A/RES/47/135, December 18, 1992.

1. Adopts the Declaration on the Rights of Persons Belonging to National or Ethnic, Religious and Linguistic Minorities,

Article 1

1. States shall protect the existence and the national or ethnic, 3–056 cultural, religious and linguistic identity of minorities within their respective territories and shall encourage conditions for the promotion of that identity.

2. States shall adopt appropriate legislative and other measures to achieve those ends.

Article 2

1. Persons belonging to national or ethnic, religious and linguistic minorities (hereinafter referred to as persons belonging to minorities) have the right to enjoy their own culture, to profess and practise their own religion, and to use their own language, in private and in public, freely and without interference or any form of discrimination.

2. Persons belonging to minorities have the right to participate effectively in cultural, religious, social, economic and public life.

3. Persons belonging to minorities have the right to participate effectively in decisions on the national and, where appropriate, regional level concerning the minority to which they belong or the regions in which they live, in a manner not incompatible with national legislation.

4. Persons belonging to minorities have the right to establish and maintain their own associations.

5. Persons belonging to minorities have the right to establish and maintain, without any discrimination, free and peaceful contacts with other members of their group and with persons belonging to other minorities, as well as contacts across frontiers with citizens of other States to whom they are related by national or ethnic, religious or linguistic ties.

Article 3

1. Persons belonging to minorities may exercise their rights, 3–057 including those set forth in the present Declaration, individually as well as in community with other members of their group, without any discrimination.

2. No disadvantage shall result for any person belonging to a minority as the consequence of the exercise or non-exercise of the rights set forth in the present Declaration.

Article 4

1. States shall take measures where required to ensure that persons belonging to minorities may exercise fully and effectively all their human rights and fundamental freedoms without any discrimination and in full equality before the law.

2. States shall take measures to create favourable conditions to enable persons belonging to minorities to express their characteristics and to develop their culture, language, religion, traditions and customs, except where specific practices are in violation of national law and contrary to international standards.

3. States should take appropriate measures so that, wherever possible, persons belonging to minorities may have adequate opportunities to learn their mother tongue or to have instruction in their mother tongue.

4. States should, where appropriate, take measures in the field of education, in order to encourage knowledge of the history, traditions, language and culture of the minorities existing within their territory. Persons belonging to minorities should have adequate opportunities to gain knowledge of the society as a whole.

5. States should consider appropriate measures so that persons belonging to minorities may participate fully in the economic progress and development in their country.

Article 5

3–058   **1.** National policies and programmes shall be planned and implemented with due regard for the legitimate interests of persons belonging to minorities.

2. Programmes of co-operation and assistance among States should be planned and implemented with due regard for the legitimate interests of persons belonging to minorities.

Article 6

States should co-operate on questions relating to persons belonging to minorities, *inter alia*, exchanging information and experiences, in order to promote mutual understanding and confidence.

Article 7

3–059   States should co-operate in order to promote respect for the rights set forth in the present Declaration.

Article 8

1. Nothing in the present Declaration shall prevent the fulfilment of international obligations of States in relation to persons belonging to minorities. In particular, States shall fulfil in good faith the obligations and commitments they have assumed under international treaties and agreements to which they are parties.

2. The exercise of the rights set forth in the present Declaration shall not prejudice the enjoyment by all persons of universally recognised human rights and fundamental freedoms.

3. Measures taken by States to ensure the effective enjoyment of the rights set forth in the present Declaration shall not prima facie be considered contrary to the principle of equality contained in the Universal Declaration of Human Rights.

4. Nothing in the present Declaration may be construed as permitting any activity contrary to the purposes and principles of the United Nations, including sovereign equality, territorial integrity and political independence of States.

Article 9

The specialised agencies and other organisations of the United 3–060 Nations system shall contribute to the full realisation of the rights and principles set forth in the present Declaration, within their respective fields of competence.

THIRD DECADE TO COMBAT RACISM AND RACIAL DISCRIMINATION[29]

The General Assembly,

Reaffirming also its firm determination and its commitment to 3–061 eradicate totally and unconditionally racism in all its forms, racial discrimination and apartheid,

. . .

. . .

Welcoming the outcome of the World Conference on Human Rights, and, in particular, the attention given in the Vienna Declaration and Programme of Action to the elimination of racism, racial discrimination, xenophobia and other forms of intolerance, Welcoming also the decision taken by the Economic and Social Council on July 28, 1993 concerning the appointment of a special rapporteur on contemporary forms of racism, racial discrimination, xenophobia and related intolerance,

. . .

Deeply concerned about the current trend of the evolution of racism into discriminatory practices based on culture, nationality, religion or language,

. . .

Recognising the importance of strengthening national legislation and institutions for the promotion of racial harmony,

[29] A/RES/48/91, 84th Plenary Meeting, December 20, 1993.

. . .,

Acknowledging that indigenous people are at times victims of particular forms of racism and racial discrimination,

3–062   **1.** Declares once again that all forms of racism and racial discrimination, whether in their institutionalised form, such as apartheid, or resulting from official doctrines of racial superiority and/or exclusivity, such as ethnic cleansing, are among the most serious violations of human rights in the contemporary world and must be combated by all available means;

2. Decides to proclaim the ten-year period beginning in 1993 as the Third Decade to Combat Racism and Racial Discrimination,[30] and to adopt the Programme of Action proposed for the Third Decade contained in the annex to the present resolution;

3. Calls upon Governments to co-operate with the Special Rapporteur on contemporary forms of racism, racial discrimination, xenophobia and related intolerance to enable him to fulfil his mandate;

4. Urges all Governments to take all necessary measures to combat new forms of racism, in particular by adapting constantly the methods provided to combat them, especially in the legislative, administrative, educational and information fields;

5. Decides that the international community, in general, and the United Nations, in particular, should continue to give the highest priority to programmes for combating racism, racial discrimination and apartheid and intensify their efforts, during the Third Decade, to provide assistance and relief to the victims of racism and all forms of racial discrimination and apartheid;

3–063   **6.** Requests the Secretary-General to continue to accord special attention to the situation of migrant workers and members of their families and to include regularly in his reports all information on such workers[31];

7. Calls upon all Member States to consider signing and ratifying or acceding to the International Convention on the Protection of the Rights of All Migrant Workers and Members of Their Families as a matter of priority, to enable its entry into force[32];

8. Also requests the Secretary-General to continue the study on the effects of racial discrimination on the children of minorities, in particular those of migrant workers, in the fields of education, training and employment, and to submit, *inter alia*, specific recommendations for the implementation of measures to combat the effects of that discrimination[33];

---

[30] See below, para. 3–067.
[31] See Chapter on Migrant Workers.
[32] *ibid.*
[33] *ibid.*

9. Urges the Secretary-General, United Nations bodies, the 3–064 specialised agencies, all Governments, intergovernmental organisations and relevant non-governmental organisations, in implementing the Programme of Action for the Third Decade, to pay particular attention to the situation of indigenous people[34];

10. . . .,

11. Renews its invitation to the United Nations Educational, Scientific and Cultural Organisation to expedite the preparation of teaching materials and teaching aids to promote teaching, training and educational activities on human rights and against racism and racial discrimination, with particular emphasis on activities at the primary and secondary levels of education;

12. Considers that all the parts of the Programme of Action for the Third Decade should be given equal attention in order to attain the objectives of the Third Decade[35];

13. . . .,

14. . . .,

15. . . .,

16. Further requests the Secretary-General to submit each year 3–065 to the Economic and Social Council a detailed report on all activities of United Nations bodies and the specialised agencies containing an analysis of information received on such activities to combat racism and racial discrimination;

17. Invites the Secretary-General to submit proposals to the General Assembly with a view to supplementing, if necessary, the Programme of Action for the Third Decade;

18. Invites all governments, United Nations bodies, the specialised agencies and other intergovernmental organisations, as well as interested non-governmental organisations in consultative status with the Economic and Social Council, to participate fully in the Third Decade;

19. Invites all governments, intergovernmental and non-governmental organisations and individuals in a position to do so to contribute generously to the Trust Fund for the Programme for the Decade for Action to Combat Racism and Racial Discrimination, and to this end requests the Secretary-General to continue to undertake appropriate contacts and initiatives;

20. Decides to keep the item entitled "Elimination of racism and 3–066 racial discrimination" on its agenda and to consider it as a matter of the highest priority at its 49th session.

---

[34] See Chapter on Indigenous People.
[35] See below, para. 3–067.

Annex

Programme of Action for the Third Decade to Combat Racism and Racial Discrimination (1993–2003)

Introduction

3–067   **1.** The goals and objectives of the Third Decade to Combat Racism and Racial Discrimination are those adopted by the General Assembly for the first Decade and contained in paragraph 8 of the annex to its resolution 3057 (XXVIII) of November 2, 1973:

> "The ultimate goals of the Decade are to promote human rights and fundamental freedoms for all, without distinction of any kind on grounds of race, colour, descent or national or ethnic origin, especially by eradicating racial prejudice, racism and racial discrimination; to arrest any expansion of racist policies, to eliminate the persistence of racist policies and to counteract the emergence of alliances based on mutual espousal of racism and racial discrimination; to resist any policy and practices which lead to the strengthening of the racist regimes and contribute to the sustainment of racism and racial discrimination; to identify, isolate and dispel the fallacious and mythical beliefs, policies and practices that contribute to racism and racial discrimination; and to put an end to racist regimes."

2. In drawing up suggested elements for the Programme of Action for the Third Decade, account has been taken of the fact that current global economic conditions have caused many Member States to call for budgetary restraint, which in turn requires a conservative approach to the number and type of programmes of action that may be considered at this time. The Secretary- General also took into account the relevant suggestions made by the Committee on the Elimination of Racial Discrimination at its 41st session. The elements presented below have been suggested as those which are essential, should resources be made available to implement them.

. . ."

Action at the International Level

3–068   **9.** During the discussion at the substantive session of 1992 of the Economic and Social Council concerning the Second Decade to Combat Racism and Racial Discrimination, many delegations expressed their concern with regard to new expressions of racism, racial discrimination, intolerance and xenophobia in various parts of the world. In particular, these affect minorities, ethnic groups, migrant workers, indigenous populations, nomads, immigrants and refugees.

10. The biggest contribution to the elimination of racial discrimination will be that which results from the actions of States within their own territories. International action undertaken as part of any programme for the Third Decade should therefore be directed so as to assist States to act effectively. The International Convention on the Elimination of All Forms of Racial Discrimination has established standards for States, and every opportunity should be seized to ensure that these are universally accepted and applied.

11. The General Assembly should consider more effective action to ensure that all States parties to the International Convention on the Elimination of All Forms of Racial Discrimination fulfil their reporting and financial obligations. National action against racism and racial discrimination should be monitored and improved by requesting an expert member of the Committee on the Elimination of Racial Discrimination to prepare a report on obstacles encountered with respect to the effective implementation of the Convention by States parties and suggestions for remedial measures.

. . .,

13. The General Assembly requests the Department of Public 3–069
Information of the Secretariat to undertake specific activities that could be carried out by Governments and relevant national non-governmental organisations to commemorate the International Day for the Elimination of Racial Discrimination on March 21 each year.

. . .,

Action at the National and Regional Levels

21. The General Assembly recommends that Member States 3–070
review their national programmes to combat racial discrimination and its effects in order to identify and to seize opportunities to close gaps between different groups, and especially to undertake housing, educational and employment programmes that have proved to be successful in combating racial discrimination and xenophobia.

22. The General Assembly recommends that Member States encourage the participation of journalists and human rights advocates from minority groups and communities in the mass media. Radio and television programmes should increase the number of broadcasts produced by and in co-operation with racial and cultural minority groups. Multicultural activities of the media should also be encouraged where they can contribute to the suppression of racism and xenophobia.

23. The General Assembly recommends that regional organisations co-operate closely with United Nations efforts to combat racism and racial discrimination. Regional organisations dealing with human rights issues could mobilise public opinion in their regions against the evils of racism and racial prejudices directed towards disadvantaged racial and ethnic groups. These institutions could serve an important function in assisting governments to enact national legislation against racial discrimination and promote adoption and application of international conventions. Regional human rights commissions should be called upon to publicise widely basic texts on existing human rights instruments.

Basic Research and Studies

3–071   **24.** The long-term viability of the United Nations programme against racism and racial discrimination will depend in part on continuing research into the causes of racism and into the new manifestations of racism and racial discrimination. The General Assembly may wish to examine the importance of preparing studies on racism. The following are some aspects to be studied:

(a) Application of Article 2 of the International Convention on the Elimination of All Forms of Racial Discrimination. Such a study might assist States to learn from one another the national measures taken to implement the Convention;

(b) Economic factors contributing to perpetuation of racism and racial discrimination;

(c) Integration or preservation of cultural identity in a multiracial or multi-ethnic society;

(d) Political rights, including the participation of various racial groups in political processes and their representation in government service;

(e) Civil rights, including migration, nationality and freedom of opinion and association;

(f) Educational measures to combat racial prejudice and discrimination and to propagate the principles of the United Nations;

(g) Socio-economic costs of racism and racial discrimination;

(h) Global integration and the question of racism and the nation State;

(i) National mechanisms against racism and racial discrimination in the fields of immigration, employment, salary, housing, education and ownership of property.

Co-ordination and Reporting

25. . . . The Assembly decides that the following steps should 3–072 be taken to strengthen the United Nations input into the Third Decade to Combat Racism and Racial Discrimination:

(a) The General Assembly entrusts the Economic and Social Council and the Commission on Human Rights, in co-operation with the Secretary-General, with the responsibility for co-ordinating the programmes and evaluating the activities undertaken in connection with the Third Decade;

(b) The Secretary-General is invited to provide specific information on activities against racism, to be contained in one annual report, which should be comprehensive in nature and allow a general overview of all mandated activities. This will facilitate co-ordination and evaluation;

(c) An open-ended working group of the Commission on Human Rights, or other appropriate arrangements under the Commission, may be established to review decade-related information on the basis of the annual reports referred to above, as well as relevant studies and reports of seminars, to assist the Commission in formulating appropriate recommendations to the Economic and Social Council on particular activities, allocation of priorities and so on.

26. Furthermore, an inter-agency meeting should be organised immediately after the proclamation of the Third Decade, in 1994, with a view to planning working meetings and other activities.

Regular System-Wide Consultations

27. On an annual basis, consultations between the United 3–073 Nations, specialised agencies and non-governmental organisations should take place to review and plan decade-related activities. In this framework, the Centre for Human Rights should organise inter-agency meetings to consider and discuss further measures to strengthen the co-ordination and co-operation of programmes related to the issues of combating racism and racial discrimination.

28. The Centre should also strengthen the relationship with non-governmental organisations fighting against racism and racial discrimination by holding consultations and briefings with the non-governmental organisations. Such meetings could help them to initiate, develop and present proposals regarding the struggle against racism and racial discrimination.

IMPLEMENTATION OF THE PROGRAMME OF ACTION FOR THE THIRD DECADE TO COMBAT RACISM AND RACIAL DISCRIMINATION[36]

3–074 The Economic and Social Council,

. . .,

Reaffirming its firm determination and its commitment to eradicate totally and unconditionally racism in all its forms and racial discrimination,

. . .,

Welcoming the outcome of the World Conference on Human Rights, held at Vienna from June 14–25, 1993, and, in particular, the attention given in the Vienna Declaration and Programme of Action to the elimination of racism, racial discrimination, xenophobia and related intolerance,

Aware of the importance and magnitude of the phenomenon of migrant workers, as well as the efforts made by the international community to improve the protection of the fundamental rights of migrant workers and members of their families,[37] . . . Aware that indigenous populations are at times victims of particular forms of racism and racial discrimination,

Welcoming General Assembly resolution 48/91 of December 20, 1993, . . .

3–075   1. Declares that all forms of racism or racial discrimination, whether institutionalised or resulting from official doctrines of racial superiority or exclusivity, such as "ethnic cleansing", are among the most serious violations of human rights in the contemporary world and must be combated by all possible means;

2. Commends all States that have ratified or acceded to the international instruments to combat racism and racial discrimination;

3. Appeals to those States that have not yet done so to consider ratifying, acceding to and implementing the relevant international instruments, particularly the International Convention on the Elimination of All Forms of Racial Discrimination and the Convention against Discrimination in Education[38];

4. Urges all governments to take all requisite measures to combat new forms of racism, in particular by ongoing adjustment of the methods used to combat them;

5. Invites all governments and international and non-governmental organisations to increase and intensify their

---

[36] Resolution 1995/59, 57th Plenary Meeting, July 28, 1995 *Note*: The General Assembly declared 1995 as the UN Year of Tolerance, A/RES/48/126, 85th Plenary Meeting, December 20, 1993.

[37] See below, Chapter 8.

[38] UNESCO Records of the General Conference, 11th Session, Res., p. 119, December 14, 1960.

activities to combat racism and racial discrimination and to provide relief and assistance to victims of these evils;

6. Invites the Secretary-General to take action to co-ordinate all the programmes currently being implemented by United Nations bodies with a view to achieving the objectives of the Third Decade to Combat Racism and Racial Discrimination;

7. Requests the Secretary-General to continue to accord special 3–076 attention to the situation of migrant workers and members of their families and to include regularly in his reports full information on such workers;

8. Also requests the Secretary-General to continue the study on the effects of racial discrimination on the children of minorities, particularly those of migrant workers, in the fields of education, training and employment and to submit, *inter alia*, specific recommendations for the implementation of measures to combat the effects of that discrimination;

9. Calls upon all Member States to consider signing and ratifying or acceding to the International Convention on the Protection of the Rights of All Migrant Workers and Members of Their Families as a matter of priority, so that it can enter into force as soon as possible;

10. Urges the Secretary-General, United Nations bodies and specialised agencies, all governments, intergovernmental organisations and relevant non-governmental organisations, in implementing the Programme of Action for the Third Decade, to pay particular attention to the situation of indigenous peoples;

11. Requests the Secretary-General to publish and distribute as soon as possible the model legislation on racism and racial discrimination for the guidance of governments in the enactment of further legislation against racial discrimination;

12. Invites the United Nations Educational, Scientific and 3–077 Cultural Organisation to expedite the preparation of teaching materials and teaching aids to promote teaching, training and education activities on human rights and against racism and racial discrimination, with particular emphasis on activities at the primary and secondary levels of education;

13. Regrets that some of the activities for the Second Decade to Combat Racism and Racial Discrimination have not been implemented for lack of adequate resources;

14. Calls upon the international community to provide the Secretary-General with appropriate financial resources for efficient action against racism and racial discrimination;

15. Invites all governments, United Nations bodies, the specialised agencies and other intergovernmental organisations, as well as interested non-governmental organisations in consultative status with the Economic and Social Council, to participate fully in the Third Decade;

16. Considers that voluntary contributions to the Trust Fund for the Programme for the Decade to Combat Racism and Racial Discrimination are indispensable for the implementation of the Programme;

3–078 **17.** Strongly appeals, therefore, to all governments, organisations and individuals in a position to do so to contribute generously to the Trust Fund, and to this end requests the Secretary-General to continue to undertake appropriate contacts and initiatives to encourage contributions;

18. Requests the Secretary-General to ensure that the necessary financial resources are provided for the implementation of the activities of the Third Decade during the bienniums 1994–95 and 1996–97;

19. Takes note of the report of the Secretary-General on the Programme of Action for the Third Decade to Combat Racism and Racial Discrimination[39];

20. Recommends that the activities mentioned in the plan of activities to be carried out during the first third of the Third Decade (1994–97), as set out in the previous report of the Secretary-General,[40] should be implemented;

21. Invites the Secretary-General to do his utmost to establish a focal point within the Centre for Human Rights of the Secretariat, which will be responsible for reviewing information concerning specific recommendations on activities to be undertaken;

3–079 **22.** Decides to maintain the item entitled "Third Decade to Combat Racism and Racial Discrimination" in its agenda and to give it the highest priority at its substantive session of 1996.

NOTE: The issue of minorities has been addressed at a regional level. The Conference on Security and Co-operation in Europe (CSCE) in the Helsinki Document 1992/The Challenges of Change stated . . .

12. This is a time of promise but also a time of instability and insecurity. Economic decline, social tension, aggressive nationalism, intolerance, xenophobia and ethnic conflicts threaten stability in the CSCE area. Gross violations of CSCE commitments in the field of human rights and fundamental freedoms, including those related to national minorities, pose a special threat to the peaceful development of society, in particular in new democracies.

There is still much work to be done in building democratic and pluralistic societies, where diversity is fully protected and respected in practice. Consequently we reject racial,

[39] E/1995/111 and Add.1.
[40] E/1994/97.

ethnic and religious discrimination in any form, Freedom and tolerance must be taught and practised.[41]

In decisions taken at Helskini (*i.e.* the Helsinki Decisions) it was decided to appoint a High Commissioner on National Minorities.[42]

CSCE HIGH COMMISSIONER ON NATIONAL MINORITIES[43]

1. . . .

Mandate

2. The High Commissioner will act under the aegis of the CSO[44] **3–080** and will thus be an instrument of conflict prevention at the earliest possible stage.

3. The High Commissioner will provide "early warning" and as appropriate, "early action" at the earliest possible stage in regard to tensions involving national minority issues which have not yet developed beyond an early warning stage, but in the judgment of the High Commissioner, have the potential to develop into a conflict within the CSCE area, affecting peace, stability, or relations between participating States, requiring the action of the Council or the CSO.

4. Within the mandate, based on CSCE principles and commitments, the High Commissioner will work in confidence and independently of all parties directly involved in the tensions.

5. (a) . . .

   (b) The High Commissioner will not consider national minority issues in situations involving organised acts of terrorism.

   (c) . . .

6. In considering a situation, the High Commissioner will take fully into account availability of democratic means and international instruments to respond to it, and their utilisation by the parties involved . . .

[41] For text of the Helsinki Declaration see 13 H.R.L.J. 284 (1992).
[42] Decision 23. For text of Helskini Decisions see *ibid.* at 288.
[43] M. Van der Stoel, is the High Commissioner on National Minorities.
[44] Committee of Senior Officials.

CHAPTER 4

INDIGENOUS PEOPLE[1]

INTRODUCTION

4–001   Certain issues pertaining to the interests of indigenous people have been addressed over the last four years. A Permanent Forum for Indigenous People has now been created within the United Nations system. At a national level there has been government recognition that historically the Aboriginal population was the target of discrimination. A resolution to appoint a Special Rapporteur on human rights and indigenous issues was passed on April 24, 2001. The Resolution is a response to the absence of a dedicated mechanism designed to deal with indigenous issues. The functions of the Rapporteur will include the competence to make an immediate response to alleged violations of human rights and to make site visits as and when appropriate. What would appear to be envisaged is a somewhat proactive role for the Rapporteur. Notwithstanding these developments the progress towards the adoption of the Declaration on the Rights of Indigenous Peoples is slow.

WORLD CONFERENCE ON HUMAN RIGHTS (JUNE 1993) VIENNA DECLARATION

4–002   **20.** The World Conference on Human Rights recognises the inherent dignity and the unique contribution of indigenous people to the development and plurality of society and strongly reaffirms the commitment of the international community to their economic, social and cultural well-being and their enjoyment of the fruits of sustainable development. States should ensure the

---

[1] "Indigenous communities, peoples and nations are those which, having a historical continuity with pre-invasion and pre-colonial societies that developed on their territory, consider themselves distinct from the sectors of the societies now prevailing in those territories, or parts of them. They form at present non-dominant sectors of society and are determined to preserve, develop and transmit to future generations their ancestral territories and their ethnic identity, as the base of their continued existence as peoples, in accordance with their own cultural patterns, social institutions and legal systems. Definition of indigenous persons, 1983 United Nations Sub-Committee on Prevention of Discrimination and Protection of Minorities, E/Cn.4/Sub 2/1983/21/Add 8. It is estimated that there are 300 million indigenous inhabitants worldwide. See commentary note below re characterisation as a people(s).

full and free participation of indigenous people in all aspects of society, in particular in matters of concern to them. Considering the importance of the promotion and protection of the rights of indigenous people, and the contribution of such promotion and protection to the political and social stability of the States in which such people live, States should, in accordance with international law, take concerted positive steps to ensure respect for all human rights and fundamental freedoms of indigenous people, on the basis of equality and non-discrimination, and recognise the value and diversity of their distinct identities, cultures and social organisation.

Indigenous people

28. The World Conference on Human Rights calls on the 4–003 Working Group on Indigenous Populations of the Sub-Commission on Prevention of Discrimination and Protection of Minorities to complete the drafting of a declaration on the rights of indigenous people at its 11th session.

29. The World Conference on Human Rights recommends that the Commission on Human Rights consider the renewal and updating of the mandate of the Working Group on Indigenous Populations upon completion of the drafting of a declaration on the rights of indigenous people.

30. The World Conference on Human Rights also recommends that advisory services and technical assistance programmes within the United Nations system respond positively to requests by States for assistance which would be of direct benefit to indigenous people. The World Conference on Human Rights further recommends that adequate human and financial resources be made available to the Centre for Human Rights within the overall framework of strengthening the Centre's activities as envisaged by this document.

31. The World Conference on Human Rights urges States to 4–004 ensure the full and free participation of indigenous people in all aspects of society, in particular in matters of concern to them.

32. The World Conference on Human Rights recommends that the General Assembly proclaim an international decade of the world's indigenous people, to begin from January 1994, including action-orientated programmes, to be decided upon in partnership with indigenous people. An appropriate voluntary trust fund should be set up for this purpose. In the framework of such a decade, the establishment of a permanent forum for indigenous people in the United Nations system should be considered.

UNITED NATIONS DRAFT DECLARATION ON THE RIGHTS OF INDIGENOUS PEOPLES[2]

PART 1

Article 1

4–005 Indigenous peoples have the right to the full and effective enjoyment of all human rights and fundamental freedoms recognised in the Charter of the United Nations, The Universal Declaration of Human Rights and International human rights law.

Article 2

Indigenous individuals and peoples are free and equal to all other individuals and peoples in dignity and rights, and have the right to be free from any kind of adverse discrimination, in particular that based on their indigenous origin or identity.

Article 3

Indigenous peoples have the right of self-determination. By virtue of that right they freely determine their political status and freely pursue their economic, social and cultural development.

The United Nations Charter recognised the principle of "equal rights and self-determination" but the subsequent development of international law has been such so that self-determination is now recognised as a right under customary international law— see, for example, the *Namibia Case*,[3] ". . . the subsequent development of international law in regard to non-self governing territories, as enshrined in the Charter of the United Nations, made the principle of self-determination applicable to all of them";[4] see also the *Western Sahara Case*.[5] See also Article 1 of both the 1966 UN Covenants "All peoples have the right of self-determination. By that right they freely determine their political status and freely

---

[2] Resolution 1994/45, adopted August 26, 1994 by the UN Sub-Commission on Prevention of Discrimination and Protection of Minorities, 46th Session, 1994. The draft declaration is the culmination of work initiated over a decade ago. In 1982 the Working Group on Indigenous Populations (WGIP) was established under the auspices of the Sub-Commission on Prevention of Discrimination and Protection of Minorities with the mandate of examining annually the situation of indigenous peoples throughout the world and the development of new international standards for the realisation of indigenous rights. WGIP is made up of five (reflecting the regional groupings of the UN) experts members of the Sub-Commission. WGIP quickly became a forum of discussion and in 1987 initiated the move to produce an international instrument designed to meet the needs of indigenous peoples. The text of the Draft Declaration along with an introductory note is published in 34 I.L.M.541 (1995).

[3] I.C.J. Rep. 1971, p. 16.

[4] *ibid* at p. 31.

[5] I.C.J. Rep. 1975, p. 12 at 16.

pursue their economic, social and cultural development"; for clarification of Article see General Comment 12 Human Rights Committee,[6] see also 1970 "Declaration on Principles of International Law concerning Friendly Relations and Co-operation among States in Accordance with the Charter of the United Nations." The right of self-determination developed and evolved during decolonisation the scope of the right post colonisation has been the subject of considerable debate and controversy.[7] Note the right to self-determination recognised in the Vienna Declaration, "All peoples have the right of self-determination. By virtue of that right they freely determine their political status, and freely pursue their economic, social and cultural development. Taking into account the particular situation of peoples under colonial or other forms of alien domination or foreign occupation, the World Conference on Human Rights recognises the right of *peoples* (emphasis added) to take any legitimate action, in accordance with the Charter of the United Nations, to realise their inalienable right of self-determination. The World Conference on Human Rights considers the denial of the right of self-determination as a violation of human rights and underlines the importance of the effective realisation of this right."[8]

This is not to be construed as authorising or encouraging any action which would dismember or impair, totally or in part, the territorial integrity or political unity of sovereign and independent States conducting themselves in compliance with the principle of equal rights and self-determination of peoples and thus possessed of a Government representing the whole people belonging to the territory without distinction of any kind." The Vienna Declaration dropped the "s" from peoples. This was defeat for indigenous leaders and success for states such as Canada. The latter had lobbied for the removal of the "s" on the grounds that self-determination could be interpreted to include secession and separatism. The former had wanted the retention of "peoples" with its attendant rights and privileges, including that of self-determination.[9] The right of indigenous people to self-determination is a thorny issue particularly as that right is perceived as one which gives a right of secession, *e.g.* Canada is an

4–006

[6] 39 UN G.A.O.R., Supp. 40 (A/39/40) pp. 142–43; 1 I.H.R.R. (1994), pp. 10–11.
[7] G.A. Res. 2625 (XXV) October 24, 1975 UN Doc. A/8028(1970), 25 UN G.A.O.R. Supp.
[8] UN World Conference on Human Rights (Vienna Declaration and Programme of Action) Part I, para 2.
[9] See also Article 1(3) I.L.O. No. 169 below; See also paras 122 and 124 the Canadian Supreme Court decision in Reference Re Secession of Quebec [August 20, 1998] 37.I.LM. 1340. "International law grants the right of self-determination to "peoples". Accordingly, access to the right requires the threshold step of characterising as a people the group seeking self-determination. However, as the right to self-determination has developed by virtue of a combination of international agreements and conventions coupled with state practice, with little formal elaboration of the definition of "peoples", the result has been that the precise meaning of the term "people" remains somewhat uncertain. It is clear that "a people" may include only a portion of the population of an existing state. The right to self-determination has developed largely as a human right, and is generally used in documents that simultaneously contain references to "nation" and "state".

example of one country with strong reservations over Article 3 although the change of government in 1993 brought about a number of far-reaching initiatives with respect to native self-government, *e.g.* In 1993, Canada made a lands right agreement with *inter alia* the Inuit regarding the area which is to be known as Nanavit. The Nanavit Land Claim Agreement was ratified by the Inuit in November 1992 and signed by the Canadian Prime Minister on May 25, 1993 and was passed by the Canadian legislature the following month. The agreement which *inter alia* established a form of self government for Nanavit Inuit represents the largest native land claim in Canadian history and gives the Nanavit Inuit title to some 350,000 square kilometres in the east Arctic. Australia, a country much criticised for its treatment of its indigenous people, passed a motion of reconciliation which acknowledged regret at the injustice suffered by individual aboriginals[10] and was reiterated by Prime Minister in the Federal Address of January 2000. The plight of indigeneous people, particularly in Australia, has been the highlighted by the Committee on the Elimination of Racial Discrimination, *e.g* with respect to the Amended Native Title Act.[11] As to what constitutes a people for the rights of people in international law, including the right to self-determination see, for instance, Final Report and Recommendations of an International Meeting of Experts on the Further Study of the Concept of Right of People for UNESCO February 22, 1990,[12] which characterises a people as:

(a) A group of individual human beings who enjoy some or all of the following common features: (i) A common historical tradition; (ii) Racial or ethnic identity; (iii) Cultural homogeneity; (iv) Linguistic unity; (v) Religious or ideological affinity; (vi) Territorial connection; (vii) Common economic life.

(b) The group must be of a certain number who need not be large—but must be more than a mere association of individuals within a State.

(c) The group as a whole must have the will to be identified as a people or the consciousness of being a people— allowing that groups or some members of such groups, though sharing the foregoing characteristics, may not have the will or consciousness.

(d) Possibly the group must have institutions or other means of expressing its common characteristics and will for identity.

---

[10] Para. 12, CERD/C/SR 1393 March 29, 2000 Consideration of Reports, Comments and Information Submitted by State Parties Under Article 9 of the Convention: Tenth to Twelfth Report of Australia.

[11] For the Australian response see para. 14 *et seq. ibid.*

[12] SNS-89/CONF. 602/7.

See (CERD) General Recommendation XXI(1996) on self-determination.[13]

The Supreme Court of Canada considered the scope of the right to   **4–007**
self-determination in Reference Re Secession of Quebec[14] and
observed that :
"In summary, the international law right to self-determination
only generates, at best, a right to external self-determination in
situation of former colonies, where a people is oppressed, as for
example under foreign military occupation; or where a definable
group is denied meaningful access to government to pursue their
political, economic, social and cultural development. In all three
situations, the people in question are entitled to a right to external
self-determination because they have been denied the ability to
exert internally their right to self-determination". [*Note* The Court
concluded that "neither the population of the province of Quebec,
even if characterised in terms of "people" or "peoples", nor its
representative institution, the National Assembly, the legislature or
government of Quebec, possess a right, under international law, to
secede unilaterally from Canada. And that ". . . the concern of
aboriginal peoples is precipitated by the asserted right of Quebec
to unilateral secession. In light of our finding that there is no such
right applicable to the population of Quebec, either under the
Constitution of Canada or at international law but that on the
contrary a clear democratic expression of support for secession
would lead under the Constitution to negotiations in which
aboriginal interests would be taken into account, it becomes
unnecessary to explore further the concerns of the aboriginal
peoples in this Reference." In considering the scope of the right to
self-determination the Court emphasised that the international law
principle of self-determination had evolved within a framework of
respect for the territorial integrity of existing states.
    In another decision the Supreme Court of Canada handed down   **4–008**
what has been heralded as a pivotal decision in the evolution of
Canadian law on the Aboriginals.[15] The case related to the aboriginal title claimed by Gitksan and Wet'suwet hereditary chiefs
over the lands in British Columbia. The Province claimed that the
chiefs and their "Houses" had no right or interest in the territory,
or alternatively, that they were only due compensation and not
territory. The chiefs offered evidence of historical use and ownership in the form of shared oral traditions and spiritual songs. The
trial judge refused to accept such evidence and dismissed the
appeal against Canada. The appeal was also dismissed by the
Court of Appeal. The Supreme Court in finding that the trial court

---

[13] See Chapter on Minorities: Section Minorities and Self-Determination. For further
discussion of the right of indigenous peoples to self-determination see "H. Hannum,
minorities, indigenous peoples, and self-determination", pp. 1–16 in *Human Rights; An
Agenda for the Next Century* (L. Henkin and J. Hargrove. (eds) (1994).
[14] August 20, 1998 37 I.L.M. 1340 (1998); *supra* n. 9
[15] *Delgamuukw v. British Columbia*, December 1997, 37 I.L.M. 261.

should have allowed the oral histories as evidence of occupation and use of the disputed territory highlighted "the nature of the claimants' attachment to those lands". "Constitutionally recognised aborginal rights fall along a spectrum with respect to their degree of connection with the land. At the one end are those aboriginal rights which are practices, customs and tradition integral to the distinctive aboriginal culture of the group claiming the right but where the use and occupation of the land where the activity is taking place is not sufficient to support a claim of title to the land, it may nevertheless have a site-specific right to engage in a particular activity. At the other end of the spectrum is aboriginal title itself which confers more than the right to engage in site-specific activities which are aspects of the practices, customs and traditions of distinctive aboriginal cultures. Site-specific rights (*e.g.* hunting) can be made out even if title cannot. Because aboriginal rights can vary with respect to their degree of connection with the land, some aboriginal groups may be unable to make out a claim to title, but will nevertheless possess aboriginal rights that are recognised and affirmed—including site-specific rights to engage in particular activities".[16] The Court held that British Columbia had no authority to extinguish aborginal rights either under the Constitutional Act 1867 or by virtue of the Indian Act. The Appeal was allowed in part, the cross appeal was dismissed and a new trial ordered. The decision has been regarded as an important vehicle for further discussion of more fundamental issues such as the appropriateness of selecting the judicial form to resolve aboriginal title claims and the role of legal reasoning in furthering the process of colonisation.[17]

Article 4

4–009 Indigenous peoples have the right to maintain and strengthen their distinct political, economic, social and cultural characteristics, as well as their legal systems, while retaining their rights to participate fully, if they so choose, in the political, economic, social and cultural life of the State.

Article 5

Every indigenous individual has the right to a nationality.

PART II

Article 6

Indigenous peoples have the collective right to live in freedom, peace and security as distinct peoples and to full guarantees

---

[16] *per* Lamer C.J. and Cory, McLachlin and Majoe JJ: *supra* n. at p. 271.
[17] *Supra* n. Introductory Note, C Bell.

against genocide or any other act of violence, including the removal of indigenous children from their families and communities under any pretext.

In addition, they have the individual rights to life, physical and mental integrity, liberty and security of person.

Article 7

Indigenous peoples have the collective and individual right not to **4–010** be subjected to ethnocide and cultural genocide, including prevention of and redress for:

(a) Any action which has the aim or effect of depriving them of their integrity as distinct peoples, or of their cultural values or ethnic identities;

(b) Any action which has the aim or effect of dispossessing them of their lands, territories or resources;

(c) Any form of population transfer which has the aim or effect of violating or undermining any of their rights;

(d) Any form of assimilation or integration by other cultures or ways of life imposed on them by legislative, administrative or other measures;

(e) Any form of propaganda directed against them.

Article 8

Indigenous peoples have the collective and individual right to maintain and develop their distinct identities and characteristics, including the right to identity themselves as indigenous and to be recognised as such.

Article 9

Indigenous peoples and individuals have the right to belong to an **4–011** indigenous community or nation, in accordance with the traditions and customs of the community or nation concerned. No disadvantage of any kind may arise from the exercise of such a right.

Article 10

Indigenous peoples shall not be forcibly removed from their lands or territories. No relocation shall take place without the free and informed consent of the indigenous peoples concerned and after agreement on just and fair compensation and, where possible, with the option of return.

Article 11

Indigenous peoples have the right to special protection and security in periods of armed conflict. States shall observe international standards, in particular the Fourth Geneva Convention of 1949, for the protection of civilian populations in circumstances of emergency and armed conflict, and shall not:

(a) Recruit indigenous individuals against their will into the armed forces and, in particular, for use against other indigenous peoples;

(b) Recruit indigenous children into the armed forces under any circumstances;

(c) Force indigenous individuals to abandon their lands, territories or means of subsistence, or relocate them in special centres for military purposes;

(d) Force indigenous individuals to work for military purposes under any discriminatory conditions.

PART III

Article 12

4–012 Indigenous peoples have the right to practise and revitalise their cultural traditions and customs. This includes the right to maintain, protect and develop the past, present and future manifestations of their culture, such as archaeological and historical sites, artifacts, designs, ceremonies, technologies and visual and performing arts and literature, as well as the right to the restitution of cultural, intellectual, religious and spiritual property taken without their free and informed consent or in violation of their laws, traditions and customs.

Article 13

Indigenous peoples have the right to manifest, practise, develop and teach their spiritual and religious traditions, customs and ceremonies; the right to maintain, protect, and have access in privacy to their religious and cultural sites; the right to the use and control of ceremonial objects; and the right to the repatriation of human remains.

States shall take effective measures, in conjunction with the indigenous peoples concerned, to ensure that indigenous sacred places, including burial sites, be preserved, respected and protected.

Article 14

Indigenous peoples have the right to revitalise, use, develop and transmit to future generations their histories, languages, oral traditions, philosophies, writing systems and literatures, and to designate and retain their own names for communities, places and persons.

States shall take effective measures, whenever any right of indigenous peoples may be threatened, to ensure this right is protected and also to ensure that they can understand and be understood in political, legal and administrative proceedings, where necessary through the provision of interpretation or by other appropriate means.

PART IV

Article 15

Indigenous children have the right to all levels and forms of 4–013 education of the State. All indigenous peoples also have this right and the right to establish and control their educational systems and institutions providing education in their own language, in a manner appropriate to their cultural methods of teaching and learning.

Indigenous children living outside their communities have the right to be provided access to education in their own culture and language.

States shall take effective measures to provide appropriate resources for these purposes.

Article 16

Indigenous peoples have the right to have the dignity and diversity of their cultures, traditions, histories and aspirations appropriately reflected in all forms of education and public information.

States shall take effective measures, in consultation with the indigenous peoples concerned, to eliminate prejudice and dis-crimination and to promote tolerance, understanding and good relations among indigenous peoples and all segments of society.

Article 17

Indigenous peoples have the right to establish their own media in their own languages. They also have the right to equal access to all forms of non-indigenous media.

States shall take effective measures to ensure that State-owned media duly reflect indigenous cultural diversity.

Article 18

Indigenous peoples have the right to enjoy fully all rights established under international labour law and national labour legislation.

Indigenous individuals have the right not to be subjected to any discriminatory conditions of labour, employment or salary.

PART V

Article 19

4–014 Indigenous peoples have the right to participate fully, if they so choose, at all levels of decision-making in matters which may affect their rights, lives and destinies through representatives chosen by themselves in accordance with their own procedures, as well as to maintain and develop their own indigenous decision-making institutions.

Article 20

Indigenous peoples have the right to participate fully, if they so choose, through procedures determined by them, in devising legislative or administrative measures that may affect them.

States shall obtain the free and informed consent of the peoples concerned before adopting and implementing such measures.

Article 21

Indigenous peoples have the right to maintain and develop their political, economic and social systems, to be secure in the enjoyment of their own means of subsistence and development, and to engage freely in all their traditional and other economic activities. Indigenous peoples who have been deprived of their means of subsistence and development are entitled to just and fair compensation.

Article 22

Indigenous peoples have the right to special measures for the immediate, effective and continuing improvement of their economic and social conditions, including in the areas of employment, vocational training and retraining, housing, sanitation, health and social security. Particular attention shall be paid to the rights and special needs of indigenous elders, women, youth, children and disabled persons.

Article 23

Indigenous peoples have the right to determine and develop priorities and strategies for exercising their right to development. In particular, indigenous peoples have the right to determine and develop all health, housing and other economic and social programmes affecting them and, as far as possible, to administer such programmes through their own institutions.

Article 24

Indigenous peoples have the right to their traditional medicines and health practices, including the right to the protection of vital medicinal plants, animals and minerals.

They also have the right to assess, without any discrimination, to all medical institutions, health services and medical care.

PART VI

Article 25

Indigenous peoples have the right to maintain and strengthen 4–015 their distinctive spiritual and material relationship with the lands, territories, waters and coastal seas and other resources which they have traditionally owned or otherwise occupied or used, and to uphold their responsibilities to future generations in this regard.

Article 26

Indigenous peoples have the right to own, develop, control and use the lands and territories, including the total environment of the lands, air, waters, coastal seas, sea-ice, flora and fauna and other resources which they have traditionally owned or otherwise occupied or used. This includes the right to the full recognition of their laws, traditions and customs, land-tenure systems and institutions for the development and management of resources, and the right to effective measures by States to prevent any interference with, alienation of or encroachment upon these rights.

Article 27

Indigenous peoples have the right to the restitution of the lands, territories and resources which they have traditionally owned or otherwise occupied or used, and which have been confiscated, occupied, used or damage without their free and informed consent. Where this is not possible, they have the right to just and fair compensation. Unless otherwise freely agree upon by the peoples concerned, compensation shall take the form of lands, territories and resources equal in quality, size and legal status.

Article 28

Indigenous peoples have the right to the conservation, restoration and protection of the total environment and the productive capacity of their lands, territories and resources, as well as to assistance for this purpose from States and through international co-operation. Military activities shall not take place in the lands and territories of indigenous peoples, unless otherwise freely agreed upon by the peoples concerned.

States shall take effective measures to ensure that no storage or disposal of hazardous materials shall take place in the lands and territories of indigenous peoples.

States shall also take effective measures to ensure, as needed, that programmes for monitoring, maintaining and restoring the health of indigenous peoples, as developed and implemented by the peoples affected by such materials, are duly implemented.

Article 29

Indigenous peoples are entitled to the recognition of the full ownership, control and protection of their cultural and intellectual property.

They have the right to special measures to control, develop and protect their sciences, technologies and cultural manifestations, including human and other genetic resources, seeds, medicines, knowledge of the properties of fauna and flora, oral traditions, literatures, designs and visual and performing arts.

Article 30

Indigenous peoples have the right to determine and develop priorities and strategies for the development of use of their lands, territories and other resources, including the right to require that States obtain their free and informed consent prior to the approval of any project affecting their lands, territories and other resources, particularly in connection with the development, utilisation or exploitation or mineral, water or other resources. Pursuant to agreement with the indigenous peoples concerned, just and fair compensation shall be provided for any such activities and measures taken to mitigate adverse environmental, economic, social, cultural or spiritual impact.

PART VII

Article 31

4–016   Indigenous peoples, as a specific form of exercising their right to self-determination, have the right to autonomy or self-government in matters relating to their internal and local affairs, including culture, religion, education, information, media, health, housing, employment, social welfare, economic activities, land

and resources management, environment and entry by non-members, as well as ways and means for financing these autonomous functions.

Article 32

Indigenous peoples have the collective right to determine their own citizenship in accordance with their customs and traditions. Indigenous citizenship does not impair the right of indigenous individuals to obtain citizenship of the States in which they live.

Indigenous people have the right to determine the structures and to select the membership of their institutions in accordance with their own procedures.

Article 33

Indigenous peoples have the right to promote, develop and maintain their institutional structures and their distinctive juridical customs, traditions, procedures and practices, in accordance with international recognised human rights standards.

Article 34

Indigenous peoples have the collective right to determine the responsibilities of individuals to their communities.

Article 35

Indigenous peoples, in particular those divided by international borders, have the right to maintain and develop contacts, relations and co-operation, including activities for spiritual, cultural, political, economic and social purposes, with other peoples across borders.

States shall take effective measures to ensure the exercise and implementation of this right.

Article 36

Indigenous peoples have the right to the recognition, observance and enforcement of treaties, agreements and other constructive arrangements concluded with States or their successors, according to their original spirit and intent, and to have States honour and respect such treaties, agreements and other constructive arrangements. Conflicts and disputes which cannot otherwise be settled should be submitted to competent international bodies agreed to by all parties concerned.

PART VIII

Article 37

State shall take effective and appropriate measures, in consultation with the indigenous peoples concerned, to give full effect to the provisions of this Declaration. The rights recognised herein 4–017 shall be adopted and included in national legislation in such a manner that indigenous peoples can avail themselves of such rights in practice.

Article 38

Indigenous peoples have the right to have access to adequate financial and technical assistance, from States and through international co-operation, to pursue freely their political, economic, social, cultural and spiritual development and for the enjoyment of the rights and freedoms recognised in this Declaration.

Article 39

Indigenous peoples have the right to have access to and prompt decision through mutually acceptable and fair procedures for the resolution of conflicts and disputes with States, as well as to effective remedies for all infringements of their individual and collective rights. Such a decision shall take into consideration in the customs, traditions, rules and legal systems of the indigenous peoples concerned.

Article 40

The organs and specialised agencies of the United Nations system and other intergovernmental organisations shall contribute to the full realisation of the provisions of this Declaration through the mobilisation, *inter alia*, of financial co-operation and technical assistance. Ways and means of ensuring participation of indigenous peoples on issues affecting them shall be established.

Article 41

The United Nations shall take the necessary steps to ensure the implementation of this Declaration including the creation of a body at the highest level with special competence in this field and with the direct participation of indigenous peoples. All United Nations bodies shall promote respect for and full application of the provisions of this Declaration.

PART IX

Article 42

4–018 The rights recognised herein constitute the minimum standards for the survival, dignity and well-being of the indigenous peoples of the world.

Article 43

All the rights and freedoms recognised herein are equally guaranteed to male and female indigenous individuals.

Article 44

Nothing in this Declaration may be construed as diminishing or extinguishing existing or future rights indigenous peoples may have or acquire.

Article 45

Nothing in this Declaration may be interpreted as implying for any State, group or person any right to engage in any activity or to perform any act contrary to the Charter of the United Nations.

On March 3, 1995, the United Nations Commission on Human Rights decided to set up an intergovernmental working group to elaborate upon the draft Declaration.[18] The group's establishment was subject to approval by the Economic and Social Council—such approval was given in Resolution 1995/32 July 25, 1995. Provision is made for the participation of organisations of indigenous people not in consultative status with the Economic and Social Council.

ILO CONVENTION (No. 169) CONCERNING INDIGENOUS AND TRIBAL PERSONS IN INDEPENDENT COUNTRIES, 1989[19]

PART I

General Policy

Article 1

1. This Convention applies to:
(a) tribal peoples in independent countries whose social, 4–019 cultural and economic conditions distinguish them from other sections of the national community, and whose status is regulated wholly or partially by their own customs or traditions or by special laws or regulations;

---

[18] Resolution 1995/32 see 34 I.L.M. 535 (1995).
[19] This Convention was adopted during the 76th Session of the International Labour Organisation and revises the provisions of the earlier relevant instrument, Indigenous and Tribal Populations Convention (No. 107). Currently there are 14 Ratifying States.

(b) peoples in independent countries who are regarded as indigenous on account of their descent from the populations which inhabited the country, or a geographical region to which the country belongs, at the time of conquest or colonisation or the establishment of present state boundaries and who, irrespective of their legal status, retain some or all of their own social, economic, cultural and political institutions.

2. Self-identification as indigenous or tribal shall be regarded as a fundamental criterion for determining the groups to which the provisions of this Convention apply.

3. The use of the term "peoples" in this Convention shall not be construed as having any implications as regards the rights which may attach to the term under international law.

Article 2

4–020   1. Governments shall have the responsibility for developing, with the participation of the peoples concerned, co-ordinated and systematic action to protect the rights of these peoples and to guarantee respect for their integrity.

2. Such action shall include measures for:

(a) ensuring that members of these peoples benefit on an equal footing from the rights and opportunities which national laws and regulations grant to other members of the population.;

(b) promoting the full realisation of the social, economic and cultural rights of these peoples with respect for their social and cultural identity, their customs and traditions and their institutions;

(c) assisting the members of the peoples concerned to eliminate socio-economic gaps that may exist between indigenous and other members of the national community, in a manner compatible with their aspirations and ways of life.

Article 3

4–021   1. Indigenous and tribal peoples shall enjoy the full measure of human rights and fundamental freedoms without hindrance or discrimination. The provisions of the Convention shall be applied without discrimination to male and female members of these peoples.

2. No form of force or coercion shall be used in violation of the human rights and fundamental freedoms of the peoples concerned, including the rights contained in this Convention.

Article 4

1. Special measures shall be adopted as appropriate for safe- 4–022
guarding the persons, institutions, property, labour, cultures and
environment of the peoples concerned.

2. Such special measures shall not be contrary to the freely-
expressed wishes of the peoples concerned.

3. Enjoyment of the general rights of citizenship, without
discrimination, shall not be prejudiced in any way by such special
measures.

Article 5

In applying the provisions of this Convention: 4–023

  (a) the social, cultural, religious and spiritual values and prac-
      tices of these peoples shall be recognised and protected,
      and due account shall be taken of the nature of the
      problems which face them both as groups and as
      individuals;

  (b) the integrity of the values, practices and institutions of
      these peoples shall be respected;

  (c) policies aimed at mitigating the difficulties experience by
      these peoples in facing new conditions of life and work
      shall be adopted, with the participation and co-operation of
      the peoples affected.

Article 6

1. In applying the provisions of this Convention, governments 4–024
shall:

  (a) consult the peoples concerned, through appropriate pro-
      cedures and in particular through their representative
      institutions, whenever consideration is being given to legis-
      lative or administrative measures which may affect them
      directly;

  (b) establish means by which these peoples can freely particip-
      ate, to at least the same extent as other sectors of the
      population, at all levels of decision-making in elective
      institutions and administrative and other bodies respon-
      sible for policies and programmes which concern them;

  (c) establish means for the full development of these peoples'
      own institutions and initiatives, and in appropriate cases
      provide the resources necessary for this purpose.

2. The consultations carried out in application of this Convention shall be undertaken, in good faith and in a form appropriate to the circumstances, with the objective of achieving agreement or consent to the proposed measures.

Article 7

4–025   **1.** The peoples concerned shall have the right to decide their own priorities for the process of development as it affects their lives, beliefs, institutions and spiritual well-being and the lands they occupy or otherwise use, and to exercise control, to the extent possible, over their own economic, social and cultural development. In addition, they shall participate in the formulation, implementation and evaluation of plans and programmes for national and regional development which may affect them directly.

2. The improvement of the conditions of life and work and levels of health and education of the peoples concerned, with their participation and co-operation, shall be a matter of priority in plans for the overall economic development of areas they inhabit. Special projects for development of the areas in question shall also be so designed as to promote such improvement.

3. Governments shall ensure that, whenever appropriate, studies are carried out, in co-operation with the peoples concerned, to assess the social, spiritual, cultural and environmental impact on them of planned development activities. The results of these studies shall be considered as fundamental criteria for the implementation of these activities.

4. Governments shall take measures, in co-operation with the peoples concerned, to protect and preserve the environment of the territories they inhabit.

Article 8

4–026   **1.** In applying national laws and regulations to the peoples concerned, due regard shall be had to their customs or customary laws.

2. These peoples shall have the right to retain their own customs and institutions, where these are not incompatible with fundamental rights defined by the national legal system and with international recognised human rights. Procedures shall be established, whenever necessary, to resolve conflicts which may arise in the application of this principle.

3. The application of paragraphs 1 and 2 of this Article shall not prevent members of these peoples from exercising the rights granted to all citizens and from assuming the correspondence duties.

Article 9

1. To the extent compatible with the national legal system and internationally recognised human rights, the methods customarily practised by the peoples concerned for dealing with offences committed by their members shall be respected.

2. The customs of these peoples in regard to penal matters shall be taken into consideration by the authorities and courts dealing with such cases.

Article 10

1. In imposing penalties laid down by general law on members 4–027 of these peoples account shall be taken of their economic, social and cultural characteristics.

2. Preference shall be given to methods of punishment other than confinement in prison.

Article 11

The exaction from members of the peoples concerned of compulsory personal services in any form, whether paid or unpaid, shall be prohibited and punishable by law, except in cases prescribed by law for all citizens.

Article 12

The peoples concerned shall be safeguarded against the abuse of their rights and shall be able to take legal proceedings, either individually or through their representative bodies, for the effective protection of these rights. Measures shall be taken to ensure that members of these peoples can understand and be understood in legal proceedings, where necessary through the provision of interpretation or by other effective means.

PART II

Land

Article 13

1. In applying the provisions of this Part of the Convention 4–028 governments shall respect the special importance for the cultures and spiritual values of the peoples concerned of their relationship with the lands or territories, or both as applicable, which they occupy of otherwise use, and in particular the collective aspects of this relationship.

2. The use of the term 'lands' in Article 15 and 16 shall include the concept of territories, which covers the total environment of the areas which the peoples concerned occupy or otherwise use.

Article 14

1. The rights of ownership and possession of the peoples concerned over the lands which they traditionally occupy shall be recognised. In addition, measures shall be taken in appropriate cases to safeguard the right of the peoples concerned to use lands not exclusively occupied by them, but to which they have traditionally had access for their subsistence and traditional activities. Particular attention shall be paid to the situation of nomadic peoples and shifting cultivators in this respect.

2. Governments shall take steps as necessary to identify the lands which the peoples concerned traditionally occupy, and to guarantee effective protection of their rights or ownership and possession.

3. Adequate procedures shall be established within the national legal system to resolve land claims by the peoples concerned.

Article 15

4–029   **1.** The rights of the peoples concerned to the natural resources pertaining to their lands shall be specially safeguarded. These rights include the right of these peoples to participate in the use, management and conservation of these resources.

2. In cases in which the State retains the ownership of mineral or sub-surface or rights to other resources pertaining to lands, governments shall establish or maintain procedures through which they shall consult these peoples, with a view of ascertaining whether and to what degree their interests would be prejudiced, before undertaking or permitting any programmes for the exploration of such resources pertaining to their lands. The peoples concerned shall wherever possible participate in the benefits of such activities, and shall receive fair compensation for any damages which they may sustain as a result of such activities.

Article 16

1. Subject to the following paragraphs of this Article, the peoples concerned shall not be removed from the lands which they occupy.

2. Where the relocation of these peoples is considered necessary as an exceptional measure, such relocation shall take place only with their free and informed consent. Where their consent cannot be obtained, such relocation shall take place only following appropriate procedures established by national laws and regulations, including public inquiries where appropriate, which provide the opportunity for effective representation of the peoples concerned.

3. Whenever possible, these peoples shall have the right to return to their traditional lands, as soon as the grounds for relocation cease to exist.

4. When such return is not possible, as determined by agreement or, in the absence of such agreement, through appropriate procedures, these peoples shall be provided in all possible cases with lands of quality and legal status at least equal to that of the lands previously occupied by them, suitable to provide for their present needs and future development. Where the peoples concerned express a preference for compensation in money or in kind, they shall be so compensated under appropriate guarantees.

5. Persons thus relocated shall be fully compensated for any resulting loss or injury.

Article 17

1. Procedures established by the peoples concerned for the 4–030 transmission of land rights among members of these peoples shall be respected.

2. The peoples concerned shall be consulted whenever consideration is being given to their capacity to alienate their lands or otherwise transmit their rights outside their own community.

3. Persons not belonging to these peoples shall be prevented from taking advantage of their customs or of lack of understanding of the laws on the part of their members to secure the ownership, possession or use of land belonging to them.

Article 18

Adequate penalties shall be established by law for unauthorised 4–031 intrusion upon, or use of, the lands of the peoples concerned, and governments shall take measures to prevent such offences.

Article 19

National agrarian programmes shall secure to the peoples concerned treatment equivalent to that accorded to other sectors of the population with regard to:

(a) the provision of more land for these peoples when they have not the area necessary for providing the essentials of a normal existence, or for any possible increase in their numbers;

(b) the provision of the means required to promote the development of the lands which these peoples already possess.

PART III

Recruitment and conditions of employment

Article 20

4–032   **1.** Governments shall, within the framework of national laws and regulations, and in co-operation with the peoples concerned, adopt special measures to ensure the effective protection with regard to recruitment and conditions of employment of workers belonging to these peoples, to the extent that they are not effectively protected by laws applicable to workers in general.

2. Governments shall do everything possible to prevent any discrimination between workers belonging to the peoples concerned and other workers, in particular as regards:

(a) admission to employment, including skilled employment, as well as measures for promotion and advancement;

(b) equal remuneration for work of equal value;

(c) medical and social assistance, occupational safety and health, all social security benefits and any other occupationally related benefits, and housing;

(d) the right of association and freedom for all lawful trade union activities, and the right to conclude collective agreements with employers or employers' organisations.

3. The measures taken shall include measures to ensure:

(a) that workers belonging to the peoples concerned, including seasonal, casual and migrant workers in agricultural and other employment, as well as those employed by labour contractors, enjoy the protection afforded by national law and practice to other such workers in the same sectors, and that they are fully informed of their rights under labour legislation and of means of redress available to them;

(b) that workers belonging to these peoples are not subjected to working conditions hazardous to their health, in particular through exposure to pesticides or other toxic substances;

(c) that workers belonging to these peoples are not subjected to coercive recruitment systems, including bonded labour and other forms of debt servitude;

(d) that workers belonging to these peoples enjoy equal opportunities and equal treatment in employment for men and
women, and protection from sexual harassment.

4. Particular attention shall be paid to the establishment of
adequate labour inspection services in areas where workers
belonging to the peoples concerned undertake wage employment,
in order to ensure compliance with the provisions of this Part of
this Convention.

PART IV

Vocational training, handicrafts and rural industries

Article 21

Members of the peoples concerned shall enjoy opportunities at 4–033
least equal to those of other citizens in respect of vocational
training measures.

Article 22

1. Measures shall be taken to promote the voluntary participation of members of the peoples concerned in vocational training
programmes of general application.
2. Whenever existing programmes of vocational training of
general application do not meet the special needs of the peoples
concerned, governments shall, with the participation of these
peoples, ensure the provision of special training programmes and
facilities.
3. Any special training programmes shall be based on the
economic environment, social and cultural conditions and practical needs of the peoples concerned. Any studies made in this
connection shall be carried out in co-operation with these peoples,
who shall be consulted on the organisation and operation of such
programmes. Where feasible, these peoples shall progressively
assume responsibility for the organisation and operation of such
special training programmes, if they so decide.

Article 23

1. Handicrafts, rural and community-based industries, and
subsistence economy and traditional activities of the peoples
concerned, such as hunting, fishing, trapping and gathering, shall
be recognised as important factors in the maintenance of their
cultures and in their economic self-reliance and development.
Governments shall, with the participation of these peoples and

whenever appropriate, ensure that these activities are strengthened and promoted.

2. Upon the request of the peoples concerned, appropriate technical and financial assistance shall be provided wherever possible, taking into account the traditional technologies and cultural characteristics of these peoples, as well as the importance of sustainable and equitable development.

PART V

Social security and health

Article 24

4-034 Social security schemes shall be extended progressively to cover the peoples concerned, and applied without discrimination against them.

Article 25

1. Governments shall ensure that adequate health services are made available to the peoples concerned, or shall provide them with resources to allow them to design and deliver such services under their own responsibility and control, so that they may enjoy the highest attainable standard of physical and mental health.

2. Health services shall, to the extend possible, be community-based. These services shall be planned and administered in co-operation with the peoples concerned and take into account their economic, geographic, social and cultural conditions as well as their traditional preventive care, healing practices and medicines.

3. The health care system shall give preference to the training and employment of local community health workers, and focus on primary health care while maintaining strong links with other levels of health care services.

4. The provision of such health services shall be co-ordinate with other social, economic and cultural measures in the country.

PART VI

Education and means of communication

Article 26

4-035 Measures shall be taken to ensure that members of the peoples concerned have the opportunity to acquire education at all levels on at least an equal footing with the rest of the national community.

Article 27

1. Education programmes and services for the peoples concerned shall be developed and implemented in co-operation with them to address their special needs, and shall incorporate their histories, their knowledge and technologies, their value systems and their further social, economic and cultural aspirations.

2. The competent authority shall ensure the training of members of these peoples and their involvement in the formulation and implementation of education programmes, with a view to the progressive transfer of responsibility for the conduct of these programmes to these peoples as appropriate.

3. In addition, governments shall recognise the right of these peoples to establish their own educational institutions and facilities, provided that such institutions meet minimum standards established by the competent authority in consultation with these peoples. Appropriate resources shall be provided for this purpose.

Article 28

1. Children belonging to the peoples concerned shall, wherever **4–036** practicable, be taught to read and write in their own indigenous language or in the language most commonly used by the group to which they belong. When this is not practicable, the competent authorities shall undertake consultations with these peoples with a view to the adoption of measures to achieve this objective.

2. Adequate measures shall be taken to ensure that these peoples have the opportunity to attain fluency in the national language or in one of the official languages of the country.

3. Measures shall be taken to preserve and promote the development and practice of the indigenous languages of the peoples concerned.

Article 29

The imparting of general knowledge and skills that will help children belonging to the peoples concerned to participate fully and on an equal footing in their own community and in the national community shall be an aim of education for these peoples.

Article 30

1. Governments shall adopt measures appropriate to the traditions and cultures of the peoples concerned, to make known to them their rights and duties, especially in regard to labour, economic opportunities, education and health matters, social welfare and their rights deriving from this Convention.

2. If necessary, this shall be done by means of written translations and through the use of mass communications in the languages of these peoples.

Article 31

Educational measures shall be taken among all sections of the national community, and particularly among those that are in most direct contact with the peoples concerned, with the object of eliminating prejudices that they may harbour in respect of these peoples. To this end, efforts shall be made to ensure that history textbooks and other educational materials provide a fair, accurate and informative portrayal of the societies and cultures of these peoples.

PART VII

Contacts and co-operation across borders

Article 32

4–037 Governments shall take appropriate measures, including by means of international agreements, to facilitate contacts and co-operation between indigenous and tribal peoples across borders, including activities in the economic, social, cultural, spiritual and environmental fields.

PART VIII

Administration

Article 33

4–038 1. The governmental authority responsible for the matters covered in this Convention shall ensure that agencies or other appropriate mechanisms exist to administer the programmes affecting the peoples concerned, and shall ensure that they have the means necessary for the proper fulfilment of the functions assigned to them.

2. These programmes shall include:

(a) the planning, co-ordination, execution and evaluation, in co-operation with the peoples concerned, of the measures provided for in this Convention.

(b) the proposing of legislative and other measures to the competent authorities and supervision of the application of the measures taken, in co-operation with the peoples concerned.

INTERNATIONAL DECADE FOR THE WORLD'S INDIGENOUS PEOPLE

The General Assembly accepted the recommendation of the 4–039 World Conference (see above para. 32) and declared the 1994–2004 the International Decade for the World's Indigenous People.[20] The declaration of the Decade is welcomed by many indigenous leaders as it is seen as an opportunity to focus public opinion on the particular needs of indigenous people. It has been suggested that there should be established a High Commissioner for Indigenous peoples and that a UN fund created for the financing of the development projects of indigenous peoples. As yet there is no High Commissioner for Indigenous People—the office not having been established. Although no UN fund for development projects of indigenous people has been created two voluntary funds to assist indigenous people have been established: travel grants for those indigenous people wanting to attend the working group on indigenous populations or working group on the draft declaration; and a fellowship programme for indigenous people.

INTERNATIONAL DAY OF THE WORLD'S INDIGENOUS PEOPLE

August 9, has been designated as International Day of the World's Indigenous People and is to be celebrated as such annually.

Indigenous Peoples' Day in August 2000 had particular reason for celebration because of the adoption by ECOSOC of a resolution to establish a Permanent Forum for Indigenous Issues.[21] The Forum was first proposed at the Vienna World Conference on Human Rights, and will give a high-level forum for the representatives of indigenous peoples for the first time. The High Commissioner for Human Rights, Mary Robinson has hailed the move as a "historic step forward".

The Forum will be a subsidiary organ of ECOSOC, consisting of 16 representatives. It is expected to come into operation in 2002.

---

[20] A/Res/47/75, December 14, 1992. 1993 was the UN Year of the *"Indigenous Peoples – A New Partnership"*. However the year was regarded as being of limited success in focusing on the needs of the world's indigenous population.

[21] Res 2000/22, July 28, 2000.

The Economic and Social Council,

4–040 *Recalling* the provision contained in the final document of the World Conference on Human Rights, held in Vienna in June 1993, according to which the establishment of a permanent forum for indigenous people within the United Nations system should be considered.

Recalling also that consideration of the establishment of a permanent forum is recognised as one of the important objectives of the programme of activities for the International Decade of the World's Indigenous People,

1. *Decides* to establish as a subsidiary organ of the Council a permanent forum on indigenous issues, consisting of 16 members, eight members to be nominated by Governments and elected by the Council, and eight members to be appointed by the President of the Council following formal consultation with the Bureau and the regional groups through their co-ordinators, on the basis of broad consultations with indigenous organisations, taking into account the diversity and geographical distribution of the indigenous people of the world as well as the principles of transparency, representativity and equal opportunity for all indigenous people, including internal processes, when appropriate, and local indigenous consultation processes, with all members serving in their personal capacity as independent experts on indigenous issues for a period of three years with the possibility of re-election or reappointment for one further period; States, United Nations bodies and organs, intergovernmental organisations and non-governmental organisations in consultative status with the Council may participate as observers; in accordance with the procedures which have been applied in the Working Group on Indigenous Populations of the Subcommission on the Promotion and Protection of Human Rights;

2. *Also decides* that the Permanent Forum on Indigenous Issues shall serve as an advisory body to the Council with a mandate to discuss indigenous issues within the mandate of the Council relating to economic and social development, culture, the environment, education, health and human rights; in so doing the Permanent Forum shall:

(a) Provide expert advice and recommendations on indigenous issues to the Council, as well as to programmes, funds and agencies of the United Nations, through the Council.

(b) Raise awareness and promote the integration and co-ordination of activities relating to indigenous issues within the United Nations system.

(c) Prepare and dissemmate information on indigenous issues.

CHAPTER 5

CHILDREN

WORLD CONGRESS ON HUMAN RIGHTS (JUNE 1993)
VIENNA DECLARATION[1]

"Children are our most valuable natural resource"[2]

Today the most widely adopted international human rights 5–001
instrument is the UN Convention on the Rights of the Child.
Indeed its almost universal acceptance can be invoked to sustain a
case that at least some, if not all, of the Convention's provisions
have acquired the status of customary international law. Domestic
courts have called for cognisance to be given to the Convention
even where the Convention has not been incorporated into the
relevant domestic law. Yet in spite of this the lives of many
thousands of children are blighted by abject poverty, forced
labour, child prostitution, service as child soldiers . . . These
problems have got to be met and addressed through concerted
international action and co-operation.

Two new Optional Protocols to the Convention on the Rights of
the Child reflect areas of significant concern which are being
addressed by the international community. Child pornography
and trafficking in children remain serious problems throughout
the world, both in developed and developing nations. Such
exploitation requires to be addressed at an international level if
progress is to be achieved towards its eradication. The use of
child soldiers is another matter of considerable concern. Although
principally an issue in developing nations, it would be wrong for
Western nations to ignore the problem, which may be closer to
their own doorstep than is immediately apparent.

A change in attitude towards children is required before they
can truly be said to have recognition for their human rights. Such
a change requires the message to be promulgated that children
require additional protection for their rights and more fundamentally that they are entitled to human rights in the first place. The
ratification of and compliance with the major international instruments concerning children by the developed Western world will
send out a positive message that the rights of children are to be
recognised, and are worthy of such recognition.

[1] 32 I.L.M. 1661 (1993).
[2] Herbert Hoover.

5–002   **21.** The World Conference on Human Rights, welcoming the early ratification of the Convention on the Rights of the Child by a large number of States and noting the recognition of the human rights of children in the World Declaration on the Survival, Protection and Development of Children and Plan of Action adopted by the World Summit for Children, urges universal ratification of the Convention by 1995 and its effective implementation by States parties through the adoption of all the necessary legislative, administrative and other measures and the allocation to the maximum extent of the available resources. In all actions concerning children, non-discrimination and the best interest of the child should be primary considerations and the views of the child given due weight. National and international mechanisms and programmes should be strengthened for the defence and protection of children, in particular, the girl-child, abandoned children, street children, economically and sexually exploited children, including through child pornography, child prostitution or sale of organs, children victims of diseases including acquired immunodeficiency syndrome, refugee and displaced children, children in detention, children in armed conflict, as well as children victims of famine and drought and other emergencies.

International co-operation and solidarity should be promoted to support the implementation of the Convention and the rights of the child should be a priority in the United Nations system-wide action on human rights.

The World Conference on Human Rights also stresses that the child for the full and harmonious development of his or her personality should grow up in a family environment which accordingly merits broader protection.

The realisation of universal ratification urged by the Vienna Declaration has virtually been achieved in that only two states, the USA and Somalia have not yet ratified the Convention. Somalia has no recognised government while the U.S. has indicated an intention to ratify by formally signing the Convention. Arguably at least of the some of the rights enshrined in the Convention have now obtained the status of customary international law. The Convention has been supplemented by the adoption of two optional protocols which were adopted by the General Assembly on May 25, 2000. The optional protocols concern children in armed conflict and the sale of children, child prostitution and child pornography.

Part II(B) 4. The rights of the child

5–003   **45.** The World Conference on Human Rights reiterates the principle of "First Call for Children" and, in this respect, underlines the importance of major national and international efforts, especially those of the United Nations Children's Fund, for promoting respect for the rights of the child to survival, protection, development and participation.

46. Measures should be taken to achieve universal ratification of the Convention on the Rights of the Child by 1995 and the universal signing of the World Declaration on the Survival, Protection and Development of Children and Plan of Action adopted by the World Summit for Children, as well as their effective implementation. The World Conference on Human Rights urges States to withdraw reservations to the Convention on the Rights of the Child contrary to the object and purpose of the Convention or otherwise contrary to international treaty law.

47. The World Conference on Human Rights urges all nations to undertake measures to the maximum extent of their available resources, with the support of international co-operation, to achieve the goals in the World Summit Plan of Action. The Conference calls on States to integrate the Convention on the Rights of the Child into their national action plans. By means of these national action plans and through international efforts, particular priority should be placed on reducing infant and maternal mortality rates, reducing malnutrition and illiteracy rates and providing access to safe drinking water and to basic education. Whenever so called for, national plans of action should be devised to combat devastating emergencies resulting from natural disasters and armed conflicts and the equally grave problem of children in extreme poverty.

48. The World Conference on Human Rights urges all States, 5–004 with the support of international co-operation, to address the acute problem of children under especially difficult circumstances. Exploitation and abuse of children should be actively combated, including by addressing their root causes. Effective measures are required against female infanticide, harmful child labour, sale of children and organs, child prostitution, child pornography, as well as other forms of sexual abuse.

49. The World Conference on Human Rights supports all measures by the United Nations and its specialised agencies to ensure the effective protection and promotion of human rights of the girl-child. The World Conference on Human Rights urges States to repeal existing laws and regulations and remove customs and practices which discriminate against and cause harm to the girl-child.

50. The World Conference on Human Rights strongly supports the proposal that the Secretary-General initiate a study into means of improving the protection of children in armed conflicts. Humanitarian norms should be implemented and measures taken in order to protect and facilitate assistance to children in war zones. Measures should include protection for children against indiscriminate use of all weapons of war, especially anti-personnel mines. The need for aftercare and rehabilitation of children traumatised by war must be addressed urgently. The Conference calls on the Committee on the Rights of the Child to study the question of raising the minimum age of recruitment into armed forces.

5–005   **51.** The World Conference on Human Rights recommends that matters relating to human rights and the situation of children be regularly reviewed and monitored by all relevant organs and mechanisms of the United Nations system and by the supervisory bodies of the specialised agencies in accordance with their mandates.

52. The World Conference on Human Rights recognises the important role played by non-governmental organisations in the effective implementation of all human rights instruments and, in particular, the Convention on the Rights of the Child.

53. The World Conference on Human Rights recommends that the Committee on the Rights of the Child, with the assistance of the Centre for Human Rights, be enabled expeditiously and effectively to meet its mandate, especially in view of the unprecedented extent of ratification and subsequent submission of country reports.

As is apparent from the Vienna Declaration children are especially vulnerable in a variety of situations and this necessitates protection at an international level. Accordingly this chapter will examine the international protection afforded to children in the situations so identified, namely:

- child labour;
- adoption;
- armed conflict;
- refugee children;
- child prostitution and sexual exploitation;
- health;
- rights within the family;

5–006   The special vulnerability of children prompted the adoption of a comprehensive international instrument, the UN Convention on the Rights of the Child 1989 which is the successor to the 1924 Geneva Declaration of the Rights of the Child[3] and the General Assembly Declaration on the Rights of the Child, 1959.[4]

The Convention was adopted without a vote by the General Assembly of the United Nations on November 20, 1989 and

---

[3] See below, para. 5–007.
[4] See below, para. 5–009.

entered into force on September 2, 1990. The Convention has been adopted by 191[5] States making it of almost universal application and highlighting that children do merit protection. The Convention is unique amongst international human rights instruments in that it applies both in times of peace and during hostilities. The Convention comprises a preamble and 41 substantive articles. The Convention identifies certain rights of the child as well articles affording protection in circumstances where children are especially vulnerable—for example during armed conflict. The Convention is comprehensive in that it addresses economic, social and cultural rights as well as civil and political rights. It is to date the most comprehensive instrument dealing exclusively with the issues pertinent to children. Children are encompassed within the ambit of general international human rights instruments and certain provisions within the latter deal specifically with issues particularly applicable to children.

1924 GENEVA DECLARATION OF THE RIGHTS OF THE CHILD

The 1924 Declaration endorsed protection of the child, *i.e.* economic, psychological and social. The Declaration did not grant legal rights to children or impose obligations on States.[6] The Declaration spelt out seven principles: **5–007**

(i) the Child must be protected beyond and above all considerations of race, nationality or creed;

(ii) the Child must be cared for with due respect for the family as an entity;

(iii) the Child must be given the means requisite for its normal development, materially, morally and spiritually;

(iv) the Child that is hungry must be fed, the child that is sick must be nursed, the child that is mentally or physically handicapped must be helped, the maladjusted child must be re-educated, the orphan and waif must be sheltered and succoured;

(v) the Child must be the first to receive relief in time of distress;

(vi) the Child must enjoy the full benefits provided by social welfare and social security schemes, must receive a training which will enable it, at the right time, to earn a livelihood, and must be protected against every form of exploitation;

---

[5] The United States has signed but not ratified while Somalia because of the absence of an government has neither signed or ratified.

[6] Unlike the UN Convention on the Rights of the Child, 1989—see below, para 5–010.

(vii) the Child must be brought up in the consciousness that its talents must be devoted to the service of its fellow men.[7]

INTERNATIONAL COVENANT ON ECONOMIC, SOCIAL AND CULTURAL RIGHTS, 1966

Article 10(3)

5–008 Special measures of protection and assistance should be taken on behalf of all children and young persons without any discrimination for reasons of parentage or other conditions. Children and young persons should be protected from economic and social exploitation. Their employment in work harmful to their morals or health or dangerous to life or likely to hamper their normal development should be punishable by law. States should also set age limits below which the paid employment of child labour should be prohibited and punishable by law.

UN GENERAL ASSEMBLY DECLARATION ON THE RIGHTS OF THE CHILD, 1959[8]

Preamble

5–009 Whereas the peoples of the United Nations have, in the Charter, reaffirmed their faith in fundamental human rights and in the dignity and worth of the human person, and have determined to promote social progress and better standards of life in larger freedom,

Whereas the United Nations has, in the Universal Declaration of Human Rights, proclaimed that everyone is entitled to all the rights and freedoms set forth therein, without distinction of any kind, such as race, colour, sex, language, religion, political or other opinion, national or social origin, property, birth or other status,

Whereas the child, by reason of his physical and mental immaturity, needs special safeguards and care, including appropriate legal protection, before as well as after birth,

Whereas the need for such special safeguards has been stated in the Geneva Declaration of the Rights of the Child of 1924, and recognised in the Universal Declaration of Human Rights and in

---

[7] The 1924 Declaration was based the on the philosophy of Eglantyne Jebb, the British founder of Save the Children Union.

[8] The Declaration was adopted unanimously by the General Assembly on November 20, 1959.

the statutes of specialised agencies and international organisations concerned with the welfare of children,

Whereas mankind owes to the child the best it has to give,

Now therefore, The General Assembly Proclaims this Declaration of the Rights of the Child to the end that he may have a happy childhood and enjoy for his own good and for the good of society the rights and freedoms herein set forth, and calls upon parents, upon men and women as individuals, and upon voluntary organisations, local authorities and national Governments to recognise these rights and strive for their observance by legislative and other measures progressively taken in accordance with the following principles:

Article 1

The child shall enjoy all the rights set forth in this Declaration. Every child, without any exception whatsoever, shall be entitled to these rights, without distinction or discrimination on account of race, colour, sex, language, religion, political or other opinion, national or social origin, property, birth or other status, whether of himself or of his family.

UN CONVENTION ON THE RIGHTS OF THE CHILD, 1989

Preamble

The States Parties to the present Convention,   **5–010**

Considering that, in accordance with the principles proclaimed in the Charter of the United Nations, recognition of the inherent dignity and of the equal and inalienable rights of all members of the human family is the foundation of freedom, justice and peace in the world,

Bearing in mind that the peoples of the United Nations have, in the Charter, reaffirmed their faith in fundamental human rights and in the dignity and worth of the human person, and have determined to promote social progress and better standards of life in larger freedom,

Recognising that the United Nations has, in the Universal Declaration of Human Rights and in the International Covenants on Human Rights, proclaimed and agreed that everyone is entitled to all the rights and freedoms set forth therein, without distinction of any kind, such as race, colour, sex, language, religion, political or other opinion, national or social origin, property, birth or other status,

Recalling that, in the Universal Declaration of Human Rights, the United Nations has proclaimed that childhood is entitled to special care and assistance,

Convinced that the family, as the fundamental group of society and the natural environment for the growth and well-being of all its members and particularly children, should be afforded the necessary protection and assistance so that it can fully assume its responsibilities within the community,

Recognising that the child, for the full and harmonious development of his or her personality, should grow up in a family environment, in an atmosphere of happiness, love and understanding,

Considering that the child should be fully prepared to live an individual life in society, and brought up in the spirit of the ideals proclaimed in the Charter of the United Nations, and in particular in the spirit of peace, dignity, tolerance, freedom, equality and solidarity,

5–011 Bearing in mind that the need to extend particular care to the child has been stated in the Geneva Declaration of the Rights of the Child of 1924 and in the Declaration of the Rights of the Child adopted by the United Nations on November 20, 1959 and recognised in the Universal Declaration of Human Rights, in the International Covenant on Civil and Political Rights (in particular in Articles 23 and 24), in the International Covenant on Economic, Social and Cultural Rights (in particular in Article 10) and in the statutes and relevant instruments of specialised agencies and international organisations concerned with the welfare of children,

Bearing in mind that, as indicated in the Declaration of the Rights of the Child, "the child, by reason of his physical and mental immaturity, needs special safeguards and care, including appropriate legal protection, before as well as after birth", Recalling the provisions of the Declaration on Social and Legal Principles relating to the Protection and Welfare of Children, with Special Reference to Foster Placement and Adoption Nationally and Internationally; the United Nations Standard Minimum Rules for the Administration of Juvenile Justice ("The Beijing Rules"); and the Declaration on the Protection of Women and Children in Emergency and Armed Conflict,

Recognising that, in all countries in the world, there are children living in exceptionally difficult conditions, and that such children need special consideration,

Taking due account of the importance of the traditions and cultural values of each people for the protection and harmonious development of the child,

Recognising the importance of international co-operation for improving the living conditions of children in every country, in particular in the developing countries,

"Best Interests of Child"

The guiding principle reflected both in the 1959 Declaration 5–012 and 1989 Convention is that of "best interests of the child":

The Convention provides no guidance on how the term is to be interpreted. Although it is increasingly recognised that the concept is not one which lends itself to uniform and universal application. Rather it has to be applied to the individual circumstances peculiar to each child, as was observed by Madame Justice McLachlin in the Canadian Supreme Court case of *Gordon v. Goertz.*[9]

"The best interest of the child test has been characterised as 'indeterminate' and 'more useful as legal aspiration than as legal analysis'. The multitude of factors that may impinge on the child's best interest make a measure of indeterminacy inevitable. A more precise test would risk sacrificing the child's best interest to expediency and certainty."

The significance of the obligation incumbent on States to give cognisance to the best interests of the child was highlighted in the case of *Baker v. Canada (Minister of Citizenship and Immigration (No. 25823 (July 9, 1999))* even where the international convention had not been incorporated into domestic legislation.

UN GENERAL ASSEMBLY DECLARATION ON THE RIGHTS OF THE CHILD, 1959

Principle 2

The child shall enjoy special protection, and shall be given 5–013 opportunities and facilities, by law and by other means, to enable him to develop physically, mentally, morally, spiritually and socially in a healthy and normal manner and in conditions of freedom and dignity. In the enactment of laws for this purpose, the best interests of the child shall be the paramount consideration.

UN CONVENTION ON THE RIGHTS OF THE CHILD, 1989

Article 3

1. In all actions concerning children, whether undertaken by 5–014 public or private social welfare institutions, courts of law, administrative authorities or legislative bodies, the best interests of the child shall be a primary consideration.

[9] S.C.C, No. 24622.

2. States Parties undertake to ensure the child such protection and care as is necessary for his or her well-being, taking into account the rights and duties of his or her parents, legal guardians, or other individuals legally responsible for him or her, and, to this end, shall take all appropriate legislative and administrative measures.

3. States Parties shall ensure that the institutions, services and facilities responsible for the care or protection of children shall conform with the standards established by competent authorities, particularly in the areas of safety, health, in the number and suitability of their staff, as well as competent supervision.

DEFINITION OF CHILD

Article 1

Article 1 defines child for the purposes of the Convention, as every human being below the age of 18 years unless, under the law applicable to the child, majority is attained earlier.

Article 1 was left deliberately vague so as to allow each Contracting Party flexibility in interpretation of "child". Article 1 is silent on the issue of when rights may be afforded. Is it at the point of birth or before? This is in spite of the fact that in the Preamble to the Convention reference is made to the need for "special safeguards and care, including appropriate legal protection, before as well as after birth",

Likewise States are free to determine when childhood ends. The Convention confines itself to guaranteeing the right to life.

Article 6

1. States Parties recognise that every child has the inherent right to life.

2. States Parties shall ensure to the maximum extent possible the survival and development of the child.

OBLIGATION ON CONTRACTING PARTIES

Article 2

5–015 Article 2 demands that Contracting Parties respect and ensure the rights contained in the Convention of all children within their jurisdiction without discrimination of any kind, irrespective of the child's or his or her parent's or legal guardian's race, colour, sex, language, religion, political or other opinion, national, ethnic or social origin, property, disability, birth or other status.[10] To this end States are required to take all appropriate measures to ensure that the child is protected against all forms of discrimination or punishment on the basis of the status, activities, expressed opinions, or beliefs of the child's parents, legal guardians, or family members.[11]

Article 2 is complemented by Article 4 which requires a Contracting Party to introduce all appropriate legislative, administrative, and other measures for the implementation of the rights recognised in the present Convention. However with respect to economic, social and cultural rights, Contracting Parties are obliged to undertake such measures to the maximum extent of their available resources and, where needed, within the framework of international co-operation.

1. CHILD LABOUR

The plight of children and its severity has been recognised by the **5–016** Human Rights Commission[12]:

1. . . . the exploitation of child labour still remains a current and widespread phenomenon of a serious nature in various parts of the world.

2. This phenomenon, which is both complex and worldwide, varies from one country to another. Although the industrialised countries are not spared, it affects the developing countries more particularly, and within each country the more vulnerable groups of the population. Poverty is often the main cause of child labour, but generations of children should not be condemned, until poverty is overcome, to exploitation. Underdevelopment cannot justify exploitation of which children are the victims. The governments concerned and the international community as a whole must not wait for development problems to be adequately solved before attacking the phenomenon of the exploitation of child labour . . . it is essential that urgent measures and medium and short-term action be taken to meet the immediate needs of the children who are exposed to the gravest dangers, while making sure that such action is integrated into economic and social development strategies."

---

[10] Article 2.1.
[11] Article 2.2.
[12] Programme of Action for the Elimination of the Exploitation of Child Labour—I.H.R.R. Vol. 1, No. 1 (1994) 227.

In particular the Commission calls for high priority to be given to the elimination of child prostitution, pornography, the sale of children, the employment of children in dangerous occupations or for enforced begging and debt bondage[13] and urges the international community to place "particular emphasis on the new phenomena of the exploitation of child labour, such as the use of children for illegal, clandestine or criminal purposes, including their implication in the narcotic drugs traffic of in armed conflicts or military activities."[14] The Commission perceives the initial task as being the elimination of work by children under 10 years of age with a view to achieving compliance with all relevant international instruments.[15]

Where most children live and numbers at work

	Number of 16-year-olds (million)	Number working (million)
CHINA	340	no data
INDIA	340	17.5 (government figure) 100 (1994 independent estimate)
PAKISTAN	62	17.3 in bonded labour (ILO estimate) 19 (1994 independent estimate)
UNITED STATES	60	5.5 (1993 figures for 12–17-year-olds)
BRAZIL	55	7.0 (1994 UNHCR estimate)
NIGERIA	50	12 (1994 UNHCR estimate)
BANGLADESH	49	15 (1993 Union estimate)
MEXICO	35	11 (1994 government estimate)
RUSSIAN FED.	35	no data
IRAN	30	no data
VIETNAM	29	no data
PHILIPPINES	27	5 (1994 government estimate)
EGYPT	25	0.4 (1991 ILO estimate)

SOURCE: *The Progress of Nations* (UNICEF 1995).

Subsequent UNICEF annual reports have focused on living conditions around the world (1997): over-population, polio and the toll of debt crisis (1999), AIDS, immigration and early childhood care (2000).

[13] *ibid.* pt. 3.
[14] *ibid.* pt. 4.
[15] *ibid.* pt. 5.

In Britain at least 40,000 children under 18 years have primary 5–017
responsibility for the care of their parents or brothers and sisters.
The numbers are increasing with the average age of the young
carer being 12 but currently it is estimated that 28 per cent of
young carers are under the age of 10. In Edinburgh 500 children
have been left to care for their AIDS disabled parent and 29 per
cent of young carers are looking after mentally ill parents. 61 per
cent are children of lone parents who have become sick or
disabled.[16]

The most vulnerable categories of children are identified as
including the children of immigrants, street children, children of
minority groups, indigenous children, refugee children and children in occupied territories.[17]

The Commission recognises that to combat poverty increased
resources are required along with "deep structural reforms in the
economic, social and cultural spheres,[18] and calls for action at all
levels of government.[19]

The Commission highlights the need for information, education
and vocational training, social action and development aid as well
as greater adherence to international labour standards already in
force.

Points 15–25 of the Resolution outline duties on States, namely:

- *adherence to the Declaration on the Rights of the Child 1959;*

- *ratification of the Convention on the Rights of the Child and the
  Minimum Age Convention;*

- *the adoption and implementation of policies and programmes to
  narrow the gap between legislation and its implementation in
  practice, a review of legislation in the area of child labour with a
  view to the absolute prohibition of the employment of children in
  certain areas such as night work, work in connection with drug
  trafficking and production of the same and underage maid service
  and the prostitution, pornography and sexual exploitation industry; the adoption of preventive and curative measures to combat
  the phenomena of the exploitation of child labour such as the use
  of children for illegal, clandestine or criminal purposes,including
  the traffic in narcotic drugs, or in armed conflicts or military
  activities, or any other form of conflict;*

- *provision of free primary and compulsory education[20];*

---

[16] Findings of the First National Survey of Young Carers conducted by Loughborough
University for the magazine *Community Care* and featured in "Too Much, Too Young"—
World in Action, Granada Television, October 1995.

[17] Programme of Action *supra* n. pt. 6.

[18] *ibid.* pt 7.

[19] *ibid.* pts 8 and 9.

[20] See below para. 5–047.

- *improvement of child medical services;*

- *improvement of training programmes for professionals in the field of child labour;*

- *establishment of national bodies to promote children's rights and to protect from exploitation with particular efforts being made to stress the importance of family values.*

The remaining points deal with the role of the United Nations, and that of bodies/specialised agencies in combatting child exploitation. The creation of an international child welfare fund is called for with the resources being allocated to afford protection to children who are in particularly vulnerable circumstances.

UN GENERAL ASSEMBLY DECLARATION ON THE RIGHTS OF THE CHILD, 1959

Principle 9

5–018 The child shall not be admitted to employment before an appropriate minimum age; he shall in no case be caused or permitted to engage in any occupation or employment which would prejudice his health or education, or interfere with his physical, mental or moral development.

UN CONVENTION ON THE RIGHTS OF THE CHILD, 1989

Article 32

1. States Parties recognise the right of the child to be protected from economic exploitation and from performing any work that is likely to be hazardous or to interfere with the child's education, or to be harmful to the child's health or physical, mental, spiritual, moral or social development.

2. States Parties shall take legislative, administrative, social and educational measures to ensure the implementation of the present article. To this end, and having regard to the relevant provisions of other international instruments, States Parties shall in particular:

(a) Provide for a minimum age or minimum ages for admissions to employment;

(b) Provide for appropriate regulation of the hours and conditions of employment;

(c) Provide for appropriate penalties or other sanctions to ensure the effective enforcement of the present article.

2. ADOPTION

CONVENTION ON THE RIGHTS OF THE CHILD, 1989

Article 21

1. States Parties shall take appropriate measures to ensure that 5–019 a child who is seeking refugee status or who is considered a refugee in accordance with applicable international or domestic law and procedures shall, whether unaccompanied or accompanied by his or her parents or by any other person, receive appropriate protection and humanitarian assistance in the enjoyment of applicable rights set forth in the present Convention and in other international human rights or humanitarian instruments to which the said States are Parties.

2. For this purpose, States Parties shall provide, as they consider appropriate, co-operation in any efforts by the United Nations and other competent intergovernmental organisations or non-governmental organisations co-operating with the United Nations to protect and assist such a child and to trace the parents or other members of the family of any refugee child in order to obtain information necessary for reunification with his or her family. In cases where no parents or other members of the family can be found, the child shall be accorded the same protection as any other child permanently or temporarily deprived of his or her family environment for any reason, as set forth in the present Convention.

States Parties that recognise and/or permit the system of adoption shall ensure that the best interests of the child shall be the paramount consideration and they shall:

(a) Ensure that the adoption of a child is authorised only by competent authorities who determine, in accordance with applicable law and procedures and on the basis of all pertinent and reliable information, that the adoption is permissible in view of the child's status concerning parents, relatives and legal guardians and that, if required, the persons concerned have given their informed consent to the adoption on the basis of such counselling as may be necessary;

(b) Recognise that inter-country adoption may be considered as an alternative means of child's care, if the child cannot be placed in a foster or an adoptive family or cannot in any suitable manner be cared for in the child's country of origin;

(c) Ensure that the child concerned by intercountry adoption enjoys safeguards and standards equivalent to those existing in the case of national adoption;

(d) Take all appropriate measures to ensure that, in intercountry adoption, the placement does not result in improper financial gain for those involved in it;

(e) Promote, where appropriate, the objectives of the present article by concluding bilateral or multilateral arrangements or agreements, and endeavour, within this framework, to ensure that the placement of the child in another country is carried out by competent authorities or organs.[21]

5–020   In addition to Article 21 the Convention on Protection of Children and Co-operation in Respect of Intercountry Adoption[22] seeks to regulate intercountry adoption. The Convention recognises that intercountry adoption may offer the advantage of a permanent family to a child for whom a suitable family cannot be found in his or her State of origin, and recognises the need in such situations to take account of the of the best interests of the child and so ensure "respect for his or her fundamental rights, and to prevent the abduction, the sale of, or traffic in children".[23] The essence of the Convention is to set out various requirements in cases of intercountry adoption, such as the eligibility of the child for adoption,[24] ensuring the relevant consents are obtained freely and not induced by payment or compensation,[25] receiving consent of the mother subsequent to the birth,[26] due consideration where appropriate to the child's opinion and the suitability of prospective adoptive parents.[27] The other issues addressed by the Convention fall within the domain of the conflict of laws for example, procedural requirements, exchange of information between central authorities and the recognition and effects of adoption.

3. Armed Conflict

"It is our Children who pay the Heaviest Price for our Short Sighted Economic Policy, Our Political Blunders, Our Wars."[28]

CONVENTION ON THE RIGHTS OF THE CHILD, 1989

Article 38

5–021   **1.** States Parties undertake to respect and to ensure respect for rules of international humanitarian law applicable to them in armed conflicts which are relevant to the child.

---

[21] Note that Art. 21 takes account of the fact that not all states recognise adoption, *e.g.* Islamic states which the utilise the concept of *Kafala* which resembles the Western practice of fostering.

[22] May 29, 1993.

[23] Preamble.

[24] Art. 4(a).

[25] Art. 4(c) 3.

[26] Art. 4(d)4.

[27] Art. 5(a).

[28] Eglantyne Jebb cited in Thomas Hammarberg, "The UN Convention on the Rights of the Child—And How to Make it Work" (1990) 12. H.R.Q.

2. States Parties shall take all feasible measures to ensure that persons who have not attained the age of 15 years do not take a direct part in hostilities.

3. States Parties shall refrain from recruiting any person who has not attained the age of 15 years into their armed forces. In recruiting among those persons who have attained the age of 15 years but who have not attained the age of 18 years, States Parties shall endeavour to give priority to those who are oldest.

4. In accordance with their obligations under international humanitarian law to protect the civilian population in armed conflicts, States Parties shall take all feasible measures to ensure protection and care of children who are affected by an armed conflict.

Under the Convention it is a violation to recruit a child under 15 years to be a soldier. States are also under an obligation to ensure that a child under 15 years does not "take a direct part in hostilities." It is a violation regardless of whether the child volunteered or was conscripted, or whether the war is an international or civil war or whether it is a government or opposition army. This is provided for in the 1977 Protocols 1 and 11 to the 1949 Geneva Conventions, – *i.e.* Article 77 and Article 4, respectively.

International law permits each state to decide whether adolescents 15 years and over can be soldiers but when this happens older adolescents must be recruited in preference to younger ones. An increase in the minimum age from 15 to 18 years was proposed but not adopted due to the objection of the United States—primarily on the grounds apparently that this was an inappropriate forum for amending existing humanitarian law.

Note: The United Nations High Commissioner for Refugees advocates that no refugee, adult, adolescent, or child be conscripted and that forcing refugees to be soldiers violates the principle that refugees are a neutral population in an asylum country. As a rule once a refugee voluntarily takes up arms or otherwise takes direct part in hostilities (s)he no longer can invoke the protection of the UNHCR. However, children who are constrained to take up arms even voluntarily will not be regarded as responsible for their own actions by virtue of their status as a minor.[29]

Effects of War: Landmines

Landmines are a legacy of hostilities and children are particularly **5–022** likely to be killed or maimed. Landmines laid during the Second World War are still claiming victims today with with eight per cent

---

[29] UNHCR, "Refugee Children: Guidelines on Protection and Care," (1994), p. 85.

of the casualties and fatalities being children. It is estimated that land mines kill some 10,000 civilians every year and maim or blind thousands more. Modern landmines are designed to shred limbs rather than kill and, because they contain no metal parts, the one hundred million mines adults have planted in the soil of 62 countries around the world are virtually undetectable. Although the majority of the countries so affected are on the African continent the most heavily mined country is Afganistan with nearly ten million mines laid mainly by Soviet forces.[30] In addition to the obvious physical effects land mines render agricultural land useless thereby exacerbating the problem of malnutrition. The former Yugoslavia is creeping up the list of most mined countries with UN officials estimating more than three million land mines since 1991. New minefields are also reported in Georgia, Armenia, Azerbaijan and Tajikistan. Human Rights Watch reports that there are 96 manufacturers in 48 countries producing in the region of ten million anti-personnel landmines each year worth approximately three hundred million pounds in sales. UN estimates present landmine areas would take 1,000 years to clear and this does not include areas currently being mined or which will be mined in the future. There is a growing international movement for a ban on the production of use of landmines and on exporting and stockpiling. Some countries have already decided not to export mines. The United States passed a moratorium on mine exporting in 1992 and recently this example has been followed by Italy. France, Sweden, Germany, Belgium, Spain and Ireland no longer export mines and Belgium has declared a ban on production. The United Kingdom justifies the production of landmines on the grounds that it produces "smart mines" which deactivate after three months.[31] At the International Meeting on Mine Clearance held in Geneva on July 6, 1995, UN Secretary General Boutros Boutros-Ghali called for a global ban on the production and use of landmines and the destruction of stockpiles. The current applicable international instrument is Protocol 11[32] to the Convention on Certain Conventional Weapons.[33] A review conference of Protocol 11 was convened in April/May 1996, however, although some amendments were adopted the end product in the words of the International Red Cross was "woefully inadequate". The measures adopted include an extension of the scope of Protocol II to non-international

[30] Angola nine million mines; Cambodia four–seven million mines.
[31] Source: Save the Children Fund.
[32] Protocol on Prohibitions or Restrictions on the Use of Mines, Booby Traps and other Devices cited below.
[33] "Convention Prohibitions or Restrictions on the Use of Certain Conventional Weapons which may be Deemed to be Excessively Injurious or to have Indiscriminate Effects", UN Doc. A/CONF/.95/15 and Corr. 1–5; Misc. 23 (1981), Cmnd. 8370; 19 I.L.M. 1523.

conflicts, assignment of responsibility for mine clearance to those who lay them, improved recording requirements and improved protection for humanitarian workers. ICRC is critical because it believes that "measures have been adopted which, instead of entirely prohibiting use of an indiscriminate weapon, both permit its continued use and implicitly promote the use of new models which will have virtually the same effects".[34] To help defray the cost of mine clearance a United Nations Voluntary Trust Fund for Assistance in Mine Clearance has been established.[35]

The General Assembly of the United Nations adopted an **5–023** Optional Protocol to the Convention on May 25, 2000. The Optional Protocol concerns children in armed conflict. Upon ratification, states are required to declare the minimum age at which voluntary recruitment is countenanced. While 18 is the minimum age for compulsory recruitment, there is no such limit where the enlisting is voluntary. In July 2001, there were 76 signatories to the Protocol and four states had ratified it.

The States Parties to the present Protocol.

Encouraged by the overwhelming support for the Convention on the Rights of the Child, demonstrating the widespread commitment that exists to strive for the promotion and protection of the rights of the child,

Reaffirming that the rights of children require special protection, and calling for continuous improvement of the situation of children without distinction, as well as for their development and education in conditions of peace and security,

Disturbed by the harmful and widespread impact of armed conflict on children and the long-term consequences it has for durable peace, security and development,

Condemning the targeting of children in situations of armed conflict and direct attacks on objects protected under international law, including places that generally have a significant presence of children, such as schools and hospitals.

Noting the adoption of the Rome Statute of the International Criminal Court, in particular, the inclusion therein as a war crime, of conscripting or enlisting children under the age of 15 years or using them to participate actively in hostilities in both international and non-international armed conflicts.

Considering therefore that to strengthen further the implementation of rights recognised in the Convention on the Rights of the Child there is a need to increase the protection of children from involvement in armed conflict.

Noting that Article 1 of the Convention on the Rights of the Child specifies that, for the purposes of that Convention, a child

---

[34] ICRC Press Release, May 1996.
[35] For every mine laid at a cost of U.S. $3, it costs an estimated U.S. $1,000 to detect and destroy.

means every human being below the age of 18 years unless, under the law applicable to the child, majority is attained earlier.

Convinced that an optional protocol to the Convention that raises the age of possible recruitment of persons into armed forces and their participation in hostilities will contribute effectively to the implementation of the principle that the best interests of the child are to be a primary consideration in all actions concerning children.

Noting that the 26th International Conference of the Red Cross and Red Crescent in December 1995 recommended, *inter alia*, that parties to conflict take every feasible step to ensure that children below the age of 18 years do not take part in hostilities.

5–024   Welcoming the unanimous adoption, in June 1999, of International Labour Organisation Convention No. 182 on the Prohibition and Immediate Action for the Elimination of the Worst Forms of Child Labour, which prohibits, *inter alia*, forced or compulsory recruitment of children for use in armed conflict.

Condemning with the gravest concern the recruitment, training and use within and across national borders of children in hostilities by armed groups distinct from the armed forces of a State, and recognising the responsibility of those who recruit, train and use children in this regard.

Recalling the obligation of each party to an armed conflict to abide by the provisions of international humanitarian law.

Stressing that the present Protocol is without prejudice to the purposes and principles contained in the Charter of the United Nations, including Article 51, and relevant norms of humanitarian law.

Bearing in mind that conditions of peace and security based on full respect of the purposes and principles contained in the Charter and observance of applicable human rights instruments are indispensable for the full protection of children, in particular during armed conflicts and foreign occupation.

Recognising the special needs of those children who are particularly vulnerable to recruitment or use in hostilities contrary to the present Protocol owing to their economic or social status or gender.

Mindful of the necessity of taking into consideration the economic, social and political root causes of the involvement of children in armed conflicts.

Convinced of the need to strengthen international co-operation in the implementation of the present Protocol, as well as the physical and psychosocial rehabilitation and social reintegration of children who are victims of armed conflict.

Encouraging the participation of the community and, in particular, children and child victims in the dissemination of informational and educational programmes concerning the implementation of the Protocol.

Have agreed as follows:

Article 1

States Parties shall take all feasible measures to ensure that 5–025
members of their armed forces who have not attained the age of
18 years do not take a direct part in hostilities.

Article 2

States Parties shall ensure that persons who have not attained the
age of 18 years are not compulsorily recruited into their armed
forces.

Article 3

1. States Parties shall raise the minimum age for the voluntary
recruitment of persons into their national armed forces from that
set out in Article 38, paragraph 3, of the Convention on the Rights
of the Child, taking account of the principles contained in that
article and recognising that under the Convention persons under
the age of 18 years are entitled to special protection.

2. Each State Party shall deposit a binding declaration upon
ratification of or accession to the present Protocol that sets forth
the minimum age at which it will permit voluntary recruitment
into its national armed forces and a description of the safeguards
it has adopted to ensure that such recruitment is not forced or
coerced.

3. States Parties that permit voluntary recruitment into their
national armed forces under the age of 18 years shall maintain
safeguards to ensure, as a minimum, that:

(a) Such recruitment is genuinely voluntary;

(b) Such recruitment is carried out with the informed consent
of the person's parents or legal guardians;

(c) Such persons are fully informed of the duties involved in
such military service;

(d) Such persons provide reliable proof of age prior to acceptance into national military service;

4. Each State Party may strengthen its declaration at any time
by notification to that effect addressed to the Secretary-General of
the United Nations, who shall inform all States Parties. Such
notification shall take effect on the date on which it is received by
the Secretary-General.

5. The requirement to raise the age in paragraph 1 of the
present article does not apply to schools operated by or under the

control of the armed forces of the States Parties, in keeping with Articles 28 and 29 of the Convention on the Rights of the Child.

Article 4

5–026   **1.** Armed groups that are distinct from the armed forces of a State should not, under any circumstances, recruit or use in hostilities persons under the age of 18 years.

2. States Parties shall take all feasible measures to prevent such recruitment and use, including the adoption of legal measures necessary to prohibit and criminalise such practices.

3. The application of the present article shall not affect the legal status of any party to an armed conflict.

Article 5

Nothing in the present Protocol shall be construed as precluding provisions in the law of a State Party or in international instruments and international humanitarian law that are more conducive to the realisation of the rights of the child.

Article 6

1. Each State Party shall take all necessary legal, administrative and other measures to ensure the effective implementation and enforcement of the provisions of the present Protocol within its jurisdiction.

2. States Parties undertake to make the principles and provisions of the present Protocol widely known and promoted by appropriate means, to adults and children alike.

3. States Parties shall take all feasible measures to ensure that persons within their jurisdiction recruited or used in hostilities contrary to the present Protocol are demobilised or otherwise released from service. States Parties shall, when necessary, accord to such persons all appropriate assistance for their physical and psychological recovery and their social reintegration.

Article 7

5–027   **1.** States Parties shall co-operate in the implementation of the present Protocol, including in the prevention of any activity contrary thereto and in the rehabilitation and social reintegration of persons who are victims of acts contrary thereto, including through technical co-operation and financial assistance. Such assistance and co-operation will be undertaken in consultation with the States Parties concerned and the relevant international organisations.

2. States Parties in a position to do so shall provide such assistance through existing multilateral, bilateral or other programmes or, *inter alia*, through a voluntary fund established in accordance with the rules of the General Assembly.

Article 8

1. Each State Party shall, within two years following the entry into force of the present Protocol for that State Party, submit a report to the Committee on the Rights of the Child providing comprehensive information on the measures it has taken to implement the provisions of the Protocol, including the measures taken to implement the provisions on participation and recruitment.

2. Following the submission of the comprehensive report, each State Party shall include in the reports it submits to the Committee on the Rights of the Child, in accordance with Article 44 of the Convention, any further information with respect to the implementation of the Protocol. Other States Parties to the Protocol shall submit a report every five years.

3. The Committee on the Rights of the Child may request from States Parties further information relevant to the implementation of the present Protocol.

4. Juvenile Justice[36]

UN COVENANT ON CIVIL AND POLITICAL RIGHTS, 1966

Article 6(5)

Sentence of death shall not be imposed for crimes committed by 5–028 persons below 18 years of age . . . One notable reservation to this Article is that made by the United States as in approximately one half of states allowing the death penalty juveniles of 16 and 17 may be prosecuted as adults and punished for the perpetration of capital crimes.

Article 10(3)

The penitentiary system shall comprise treatment of prisoners the essential aim of which shall be their reformation and social rehabilitation. Juvenile offenders shall be segregated from adults and shall be accorded treatment appropriate to their age and legal status.

Article 14

1. All persons shall be equal before the Courts and tribunals . . .

---

[36] See Chapter on Prisoners.

4. In the case of juvenile persons, the procedures shall be such as will take account of their age and desirability of promoting their rehabilitation.

CONVENTION ON THE RIGHTS OF THE CHILD, 1989

Article 37

5–029 States Parties shall ensure that:

(a) No child shall be subjected to torture or other cruel, inhuman or degrading treatment or punishment. Neither capital punishment nor life imprisonment without possibility of release shall be imposed for offences committed by persons below 18 years of age;

(b) No child shall be deprived of his or her liberty unlawfully or arbitrarily. The arrest, detention or imprisonment of a child shall be in conformity with the law and shall be used only as a measure of last resort and for the shortest appropriate period of time;

(c) Every child deprived of liberty shall be treated with humanity and respect for the inherent dignity of the human person, and in a manner which takes into account the needs of persons of his or her age. In particular every child deprived of liberty shall be separated from adults unless it is considered in the child's best interest not to do so and shall have the right to maintain contact with his or her family through correspondence and visits, save in exceptional circumstances;

(d) Every child deprived of his or her liberty shall have the right to prompt access to legal and other appropriate assistance, as well as the right to challenge the legality of the deprivation of his or her liberty before a court or other competent, independent and impartial authority, and to a prompt decision on any such action.

Article 40

5–030   **1.** States Parties recognise the right of every child alleged as, accused of, or recognised as having infringed the penal law to be treated in a manner consistent with the promotion of the child's sense of dignity and worth, which reinforces the child's respect for the human rights and fundamental freedoms of others and which takes into account the child's age and the desirability of promoting the child's reintegration and the child's assuming a constructive role in society.

2. To this end, and having regard to the relevant provisions of international instruments, States Parties shall, in particular, ensure that:

(a) No child shall be alleged as, be accused of, or recognised as having infringed the penal law by reason of acts or omissions that were not prohibited by national or international law at the time they were committed;

(b) Every child alleged as or accused of having infringed the penal law has at least the following guarantees:

   (i) To be presumed innocent until proven guilty according to law;

   (ii) To be informed promptly and directly of the charges against him or her, and, if appropriate, through his or her parents or legal guardians, and to have legal or other appropriate assistance in the preparation and presentation of his or her defence;

   (iii) To have the matter determined without delay by a competent, independent and impartial authority or judicial body in a fair hearing according to law, in the presence of legal or other appropriate assistance and, unless it is considered not to be in the best interest of the child, in particular, taking into account his or her age or situation, his or her parents or legal guardians;

   (iv) Not to be compelled to give testimony or to confess guilt; to examine or have examined adverse witnesses and to obtain the participation and examination of witnesses on his or her behalf under conditions of equality;

   (v) If considered to have infringed the penal law, to have this decision and any measures imposed in consequence thereof reviewed by a higher competent, independent and impartial authority or judicial body according to law;

   (vi) To have the free assistance of an interpreter if the child cannot understand or speak the language used;

   (vii) To have his or her privacy fully respected at all stages of the proceedings.

3. States Parties shall seek to promote the establishment of laws, procedures, authorities and institutions specifically applicable to children alleged as, accused of, or recognised as having infringed the penal law, and, in particular:

(a) the establishment of a minimum age below which children shall be presumed not to have the capacity to infringe the penal law;

(b) whenever appropriate and desirable, measures for dealing with such children without resorting to judicial proceedings, providing that human rights and legal safeguards are fully respected.

4. A variety of dispositions, such as care, guidance and supervision orders; counselling; probation; foster care; education and vocational training programmes and other alternatives to institutional care shall be available to ensure that children are dealt with in a manner appropriate to their well-being and proportionate both to their circumstances and the offence.

NOTE: "In Rwanda, where the 1994 genocide and war claimed up to one million lives, the Convention has been a vital instrument in protecting the rights of children and youngsters under the age of 18 who are in the unusual and desperate situation of being accused of genocide and murder. Citing Convention clauses that protect children in conflict with the law UNICEF and the International Committee of the Red Cross[37] are working with the Government to transfer most of the remaining 2,300 child prisoners still being held in overcrowded adult prisons. Some 200 have already been moved to UNICEF-run rehabilitation centres.—UNICEF also hired five lawyers to represent the children".[38]

5. REFUGEE CHILDREN

CONVENTION ON THE RIGHTS OF THE CHILD, 1989

Article 22

5–031 **1.** States Parties shall take appropriate measures to ensure that a child who is seeking refugee status or who is considered a refugee in accordance with applicable international or domestic law and procedures shall, whether unaccompanied or accompanied by his or her parents or by any other person, receive appropriate protection and humanitarian assistance in the enjoyment of applicable rights set forth in the present Convention and in other international human rights or humanitarian instruments to which the said States are Parties.

2. For this purpose, States Parties shall provide, as they consider appropriate, co-operation in any efforts by the United Nations and other competent intergovernmental organisations or

---

[37] For information on the International Committee see Chapter on the Protection of Civilians.
[38] UNICEF, *The Progress of Nations*, 1996.

non-governmental organisations co-operating with the United Nations to protect and assist such a child and to trace the parents or other members of the family of any refugee child in order to obtain information necessary for reunification with his or her family. In cases where no parents or other members of the family can be found, the child shall be accorded the same protection as any other child permanently or temporarily deprived of his or her family environment for any reason, as set forth in the present Convention.

It is estimated that children constitute approximately half of any refugee population. Refugee children are particularly vulnerable—they are vulnerable as children and they are vulnerable as refugees. Recognition of this has precipitated UNHCR initiatives and in particular Guidelines on Protection and Care of Refugee Children.[39] The initial guidelines were published in 1988 and were revised in 1994 and the latter have been described as "the result of combining the concept of children's rights with UNHCR's ongoing efforts to protect and assist refugee children".[40] The guiding principles of the UNHCR policy on refugee children are spelt out in a document which is reproduced as Annex A of the Guidelines.[41]

The UNHCR's primary goals with regard to refugee children 5–032 are as follows:

a. to ensure the protection and healthy development of refugee children;

b. to achieve durable solutions which are appropriate to the immediate and long-term developmental needs of refugee children.

In addition the UNHCR has identified central principles to serve as guidance in the pursuit of the above, namely:

a. in all actions taken concerning refugee children, the human rights of the child, in particular his of her best interests, are to be given primary consideration;

b. preserving and restoring family unity are of fundamental concern;

c. actions to benefit refugee children should be directed primarily at enabling their primary care givers to fulfil their principal responsibility to meet their children's needs;

---

[39] UNHCR Geneva, 1988; revised 1994. Such guidelines were initially requested by the Executive Committee (UNHCR) in Executive Committee Conclusion No. 47 (XXXVIII) 1987, Refugee Children.
[40] Introduction, 1994 Guidelines.
[41] Doc. EC/SCP/82.

d. where the special needs of refugee children can only be met effectively through child-focused activities, these should be carried out with the full participation of their families and communities;

e. refugee girls and boys must be assured protection and assistance of a basis of equality;

f. unaccompanied refugee children must be the particular focus of protection and care[42];

g. UNHCR staff are required to make their best efforts both to prevent risk to refugee children and to take additional action to ensure the survival and safety of refugee children at particular risk.

Objectives

5-033 On the basis of these principles, UNHCR staff should endeavour to ensure that the protection of children's rights as recognised under national and international law, including their rights to personal security and special assistance, are adequately and consistently addressed in the Office's protection and assistance activities.

To this effect UNHCR staff will pursue the following specific objectives:

a. the protection of refugee children at risk from detention, armed conflict, military recruitment, sexual assault or abuse, prostitution, torture, hazardous working conditions or any other form of violence, abuse or neglect;

b. the diligent enforcement of national laws regarding all forms of violence and abuse against refugee children, in accordance with the relevant international legal obligations of the States concerned;

c. the consistent incorporation, from the beginning of a refugee situation, of protection and assistance criteria, monitoring and addressing the needs and vulnerabilities of refugee children;

d. the compilation and updating of a statistical profile on each refugee population of concern to the High Commissioner, including age/gender disaggregation and identification of unaccompanied minors, for use and planning protection and assistance measures;

---

[42] The plight of such children has been highlighted by the Committee on the Rights of the Child in its recommendations to certain Contracting Parties on receipt of their reports, *e.g.* Poland, France and Belgium.

e. the identification, and provision for the special protection and care, of unaccompanied children in every refugee situation, as well as their reunification with their families;

f. the training of UNHCR and implementing partner staff to understand and address appropriately within their areas of competence the particular needs of refugee children in ways consistent with this policy and the UNHCR Guidelines on refugee children;

g. the training of police and military forces, other government employees involved with refugee protection and assistance, adults and leaders regarding the specific human rights most relevant to the well-being of refugee chldren;

h. the sensitisation of refugee children themselves to their specific rights;

i. the promotion of awareness of, and response to, the particular needs of refugee children through information strategies directed at the governments of both countries of asylum and countries of origin, donors, · NGOs, other United Nations bodies and the public at large;

j. the promotion and facilitation by UNHCR of the technically competent co-operation of governmental and non-governmental organisations and other United Nations bodies in providing for the protection and care of refugee children.

The UNHCR acknowledges that periodic review is necessary and that no set of goals or objectives should be regarded as definitive. The hope of UNHCR is that future efforts on behalf of children will have become so well integrated into all aspects of protection and programme planning and implementation that a separate policy for children will cease to be necessary.

UNHCR Guidelines:

The Guidelines are presented in the form of a book and are   5–034
primarily written for UNHCR staff but also for voluntary organisations, UN agencies and governments. The Guidelines are not
intended to be a practice manual but rather a tool for reaching
policy objectives such that there must be good reason for not
following them in a specific situation. Most of the guidelines are
universal in application and apply in an emergency situation as
well as in ongoing refugee assistance programmes both in the
country of asylum and country of return. The guidelines address
such issues as psychosocial well-being; health and nutrition; prevention and treatment of disabilities; personal liberty and security;
education and the particular needs of unaccompanied children.

The Guidelines also contain a chapter headed "Durable Solutions" before concluding with an "operational framework."[43]

The Convention on the Rights of the Child applies to refugee children and contracting parties to the Convention are required to apply its provisions to refugee children within their territory and where a State has not ratified the 1989 Convention UNHCR advocates its observance "because its standards are universal."[44] The UNHCR has recognised the Convention as constituting a "normative frame or reference for UNHCR's policy."[45]

Refugee children also come within the ambit of the 1951 Geneva Convention Relating to the Status of Refugees and the 1967 Protocol.[46]

6. EXPLOITATION

UN GENERAL ASSEMBLY DECLARATION ON THE RIGHTS OF THE CHILD, 1959.

Principle 9

5–035 The child shall be protected against all forms of neglect, cruelty and exploitation. He shall not be the subject of traffic, in any form . . .

UN CONVENTION ON THE RIGHTS OF THE CHILD, 1989

Article 19

5–036   **1.** States Parties shall take all appropriate legislative, administrative, social and educational measures to protect the child from all forms of physical or mental violence, injury or abuse, neglect or negligent treatment, maltreatment or exploitation, including sexual abuse, while in the care of parent(s), legal guardian(s) or any other person who has the care of the child.
    2. Such protective measures should, as appropriate, include effective procedures for the establishment of social programmes to provide necessary support for the child and for those who have the care of the child, as well as for other forms of prevention and for identification, reporting, referral, investigation, treatment and follow-up of instances of child maltreatment described heretofore, and, as appropriate, for judicial involvement.

---

[43] See also Executive Committee Conclusion No. 59 (XL), 1959 highlighting the particular needs of refugee children and especially the right of refugee children to education, protection from military recruitment and irregular adoption.
[44] *Refugee Children, Protection and Care*, 1994, p. 19.
[45] See, for example, 1993 UNHCR Policy on Refugee Children, para. 17.
[46] See Chapter 7 on Refugees.

Article 34

States Parties undertake to protect the child from all forms of sexual exploitation and sexual abuse for these purposes, States Parties shall in particular take all appropriate national, bilateral and multilateral measures to prevent:

(a) The inducement or coercion of a child to engage in any unlawful sexual activity;

(b) The exploitative use of children in prostitution or other unlawful sexual practices;

(c) The exploitative use of children in pornographic performances and materials.

Article 35

States Parties shall take all appropriate national, bilateral and multilateral measures to prevent the abduction of, the sale of or traffic in children for any purpose or in any form.

Article 36

States Parties shall protect the child against all other forms of exploitation prejudicial to any aspects of the child's welfare.

Article 39

States Parties shall take all appropriate measures to promote 5–037 physical and psychological recovery and social reintegration of a child victim of: any form of neglect, exploitation, or abuse; torture or any other form of cruel, inhuman or degrading treatment or punishment; or armed conflicts. Such recovery and reintegration shall take place in an environment which fosters the health, self-respect and dignity of the child.

Sex Tourist Trade

A review of 160 foreigners arrested in Asia for sexual abuse of children between 1992–94 showed the accused to be 25 per cent American, 18 per cent German, 14 per cent Australian, 12 per cent British and 6 per cent French.[47]

According to UNICEF, 60,000 children under 18 years of age are caught up in the sex trade in the Philippines. The sex trade is prevalent throughout Asia involving at least a million young girls.

[47] UNICEF, *The Progress of Nations* (1995).

Thailand is the capital of the world sex tourist industry with estimates of 100,000 children under 18 years working as prostitutes including 20 per cent of girls in the 11–17 years age group.[48] Although a number of governments are taking steps to apprehend foreigners who abuse children there is a reluctance to do anything which may adversely affect tourism on which so many of these countries economically depend.[49] Countries whose nationals are the alleged principal offenders have taken legislative measures in efforts to eradicate this form of tourism by way of extending the territorial application of legislation—*e.g.* The Australian Crimes (Child Sex Tourism Amendment Act) whereby an Australian who commits abuses against children may be prosecuted on returning to Australia. This pioneering legislation has served as a blueprint for a number of other states including *inter alia* Sweden, Norway, France and Japan. Efforts to introduce similar legislation in the United Kingdom were unsuccessful when the private bill, Sexual Offences (Amendment) Bill introduced by Lord Hylton failed to get through. The Home Secretary, Michael Howard then promised a review of the law relating to organisers of "sex tours".[50] The British Government believes that the Criminal Justice (International Co-operation) Act 1990 and current extradition arrangements whereby a British national may be extradited (contrary to Swedish practice whereby Swedish nationals are not extradited) are adequate to combat the problem.

The United Nations Economic and Social Council on July 22, 1994[51] authorised the establishment of an open-ended intersessional working group responsible for elaborating as a matter of priority and in close collaboration with the Special Rapporteur on the Sale of Children, Child Prostitution and Child Pornography to consider the adoption of a possible draft optional protocol. Note the Council of Europe adopted recommendations in 1991 to counter the sexual exploitation, pornography and prostitution of, and trafficking in young children and adults.

Article 11

5–038   **1.** States Parties shall take measures to combat the illicit transfer and non-return of children abroad.

[48] UNICEF figures; Child Prostitution in Asian Tourism (ECPAT) established in 1990 a three-year campaign against sex tourism but the programme was extended as the magnitude of the problem became apparent. A congress on the issue was held in Stockholm in 1996. Nor is the problem one exclusively affecting young girls. Girl prostitution is, in the words of the UN Economic and Social Commission for Asia, an "alarming problem" but also notes that "boy prostitution, also closely associated with tourism, is also assuming alarming proportions."

[49] Thailand in 1990 earned more than U.S.$4.5 billion from tourism (more than any other sector of the economy) from some five million visitors of whom 70 per cent are male.

[50] Response to Written Question No. 366, July 12, 1995.

[51] Resolution 1994/9 42nd Plenary Meeting on the Question of a Draft Optional Protocol on the "Convention on the Rights of the Child on the Sale of Children, Child Prostitution and Child Pornography as Well as the Basic Measures Needed for their Prevention and Eradication".

2. To this end, States Parties shall promote the conclusion of bilateral or multilateral agreements or accession to existing agreements.

An Optional Protocol to the Convention on the Rights of the Child, concerning the sale of children, child prostitution and child pornography was adopted by the General Assembly on May 25, 2000. In July 2001, there were 70 signatures and three ratifications to the Protocol.

OPTIONAL PROTOCOL TO THE CONVENTION ON THE RIGHTS OF THE CHILD CONCERNING THE SALE OF CHILDREN, CHILD PROSTITUTION AND CHILD PORNOGRAPHY

The States Parties to the present Protocol,

Considering that, in order further to achieve the purposes of the Convention on the Rights of the Child and the implementation of its provisions, especially Articles 1, 11, 21, 32, 33, 34, 35 and 36 it would be appropriate to extend the measures that States Parties should undertake in order to guarantee the protection of the child from the sale of children, child prostitution and child pornography,

Considering also that the Convention on the Rights of the Child recognises the right of the child to be protected from economic exploitation and from performing any work that is likely to be hazardous or to interfere with the child's education, or to be harmful to the child's health or physical, mental, spiritual, moral or social development,

Gravely concerned at the significant and increasing international traffic in children for the purpose of the sale of children, child prostitution and child pornography,

Deeply concerned at the widespread and continuing practice of sex tourism, to which children are especially vulnerable, as it directly promotes the sale of children, child prostitution and child pornography,

Recognising that a number of particularly vulnerable groups, including girl children, are at greater risk of sexual exploitation and that girl children are disproportionately represented among the sexually exploited,

Concerned about the growing availability of child pornography on the Internet and other evolving technologies, and recalling the "International Conference on Combating Child Pornography on the Internet", held in Vienna in 1999, in particular its conclusion calling for the worldwide criminalisation of the production, distribution, exportation, transmission, importation, intentional possession and advertising of child pornography, and stressing the importance of closer co-operation and partnership between governments and the Internet industry,

Believing that the elimination of the sale of children, child prostitution and child pornography will be facilitated by adopting a holistic approach, addressing the contributing factors, including underdevelopment, poverty, economic disparities, inequitable socio-economic structure, dysfunctioning families, lack of education, urban-rural migration, gender discrimination, irresponsible adult sexual behaviour, harmful traditional practices, armed conflicts and trafficking in children,

Believing also that efforts to raise public awareness are needed to reduce consumer demand for the sale of children, child prostitution and child pornography, and believing further in the importance of strengthening global partnership among all actors and of improving law enforcement at the national level,

Noting the provisions of international legal instruments relevant to the protection of children, including the Hague Convention on Protection of Children and Co-operation in Respect of Intercountry Adoption, the Hague Convention on the Civil Aspects of International Child Abduction, the Hague Convention on Jurisdiction, Applicable Law, Recognition, Enforcement and Co-operation in Respect of Parental Responsibility and Measures for the Protection of Children, and International Labour Organisation Convention No. 182 on the Prohibition and Immediate Action for the Elimination of the Worst Forms of Child Labour,

Encouraged by the overwhelming support for the Convention on the Rights of the Child, demonstrating the widespread commitment that exists for the promotion and protection of the rights of the child,

Recognising the importance of the implementation of the provisions of the Programme of Action for the Prevention of the Sale of Children, Child Prostitution and Child Pornography and the Declaration and Agenda for Action adopted at the World Congress against Commercial Sexual Exploitation of Children, held in Stockholm from August 27–31, 1996, and the other relevant decisions and recommendations of pertinent international bodies,

Taking due account of the importance of the traditions and cultural values of each people for the protection and harmonious development of the child,

Have agreed as follows:

Article 1

5–039 States Parties shall prohibit the sale of children, child prostitution and child pornography as provided for by the present Protocol.

Article 2

For the purposes of the present Protocol:

(a) Sale of children means any act or transaction whereby a child is transferred by any person or group of persons to another for remuneration or any other consideration;

(b) Child prostitution means the use of a child in sexual activities for remuneration or any other form of consideration;

(c) Child pornography means any representation, by whatever means, of a child engaged in real or simulated explicit sexual activities or any representation of the sexual parts of a child for primarily sexual purposes.

Article 3

1. Each State Party shall ensure that, as a minimum, the following acts and activities are fully covered under its criminal or penal law, whether such offences are committed domestically or transnationally or on an individual or organised basis:

(a) In the context of sale of children as defined in Article 2:

    (i) Offering, delivering or accepting, by whatever means, a child for the purpose of:
- Sexual exploitation of the child
- Transfer of organs of the child for profit
- Engagement of the child in forced labour

    (ii) Improperly inducing consent, as an intermediary, for the adoption of a child in violation of applicable international legal instruments on adoption;

(b) Offering, obtaining, procuring or providing a child for child prostitution, as defined in Article 2;

(c) Producing, distributing, disseminating, importing, exporting, offering, selling or possessing for the above purposes child pornography as defined in Article 2.

2. Subject to the provisions of the national law of a State Party, the same shall apply to an attempt to commit any of the said acts and to complicity or participation in any of the said acts.

3. Each State Party shall make such offences punishable by appropriate penalties that take into account their grave nature.

4. Subject to the provisions of its national law, each State Party shall take measures, where appropriate, to establish the liability of legal persons for offences established in paragraph 1 of the present article. Subject to the legal principles of the State Party, such liability of legal persons may be criminal, civil or administrative.

5. States Parties shall take all appropriate legal and administrative measures to ensure that all persons involved in the adoption of a child act in conformity with applicable international legal instruments.

Article 4

5–040   1. Each State Party shall take such measures as may be necessary to establish its jurisdiction over the offences referred to in Article 3, paragraph 1, when the offences are commited in its territory or on board a ship or aircraft registered in that State.

2. Each State Party may take such measures as may be necessary to establish its jurisdiction over the offences referred to in Article 3, paragraph 1, in the following cases.

(a) When the alleged offender is a national of that State or a person who has his habitual residence in its territory;

(b) When the victim is a national of that State.

3. Each State Party shall also take such measures as may be necessary to establish its jurisdiction over the aforementioned offences when the alleged offender is present in its territory and it does not extradite him or her to another State Party on the ground that the offence has been committed by one of its nationals.

4. The present Protocol does not exclude any criminal jurisdiction exercised in accordance with internal law.

Article 5

1. The offences referred to in Article 3, paragraph 1, shall be deemed to be included as extraditable offences in any extradition treaty existing between States Parties and shall be included as extraditable offences in every extradition treaty subsequently concluded between them, in accordance with the conditions set forth in such treaties.

2. If a State Party that makes extradition conditional on the existence of a treaty receives a request for extradition from another State Party with which it has no extradition treaty, it may consider the present Protocol to be a legal basis for extradition in respect of such offences. Extradition shall be subject to the conditions provided by the law of the requested State.

3. States Parties that do not make extradition conditional on the existence of a treaty shall recognise such offences as extraditable offences between themselves subject to the conditions provided by the law of the requested State.

4. Such offences shall be treated, for the purpose of extradition between States Parties, as if they had been committed not only in the place in which they occurred but also in the territories of the

States required to establish their jurisdiction in accordance with Article 4.

5. If an extradition request is made with respect to an offence described in Article 3, paragraph 1, and the requested State Party does not or will not extradite on the basis of the nationality of the offender, that State shall take suitable measures to submit the case to its competent authorities for the purpose of prosecution.

Article 6

1. States Parties shall afford one another the greatest measure of **5–041** assistance in connection with investigations or criminal or extradition proceedings brought in respect of the offences set forth in Article 3, paragraph 1, including assistance in obtaining evidence at their disposal necessary for the proceedings.

2. States Parties shall carry out their obligations under paragraph 1 of the present article in conformity with any treaties or other arrangements on mutual legal assistance that may exist between them. In the absence of such treaties or arrangements, States Parties shall afford one another assistance in accordance with their domestic law.

Article 7

States Parties shall, subject to the provisions of their national law:

(a) Take measures to provide for the seizure and confiscation, as appropriate, of:

   (i) Goods, such as materials, assets and other instrumentalities used to commit or facilitate offences under the present protocol;

   (ii) Proceeds derived from such offences;

(b) Execute requests from another State Party for seizure or confiscation of goods or proceeds referred to in subparagraph (a) (i) and (ii);

(c) Take measures aimed at closing, on a temporary or definitive basis, premises used to commit such offences.

Article 8

1. States Parties shall adopt appropriate measures to protect the rights and interests of child victims of the practices prohibited under the present Protocol at all stages of the criminal justice process, in particular by:

(a) Recognising the vulnerability of child victims and adapting procedures to recognise then special needs, including their special needs as witnesses;

(b) Informing child victims of their rights, their role and the scope, timing and progress of the proceedings and of the disposition of their cases;

(c) Allowing the views, needs and concerns of child victims to be presented and considered in proceedings where their personal interests are affected, in a manner consistent with the procedural rules of national law;

(d) Providing appropriate support services to child victims throughout the legal process;

(e) Protecting, as appropriate, the privacy and identity of child victims and taking measures in accordance with national law to avoid the inappropriate dissemination of information that could lead to the identification of child victims;

(f) Providing, in appropriate cases, for the safety of child victims, as well as that of their families and witnesses on their behalf, from intimidation and retaliation;

(g) Avoiding unnecessary delay in the disposition of cases and the execution of orders or decrees granting compensation to child victims.

2. States Parties shall ensure that uncertainty as to the actual age of the victim shall not prevent the initiation of criminal investigations, including investigations aimed at establishing the age of the victim.

3. States Parties shall ensure that, in the treatment by the criminal justice system of children who are victims of the offences described in the present Protocol, the best interest of the child shall be a primary consideration.

4. States Parties shall take measures to ensure appropriate training, in particular legal and psychological training, for the persons who work with victims of the offences prohibited under the present Protocol.

5. States Parties shall, in appropriate cases, adopt measures in order to protect the safety and integrity of those persons and/or organisations involved in the prevention and/or protection and rehabilitation of victims of such offences.

6. Nothing in the present article shall be construed to be prejudicial to or inconsistent with the rights of the accused to a fair and impartial trial.

Article 9

5–042   **1.** States Parties shall adopt or strengthen, implement and disseminate laws, administrative measures, social policies and programmes to prevent the offences referred to in the present

Protocol. Particular attention shall be given to protect children who are especially vulnerable to such practices.

2. States Parties shall promote awareness in the public at large, including children, through information by all appropriate means, education and training, about the preventive measures and harmful effects of the offences referred to in the present Protocol. In fulfilling their obligations under this article, States Parties shall encourage the participation of the community and, in particular, children and child victims, in such information and education and training programmes, including at the international level.

3. States Parties shall take all feasible measures with the aim of ensuring all appropriate assistance to victims of such offences, including their full social reintegration and their full physical and psychological recovery.

4. States Parties shall ensure that all child victims of the offences described in the present Protocol have access to adequate procedures to seek, without discrimination, compensation for damages from those legally responsible.

5. States Parties shall take appropriate measures aimed at effectively prohibiting the production and dissemination of material advertising the offences described in the present Protocol.

Article 10

1. States Parties shall take all necessary steps to strengthen 5–043 international co-operation by multilateral, regional and bilateral arrangements for the prevention, detection, investigation, prosecution and punishment of those responsible for acts involving the sale of children, child prostitution, child pornography and child sex tourism. States Parties shall also promote international co-operation and co-ordination between their authorities, national and international non-governmental organisations and international organisations.

2. States Parties shall promote international co-operation to assist child victims in their physical and psychological recovery, social reintegration and repatriation.

3. States Parties shall promote the strengthening of international co-operation in order to address the root causes, such as poverty and underdevelopment, contributing to the vulnerability of children to the sale of children, child prostitution, child pornography and child sex tourism.

4. States Parties in a position to do so shall provide financial, technical or other assistance through existing multilateral, regional, bilateral or other programmes.

Article 11

Nothing in the present Protocol shall affect any provisions that are more conducive to the realisation of the rights of the child and that may be contained in:

(a) The law of a State Party;

(b) International law in force for that State.

Article 12

1. Each State Party shall, within two years following the entry into force of the present Protocol for that State Party, submit a report to the Committee on the Rights of the Child providing comprehensive information on the measures it has taken to implement the provisions of the Protocol.

2. Following the submission of the comprehensive report, each State Party shall include in the reports they submit to the Committee on the Rights of the Child, in accordance with Article 44 of the Convention, any further information with respect to the implementation of the present Protocol. Other States Parties to the Protocol shall submit a report every five years.

3. The Committee on the Rights of the Child may request from States Parties further information relevant to the implementation of the present Protocol.

7. HEALTH

UN GENERAL ASSEMBLY DECLARATION ON THE RIGHTS OF THE CHILD, 1959

Principle 4

5–044 The child shall enjoy the benefits of social security. He shall be entitled to grow and develop in health; to this end, special care and protection shall be provided both to him and to his mother, including adequate pre-natal and post-natal care. The child shall have the right to adequate nutrition, housing, recreation and medical services.

Article 5

The child who is physically, mentally or socially handicapped shall be given the special treatment, education and care required by his particular condition.

UN CONVENTION ON THE RIGHTS OF THE CHILD, 1989

Article 24

1. States Parties recognise the right of the child to the enjoy- 5–045
ment of the highest attainable standard of health and to facilities
for the treatment of illness and rehabilitation of health. States
Parties shall strive to ensure that no child is deprived of his or her
right of access to such health care services.

2. States Parties shall pursue full implementation of this right
and, in particular, shall take appropriate measures:

(a) To diminish infant and child mortality;

(b) To ensure the provision of necessary medical assistance and
    health care to all children with emphasis on the develop-
    ment of primary health care;

(c) To combat disease and malnutrition including within the
    framework of primary health care, through *inter alia* the
    application of readily available technology and through the
    provision of adequate nutritious foods and clean drinking
    water, taking into consideration the dangers and risks of
    environmental pollution;

(d) To ensure appropriate pre-natal and post-natal health care
    for mothers;

(e) To ensure that all segments of society, in particular parents
    and children, are informed, have access to education and
    are supported in the use of basic knowledge of child health
    and nutrition, the advantages of breast-feeding, hygiene
    and environmental sanitation and the prevention of
    accidents;

(f) To develop preventive health care, guidance for parents
    and family planning education and services.

3. States Parties shall take all effective and appropriate measures with a view to abolishing traditional practices prejudicial to
the health of children.

4. States Parties undertake to promote and encourage international co-operation with a view to achieving progressively the
full realisation of the right recognised in the present article. In this
regard, particular account shall be taken of the needs of developing countries.

The prime example of a traditional practice "prejudicial to the
health of children" is female circumcision (more commonly
referred to as female genital mutilation (f.g.m.). According to the

World Health Organisation it is estimated that 90 million females have undergone genital mutilation which is usually performed without anaesthetic in unhygienic conditions.[52] Currently the practice is still performed on more than two million girls annually. The practice is one peculiar primarily to African countries but is performed in certain Asian and Middle Eastern Countries.[53] Somalia has one of the highest percentages of women having undergone this procedure—it is estimated that 98 per cent of Somali women experience f.g.m. Female circumcision has been characterised as "persecution" for the purposes of granting refugee status under the 1951 Refugee Convention. Such an opportunity was afforded to the Canadian Immigration and Refugee Board in 1994 when a Somali woman sought refugee status for herself and her daughter on the grounds *inter alia* that if she were returned to Somalia she would lose custody of her daughter and would be powerless to prevent her from being subjected to f.g.m.[54] Infibulation is the most intrusive form of f.g.m. and can cause long term physchological trauma and physical impairment. Although legislation and the granting of refugee status go some way towards demonstrating condemnation of the practice, they cannot be regarded as the most effective way of combatting the practice. Legislation demands the co-operation of the individual victim in that she would be required to implicate in criminal proceedings members of her own family whilst refugee decisions are specific to the applicant alone. Accordingly, education would be the more effective means of dealing with this issue, for instance UK FOR-WARD (Foundation for Women's Health) seeks to promote awareness in countering traditional practices prejudicial to the health of women and children.

Article 25

5–046 States Parties recognise the right of a child who has been placed by the competent authorities for the purposes of care, protection or treatment of his or her physical or mental health, to a periodic review of the treatment provided to the child and all other circumstances relevant to his or her placement.

[52] The practice is one normally performed by women, usually a relative of the girl. The majority of those concerned believe the practice to be essential on moral and/or religious grounds.

[53] A consequence of migration is that the practice is performed in Europe and North America. More than 20,000 women in the U.K. have undergone the procedure and 10,000 children from ethnic groups living in Britain are estimated to be at risk. Female genital mutilation was made illegal in Britain by the Prohibition of Female Circumcision Act in 1985 but as yet there have been no instances of prosecutions brought under the Act in British Courts.

[54] Decision T93–12197/12199, *Ramirez, McCaffrey* July 13, 1994]. In reaching its decision the panel took cognisance of the provisions of the Convention on the Rights of the Child and in particular highlighted Articles 3, 9, ("best interests of child") 12 (account of child's views) 19 and 24.

Article 33

States Parties shall take all appropriate measures, including legislative, administrative, social and educational measures, to protect children from the illicit use of narcotic drugs and psychotropic substances as defined in the relevant international treaties, and to prevent the use of children in the illicit production and trafficking of such substances.

Disabled children

Article 23

1. States Parties recognise that a mentally or physically disabled child should enjoy a full and decent life, in conditions which ensure dignity, promote self-reliance, and facilitate the child's active participation in the community.

2. States Parties recognise the right of the disabled child to special care and shall encourage and ensure the extension, subject to available resources, to the eligible child and those responsible for his or her care, of assistance for which application is made and which is appropriate to the child's condition and to the circumstances of the parents or others caring for the child.

3. Recognising the special needs of a disabled child, assistance extended in accordance with paragraph 2 of the present article shall be provided free of charge, whenever possible, taking into account the financial resources of the parents or others caring for the child, and shall be designed to ensure that the disabled child has effective access to and receives education, training, health care services, rehabilitation services, preparation for employment and recreation opportunities in a manner conducive to the child's achieving the fullest possible social integration and individual development, including his or her cultural and spiritual development.

4. States Parties shall promote, in the spirit of international cooperation, the exchange of appropriate information in the field of preventive health care and of medical, psychological and functional treatment of disabled children, including dissemination of and access to information concerning methods of rehabilitation, education and vocational services, with the aim of enabling States Parties to improve their capabilities and skills and to widen their experience in these areas. In this regard, particular account shall be taken of the needs of developing countries.[55]

---

[55] See below Article III.5. of the World Declaration on Education for All, 1990.

8. EDUCATION

UNIVERSAL DECLARATION OF HUMAN RIGHTS, 1948

Article 26

5–047 (1) Everyone has the right to education. Education shall be free, at least in the elementary and fundamental stages. Elementary education shall be compulsory. Technical and professional education shall be made generally available and shall be equally accessible to all on the basis of merit.

(2) Education shall be directed to the full development of the human personality and to strengthening of respect for human rights and fundamental freedoms. It shall promote understanding, tolerance and friendship among all nations, racial or religious groups, and shall further the activities of the United Nations for the maintenance of peace.

(3) Parents have a prior right to choose the kind of education that shall be given to their children.

UN COVENANT ON ECONOMIC, SOCIAL AND CULTURAL RIGHTS

Article 13

1. The States Parties to the present Covenant recognise the right of everyone to education. They agree that education shall be directed to the full development of the human personality and the sense of its dignity, and shall strengthen the respect for human rights and fundamental freedoms. They further agree that education shall enable all persons to participate effectively in a free society, promote understanding, tolerance and friendship among all nations and all racial, ethnic or religious groups and further the activities of the United nations for the maintenance of peace.

2. States Parties to the present Covenant recognise that, with a view to achieving the full realisation of this right:

(a) primary education shall be compulsory and available free to all;

(b) secondary education in its different forms including technical and vocational secondary education shall be made generally available and accessible to all by every appropriate means and in particular by the progressive introduction of free education;

(c) higher education shall be equally accessible to all on the basis of capacity by every appropriate means, and in particular by the progressive of the introduction of free education;

(d) fundamental education shall be encouraged or intensified as far as possible for those persons who have not received or completed the whole period of their primary education;

(e) the development of a system of schools at all levels shall be actively pursued, an adequate fellowship system shall be established and the material conditions of teaching staff shall be continuously improved.

3. The States Parties to the present Covenant undertake to have respect for the liberty of parents and, when applicable, legal guardians, to choose for their children schools, other than those established by the public authorities which conform to such minimum educational standards as may be laid down or improved by the state and to ensure the religious and moral education of their children in conformity with their own convictions.

4. No part of this article shall be construed so as to interfere with the liberty of individuals and bodies to establish and direct educational institutions, subject always to the observance of the principles set forth in paragraph 1 of this Article and to the requirement that the education given in such institutions shall conform to such minimum standards as may be laid down by the state.

Article 14

Each State Party to the present Covenant which, at the time of 5–048 becoming a party, has not been able to secure in its metropolitan territory or other territories under its jurisdiction compulsory primary education, free of charge, undertakes, within two years, to work out and adopt a detailed plan of action for the progressive implementation, within a reasonable number of years, to be fixed in the plan, of the principle of compulsory education free of charge for all.

UN GENERAL ASSEMBLY DECLARATION ON THE RIGHTS OF THE CHILD, 1959

Article 7

The child is entitled to receive education, which shall be free and compulsory, at least in the elementary stages. He shall be given an education which will promote his general culture and enable him, on a basis of equal opportunity, to develop his abilities, his individual judgment, and his sense of moral and social responsibility, and to become a useful member of society. The best interests of the child shall be the guiding principle of those responsible for his education and guidance; that responsibility lies in the first place with his parents.

The child shall have full opportunity for play and recreation, which should be directed to the same purposes as education; society and the public authorities shall endeavour to promote the enjoyment of this right.

UN CONVENTION ON THE RIGHTS OF THE CHILD, 1989

Article 28

5–049   **1.** States Parties recognise the right of the child to education, and with a view to achieving this right progressively and on the basis of equal opportunity, they shall, in particular:

(a) Make primary education compulsory and available free to all;

(b) Encourage the development of different forms of secondary education, including general and vocational education, make them available and accessible to every child, and take appropriate measures such as the introduction of free education and offering financial assistance in case of need;

(c) Make higher education accessible to all on the basis of capacity by every appropriate means;

(d) Make educational and vocational information and guidance available and accessible to all children;

(e) Take measures to encourage regular attendance at schools and the reduction of drop-out rates.

2. States Parties shall take all appropriate measures to ensure that school discipline is administered in a manner consistent with the child's human dignity and in conformity with the present Convention.

3. States Parties shall promote and encourage international co-operation in matters relating to education, in particular with a view to contributing to the elimination of ignorance and illiteracy throughout the world and facilitating access to scientific and technical knowledge and modern teaching methods. In this regard, particular account shall be taken of the needs of developing countries.

Article 29

1. States Parties agree that the education of the child shall be 5–050
directed to:

(a) The development of the child's personality, talents and
mental and physical abilities to their fullest potential;

(b) The development of respect for human rights and fundamental freedoms, and for the principles enshrined in the
Charter of the United Nations;

(c) The development of respect for the child's parents, his or
her own cultural identity, language and values, for the
national values of the country in which the child is living,
the country from which he or she may originate, and for
civilisations different from his or her own;

(d) The preparation of the child for responsible life in a free
society, in the spirit of understanding, peace, tolerance,
equality of sexes, and friendship among all peoples, ethnic,
national and religious groups and persons of indigenous
origin;

(e) The development of respect for the natural environment.

2. No part of the present Article or Article 28 shall be construed
so as to interfere with the liberty of individuals and bodies to
establish and direct educational institutions, subject always to the
observance of the principles set forth in paragraph 1 of the
present article and to the requirements that the education given in
such institutions shall conform to such minimum standards as
may be laid down by the State.

Half a century after the promulgation of the Universal Declaration the right to education is not a right enjoyed by all children as
the following statistics reveal.[56] More than 100 million children,
including at least 60 million girls, have no access to primary
schooling. More than 90 million adults, two-thirds of whom are
women are illiterate, and functional literacy is a significant
problem in all countries, industrialised and developing. More
than one-third of the world's adults have no access to the printed
knowledge, new skills and technologies. More than 100 million
children fail to complete basic education programmes. Efforts on
the part of governments to meet educational needs have been
hampered by such factors as mounting debt burdens, rapid

[56] Released by UNICEF in 1990.

population growth, civil strife, war and widespread environmental degradation. Accordingly at the World Conference on Education for All,[57] reaffirmed that education is a fundamental right for all people, women and men, of all ages, throughout the world and adopted a declaration entitled "Education for All: Meeting Basic Learning Needs." and agreed on a Framework for Action to Meet Basic Learning Needs to achieve the goals spelt out in the Declaration. These goals included universal access to and completion of primary education by the year 2000, improvement in learning achievement such that an agreed percentage of an appropriate cohort (for example 80 per cent of 14-year-olds) attains or surpasses a defined level of necessary learning achievement. A key article in the declaration is Article 111 entitled "Universalising Access and Promoting Equity":

1. Basic education should be provided to all children, youth and adults. To this end, basic education services of quality should be expanded and consistent measures must be taken to reduce disparities.

2. For basic education to be equitable all children, youth and adults must be given the opportunity to achieve and maintain an acceptable level of learning.

3. The most urgent priority is to ensure access to, and improve the quality of education for girls and women, and to remove every obstacle that hampers their active participation. All gender stereotyping in education should be eliminated.

4. An active commitment must be made to removing educational disparities. Undeserved groups, the poor; street and working children; rural and remote publications; nomads and migrant workers; indigenous peoples; ethnic, racial and linguistic minorities; refugees; those displaced by war and people under occupation should not suffer any discrimination in access to learning opportunities.

5. The learning needs of the disabled demand special attention. Steps need to be taken to provide equal access to every category of disabled persons as an integral part of the education system.

Article I addresses the issue of meeting basic learning needs and provides:

5–051   1. Every person—child, youth and adult—shall be able to benefit from educational opportunities designed to meet

---

[57] A conference which brought together representatives of governments, international and bilateral development agencies, and non-governmental organisations. The Conference was organised under the auspices of UNESCO—Jomtien, Thailand, March 5–9, 1990.

their basic learning needs. These needs comprise both essential learning tools (such as literacy, oral expression, numeracy, and problem solving) and the basic learning content (such as knowledge, skills, values, and attitudes) required by human beings to be able to survive, to develop their full capacities to live and work in dignity, to participate fully in development, to improve the quality of their lives, to make informed decisions, and to continue learning. The scope of basic learning needs and how they should be met varies with individual countries, and cultures and inevitably changes with the passage of time.

2. The satisfaction of these needs empowers individuals in any society and confers upon them a responsibility to respect and build upon their collective culture, linguistic and spiritual heritage, to promote the education, to promote the education of others, to further the cause of social justice, to achieve environmental protection, to be tolerant towards social, political and religious systems which differ from their own, ensuring that commonly accepted humanistic values and human rights are upheld and to work for international peace and solidarity in an interdependent world.

3. Another and no less fundamental aim of education development is the transmission and enrichment of common cultural and moral values. It is in these values that the individual and society find their identity and worth.

4. Basic education is more than an end in itself. It is the foundation for life learning and human development on which countries may build, systematically, further levels and types of education and training.

Article II "Shaping the Vision" states:

To serve the basic learning needs of all requires more than a 5–052 recommitment to basic education as it now exists. What is needed is an expanded vision that surpasses present resource levels, institutional structures, curricula, and conventional delivery systems which building on the best in current practices. New possibilities exist today which result from the convergence of the increase in information and the unprecedented capacity to communicate. We must seize them with creativity and a determination for increased effectiveness . . .

Articles IV to X address the following:

- Focusing on Learning;
- Broadening the Means and the Scope of Basic Education;

- Enhancing the Environment for Learning;
- Strengthening Partnerships;
- Developing a Supportive Policy Context;
- Mobilising Resources;
- Strengthening International Solidarity.

The Girl-Child

5–053 As already highlighted girls and women make up two thirds of the world's illiterate population and it is estimated that if universal primary education is to be achieved in the forseeable future, then three additional girls have to be enrolled in school for each boy. Obviously this requires a change in social attitudes, a greater awareness of the importance of educating women and an increase in public spending.[58]
  The principal obstacles to the education of girls are said to be:

- heavy workloads;
- deep-seated cultural beliefs that favour the education of boys and deem girls as inferior and destined to the roles of wife and mother;
- pregnancy and early marriage[59];
- long distances to the nearest school, leading parents to fear for their daughter's safety;
- effects of war.[60]

Strategies suggested to combat the difficulties associated with access to education of the girl-child include:

- locating schools closer to homes and improving facilities;
- reducing the cost to families of girls' schooling through the provision of scholarships, food aid, books, uniforms, hostels, free accommodation and boarding schools;

[58] UNESCO notes that in African countries that education budgets have increased at a slower rate than population growth. Poverty is on the rise and the quality of education is rapidly declining.
[59] In Africa about 18 per cent of the female population between the ages of 15 and 19 gives birth annually compared with 8 per cent in Latin America and 3 per cent in Asia among the same age group. Child brides, as young as 12, are not uncommon in certain parts of the United States, *e.g.* Kentucky.
[60] War in Angola, Mozambique, Sudan and Ethopia has resulted in an entire generation of children in these countries being deprived of education. Refugee women and children are frequently denied access to education.

- adjusting the school calendar to the realities of rural life and demands of rural economies;

- providing day care facilities to free girls from caring for siblings during school hours, making the curriculum and learning materials more gender sensitive and attuned to the local environment so that students learn life's skills;

- sensitising and mobilising public opinion, especially of parents, to the value of educating girls;

- reinforcing and reorienting guidance and counselling programmes in schools towards girls' needs and expectations;

- giving girls who interrupt their schooling due to marriage or pregnancy the opportunity to continue their education.

Disabled children

NOTE: Standard Rules on the Equalisation of Opportunities for **5–054** Person with Disabilities, rule 6 on education; rule 12(2) on provision of religious education; General Comment No. 5 of Committee on Economic, Social and Cultural Rights, Section G, Right to Education—see Chapter on Persons with Disabilities.

9. THE FAMILY[61]

UNIVERSAL DECLARATION OF HUMAN RIGHTS ARTICLE 16.3. and INTERNATIONAL COVENANT ON CIVIL AND POLITICAL RIGHTS ARTICLE 23.1

The family is the natural and fundamental group unit of society **5–055** and is entitled to protection by society and the State.

Article 23.4

States Parties to the present Covenant shall take appropriate steps to ensure equality of rights and responsibilities of spouses as to

---

[61] 1994 was declared the Year of the Family ("1 YF") in General Assembly Resolution 44/82, December 9, 1989. The theme of the year was "Family: resources and responsibilities in a changing world." with the motto "Building the Smallest Democracy at the Heart of Society." The objectives of IYF were to stimulate local, national and international action as part of a sustained long-term effort to increase awareness of family issues amongst governments as well as in the private sector; strengthen national institutions to formulate, implement and monitor policies in respect of families; stimulate efforts to respond to problems affecting, and affected by, the situation of families; enhance the effectiveness of local, regional and national efforts to carry out specific programmes, concerning families by generating new activities and strengthening existing ones; improve the collaboration among national and international non-governmental organisations in support of multi-sectoral activities; build upon the results of international activities concerning women, children, the aged, the disabled as well as other major events of concern to the family or its individual members. The UN organ responsible for observance of IYF was the Department for Policy, Co-ordination and Sustainable Development, Vienna.

marriage and at its dissolution. In the case of dissolution pro-vision shall be made for the necessary protection of any children.

UN GENERAL ASSEMBLY DECLARATION ON THE RIGHTS OF THE CHILD, 1959

Principle 6

5–056 The child, for the full and harmonious development of his personality, needs love and understanding. He shall, wherever possible, grow up in the care and under the responsibility of his parents, and, in any case, in an atmosphere of affection and of moral and material security; a child of tender years shall not, save in exceptional circumstances, be separated from his mother. Society and the public authorities shall have the duty to extend particular care to children without a family and to those without adequate means of support. Payment of State and other assistance towards the maintenance of children of large families is desirable.

UN CONVENTION ON THE RIGHTS OF THE CHILD, 1989

Article 5

States Parties shall respect the responsibilities, rights and duties of parents or, where applicable, the members of the extended family or community as provided for by local custom, legal guardians or other persons legally responsible for the child, to provide, in a manner consistent with the evolving capacities of the child, appropriate direction and guidance in the exercise by the child of the rights recognised in the present Convention.

Article 9

5–057 **1.** States Parties shall ensure that a child shall not be separated from his or her parents against their will, except when competent authorities subject to judicial review determine, in accordance with applicable law and procedures, that such separation is necessary for the best interests of the child. Such determination may be necessary in a particular case such as one involving abuse or neglect of the child by the parents, or one where the parents are living separately and a decision must be made as to the child's place of residence.

2. In any proceedings pursuant to paragraph 1 of the present article, all interested parties shall be given an opportunity to participate in the proceedings and make their views known.

3. States Parties shall respect the right of the child who is separated from one or both parents to maintain personal relations and direct contact with both parents on a regular basis, except if it is contrary to the child's best interests.

4. Where such separation results from any action initiated by a State Party, such as the detention, imprisonment, exile, deportation or death (including death arising from any cause while the person is in the custody of the State) of one or both parents or of the child, that State Party shall, upon request, provide the parents, the child or, if appropriate, another member of the family with the essential information concerning the whereabouts of the absent member(s) of the family unless the provision of the information would be detrimental to the well-being of the child. States Parties shall further ensure that the submission of such a request shall of itself entail no adverse consequences for the person(s) concerned.

Article 10

1. In accordance with the obligation of States Parties under 5–058 Article 9, paragraph 1, applications by a child or his or her parents to enter or leave a State Party for the purpose of family reunification shall be dealt with by States Parties in a positive, humane and expeditious manner. States Parties shall further ensure that the submission of such a request shall entail no adverse consequences for the applicants and for the members of their family.

2. A child whose parents reside in different States shall have the right to maintain on a regular basis, save in exceptional circumstances personal relations and direct contacts with both parents. Towards that end and in accordance with the obligation of States Parties under Article 9, paragraph 1, States Parties shall respect the right of the child and his or her parents to leave any country, including their own, and to enter their own country. The right to leave any country shall be subject only to such restrictions as are prescribed by law and which are necessary to protect the national security, public order (ordre public), public health or morals or the rights and freedoms of others and are consistent with the other rights recognised in the present Convention.

Article 18

1. States Parties shall use their best efforts to ensure recognition 5–059 of the principle that both parents have common responsibilities for the upbringing and development of the child. Parents or, as the case may be, legal guardians, have the primary responsibility for the upbringing and development of the child. The best interests of the child will be their basic concern.

2. For the purpose of guaranteeing and promoting the rights set forth in the present Convention, States Parties shall render appropriate assistance to parents and legal guardians in the performance of their child-rearing responsibilities and shall ensure the development of institutions, facilities and services for the care of children.

3. States Parties shall take all appropriate measures to ensure that children of working parents have the right to benefit from child-care services and facilities for which they are eligible.

Article 20

5–060 **1.** A child temporarily or permanently deprived of his or her family environment, or in whose own best interests cannot be allowed to remain in that environment, shall be entitled to special protection and assistance provided by the State.

2. States Parties shall in accordance with their national laws ensure alternative care for such a child.

3. Such care could include, *inter alia*, foster placement, Kafala of Islamic law, adoption, or if necessary placement in suitable institutions for the care of children. When considering solutions, due regard shall be paid to the desirability of continuity in a child's upbringing and to the child's ethnic, religious, cultural and linguistic background.

Disabled Children

NOTE: Standard Rules on the Equalisation of Opportunities for Person with Disabilities, above, rule 9 on Family Life and Personal Integrity.

UN GENERAL ASSEMBLY DECLARATION ON THE RIGHTS OF THE CHILD, 1959

Principle 3

The child shall be entitled from his birth to a name and a nationality.

UN CONVENTION ON THE RIGHTS OF THE CHILD, 1989

Article 7

5–061 **1.** The child shall be registered immediately after birth and shall have the right from birth to a name, the right to acquire a nationality and, as far as possible, the right to know and be cared for by his or her parents.

Article 8

1. States Parties undertake to respect the right of the child to preserve his or her identity, including nationality, name and family relations as recognised by law without unlawful interference.

2. Where a child is illegally deprived of some or all of the elements of his or her identity, States Parties shall provide appropriate assistance and protection, with a view to speedily re-establishing his or her identity.

10. CIVIL RIGHTS

UN GENERAL ASSEMBLY DECLARATION ON THE RIGHTS OF THE CHILD, 1959

Principle 10

The child shall be protected from practices which may foster 5–062 racial, religious and any other form of discrimination. He shall be brought up in a spirit of understanding, tolerance, friendship among peoples, peace and universal brotherhood, and in full consciousness that his energy and talents should be devoted to the service of his fellow men.

UN CONVENTION ON THE RIGHTS OF THE CHILD, 1989

Article 12

1. States Parties shall assure to the child who is capable of forming his or her own views the right to express those views freely in all matters affecting the child, the views of the child being given due weight in accordance with the age and maturity of the child.

2. For this purpose, the child shall in particular be provided the opportunity to be heard in any judicial and administrative proceedings affecting the child, either directly, or through a representative or an appropriate body, in a manner consistent with the procedural rules of national law.

Article 13

1. The child shall have the right to freedom of expression; this right shall include freedom to seek, receive and impart information and ideas of all kinds, regardless of frontiers, either orally, in writing or in print, in the form of art, or through any other media of the child's choice.

2. The exercise of this right may be subject to certain restrictions, but these shall only be such as are provided by law and are necessary:

(a) For respect of the rights or reputations of others; or

(b) For the protection of national security or of public order (ordre public), or of public health or morals.

Article 14

5–062a   1. States Parties shall respect the right of the child to freedom of thought, conscience and religion.

2. States Parties shall respect the rights and duties of the parents and, when applicable, legal guardians, to provide direction to the child in the exercise of his or her right in a manner consistent with the evolving capacities of the child.

3. Freedom to manifest one's religion or beliefs may be subject only to such limitations as are prescribed by law and are necessary to protect public safety, order, health or morals, or the fundamental rights and freedoms of others.

Article 15

1. States Parties recognise the rights of the child to freedom of association and to freedom of peaceful assembly.

2. No restrictions may be placed on the exercise of these rights other than those imposed in conformity with the law and which are necessary in a democratic society in the interests of national security or public safety, public order (ordre public), the protection of public health or morals or the protection of the rights and freedoms of others.

Article 16

1. No child shall be subjected to arbitrary or unlawful interference with his or her privacy, family, home or correspondence, nor to unlawful attacks on his or her honour and reputation.

2. The child has the right to the protection of the law against such interference or attacks.

Article 17

1. States Parties recognise the important function performed by the mass media and shall ensure that the child has access to information and material from a diversity of national and international sources, especially those aimed at the promotion of his or her social, spiritual and moral well-being and physical and mental health. To this end, States Parties shall:

(a) Encourage the mass media to disseminate information and material of social and cultural benefit to the child and in accordance with the spirit of Article 29;

(b) Encourage international co-operation in the production, exchange and dissemination of such information and material from a diversity of cultural, national and international sources;

(c) Encourage the production and dissemination of children's books;

(d) Encourage the mass media to have particular regard to the linguistic needs of the child who belongs to a minority group or who is indigenous;

(e) Encourage the development of appropriate guidelines for the protection of the child from information and material injurious to his or her well-being, bearing in mind the provisions of Articles 13 and 18.

2. States Parties shall ensure the implementation of these rights in accordance with their national law and their obligations under the relevant international instruments in this field, in particular where the child would otherwise be stateless.

11. ECONOMIC, SOCIAL AND CULTURAL RIGHTS

UN CONVENTION ON THE RIGHTS OF THE CHILD, 1989

Article 26

1. States Parties shall recognise for every child the right to 5–063 benefit from social security, including social insurance, and shall take the necessary measures to achieve the full realisation of this right in accordance with their national law.

2. The benefits should, where appropriate, be granted, taking into account the resources and the circumstances of the child and persons having responsibility for the maintenance of the child, as well as any other consideration relevant to an application for benefits made by or on behalf of the child.

Article 27

1. States Parties recognise the right of every child to a standard of living adequate for the child's physical, mental, spiritual, moral and social development.

2. The parent(s) or others responsible for the child have the primary responsibility to secure, within their abilities and finan-

cial capacities, the conditions of living necessary for the child's development.

3. States Parties, in accordance with national conditions and within their means, shall take appropriate measures to assist parents and others responsible for the child to implement this right and shall in case of need provide material assistance and support programmes, particularly with regard to nutrition, clothing and housing.

4. States Parties shall take all appropriate measures to secure the recovery of maintenance for the child from the parents or other persons having financial responsibility for the child, both within the State Party and from abroad. In particular, where the person having financial responsibility for the child lives in a State different from that of the child, States Parties shall promote the accession to international agreements or the conclusion of such agreements, as well as the making of other appropriate arrangements.

NOTE: The obligation on Contracting Parties with respect to economic, social and cultural rights is in accordance with Article 4, namely "States Parties shall undertake such measures to the maximum extent of their available resources and, where needed, within the framework of international co-operation."

ENFORCEMENT OF THE CONVENTION

Article 43

5–064 **1.** For the purpose of examining the progress made by States Parties in achieving the realisation of the obligations undertaken in the present Convention, there shall be established a Committee on the Rights of the Child, which shall carry out the functions hereinafter provided.

2. The Committee shall consist of ten experts of high moral standing and recognised competence in the field covered by this Convention. The members of the Committee shall be elected by States Parties from among their nationals and shall serve in their personal capacity, consideration being given to equitable geographical distribution, as well as to the principal legal systems.

3. The members of the Committee shall be elected by secret ballot from a list of persons nominated by States Parties. Each State Party may nominate one person from among its own nationals.

4. The initial election to the Committee shall be held no later than six months after the date of the entry into force of the present Convention and thereafter every second year. At least four months before the date of each election, the Secretary-General of the United Nations shall address a letter to States Parties inviting them to submit their nominations within two months. The Secretary-General shall subsequently prepare a list in alphabetical order of all persons thus nominated, indicating States Parties which have nominated them, and shall submit it to the States Parties to the present Convention.

5. The elections shall be held at meetings of States Parties convened by the Secretary-General at United Nations Headquarters. At those meetings, for which two thirds of States Parties shall constitute a quorum, the persons elected to the Committee shall be those who obtain the largest number of votes and an absolute majority of the votes of the representatives of States Parties present and voting.

6. The members of the Committee shall be elected for a term of 5–065 four years. They shall be eligible for re-election if renominated. The term of five of the members elected at the first election shall expire at the end of two years; immediately after the first election, the names of these five members shall be chosen by lot by the Chairman of the meeting.

7. If a member of the Committee dies or resigns or declares that for any other cause he or she can no longer perform the duties of the Committee, the State Party which nominated the member shall appoint another expert from among its nationals to serve for the remainder of the term, subject to the approval of the Committee.

8. The Committee shall establish its own rules of procedure.

9. The Committee shall elect its officers for a period of two years.

10. The meetings of the Committee shall normally be held at United Nations Headquarters or at any other convenient place as determined by the Committee. The Committee shall normally meet annually. The duration of the meetings of the Committee shall be determined, and reviewed, if necessary, by a meeting of the States Parties to the present Convention, subject to the approval of the General Assembly.

11. The Secretary-General of the United Nations shall provide the necessary staff and facilities for the effective performance of the functions of the Committee under the present Convention.

12. With the approval of the General Assembly, the members of the Committee established under the present Convention shall receive emoluments from the United Nations resources on such terms and conditions as the Assembly may decide.

Article 44

1. States Parties undertake to submit to the Committee, through 5–066 the Secretary-General of the United Nations, reports on the measures they have adopted which give effect to the rights recognised herein and on the progress made on the enjoyment of those rights:

(a) Within two years of the entry into force of the Convention for the State Party concerned,

(b) Thereafter every five years.

2. Reports made under the present article shall indicate factors and difficulties, if any, affecting the degree of fulfilment of the obligations under the present Convention. Reports shall also contain sufficient information to provide the Committee with a comprehensive understanding of the implementation of the Convention in the country concerned.

3. A State Party which has submitted a comprehensive initial report to the Committee need not in its subsequent reports submitted in accordance with paragraph 1(b) of the present article repeat basic information previously provided.

4. The Committee may request from States Parties further information relevant to the implementation of the Convention.

5. The Committee shall submit to the General Assembly, through the Economic and Social Council, every two years, reports on its activities.

6. States Parties shall make their reports widely available to the public in their own countries.

Article 45

5–067 In order to foster the effective implementation of the Convention and to encourage international co-operation in the field covered by the Convention:

(a) The specialised agencies, the United Nations Children's Fund and other United Nations organs shall be entitled to be represented at the consideration of the implementation of such provisions of the present Convention as fall within the scope of their mandate. The Committee may invite the specialised agencies, the United Nations Children's Fund and other competent bodies as it may consider appropriate to provide expert advice on the implementation of the Convention in areas falling within the scope of their respective mandates. The Committee may invite the specialised agencies, the United Nations Children's Fund and other United Nations organs to submit reports on the implementation of the Convention in areas falling within the scope of their activities;

(b) The Committee shall transmit, as it may consider appropriate, to the specialised agencies, the United Nations Children's Fund and other competent bodies, any reports from States Parties that contain a request, or indicate a need, for technical advice or assistance, along with the Committee's observations and suggestions, if any, on these requests or indications;

(c) The Committee may recommend to the General Assembly to request the Secretary-General to undertake on its behalf studies on specific issues relating to the rights of the child;

(d) The Committee may make suggestions and general recommendations based on information received pursuant to Articles 44 and 45 of the present Convention. Such suggestions and general recommendations shall be transmitted to any State Party concerned and reported to the General Assembly, together with comments, if any, from States Parties.

The first election for the Committee members was held in **5–068** February 1991.[62] The Committee held its first session from September 30, – October 18, 1991. During this time a set of provisional rules of procedure were adopted to govern the future work of the Treaty. General guidelines were also adopted for state parties to follow when reporting on the steps taken by them to put the Convention into effect as well as progress made in the enjoyment of children's rights. The Committee also discussed how the specialised agencies, UNICEF, other United Nations organs as well as other competent bodies as non-governmental organisations, could contribute to its work. In accordance with the Convention and the Committee's provisional rules of procedures, all competent organisation can take part in the Committee's discussions, submit their views and be consulted. By the end of June 2001 the Committee had held 27 sessions and had examined over 100 reports from Contracting Parties. The Committee in accordance with Article 45(d) makes general recommendations and suggestions: for example with respect to the United Kingdom the Committee recommended withdrawal from reservations on immigration and nationality, and child labour and serious consideration given to raising the age of criminal responsibility as well as the introduction of a comprehensive national and interdepartmental mechanism for children's rights; in Poland the Committee recommends that steps should be taken to prevent a rise in discriminatory attitudes towards vulnerable children and national legislation should reflect a ban on corporal punishment

---

[62] The ten members elected were from Burkina Faso, Peru, Sweden, the former USSR now the Russian Federation, Barbados, Zimbabwe, the Philippines, Egypt, Brazil and Portugal.

within the family as well as a comprehensive reform of juvenile justice.

"At the suggestion of the Committee on the Rights of the Child, Vietnam's Ministry of Justice, working with the Centre for Human Rights, UNICEF, NGOs and the National Committee for the Protection and Care of Children, is reviewing the judicial process for juveniles, training judges, policemen, and other legal professionals on how to apply the Convention."[63]

12. INTO THE TWENTY-FIRST CENTURY: THE WAY FORWARD

UNITED NATIONS FOURTH WORLD CONFERENCE ON WOMEN[64]

5–069 Prior to the Beijing Conference, a Conference on Social Development was held in March 1995 which, *inter alia*, laid down 10 commitments, the sixth of which calls on States:

> *"to promote and attain universal and equitable access to quality education and health. . . . Delegates added emphasis to gender issues and the priority of women and girls in . . . lifelong learning, completing school, access to education and health education . . . called for children's access to education, adequate nutrition and health care, consistent with the Convention on the Rights of the Child."*

Reference was also made to the need "for co-ordinated actions against major diseases; promotion of technology transfer related to education, training and health programmes and policies; and support for programmes to protect all women and children against exploitation, trafficking, child prostitution, female genital mutilation and child marriages."

The extracts included below pertain specifically to the girl-child.[65] Paragraphs 259–273 outline the particular difficulties encountered by the girl-child in education, health, exploitation and the plight of street children, children caught up in hostilities, disabled children, those discriminated against by virtue of membership of a minority group whether ethnic or racial.

> *Strategic objective L.1. Eliminate all forms of discrimination against the girl-child*

Actions to be taken

274. By Governments:

---

[63] UNICEF, *The Progress of Nations*.

[64] The Fourth UN Conference on Women was held in Beijing, China from September 4–15, 1995—for discussion of background to the Conference and the Declaration and Programme for Action adopted at the end of the Conference see Chapter Two on Women.

[65] Programme for Action, paras 259–285.

(a) By States that have not signed or ratified the Convention on 5–070
   the Rights of the Child, take urgent measures towards
   signing and ratifying the Convention, bearing in mind the
   strong exhortation made at the World Conference on
   Human Rights to sign it before the end of 1995, and by
   States that have signed and ratified the Convention, ensure
   its full implementation through the adoption of all necessary legislative, administrative and other measures and by
   fostering an enabling environment that encourages full
   respect for the rights of children;

(b) Consistent with Article 7 of the Convention on the Rights of
   the Child, take measures to ensure that a child is registered
   immediately after birth and has the right from birth to a
   name, the right to acquire a nationality and, as far as
   possible, the right to know and be cared for by his or her
   parents;

(c) Take steps to ensure that children receive appropriate
   financial support from their parents, by, among other
   measures, enforcing child-support laws;

(d) Eliminate the injustice and obstacles in relation to inheritance faced by the girl-child so that all children may enjoy
   their rights without discrimination, by, *inter alia*, enacting,
   as appropriate, and enforcing legislation that guarantees
   equal right to succession and ensures equal right to inherit,
   regardless of the sex of the child;

(e) Enact and strictly enforce laws to ensure that marriage is
   only entered into with the free and full consent of the
   intending spouses; in addition, enact and strictly enforce
   laws concerning the minimum legal age of consent and the
   minimum age for marriage and raise the minimum age for
   marriage where necessary;

(f) Develop and implement comprehensive policies, plans of
   action and programmes for the survival, protection,
   development and advancement of the girl-child to promote
   and protect the full enjoyment of her human rights and to
   ensure equal opportunities for girls; these plans should
   form an integral part of the total development process;

(g) Ensure the disaggregation by sex and age of all data related
   to children in the health, education and other sectors in
   order to include a gender perspective in planning, implementation and monitoring of such programmes.

275. By Governments and international and non-governmental
organisations:

(a) Disaggregate information and data on children by sex and age, undertake research on the situation of girls and integrate, as appropriate, the results in the formulation of policies, programmes and decision-making for the advancement of the girl-child;

(b) Generate social support for the enforcement of laws on the minimum legal age for marriage, in particular by providing educational opportunities for girls.

Strategic objective L.2. Eliminate negative cultural attitudes and practices against girls

Actions to be taken

276. By Governments:

5–071

(a) Encourage and support, as appropriate, non-governmental organisations and community-based organisations in their efforts to promote changes in negative attitudes and practices towards girls;

(b) Set up educational programmes and develop teaching materials and textbooks that will sensitise and inform adults about the harmful effects of certain traditional or customary practices on girl-children;

(c) Develop and adopt curricula, teaching materials and textbooks to improve the self-image, lives and work opportunities of girls, particularly in areas where women have traditionally been underrepresented, such as mathematics, science and technology;

(d) Take steps so that tradition and religion and their expressions are not a basis for discrimination against girls.

277. By Governments and, as appropriate, international and non-governmental organisations:

(a) Promote an educational setting that eliminates all barriers that impede the schooling of married and/or pregnant girls and young mothers, including, as appropriate, affordable and physically accessible child-care facilities and parental education to encourage those who have responsibilities for the care of their children and siblings during their school years to return to, or continue with, and complete schooling;

(b) Encourage educational institutions and the media to adopt and project balanced and non-stereotyped images of girls and boys, and work to eliminate child pornography and degrading and violent portrayals of the girl-child;

(c) Eliminate all forms of discrimination against the girl-child and the root causes of son preference, which result in harmful and unethical practices such as pre-natal sex selection and female infanticide; this is often compounded by the increasing use of technologies to determine foetal sex, resulting in abortion of female foetuses;

(d) Develop policies and programmes, giving priority to formal and informal education programmes that support girls and enable them to acquire knowledge, develop self-esteem and take responsibility for their own lives; and place special focus on programmes to educate women and men, especially parents, on the importance of girls' physical and mental health and well-being, including the elimination of discrimination against girls in food allocation, early marriage, violence against girls, female genital mutilation, child prostitution, sexual abuse, rape and incest.

Strategic objective L.3. Promote and protect the rights of the girl-child and increase awareness of her needs and potential.

Actions to be taken

278. By Governments and international and non-governmental 5–072 organisations:

(a) Generate awareness of the disadvantaged situation of girls among policy makers, planners, administrators and implementors at all levels, as well as within households and communities;

(b) Make the girl-child, particularly the girl-child in difficult circumstances, aware of her own potential, educate her about the rights guaranteed to her under all international human rights instruments, including the Convention on the Rights of the Child, legislation enacted for her and the various measures undertaken by both governmental and non-governmental organisations working to improve her status;

(c) Educate women, men, girls and boys to promote girls' status and encourage them to work towards mutual respect and equal partnership between girls and boys;

(d) Facilitate the equal provision of appropriate services and devices to girls with disabilities and provide their families with related support services, as appropriate.

Strategic objective L.4. Eliminate discrimination against girls in education,
skills development and training.

Actions to be taken

279. By Governments:

5–073   (a) Ensure universal and equal access to and completion of primary education by all children and eliminate the existing gap between girls and boys, as stipulated in Article 28 of the Convention on the Rights of the Child; similarly, ensure equal access to secondary education by the year 2005 and equal access to higher education, including vocational and technical education, for all girls and boys, including the disadvantaged and gifted;

    (b) Take steps to integrate functional literacy and numeracy programmes, particularly for out-of-school girls in development programmes;

    (c) Promote human rights education in educational programmes and include in human rights education the fact that the human rights of women and the girl child are an inalienable, integral and indivisible part of universal human rights;

    (d) Increase enrolment and improve retention rates of girls by allocating appropriate budgetary resources and by enlisting the support of the community and parents through campaigns and flexible school schedules, incentives, scholarships, access programmes for out-of-school girls and other measures;

    (e) Develop training programmes and materials for teachers and educators, raising awareness about their own role in the educational process, with a view to providing them with effective strategies for gender-sensitive teaching;

    (f) Take actions to ensure that female teachers and professors have the same possibilities and status as male teachers and professors.

280. By Governments and international and non-governmental organisations:

    (a) Provide education and skills training to increase girls' opportunities for employment and access to decision-making processes;

    (b) Provide education to increase girls' knowledge and skills related to the functioning of economic, financial and political systems;

(c) Ensure access to appropriate education and skills-training for girl children with disabilities for their full participation in life;

(d) Promote the full and equal participation of girls in extracurricular activities, such as sports, drama and cultural activities.

Strategic objective L.5. Eliminate discrimination against girls
in health and nutrition.

Actions to be taken

281. By Governments and international and non-governmental 5–074 organisations:

(a) Provide public information on the removal of discriminatory practices against girls in food allocation, nutrition and access to health services;

(b) Sensitise the girl-child, parents, teachers and society concerning good general health and nutrition and raise awareness of the health dangers and other problems connected with early pregnancies;

(c) Strengthen and reorient health education and health services, particularly primary health care programmes, including sexual and reproductive health, and design quality health programmes that meet the physical and mental needs of girls and that attend to the needs of young, expectant and nursing mothers;

(d) Establish peer education and outreach programmes with a view to strengthening individual and collective action to reduce the vulnerability of girls to HIV/AIDS and other sexually transmitted diseases, as agreed to in the Programme of Action of the International Conference on Population and Development and as established in the report of that Conference, recognizing the parental roles referred to in paragraph 267 of the present Platform for Action;

(e) Ensure education and dissemination of information to girls, especially adolescent girls, regarding the physiology of reproduction, reproductive and sexual health, as agreed to in the Programme of Action of the International Conference on Population and Development and as established in the report of that Conference, responsible family planning practice, family life, reproductive health, sexually transmitted diseases, HIV infection and AIDS prevention, recognising the parental roles referred to in paragraph 267;

(f) Include health and nutritional training as an integral part of literacy programmes and school curricula starting at the primary level for the benefit of the girl-child;

(g) Emphasise the role and responsibility of adolescents in sexual and reproductive health and behaviour through the provision of appropriate services and counselling, as discussed in paragraph 267;

(h) Develop information and training programmes for health planners and implementors on the special health needs of the girl-child;

(i) Take all the appropriate measures with a view to abolishing traditional practices prejudicial to the health of children, as stipulated in Article 24 of the Convention on the Rights of the Child.

Strategic objective L.6. Eliminate the economic exploitation of child labour and protect young girls at work.

Actions to be taken

282. By Governments:

5–075
(a) In conformity with Article 32 of the Convention on the Rights of the Child, protect children from economic exploitation and from performing any work that is likely to be hazardous or to interfere with the child's education, or to be harmful to the child's health or physical, mental, spiritual, moral or social development;

(b) Define a minimum age for a child's admission to employment in national legislation, in conformity with existing international labour standards and the Convention on the Rights of the Child, including girls in all sectors of activity;

(c) Protect young girls at work, *inter alia*, through:

(i) A minimum age or ages for admission to employment;
(ii) Strict monitoring of work conditions (respect for work time, prohibition of work by children not provided for by national legislation, and monitoring of hygiene and health conditions at work);
(iii) Application of social security coverage;
(iv) Establishment of continuous training and education;

(d) Strengthen, where necessary, legislation governing the work of children and provide for appropriate penalties or other sanctions to ensure effective enforcement of the legislation;

(e) Use existing international labour standards, including, as appropriate, ILO standards for the protection of working children, to guide the formulation of national labour legislation and policies.

Strategic objective L.7. eradicate violence against the girl-child.

Actions to be taken

283. By Governments and, as appropriate, international and non-governmental organisations:

(a) Take effective actions and measures to enact and enforce legislation to protect the safety and security of girls from all forms of violence at work, including training programmes and support programmes, and take measures to eliminate incidents of sexual harassment of girls in educational and other institutions;

(b) Take appropriate legislative, administrative, social and educational measures to protect the girl-child, in the household and in society, from all forms of physical or mental violence, injury or abuse, neglect or negligent treatment, maltreatment or exploitation, including sexual abuse;

(c) Undertake gender sensitisation training for those involved in healing and rehabilitation and other assistance programmes for girls who are victims of violence and promote programmes of information, support and training for such girls;

(d) Enact and enforce legislation protecting girls from all forms of violence, including female infanticide and prenatal sex selection, genital mutilation, incest, sexual abuse, sexual exploitation, child prostitution and child pornography, and develop age-appropriate safe and confidential programmes and medical, social and psychological support services to assist girls who are subjected to violence.

Strategic objective L.8. promote the girl child's awareness of and participation in social, economic and political life.

Actions to be taken

284. By Governments and international and non-governmental organisations:

(a) Provide access for girls to training, information and the media on social, cultural, economic and political issues and enable them to articulate their views;

(b) Support non-governmental organisations, in particular youth non-governmental organisations, in their efforts to promote the equality and participation of girls in society.

Strategic objective L.9. strengthen the role of the family in improving the status of the girl-child.

Actions to be taken

285. By Governments, in co-operation with non-governmental organisations:

(a) (a) Formulate policies and programmes to help the family, . . . above, in its supporting, educating and nurturing roles, with particular emphasis on the elimination of intra-family discrimination against the girl-child;

(b) Provide an environment conducive to the strengthening of the family, . . . with a view to providing supportive and preventive measures which protect, respect and promote the potential of the girl-child;

(c) Educate and encourage parents and caregivers to treat girls and boys equally and to ensure shared responsibilities between girls and boys in the family, . . .

CHAPTER 6

PERSONS WITH DISABILITIES[1]

"Societies which accommodate human diversity not only respect fundamental freedoms, but mobilise people's full potential. Disabled persons challenge the world to grow, and to build a society which advanced freedoms and addressed the needs and contributions of all its members."[2]

INTRODUCTION

The thrust of international measures to promote the rights of persons with disabilities has been to encourage the promulgation of national legislation which ensures equal access to human rights for such persons. The third quinquennial review of the Programme of Action Concerning Disabled Persons is scheduled to take place in 2002 and it will show that many States have implemented measures designed to guarantee equality of opportunity and treatment for such individuals. This is encouraging although it is recognised that persons with disabilities still encounter discrimination in employment, education and health care. Raising the profile of persons with disabilities on the political agenda has reaped benefits which will ultimately permeate all strata of society.

WORLD CONFERENCE ON HUMAN RIGHTS, (JUNE 1993) VIENNA DECLARATION[3]

22. Special attention needs to be paid to ensuring non- **6–001** discrimination, and the equal enjoyment of all human rights and fundamental freedoms by disabled persons, including their active participation in all aspects of society.

Part II(B) 6. The Rights of the Disabled Person

63. The World Conference On Human Rights reaffirms that all human rights and fundamental freedoms are universal and thus

---

[1] The term "persons with disabilities" is now favoured in preference to the older term "disabled persons." The latter term is liable to be misinterpreted so as to imply that the ability of the individual to function as a person has been disabled. See below "Disability and Handicap."

[2] Secretary-General Boutros Boutros-Ghali, December 2, 1994.

[3] 32 I.L.M.1661 (1993).

unreservedly include persons with disabilities. Every person is born equal and has the same rights to life and welfare, education and work, living independently and active participation in all aspects of society. Any direct discrimination or other negative discriminatory treatment of a disabled person is therefore a violation of his or her rights. The World Conference on Human Rights calls on Governments, where necessary, to adopt or adjust legislation to assure access to these and other rights for disabled persons.

64. The place of disabled persons is everywhere. Persons with disabilities should be guaranteed equal opportunity through the elimination of all socially determined barriers, be they physical, financial, social or psychological, which exclude or restrict full participation in society.

65. Recalling the World Programme of Action concerning Disabled Persons, adopted by the General Assembly at its 37th session, the World Conference on Human Rights calls upon the General Assembly and the Economic and Social Council to adopt the draft standard rules on the equalisation of opportunities for persons with disabilities with disabilities, at their meetings in 1993.

There is as highlighted in the Vienna Declaration a paucity of international instruments affording protection to persons with disabilities. The Standard Rules on the Equalisation of Opportunities for Persons with Disabilities were adopted by the General Assembly[4] and although not binding they do serve as an important and valuable reference guide for the international community.[5] The Rules are designed to ensure that girls, boys,[6] women and men with disabilities may exercise the same rights and obligations as others and that measures are adopted to remove the obstacles which prevent persons with disabilities from participating fully in the activities of the society within which they live. Equalisation of opportunities means the process through which the various systems of society and the environment, such as services, activities, information and documentation are made availalbe to all, particularly persons with disabilities.[7] The principle of equal rights implies that the needs of each and every individual are of equal importance, that those needs must be made the basis for the planning of societies and that all resouces must be employed in such a way as to ensure that every individual has equal opportunity for participation.[8]

[4] G.A. Res. 48/96, December 20, 1993.

[5] See Committee on Economic, Social and Cultural Rights, General Comment no. 5 "Persons with disabilities" (11th Session, 1994) [UN Doc. E/C.12/1994/13] adopted November 25, 1994; I.H.R.R. Vol. 2 No. 2 (1995) 261.

[6] Specific measures for the international protection of the disabled child see Chapter on Children p. 180.

[7] Standard Rules, Introduction, para. 24.

[8] *ibid.*, para. 25.

Disability and Handicap

The term disability summarises a great number of different func-   **6–002**
tional limitations occurring in any population in all countries of the
world. People may be disabled by physical, intellectual or sensory
impairment, medical conditions or mental illness. Such impairments, conditions or illnesses may be permanent or transitory in
nature.[9] Handicap is the loss or limitation of opportunites to take
part in the life of the community on any equal level with others.
The term handicap describes the encounter between the person
with the disability and the environment. The purpose of this term
is to emphasise the focus on the shortcomings in the environment
and in many organised activities in society, for example, information, communication and education, which prevent persons with
disabilities from participating on equal terms.[10] Current terminology recognises the necessity of addressing both the individual
needs (such as rehabilitation and technical aids) and the shortcomings of the society (various obstacles for participation).[11]
It is estimated that there are more than 500 million persons in
the world with disabilities and according to UN sources some 80
per cent of that figure live in developing countries whilst some 70
per cent of the total figure have no access to the services they
require. The General Assembly in the Introduction to the Standard
Rules recognises that there is an ever increasing number of persons
with disabilities in all parts of the world and at all levels in every
society[12] and that both the causes and the consequences of disability vary throughout the world as a result of different socio-
economic circumstances and the different provisions that States
make for the well-being of their citizens.[13]
The introduction also contains the following observations;

3. Present disability policy is the result of developments over   **6–003**
   the past 200 years. In many ways it reflects the general
   living conditions and social and economic policies of different times. In the disability field, however, there are also
   many specific circumstances that have influenced the living
   conditions of persons with disabilities. Ignorance, neglect,
   superstition and fear are social factors that throughout the
   history of disability have isolated persons with disabilities
   and delayed their development.

4. Over the years disability policy developed from elementary
   care at institutions to education for children with disabilities and rehabilitation for persons who became dis-

[9] *ibid.*, para. 17.
[10] *ibid.*, para. 18.
[11] *ibid.*, para. 221.
[12] *ibid.*, para. 1.
[13] *ibid.*, para. 2.

abled during adult life. Through education and rehabilitation, persons with disabilities became more active and a driving force in the further development of disability policy. Organisations of persons with disabilities, their families and advocates were formed, which advocated better conditions for persons with disabilities. After the Second World War the concepts of integration and normalisation were introduced, which reflected a growing awareness of the capabilities of persons with disabilities.

5. Towards the end of the 1960s organisations of persons with disabilities in some countries started to formulate a new concept of disability. That new concept indicated the close connection between the limitation experienced by individuals with disabilities, the design and structure of their environments and the attitude of the general population. At the same time the problems of disability in developing countries were more and more highlighted. In some of those countries the percentage of the population with disabilities was estimated to be very high and, for the most part, persons with disabilities were extremely poor.

The Standard Rules have six specific objectives:

(a) To stress that all action in the field of disability presupposes adequate knowledge and experience of the conditions and special needs of persons with disabilities;

(b) To emphasise the processes through which every aspect of social organisation is made accessible to all is a basic objective of socio-economic development;

(c) To outline crucial aspects of social politiies in the field of disability, including as appropriate, the active encouragemnt of technical and economic co-operation;

(d) To provide models for the political decision-making process required for the attainment of equal opportunities, bearing in mind the widely differing technical and economic levels, the fact that the process must reflect keen understanding of the cultural context within which it takes place and the crucial role of persons with disabilities in it;

(e) To propose national mechanism for close collaboration among States, the organs of the United Nations system, other intergovernmental bodies and organisations of persons with disabilities;

(f) To propose an effective machinery for monitoring the process by which States seek to attain the equalisation of opportunities for persons with disabilities.[14]

---

[14] *ibid.*, Preamble.

STANDARD RULES ON THE EQUALISATION OF OPPORTUNITIES FOR PERSONS WITH DISABILITIES 1993.

I. PRECONDITIONS FOR EQUAL PARTICIPATION

Rule 1. Awareness-raising

States should take action to raise awareness in society about 6–004 persons with disabilities, their rights, their needs, their potential and their contribution.

1. States should ensure that responsible authorities distribute up-to-date information on available programmes and services to persons with disabilities,their families, professionals in the field and the general public.

Information to persons with disabilities should be presented in accessible form.

2. States should initiate and support information campaigns concerning persons with disabilities and disability policies, conveying the message that persons with disabilities are citizens with the same rights and obligations as others, thus justifying measures to remove all obstacles to full participation.

3. States should encourage the portrayal of persons with disabilities by the mass media in a positive way; organisations of persons with disabilities should be consulted on this matter.

4. States should ensure that public education programmes reflect in all their aspects the principle of full participation and equality.

5. States should invite persons with disabilities and their families and organisations to participate in public education programmes concerning disability matters.

6. States should encourage enterprises in the private sector to include disability issues in all aspects of their activity.

7. States should initiate and promote programmes aimed at raising the level of awareness of persons with disabilities concerning their rights and potential. Increased self-reliance and empowerment will assist persons with disabilities to take advantage of the opportunities available to them.

8. Awareness-raising should be an important part of the education of children with disabilities and in rehabilitation programmes. Persons with disabilities could also assist one another in awareness-raising through the activities of their own organisations.

9. Awareness-raising should be part of the education of all children and should be a component of teacher-training courses and training of all professionals.

Rule 2. Medical care

States should ensure the provision of effective medical care to 6–005 persons with disabilities.

1. States should work towards the provision of programmes run by multidisciplinary teams of professionals for early detection, assessment and treatment of impairment. This could prevent, reduce or eliminate disabling effects. Such programmes should ensure the full participation of persons with disabilities and their families at the individual level, and of organisations of persons with disabilities at the planning and evaluation level.

2. Local community workers should be trained to participate in areas such as early detection of impairments, the provision of primary assistance and referral to appropriate services.

3. States should ensure that persons with disabilities, particularly infants and children, are provided with the same level of medical care within the same system as other members of society.

4. States should ensure that all medical and paramedical personnel are adequately trained and equipped to give medical care to persons with disabilities and that they have access to relevant treatment methods and technology.

5. States should ensure that medical, paramedical and related personnel are adequately trained so that they do not give inappropriate advice to parents,thus restricting options for their children. This training should be an ongoing process and should be based on the latest information available.

6. States should ensure that persons with disabilities are provided with any regular treatment and medicines they may need to preserve or improve their level of functioning.

Rule 3. Rehabilitation[15]

States should ensure the provision of rehabilitation services to persons with disabilities in order for them to reach and sustain their optimum level of independence and functioning.

1. States should develop national rehabilitation programmes for all groups of persons with disabilities. Such programmes should be based on the actual individual needs of persons with disabilities and on the principles of full participation and equality.

2. Such programmes should include a wide range of activities, such as basic skills training to improve or compensate for an affected function, counselling of persons with disabilities and their families, developing self-reliance, and occasional services such as assessment and guidance.

[15] The term "rehabilitation" refers to a process aimed at enabling persons with disabilities to reach and maintain their optimal physical, sensory, intellectual, psychiatric and/or social functional levels, thus providing them with the tools to change their lives towards a higher level of independence. Rehabilitation may include measures to provide and/or restore functions, or compensate for the loss or absence of a function or for a functional limitation. The rehabilitation process does not involve initial medical care. It includes a wide range of measures and activities from more basic and general rehabilitation to goal-oriented activities, for instance vocational rehabilitation (Standard Rules, para. 23).

3. All persons with disabilities, including persons with severe and/or multiple disabilities, who require rehabilitation should have access to it.

4. Persons with disabilities and their families should be able to participate in the design and organisation of rehabilitation services concerning themselves.

5. All rehabilitation services should be available in the local community where the person with disabilities lives. However, in some instances, in order to attain a certain training objective, special time-limited rehabilitation courses may be organised, where appropriate, in residential form.

6. Persons with disabilities and their families should be encouraged to involve themselves in rehabilitation, for instance as trained teachers, instructors or counsellors.

7. States should draw upon the expertise of organisations of persons with disabilities when formulating or evaluating rehabilitation programmes.

Rule 4. Support services

States should ensure the development and supply of support 6–006 services, including assistive devices for persons with disabilities, to assist them to increase their level of independence in their daily living and to exercise their rights.

1. States should ensure the provision of assistive devices and equipment, personal assistance and interpreter services, according to the needs of persons with disabilities, as important measures to achieve the equalisation of opportunities.

2. States should support the development, production, distribution and servicing of assistive devices and equipment and the dissemination of knowledge about them.

3. To achieve this, generally available technical know-how should be utilised. In States where high-technology industry is available, it should be fully utilised to improve the standard and effectiveness of assistive devices and equipment. It is important to stimulate the development and production of simple and inexpensive devices, using local material and local production facilities when possible. Persons with disabilities themselves could be involved in the production of those devices.

4. States should recognise that all persons with disabilities who need assistive devices should have access to them as appropriate, including financial accessibility. This may mean that assistive devices and equipment should be provided free of charge or at such a low price that persons with disabilities or their families can afford to buy them.

5. In rehabilitation programmes for the provision of assistive devices and equipment, States should consider the special requirements of girls and boys with disabilities concerning the design, durability and age-appropriateness of assistive devices and equipment.

6. States should support the development and provision of personal assistance programmes and interpretation services, especially for persons with severe and/or multiple disabilities. Such programmes would increase the level of participation of persons with disabilities in everyday life at home, at work, in school and during leisure-time activities.

7. Personal assistance programmes should be designed in such a way that the persons with disabilities using the programmes have a decisive influence on the way in which the programmes are delivered.

II. Target areas for Equal Participation

Rule 5. Accessibility

6–007 States should recognise the overall importance of accessibility in the process of the equalisation of opportunities in all spheres of society. For persons with disabilities of any kind, States should (a) introduce programmes of action to make the physical environment accessible; and (b) undertake measures to provide access to information and communication.

(a) Access to the Physical Environment

1. States should initiate measures to remove the obstacles to participation in the physical environment. Such measures should be to develop standards and guidelines and to consider enacting legislation to ensure accessibility to various areas in society, such as housing, buildings, public transport services and other means of transportation, streets and other outdoor environments.

2. States should ensure that architects, construction engineers and others who are professionally involved in the design and construction of the physical environment have access to adequate information on disability policy and measures to achieve accessibility.

3. Accessibility requirements should be included in the design and construction of the physical environment from the beginning of the designing process.

4. Organisations of persons with disabilities should be consulted when standards and norms for accessibility are being developed. They should also be involved locally from the initial planning stage when public construction projects are being designed, thus ensuring maximum accessibility.

(b) Access to Information and Communication

6–008 **5.** Persons with disabilities and, where appropriate, their families and advocates should have access to full information on diagnosis, rights and available services and programmes, at all stages. Such information should be presented in forms accessible to persons with disabilities.

6. States should develop strategies to make information services and documentation accessible for different groups of persons with disabilities.

Braille, tape services, large print and other appropriate technologies should be used to provide access to written information and documentation for persons with visual impairments. Similarly, appropriate technologies should be used to provide access to spoken information for persons with auditory impairments or comprehension difficulties.

7. Consideration should be given to the use of sign language in the education of deaf children, in their families and communities. Sign language interpretation services should also be provided to facilitate the communication between deaf persons and others.

8. Consideration should also be given to the needs of people with other communication disabilities.

9. States should encourage the media, especially television, radio and newspapers, to make their services accessible.

10. States should ensure that new computerised information and service systems offered to the general public are either made initially accessible or are adapted to be made accessible to persons with disabilities.

11. Organisations of persons with disabilities should be consulted when measures to make information services accessible are being developed.

Rule 6. Education[16]

States should recognise the principle of equal primary, secondary   6–009
and tertiary educational opportunities for children, youth and adults with disabilities, in integrated settings. They should ensure that the education of persons with disabilities is an integral part of the educational system.

1. General educational authorities are responsible for the education of persons with disabilities in integrated settings. Education for persons with disabilities should form an integral part of national educational planning, curriculum development and school organisation.

2. Education in mainstream schools presupposes the provision of interpreter and other appropriate support services. Adequate accessibility and support services, designed to meet the needs of persons with different disabilities, should be provided.

3. Parent groups and organisations of persons with disabilities should be involved in the education process at all levels.

---

[16] See also Chapter on Children p. 173 *et seq.*

4. In States where education is compulsory it should be provided to girls and boys with all kinds and all levels of disabilities, including the most severe.

5. Special attention should be given in the following areas:

(a) Very young children with disabilities;

(b) Pre-school children with disabilities;

(c) Adults with disabilities, particularly women.

6. To accommodate educational provisions for persons with disabilities in the mainstream, States should:

(a) Have a clearly stated policy, understood and accepted at the school level and by the wider community;

(b) Allow for curriculum flexibility, addition and adaptation;

(c) Provide for quality materials, ongoing teacher training and support teachers.

7. Integrated education and community-based programmes should be seen as complementary approaches in providing cost-effective education and training for persons with disabilities. National community-based programmes should encourage communities to use and develop their resources to provide local education to persons with disabilities.

8. In situations where the general school system does not yet adequately meet the needs of all persons with disabilities, special education may be considered. It should be aimed at preparing students for education in the general school system. The quality of such education should reflect the same standards and ambitions as general education and should be closely linked to it. At a minimum, students with disabilities should be afforded the same portion of educational resources as students without disabilities. States should aim for the gradual integration of special education services into mainstream education. It is acknowledged that in some instances special education may currently be considered to be the most appropriate form of education for some students with disabilities.

9. Owing to the particular communication needs of deaf and deaf/blind persons, their education may be more suitably provided in schools for such persons or special classes and units in mainstream schools. At the initial stage, in particular, special attention needs to be focused on culturally sensitive instruction that will result in effective communication skills and maximum independence for people who are deaf or deaf/blind.

Rule 7. Employment

6–010 States should recognise the principle that persons with disabilities must be empowered to exercise their human rights, particularly in the field of employment. In both rural and urban areas they must have equal opportunities for productive and gainful employment in the labour market.

1. Laws and regulations in the employment field must not discriminate against persons with disabilities and must not raise obstacles to their employment.

2. States should actively support the integration of persons with disabilities into open employment. This active support could occur through a variety of measures, such as vocational training, incentive-oriented quota schemes, reserved or designated employment, loans or grants for small business, exclusive contracts or priority production rights, tax concessions, contract compliance or other technical or financial assistance to enterprises employing workers with disabilities. States should also encourage employers to make reasonable adjustments to accommodate persons with disabilities.

3. States' action programmes should include:

(a) Measures to design and adapt workplaces and work premises in such a way that they become accessible to persons with different disabilities;

(b) Support for the use of new technologies and the development and production of assistive devices, tools and equipment and measures to facilitate access to such devices and equipment for persons with disabilities to enable them to gain and maintain employment;

(c) Provision of appropriate training and placement and ongoing support such as personal assistance and interpreter services.

4. States should initiate and support public awareness-raising campaigns designed to overcome negative attitudes and prejudices concerning workers with disabilities.

5. In their capacity as employers, States should create favourable conditions for the employment of persons with disabilities in the public sector.

6. States, workers' organisations and employers should co-operate to ensure equitable recruitment and promotion policies, employment conditions, rates of pay, measures to improve the work environment in order to prevent injuries and impairments and measures for the rehabilitation of employees who have sustained employment-related injuries.

7. The aim should always be for persons with disabilities to obtain employment in the open labour market. For persons with disabilities whose needs cannot be met in open employment, small units of sheltered or supported employment may be an alternative. It is important that the quality of such programmes be assessed in terms of their relevance and sufficiency in providing opportunities for persons with disabilities to gain employment in the labour market.

8. Measures should be taken to include persons with disabilities in training and employment programmes in the private and informal sectors.

9. States, workers' organisations and employers should co-operate with organisations of persons with disabilities concerning all measures to create training and employment opportunities, including flexible hours, part-time work, job-sharing, self-employment and attendant care for persons with disabilities.

Rule 8. Income maintenance and social security

States are responsible for the provision of social security and income maintenance for persons with disabilities.

1. States should ensure the provision of adequate income support to persons with disabilities who, owing to disability or disability-related factors, have temporarily lost or received a reduction in their income or have been denied employment opportunities. States should ensure that the provision of support takes into account the costs frequently incurred by persons with disabilities and their families as a result of the disability.

2. In countries where social security, social insurance or other social welfare schemes exist or are being developed for the general population, States should ensure that such systems do not exclude or discriminate against persons with disabilities.

3. States should also ensure the provision of income support and social security protection to individuals who undertake the care of a person with a disability.

4. Social security systems should include incentives to restore the income-earning capacity of persons with disabilities. Such systems should provide or contribute to the organisation, development and financing of vocational training. They should also assist with placement services.

5. Social security programmes should also provide incentives for persons with disabilities to seek employment in order to establish or re-establish their income-earning capacity.

6. Income support should be maintained as long as the disabling conditions remain in a manner that does not discourage persons with disabilities from seeking employment. It should only be reduced or terminated when persons with disabilities achieve adequate and secure income.

7. States, in countries where social security is to a large extent provided by the private sector, should encourage local communities, welfare organisations and families to develop self-help measures and incentives for employment or employment-related activities for persons with disabilities.

Rule 9. Family life and personal integrity

States should promote the full participation of persons with 6–011
disabilities in family life. They should promote their right to
personal integrity and ensure that laws do not discriminate
against persons with disabilities with respect to sexual relationships, marriage and parenthood.

1. Persons with disabilities should be enabled to live with their
families.

States should encourage the inclusion in family counselling of
appropriate modules regarding disability and its effects on family
life. Respite-care and attendant-care services should be made
available to families which include a person with disabilities.
States should remove all unnecessary obstacles to persons who
want to foster or adopt a child or adult with disabilities.

2. Persons with disabilities must not be denied the opportunity
to experience their sexuality, have sexual relationships and experience parenthood. Taking into account that persons with disabilities may experience difficulties in getting married and setting
up a family, States should encourage the availability of appropriate counselling. Persons with disabilities must have the same
access as others to family-planning methods, as well as to
information in accessible form on the sexual functioning of their
bodies.

3. States should promote measures to change negative attitudes
towards marriage, sexuality and parenthood of persons with
disabilities, especially of girls and women with disabilities, which
still prevail in society. The media should be encouraged to play
an important role in removing such negative attitudes.

4. Persons with disabilities and their families need to be fully
informed about taking precautions against sexual and other forms
of abuse. Persons with disabilities are particularly vulnerable to
abuse in the family, community or institutions and need to be
educated on how to avoid the occurrence of abuse, recognise
when abuse has occurred and report on such acts.

Rule 10. Culture

States will ensure that persons with disabilities are integrated into 6–012
and can participate in cultural activities on an equal basis.

1. States should ensure that persons with disabilities have the
opportunity to utilise their creative, artistic and intellectual potential, not only for their own benefit, but also for the enrichment of
their community, be they in urban or rural areas. Examples of
such activities are dance, music, literature, theatre, plastic arts,
painting and sculpture. Particularly in developing countries,
emphasis should be placed on traditional and contemporary art
forms, such as puppetry, recitation and story-telling.

2. States should promote the accessibility to and availability of places for cultural performances and services, such as theatres, museums, cinemas and libraries, to persons with disabilities.

3. States should initiate the development and use of special technical arrangements to make literature, films and theatre accessible to persons with disabilities.

Rule 11. Recreation and sports

States will take measures to ensure that persons with disabilities have equal opportunities for recreation and sports.

1. States should initiate measures to make places for recreation and sports, hotels, beaches, sports arenas, gym halls, etc., accessible to persons with disabilities. Such measures should encompass support for staff in recreation and sports programmes, including projects to develop methods of accessibility, and participation, information and training programmes.

2. Tourist authorities, travel agencies, hotels, voluntary organisations and others involved in organising recreational activities or travel opportunities should offer their services to all, taking into account the special needs of persons with disabilities. Suitable training should be provided to assist that process.

3. Sports organisations should be encouraged to develop opportunities for participation by persons with disabilities in sports activities. In some cases, accessibility measures could be enough to open up opportunities for participation. In other cases, special arrangements or special games would be needed. States should support the participation of persons with disabilities in national and international events.

4. Persons with disabilities participating in sports activities should have access to instruction and training of the same quality as other participants.

5. Organisers of sports and recreation should consult with organisations of persons with disabilities when developing their services for persons with disabilities.

Rule 12. Religion

6–013 States will encourage measures for equal participation by persons with disabilities in the religious life of their communities.

1. States should encourage, in consultation with religious authorities, measures to eliminate discrimination and make religious activities accessible to persons with disabilities.

2. States should encourage the distribution of information on disability matters to religious institutions and organisations. States should also encourage religious authorities to include information on disability policies in the training for religious professions, as well as in religious education programmes.

3. They should also encourage the accessibility of religious literature to persons with sensory impairments.

4. States and/or religious organisations should consult with organisations of persons with disabilities when developing measures for equal participation in religious activities.

III. IMPLEMENTATION MEASURES

Rule 13. Information and research

States assume the ultimate responsibility for the collection and 6–014 dissemination of information on the living conditions of persons with disabilities and promote comprehensive research on all aspects, including obstacles that affect the lives of persons with disabilities.

1. States should, at regular intervals, collect gender-specific statistics and other information concerning the living conditions of persons with disabilities. Such data collection could be conducted in conjunction with national censuses and household surveys and could be undertaken in close collaboration, *inter alia*, with universities, research institutes and organisations of persons with disabilities. The data collection should include questions on programmes and services and their use.

2. States should consider establishing a data bank on disability, which would include statistics on available services and programmes as well as on the different groups of persons with disabilities.

They should bear in mind the need to protect individual privacy and personal integrity.

3. States should initiate and support programmes of research on social, economic and participation issues that affect the lives of persons with disabilities and their families. Such research should include studies on the causes, types and frequencies of disabilities, the availability and efficacy of existing programmes and the need for development and evaluation of services and support measures.

4. States should develop and adopt terminology and criteria for the conduct of national surveys, in co-operation with organisations of persons with disabilities.

5. States should facilitate the participation of persons with disabilities in data collection and research. To undertake such research States should particularly encourage the recruitment of qualified persons with disabilities.

6. States should support the exchange of research findings and experiences.

7. States should take measures to disseminate information and knowledge on disability to all political and administration levels within national, regional and local spheres.

Rule 14. Policy-making and planning

States will ensure that disability aspects are included in all relevant policy-making and national planning.

1. States should initiate and plan adequate policies for persons with disabilities at the national level, and stimulate and support action at regional and local levels.

2. States should involve organisations of persons with disabilities in all decision-making relating to plans and programmes concerning persons with disabilities or affecting their economic and social status.

3. The needs and concerns of persons with disabilities should be incorporated into general development plans and not be treated separately.

4. The ultimate responsibility of States for the situation of persons with disabilities does not relieve others of their responsibility. Anyone in charge of services, activities or the provision of information in society should be encouraged to accept responsibility for making such programmes available to persons with disabilities.

5. States should facilitate the development by local communities of programmes and measures for persons with disabilities. One way of doing this could be to develop manuals or check-lists and provide training programmes for local staff.

Rule 15. Legislation

6–015 States have a responsibility to create the legal bases for measures to achieve the objectives of full participation and equality for persons with disabilities.

1. National legislation, embodying the rights and obligations of citizens, should include the rights and obligations of persons with disabilities.

States are under an obligation to enable persons with disabilities to exercise their rights, including their human, civil and political rights, on an equal basis with other citizens. States must ensure that organisations of persons with disabilities are involved in the development of national legislation concerning the rights of persons with disabilities, as well as in the ongoing evaluation of that legislation.

2. Legislative action may be needed to remove conditions that may adversely affect the lives of persons with disabilities, including harassment and victimisation. Any discriminatory provisions against persons with disabilities must be eliminated. National legislation should provide for appropriate sanctions in case of violations of the principles of non-discrimination.

3. National legislation concerning persons with disabilities may appear in two different forms. The rights and obligations may be incorporated in general legislation or contained in special legislation. Special legislation for persons with disabilities may be established in several ways:

(a) By enacting separate legislation, dealing exclusively with disability matters;

(b) By including disability matters within legislation on particular topics;

(c) By mentioning persons with disabilities specifically in the texts that serve to interpret existing legislation.

A combination of those different approaches might be desirable. Affirmative action provisions may also be considered.

4. States may consider establishing formal statutory complaints mechanisms in order to protect the interests of persons with disabilities.

Rule 16. Economic policies

States have the financial responsibility for national programmes 6–016 and measures to create equal opportunities for persons with disabilities.

1. States should include disability matters in the regular budgets of all national, regional and local government bodies.

2. States, non-governmental organisations and other interested bodies should interact to determine the most effective ways of supporting projects and measures relevant to persons with disabilities.

3. States should consider the use of economic measures (loans, tax exemptions, earmarked grants, special funds, and so on) to stimulate and support equal participation by persons with disabilities in society.

4. In many States it may be advisable to establish a disability development fund, which could support various pilot projects and self-help programmes at the grass-roots level.

Rule 17. Co-ordination of work

States are responsible for the establishment and strengthening of national co-ordinating committees, or similar bodies, to serve as a national focal point on disability matters.

1. The national co-ordinating committee or similar bodies should be permanent and based on legal as well as appropriate administrative regulation.

2. A combination of representatives of private and public organisations is most likely to achieve an intersectoral and

multidisciplinary composition. Representatives could be drawn from concerned government ministries organisations of persons with disabilities and non-governmental organisations.

3. Organisations of persons with disabilities should have considerable influence in the national co-ordinating committee in order to ensure proper feedback of their concerns.

4. The national co-ordinating committee should be provided with sufficient autonomy and resources to fulfil its responsibilities in relation to its decision-making capacities. It should report to the highest governmental level.

Rule 18. Organisations of persons with disabilities

6–017 States should recognise the right of the organisations of persons with disabilities to represent persons with disabilities at national, regional and local levels. States should also recognise the advisory role of organisations of persons with disabilities in decision-making on disability matters.

1. States should encourage and support economically and in other ways the formation and strengthening of organisations of persons with disabilities, family members and/or advocates. States should recognise that those organisations have a role to play in the development of disability policy.

2. States should establish ongoing communication with organisations of persons with disabilities and ensure their participation in the development of government policies.

3. The role of organisations of persons with disabilities could be to identify needs and priorities, to participate in the planning, implementation and evaluation of services and measures concerning the lives of persons with disabilities, and to contribute to public awareness and to advocate change.

4. As instruments of self-help, organisations of persons with disabilities provide and promote opportunities for the development of skills in various fields, mutual support among members and information sharing.

5. Organisations of persons with disabilities could perform their advisory role in many different ways such as having permanent representation on boards of government-funded agencies, serving on public commissions and providing expert knowledge on different projects.

6. The advisory role of organisations of persons with disabilities should be ongoing in order to develop and deepen the exchange of views and information between the State and the organisations.

7. Organisations should be permanently represented on the national co-ordinating committee or similar bodies.

8. The role of local organisations of persons with disabilities should be developed and strengthened to ensure that they influence matters at the community level.

Rule 19. Personnel training

States are responsible for ensuring the adequate training of 6–018
personnel, at all levels, involved in the planning and provision of
programmes and services concerning persons with disabilities.

1. States should ensure that all authorities providing services in
the disability field give adequate training to their personnel.

2. In the training of professionals in the disability field, as well
as in the provision of information on disability in general training
programmes, the principle of full participation and equality
should be appropriately reflected.

3. States should develop training programmes in consultation
with organisations of persons with disabilities, and persons with
disabilities should be involved as teachers, instructors or advisers
in staff training programmes.

4. The training of community workers is of great strategic
importance, particularly in developing countries. It should
involve persons with disabilities and include the development of
appropriate values, competence and technologies as well as skills
which can be practised by persons with disabilities, their parents,
families and members of the community.

**Rule 20. National monitoring and evaluation of disability pro-
grammes in the implementation of the Rules**

States are responsible for the continuous monitoring and evaluation of the implementation of national programmes and services
concerning the equalisation of opportunities for persons with
disabilities.

1. States should periodically and systematically evaluate
national disability programmes and disseminate both the bases
and the results of the evaluations.

2. States should develop and adopt terminology and criteria for
the evaluation of disability-related programmes and services.

3. Such criteria and terminology should be developed in close
co-operation with organisations of persons with disabilities from
the earliest conceptual and planning stages.

4. States should participate in international co-operation in
order to develop common standards for national evaluation in the
disability field.

States should encourage national co-ordinating committees to
participate also.

5. The evaluation of various programmes in the disability field
should be built in at the planning stage, so that the overall
efficacy in fulfilling their policy objectives can be evaluated.

Rule 21. Technical and economic co-operation

6–019 States, both industrialised and developing, have the responsibility to co-operate in and take measures for the improvement of the living conditions of persons with disabilities in developing countries.

1. Measures to achieve the equalisation of opportunities of persons with disabilities, including refugees with disabilities, should be integrated into general development programmes.

2. Such measures must be integrated into all forms of technical and economic co-operation, bilateral and multilateral, governmental and non-governmental. States should bring up disability issues in discussions on such co-operation with their counterparts.

3. When planning and reviewing programmes of technical and economic co-operation, special attention should be given to the effects of such programmes on the situation of persons with disabilities. It is of the utmost importance that persons with disabilities and their organisations are consulted on any development projects designed for persons with disabilities. They should be directly involved in the development, implementation and evaluation of such projects.

4. Priority areas for technical and economic co-operation should include:

(a) The development of human resources through the development of skills, abilities and potentials of persons with disabilities and the initiation of employment-generating activities for and of persons with disabilities;

(b) The development and dissemination of appropriate disability-related technologies and know-how.

5. States are also encouraged to support the formation and strengthening of organisations of persons with disabilities.

6. States should take measures to improve the knowledge of disability issues among staff involved at all levels in the administration of technical and economic co-operation programmes.

Rule 22. International co-operation

6–020 States will participate actively in international co-operation concerning policies for the equalisation of opportunities for persons with disabilities.

1. Within the United Nations, the specialised agencies and other concerned intergovernmental organisations, States should participate in the development of disability policy.

2. Whenever appropriate, States should introduce disability aspects in general negotiations concerning standards, information exchange, development programmes, etc.

3. States should encourage and support the exchange of knowledge and experience among:

(a) Non-governmental organisations concerned with disability issues;

(b) Research institutions and individual researchers involved in disability issues;

(c) Representatives of field programmes and of professional groups in the disability field;

(d) Organisations of persons with disabilities;

(e) National co-ordinating committees.

4. States should ensure that the United Nations and the specialised agencies, as well as all intergovernmental and inter-parliamentary bodies, at global and regional levels, include in their work the global and regional organisations of persons with disabilities.

IV. MONITORING MECHANISM

1. The purpose of a monitoring mechanism is to further the 6–021 effective implementation of the Rules. It will assist each State in assessing its level of implementation of the Rules and in measuring its progress. The monitoring should identify obstacles and suggest suitable measures that would contribute to the successful implementation of the Rules. The monitoring mechanism will recognise the economic, social and cultural features existing in individual States. An important element should also be the provision of advisory services and the exchange of experience and information between States.

2. The Rules shall be monitored within the framework of the sessions of the Commission for Social Development. A Special Rapporteur with relevant and extensive experience in disability issues and international organisations shall be appointed, if necessary, funded by extrabudgetary resources, for three years to monitor the implementation of the Rules.

3. International organisations of persons with disabilities having consultative status with the Economic and Social Council and organisations representing persons with disabilities who have not yet formed their own organisations should be invited to create among themselves a panel of experts, on which organisations of persons with disabilities shall have a majority, taking into account the different kinds of disabilities and necessary equitable geographical distribution, to be consulted by the Special Rapporteur and, when appropriate, by the Secretariat.

4. The panel of experts will be encouraged by the Special Rapporteur to review, advise and provide feedback and suggestions on the promotion, implementation and monitoring of the Rules.

5. The Special Rapporteur shall send a set of questions to States, entities within the United Nations system, and intergovernmental and non-governmental organisations, including organisations of persons with disabilities. The set of questions should address implementation plans for the Rules in States. The questions should be selective in nature and cover a number of specific rules for in-depth evaluation. In preparing the questions the Special Rapporteur should consult with the panel of experts and the Secretariat.

6. The Special Rapporteur shall seek to establish a direct dialogue not only with States but also with local non-governmental organisations, seeking their views and comments on any information intended to be included in the reports. The Special Rapporteur shall provide advisory services on the implementation and monitoring of the Rules and assistance in the preparation of replies to the sets of questions.

7. The Department for Policy Co-ordination and Sustainable Development of the Secretariat, as the United Nations focal point on disability issues, the United Nations Development Programme and other entities and mechanisms within the United Nations system, such as the regional commissions and specialised agencies and inter-agency meetings, shall co-operate with the Special Rapporteur in the implementation and monitoring of the Rules at the national level.

8. The Special Rapporteur, assisted by the Secretariat, shall prepare reports for submission to the Commission for Social Development at its 34th and 35th sessions. In preparing such reports, the Rapporteur should consult with the panel of experts.

9. States should encourage national co-ordinating committees or similar bodies to participate in implementation and monitoring. As the focal points on disability matters at the national level, they should be encouraged to establish procedures to co-ordinate the monitoring of the Rules. Organisations of persons with disabilities should be encouraged to be actively involved in the monitoring of the process at all levels.

10. Should extra budgetary resources be identified, one or more positions of interregional adviser on the Rules should be created to provide direct services to States, including:

(a) The organisation of national and regional training seminars on the content of the Rules;

(b) The development of guidelines to assist in strategies for implementation of the Rules;

(c) Dissemination of information about best practices concerning implementation of the Rules.

11. At its 34th session, the Commission for Social Development **6–022** should establish an open-ended working group to examine the Special Rapporteur's report and make recommendations on how to improve the application of the Rules. In examining the Special Rapporteur's report, the Commission, through its open-ended working group, shall consult international organisations of persons with disabilities and specialised agencies, in accordance with rules 71 and 76 of the rules of procedure of the functional commissions of the Economic and Social Council.

12. At its session following the end of the Special Rapporteur's mandate, the Commission should examine the possibility of either renewing that mandate appointing a new Special Rapporteur or considering another monitoring mechanism, and should make appropriate recommendations to the Economic and Social Council.

13. States should be encouraged to contribute to the United Nations Voluntary Fund on Disability in order to further the implementation of the Rules.

NOTE: Attempts to draw up a Convention on the Elimination of all Forms of Discrimination against Persons with Disabilities at the conclusion of the United Nations Decade of Disabled Person, 1983–92 were unsuccessful. A draft Convention was prepared by Italy and presented to the 42nd session of the General Assembly with further presentations being submitted by Sweden at the 44th session. On neither occasion was a concensus achieved, many representatives maintaining that the rights of disabled persons were guaranteed under existing international human rights instruments. As a consequence the Economic and Social Council of the United Nations agreed to consider an alternative, an international instrument of a different type. The Standard Rules on the Equalisation of Opportunites for Persons with Disabilities are the result.

INTERNATIONAL YEAR OF THE DISABLED 1981

An important outcome of the International Year of the Disabled was the adoption by the General Assembly of the World Programme of Action Concerning Disabled Persons.[17] The principal thrust of the Action Programme was the emphaisis placed on the rights of persons with disabilities to the same opportunites as

[17] G.A. Res. 37/52 of December 3, 1982

other citizens and to an equal share in the improvements in living conditions resulting from economic and social development. Handicap was also defined for the first time as a function of the relationship between persons with disabilities and their environment.

International Day of Disabled Persons

6–023 December 3 was proclaimed International Day of Disabled Persons by the General Assembly on October 14, 1992[18] and was celebrated for the first time on December 3 of that year. The objective of such a day is to provide an opportunity to awaken the "consciousness of populations regarding the gains to be derived by individuals and society from the integration of disabled persons into every area of social, economic and political life."

Other General Assembly resolutions include *inter alia* the following;

— G.A. Res. 48/99 towards full integration of persons with disabilities into society: a continuing world programme of action[19];

— Declaration on the Rights of Mentally Retarded Persons[20];

— Principles for the protection of persons with Mental Illness and the Improvement of Mental Health Care.[21]

COMMITTEE ON ECONOMIC, SOCIAL AND CULTURAL RIGHTS GENERAL COMMENT NO. 5 "PERSONS WITH DISABILITIES"

6–024 The Committee on Economic, Social and Cultural Rights the body now responsible for overviewing Contracting Parties adherence to the Covenant on Economic, Social and Cultural Rights has been specifically charged "to monitor the compliance of States parties to the Convenant with their obligation to ensure the full enjoyment of the relevant rights by persons with disabilities."[22] Indications that States parties have given little credence to this issue in the reports submitted to the Committee led the Committee to conclude that it was appropriate to review, and to emphasise,

[18] G.A. Res. 47/3.
[19] Adopted December 20, 1993.
[20] UN Doc. A/8429 (1971).
[21] see below para. 6–031.
[22] See para. 165 of the World Programme of Action concerning Disabled Persons *supra* n. 17; Commission on Human Rights, Resolution 1992/48, para. 4 and 1993/29, para. 7.

some of the ways in which issues concerning persons with disabilities arise in connection with the obligations contained in the Covenant.[23] The Covenant on Economic, Social and Cultural Rights does not refer explicitly to persons with disabilites and the Committee is of the view that the "absence of an explicit, disability related provision in the Covenant can be attributed to the lack of awareness of the importance of addressing this issue explicitly, rather than only by implication, at the time of the drafting the Covenant . . ."[24]

The Comment initially spells out the general obligations of states parties to the Covenant.[25]

9. The obligation of States parties to the Covenant to promote **6–025** progressive realisation of the relevant rights to the maximum of their available resources clearly requires governments to do much more than merely abstain from taking measures which might have a negative impact on persons with disabilities. The obligation in the case of such a vulnerable and disadvantaged group is to take positive action to reduce structural disadvantages and to give appropriate prefential treatment to people with disabilities in order to achieve the objectives of full participation and equality within society for all persons with disabilities. This almost invariably means that additional resources will need to be made for this purpose and that a wide range of specially tailored measures will be required.

10. According to a report by the Secretary General, developments over the past decade in both developed and developing countries have been especially unfavourable from the perspective of persons with disabilities:

"... current economic and social deterioration, marked by low-growth rates, high unemployment, reduced public expenditure, current structural adjustment programmes and privatisation, have negatively affected programmes and services ... If the present negative trends continue, there is a risk that [persons with disabilities] may increasingly be relegated to the margins of society, dependent on ad hoc support."[26]

As the Committee has previously observed . . ., the duty of States parties to protect the vulnerable members of their societies assumes greater rather than less importance in times of severe resource contraints.

11. Given the increasing commitment of governments around the world to market-based policies it is appropriate in that context

---

[23] General Comment, UN Doc. E/C.12/1994/13, para. 2.
[24] *ibid.* para. 6.
[25] Footnotes from the original text have been omitted
[26] A/47/415, para. 5.

to emphasise certain aspects of States Parties' obligations. One is the need to ensure that not only the public sphere, but also the private sphere, are, within appropriate limits, subject to regulation to ensure the equitable treatment of persons with disabilities . . ., it is essential that private employers, private suppliers of goods and services, and other non-public entities be subject to both non-discrimination and equality norms in relation to persons with disabilities.

In circumstances where such protection does not extend beyond the public domain, the ability of persons with disabilities to participate in the mainstream of community activities and to realise their full potential as active members of society will be severely and often arbitrarily constrained. This is not to imply that legislative measures will always be the most effective means of seeking to eliminate discrimination within the private sphere. Thus for example, the Standard Rules place particular emphasis on the need for States to "take action to raise awareness in society about persons with disabilities, their rights, their needs, their potential and their contribution."

6–026   12. In the absence of government intervention there will always be instances, in which the operation of the free market will produce unsatisfactory results for persons with disabilities either individually or as a group, and in such circumstances it is incumbent on governments to step in and take appropriate measure to temper, complement, compensate for, or override the results produced by market forces. Similarly, while it is appropriate for governments to rely on private, voluntary groups to assist persons with disabilities in various ways, such arrangements can never absolve governments from their duty to ensure full compliance with their obligations under the Covenant. As the World Programme of Action . . . states, "the ultimate responsibility for remedying the conditions that lead to impairment and for dealing with the consequences of disability rests with Governments".
The Comment then addresses the issue of discrimination on grounds of disability with regard to specific provisions of the Covenant[27]

A. ARTICLE 3—EQUAL RIGHTS FOR MEN AND WOMEN

19. Persons with disabilities are sometimes treated as genderless human beings. As a result, the double discrimination suffered by women with disabilities is often neglected . . . The Committee therefore urges States parties to address the situation of women with disabilities, with high priority being given in future to the

---

[27] Part IV, Sections A-H, paras 19–38.

implementation of economic, social and cultural rights-related programmes.[28]

B. ARTICLES 6–8—RIGHTS RELATING TO WORK

20. The field of employment is one in which disability-based **6–027** discrimination has been prominent and persistent . . . The integration of persons with disabilities into the regularly labour market should be actively supported by States.

21. The "right of everyone to the opportunity to gain his living by work which he freely chooses or accepts" (Article 6(1)) is not realised where the only real opportunity open to disabled workers is to work in so-called "sheltered" facilities under substandard conditions. Arrangements whereby persons with a certain category of disability are effectively confined to certain occupations or to the production of certain goods may violate this right. Similarily, in the light of the Principles for the Protection of Persons with Mental Illness and for the Improvement of Mental Health Care,[29] "therapeutical treatment" in institutions which amounts to forced labour contained in the International Covenant on Civil and Political Rights is also of potential relevance.

22. . . . .

. . . it is particularly important that artificial barriers to integra- **6–028** tion in general, and to employment in particular, be removed . . ., it is very often the physical barriers that society has erected in areas such as transport, housing and workplace which are then cited as the reason why persons with disabilities cannot be employed . . ., as long as workplaces are designed and built in ways that make them inaccessible to wheelchairs, employers will be able to "justify" their failure to employ wheelchair users. Governments should also develop policies which promote and regulate flexible and alternative work arrangements that reasonably accommodate the needs of disabled workers.

23. . . . .

. . . Indeed, the provision of access to appropriate and, where necessary, specially tailored forms of transportation is crucial to the realisation by persons with disabilities of virtually all the rights recognised in the Covenant.

24. The "technical and vocational guidance and training programmes" required under Article 6(2) of the Covenant should

---

[28] See also Beijing Programme for Action, para. 232 (p) which calls upon government to take action to "[s]trengthen and encourage the implementation of the recommendations contained in the Standard Rules on the Equalisation of Opportunities for Persons with Disabilities, paying special attention to ensure non-discrimination and equal enjoyment of all human rights and fundamental freedoms by women and girls with disabilities, including their access to information and services in the field of violence against women, as well as their active participation in and economic contribution to all aspects of society."

[29] See below para. 6–031 *et seq.*

reflect the needs of all persons with disabilities, take place in integrated settings, and be planned and implemented with the full involvement of representatives of persons with disabilities.

25. The right to "the enjoyment of just and favourable conditions of work" (Article 7) applies to all disabled workers, whether they work in sheltered facilities or in the open labour market. Disabled workers may not be discriminated against with respect to wages or other conditions if their work is equal to that of non-disabled workers. States parties have a responsibility to ensure that disability is not used as an excuse for creating low standards of labour protection or for paying below minimum wages.

26. Trade union-related rights (Article 8) apply equally to workers with disabilities and regardless of whether they work in special work facilities or in the open labour market. In addition, Article 8, read in conjunction with other rights such as the right to freedom of association serves to emphasise the importance of the rights of persons with disabilities to form their own organisations. If these organisations are to be effective in "the promotion and protection of [the] economic and social interest" (Article 8(1)(a)) of such persons, they should be consulted regularly by government bodies and others in relation to all matters affecting them; it may also be necessary that they be supported financially and otherswise so as to ensure their viability.

27. The International Labour Organisation has developed valuable and comprehensive instruments with respect to the work-related rights of persons with disabilities, including in particular Convention No. 159 (1983) concerning vocational rehabilitation and employment of persons with disabilities. The Committee encourages States parties to the Covenant to consider ratifying that Convention.

C. ARTICLE 9—SOCIAL SECURITY

6–029   **28.** Social security and income-maintenance schemes are of particular importance for persons with disabilities . . . Such support should reflect the special needs for assistance and other expenses often associated with disability . . ., as far as possible, the support provided should also cover individuals (who are overwhelmingly female) who undertake care of a person with disabilities. Such persons, including members of the families of persons with disabilities, are often in urgent need of financial support because of their assistant role.

29. Institutionalisation of persons with disabilities, unless rendered necessary for other reasons, cannot be regarded as an adequate substitute for the social security and income-support rights of such persons.

D. ARTICLE 10—PROTECTION OF THE FAMILY AND OF MOTHERS AND CHILDREN

30. In the case of persons with disabilities, the Covenant's requirements that "protection and assistance" should be rendered to the family means that everything possible should be done to enable such persons, when they so wish, to live with their families . . .,

. . . the term "family" should be interpreted broadly and in accordance with appropriate local usage. States parties should ensure that laws and social policies and practices do not impede the realisation of these rights. Persons with disabilities should have access to necessary counselling services in order to fulfil their rights and duties within the family.

31. Women with disabilities also have a right to protection and support in relation to motherhood and pregnancy . . .

Both the sterilisation of, and the performance of an abortion on, a woman with disabilities without her prior informed consent are serious violations of Article 10(2).

32. Children with disabilities are especially vulnerable to exploitation, abuse and neglect and are, in accordance with Article 10(3) of the Covenant (reinforced by the corresponding provisions of the Convention on the Rights of the Child),[30] entitled to special protection.

E. ARTICLE 11—THE RIGHT TO AN ADEQUATE STANDARD OF LIVING

33. In addition, to the need to ensure that persons with 6–030 disabilities have access to adequate food, accessible housing and other basic material needs, . . . The right to adequate clothing also assumes a special significance in the context of persons with disabilities who have particular clothing needs assumes a special significance in the context of persons with disabilities, so as to enable them to function fully and effectively in society. Wherever possible, appropriate personal assistance should also be provided in this connection. Such assistance should be undertaken in a manner and spirit which fully respect the human rights of the person(s) concerned . . .

F. ARTICLE 12—THE RIGHT TO PHYSICAL AND MENTAL HEALTH

34.. . . The right to physical and mental health also implies the right to have access to, and to benefit from, those medical and

---

[30] See Chapter on Children.

social services—including orthopaedic devices—which enable persons with disabilities to become independent, prevent further disabilities and support their social integration . . . All such services should be provided in such a way that the persons concerned are able to maintain full respect for their rights and dignity.

G. ARTICLES 13 AND 14—THE RIGHT TO EDUCATION

. . ., States should ensure that teachers are trained to educate children with disabilities within regular schools and that the necessary equipment and support are available to bring persons with disabilities up to the same level of education as their non-disabled peers. In the case of deaf children, for example, sign language should be recognised as a separate language to which the children should have access and whose importance should be acknowledged in their overall social environment.

H. ARTICLE 15—THE RIGHT TO TAKE PART IN CULTURAL LIFE AND ENJOY THE BENEFITS OF SCIENTIFIC PROGRESS

6–031   38. . . . In order to facilitate the equal participation in cultural life of persons with disabilities, governments should inform and educate the general public about disability. In particular, measures must be taken to dispel prejudices or superstitious beliefs against persons with disabilities, for example those that view epilepsy as a form of spirit possession or a child with disabilities as a form of punishment visited upon the family. Similarly, the general public should be educated to accept that persons with disabilities have as much right as any other person to make use of restaurants, hotels, recreation centres and cultural venues.

THE PROTECTION OF PERSONS WITH MENTAL ILLNESS AND THE IMPROVEMENT OF MENTAL HEALTH CARE

The General Assembly adopted 25 principles for the protection of persons with mental illness and for the improvement of mental health care on December 17, 1991.[31] The principles are to be applied without discrimination on any grounds, such as disability, race, colour, sex, language, religion, political or other opinion, national, ethnic or social origin, legal or social status, age, property or birth. The exercise of the rights spelt out may be subject only to such limitations as are prescribed by law and are

---

[31] A/RES/46/119.

necessary to protect the health or safety of the person concerned or of others, or otherwise to protect public safety, order, health or morals or the fundamental rights and freedoms of others.

The General Assembly,

1. Adopts the Principles for the Protection of Persons with Mental Illness and for the Improvement of Mental Health Care, . . .

2. Requests the Secretary-General to include the text of the Principles, together with the introduction, in the next edition of the publication entitled *"Human Rights: A Compilation of International Instruments"*;

3. Requests the Secretary-General to give the Principles the widest possible dissemination and to ensure that the introduction is published at the same time as an accompanying document for the benefit of governments and the public at large . . .

Principle 1. Fundamental Freedoms and Basic Rights

1. All persons have the right to the best available mental health 6–032 care, which shall be part of the health and social care system.

2. All persons with a mental illness, or who are being treated as such persons, shall be treated with humanity and respect for the inherent dignity of the human person.

3. All persons with a mental illness, or who are being treated as such persons, have the right to protection from economic, sexual and other forms of exploitation, physical or other abuse and degrading treatment.

4. There shall be no discrimination on the grounds of mental illness. "Discrimination" means any distinction, exclusion or preference that has the effect of nullifying or impairing equal enjoyment of rights. Special measures solely to protect the rights, or secure the advancement, of persons with mental illness shall not be deemed to be discriminatory. Discrimination does not include any distinction, exclusion or preference undertaken in accordance with the provisions of the present Principles and necessary to protect the human rights of a person with a mental illness or of other individuals.

5. Every person with a mental illness shall have the right to exercise all civil, political, economic, social and cultural rights as recognised in the Universal Declaration of Human Rights, the International Covenant on Economic, Social and Cultural Rights, the International Covenant on Civil and Political Rights and in other relevant instruments, such as the Declaration on the Rights of Disabled Persons and the Body of Principles for the Protection of All Persons under Any Form of Detention or Imprisonment.

6. Any decision that, by reason of his or her mental illness, a person lacks legal capacity, and any decision that, in consequence of such incapacity, a personal representative shall be appointed, shall be made only after a fair hearing by an independent and impartial tribunal established by domestic law. The person whose capacity is at issue shall be entitled to be represented by a counsel. If the person whose capacity is at issue does not himself or herself secure such representation, it shall be made available without payment by that person to the extent that he or she does not have sufficient means to pay for it. The counsel shall not in the same proceedings represent a mental health facility or its personnel and shall not also represent a member of the family of the person whose capacity is at issue unless the tribunal is satisfied that there is no conflict of interest. Decisions regarding capacity and the need for a personal representative shall be reviewed at reasonable intervals prescribed by domestic law. The person whose capacity is at issue, his or her personal representative, if any, and any other interested person shall have the right to appeal to a higher court against any such decision.

7. Where a court or other competent tribunal finds that a person with mental illness is unable to manage his or her own affairs, measures shall be taken, so far as is necessary and appropriate to that person's condition, to ensure the protection of his or her interests.

Principle 2. Protection of Minors

6–033 Special care should be given within the purposes of the Principles and within the context of domestic law relating to the protection of minors to protect the rights of minors, including, if necessary, the appointment of a personal representative other than a family member.

Principle 3. Life in the Community

Every person with a mental illness shall have the right to live and work, to the extent possible, in the community.

Principle 4. Determination of Mental Illness

1. A determination that a person has a mental illness shall be made in accordance with internationally accepted medical standards.

2. A determination of mental illness shall never be made on the basis of political, economic or social status, or membership in a cultural, racial or religious group, or for any other reason not directly relevant to mental health status.

3. Family or professional conflict, or non-conformity with moral, social, cultural or political values or religious beliefs

prevailing in a person's community, shall never be a determining factor in the diagnosis of mental illness.

4. A background of past treatment or hospitalisation as a patient shall not of itself justify any present or future determination of mental illness.

5. No person or authority shall classify a person as having, or otherwise indicate that a person has, a mental illness except for purposes directly relating to mental illness or the consequences of mental illness.

Principle 5. Medical Examination

No person shall be compelled to undergo medical examination 6–034 with a view to determining whether or not he or she has a mental illness except in accordance with a procedure authorised by domestic law.

Principle 6. Confidentiality

The right of confidentiality of information concerning all persons to whom the present Principles apply shall be respected.

Principle 7. Role of Community and Culture

1. Every patient shall have the right to be treated and cared for, as far as possible, in the community in which he or she lives.

2. Where treatment takes place in a mental health facility, a patient shall have the right, whenever possible, to be treated near his or her home or the home of his or her relatives or friends and shall have the right to return to the community as soon as possible.

3. Every patient shall have the right to treatment suited to his or her cultural background.

Principle 8. Standards of Care

1. Every patient shall have the right to receive such health and social care as is appropriate to his or her health needs, and is entitled to care and treatment in accordance with the same standards as other ill persons.

2. Every patient shall be protected from harm, including unjustified medication, abuse by other patients, staff or others or other acts causing mental distress or physical discomfort.

Principle 9. Treatment

1. Every patient shall have the right to be treated in the least restrictive environment and with the least restrictive or intrusive treatment appropriate to the patient's health needs and the need to protect the physical safety of others.

2. The treatment and care of every patient shall be based on an individually prescribed plan, discussed with the patient, reviewed regularly, revised as necessary and provided by qualified professional staff.

3. Mental health care shall always be provided in accordance with applicable standards of ethics for mental health practitioners, including internationally accepted standards such as the Principles of Medical Ethics relevant to the role of health personnel, particularly physicians, in the protection of prisoners and detainees against torture and other cruel, inhuman or degrading treatment or punishment, adopted by the United Nations General Assembly. Mental health knowledge and skills shall never be abused.

4. The treatment of every patient shall be directed towards preserving and enhancing personal autonomy.

Principle 10. Medication

6–035   **1.** Medication shall meet the best health needs of the patient, shall be given to a patient only for therapeutic or diagnostic purposes and shall never be administered as a punishment or for the convenience of others. Subject to the provisions of paragraph 15 of principle 11 below, mental health practitioners shall only administer medication of known or demonstrated efficacy.

2. All medication shall be prescribed by a mental health practitioner authorised by law and shall be recorded in the patient's records.

Principle 11. Consent to Treatment

1. No treatment shall be given to a patient without his or her informed consent, except as provided for in paragraphs 6, 7, 8, 13 and 15 of the present principle.

2. Informed consent is consent obtained freely, without threats or improper inducements, after appropriate disclosure to the patient of adequate and understandable information in a form and language understood by the patient on:

(a) The diagnostic assessment;

(b) The purpose, method, likely duration and expected benefit of the proposed treatment;

(c) Alternative modes of treatment, including those less intrusive;

(d) Possible pain or discomfort, risks and side-effects of the proposed treatment.

3. A patient may request the presence of a person or persons of the patient's choosing during the procedure for granting consent.

4. A patient has the right to refuse or stop treatment, except as provided for in paragraphs 6, 7, 8, 13 and 15 of the present principle. The consequences of refusing or stopping treatment must be explained to the patient.

5. A patient shall never be invited or induced to waive the right to informed consent. If the patient should seek to do so, it shall be explained to the patient that the treatment cannot be given without informed consent.

6. Except as provided in paragraphs 7, 8, 12, 13, 14 and 15 of 6–036 the present principle, a proposed plan of treatment may be given to a patient without a patient's informed consent if the following conditions are satisfied:

(a) The patient is, at the relevant time, held as an involuntary patient;

(b) An independent authority, having in its possession all relevant information, including the information specified in paragraph 2 of the present principle, is satisfied that, at the relevant time, the patient lacks the capacity to give or withhold informed consent to the proposed plan of treatment or, if domestic legislation so provides, that, having regard to the patient's own safety or the safety of others, the patient unreasonably withholds such consent;

(c) The independent authority is satisfied that the proposed plan of treatment is in the best interest of the patient's health needs.

7. Paragraph 6 above does not apply to a patient with a personal representative empowered by law to consent to treatment for the patient; but, except as provided in paragraphs 12, 13, 14 and 15 of the present principle, treatment may be given to such a patient without his or her informed consent if the personal representative, having been given the information described in paragraph 2 of the present principle, consents on the patient's behalf.

8. Except as provided in paragraphs 12, 13, 14 and 15 of the present principle, treatment may also be given to any patient without the patient's informed consent if a qualified mental health practitioner authorised by law determines that it is urgently necessary in order to prevent immediate or imminent harm to the patient or to other persons. Such treatment shall not be prolonged beyond the period that is strictly necessary for this purpose.

9. Where any treatment is authorised without the patient's informed consent, every effort shall nevertheless be made to inform the patient about the nature of the treatment and any possible alternatives and to involve the patient as far as practicable in the development of the treatment plan.

10. All treatment shall be immediately recorded in the patient's medical records, with an indication of whether involuntary or voluntary.

11. Physical restraint or involuntary seclusion of a patient shall not be employed except in accordance with the officially approved procedures of the mental health facility and only when it is the only means available to prevent immediate or imminent harm to the patient or others. It shall not be prolonged beyond the period which is strictly necessary for this purpose. All instances of physical restraint or involuntary seclusion, the reasons for them and their nature and extent shall be recorded in the patient's medical record. A patient who is restrained or secluded shall be kept under humane conditions and be under the care and close and regular supervision of qualified members of the staff. A personal representative, if any, and if relevant, shall be given prompt notice of any physical restraint or involuntary seclusion of the patient.

6–037   **12.** Sterilisation shall never be carried out as a treatment for mental illness.

13. A major medical or surgical procedure may be carried out on a person with mental illness only where it is permitted by domestic law, where it is considered that it would best serve the health needs of the patient and where the patient gives informed consent, except that, where the patient is unable to give informed consent, the procedure shall be authorised only after independent review.

14. Psychosurgery and other intrusive and irreversible treatments for mental illness shall never be carried out on a patient who is an involuntary patient in a mental health facility and, to the extent that domestic law permits them to be carried out, they may be carried out on any other patient only where the patient has given informed consent and an independent external body has satisfied itself that there is genuine informed consent and that the treatment best serves the health needs of the patient.

15. Clinical trials and experimental treatment shall never be carried out on any patient without informed consent, except that a patient who is unable to give informed consent may be admitted to a clinical trial or given experimental treatment, but only with the approval of a competent, independent review body specifically constituted for this purpose.

16. In the cases specified in paragraphs 6, 7, 8, 13, 14 and 15 of the present principle, the patient or his or her personal representative, or any interested person, shall have the right to appeal to a judicial or other independent authority concerning any treatment given to him or her.

Principle 12. Notice of Rights

1. A patient in a mental health facility shall be informed as soon as possible after admission, in a form and a language which the patient understands, of all his or her rights in accordance with the present Principles and under domestic law, and the information shall include an explanation of those rights and how to exercise them.

2. If and for so long as a patient is unable to understand such information, the rights of the patient shall be communicated to the personal representative, if any and if appropriate, and to the person or persons best able to represent the patient's interests and willing to do so.

3. A patient who has the necessary capacity has the right to 6–038 nominate a person who should be informed on his or her behalf, as well as a person to represent his or her interests to the authorities of the facility.

Principle 13. Rights and Conditions in Mental Health Facilities

1. Every patient in a mental health facility shall, in particular, have the right to full respect for his or her:

(a) Recognition everywhere as a person before the law;

(b) Privacy;

(c) Freedom of communication, which includes freedom to communicate with other persons in the facility; freedom to send and receive uncensored private communications; freedom to receive, in private, visits from a counsel or personal representative and, at all reasonable times, from other visitors; and freedom of access to postal and telephone services and to newspapers, radio and television;

(d) Freedom of religion or belief.

2. The environment and living conditions in mental health facilities shall be as close as possible to those of the normal life of persons of similar age and in particular shall include:

(a) Facilities for recreational and leisure activities;

(b) Facilities for education;

(c) Facilities to purchase or receive items for daily living, recreation and communication;

(d) Facilities, and encouragement to use such facilities, for a patient's engagement in active occupation suited to his or her social and cultural background, and for appropriate vocational rehabilitation measures to promote reintegration in the community. These measures should include vocational guidance, vocational training and placement services to enable patients to secure or retain employment in the community.

3. In no circumstances shall a patient be subject to forced labour. Within the limits compatible with the needs of the patient and with the requirements of institutional administration, a patient shall be able to choose the type of work he or she wishes to perform.

4. The labour of a patient in a mental health facility shall not be exploited. Every such patient shall have the right to receive the same remuneration for any work which he or she does as would, according to domestic law or custom, be paid for such work to a non-patient. Every such patient shall, in any event, have the right to receive a fair share of any remuneration which is paid to the mental health facility for his or her work.

Principle 14. Resources for Mental Health Facilities

6–039 **1.** A mental health facility shall have access to the same level of resources as any other health establishment, and in particular:

(a) Qualified medical and other appropriate professional staff in sufficient numbers and with adequate space to provide each patient with privacy and a programme of appropriate and active therapy;

(b) Diagnostic and therapeutic equipment for the patient;

(c) Appropriate professional care;

(d) Adequate, regular and comprehensive treatment, including supplies of medication.

2. Every mental health facility shall be inspected by the competent authorities with sufficient frequency to ensure that the conditions, treatment and care of patients comply with the present Principles.

Principle 15. Admission Principles

1. Where a person needs treatment in a mental health facility, every effort shall be made to avoid involuntary admission.

2. Access to a mental health facility shall be administered in the same way as access to any other facility for any other illness.

3. Every patient not admitted involuntarily shall have the right to leave the mental health facility at any time unless the criteria for his or her retention as an involuntary patient, as set forth in Principle 16 below, apply, and he or she shall be informed of that right.

Principle 16. Involuntary Admission

1. A person may be admitted involuntarily to a mental health facility as a patient or,) having already been admitted voluntarily as a patient, be retained as an involuntary patient in the mental health facility if, and only if, a qualified mental health practitioner authorised by law for that purpose determines, in accordance with Principle 4 above, that that person has a mental illness and considers:

(a) That, because of that mental illness, there is a serious likelihood of immediate or imminent harm to that person or to other persons; or

(b) That, in the case of a person whose mental illness is severe and whose judgment is impaired, failure to admit or retain that person is likely to lead to a serious deterioration in his or her condition or will prevent the giving of appropriate treatment that can only be given by admission to a mental health facility in accordance with the principle of the least restrictive alternative.

In the case referred to in sub-paragraph (b), a second such mental health practitioner, independent of the first, should be consulted where possible. If such consultation takes place, the involuntary admission or retention may not take place unless the second mental health practitioner concurs.

2. Involuntary admission or retention shall initially be for a short period as specified by domestic law for observation and preliminary treatment pending review of the admission or retention by the review body. The grounds of the admission shall be communicated to the patient without delay and the fact of the admission and the grounds for it shall also be communicated promptly and in detail to the review body, to the patient's personal representative, if any, and, unless the patient objects, to the patient's family.

3. A mental health facility may receive involuntarily admitted patients only if the facility has been designated to do so by a competent authority prescribed by domestic law.

Principle 17. Review Body

1. The review body shall be a judicial or other independent and 6–040 impartial body established by domestic law and functioning in accordance with procedures laid down by domestic law. It shall, in formulating its decisions, have the assistance of one or more qualified and independent mental health practitioners and take their advice into account.

2. The initial review of the review body, as required by paragraph 2 of Principle 16 above, of a decision to admit or retain a person as an involuntary patient shall take place as soon as possible after that decision and shall be conducted in accordance with simple and expeditious procedures as specified by domestic law.

3. The review body shall periodically review the cases of involuntary patients at reasonable intervals as specified by domestic law.

4. An involuntary patient may apply to the review body for release or voluntary status, at reasonable intervals as specified by domestic law.

5. At each review, the review body shall consider whether the criteria for involuntary admission set out in paragraph 1 of Principle 16 above are still satisfied, and, if not, the patient shall be discharged as an involuntary patient.

6. If at any time the mental health practitioner responsible for the case is satisfied that the conditions for the retention of a person as an involuntary patient are no longer satisfied, he or she shall order the discharge of that person as such a patient.

7. A patient or his personal representative or any interested person shall have the right to appeal to a higher court against a decision that the patient be admitted to, or be retained in, a mental health facility.

Principle 18. Procedural Safeguards

6–041 **1.** The patient shall be entitled to choose and appoint a counsel to represent the patient as such, including representation in any complaint procedure or appeal. If the patient does not secure such services, a counsel shall be made available without payment by the patient to the extent that the patient lacks sufficient means to pay.

2. The patient shall also be entitled to the assistance, if necessary, of the services of an interpreter. Where such services are necessary and the patient does not secure them, they shall be made available without payment by the patient to the extent that the patient lacks sufficient means to pay.

3. The patient and the patient's counsel may request and produce at any hearing an independent mental health report and any other reports and oral, written and other evidence that are relevant and admissible.

4. Copies of the patient's records and any reports and documents to be submitted shall be given to the patient and to the patient's counsel, except in special cases where it is determined that a specific disclosure to the patient would cause serious harm to the patient's health or put at risk the safety of others. As domestic law may provide, any document not given to the patient should, when this can be done in confidence, be given to the patient's personal representative and counsel. When any part of a document is withheld from a patient, the patient or the patient's counsel, if any, shall receive notice of the withholding and the reasons for it and it shall be subject to judicial review.

5. The patient and the patient's personal representative and counsel shall be entitled to attend, participate and be heard personally in any hearing.

6. If the patient or the patient's personal representative or counsel requests that a particular person be present at a hearing, that person shall be admitted unless it is determined that the person's presence could cause serious harm to the patient's health or put at risk the safety of others.

7. Any decision on whether the hearing or any part of it shall be in public or in private and may be publicly reported shall give full consideration to the patient's own wishes, to the need to respect the privacy of the patient and of other persons and to the need to prevent serious harm to the patient's health or to avoid putting at risk the safety of others.

8. The decision arising out of the hearing and the reasons for it shall be expressed in writing. Copies shall be given to the patient and his or her personal representative and counsel. In deciding whether the decision shall be published in whole or in part, full consideration shall be given to the patient's own wishes, to the need to respect his or her privacy and that of other persons, to the public interest in the open administration of justice and to the need to prevent serious harm to the patient's health or to avoid putting at risk the safety of others.

Principle 19. Access to Information

1. A patient (which term in the present Principle includes a 6–042 former patient) shall be entitled to have access to the information concerning the patient in his or her health and personal records maintained by a mental health facility. This right may be subject to restrictions in order to prevent serious harm to the patient's health and avoid putting at risk the safety of others. As domestic law may provide, any such information not given to the patient should, when this can be done in confidence, be given to the patient's personal representative and counsel. When any of the information is withheld from a patient, the patient or the patient's counsel, if any, shall receive notice of the withholding and the reasons for it and it shall be subject to judicial review.

2. Any written comments by the patient or the patient's personal representative or counsel shall, on request, be inserted in the patient's file.

Principle 20. Criminal Offenders

1. The present Principle applies to persons serving sentences of imprisonment for criminal offences, or who are otherwise detained in the course of criminal proceedings or investigations against them, and who are determined to have a mental illness or who it is believed may have such an illness.

2. All such persons should receive the best available mental health care as provided in Principle 1 above. The present Principles shall apply to them to the fullest extent possible, with only such limited modifications and exceptions as are necessary in the circumstances. No such modifications and exceptions shall prejudice the persons' rights under the instruments noted in paragraph 5 of Principle 1 above.

3. Domestic law may authorise a court or other competent authority, acting on the basis of competent and independent medical advice, to order that such persons be admitted to a mental health facility.

4. Treatment of persons determined to have a mental illness shall in all circumstances be consistent with principle 11 above.

Principle 21. Complaints

6–043 Every patient and former patient shall have the right to make a complaint through procedures as specified by domestic law.

Principle 22. Monitoring and Remedies

States shall ensure that appropriate mechanisms are in force to promote compliance with the present Principles, for the inspection of mental health facilities, for the submission, investigation and resolution of complaints and for the institution of appropriate disciplinary or judicial proceedings for professional misconduct or violation of the rights of a patient.

Principle 23. Implementation

1. States should implement the present Principles through appropriate legislative, judicial, administrative, educational and other measures, which they shall review periodically.

2. States shall make the present Principles widely known by appropriate and active means.

Principle 24. Scope of Principles Relating to Mental Health Facilities

The present Principles apply to all persons who are admitted to a mental health facility.

Principle 25. Saving of Existing Rights

There shall be no restriction upon or derogation from any existing rights of patients, including rights recognised in applicable international or domestic law, on the pretext that the present Principles do not recognise such rights or that they recognise them to a lesser extent.

CHILDREN WITH DISABILITIES

Economic and Social Council resolution 1997/20

Recalling also the Standard Rules on the Equalisation of Opportunities for Persons with Disabilities and the Long-term Strategy to Implement the World Programme of Action concerning Disabled Persons to the Year 2000 and Beyond, as well as the various resolutions and declarations adopted by the General Assembly relating to persons with physical, mental and psychological disabilities, including the Declaration on the Rights of Mentally Retarded Persons and the Declaration on the Rights of Disabled Persons. 6–044

Recalling further the disability provisions in the results of international conferences, including the World Conference on Special Needs Education: Access and Quality, held at Salamanca, Spain, in 1994 and the World Summit for Social Development, held at Copenhagen in 1995.

Welcoming the report of the Special Rapporteur on Disability of the Commission for Social Development on monitoring the implementation of the Standard Rules on the Equalisation of Opportunities for Persons with Disabilities.

Noting with appreciation the activities in support of disability issues carried out by non-governmental organisations,

Convinced that disability is not inability and that it is critically important to take a positive view of abilities as the basis of planning for persons with disabilities, in particular children with disabilities,

1. Recognises the need for special attention to be directed towards children with disabilities and their families or other caretakers;

2. Notes with concern the large numbers of children who have become disabled physically or mentally, or both, as a consequence, *inter alia*, of poverty, disease, disasters, land mines and all forms of violence;

3. Urges both governments and the Secretary-General to give full attention to the rights, special needs and welfare of children with disabilities;

4. Invites governments, concerned United Nations organisations and bodies, including the United Nations Children's Fund, the United Nations Educational, Scientific and Cultural Organisation and the World Health Organisation, and non-governmental organisations, especially those of persons with disabilities, to conduct awareness-raising activities, with a view to combating and overcoming discrimination against children with disabilities;

5. Encourages further co-operation among governments, in co-ordination, where appropriate, with the United Nations Children's Fund, other relevant United Nations organisations and non-governmental organisations, to nurture the talents and potential of children with disabilities by developing and disseminating appropriate technologies and know-how;

6. Encourages governments to include data on children when implementing Rule 13 on information and research of the Standard Rules;

7. Urges governments to ensure, in accordance with rule 6 of the Standard Rules, that children with disabilities have equal access to education and that their education is an integral part of the educational system and also urges governments to provide vocational preparatory training appropriate for children with disabilities;

8. Invites the United Nations Educational, Scientific and Cultural Organisation to continue its programme activities aimed at the integration of children and youth with disabilities into mainstream education and to provide appropriate assistance to governments, at their request, in designing and setting up programmes to encourage the creative, artistic and intellectual potential of children, including those with disabilities;

9. Calls upon governments to ensure the participation of children with disabilities in recreational activities and sports;

10. Emphasises the right of children with disabilities to the enjoyment of the highest attainable standard of physical and mental health and urges governments to ensure the provision of equal access to comprehensive health services and the adoption of holistic approaches to the total well-being of all children with disabilities, particularly children at highest risk, including refugee, displaced or migrant children, children living in situations of violence and its immediate aftermath, children living in disaster areas, street children and children in squatter colonies;

11. Encourages governments to contribute to the United Nations Voluntary Fund on Disability;

12. Requests the Special Rapporteur, in monitoring the implementation of the Standard Rules, to pay special attention to the situation of children with disabilities, to pursue close working relations with the Committee on the Rights of the Child in its monitoring role with respect to the Convention on the Rights of the Child and to include in his report to the Commission for Social Development at its 38th session his findings, views, observations and recommendations on children with disabilities.

STRENGTHENING REGIONAL SUPPORT FOR PERSONS WITH DISABILITIES INTO THE TWENTY-FIRST CENTURY

Economic and Social Council resolution 1998/4

The Economic and Social Council,   6–045
Noting the need for a stronger regional impetus to support national and local endeavours in the second half of the Decade,

1. Requests the General Assembly to endorse the present resolution and to encourage intergovernmental organisations to support its implementation in order to assist in addressing equalisation issues faced by the majority of the world's disabled persons, including disabled women and disabled children, who live in the Asia and Pacific region;

2. Urges all members and associate members of the Economic and Social Commission for Asia and the Pacific:

(a) To intensify multisectoral collaborative action towards the fulfilment of the targets for the implementation of the Agenda for Action for the Asian and Pacific Decade of Disabled Persons, 1993–2002, adopted by the Commission at its 49th session, in April 1993; [Official Records of the Economic and Social Council, 1993, Supplement No. 16 (E/1993/36), Chap. IV, resolution 49/6.];

(b) To contribute to the Economic and Social Commission for Asia and the Pacific technical co-operation trust fund for the Decade to meet capacity-building needs for information and technical assistance in multisectoral collaboration among diverse sectors, in support of the fulfilment of the targets for the Decade;

3. Also urges all governments that have not yet signed the Proclamation on the Full Participation and Equality of People with Disabilities in the Asian and Pacific Region [E/ESCAP/902, annex I. to do so before the next regional meeting to review the progress of the Decade, to be held in 1999];

4. Requests the Executive Secretary of the Economic and Social Commission for Asia and the Pacific to strengthen secretariat assistance to members and associate members by taking the following action:

(a) Harnessing the multidisciplinary potential of the secretariat of the Commission to enhance sensitivity to disabilities—

that is, by the inclusion of persons with disabilities and/or the consideration of the impact thereof on disability-related concerns—as a performance criterion of the secretariat's overall technical assistance, on a par with other criteria, such as gender sensitivity and relevance to development needs in the countries and areas of the region;

(b) Examining resource allocations within the secretariat, with a view to undertaking the adjustments required to enhance secretariat support for disability-related action;

(c) Mobilising resources to continually replenish the technical co-operation trust fund for the Decade for the purposes of documentation, exchanges and field visits, and to disseminate good practices in the implementation of the Agenda for Action for the Decade, giving special attention to the enhancement of knowledge and skills among persons with disabilities and the equal participation of disabled women and girls;

(d) Generating practical guidelines for advancing equal access by disabled persons to mainstream development opportunities, by organising and following up on two regional meetings in 1999, in close collaboration with other members of the Subcommittee on Disability-related Concerns, on the following topics:

    (i) Education and technology for the specific needs of disabled children and youth;

    (ii) Implementation of the United Nations Standard Rules on the Equalisation of Opportunities for Persons with Disabilities [General Assembly resolution 48/96, annex.] and fulfilment of the targets for the Decade;

(e) Exploring the means of organising, by the end of 2002, a high-level regional meeting to consider the lessons learned from national and area efforts towards the fulfilment of the targets for the decade, so as to lay a solid foundation for the inclusion of persons with disabilities in mainstream society into the twenty-first century;

5. Further requests the Executive Secretary to report to the Commission biennially on the progress made in the implementation of the present resolution, with emphasis on follow-up action to reinforce the impact of the above-mentioned regional meetings, and to submit recommendations to the Commission, as required, concerning continuous secretariat action to improve the opportunities for persons with disabilities to participate in the development process, until 2003, when the overall endeavours of the

Decade will be reviewed as a separate agenda item at the 59th session of the Commission, to provide a basis for further action in the new millennium.

CHAPTER 7

REFUGEES

WORLD CONFERENCE ON HUMAN RIGHTS, (JUNE 1993)
VIENNA DECLARATION

7–001 Throngs of displaced people fleeing from their homes, crossing international borders and seeking asylum has been a recurring theme in the media during the last four years. The number of refugees worldwide is estimated to be 11.7 million. The total number of persons of concern to the United Nations High Commissioner for Refugees is if account is taken of internally displaced persons between 20–25 million. As travel and communications have become easier the number of people seeking asylum has increased while simultaneously the wealthier industrial states have tightened their asylum legislation with the aim of decreasing refugee recognition status. Refugees remain amongst the most vulnerable groups and many are doubly disadvantaged as not only are they are refugees but they are also women and children. Women and children constitute 80 per cent of the total refugee population. The vulnerability of such individuals is further exacerbated by the increasing problems of human trafficking and smuggling.

Part I

7–002 23. The World Conference on Human Rights reaffirms that everyone, without distinction of any kind, is entitled to the right to seek and to enjoy in other countries asylum from persecution, as well as the right to return to one's own country. In this respect it stresses the importance of the Universal Declaration of Human Rights, the 1951 Convention relating to the Status of Refugees, its 1967 Protocol and regional instruments. It expresses its appreciation to States that continue to admit and host large numbers of refugees in their territories, and to the Office of the United Nations High Commissioner for Refugees for its dedication to its task. It also expresses its appreciation to the United Nations Relief and Works Agency for Palestine Refugees in the Near East.

The World Conference on Human Rights recognises that gross violations of human rights, including in armed conflicts, are among the multiple and complex factors leading to displacement of people.

The World Conference on Human Rights recognises that, in view of the complexities of the global refugee crisis and in accordance with the Charter of the United Nations, relevant international instruments and international solidarity and in the spirit of burden-sharing, a comprehensive approach by the international community is needed in co-ordination and co-operation with the countries concerned and relevant organisations, bearing in mind the mandate of the United Nations High Commissioner for Refugees. This should include the development of strategies to address the root causes and effects of movements of refugees and other displaced persons, the strengthening of emergency preparedness and response mechanisms, the provision of effective protection and assistance, bearing in mind the special needs of women and children, as well as the achievement of durable solutions, primarily through the preferred solution of dignified and safe voluntary repatriation, including solutions such as those adopted by the international refugee conferences. The World Conference on Human Rights underlines the responsibilities of States, particularly as they relate to the countries of origin.

In the light of the comprehensive approach, the World Conference on Human Rights emphasises the importance of giving special attention including through intergovernmental and humanitarian organisations and finding lasting solutions to questions related to internally displaced persons including their voluntary and safe return and rehabilitation.

In accordance with the Charter of the United Nations and the principles of humanitarian law, the World Conference on Human Rights further emphasises the importance of and the need for humanitarian assistance to victims of all natural and man-made disasters.

UNIVERSAL DECLARATION OF HUMAN RIGHTS 1948

Article 13

2. Everyone has the right to leave any country, including his own, and to return to his country.   7–003

Article 14

1. Everyone has the right to seek and to enjoy in other countries asylum from persecution.
2. This right may not be invoked in the case of prosecutions genuinely arising from non-political crimes or from acts contrary to the purposes and principles of the United Nations.

INTERNATIONAL COVENANT ON CIVIL AND POLITICAL RIGHTS 1966

Article 13

An alien lawfully in the territory of a state party to the present Covenant may be expelled therefrom only in pursuance of a decision reached in accordance with law and shall, except where compelling reasons of national security otherwise require, be allowed to submit the reasons against his expulsion and to have his case reviewed by, and be represented for the purpose before the competent authority or a person or persons especially designated by the competent authority.

GENERAL ASSEMBLY DECLARATION ON TERRITORIAL ASYLUM (RESOLUTION 2312 (XX11) DECEMBER 14, 1967

7–004 The General Assembly, Recalling its resolutions 1839 (XVII) of December 19, 1962, 2100 (XX) of December 20, 1965 and 2203 (XXI) of December 16, 1966 concerning a declaration on the right of asylum,

Considering the work of codification to be undertaken by the International Law Commission in accordance with General Assembly resolution 1400 (XIV) of November 21, 1959, Adopts the following Declaration: DECLARATION ON TERRITORIAL ASYLUM

The General Assembly,

Noting that the purposes proclaimed in the Charter of the United Nations are to maintain international peace and security, to develop friendly relations among all nations and to achieve international co-operation in solving international problems of an economic, social, cultural or humanitarian character and in promoting and encouraging respect for human rights and for fundamental freedoms for all without distinction as to race, sex, language or religion, Mindful of the Universal Declaration of Human Rights, which declares in Article 14[1] . . . This right may not be invoked in the case of prosecutions genuinely arising from non-political crimes or from acts contrary to the purposes and principles of the United Nations",

Recalling also Article 13, paragraph 2, of the Universal Declaration of Human Rights, . . .,[2]

Recognising that the grant of asylum by a State to persons entitled to invoke Article 14 of the Universal Declaration of

---

[1] See above, para. 7–003.
[2] See above, para. 7–003.

Human Rights is a peaceful and humanitarian act and that, as such, it cannot be regarded as unfriendly by any other State, Recommends that, without prejudice to existing instruments dealing with asylum and the status of refugees and stateless persons, States should base themselves in their practices relating to territorial asylum on the following principles:

Article 1

1. Asylum granted by a State, in the exercise of its sovereignty, to persons entitled to invoke Article 14 of the Universal Declaration of Human Rights, including persons struggling against colonialism, shall be respected by all other States.

2. The right to seek and to enjoy asylum may not be invoked by any person with respect to whom there are serious reasons for considering that he has committed a crime against peace, a war crime or a crime against humanity, as defined in the international instruments drawn up to make provision in respect of such crimes.

3. It shall rest with the State granting asylum to evaluate the grounds for the grant of asylum.

Article 2

1. The situation of persons referred to in Article 1, paragraph 1, **7–005** is, without prejudice to the sovereignty of States and the purposes and principles of the United Nations, of concern to the international community.

2. Where a State finds difficulty in granting or continuing to grant asylum, States individually or jointly or through the United Nations shall consider, in a spirit of international solidarity, appropriate measures to lighten the burden on that State.

Article 3

1. No person referred to in Article 1, paragraph 1, shall be subjected to measures such as rejection at the frontier or, if he has already entered the territory in which he seeks asylum, expulsion or compulsory return to any State where he may be subjected to persecution.

2. Exception may be made to the foregoing principle only for overriding reasons of national security or in order to safeguard the population, as in the case of a mass influx of persons.

3. Should a State decide in any case that exception to the principle stated in paragraph 1 of this article would be justified, it shall consider the possibility of granting to the person concerned, under such conditions as it may deem appropriate, an opportunity, whether by way of provisional asylum or otherwise, of going to another State.

Article 4

States granting asylum shall not permit persons who have received asylum to engage in activities contrary to the purposes and principles of the United Nations.

The granting of asylum is not required by international law and states are not obliged to grant asylum[3] and the characterisation of who meets the definition of "refugee" lies within the discretion of each state (see below). However, States are under an obligation to respect the principle of *non-refoulement*. The principle expounded in Article 33 of the 1951 Geneva Convention Relating to the Status of Refugees[4] and Article 3 of the Convention against Torture and Other Cruel, Inhuman or Degrading Treatment Punishment[5] has crystallised into customary international law[6] and there is support for the argument that the principle is one of *jus cogens*. The Articles in the respective Conventions provide:

Article 33

7–006 Prohibition of expulsion or return ("refoulement")

1. No Contracting State shall expel or return ("refouler") a refugee in any manner whatsoever to the frontiers of territories where his life or freedom would be threatened on account of his race, religion, nationality, membership of a particular social group or political opinion.

2. The benefit of the present provision may not, however, be claimed by a refugee whom there are reasonable grounds for regarding as a danger to the security of the country in which he is, or who, having been convicted by a final judgment of a particularly serious crime, constitutes a danger to the community of that country.

Article 3

1. No State Party shall expel, return ("refouler") or extradite a person to another State where there are substantial grounds for

---

[3] Article 14 of the Universal Declaration has no counterpart in either of the 1966 UN Covenants. The granting of asylum and refugee status are distinct as the former embraces the granting of asylum for humanitarian reasons and is not confined to those characterised as warranting Convention refugee status. Note, however, that under U.K. legislation the Asylum and Immigration Appeals Act 1993 Section I "asylum" is defined as meaning refugee status under the 1951 Convention and the 1967 Protocol. Note also Article 18 of the Draft Charter of Fundamental Rights of the European Union which provides: The right to asylum shall be guaranteed with due respect for the rules of the Geneva Convention of 28 July 1951 and the Protocol of 31 January 1967 relating to the status of refugees and in accordance with the Treaty establishing the European Community.

[4] 189 U.N.T.S. 150.

[5] See Chapter 10.

[6] See, for example, *Filartiga v. Pena-Irala* 630 F. 2nd 876 (1980) U.S. C.A., Second Circuit; and *Trajano v. Marcos* 978 F. 2nd 493 (1992) U.S. CA Ninth Circuit.

believing that he would be in danger of being subjected to torture.

2. For the purpose of determining whether there are such grounds, the competent authorities shall take into account all relevant considerations including, where applicable, the existence in the State concerned of a consistent pattern of gross, flagrant or mass violations of human rights.

Under the Refugee Convention the risk or threat to life is to be assessed with regard to the individual's race, religion, nationality, membership of a particular social group or political opinion[7] whereas the risk of torture is assessed by all relevant considerations and in particular evidence of a "consistent pattern of gross, flagrant or mass violations of human rights. No reservation is allowed in respect of Article 33 but Chile has lodged a reservation in respect of Article 3 on the grounds that it "discretionary and subjective."[8] In two instances individuals[9] seeking recognition as refugees[10] have successfully invoked against their "host" state Article 3 of the Torture Convention to prevent their expulsion. Note also the European Court of Human Rights decision in *Chahal v. UK*[11] in which the European Court maintained the absolute nature of the rights protected by Article 3 of the European Convention on Human Rights and Fundamental Freedoms notwithstanding the national security issues raised by the UK government. The European Court maintained that:

The prohibition provided for by Article 3—is—absolute in expulsion cases. Thus, whatever substantial grounds have been shown for believing that an individual qouls face a real risk of being subjected to treatmetn contrary to Article 3 if removed to another State, the responsibility of the Contracting State to safeguard him or her against such treatment is engaged in the event of expulsion. In these circumstances, the activities of the individual in question, however undesirable or dangerous, cannot be a material consideration. The protection afforded by Article 3 is thus wider than tht provided by Article 32 and Article 33 of the United Nations 1951 Convention on the Status of Refugees.

---

[7] *i.e.* the definition of "refugee" as contained in Article 1A(2) of the 1951 Convention Relating to the Status of Refugees—discussed below.

[8] See L. Lijnzaad, *Reservations to UN Human Rights Treaties*, p. 376.

[9] UN Committee Against Torture, Communication No. 13/1993 *Mutombo v. Switzerland*, 15 H.R.L.J. 164; UN Committee Against Torture, Communication No. 15/1994, *Khan v. Canada*, *ibid.* at p. 426.

[10] In both cases the individuals were denied Convention refugee status. The majority of communications from would be refugees maintaining a violation of the Convention against Torture and other Cruel, Inhuman or Degrading Treatment or Punishment have either been found to be inadmissible or unsubstantiated on the merits.

[11] See also *Ahmed v. Austria* (1996) 24 E.H.R.R. 278 in which the Court applied Chahal.

DEFINITION OF REFUGEE

Convention Refugee

7–007 Article 1A(2) of the 1951 Geneva Convention Relating to the Status of Refugees (hereinafter referred to as the 1951 Convention)[12] sets out the criteria which require to be fulfilled if an individual is to be granted Convention refugee status.

Article 1A(2) of the 1951 Convention provides that the term "refugee" shall apply to any person who:

"As a result of events[13] occurring before January 1, 1951 and owing to well founded fear of being persecuted for reasons of race, religion, nationality, membership of a particular social group or political opinion, is outside the country of his nationality and is unable or, owing to such fear, is unwilling to avail himself of the protection of that country; or who, not having a nationality and being outside the country of his former habitual residence as a result of such events, is unable or, owing to such fear, is unwilling to return to it."

Note: the 1967 New York Protocol[14] to the Convention removed the time limitation provision so that persons who became refugees subsequent to 1951 would similarily benefit from the provisions of the Convention).

Interpretation of terms employed in Article 1A(2)

7–008 *Note*: Guidance on the interpretation of the Convention is avail-

---

[12] The 1951 Convention was a response to the plight of persons denied the protection of any government in the aftermath of the Second World War. The Convention entered into force on April 21, 1954 following acceptance by six states. There are now 137 Contracting Parties to the Convention. Signatories to the Convention only are Madagascar, Namibia and St. Vincent and the Grenadines. Switzerland and the Holy See have signed both the Convention and the Protocol (see below).

[13] "events"—Article 1B(1) states: "For the purposes of this Convention, the words 'event occurring before 1st January 1951' in Article 1, section A, shall be understood to mean either (a) 'events occurring in Europe before January 1, 1951'; or (b) 'events occurring in Europe or elsewhere before January 1, 1951'; and each Contracting State shall make a declaration at the time of signature, ratification or accession, specifying which of these meanings it applies for the purpose of its obligations under this Convention." Accordingly under this provision states had the opportunity to restrict their obligation arising under the Convention exclusively to European refugees. Congo, Madagascar, Malta, Monaco and Turkey have made a declaration in accordance with Article 1B(1) of the 1951 Convnetion to the effect that "events occurring before January 1, 1951" should be understood to mean "events occurring in *Europe* before January 1, 1951." All other Contracting Parties apply the Convention without geographical limitation. Malta and Turkey have maintained their declarations of geographical limitation with regard to the 1951 Convention upon adhering to the 1967 Protocol. Madagascar and Monaco are not parties to the 1967 Protocol.

[14] 606 U.N.T.S. 8791 P 267. The Protocol is a separate instrument from the Convention whereby Contracting agree to apply the 1951 Convention provisions but without the 1951 date constraint. Currently there are 136 Contracting Parties to the Protocol. Signatories only to the Protocol—Cape Verde the United States of America and Venezuela. See also above at n. 14.

able in the UNHCR's *Handbook on Procedures and Criteria for Determining Refugee Status*. The first edition of the Handbook was published in 1979 following a *request* from the Executive Committee of the High Commissioner's Programme that such a manual be published "for the guidance of governments". The handbook is essentially a practical guide based on the knowledge accumulated by the High Commissioner's Office and takes into account the practice of States and the relevant literature on the subject. The current edition of the handbook was published in 1992.[15] The handbook does not enjoy the force of law although it is frequently referred to by domestic authorities[16] and the Council of the European Union have acknowledged it as being "a valuable aid to Member States in determining refugee status".[17]

Note: The discussion below is primarily a general one and is not an examination of the jurisprudence of the Contracting Parties. Only those domestic decisions which are seen as breaking new ground are identified and highlighted. Recognition of the status of refugee is based on criteria according to which the competent national bodies decide to grant an *asylum* seeker the protection provided for in the Geneva Convention.[18-19] The Joint Position of adopted by the Council of the European Union constitute guidelines for the application of criteria for recognition and admission as a refugee they do not bind the legislative authorities of affect decisions of the judicial authorities of the Member States and although notified to the relevant refugee determination bodies the latter are only requested to take them as a basis, without prejudice to member States' caselaw on asylum matters and their relevant constitutional positions.[20] The Tampere European Council in October 1999, concluded that a common European asylum system should include, in the short term, a clear and workable determination of the State responsible for the examination of an asylum application, common standards for a fair and efficient

---

[15] HCR/1P/4/Eng/REV.2.

[16] See *R v. Secretary of State ex parte Mehari* [1994] QB 474; also Lord Lloyd in *T v. Secretary State for the Home Department; House of Lords* (decision of May 22, 1996, reported in the Independent Law Report June 4, 1996) where he stated that "another important source though not having the binding force of law, was the United Nations Handbook on Procedures and Criteria for Determining Refugee Status."

[17] See below.

[18-19] Joint Position of March 4, 1996 defined by the Council on the basis of Article K.3. of the Treaty on European Union on the harmonised application of the definition of the term "refugee" in Article 1 of the Geneva Convention July 28, 1951 relating to the status of refugees (96/196/JHA) [1996] O.J. L63/2, discussed further below.

[20] The guidelines were adopted in accordance with Article K.1 of the treaty on European Union which spelt out that asylum policy was to be regarded as a matter of common interest. The guidelines are to be reviewed once a year by the Council and, if appropriate, will be adapted to meet developments in asylum applications. The guidelines relate only to the implementation of the Convention criteria for refugee status and they leave intact the discretion of a member state to allow a person to remain within its territory even although the individual concerned does not meet the criteria for Convention refugee status.

asylum procedure, common minimum conditions of reception of asylum seekers and the approximation of rules on the recognition and content of the refugee status. These would be supplemented with measures on subsidiary forms of protection offering an appropriate status to any person in need of such protection.[21] A proposal for a Council Directive on minimum standards on procedures in member States for granting and withdrawing refugee status was submitted by the Commission on October 24, 2000.[22] The proposal seeks to encapsulate the approach envisaged at Tampere namely that a common European asylum system, while including in the short term measures on asylum in accordance with the Geneva Convention of July 28, 1951 and the Protocol of January 31, 1967 relating to the status of refugees and other treaties, should lead, in the longer term, to a common asylum procedure and a uniform status for those granted asylum valid throughout the Union. The proposal spells out in Annex 1 Principles With Respect to the Designation of Safe Third Countries and in Annex 11 Principles With Respect to the designation of Safe Countries of Origin.

"Well Founded Fear of Being Persecuted"

7–009   This phrase constitutes the lynchpin of Convention refugee status. In order that this requirement be satisfied two elements must co-exist, namely a subjective element and an objective element. Fear is subjective and will accordingly "primarily require an evaluation of the applicant's statements. . . ." However, a subjective fear alone is not sufficient and hence that fear must be measured alongside the prevailing factual situation. Persecution does not have to have occurred; it is only necessary to demonstrate a fear and *that fear is ongoing* (emphasis added) and it must emanate from a stipulated Convention (see below). As the UNHCR handbook notes an evaluation of the subjective element is inseparable form an assessment of the personality of the applicant[23] "as individuals react differently to identical situations". Fear must be reasonable although exaggerated fear will not defeat a claim if such fear is can be deemed as warranted. Satisfaction may hinge on the credibility of the applicant and especially when the facts are not "sufficiently clear on the record."[24] In assessing the objective element the relevant determining authorities should make reference to the prevailing political and legal situation within the applicant's country of origin, *e.g.* the laws and in particular their application will be a relevant factor. However, each situation must be assessed on its

[21] A Proposal for a Council Directive on minimum standards for giving temporary protection in the event of a mass influx of displaced persons and on measures promoting a balance of efforts between Member States in receiving such persons and bearing the consequences thereof was presented by the Commission on May 24, 2000; see COM (2000) 303 final.

[22] COM (2000) 578 final—2000/0238(CNS) [2001] O.J. C62/27.

[23] *Handbook*, para. 40.

[24] *ibid.*, para. 41.

own merits. A person of high public profile may merit charaterisation as a Convention refugee.[25] In the words of the Handbook itself ". . . the applicant's fear should be considered well-founded if he can establish, to a reasonable degree, that his continued stay in his country of origin has become intolerable to him for the reasons stated in the definition, or would be for the same reasons be intolerable if he returned there."[26] The EU Guidelines provide:

3. Establishment of the evidence required for granting refugee status

. . . The question of whether fear of persecution is well-founded must be appreciated in the light of the circumstances of each case. It is for the asylum-seeker to submit the evidence needed to assess the veracity of the facts and the circumstances put forward. It should be understood that once the credibility of the asylum-seeker's statements has been sufficiently established, it will not be necessary to seek detailed confirmation of the facts put forward and the asylum-seeker should, unless there are good reasons to the contrary, be given the benefit of the doubt.

The fact that an individual has already been subject to persecution or to direct threats of persecution is a serious indication of the risk of persecution, unless a radical change of conditions has taken place since then in his country of origin or in his relation with his country of origin.

The fact that an individual, prior to his departure from his country of origin, was not subject to persecution or directly threatened with persecution does not *per se* mean that he cannot in asylum proceedings claim a well-founded fear of persecution.

Persecution

Although there is no universally accepted definition of "persecution". However . . . "it may be inferred[27] that a threat to life or freedom on account of . . .[28]—is always persecution."[29]   **7–010**

---

[25] *ibid.* 43.

[26] para. 42.

[27] From Article 33 of the 1951 Convention—see para. 7–006.

[28] A Convention ground.

[29] *Handbook*, para 51. Persecution is to be distinguished from punishment. As a rule a refugee is a victim—or a potential victim—of injustice and not a fugitive from justice. *Ibid*, para. 56. However, there may be occasions when excessive punishment may constitute persecution. *Ibid*, para. 57 and para 60 notes that recourse may be had to the principles set out in prevailing international instruments—see also Guidelines of Canadian Immigration and Refugee Board, March 1993 on Women Refugee Claimants Fearing Gender-Related Persecution discussed below. See also EU Guidelines 5.1.2. In respect of political offenders the UNHCR Handbook states "Where a person is subject to prosecution or punishment for a political offence, a distinction may have to be drawn according to whether the prosecution is for a political opinion or for politically-motivated acts. If the prosecution pertains to a punishable act committed out of political motives, and if the anticipated

EU Guidelines:

4. "Persecution" within the meaning of Article 1A of the Geneva Convention

7–011   . . . it is generally agreed that, in order to constitute "persecution",

. . ., acts suffered or feared must:

—be sufficiently serious, by their nature or their repetition: they must either constitute a basic attack on human rights, for example, life freedom or physical integrity, or, in the light of all the facts of the case, manifestly preclude the person who has suffered them from continuing to live in his country of origin,[30]

and

—be based on one of the grounds mentioned in Article 1A: . . . Grounds of persecution may overlap and several will often be applicable to the same person. The fact that these grounds are genuine or simply attributed to the person concerned by the persecutor is immaterial.

Several types of persecution may occur together and the combination of events each of which, taken separately, does not constitute persecution may, depending on the circumstances, amount to actual persecution or be regarded as a serious ground for fear of persecution.

The agents of the alleged persecution will normally be the authorities of a country—but the activities of others may amount to persecution when such activities are "knowingly tolerated by the authorities, or if the authorites refuse, or prove unable, to offer effective protection."[31]

---

punishment is in conformity with the general law of the country concerned, fear of such prosecution will not in itself make the applicant a refugee" (Handbook, para. 84). Whether a political offender can also be considered a refugee will depend upon various other factors. Prosecution for an offence may, depending upon the circumstances, be a pretext for punishing the offender for his political opinions or the expression thereof. Again there may be reason to believe that a political offender would be exposed to excessive or arbitrary punishment for the alleged offence. Such excessive or arbitrary punishment will amount to persecution (*ibid.* para. 85). In determining whether a political offender can be considered a refugee, regard should also be had to the following elements: personality of the applicant, his political opinion, the motive behind the act, the nature of the act committed, the nature of the prosecution and its motives; finally, also the nature of the law on which the prosecution is based. These elements may go to show that the person concerned has a fear of persecution and not merely a fear of prosecution and punishment—within the law—for an act committed by him.

[30] This is without prejudice to point 8 of the Guidelines relating to relocation within the country of origin: "Where it appears that persecution is clearly confined to a specific part of a country's territory, it may be necessary in order to check that the condition laid down in Article 1A of the Geneva Convention has been fulfilled, namely that the person concerned "is unwilling to avail himself of the protection of that country", to ascertain whether the person concerned cannot find effective protection in another part of his country, to which he may reasonably be expected to move.

[31] *ibid.* para. 65. See also *Ward v. Canada (Minister of Employment and Immigration)* [1993] 2 S.C.R 689 in which the agent of persecution was INLA (Irish National Liberation Army); see also jurisprudence relating to women below. See also EU Guidelines 5.2. below.

5. Origins of persecution

5.1. Persecution by the State

Persecution is generally the act of a State organ (central State or federal States, regional and local authorities) whatever its status in international law, or of parties or organisations controlling the State.   **7–012**

In addition to cases in which persecution takes the form of the use of brute force, it may also take the form of administrative and/or judicial measures which either have the appearance of legality are misused for the purposes of persecution, or are carried out in breach of the law.

5.1.1. Legal, administrative and police measures

(a) **General measures**. The official authorities of a country are sometimes moved to take general measure to maintain public order, safeguard State security, preserve public health, etc. As required, such measures may included restriction on the exercise of certain freedoms. They may also be accompanied by the use of force, but such restriction or use of force do not in themselves constitute sufficient grounds for granting refugee status to the individuals against whom the measures are directed. However, if it emerges that such measures are being implemented in a discriminatory manner on one or more of the grounds mentioned in Aritcle 1A of the Geneva Convention and may have sufficiently serious consequences, they may rise to a well-founded fear of persecution on the part of the individuals who are victims of their improper application. Such is the case, in particular, where general measures are used to camouflage individual measures taken against persons who, for the reasons mentioned in Article 1A are likely to be threatened by their authorities.   **7–013**

(b) **Measures directed against certain categories**. Measures directed against one or more specific categories or the population may even be legitimate in a society, even when they impose particular constraints or restrictions on certain freedoms.

However, they may be considered as justifying fears of persecution, in particular where the aim which they pursue has been condemned by the international community, or where they are manifestly disproportionate to the end sought, or where their implementation leads to serious abuses aimed at treating a certain group differently and less favourably than the population as a whole.

(c) **Individual measures**. Any administrative measure taken against an individual, leaving aside any consideration of general interest referred to above, on one of the grounds mentioned in Article 1A, which is sufficiently severe in the light of the criteria referred to in section 4 of this Joint Position, may be regarded as persecution, in particular where it is intentional, systematic and lasting.

It is important, therefore, to take account of all the circumstances surrounding the individual measure reported by the asylum-seeker, in order to assess whether his fears of persecution are well-founded.

In all cases referred to above, consideration must be given to whether there is an effective remedy or remedies which would put an end to the situation of abuse. As a general rule, persectuion will be indicated by the fact that no redress exists or, if there are means of redress, that the individual or individuals concerned are deprived of the opportunity of having access to them or by the fact that the decisions of the competent authority are not imparial (see 5.1.2)[33] or have no effect.

5.1.2. Prosecution[34]

7-014 Whilst appearing to be lawful, prosecution or court sentences may amount to persecution where they include a discriminatory element and where they are sufficiently severe in the light of the criteria referred to in section 4 of this Joint Position. This is particularly true in the event of:

(a) **Discriminatory prosecution.** This concerns a situation in which the criminal law provision is applicable to all but where only certain persons are prosecuted on grounds of characteristics likely to lead to the award of refugee status. It is therefore the discriminatory element in the implementation of prosecution policy which is essential for recognising a person as a refugee.

(b) **Discriminatory punishment.** Punishment or the threat thereof on the basis of a universally applicable criminal law provision will be discriminatory if persons who breach the law are punished but certain persons are subject to more severe punishment on account of characteristics likely to lead to the award of refugee status. The discriminatory element in the punishment imposed is essential. Persecution may be deemed to exist in the event of a disproportionate sentence, provided that there is link with one of the grounds of persecution referred to in Article 1A.

(c) **Breach of a criminal law provision on account of the grounds of persecution.** Intentional breach of a criminal law provision—whether applicable universally or to certain categories

---

[33] See below.
[34] See *supra* n. 24.

of persons—on account of the grounds of persecution must be clearly the result of pronouncements or participation in certain activities in the country of origin or be the objective consequence of characteristics of the asylum-seeker liable to to lead to the grant of refugee status. The deciding factors are the nature of the punishment, the severity of the punishment in relation to the offence committed, the legal system and the human rights situation in the country of origin. Consideration should be given to whether the intentional breach of the criminal law provision can be deemed unavoidable in the light of the individual circumstances of the person involved and the situation in the country of origin.

5.2. Persecution by Third Parties

Persecution by third parties will be considered to fall within the scope of the Geneva Convention where it is based on one of the grounds in Article 1A of that Convention, is individual in nature and is encouraged or permitted by the authorities. Where the official authorities fail to act, such persecution should give rise to individual examination of each application for refugee status, in accordance with national judicial practice, in the light in particular of whether or not the failure to act was deliberate. The persons concerned may be eligible in any event for appropriate forms for protection under national law.

Grounds of Persecution

As indicated above there must be an obvious nexus between the alleged persecution and one or more than one of the five enumerated Convention grounds.

(a) Race

Race for the purposes of the Convention is to be interpreted in its **7–015** widest sense "to include all kinds of ethnic groups that are referred to as races" in common usage. Frequently it will also entail membership of a specific social group of common descent forming a minority within a larger population . . . Racial discrimination, therefore, represents an important element in determining the existence of persecution.[35]

Racial discrimination will constitute persecution in the sense of the 1951 Convention. This if, as a result . . ., a person's human dignity is affected to such an extent as to be incompatible with the most elementary and inalienable human rights, or where the disregard of racial barriers is subject to serious consequences.[36]

---

[35] Handbook, para. 68.
[36] *ibid.* para. 69. Membership alone of a racial group will not normally consitute persecution unless there are particular circumstances affecting the group. *Ibid.* para. 70.

EU Guidelines

7.1. Race

The concept of race should be understood in the broad sense and include membership of different ethnic groups. As a general rule, persecution should be deemed to be founded on racial grounds where the persecutor regards the victim of his persecution as belonging to a racial group other than his own, by reason of a real or supposed difference, and this forms the grounds for his action.

(b) Religion

Persecution for "reasons of religion" may assume various forms, *e.g.* prohibition of membership of a religious community, of worship in private or in public, of religious instruction, or serious measures of discrimination imposed on persons because they practise their religion or belong to a particular religious community.[37]

EU Guidelines

7.2. Religion

The concept of religion may be understood in the broad sense and include theitic, non-theistic and atheistic beliefs.

Persecution on religious grounds may take various forms, such as a total ban on worship and religious instruction, or severe discriminatory measures against persons belonging to a particular religious group. For persecution to occur, the interference and impairment suffered must be sufficiently severe in the light of the criteria referred to in section 4 of this Joint Postion. This may apply where, over and above measures essential to maintain public order, the State also prohibits or penalises religious activity even in private life.

Persecution on religious grounds may also occur where such interference targets a person who does not wish to profess any religion, refuses to take up a particular religion or does not wish to comply with all or part of the rites and customs relating to a religion.[38]

---

[37] *ibid*. para. 72. Although mere membership of a particular religious community will not normally be sufficient to warrant the granting of Convention refugee status there may be instances where due to special circumstances mere membership will be sufficient. *Ibid* para. 73.

[38] Refusal to perform military service may also be based on religious convictions. If an applicant is able to show that his religious convictions are genuine, and that such conviction is not taken into account by the authorities of his country in requiring him to perform military sevice, he may be able to establish a claim to refugee status (*Handbook*, para. 172). Such a claim would require to be substantiated by evidence that the applicant and/or his family had encountered difficulties due to their religious convictions (*ibid*).

(c) Nationality

Nationality extends beyond "citizenship". It refers also to mem-   7–016
bership of an ethnic or linguistic group and may occasionally
overlap with the term "race". Persecution for reasons of
nationality may consist of adverse attitudes and measures directed against a national (ethnic, linguistic) minority and in certain
circumstances the fact of belonging to such a minority may in
itself give rise to well founded fear of persecution.[39]

The UNHCR handbook acknowledges that the co-existence
within a State of two or more national (ethnic, linguistic) groups
may create situations of conflict and also situations of persecution or danger of persecution. At times, *e.g.* when a conflict
between national groups is combined with political movements,
persecution for reasons of nationality may not be readily distinguished from persecution because of political opinion.[40] Persecution on grounds of nationality is in most instances feared by
members of a national minority but it is possible for a person
belonging to a majority group to fear persecution by a dominant
minority.[41]

75. The co-existence within the boundaries of a State of two or
more national (ethnic, linguistic) groups may create situations of
conflict and also situations of persecution or danger of persecution. It may not always be easy to distinguish between persecution for reasons of nationality and persecution for reasons of
political opinion when a conflict between national groups is
combined with political movements, particularly where a political movement is identified with a specific "nationality".

76. Whereas in most cases persecution for reason of
nationality is feared by persons belonging to a national minority,
there have been many cases in various continents where a
person belonging to a majority group may fear persecution by a
dominant minority.

EU Guidelines

7.3. Nationality

This should not be confined exclusively to the idea of citizenship
but should also include membership of a group determined by its
cultural or linguistic identity or its relationship with the population of another State.

[39] *ibid.* para. 74.
[40] *ibid.* para. 75.
[41] *ibid.* para. 76.

(d) Membership of a Particular Social Group

7–017 The Refugee Convention does not provide a definition or indeed any guidance as to the interpretation to be given to "particular social group".[42] The UNHCR handbook provides that a "particular social group" normally comprises persons of similar background, habits or social status. and that a claim of persecution invoked under this heading may frequently overlap with a claim to fear of persecution on other grounds, *i.e.* race, religion or nationality.[43] The UNHCR then simply states that "[M]embership of such a particular social group may be at the root of persecution because there is no confidence in the group's loyalty to the Government or because the political outlook, antecedents or economic activity of its members, or the very existence of the social group as such, is held to be an obstacle to the Government's policies[44]; and that mere membership of a particular social group will not normally be enough to substantiate a claim to refugee status. There may, however, be special circumstances where mere membership can be a sufficient ground to fear persecution.[45]

There is no guidance given as to how a particular group may attain the characterisation of a "particular social group" although the imprecision of the definition tends to suggest that a narrow interpretation of the term should be avoided.

The EU Guidelines essentially reiterate the position adopted in the UNHCR Handbook.

EU Guidelines

7.5. Social Group

7–018 A specific social group normally comprises persons from the same background, with the same customs or the same social status, etc.

Fear of persecution cited under this heading may frequently overlap with fear of persecution on other grounds, for example, race, religion or nationality.

Membership of a social group may simply be attributed to the victimised person or group by the persecutor.

In some cases, the social group may not have existed previously but may be determined by the common characteristcis of

---

[42] The term was included at the 11th hour following a proposal from a Swedish delegate on the grounds that "experience has shown that certain refugees were persecuted because they belonged to particular social groups". The amendment was passed by 14 votes with eight abstentions. There was no discussion of the term.

[43] Handbook, para 77.

[44] *ibid.* para. 78.

[45] *ibid.* para. 79.

the victimised persons because the persecutor sees them as an obstacle to achieving his aims.

Historically there had been relatively limited judicial authority on the scope of "membership of a particular social group" although the term has increasingly been the focus of judicial thinking.[46]

The issue of "particular social group" has been addressed to some extent in a number of Immigration Appeal Tribunal cases. The majority of these are unreported. However, for a brief but comprehensive survey of these decisions, British position, see Michael Haran, "Social group for the Purposes of Ayslum Claims" (1995) 9 Imm. and Nat.L and P. 64. Of the foregoing *Ward* is regarded as the most authoritative in that La Forest J. set forth general guidlelines[47] for determining three possible groups of "particular social group," namely "(1) groups defined by an innate or unchangeable characteristic; (2) groups whose members voluntary associate for reasons so fundamental to their human dignity that they should not be forced to forsake the association; and (3) groups associated by a former voluntary status unalterable due to its historical permanence. The first category would embrace individuals fearing persecution on such bases as gender, linguistic background and sexual orientation, while the second would encompass, for example, human rights activists. The third branch is included more because of historical intention, although it is also relevant to the anti-discrimination influences, in that one's past is an immutable part of the person."[47] But see also La Forest's own view as to what *Ward* provided, "only a working rule was enunciated in *Ward*, not an unyielding deterministic approach to resolving whether a refugee claimant could be classified within a particular social group. The general underlying themes of the defence of human rights and non-discrimination were to remain the paramount consideration in determining a claimant's membership in any particular social group." (dissenting opinion in decision of *Chan v. Minister of Employment and Immigration* Supreme Court of Canada, decision of October 19, 1995 at para. 83.)

---

[46] Cases of note include *inter alia*, *Sanchez-Trujillo v. INS*, 801 F 2d 1571 (1986); *Matter of Acosta* (Interim Decision 2986, 919850 WL 56042 BIA); *Re FA Toboso-Alfonso, Cheung v. Canada (Minister of Employment and Immigration)* [1993] 2 F.C. 314; *Canada v. Mayers* (1992) 97 D.L.R. (4th) 729; *Ward v. Canada (Minister of Employment and Immigration)* [1993] 2 S.C.R. 689; *Pizarro v. Canada (Minister of Employment and Immigration)* [1994] F.C.J. No. 320; *Morato v. Minister for Immigration* (1992) 106 A.L.R. 367; *Minister for Immigration Ethnic Affairs v. Respondent A and Others* Federal Court of Australia, New South Wales District Registry General Division, No. NG 327 of 1994, *SSHD v. Savchenkov* (CA) [1996] Imm. AR 28, and Re ZWD Refugee Appeal No 3/91 (New Zealand Refugee Review Board).

[47] These guidelines were deduced from the tests proposed in *Mayers, Cheung and Matter of Acosta.*

[47] *ibid.* at para. 77.

See also the UK House of Lords decision in *ISLAM (AP.) v. Secretary of State for the Home Department* and *R. v. Immigration Appeal Tribunal and Another Ex Parte Shah* (A.P)[48] in which Lord Hope stated that "In general terms a social group may be said to exist when a group of people with a particular characteristic is recognised as a distinct group by society. The concept of a group means that we are dealing here with people who are grouped together because they share a characteristic not shared by other, not with individual. The word "social" means that we are being asked to identify a group of people which is recognised as a particular group by society. As social customs and social attitudes differ from one country to an another, the context for this inquiry is the country of the person's nationality. The phrase can thus accommodate particular social groups which may be recognisable as such in one country but not in others or which, in any given country, have not previously been recognised.[49] See also the U.S. decision of the *Ninth Circuit Court of Appeal in Aguirre-Cervantes v. INS* discussed below at n. 58 in which immediate family was held to a protected particular social group.

(e) Gender-Based Social Groups

7–019 The Refugee Convention is silent on gender—it is gender neutral and does not include gender as an independent enumerated ground warranting characterisation of Convention refugee status. The problem with respect to women has been a reluctance until relatively recently to acknowledge that women or at least a sub-group of women can constitute a "particular social group".

ExCOM CONCLUSION[50] (UNHCR EXECUTIVE COMMITTEE) NO. 39 (XXXVI)—1985

REFUGEE WOMEN AND INTERNATIONAL PROTECTION

The Executive Committee,
(k) Recognised that States, in the exercise of their sovereignty, are free to adopt the interpretation that women asylum-seekers who face harsh or inhuman treatment due to their having transgressed the social mores of the society in which they live may be considered as a "particular social group" within the meaning of Article 1A(2) of the 1951 United Nations Refugee Convention.

---

[48] (HL) [1999] I.N.L.R. 144, [1999] Imm. AR 283.
[49] See also Opinions of Lord Hoffmann and Lord Millett. See also below in respect of gender-related persecution.
[50] For the status of ExCOM conclusions see below.

Excom Conclusion No. 39 (Executive Committee) UNHCR provides States:

"are free to adopt the interpretation according to which women ayslum-seekers, who are the object of inhuman or degrading treatment because they have trangressed social rules of the society in which they live, can be seen as constituting a partiuclar social group in the sense of Article 1A(2) of the 1951 Convention . . ."[51]

ExCOM CONCLUSION (UNHCR EXECUTIVE COMMITTEE) NO. 73 (XLIV)—1993

REFUGEE PROTECTION AND SEXUAL VIOLENCE

The Executive Committee,

Noting with grave concern the widespread occurrence of sexual **7–020** violence in violation of the fundamental right to personal security as recognised in international human rights and humanitarian law, which inflicts serious harm and injury to the victims, their families and communities, and which has been a cause of coerced displacement including refugee movements in some areas of the world,

Noting also distressing reports that refugees and asylum-seekers, including children, in many instances have been subjected to rape or other forms of sexual violence during their flight or following their arrival in countries where they sought asylum, including sexual extortion in connection with the granting of basic necessities, personal documentation or refugee status,

Recognising the need for concrete action to detect, deter and redress instances of sexual violence to effectively protect asylum-seekers and refugees,

Recognising further that the prevention of sexual violence can contribute to averting coerced displacement including refugee situations and to facilitating solutions,

Stressing the importance of international instruments relating to refugees, human rights and humanitarian law for the protection of asylum-seekers, refugees and returnees against sexual violence,

Bearing in mind the draft Declaration on the Elimination of Violence against Women adopted by the Commission on the Status of Women[52] as well as other measures being taken by the

---

[51] UNHCR EXCOM Conclusions No. 39 (XXXVI) (1985); see also Resolution of the European Parliament, April, 13 1984, [1984] O.J. C127/137.

[52] Adopted by the UN General Assembly, February 1994, see Chapter 2.

Commission on the Status of Women, the Committee on the Elimination of Discrimination against Women, the Commission on Human Rights, the Security Council and other bodies of the United Nations to prevent, investigate and, as appropriate, according to their mandates, punish sexual violence,

7–021   Reaffirming its Conclusions No. 39 (XXXVI),[53] No. 54 (XXXIX),[54] No. 60 (XL)[55] and No. 64 (XLI)[56] concerning refugee women:

(a) Strongly condemns persecution through sexual violence, which not only constitutes a gross violation of human rights, as well as, when committed in the context of armed conflict, a grave breach of humanitarian law, but is also a particularly serious offence to human dignity;

(b) Urges States to respect and ensure the fundamental right of all individuals within their territory to personal security, *inter alia* by enforcing relevant national laws in compliance with international legal standards and by adopting concrete measures to prevent and combat sexual violence, including:

(i) the development and implementation of training programmes aimed at promoting respect by law enforcement officers and members of military forces of the right of every individual, at all times and under all circumstances, to security of person, including protection from sexual violence,

(ii) implementation of effective, non-discriminatory legal remedies including the facilitation of the filing and investigation of complaints against sexual abuse, the prosecution of offenders, and timely and proportional disciplinary action in cases of abuse of power resulting in sexual violence,

(iii) arrangements facilitating prompt and unhindered access to all asylum-seekers, refugees and returnees

[53] See para. 7–019.

[54] Refugee Women, adopted by the Executive Committee at its 39th Session in 1988. The conclusion highlighted the vulnerability of refugee women and the need the particular problems confronting such women, notably in the area of physical security. The conclusion also stressed the need for an active senior level steering committee on refugee women to co-ordinate, integrate and oversee the assessment, reorientation and strengthening of existing policies and programmes in favour of refugee women, whilst ensuring that such efforts were culturally appropriate and led to the full integration of such women. There was also a call for increased public awareness on the needs of refugee women and the need for there to be training modules to be offered to *inter alia* UNHCR's staff so as to increase their awareness of the specific needs of refugee women.

[55] Refugee Women, Conclusion adopted at the Executive Committee's 40th Session in 1989 calling for further action such as the expansion of training, aimed at addressing gender issues.

[56] Refugee Women and International Protection, calling for the development of comprehensive guidelines on protection of refugee women as a matter of urgency.

for UNHCR and, as appropriate, other organisations approved by the Governments concerned, and

(iv) activities aimed at promoting the rights of refugee women, including through the dissemination of the Guidelines on the Protection of Refugee Women and their implementation, in close co-operation with refugee women, in all sectors of refugee programmes,

(c) Calls upon States and UNHCR to ensure the equal access of women and men to refugee status determination procedures and to all forms of personal documentation relevant to refugees' freedom of movement, welfare and civil status, and to encourage the participation of refugee women as well as men in decisions relating to their voluntary repatriation or other durable solutions;

(d) Supports the recognition as refugees of persons whose claim to refugee status is based upon a well-founded fear of persecution, through sexual violence, for reasons of race, religion, nationality, membership of a particular social group or political opinion;

(e) Recommends the development by States of appropriate **7–021a** guidelines on women asylum-seekers, in recognition of the fact that women refugees often experience persecution differently from refugee men;

(f) Recommends that refugee victims of sexual violence and their families be provided with adequate medical and psycho-social care, including culturally appropriate counselling facilities, and generally be considered as persons of special concern to States and to UNHCR with respect to assistance and the search for durable solutions;

(g) Recommends that in procedures for the determination of refugee status, asylum-seekers who may have suffered sexual violence be treated with particular sensitivity;

(h) Reiterates the importance of ensuring the presence of female field staff in refugee programmes, including emergency operations, and the direct access of refugee women to them:

(i) Supports the High Commissioner's efforts, in co-ordination with other intergovernmental and non-governmental organisations competent in this area, to develop and organise training courses for authorities, including camp officials, eligibility officers, and others dealing with refugees on practical protection measures for preventing and responding to sexual violence;

(j) Recommends the establishment by States of training programmes designed to ensure that those involved in the

refugee status determination process are adequately sensitised to issues of gender and culture;

(k) Encourages the High Commissioner to pursue actively her
efforts, in co-operation with bodies and organisations dealing with human rights, to increase awareness of the rights
of refugees and the specific needs and abilities of refugee
women and girls and to promote the full and effective
implementation of the Guidelines on the Protection of
Refugee Women[57];

(l) Calls upon the High Commissioner to include the issue of
sexual violence in future progress reports on the implementation of the Guidelines on the Protection of Refugee
Women;

(m) Requests the High Commissioner to issue as an Executive
Committee document and disseminate widely the Note on
Certain Aspects of Sexual Violence against Refugee
Women.

7–022 Recently in the context of the international concern to combat
violence against women, refugee claimants alleging gender-
related violence have been successful in establishing their membership of a "particular social group."[58]

---

[57] Guidelines on the Protection of Refugee Women, prepared by the Office of the
UNHCR, Geneva, July 1991. The purpose of the Guidelines as outlined in para. 16 was to
help the staff of UNHCR and its implementing partners to identify the specific protection
issues, problems and risks facing refugee women. In doing so, they cover traditional
protection concerns such as the determination of refugee status and the provision of
physical security. They outline various measures that can be taken to improve the
protection of refugee women and suggest action that can be taken particularly within
traditional assistance sectors, to prevent or deter protection problems from arising. They
present approaches for helping women whose rights have been violated and outline steps
that can be taken to ameliorate and report about protection problems that do arise.

[58] This has been particularly reflected in Canadian IRB decisions see *e.g. inter alia*
C.R.D.D. No. U92–08714, *Maraj and Shuter*, June 4, 1993, (particular social group was
"unprotected Ecuadoran women subject to wife abuse"), *Cheung v. Canada (Minister of
Employment and Immigration)*, *supra* in which the particular social group was identified as
"women who have more than one child and are faced with forced sterilisation"); T93–
12197/12198/12199—*Ramirez, McCaffrey* July 13, 1994 the particular social group being
"women"; *Litinov v. Secretary of State of Canada*, Decision of Federal Court of Canada, June
30, 1994 in which the particular social group was defined as "new citizens of Israel who
are women recently arrived from elements of the former Soviet Union and who are not yet
well integrated into Israeli society, despite the generous support of the Israeli government,
who are lured into prostitution and threatened and exploited by individuals not connected
to the government, and who can demonstrate indifference to their plight by front line
authorities to whom they would normally be expected to turn for protection". The
persecution in the foregoing instances was "wife abuse"; "forced sterilisation"; "female
genital mutilation" and "forced prostitution" respectively. See also U.S. case of *Fatin v.
INS*, 12 F.3d 1233 (3rd Cir. 1993); and Judge Paul A. Najelski's decision according
Convention refugee status to a Jordanian woman whose "government had failed to
protect her from over three decades of physical and mental abuse by her husband,"

A number of states have now issued[59] guidelines for the handling of claims from women seeking refugee status on the basis of gender-related persecution. Canada in March 1993 promulated guidelines and became the first country to recognise formally that gender-related persecution warranted cognisance.

CANADIAN GUIDELINES ON WOMEN REFUGEE CLAIMANTS FEARING GENDER-RELATED PERSECUTION.[60]

THE ISSUE

The definition of a Convention refugee in the Immigration Act does not include gender as an independent enumerated ground for a well-founded fear of persecution warranting the recognition of Convention refugee status. As a developing area of the law, it has been more widely recognised that gender-related persecution is a form of persecution which can and should be assessed by the Refugee Division panel hearing the claim. Where a woman claims to have a gender-related fear of persecution, the central issue is thus the need to determine the linkage between gender, the feared persecution and one or more of the definition grounds.[61]

Washington Post, June 3, 1995. In the United States the BIA held that the practice of female genital mutilation can form the basis of persecution—see the Matter of Kasinga decided June 13, 1996. In the UK The House of Lords held in *ISLAM (A.P.) v. Secretary of State for the Home Department and R. v. Immigration Appeal Tribunal and Another Ex Parte Shah* (A.P) that "Women in Pakistan are a social group". In these two cases the applicants had been granted exceptional leave to remain and the importance of the case lies in the consideration given as to whether they were members of a particular social group within the meaning of Article 1 A(2) of the Convention. In March 2001, the Ninth Circuit Court of Appeals ruled against deporting a Mexican woman who maintained she would be abused by her father should be forced to return. The decision (*Aguirre-Cervantes v. INS*) which sets a legal precedent in the nine Western states covered by the circuit has been heralded as one which "will open the path for other claims of persecution based on domestic violence in places where the government is unable to control the persecutor" Daniel Levy, attorney at Public Counsel in Los Angeles which represented the petitioner as quoted in the *Los Angeles Times*, March 22, 2001. The principal difficulty in the petitioner's case was not establishing that she had been the victim of persecution but rather whether her immediate family, all of whose members lived together and were subjected to abuse by the her father, constituted a protected particular social group. The Ninth Circuit Court decided in the affirmative and concluded that the petitioner was persecuted by her father on account of her membership in that social group.

[59] Canada, the United States (Considerations Asylum Officers Adjudicating Asylum Claims from Women, May 1995) Australia (Guidelines on Gender Issues for Decision Makers, July 1996) and most recently in late 2000 the United Kingdom (Asylum Gender Guidelines).

[60] Issued March 8, 1993, by the Chairperson (Mrs Mawani) pursuant to section 65(3) of the Immigration Act, Immigration and Refugee Board, Ottawa, Canada. The Guidelines were updated in November 1996.

[61] Canadian Guidelines, p. 1. For further discussion of the Canadian Guidelines, their application and impact see R.M.M. Wallace: "Making the Refugee Convention Gender Sensitive: The Canadian Guidelines" [1996] 45 I.C.L.Q. at p. 702. The text of the Update is reproduced in the Appendix. For consideration of the U.S. Guidelines see R.M.M. Wallace, "Considerations for Asylum Officers, Adjudicating Asylum Claims from Women American Guideliens" [1995] 9 Imm. Nat L&P 112.

7–023   All Guidelines seek to provide a framework for adjudicators in the handling of claims and address *inter alia* the problem of eliciting evidence of alleged gender-related persecution and the problems peculiar to women which may be encountered at determination hearings. The aim is not to lower the standard which has to be fulfilled for the granting of Convention refugee status but rather to allow the Convention to be interpreted in such a way so as to take account of the special circumstances which may be encountered by a woman by virtue of her sex. The most recently adopted Guidelines, those of the United Kingdom,[62] state their aims as being: To provide the judiciary of the IAA with the tools to enable them to fully and effectively consider and decide the asylum claims under the Refugee Convention. Specific focus on the role of gender is intended to ensure that all aspects of asylum clams are fully and fairly considered. In particular they have the following aims:

- Jurisprudence—to ensure that women's asylum claims are fully considered under the Refugee Convention so that jurisprudence properly reflects the experience of both female and male refugees.

- Procedures—to ensure that the asylum determination process is accessible to both women and men and that the procedures used do not prejudice women asylum seekers or make it more difficult for them to present their asylum claims.

- Evidential requirements—to ensure that the judiciary are aware of particular evidential problems which may be faced by women asylum seekers and that appropriate steps are taken to overcome them.[63]

(f) Political Opinion

The basic principle from an international perspective is that outlined in Article 19 of the Universal Declaration on Human Rights and Article 19 of the Covenant on Civil and Political Rights.[64]

7–024   80. Holding political opinions different from those of the Government is not in itself a ground for claiming refugee status, and an applicant must show that he has a fear of persecution for holding such opinions. This presupposes that the applicant holds opinions not tolerated by the authorities, which are critical of

---

[62] Asylum Gender Guidelines, Immigration Appellate Authority, November 2000.

[63] *ibid*, 1.8. page 2.

[64] *i.e.* Everyone has the right to freedom of opinion and expression, the right includes freedom to hold opinion without interference and to seek, receive and impart information and ideas to any media regardless of frontier.

their policies or methods. It also presupposes that such opinions have come to the notice of the authorities or are attributed by them to the applicant. The political opinions of a teacher or writer may be more manifest than those of a person in a less exposed position. The relative importance or tenacity of the applicant's opinions—in so far as this can be established from all the circumstances of the case—will also be relevant.

81. While the definition speaks of persecution "for reasons of political opinion" it may not always be possible to establish a causal link between the opinion expressed and the related measures suffered or feared by the applicant. Such measures have only rarely been based expressly on "opinion". More frequently, such measures take the form of sanctions for alleged criminal acts against the ruling power. It will, therefore, be necessary to establish the applicant's political opinion, which is at the root of his behaviour, and the fact that it has led or may lead to the persecution that he claims to fear.

82. As indicated above, persecution "for reasons of political **7–025** opinion" implies that an applicant holds an opinion that either has been expressed or has come to the attention of the authorities. There may, however, also be situations in which the applicant has not given any expression to his opinions. Due to the strength of his convictions, however, it may be reasonable to assume that his opinions will sooner or later find expression and that the applicant will, as a result, come into conflict with the authorities. Where this can reasonably be assumed, the applicant can be considered to have fear of persecution for reasons of political opinion.

83. An applicant claiming fear of persecution because of political opinion need not show that the authorities of his country of origin knew of his opinions before he left the country. He may have concealed his political opinion and never have suffered any discrimination or persecution. However, the mere fact of refusing to avail himself of the protection of his Government, or a refusal to return, may disclose the applicant's true state of mind and give rise to fear of persecution. In such circumstances the test of well-founded fear would be based on an assessment of the consequences that an applicant having certain political dispositions would have to face if he returned. This applies particularly to the so-called refugee "*sur place*".

84. Where a person is subject to prosecution or punishment for **7–026** a political offence, a distinction may have to be drawn according to whether the prosecution is for political opinion or for politically-motivated acts. If the prosecution pertains to a punishable act committed out of political motives, and if the anticipated punishment is in conformity with the general law of the country concerned, fear of such prosecution will not in itself make the applicant a refugee.

85. Whether a political offender can also be considered a refugee will depend upon various other factors. Prosecution for an offence may, depending upon the circumstances, be a pretext for punishing the offender for his political opinions or the expression thereof. Again, there may be reason to believe that a political offender would be exposed to excessive or arbitrary punishment for the alleged offence. Such excessive or arbitrary punishment will amount to persecution.

86. In determining whether a political offender can be considered a refugee, regard should also be had to the following elements: personality of the applicant, his political opinion, the motive behind the act, the nature of the act committed, the nature of the prosecution and its motives; finally, also, the nature of the law on which the prosecution is based. These elements may go to show that the person concerned has a fear of persecution and not merely a fear of prosecution and punishment—within the law— for an act committed by him.

EU Guidelines

7.4. Political Opinions

7–027 Holding political opinions different from those of the government is not in itself a sufficient ground for securing refugee status; the applicant must show that:

— the authorities know about his political opinions or attribute them to him,

— those opinions are not tolerated by the authorities,

— given the situation in his country he would be likely to be persecuted for holding such opinions.

EU Guidelines

6. Civil War and Other Internal of Generalised Armed Conflicts

Reference to civil war or internal or generalised armed conflict and the dangers which it entails is not in itself sufficient to warrant the grant of refugee status. Fear of persecution must in all cases be based on one of the grounds in Article 1A of the Geneva Convention and be individual in nature.

In such situations, persecution may stem either from the legal authorities or third parties encouraged or tolerated by them, or *de facto* authorities in control of part of the territory within which the State cannot afford its nationals protection.

In principle, use of the armed forces does not constitute persecution where it is in accordance with international rules of war and internationally recognised practice; however, it becomes persecution where, for instance, authority is established over a particular area and its attacks on opponents or on the population fulfil the criteria in section 4.

In other cases, other forms of protection may be provided under national legislation.

9. Refugee *sur place*

The fear of persecution need not necessarily have existed at the 7–028 time of an asylum-seeker's departure from his country of origin. An individual who had no reason to fear persecution on leaving his country of origin may subsequently become a refugee *sur place*. A well-founded fear of persecution may be based on the fact that the situation in his country of origin has changed since his departure, with serious consequences for him, or on his own actions.

In any event the asylum-related characteristics of the individual should be such that the authorities in the country of origin know or could come to know of them before the individual's fear of persecution can be justified.

9.1. Fear Arising from a New Situation in the Country of Origin After Departure

Political changes in the country of origin may justify fear of persecution, but only if the asylum-seeker can demonstrate that as a result of those changes he would personally have grounds to fear persecution if he returned.

9.2. Fear on Account of Activities Outside the Country of Origin

Refugee status may be granted if the activities which gave rise to the asylum-seeker's fear of persecution constitute the expression and continuation of convictions which he had held in his county of origin or can objectively be regarded as the consequence of asylum-related characteristics of the individual. However, such continuity must not be a requirement where the person concerned was not yet able to establish convictions because of age.

On the other hand if it is clear that he expressed his convictions mainly for the purpose of creating the necessary conditions for being admitted as a refugee, his activities cannot, in principle, furnish grounds for admission as a refugee; this does not prejudice his right not to be returned to a country where his life, physical integrity or freedom would be in danger.

10. Conscientious Objection, Absence Without Leave and Desertion

The fear of punishment for conscientious objection, absence 7–029 without leave or desertion is investigated on an individual basis. It should in itself be insufficient to justify recognition of refugee status. The penalty must be assessed in particular in accordance with the principles set out in point 5.

In cases of absence without leave or desertion, the person concerned must be accorded refugee status if the conditions under which military duties are performed themselves constitute persecution.

Similarly, refugee status may be granted, in the light of all the other requirements of the definition, in cases of punishment of conscientious objection or deliberate absence without leave and desertion on grounds of conscience if the performance of his military duties were to have the effect of leading person concerned to participate in acts falling under the exclusion clauses in Article 1F of the Geneva Convention.

11. Cessation of Refugee Status (Article 1C)

Whether or not refugee status may be withdrawn on the basis of Article 1C of the Convention is always investigated on an individual basis.

The Member States should make evey effort, by exchanging information, to harmonise their practice with regard to the application of the cessation clauses of Article 1C wherever possible.

The circumstances in which the cessation clause in Article 1C may be applied should be of a fundamental nature and should be determined in an objective and verifiable manner. Information provided by the Centre for Information, Discussion and Exchange on Asylum (Cirea) and the UNHCR may be of considerable relevance here.

12. Article 1D of the Geneva Convention

Any person who deliberately removes himself from the protection and assistance referred to in Article 1D of the Geneva Convention is no longer automatically covered by that Convention. In such cases, refugee status is in principle to be determined in accordance with Article 1A.

13. Article 1F of the Geneva Convnetion

7–030 The clauses in Article 1F of the Geneva Convention are designed to exclude from protection under that Convention persons who cannot enjoy international protection because of the seriousness of the crimes which they have committed.

They may also be applied where the acts become known after the grant of refugee status (see point 11).

In view of the serious consequences of such a decision for the asylum-seeker, Article 1F must be used with care and after thorough consideration, and in accordance with the procedures laid down in national law.

13.1. Article 1F(a)

The crimes referred to in Article 1F(a) are those referred to international instruments to which the Member States have acceded, and in resolutions adopted by the United Nations or other international or regional organisations to the extent that they have been accepted by the Member States.

13.2. Article 1F(b)

The severity of the expected persecution is to be weighed against the nature of the criminal offence of which the person concerned is suspected.

Particular cruel actions, even if committed with an allegedly political objective, may be classified as serious non-political crimes. This applies both to the participants in the crime and to its instigators.

13.3 Article 1F(c)

The purposes and principles referred to in Article 1F(c) are in the first instance those laid down in the Charter of the United Nations, which determines the obligations of the States party to it in their mutual relations, particularly for the purpose of maintaining peace, and with regard to human rights and fundamental freedoms.

Article 1F(c) applies to cases in which those principles have been breached and is directed notably at persons in senior positions in the State, who, by virtue of their responsibilities, have ordered or lent their authority to action at variance with those purposes and principles as well as at persons who, as members of the security forces, have been prompted to assume personal responsibility for the performance of such action.

In order to determine whether an action may be contrary to the purposes and principles of the United Nations, Member States should take account of the conventions and resolutions adopted in this connection under the auspices of the United Nations.

Contracting Parties may not make a reservation to Article 1.[65]

---

[65] Convention, Article 42. Reservations are prohibited in respect of Articles 3,4, 16(1), 33 and 36 to 46 inclusive.

Procedures for the Determination of Refugee Status

7–031 The procedures for the determination of refugee status are not prescribed by international law and the procedures adopted by states vary considerably. Given the slim possibility of all Contracting Parties to the 1951 Convention and 1967 Protocol adopting identical procedures the Executive Committee of the UNHCR in 1977[66] identified the basic requirements which procedures for the determination of refugee status should satisfy, namely.

1. The competent official (*e.g.* immigration officer or border police officer) to whom the applicant addresses himself at the border or in the territory of a Contracting State, should have clear instructions for dealing with cases which might be within the purview of the relevant international instruments. He should be required to act in accordance with the principle of non-refoulement and to refer such cases to a higher authority.

2. The applicant should receive the necessary guidance as to the procedure to be followed.

3. There should be a clearly identified authority—wherever possible a single central authority—with responsibility for examining requests for refugee status and taking a decision in the first instance.

4. The applicant should be given the necessary facilities, including the services of a competent interpreter, for submitting his case to the authorities concerned. Applicants should also be given the opportunity, of which they should be duly informed, to contact a representative of UNHCR

5. If the applicant is recognised as a refugee, he should be informed accordingly and issued with documentation certifying his refugee status.

6. If the applicant is not recognised, he should be given a reasonable time to appeal for a formal reconsideration of the decision, either to the same or to a different authority, whether administrative or judicial, according to the prevailing stem.

7. The applicant should be permitted to remain in the country pending a decision on his initial request by the competent authority referred to in paragraph 3 above, unless it has been established by that authority that his request is clearly abusive. He should also be permitted to remain in the

---

[66] ExCOM No 8 (XXVIII), 1977, Determination of Refugee Status.

country while an appeal to a higher administrative authority or to the courts is pending[67]

LEGAL STATUS OF REFUGEES

Article 2. General Obligations

Every refugee has duties to the country in which he finds himself,   7–032
which require in particular that he conform to its laws and
regulations as well as to measures taken for the maintenance of
public order.

Article 3. Non-Discrimination

The Contracting States shall apply the provisions of this Convention to refugees without discrimination as to race, religion or country of origin.

Article 4. Religion

The Contracting States shall accord to refugees within their territories treatment at least as favourable as that accorded to their nationals with respect to freedom to practice their religion and freedom as regards the religious education of their children.

Article 5. Rights granted apart from this Convention

Nothing in this Convention shall be deemed to impair any rights and benefits granted by a Contracting State to refugees apart from this Convention.

Article 6. The Term "In the Same Circumstances"

For the purpose of this Convention, the term "in the same circumstances" implies that any requirements (including requirements as to length and conditions of sojourn or residence) which the particular individual would have to fulfil for the enjoyment of the right in question, if he were not a refugee, must be fulfilled by him, with the exception of requirements which by their nature a refugee is incapable of fulfilling.

Article 7. Exemption from Reciprocity

1. Except where this Convention contains more favourable provisions, a Contracting State shall accord to refugees the same treatment as is accorded to aliens generally

---

[67] Note Amnesty International's criteria for fair and efficient asylum procedures. Europe: The need for minimum standards in asylum procedures (Amnesty International, June 1994—Paper EU ASS/01/94).

2. After a period of three years' residence, all refugees shall enjoy exemption from legislative reciprocity in the territory of the Contracting States.

3. Each Contracting State shall continue to accord to refugees the rights and benefits to which they were already entitled, in the absence of reciprocity, at the date of entry into force of this Convention for that State.

4. The Contracting States shall consider favourably the possibility of according to refugees, in the absence of reciprocity, rights and benefits beyond those to which they are entitled according to paragraphs 2 and 3, and to extending exemption from reciprocity to refugees who do not fulfil the conditions provided for in paragraphs 2 and 3.

5. The provisions of paragraphs 2 and 3 apply both to the rights and benefits referred to in articles 13, 18, 19, 21 and 22 of this Convention and to rights and benefits for which this Convention does not provide.

Article 8. Exemption from Exceptional Measures

7–033 With regard to exceptional measures which may be taken against the person, property or interests of nationals of a foreign State, the Contracting States shall not apply such measures to a refugee who is formally a national of the said State solely on account of such nationality. Contracting States which, under their legislation, are prevented from applying the general principle expressed in this article, shall, in appropriate cases, grant exemptions in favour of such refugees.

Article 9. Provisional Measures

Nothing in this Convention shall prevent a Contracting State, in time of war or other grave and exceptional circumstances, from taking provisionally measures which it considers to be essential to the national security in the case of a particular person, pending a determination by the Contracting State that person is in fact a refugee and that the continuance of such measures is necessary in his case in the interests of national security.

Article 10. Continuity of Residence

1. Where a refugee has been forcibly displaced during the Second World War and removed to the territory of a Contracting State, and is resident there, the period of such enforced sojourn shall be considered to have been lawful residence within that territory

2. Where a refugee has been forcibly displaced during the Second World War from the territory of a Contracting State and has, prior to the date of entry into force of this Convention, returned there for the purpose taking up residence, the period of residence before and after such enforced displacement shall be regarded as one uninterrupted period for any purposes for which uninterrupted residence is required.

Article 11. Refugee Seamen

In the case of refugees regularly serving as crew members on board a ship flying the flag of a Contracting State, that state shall give sympathetic consideration to their establishment on its territory and the issue of travel documents to them on their temporary admissions to its territory particularly with a view to facilitating their establishment in another country. 7–034

Article 12. Personal Status

1. The personal status of a refugee shall be governed by the law of the country of his domicile or, if he has no domicile, by the law of the country of his residence.

2. Rights previously acquired by a refugee and dependent on personal status, more particularly rights attaching to marriage, shall be respected by a Contracting State, subject to compliance, if this be necessary, with the formalities required by the law of that State, provided that the right in question is one which would have been recognised by the law of that State had he not become a refugee

Article 13. Movable and Immovable Property

The Contracting States shall accord to a refugee treatment as favourable as possible and, in any event, not less favourable than that accorded to aliens generally in the same circumstances as regards the acquisition of movable and immovable property and other rights pertaining thereto, and to leases and other contracts relating to movable and immovable property.

Article 14. Artistic Rights and Industrial Property

In respect of the protection of industrial property, such as inventions, designs or models, trade marks, trade names, and of rights in literary, artistic and scientific works, a refugee shall be accorded in the country in which he has his habitual residence the same protection as is accorded to nationals of that country. In the territory of any other Contracting State, he shall be accorded the same protection as is accorded in that territory to nationals of the country in which he has habitual residence.

Article 15. Right of Association

7–035 As regards non-political and non-profit-making associations and trade unions the Contracting States shall accord to refugees lawfully staying in their territory the most favourable treatment accorded to nationals of a foreign country, in the same circumstances

Article 16. Access to Courts

1. A refugee shall have free access to the courts of law on the territory of all Contracting States.

2. A refugee shall enjoy in the Contracting State in which he has his habitual residence the same treatment as a national in matters pertaining to access to the Courts, including legal assistance and exemption from *cautio judicatum solvi*.

3. A refugee shall be accorded in the matters referred to in paragraph 2 in countries other than that in which he has his habitual residence the treatment granted to a national of the country of his habitual residence.

Article 17. Wage-earning Employment

1. The Contracting State shall accord to refugees lawfully staying in their territory the most favourable treatment accorded to nationals of a foreign country in the same circumstances, as regards the right to engage in wage-earning employment.

2. In any case, restrictive measures imposed on aliens or the employment of aliens for the protection of the national labour market shall not be applied to a refugee who was already exempt from them at the date of entry into force of this Convention for the Contracting States concerned, or who fulfils one of the following conditions:

(a) He has completed three years residence in the country;

(b) He has a spouse possessing the nationality of the country of residence. A refugee may not invoke the benefits of this provision if he has abandoned his spouse;

(c) He has one or more children possessing the nationality of the country of residence.

3. The Contracting States shall give sympathetic consideration to assimilating the rights of all refugees with regard to wage-earning employment to those of nationals, and in particular of those refugees who have entered their territory pursuant to programmes of labour recruitment or under immigration schemes.

Article 18. Self-employment

The Contracting States shall accord to a refugee lawfully in their 7–036 territory treatment as favourable as possible and, in any event, not less favourable than that accorded to aliens generally in the same circumstances, as regards the right to engage on his own account in agriculture, industry, handicrafts and commerce and to establish commercial and industrial companies.

Article 19. Liberal Professions

1. Each Contracting State shall accord to refugees lawfully staying in their territory who hold diplomas recognised by the competent authorities of that State, and who are desirous of practising a liberal profession, treatment as favourable as possible and, in any event, not less favourable than that accorded to aliens generally in the same circumstances.

2. The Contracting States shall use their best endeavours consistently with their laws and constitutions to secure the settlement of such refugees in the territories, other than the metropolitan territory, for whose international relations they are responsible.

Article 20. Rationing

Where a rationing system exists, which applies to the population at large and regulates the general distribution of products in short supply, refugees shall be accorded the same treatment as nationals

Article 21. Housing

As regards housing, the Contracting States, in so far as the matter is regulated by laws or regulations or is subject to the control of public authorities, shall accord to refugees lawfully staying in their territory treatment as favourable as possible and, in any event, not less favourable than that accorded to aliens generally in the same circumstances.

Article 22. Public Education

1. The Contracting States shall accord to refugees the same treatment as is accorded to nationals with respect to elementary education

2. The Contracting States shall accord to refugees treatment as favourable as possible, and, in any event, not less favourable than that accorded to aliens generally in the same circumstances, with respect to education other than elementary education and, in particular, as regards access to studies, the recognition of foreign school certificates, diplomas and degrees, the remission of fees and charges and the award of scholarships.

Article 23. Public Relief

7–037 The Contracting States shall accord to refugees lawfully staying in their territory the same treatment with respect to public relief and assistance as is accorded to their nationals.

Article 24. Labour Legislation and Social Security

1. The Contracting States shall accord to refugees lawfully staying in their territory the same treatment as is accorded to nationals in respect of the following matters:

(a) In so far as such matters are governed by laws or regulations or are subject to the control of administrative authorities: remuneration, including family allowances where these form part of remuneration, hours of work, overtime arrangements, holidays with pay, restrictions on home work, minimum age of employment, apprenticeship and training, women's work and the work of young persons, and the enjoyment of the benefits of collective bargaining;

(b) Social security (legal provisions in respect of employment injury, occupational diseases, maternity, sickness, disability, old age, death, unemployment, family responsibilities and any other contingency which, according to national laws or regulations, is covered by a social security scheme), subject to the following limitations:

(i) There may be appropriate arrangements for the maintenance of acquired rights and rights in course of acquisition;

(ii) National laws or regulations of the country of residence may prescribe special arrangements concerning benefits or portions of benefits which are payable wholly out of public funds, and concerning allowances paid to persons who do not fulfil the contribution conditions prescribed for the award of a normal pension.

2. The right to compensation for the death of a refugee resulting from employment injury or from occupational disease shall not be affected by the fact that the residence of the beneficiary is outside the territory of the Contracting State.

3. The Contracting States shall extend to refugees the benefits of agreements concluded between them, or which may be concluded between them in the future, concerning the maintenance of acquired rights and rights in the process of acquisition in regard to social security, subject only to the conditions which apply to nationals of the States signatory to the agreements in question.

4. The Contracting States will give sympathetic consideration to extending to refugees so far as possible the benefits of similar agreements which may at any time be in force between such Contracting States and non-contracting States.

Article 25. Administrative Assistance

1. When the exercise of a right by a refugee would normally 7–038 require the assistance of authorities of a foreign country to whom he cannot have recourse, the Contracting States in whose territory he is residing shall arrange that such assistance be afforded to him by their own authorities or by an international authority.

2. The authority or authorities mentioned in paragraph 1 shall deliver or cause to be delivered under their supervision to refugees such documents or certifications as would normally be delivered to aliens by or through their national authorities.

3. Documents or certifications so delivered shall stand in the stead of the official instruments delivered to aliens by or through their national authorities, and shall be given credence in the absence of proof to the contrary.

4. Subject to such exceptional treatment as may be granted to indigent persons, fees may be charged for the services mentioned herein, but such fees shall be moderate and commensurate with those charged to nationals for similar services.

5. The provisions of this article shall be without prejudice to articles 27 and 28.

Article 26 Freedom of Movement

Each Contracting State shall accord to refugees lawfully in its territory the right to choose their place of residence and to move freely within its territory, subject to any regulations applicable to aliens generally in the same circumstances.

Article 27. Identity Papers

The Contracting States shall issue identity papers to any refugee in their territory who does not possess a valid travel document

Article 28. Travel Documents

1. The Contracting States shall issue to refugees lawfully 7–039 staying in their territory travel documents for the purpose of travel outside their territory unless compelling reasons of national security or public order otherwise require, and the provisions of the Schedule to this Convention shall apply with respect to such document. The Contracting States may issue such a travel document to any other refugee in their territory; they shall in particular give sympathetic consideration to the issue of such a travel document to refugees in their territory who are unable to obtain a travel document from the country of their lawful residence.

2. Travel documents issued to refugees under previous international agreements by parties thereto shall be recognised and treated by the Contracting States in the same way as if they had been issued pursuant to this article.

Article 29. Fiscal Charges

1. The Contracting States shall not impose upon refugees duties, charges or taxes, of any description whatsoever, other or higher than those which are or may be levied on their nationals in similar situations.

2. Nothing in the above paragraph shall prevent the application to refugees of the laws and regulations concerning charges in respect of the issue to aliens of administrative documents including identity papers.

Article 30. Transfer of Assets

1. A Contracting State shall, in conformity with its laws and regulations permit refugees to transfer assets which they have brought into its territory, to another country where they have been admitted for the purposes of resettlement.

2. A Contracting State shall give sympathetic consideration to the application of refugees for permission to transfer assets wherever they may be and which are necessary for their resettlement in another country to which they have been admitted.

Article 31. Refugees Unlawfully in the Country of Refuge

1. The Contracting States shall not impose penalties, on account of their illegal entry or presence, on refugees who, coming directly from a territory where their life or freedom was threatened in the sense of Article 1, enter or are present in their territory without authorisation, provided they present themselves without delay to the authorities and show good cause for their illegal entry or presence.

2. The Contracting States shall not apply to the movements of such refugees restrictions other than those which are necessary and such restrictions shall only be applied until their status in the country is regularised or they obtain admission into another

country. The Contracting States shall allow such refugees a reasonable period and all the necessary facilities to obtain admission into another country.

Article 32. Expulsion

1. The Contracting States shall not expel a refugee lawfully in 7–040 their territory save on grounds of national security or public order.

2. The expulsion of such a refugee shall be only in pursuance of a decision reached in accordance with due process of law. Except where compelling reasons of national security otherwise require, the refugee shall be allowed to clear himself, and to appeal to and be represented for the purpose before competent authority or a person or persons specially designated by the competent authority.

3. The Contracting States shall allow such a refugee a reasonable period within which to seek legal admission into another country. The Contracting States reserve the right to apply during that period such internal measures as they may deem necessary.

Article 33. Prohibition of Expulsion or Return ("Refoulement")[68]

Article 34. Naturalisation

The Contracting States shall as far as possible facilitate the assimilation and naturalisation of refugees. They shall in particular make every effort to expedite naturalisation proceedings and to reduce as far as possible the charges and cost of such proceedings.

CHAPTER VI EXECUTRY AND TRANSITORY PROVISIONS

Article 35. Co-operation of the National Authorities with the United Nations

1. The Contracting States undertake to co-operate with the Office of the United Nations High Commissioner for Refugees, or any other agency of the United Nations which may succeed it, in the exercise of its functions, and shall in particular facilitate its duty of supervising the application of the provisions of this Convention.

2. In order to enable the Office of the High Commissioner or any other agency of the United Nations which may succeed it, to make reports to the competent organs of the United Nations, the

---

[68] See above, p. 310 for text.

Contracting States undertake to provide them in the appropriate form with information and statistical data requested concerning:

(a) the condition of refugees,

(b) the implementation of this Convention, and

(c) laws, regulations and decrees which are, or may hereafter be, in force relating to refugees.

Article 36. Information on National Legislation

7–041 The Contracting States shall communicate to the Secretary-General of the United Nations the laws and regulations which they may adopt to ensure the application of this Convention

Article 37. Relation to Previous Conventions

. . .

Article 38. Settlement of Disputes

Any dispute between parties to this Convention relating to its interpretation or application, which cannot be settled by other means, shall be referred to the International Court of Justice at the request of any one of the parties to the dispute.

Article 39. Signature, Ratification and Accession

1. . . .

Article 40. Territorial Application Clause

1. . . .

Article 41. Federal Clause

. . .

Article 42. Reservations

1.[69]
2. Any State making a reservation in accordance with paragraph 1 of this article may at any time withdraw the reservation by a communication to that effect addressed to the Secretary-General of the United Nations.

[69] See p. 337, n. 82.

Article 43. Entry into Force

1.

Article 44. Denunciation

1. Any Contracting State may denounce this Convention at any 7–042
time by a notification addressed to the Secretary-General of the
United Nations.

2. Such denunciation shall take effect for the Contracting State
concerned one year from the date upon which it is received by
the Secretary-General of the United Nations.

3. Any State which has made a declaration or notification under
article 40 may, at any time thereafter, by a notification to the
Secretary-General of the United Nations, declare that the Convention shall cease to extend to such territory one year after the date
of receipt of the notification by the Secretary-General

Article 45. Revision

1. Any Contracting State may request revision of this Convention at any time by a notification addressed to the Secretary-
General of the United Nations.

2. The General Assembly of the United Nations shall recommend the steps, if any, to be taken in respect of such request

**Article 46. Notifications by the Secretary-General of the United
Nations**

The Secretary-General of the United Nations shall inform all
Members of the United Nations and non-member States referred
to in article 39

(a) of declarations and notifications in accordance with Section
B of Article 1,

(b) of signatures, ratifications and accessions in accordance
with article 39,

(c) of declarations and notifications in accordance with article
40;

(d) of reservations and withdrawals in accordance with article
42;

(e) of the date on which this Convention will come into force
in accordance with article 43;

(f) of denunciations and notifications in accordance with article 44;

(g) of requests for revision in accordance with article 45.

. . .

International response to the refugee problem dates from the League of Nations as it endeavoured to deal with the mass movements in persons which were a consequence of the Russian revolution and the collapse of the Ottoman Empire. In 1921 a High Commissioner for Russian Refugees, Dr Fridtjof Nansen, was elected by the League. His tasks were to define the legal status of the Russian refugees, to organize their repatriation or "allocation" to countries able to receive them and to undertake relief work in conjunction with "philanthropic" agencies. His mandate was subsequently extended to include Armenian, Assyrian, Assyro-Chaldean and Turkish refugees. During the League's lifetime a number of Conventions were concluded relating to specific categories of refugees.[70]

The United Nations gave recognition to the need for an international system for caring for refugees in General Resolution A/45.[71] That Resolution provided the basis for supportive activities for refugees on the part of the United Nations and stressed that no refugee or displaced person expressing valid objections to returning to his country of origin should be compelled to do so. Political objections were deemed valid by the Chairman of the Special Committee on Refugees and Displaced Persons. Furthermore, any displaced person desiring to return home was to be given assistance so to do.

INTERNATIONAL REFUGEE ORGANISATION (IRO)[72]

7–043 This intergovernmental organisation, created in 1947 as a specialised agency of the United Nations, was a noteworthy development. It was the first international agency which sought to deal comprehensively with every aspect of the refugee problem. The IRO functioned until 1951.

UNITED NATIONS HIGH COMMISSIONER FOR REFUGEES (UNHCR)

The office of the High Commissioner was created in December 1950 and came into existence as of January 1, 1951. The office was

---

[70] *e.g.* Arrangements of May 12, 1926 and June 30, 1928 concerning the issue of certificates of identity to refugees for use as travel documents, Nansen Passports Convention Relating to the International Status of Refugees (1933) which received only eight ratifications.

[71] Adopted February 12, 1946.

[72] The United Nations Relief and Rehabilitation Administration (UNRRA) which was created by the allies in 1943 organised the return of people to their countries or areas of origin.

created and is governed by the statute adopted by the General Assembly.[73] The Statute is in three chapters, general provisions, in which the functions of the Statute are spelt out in general terms; the functions of the High Commissioner, in which the persons of concern to the High Commissioner[74] are identified as are the tasks of the High Commissioner[75]; and finally, the organisation and finances of the High Commissioner's Office.

The current High Commissioner is Professor Drs Ruud Lubbers (a Dutch national who took up office in 2001).[76]

The Executive Committee of the High Commissioner was created in 1958[77] with the tasks of approving the annual assistance programmes of the High Commissioner and advising the High

---

[73] See below para. 7–044. The UNHCR was created as a subsidiary organ of the General Assembly under Article 22 of the UN Charter. The UNHCR has no formal governing board or authority however, the Executive Committee established in 1957 is responsible for approving assistance programmes and advising the High Commissioner on the exercise of functions. The Executive Committee in turn is assisted by the Sub-Committee of the Whole on International Protection established in 1975—ExCOM Conclusion No 1 (XXVI) 1975, para (h).

[74] UNHCR Statute, Chapter 11(6), below The definition of persons falling within the competence of the High Commissioner closely resembles but is not identical to the definition of the 1951 Convention. Note however that the UNHCR Statute omits any reference to membership of a particular social group, includes persons who have either a past or present fear of persecution, explicitly excludes persons whose refusal to return is for reasons of personal convenience or of an economic character, excludes from refugee definition those who are in *actual receipt* (emphasis added) of assistance from another UN agency, rather than eligibility, adopts a narrower criminal exclusion. The Statute of the High Commissioner contains no dateline or geographical limitation—however this of less relevance since the conclusion of the 1967 Protocol A person who satisfies the definition of the UNHCR Statute will warrant protection by the High Commissioner as a "mandate refugee" A mandate refugee does not depend upon the state of asylum being a Contracting Party to the 1951 Convention or the 1961 Protocol Such "mandate refugees" however, do not enjoy the full range of rights conferred by the Convention unless also recognised as "refugees" by a Contracting Party to the Convention A person can simultaneously be both a mandate refugee and a Convention refugee. The term "mandate refugee" is also used for those persons falling under the wider competencies of the High Commissioner.

[75] See UNHCR Statute, Chapter 11(8) below.

[76] The previous High Commissioners were Mr G J van Heuven Goedhart (Netherlands), December 1950-July 1956, Mr A R Lindt (Switzerland), December 1956-December 1960, Mr I Schnyder (Switzerland), December 1960-December 1965, S Adruddim Aga Khan (Ban), December 1965-December 1977, Mr P. Hartling (Denmark) January 1978 December 1985, Mr Jean-Pierre Hocke (Switzerland), January 1986-November 1989, Mr I Stoltenberg (Norway), January 1990–November 1990; Mrs Sedeico Ogata (Japan) 1990–2000.

[77] The predecessor to the Executive Committee was the Advisory Committee on Refugees, established in 1951 The task of the Advisory Committee was to guide the High Commissioner, at his/her request, in the exercise of his/her functions. The Advisory Committee remained in existence until the beginning of 1955 when the United Nations Refugee Fund (UNREF) programme was initiated (see below). The Advisory Committee was reconstituted under G.A. Res. 832 (VIII), October 1954 and ECOSOC Resn 565 (XIX), March 1955 as UNREF Executive Committee, this in turn was replaced following the decision to discontinue the UNREF programme after December 31, 1958 by the Executive Committee of the High Commissioner's Programme. The membership of the Executive Committee was originally representatives from 20–25 States, member of either the United Nations or one of its specialised agencies as elected by ECOSOC on the widest possible geographical basis from those states with a demonstrated interest in and devotion to the solution of the refugee problem. The membership of the Executive Committee has been increased to 46 governments (G.A. Res. 46/105; and ECOSOC Dec 1992/216).

Commissioner, at the latter's request, in the exercise of his statutory functions (notably international protection). As the work of the High Commissioner became increasingly more complex, it was decided in 1975 to create a Sub-Committee with the function of studying "in more detail some of the more technical aspects of the protection of refugees." The Sub-Committee meets annually prior to the plenary session of the Executive Committee and discusses specific protection issues. The conclusions adopted are subsequently submitted to the Plenary Committee for the indorsement. The Executive Committee has adopted some 76 Conclusions on a variety of issues relating to refugees.

STATUTE OF THE OFFICE OF THE UNITED NATIONS HIGH COMMISSIONER FOR REFUGEES[78]

Chapter I. General Provisions

7–044   **1.** The United Nations High Commissioner for Refugees, acting under the authority of the General Assembly, shall assume the function of providing international protection, under the auspices of the United Nations, to refugees who fall within the scope of the present Statute and of seeking permanent solutions for the problem of refugees by assisting governments and, subject to the approval of the governments concerned, private organisations to facilitate the voluntary repatriation of such refugees, of their assimilation within new national communities.

In the exercise of his functions, more particularly when difficulties arise, and for instance with regard to any controversy concerning the international status of these persons, the High Commissioner shall request the opinion of an advisory committee on refugees if it is created.

2. The work of the High Commissioner shall be of an entirely nonpolitical character; it shall be humanitarian and social and shall relate, as a rule, to groups and categories of refugees.[79]

---

[78] G.A. Res. 5/428, annex, G.A.O.R. 5th Session, Supp 20, p 46, UN Doc A/1775 (1950) adopted December 1950. The number of UNHCR Offices worldwide is 258 in 118 countries.

[79] Note the particular emphasis on the "entirely non-political" and "humanitarian and social" aspect of the High Commissioner's work.

3. The High Commissioner shall follow policy directives given him by the General Assembly or the Economic and Social Council.[80]

4. The Economic and Social Council may decide, after hearing the views of the High Commissioner on the subject, to establish an advisory committee on refugees, which shall consist of representatives of States Members and States and non-members of the United Nations, to be selected by the Council on the basis of their demonstrated interest in and devotion to the solution of the refugee problem.

5. The General Assembly shall review, not later than at its eighth regular session, the arrangements for the Office of the High Commissioner with a view to determining whether the Office should be continued beyond 31 December 1963.[81]

CHAPTER II. FUNCTIONS OF THE HIGH COMMISSIONER

6. The competence of the High Commissioner shall extend to: 7–045

A. (i) Any person who has been considered a refugee under the Arrangements of May 12, 1926 and June 30, 1928 or under the Conventions of October 28, 1933 and February 10, 1938, the Protocol of September 14, 1939 or the Constitution of the International Refugee Organisation;

(ii) Any person who, as a result of events occurring before January 1, 1951 and owing to well-founded fear of being persecuted for reasons of race, religion, nationality or political opinion, is outside the country of his nationality and is unable or, owing to such fear or for reasons other than personal convenience, is unwilling to avail himself of the protection of that country; or who, not having a nationality and being outside the country of his former habitual residence, is unable or, owing to such fear or for reasons other than personal convenience, is unwilling to return to it

Decisions as to eligibility taken by the International Refugee Organisation during the period of its activities shall not prevent the status of refugee being accorded to persons who fulfil the conditions of the present paragraph.

[80] The High Commissioner works under the policy directions of the UN General Assembly or the Economic and Social Council (ECOSOC) Annually, the High Commissioner presents a comprehensive report on his/her activities through ECOSOC to the General Assembly where it is initially scrutinised by the Third Committee Since 1970, ECOSOC considers the annual report only if it requested to do so by either the High Commissioner or one of its members. Otherwise the report is simply passed by ECOSOC to the General Assembly without debate. Administrative and financial aspects of the UNHCR's activities are dealt with by the Advisory Committee on Administrative and Budgetary Questions (ACABQ) and by the Fifth Committee of the General Assembly.

[81] The UNHCR was conceived as a temporary institution but the permanent nature of the refugee problem has dictated otherwise. The General Assembly decided to extend UNHCR's mandate for a period of five years, renewable, commencing January 1, 1954 The current mandate runs from January 1, 1999 to December 2003.

The competence of the High Commissioner shall cease to apply to any person defined in section A above if:

(a) He has voluntarily re-availed himself of the protection of the country of his nationality; or

(b) Having lost his nationality, he has voluntarily re-acquired it; or

(c) He has acquired a new nationality, and enjoys the protection of the country of his new nationality; or

(d) He has voluntarily re-established himself in the country which he left or outside which he remained owing to fear of persecution; or

(e) He can no longer, because the circumstances in connection with which he has been recognised as a refugee have ceased to exist, claim grounds other than those of personal convenience, for continuing to refuse to avail himself of the protection of the country of his nationality. Reasons of a purely economic character may not be invoked; or

(f) Being a person who has no nationality, he can no longer, because the circumstances in connection with which he has been recognised as a refugee have ceased to exist and he is able to return to the country of his former habitual residence, claim grounds other than those of personal convenience for continuing to refuse to return to that country.

7–046   B. Any other person who is outside the country of his nationality or, if he has no nationality, the country of his former habitual residence, because he has or had well-founded fear of persecution by reason of his race, religion, nationality or political opinion and is unable or, because of such fear, is unwilling to avail himself of the protection of the government of the country of his nationality, or, if he has no nationality, to return to the country of his former habitual residence.

7. Provided that the competence of the High Commissioner as defined in paragraph 6 above shall not extend to a person:

(a) Who is a national of more than one country unless he satisfies the provisions of the preceding paragraph in relation to each of the countries of which he is a national, or

(b) Who is recognised by the competent authorities of the country in which he has taken residence as having the rights and obligations which are, attached to the possession of the nationality of that country; or

(c) Who continues to receive from other organs or agencies of the United Nations protection or assistance; or

    (d) In respect of whom there are serious reasons for consider-
ing that he has committed a crime covered by the provisions of treaties of extradition or a crime mentioned in
article 6 of the London Charter of the International Military
Tribunal or by the provisions of article 14, paragraph 2, of
the Universal Declaration of Human Rights.

8. The High Commissioner shall provide for the protection of **7–047**
refugees falling under the competence of his Office by:

    (a) Promoting the conclusion and ratification of international
conventions for the protection of refugees, supervising their
application and proposing amendments thereto[82];

    (b) Promoting through special agreements with governments
the execution of any measures calculated to improve the
situation of refugees and to reduce the number requiring
protection;

    (c) Assisting governmental and private efforts to promote
voluntary repatriation or assimilation within new national
communities;

    (d) Promoting the admission of refugees, not excluding those
in the most destitute categories, to the territories of States,

    (e) Endeavouring to obtain permission for refugees to transfer
their assets and especially those necessary for their
resettlement;

    (f) Obtaining from governments information concerning the
number and conditions of refugees in their territories and
the laws and regulations concerning them,

    (g) Keeping in close touch with the governments and inter-
governmental organisations concerned;

    (h) Establishing contact in such manner as he may think best
with private organisations dealing with refugee questions;

    (i) Facilitating the co-ordination of the efforts of private organ-
isations concerned with the welfare of refugees.

9. The High Commissioner shall engage in such additional
activities, including repatriation and resettlement, as the General
Assembly may determine, within the limits of the resources
placed at his disposal.

    10. The High Commissioner shall administer any funds, public
or private, which he receives for assistance to refugees, and shall

---

[82] The High Commissioner is responsible under Article 35 of the 1951 Convention for
supervising the application of the Convention.

distribute them among the private and, as appropriate, public agencies which he deems best qualified to administer such assistance.

The High Commissioner may reject any offers which he does not consider appropriate or which cannot be utilised.

The High Commissioner shall not appeal to governments for funds or make a general appeal, without the prior approval of the General Assembly.

The High Commissioner shall include in his annual report a statement of his activities in this field.[83]

11. The High Commissioner shall be entitled to present his views before the General Assembly, the Economic and Social Council and their subsidiary bodies.

The High Commissioner shall report annually to the General Assembly through the Economic and Social Council; his report shall be considered as a separate item on the agenda of the General Assembly.

12. The High Commissioner may invite the co-operation of the various specialised agencies.

CHAPTER III. ORGANISATION AND FINANCES

7–048   **13.** The High Commissioner shall be elected by the General Assembly on the nomination of the Secretary-General. The terms of appointment of the High Commissioner shall be proposed by the Secretary-General and approved by the General Assembly. The High Commissioner shall be elected for a term of three years, from January 1, 1951.

14. The High Commissioner shall appoint, for the same term, a Deputy High Commissioner of a nationality other than his own.

15. (a) Within the limits of the budgetary appropriations provided, the staff of the Office of the High Commissioner

---

[83] G.A. Res. 538(VI)B adopted in February 1952 authorised the High Commissioner to issue an appeal for funds under paragraph 10 of the Statute, to enable UNHCR to give emergency and to the most needy groups of refugees. The United Nations Refugee Emergency Fund was thus established and remained in operation until 1954 when the UNREF Programme was established. Under G. A. Res. 832(IX) the UNREF Fund was established to undertake a four-year programme with the remit of achieving durable solutions to the problem of refugees (*e.g.* by voluntary repatriation, integration and resettlement) and the continuation of emergency aid to those in most need. Resolution 832 provides the blueprint for all subsequent UNHCR assistance activities. UNHCR expenditure is financed by a subsidy from the Regular Budget of the United Nations (used exclusively for administrative costs) and voluntary contributions from Governments, nongovernmental organisations and individuals. The High Commissioner may also make appeals for the funds (Emergency Funds) necessary to provide for refugees coming within his/her mandate and otherwise not taken into account under the conditions set by the Executive Committee of the High Commissioner's Programme. The High Commissioner's annual assistance programme is referred to as the General Programme.

shall be appointed by the High Commissioner and shall be responsible to him in the exercise of their functions.

(b) Such staff shall be chosen from persons devoted to the purposes of the Office of the High Commissioner.

(c) Their conditions of employment shall be those provided under the staff regulations adopted by the General Assembly and the rules promulgated thereunder by the Secretary-General.

(d) Provision may also be made to permit the employment of personnel without compensation.

16. The High Commissioner shall consult the governments of **7–049** the countries of residence of refugees as to the need for appointing representatives therein. In any country recognising such need, there may be appointed a representative approved by the government of that country. Subject to the foregoing, the same representative may serve in more than one country.

17. The High Commissioner and the Secretary-General shall make appropriate arrangements for liaison and consultation on matters of mutual interest.

18. The Secretary-General shall provide the High Commissioner with all necessary facilities within budgetary limitations.

19. The Office of the High Commissioner shall be located in Geneva, Switzerland.

20. The Office of the High Commission shall be financed under the budget of the United Nations. Unless the General Assembly subsequently decides otherwise, no expenditure, other than administrative expenditures relating to the functioning of the Office of the High Commissioner, shall be borne on the budget of the United Nations, and all other expenditures relating to the activities of the High Commissioner shall be financed by voluntary contributions.

21. The administration of the Office of the High Commissioner shall be subject to the Financial Regulations of the United Nations and to the financial rules promulgated thereunder by the Secretary-General.

22. Transactions relating to the High Commissioner's funds shall be subject to audit by the United Nations Board of Auditors, provided that the Board may accept audited accounts from the agencies to which funds have been allocated Administrative arrangements for the custody of such funds and their allocation shall be agreed between the High Commissioner and the Secretary-General in accordance with the Financial Regulations of the United Nations and rules promulgated thereunder by the Secretary-General.[84]

---

[84] In addition to providing protection to refugees UNHCR provides food, water, shelter medical care and emergency and to those forced to leave then homes.

EXTENDED DEFINITION OF REFUGEE

In essence the determining criterion of refugee status under the UNHCR auspices has come to be simply the existence of human suffering consequent to forced migration.[85] Extended definitions of the term refugee have been suggested by regional organisations. These definitions resemble the extended mandate of the UNHCR's mandate.

The Organisation of African Unity (OAU) Convention Governing the Specific Aspects of Refugee Problems in Africa[86]

The Convention defines refugee in terms of the 1951 Convention *but* extends protection to those "who owing to external aggression, occupation, foreign domination or events seriously disturbing public order in either part or the whole of his country of origin or nationality is compelled to leave his place of habitual residence in order to seek refugee in another place outside his country of origin or nationality".[87]

The Organisation of American States Definition of Refugee Status (Cartagena Declaration)[88]

The term refugee should be used so as to include persons who have fled their country "because their lives, safety or freedom have been threatened by generalised violence, foreign aggression, internal conflicts, massive violence of human rights or other circumstances which have seriously disturbed public order".[89]

Compare:

EU Guidelines

6. Civil war and other internal or generalised armed conflicts

7–050 Reference to civil war or internal or generalised armed conflict and the dangers which it entails is not in itself sufficient to warrant the granting of refugee status. Fear of persecution must in all cases be based on one of the grounds in Article 1A of the Geneva Convention and be individual in nature.

In such situations, persecution may stem either from the legal authorities or third parties encouraged or tolerated by them, or *de*

---

[85] James Hathaway, *The Law of Refugee Status* (1990), p. 13.
[86] U.N.T.S. 14,691 entered into force June 20, 1974.
[87] *ibid*. Article 12(2).
[88] OAS/Ser. I/V/II. 66, doc. 10, rev. 1, pp. 190–3, adopted by 10 Latin American states in 1984.
[89] *ibid*. Conclusion 3.

facto authorities in control of part of the territory within which the State cannot afford its nationals protection. In principle, use of the armed forces does not constitute persecution where it is in accordance with international rules of war and internationally recognised practice, however, it becomes persecution where, for instance, authority is established over a particular area and its attacks on opponents or on the population fulfil the criteria in section 4.

In other cases, other forms of protection may be provided under national legislation.

FAMILY REUNIFICATION

RECOMMENDATION B FINAL ACT OF THE UNITED NATIONS CONFERENCE OF PLENIPOTENTIARIES ON THE STATUS OF REFUGEES AND STATELESS PERSONS[90]

Considering that the unity of the family, the natural and fundamental group of society, is an essential right of the refugee, and that such unity is constantly threatened, and

Noting with satisfaction that, according to the official commentary of the ad hoc Committee on Statelessness and Related Problems the rights granted to a refugee are extended to members of his family,

Recommends Governments to take the necessary measures for the protection of the refugee's family, especially with a view to:

"(1) Ensuring that the unity of the refugee's family is maintained particularly in cases where the head of the family has fulfilled the necessary conditions for admission to a particular country,

(2) The problem of refugees who are minors, in particular unaccompanied children and girls, with special reference to guardianship and adoption."[91]

The 1951 Convention does not incorporate the principle of family unity.[92] However the majority of States whether or not parties to

---

[90] 189 U.N.T.S. 37.

[91] See below para. 7–052.

[92] See however, *e.g.* Articles 12 and 16 of the Universal Declaration of Human Rights, Article 23 of the UN Covenant on Civil and Political Rights, Article 10 of the UN Covenant on Economic, Social and Cultural Rights, and Article 10 of the UN Convention on the Rights of the Child.

the 1951 Convention or to the 1967. Protocol do observe the foregoing recommendation.[93]

UNHCR HANDBOOK

7–051 **184.** If the head of a family meets the criteria of the definition, his dependants are normally granted refugee status according to the principle of family unity. It is obvious, however, that formal refugee status should not be granted to a dependant if this is incompatible with his personal legal status. Thus, a dependant member of a refugee family may be a national of the country of asylum or of another country, and may enjoy that country's protection. To grant him refugee status in such circumstances would not be called for

185. As to which family members may benefit from the principle of family unity, the minimum requirement is the inclusion of the spouse and minor children. In practice, other dependants, such as aged parents of refugees, are normally considered if they are living in the same household. On the other hand, if the head of the family is not a refugee, there is nothing to prevent any one of his dependants, if they can invoke reasons on their own account, from applying for recognition as refugees under the 1951 Convention or the 1967 Protocol. In other words, the principle of family unity operates in favour of dependants, and not against them.

186. The principle of the unity of the family does not only operate where all family members become refugees at the same time. It applies equally to cases where a family unit has been temporarily disrupted through the flight of one or more of its members.

187. Where the unity of a refugee's family is destroyed by divorce, separation or death, dependants who have been granted refugee status on the basis of family unity will retain such refugee status unless they fall within the terms of a cessation clause; or if they do not have reasons other than those of personal convenience for wishing to retain refugee status; or if they themselves no longer wish to be considered as refugees.

188. If the dependant of a refugee falls within the terms of one of the exclusion clauses, refugee status should be denied to him.

In support of family reunification see also ExCOM Conclusion No. 9 (XXVIII) 1977 and ExCOM Conclusion No. 24 (XXXII) 1981.

---

[93] UNHCR Handbook, para 183.

REFUGEE CHILDREN[94]

The Convention does not make any provision for minors. The 7–052 same definition is applied irrespective of the applicant's age. The UNHCR Handbook does provide that ". . . when it is necessary to determine the refugee status of a minor, problems may arise due to the difficulty of applying the criteria of 'well-founded fear' in his case. If a minor is accompanied by one (or both) of his parents, or another family member on whom he is dependent, who requests refugee status, the minor's own refugee status will be determined according to the principle of family unity."[95] The Handbook further provides that whether or not an unaccompanied minor will quality for refugee status must in the first instance be determined according to the child's mental development and maturity.[96] The Handbook states that both a child and an adolescent[97] should, if appropriate, have a guardian appointed whose task it would be to promote a decision that will be in the minor's best interests. In the absence of parents or of a legally appointed guardian, it is for the authorities to ensure that the interests of an applicant for refugee status who is a minor are fully safeguarded.[98]

The Handbook also recognises that special problems with establishing the facts may arise when the applicant is a mentally disturbed person. Assessing such an applicant's claim may be impeded and may demand different techniques of examination from those normally employed.[99]

---

[94] See Chapter 5.

[95] Note 16 above.

[96] *ibid*. para 214 In order for this to be assessed it will generally be necessary to enrol the services of the experts conversant with child mentality *ibid*.

[97] The Handbook provides that: It can be assumed that—in the absence of indications to the contrary—a person of 16 or over may be regarded as sufficiently mature to have a well-founded fear of persecution. Minors under 16 years of age may normally be assumed not to be sufficiently mature. They may have fear and a will of their own, but these may not have the same significance as in the case of an adult (para 215). Nevertheless the foregoing is only to be treated as a general rule and a minor's mental maturity must normally be determined in the light of his personal, family and cultural background (para 216). Where the minor has not reached a sufficient degree of maturity to make it possible to establish well-founded fear in the same way as for an adult, it may be necessary to have greater regard to certain objective factors. Thus, if an unaccompanied minor finds himself in the company of a group of refugees, this may—depending on the circumstances—indicate that the minor is also a refugee (para 217). The circumstances of the parents and other family members, including their situation in the minor's country of origin, will have to be taken into account. If there is reason to believe that the parents wish their child to be outside the country of origin on grounds of well-founded fear of persecution, the child himself may be presumed to have such fear (para 218). If the will of the parents cannot be ascertained or if such will is in doubt or in conflict with the will of the child, then the examiner, in cooperation with the experts assisting him, will have to come to a decision as to the well-foundedness of the minor's fear on the basis of all the known circumstances, which may call for a liberal application of the benefit of the doubt (para. 219).

[98] *id*.

[99] *ibid*. paras 206–212.

THE CAIRO DECLARATION OF PRINCIPLES OF INTERNATIONAL LAW ON COMPENSATION TO REFUGEES[1]

THE INTERNATIONAL LAW ASSOCIATION

7–053 *Recalling* that the General Assembly in Resolution 41/70 of December 3, 1986 unanimously endorsed the Report of the Group of Governmental Experts on International Co-operation to Avert New Flows of Refugees (UN Doc. A/41/324) which calls upon Member States to respect as their "obligations," *inter alia*, "the rights of refugees to be facilitated in returning voluntarily and safely to their homes in their homelands and to receive adequate compensation therefrom, where so established, in cases of those who do not wish to return" (paragraph 66(f));

Recalling further that the General Assembly in Resolution 194(III) of December 11, 1948, which has since been reaffirmed every year, resolved that:

[T]he refugees wishing to return to their homes and live at peace with their neighbours should be permitted to do so at the earliest practical stage, and that compensation should be paid for the property of those choosing not to return and for loss or damage to property which, under principles of international law or in equity, should be made good by the Governments or authorities responsible; . . . (paragraph 11);

Noting, however, that neither the 1986 nor the 1948 resolution identifies or elaborates upon specific principles of international law governing compensation to refugees;

Recognising the need to provide such elaboration with a view both to rendering justice to refugees and to averting new flows of refugees;

Bearing in mind the significant contribution of the International Law association in adopting by consensus., the complementary Declaration of Principles of International Law on Mass Expulsion;

Declares the need for adopting the following principles, in the interest of the progressive development and codification of international law, in order to facilitate compensation, as appropriate, to persons who have been forced to leave their homes in their homelands and are unable to return to them.

---

[1] 65 ILA, Conference Report (1992), see also 87 A.J.I.L. 157 (1993). The Cairo Declaration was adopted by consensus at the International Law Association Conference in Cairo, April 20–26, 1992. The Declaration was the culmination of work initially undertaken at the ILA's Conference in Warsaw in 1988 and subsequently approved "in principle" at the next conference in Queensland in 1990. The Declaration is complementary to the ILA Declaration of Principles of International Law on Mass Expulsion, 1986 (62 ILA Conference Report at 12 (1986).

Principle 1

The responsibility for caring for the world's refugees rests 7–054 ultimately upon the countries that directly or indirectly force their own citizens to flee and/or remain abroad as refugees. The discharge of such responsibility by countries of asylum, international organisations (*e.g.*, UNHCR, UNRWA, IOM) and donors (both governmental and non-governmental), pending the return of refugees, their settlement in place, or their resettlement in third countries, shall not relieve the countries of origin of their basic responsibility, including that of paying adequate compensation to refugees

Principle 2

Since refugees are forced directly or indirectly out of their homes in their homelands, they are deprived of the full and effective enjoyment of all articles in the Universal Declaration of Human Rights that presuppose a person's ability to live in the place chosen as home. Accordingly, the State that turns a person into a refugee commits an internationally wrongful act, which creates the obligation to make good the wrong done.

Principle 3

The act of generating refugees in some situations should be 7–055 considered genocide if it is committed "with intent to destroy, in whole or in part, a national ethnical, racial or religious group, as such . . ."

Principle 4

A State is obligated to compensate its own nationals forced to leave their homes to the same extent as it is obligated by international law to compensate an lien.

Principle 5

A State that has committed an "internationally wrongful act" through the generation of refugees shall be required, as appropriate:

(a) to discontinue the act;

(b) to apply remedies provided under the municipal law;

(c) to restore the situation to that which existed prior to the act;

(d) to pay compensation in the event of the impossibility of the restoration of the pre-existing situation, and

(e) to provide appropriate guarantees against the repetition or recurrence of the act.

Principle 6

In implementing the right of refugees to compensation, States shall, directly or through the United Nations and intergovernmental organisations, tie the granting of economic or development assistance to countries of origin to their fulfilment of this right.

Principle 7

The United Nations may, in the discharge of its role as guardians of the interests of refugees, claim and administer compensation funds for refugees.

Principle 8

The possibility that refugees or UNHCR may one day successfully claim compensation from the country of origin should not serve as a pretext for withholding humanitarian assistance to refugees or refusing to join in international burden-sharing meant to meet the needs of refugees or otherwise to provide durable solutions, including mediation to facilitate voluntary repatriation in dignity and security, thereby removing or reducing the necessity to pay compensation.

CHAPTER 8

MIGRANT WORKERS[1]

WORLD CONFERENCE ON HUMAN RIGHTS (JUNE 1993)
VIENNA DECLARATION

In respect of migrant workers there have been few developments **8–001** in the last four years. The Convention on the Rights of All Migrant Workers and Members of Their Families has not yet entered into force. Although the Convention has been open for signature since 1990 there have been insufficient ratifications for it to enter into force. It is to be hoped that states will respond to the efforts of NGOs, the International Labour Organisation and the High Commissioner for Human Rights to achieve adoption of the Convention. Migrant workers are vulnerable because they may be doubly discriminated against, in that they are displaced *albeit* possibly by choice and are non-nationals of the host country.

24. Great importance must be given to the promotion and **8–002** protection of the human rights of persons belonging to groups which have been rendered vulnerable, including migrant workers, the elimination of all forms of discrimination against them, and the strengthening and making more effective the implementation of existing human rights instruments. States have an obligation to create and maintain adequate measures at the national level, in particular in the fields of education, health and social support, for the promotion and protection of the rights of persons in vulnerable sectors of their populations and to ensure the participation of those among them who are interested in finding a solution to their own problems.

Part II(B)2. Migrant workers

33. The World Conference on Human Rights urges all States to guarantee the protection of the human rights of all migrant workers and their families.

34. The World Conference on Human Rights considers that the creation of conditions to foster greater harmony and tolerance between migrant workers and the rest of the society of the State in which they reside is of particular importance.

---

[1] Namely those persons who have received or are receiving remuneration for work in a State of which they are not a national. See International Convention of the Protection of the Rights of All Migrant Workers and Members of Their Families, Article 2(1) (A/Res/45/158) below para. 8–003

35. The World Conference on Human Rights invites States to consider the possibility of signing and ratifying, at the earliest possible time, the International Convention on the Rights of All Migrant Workers and Members of Their Families.

The International Convention on the Rights of All Migrant Workers and Members of Their Families was adopted in 1990 but as yet has not entered into force.

INTERNATIONAL CONVENTION ON THE PROTECTION OF THE RIGHTS OF ALL MIGRANT WORKERS AND MEMBERS OF THEIR FAMILIES 1990[2]

Part I. Scope and definitions

Article 1

8–003   **1.** The present Convention is applicable, except as otherwise provided hereafter, to all migrant workers and members of their families without distinction of any kind such as sex, race, colour, language, religion or conviction, political or other opinion, national, ethnic or social origin, nationality, age, economic position, property, marital status, birth or other status.

2. The present Convention shall apply during the entire migration process of migrant workers and members of their families, which comprises preparation for migration, departure, transit and the entire period of stay and remunerated activity in the State of employment as well as return to the State of origin or the State of habitual residence.

Article 2

For the purposes of the present Convention:

1. The term "migrant worker" refers to a person who is to be engaged, is engaged or has been engaged in a remunerated activity in a State of which he or she is not a national.

2. (a) The term "frontier worker" refers to a migrant worker who retains his or her habitual residence in a neighbouring State to which he or she normally returns every day or at least once a week;

(b) The term "seasonal worker" refers to a migrant worker whose work by its character is dependent on seasonal conditions and is performed only during part of the year;

---

[2] A/Res/45/158 adopted December 18, 1990. Currently there have been two ratifications, Egypt and Morocco. The Convention will enter into force on receipt of the 20th ratification—see Article 87.

(c) The term "seafarer", which includes a fisherman, refers to a migrant worker employed on board a vessel registered in a State of which he or she is not a national;

(d) The term "worker on an offshore installation" refers to a migrant worker employed on an offshore installation that is under the jurisdiction of a State of which he or she is not a national;

(e) The term "itinerant worker" refers to a migrant worker who, having his or her habitual residence in one State, has to travel to another State or States for short periods, owing to the nature of his or her occupation;

(f) The term "project-tied worker" refers to a migrant worker admitted to a State of employment for a defined period to work solely on a specific project being carried out in that State by his or her employer;

(g) The term "specified-employment worker" refers to a migrant worker:

    (i) Who has been sent by his or her employer for a restricted and defined period of time to a State of employment to undertake a specific assignment or duty; or

    (ii) Who engages for a restricted and defined period of time in work that requires professional, commercial, technical or other highly specialised skill; or

    (iii) Who, upon the request of his or her employer in the State of employment, engages for a restricted and defined period of time in work whose nature is transitory or brief;

and who is required to depart from the State of employment either at the expiration of his or her authorised period of stay, or earlier if he or she no longer undertakes that specific assignment or duty or engages in that work;

(h) The term "self-employed worker" refers to a migrant worker who is engaged in a remunerated activity otherwise than under a contract of employment and who earns his or her living through this activity normally working alone or together with members of his or her family, and to any other migrant worker recognised as self-employed by applicable legislation of the State of employment or bilateral or multilateral agreements.

Article 3

8–004 The present Convention shall not apply to:

(a) Persons sent or employed by international organisations and agencies or persons sent or employed by a State outside its territory to perform official functions, whose admission and status are regulated by general international law or by specific international agreements or conventions;

(b) Persons sent or employed by a State or on its behalf outside its territory who participate in development programmes and other co-operation programmes, whose admission and status are regulated by agreement with the State of employment and who, in accordance with that agreement, are not considered migrant workers;

(c) Persons taking up residence in a State different from their State of origin as investors;

(d) Refugees and stateless persons, unless such application is provided for in the relevant national legislation of, or international instruments in force for, the State Party concerned;

(e) Students and trainees;

(f) Seafarers and workers on an offshore installation who have not been admitted to take up residence and engage in a remunerated activity in the State of employment.

Article 4

8–005 For the purposes of the present Convention the term "members of the family" refers to persons married to migrant workers or having with them a relationship that, according to applicable law, produces effects equivalent to marriage, as well as their dependent children and other dependent persons who are recognised as members of the family by applicable legislation or applicable bilateral or multilateral agreements between the States concerned.

Article 5

For the purposes of the present Convention, migrant workers and members of their families:

(a) Are considered as documented or in a regular situation if they are authorised to enter, to stay and to engage in a remunerated activity in the State of employment pursuant to the law of that State and to international agreements to which that State is a party;

(b) Are considered as non-documented or in an irregular situation if they do not comply with the conditions provided for in sub-paragraph (a) of the present article.

Article 6

For the purposes of the present Convention:

(a) The term "State of origin" means the State of which the person concerned is a national;

(b) The term "State of employment" means a State where the migrant worker is to be engaged, is engaged or has been engaged in a remunerated activity, as the case may be;

(c) The term "State of transit" means any State through which the person concerned passes on any journey to the State of employment or from the State of employment to the State of origin or the State of habitual residence.

Part II.[3] Non-discrimination with respect to rights

Article 7

States Parties undertake, in accordance with the international 8–006 instruments concerning human rights, to respect and to ensure to all migrant workers and members of their families within their territory or subject to their jurisdiction the rights provided for in the present Convention without distinction of any kind such as sex, race, colour, language, religion or conviction, political or other opinion, national, ethnic or social origin, nationality, age, economic position, property, marital status, birth or other status.

Part III. Human rights of all migrant workers and members of their families

Article 8

1. Migrant workers and members of their families shall be free to leave any State, including their State of origin. This right shall not be subject to any restrictions except those that are provided by law, are necessary to protect national security, public order (ordre public), public health or morals or the rights and freedoms of others and are consistent with the other rights recognised in the present part of the Convention.

---

[3] Many of the rights articulated in this reflect the rights and freedoms spelt out in the Universal Declaration on Human Rights and the 1966 UN Covenants, consistent with the other rights recognised in the present part of the Convention.

2. Migrant workers and members of their families shall have the right at any time to enter and remain in their State of origin.

Article 9[4]

The right to life of migrant workers and members of their families shall be protected by law.

Article 10

No migrant worker or member of his or her family shall be subjected to torture or to cruel, inhuman or degrading treatment or punishment.[5]

Article 11

8–007 **1.** No migrant worker or member of his or her family shall be held in slavery or servitude.

2. No migrant worker or member of his or her family shall be required to perform forced or compulsory labour.

3. Paragraph 2 of the present article shall not be held to preclude, in States where imprisonment with hard labour may be imposed as a punishment for a crime, the performance of hard labour in pursuance of a sentence to such punishment by a competent court.

4. For the purpose of the present article the term "forced or compulsory labour" shall not include:

(a) Any work or service not referred to in paragraph 3 of the present article normally required of a person who is under detention in consequence of a lawful order of a court or of a person during conditional release from such detention;

(b) Any service exacted in cases of emergency or calamity threatening the life or well-being of the community;

(c) Any work or service that forms part of normal civil obligations so far as it is imposed also on citizens of the State concerned.

Article 12

1. Migrant workers and members of their families shall have the right to freedom of thought, conscience and religion. This

---

[4] With respect to children see also Chapter 5.

[5] For fuller consideration on the international protection against torture see Chapter 10 on Prisoners. Note also G.A. Res. A/Res/48/110, December 20, 1993.

right shall include freedom to have or to adopt a religion or belief of their choice and freedom either individually or in community with others and in public or private to manifest their religion or belief in worship, observance, practice and teaching.

2. Migrant workers and members of their families shall not be subject to coercion that would impair their freedom to have or to adopt a religion or belief of their choice.

3. Freedom to manifest one's religion or belief may be subject only to such limitations as are prescribed by law and are necessary to protect public safety, order, health or morals or the fundamental rights and freedoms of others.

4. States Parties to the present Convention undertake to have respect for the liberty of parents, at least one of whom is a migrant worker, and, when applicable, legal guardians to ensure the religious and moral education of their children in conformity with their own convictions.

Article 13

1. Migrant workers and members of their families shall have 8–008 the right to hold opinions without interference.

2. Migrant workers and members of their families shall have the right to freedom of expression; this right shall include freedom to seek, receive and impart information and ideas of all kinds, regardless of frontiers, either orally, in writing or in print, in the form of art or through any other media of their choice.

3. The exercise of the right provided for in paragraph 2 of the present article carries with it special duties and responsibilities. It may therefore be subject to certain restrictions, but these shall only be such as are provided by law and are necessary:

(a) For respect of the rights or reputation of others;

(b) For the protection of the national security of the States concerned or of public order (ordre public) or of public health or morals;

(c) For the purpose of preventing any propaganda for war;

(d) For the purpose of preventing any advocacy of national, racial or religious hatred that constitutes incitement to discrimination, hostility or violence.

Article 14

No migrant worker or member of his or her family shall be subjected to arbitrary or unlawful interference with his or her privacy, family, home, correspondence or other communications, or to unlawful attacks on his or her honour and reputation. Each migrant worker and member of his or her family shall have the right to the protection of the law against such interference or attacks.

Article 15

No migrant worker or member of his or her family shall be arbitrarily deprived of property, whether owned individually or in association with others. Where, under the legislation in force in the State of employment, the assets of a migrant worker or a member of his or her family are expropriated in whole or in part, the person concerned shall have the right to fair and adequate compensation.

Article 16

8–009 **1.** Migrant workers and members of their families shall have the right to liberty and security of person.

2. Migrant workers and members of their families shall be entitled to effective protection by the State against violence, physical injury, threats and intimidation, whether by public officials or by private individuals, groups or institutions.

3. Any verification by law enforcement officials of the identity of migrant workers or members of their families shall be carried out in accordance with procedures established by law.

4. Migrant workers and members of their families shall not be subjected individually or collectively to arbitrary arrest or detention; they shall not be deprived of their liberty except on such grounds and in accordance with such procedures as are established by law.

5. Migrant workers and members of their families who are arrested shall be informed at the time of arrest as far as possible in a language they understand of the reasons for their arrest and they shall be promptly informed in a language they understand of any charges against them.

6. Migrant workers and members of their families who are arrested or detained on a criminal charge shall be brought promptly before a judge or other officer authorised by law to exercise judicial power and shall be entitled to trial within a reasonable time or to release. It shall not be the general rule that while awaiting trial they shall be detained in custody, but release may be subject to guarantees to appear for trial, at any other stage of the judicial proceedings and, should the occasion arise, for the execution of the judgment.

7. When a migrant worker or a member of his or her family is arrested or committed to prison or custody pending trial or is detained in any other manner:

(a) The consular or diplomatic authorities of his or her State of origin or of a State representing the interests of that State shall, if he or she so requests, be informed without delay of his or her arrest or detention and of the reasons therefor;

(b) The person concerned shall have the right to communicate with the said authorities. Any communication by the person concerned to the said authorities shall be forwarded without delay, and he or she shall also have the right to receive communications sent by the said authorities without delay;

(c) The person concerned shall be informed without delay of this right and of rights deriving from relevant treaties, if any, applicable between the States concerned, to correspond and to meet with representatives of the said authorities and to make arrangements with them for his or her legal representation.

8. Migrant workers and members of their families who are deprived of their liberty by arrest or detention shall be entitled to take proceedings before a court, in order that the court may decide without delay on the lawfulness of their detention and order their release if the detention is not lawful. When they attend such proceedings, they shall have the assistance, if necessary without cost to them, of an interpreter, if they cannot understand or speak the language used.

9. Migrant workers and members of their families who have been victims of unlawful arrest or detention shall have an enforceable right to compensation.

Article 17

1. Migrant workers and members of their families who are 8–010 deprived of their liberty shall be treated with humanity and with respect for the inherent dignity of the human person and for their cultural identity.

2. Accused migrant workers and members of their families shall, save in exceptional circumstances, be separated from convicted persons and shall be subject to separate treatment appropriate to their status as unconvicted persons. Accused juvenile persons shall be separated from adults and brought as speedily as possible for adjudication.[6]

3. Any migrant worker or member of his or her family who is detained in a State of transit or in a State of employment for violation of provisions relating to migration, shall be held, in so

---

[6] See "Juveniles" in Chapter 10, para 10–100.

far as practicable, separately from convicted persons or persons detained pending trial.

4. During any period of imprisonment in pursuance of a sentence imposed by a court of law, the essential aim of the treatment of a migrant worker or a member of his or her family shall be his or her reformation and social rehabilitation. Juvenile offenders shall be separated from adults and be accorded treatment appropriate to their age and legal status.

5. During detention or imprisonment, migrant workers and members of their families shall enjoy the same rights as nationals to visits by members of their families.

6. Whenever a migrant worker is deprived of his or her liberty, the competent authorities of the State concerned shall pay attention to the problems that may be posed for members of his or her family, in particular for spouses and minor children.

7. Migrant workers and members of their families who are subjected to any form of detention or imprisonment in accordance with the law in force in the State of employment or in the State of transit shall enjoy the same rights as nationals of those States who are in the same situation.

8. If a migrant worker or a member of his or her family is detained for the purpose of verifying any infraction of provisions related to migration, he or she shall not bear any costs arising therefrom.

Article 18

8–011   **1.** Migrant workers and members of their families shall have the right to equality with nationals of the State concerned before the courts and tribunals. In the determination of any criminal charge against them or of their rights and obligations in a suit of law, they shall be entitled to a fair and public hearing by a competent, independent and impartial tribunal established by law.

2. Migrant workers and members of their families who are charged with a criminal offence shall have the right to be presumed innocent until proven guilty according to law.

3. In the determination of any criminal charge against them, migrant workers and members of their families shall be entitled to the following minimum guarantees:

(a) To be informed promptly and in detail in a language they understand of the nature and cause of the charge against them;

(b) To have adequate time and facilities for the preparation of their defence and to communicate with counsel of their own choosing;

(c) To be tried without undue delay;

(d) To be tried in their presence and to defend themselves in person or through legal assistance of their own choosing; to be informed, if they do not have legal assistance, of this right; and to have legal assistance assigned to them, in any case where the interests of justice so require and without payment by them in any such case if they do not have sufficient means to pay;

(e) To examine or have examined the witnesses against them and to obtain the attendance and examination of witnesses on their behalf under the same conditions as witnesses against them;

(f) To have the free assistance of an interpreter if they cannot understand or speak the language used in court;

(g) Not to be compelled to testify against themselves or to confess guilt.

4. In the case of juvenile persons, the procedure shall be such as will take account of their age and the desirability of promoting their rehabilitation.

5. Migrant workers and members of their families convicted of a crime shall have the right to their conviction and sentence being reviewed by a higher tribunal according to law.

6. When a migrant worker or a member of his or her family has, by a final decision, been convicted of a criminal offence and when subsequently his or her conviction has been reversed or he or she has been pardoned on the ground that a new or newly discovered fact shows conclusively that there has been a miscarriage of justice, the person who has suffered punishment as a result of such conviction shall be compensated according to law, unless it is proved that the non-disclosure of the unknown fact in time is wholly or partly attributable to that person.

7. No migrant worker or member of his or her family shall be liable to be tried or punished again for an offence for which he or she has already been finally convicted or acquitted in accordance with the law and penal procedure of the State concerned.

Article 19

1. No migrant worker or member of his or her family shall be **8–012** held guilty of any criminal offence on account of any act or omission that did not constitute a criminal offence under national or international law at the time when the criminal offence was committed, nor shall a heavier penalty be imposed than the one that was applicable at the time when it was committed. If, subsequent to the commission of the offence, provision is made by law for the imposition of a lighter penalty, he or she shall benefit thereby.

2. Humanitarian considerations related to the status of a migrant worker, in particular with respect to his or her right of residence or work, should be taken into account in imposing a sentence for a criminal offence committed by a migrant worker or a member of his or her family.

Article 20

1. No migrant worker or member of his or her family shall be imprisoned merely on the ground of failure to fulfil a contractual obligation.

2. No migrant worker or member of his or her family shall be deprived of his or her authorisation of residence or work permit or expelled merely on the ground of failure to fulfil an obligation arising out of a work contract unless fulfilment of that obligation constitutes a condition for such authorisation or permit.

Article 21

8–013   It shall be unlawful for anyone, other than a public official duly authorised by law, to confiscate, destroy or attempt to destroy identity documents, documents authorising entry to or stay, residence or establishment in the national territory or work permits. No authorised confiscation of such documents shall take place without delivery of a detailed receipt. In no case shall it be permitted to destroy the passport or equivalent document of a migrant worker or a member of his or her family.

Article 22

1. Migrant workers and members of their families shall not be subject to measures of collective expulsion. Each case of expulsion shall be examined and decided individually.

2. Migrant workers and members of their families may be expelled from the territory of a State Party only in pursuance of a decision taken by the competent authority in accordance with law.

3. The decision shall be communicated to them in a language they understand. Upon their request where not otherwise mandatory, the decision shall be communicated to them in writing and, save in exceptional circumstances on account of national security, the reasons for the decision likewise stated. The persons concerned shall be informed of these rights before or at the latest at the time the decision is rendered.

4. Except where a final decision is pronounced by a judicial authority, the person concerned shall have the right to submit the reason he or she should not be expelled and to have his or her case reviewed by the competent authority, unless compelling reasons of national security require otherwise. Pending such review, the person concerned shall have the right to seek a stay of the decision of expulsion.

5. If a decision of expulsion that has already been executed is subsequently annulled, the person concerned shall have the right to seek compensation according to law and the earlier decision shall not be used to prevent him or her from re-entering the State concerned.

6. In case of expulsion, the person concerned shall have a reasonable opportunity before or after departure to settle any claims for wages and other entitlements due to him or her and any pending liabilities.

7. Without prejudice to the execution of a decision of expulsion, a migrant worker or a member of his or her family who is subject to such a decision may seek entry into a State other than his or her State of origin.

8. In case of expulsion of a migrant worker or a member of his or her family the costs of expulsion shall not be borne by him or her. The person concerned may be required to pay his or her own travel costs.

9. Expulsion from the State of employment shall not in itself prejudice any rights of a migrant worker or a member of his or her family acquired in accordance with the law of that State, including the right to receive wages and other entitlements due to him or her.

Article 23

Migrant workers and members of their families shall have the **8–014** right to have recourse to the protection and assistance of the consular or diplomatic authorities of their State of origin or of a State representing the interests of that State whenever the rights recognised in the present Convention are impaired. In particular, in case of expulsion, the person concerned shall be informed of this right without delay and the authorities of the expelling State shall facilitate the exercise of such right.

Article 24

Every migrant worker and every member of his or her family shall have the right to recognition everywhere as a person before the law.

Article 25

1. Migrant workers shall enjoy treatment not less favourable than that which applies to nationals of the State of employment in respect of remuneration and:

  (a) Other conditions of work, that is to say, overtime, hours of work, weekly rest, holidays with pay, safety, health, termination of the employment relationship and any other conditions of work which, according to national law and practice, are covered by this term;

  (b) Other terms of employment, that is to say, minimum age of employment, restriction on home work and any other matters which, according to national law and practice, are considered a term of employment.

2. It shall not be lawful to derogate in private contracts of employment from the principle of equality of treatment referred to in paragraph 1 of the present article.

3. States Parties shall take all appropriate measures to ensure that migrant workers are not deprived of any rights derived from this principle by reason of any irregularity in their stay or employment. In particular, employers shall not be relieved of any legal or contractual obligations, nor shall their obligations be limited in any manner by reason of any such irregularity.

Article 26

8–015　　**1.** States Parties recognise the right of migrant workers and members of their families:

  (a) To take part in meetings and activities of trade unions and of any other associations established in accordance with law, with a view to protecting their economic, social, cultural and other interests, subject only to the rules of the organisation concerned;

  (b) To join freely any trade union and any such association as aforesaid, subject only to the rules of the organisation concerned;

  (c) To seek the aid and assistance of any trade union and of any such association as aforesaid.

2. No restrictions may be placed on the exercise of these rights other than those that are prescribed by law and which are necessary in a democratic society in the interests of national security, public order (ordre public) or the protection of the rights and freedoms of others.

Article 27

1. With respect to social security, migrant workers and members of their families shall enjoy in the State of employment the same treatment granted to nationals in so far as they fulfil the requirements provided for by the applicable legislation of that State and the applicable bilateral and multilateral treaties. The competent authorities of the State of origin and the State of employment can at any time establish the necessary arrangements to determine the modalities of application of this norm.

2. Where the applicable legislation does not allow migrant workers and members of their families a benefit, the States concerned shall examine the possibility of reimbursing interested persons the amount of contributions made by them with respect to that benefit on the basis of the treatment granted to nationals who are in similar circumstances.

Article 28

Migrant workers and members of their families shall have the 8–016 right to receive any medical care that is urgently required for the preservation of their life or the avoidance of irreparable harm to their health on the basis of equality of treatment with nationals of the State concerned. Such emergency medical care shall not be refused them by reason of any irregularity with regard to stay or employment.

Article 29

Each child of a migrant worker shall have the right to a name, to registration of birth and to a nationality.

Article 30

Each child of a migrant worker shall have the basic right of access to education on the basis of equality of treatment with nationals of the State concerned. Access to public pre-school educational institutions or schools shall not be refused or limited by reason of the irregular situation with respect to stay or employment of either parent or by reason of the irregularity of the child's stay in the State of employment.

Article 31

1. States Parties shall ensure respect for the cultural identity of migrant workers and members of their families and shall not prevent them from maintaining their cultural links with their State of origin.

2. States Parties may take appropriate measures to assist and encourage efforts in this respect.

Article 32

Upon the termination of their stay in the State of employment, migrant workers and members of their families shall have the right to transfer their earnings and savings and, in accordance with the applicable legislation of the States concerned, their personal effects and belongings.

Article 33

8–017   **1.** Migrant workers and members of their families shall have the right to be informed by the State of origin, the State of employment or the State of transit as the case may be concerning:

(a) Their rights arising out of the present Convention;

(b) The conditions of their admission, their rights and obligations under the law and practice of the State concerned and such other matters as will enable them to comply with administrative or other formalities in that State.

2. States Parties shall take all measures they deem appropriate to disseminate the said information or to ensure that it is provided by employers, trade unions or other appropriate bodies or institutions. As appropriate, they shall co-operate with other States concerned.

3. Such adequate information shall be provided upon request to migrant workers and members of their families, free of charge, and, as far as possible, in a language they are able to understand.

Article 34

Nothing in the present part of the Convention shall have the effect of relieving migrant workers and the members of their families from either the obligation to comply with the laws and regulations of any State of transit and the State of employment or the obligation to respect the cultural identity of the inhabitants of such States.

Article 35

Nothing in the present part of the Convention shall be interpreted as implying the regularisation of the situation of migrant workers or members of their families who are non-documented or in an irregular situation or any right to such regularisation of their situation, nor shall it prejudice the measures intended to ensure sound and equitable conditions for international migration as provided in part VI of the present Convention.

Part IV. Other rights of migrant workers and members of their families who are documented or in a regular situation

Article 36

Migrant workers and members of their families who are documented or in a regular situation in the State of employment shall enjoy the rights set forth in the present part of the Convention in addition to those set forth in Part III.

Article 37

Before their departure, or at the latest at the time of their 8–018 admission to the State of employment, migrant workers and members of their families shall have the right to be fully informed by the State of origin or the State of employment, as appropriate, of all conditions applicable to their admission and particularly those concerning their stay and the remunerated activities in which they may engage as well as of the requirements they must satisfy in the State of employment and the authority to which they must address themselves for any modification of those conditions.

Article 38

1. States of employment shall make every effort to authorise migrant workers and members of their families to be temporarily absent without effect upon their authorisation to stay or to work, as the case may be. In doing so, States of employment shall take into account the special needs and obligations of migrant workers and members of their families, in particular in their States of origin.
2. Migrant workers and members of their families shall have the right to be fully informed of the terms on which such temporary absences are authorised.

Article 39

1. Migrant workers and members of their families shall have the right to liberty of movement in the territory of the State of employment and freedom to choose their residence there.
2. The rights mentioned in paragraph 1 of the present article shall not be subject to any restrictions except those that are

provided by law, are necessary to protect national security, public order (ordre public), public health or morals, or the rights and freedoms of others and are consistent with the other rights recognised in the present Convention.

Article 40

1. Migrant workers and members of their families shall have the right to form associations and trade unions in the State of employment for the promotion and protection of their economic, social, cultural and other interests.

2. No restrictions may be placed on the exercise of this right other than those that are prescribed by law and are necessary in a democratic society in the interests of national security, public order (ordre public) or the protection of the rights and freedoms of others.

Article 41

8–019 **1.** Migrant workers and members of their families shall have the right to participate in public affairs of their State of origin and to vote and to be elected at elections of that State, in accordance with its legislation.

2. The States concerned shall, as appropriate and in accordance with their legislation, facilitate the exercise of these rights.

Article 42

1. States Parties shall consider the establishment of procedures or institutions through which account may be taken, both in States of origin and in States of employment, of special needs, aspirations and obligations of migrant workers and members of their families and shall envisage, as appropriate, the possibility for migrant workers and members of their families to have their freely chosen representatives in those institutions.

2. States of employment shall facilitate, in accordance with their national legislation, the consultation or participation of migrant workers and members of their families in decisions concerning the life and administration of local communities.

3. Migrant workers may enjoy political rights in the State of employment if that State, in the exercise of its sovereignty, grants them such rights.

Article 43

1. Migrant workers shall enjoy equality of treatment with nationals of the State of employment in relation to:

(a) Access to educational institutions and services subject to the admission requirements and other regulations of the institutions and services concerned;

(b) Access to vocational guidance and placement services;

(c) Access to vocational training and retraining facilities and institutions;

(d) Access to housing, including social housing schemes, and protection against exploitation in respect of rents;

(e) Access to social and health services, provided that the requirements for participation in the respective schemes are met;

(f) Access to co-operatives and self-managed enterprises, which shall not imply a change of their migration status and shall be subject to the rules and regulations of the bodies concerned;

(g) Access to and participation in cultural life.

2. States Parties shall promote conditions to ensure effective 8–020 equality of treatment to enable migrant workers to enjoy the rights mentioned in paragraph 1 of the present article whenever the terms of their stay, as authorised by the State of employment, meet the appropriate requirements.

3. States of employment shall not prevent an employer of migrant workers from establishing housing or social or cultural facilities for them. Subject to Article 70 of the present Convention, a State of employment may make the establishment of such facilities subject to the requirements generally applied in that State concerning their installation.

Article 44

1. States Parties, recognising that the family is the natural and fundamental group unit of society and is entitled to protection by society and the State, shall take appropriate measures to ensure the protection of the unity of the families of migrant workers.

2. States Parties shall take measures that they deem appropriate and that fall within their competence to facilitate the reunification of migrant workers with their spouses or persons who have with the migrant worker a relationship that, according to applicable law, produces effects equivalent to marriage, as well as with their minor dependent unmarried children.

3. States of employment, on humanitarian grounds, shall favourably consider granting equal treatment, as set forth in paragraph 2 of the present article, to other family members of migrant workers.

Article 45

1. Members of the families of migrant workers shall, in the State of employment, enjoy equality of treatment with nationals of that State in relation to:

(a) Access to educational institutions and services, subject to the admission requirements and other regulations of the institutions and services concerned;

(b) Access to vocational guidance and training institutions and services, provided that requirements for participation are met;

(c) Access to social and health services, provided that requirements for participation in the respective schemes are met;

(d) Access to and participation in cultural life.

2. States of employment shall pursue a policy, where appropriate in collaboration with the States of origin, aimed at facilitating the integration of children of migrant workers in the local school system, particularly in respect of teaching them the local language.

3. States of employment shall endeavour to facilitate for the children of migrant workers the teaching of their mother tongue and culture and, in this regard, States of origin shall collaborate whenever appropriate.

4. States of employment may provide special schemes of education in the mother tongue of children of migrant workers, if necessary in collaboration with the States of origin.

Article 46

8–021 Migrant workers and members of their families shall, subject to the applicable legislation of the States concerned, as well as relevant international agreements and the obligations of the States concerned arising out of their participation in customs unions, enjoy exemption from import and export duties and taxes in respect of their personal and household effects as well as the equipment necessary to engage in the remunerated activity for which they were admitted to the State of employment:

(a) Upon departure from the State of origin or State of habitual residence;

(b) Upon initial admission to the State of employment;

(c) Upon final departure from the State of employment;

(d) Upon final return to the State of origin or State of habitual residence.

Article 47

1. Migrant workers shall have the right to transfer their earnings and savings, in particular those funds necessary for the support of their families, from the State of employment to their State of origin or any other State. Such transfers shall be made in conformity with procedures established by applicable legislation of the State concerned and in conformity with applicable international agreements.

2. States concerned shall take appropriate measures to facilitate such transfers.

Article 48

1. Without prejudice to applicable double taxation agreements, 8–022 migrant workers and members of their families shall, in the matter of earnings in the State of employment:

(a) Not be liable to taxes, duties or charges of any description higher or more onerous than those imposed on nationals in similar circumstances;

(b) Be entitled to deductions or exemptions from taxes of any description and to any tax allowances applicable to nationals in similar circumstances, including tax allowances for dependent members of their families.

2. States Parties shall endeavour to adopt appropriate measures to avoid double taxation of the earnings and savings of migrant workers and members of their families.

Article 49

1. Where separate authorisations to reside and to engage in employment are required by national legislation, the States of employment shall issue to migrant workers authorisation of residence for at least the same period of time as their authorisation to engage in remunerated activity.

2. Migrant workers who in the State of employment are allowed freely to choose their remunerated activity shall neither be regarded as in an irregular situation nor shall they lose their authorisation of residence by the mere fact of the termination of their remunerated activity prior to the expiration of their work permits or similar authorisations.

3. In order to allow migrant workers referred to in paragraph 2 of the present article sufficient time to find alternative remunerated activities, the authorisation of residence shall not be withdrawn at least for a period corresponding to that during which they may be entitled to unemployment benefits.

Article 50

1. In the case of death of a migrant worker or dissolution of marriage, the State of employment shall favourably consider granting family members of that migrant worker residing in that State on the basis of family reunion an authorisation to stay; the State of employment shall take into account the length of time they have already resided in that State.

2. Members of the family to whom such authorisation is not granted shall be allowed before departure a reasonable period of time in order to enable them to settle their affairs in the State of employment.

3. The provisions of paragraphs 1 and 2 of the present article may not be interpreted as adversely affecting any right to stay and work otherwise granted to such family members by the legislation of the State of employment or by bilateral and multi-lateral treaties applicable to that State.

Article 51

8–023 Migrant workers who in the State of employment are not permitted freely to choose their remunerated activity shall neither be regarded as in an irregular situation nor shall they lose their authorisation of residence by the mere fact of the termination of their remunerated activity prior to the expiration of their work permit, except where the authorisation of residence is expressly dependent upon the specific remunerated activity for which they were admitted. Such migrant workers shall have the right to seek alternative employment, participation in public work schemes and retraining during the remaining period of their authorisation to work, subject to such conditions and limitations as are specified in the authorisation to work.

Article 52

1. Migrant workers in the State of employment shall have the right freely to choose their remunerated activity, subject to the following restrictions or conditions.

2. For any migrant worker a State of employment may:

(a) Restrict access to limited categories of employment, functions, services or activities where this is necessary in the interests of this State and provided for by national legislation;

(b) Restrict free choice of remunerated activity in accordance with its legislation concerning recognition of occupational qualifications acquired outside its territory. However, States

Parties concerned shall endeavour to provide for recognition of such qualifications.

3. For migrant workers whose permission to work is limited in time, a State of employment may also:

(a) Make the right freely to choose their remunerated activities subject to the condition that the migrant worker has resided lawfully in its territory for the purpose of remunerated activity for a period of time prescribed in its national legislation that should not exceed two years;

(b) Limit access by a migrant worker to remunerated activities in pursuance of a policy of granting priority to its nationals or to persons who are assimilated to them for these purposes by virtue of legislation or bilateral or multilateral agreements. Any such limitation shall cease to apply to a migrant worker who has resided lawfully in its territory for the purpose of remunerated activity for a period of time prescribed in its national legislation that should not exceed five years.

4. States of employment shall prescribe the conditions under which a migrant worker who has been admitted to take up employment may be authorised to engage in work on his or her own account. Account shall be taken of the period during which the worker has already been lawfully in the State of employment.

Article 53

1. Members of a migrant worker's family who have themselves 8–024 an authorisation of residence or admission that is without limit of time or is automatically renewable shall be permitted freely to choose their remunerated activity under the same conditions as are applicable to the said migrant worker in accordance with Article 52 of the present Convention.

2. With respect to members of a migrant worker's family who are not permitted freely to choose their remunerated activity, States Parties shall consider favourably granting them priority in obtaining permission to engage in a remunerated activity over other workers who seek admission to the State of employment, subject to applicable bilateral and multilateral agreements.

Article 54

1. Without prejudice to the terms of their authorisation of residence or their permission to work and the rights provided for in Articles 25 and 27 of the present Convention, migrant workers

shall enjoy equality of treatment with nationals of the State of employment in respect of:

(a) Protection against dismissal;

(b) Unemployment benefits;

(c) Access to public work schemes intended to combat unemployment;

(d) Access to alternative employment in the event of loss of work or termination of other remunerated activity, subject to Article 52 of the present Convention.

8–025   2. If a migrant worker claims that the terms of his or her work contract have been violated by his or her employer, he or she shall have the right to address his or her case to the competent authorities of the State of employment, on terms provided for in Article 18, paragraph 1, of the present Convention.

Article 55

Migrant workers who have been granted permission to engage in a remunerated activity, subject to the conditions attached to such permission, shall be entitled to equality of treatment with nationals of the State of employment in the exercise of that remunerated activity.

Article 56

1. Migrant workers and members of their families referred to in the present part of the Convention may not be expelled from a State of employment, except for reasons defined in the national legislation of that State, and subject to the safeguards established in Part III.

2. Expulsion shall not be resorted to for the purpose of depriving a migrant worker or a member of his or her family of the rights arising out of the authorisation of residence and the work permit.

3. In considering whether to expel a migrant worker or a member of his or her family, account should be taken of humanitarian considerations and of the length of time that the person concerned has already resided in the State of employment.

Part V. Provisions applicable to particular categories of migrant workers and members of their families

Article 57

The particular categories of migrant workers and members of their families specified in the present part of the Convention who are documented or in a regular situation shall enjoy the rights set forth in Part III and, except as modified below, the rights set forth in Part IV.

Article 58

1. Frontier workers, as defined in Article 2, paragraph 2 (a), of the present Convention, shall be entitled to the rights provided for in Part IV that can be applied to them by reason of their presence and work in the territory of the State of employment, taking into account that they do not have their habitual residence in that State.

8–026

2. States of employment shall consider favourably granting frontier workers the right freely to choose their remunerated activity after a specified period of time. The granting of that right shall not affect their status as frontier workers.

Article 59

1. Seasonal workers, as defined in Article 2, paragraph 2 (b), of the present Convention, shall be entitled to the rights provided for in Part IV that can be applied to them by reason of their presence and work in the territory of the State of employment and that are compatible with their status in that State as seasonal workers, taking into account the fact that they are present in that State for only part of the year.

2. The State of employment shall, subject to paragraph 1 of the present article, consider granting seasonal workers who have been employed in its territory for a significant period of time the possibility of taking up other remunerated activities and giving them priority over other workers who seek admission to that State, subject to applicable bilateral and multilateral agreements.

Article 60

Itinerant workers, as defined in Article 2, paragraph 2 (e), of the present Convention, shall be entitled to the rights provided for in Part IV that can be granted to them by reason of their presence and work in the territory of the State of employment and that are compatible with their status as itinerant workers in that State.

Article 61

1. Project-tied workers, as defined in Article 2, paragraph 2 (f), of the present Convention, and members of their families shall be entitled to the rights provided for in Part IV except the provisions of Article 43, paragraphs 1 (b) and (c), Article 43, paragraph 1 (d),

as it pertains to social housing schemes, Article 45, paragraph 1 (b), and Articles 52 to 55.

2. If a project-tied worker claims that the terms of his or her work contract have been violated by his or her employer, he or she shall have the right to address his or her case to the competent authorities of the State which has jurisdiction over that employer, on terms provided for in Article 18, paragraph 1, of the present Convention.

3. Subject to bilateral or multilateral agreements in force for them, the States Parties concerned shall endeavour to enable project-tied workers to remain adequately protected by the social security systems of their States of origin or habitual residence during their engagement in the project. States Parties concerned shall take appropriate measures with the aim of avoiding any denial of rights or duplication of payments in this respect.

4. Without prejudice to the provisions of Article 47 of the present Convention and to relevant bilateral or multilateral agreements, States Parties concerned shall permit payment of the earnings of project-tied workers in their State of origin or habitual residence.

Article 62

8–027   **1.** Specified-employment workers as defined in Article 2, paragraph 2(g), of the present Convention, shall be entitled to the rights provided for in Part IV, except the provisions of Article 43, paragraphs 1(b) and (c), Article 43, paragraph 1(d), as it pertains to social housing schemes, Article 52, and Article 54, paragraph 1(d).

2. Members of the families of specified-employment workers shall be entitled to the rights relating to family members of migrant workers provided for in Part IV of the present Convention, except the provisions of Article 53.

Article 63

1. Self-employed workers, as defined in Article 2, paragraph 2(h), of the present Convention, shall be entitled to the rights provided for in Part IV with the exception of those rights which are exclusively applicable to workers having a contract of employment.

2. Without prejudice to Articles 52 and 79 of the present Convention, the termination of the economic activity of the self-employed workers shall not in itself imply the withdrawal of the authorisation for them or for the members of their families to stay or to engage in a remunerated activity in the State of employment except where the authorisation of residence is expressly dependent upon the specific remunerated activity for which they were admitted.

Part VI. Promotion of sound, equitable, humane and lawful conditions in connection with international migration of workers and members of their families

Article 64

1. Without prejudice to Article 79 of the present Convention, 8–028 the States Parties concerned shall as appropriate consult and co-operate with a view to promoting sound, equitable and humane conditions in connection with international migration of workers and members of their families.

2. In this respect, due regard shall be paid not only to labour needs and resources, but also to the social, economic, cultural and other needs of migrant workers and members of their families involved, as well as to the consequences of such migration for the communities concerned.

Article 65

1. States Parties shall maintain appropriate services to deal with questions concerning international migration of workers and members of their families. Their functions shall include, *inter alia*:

  (a) The formulation and implementation of policies regarding such migration;

  (b) An exchange of information, consultation and co-operation with the competent authorities of other States Parties involved in such migration;

  (c) The provision of appropriate information, particularly to employers, workers and their organisations on policies, laws and regulations relating to migration and employment, on agreements concluded with other States concerning migration and on other relevant matters;

  (d) The provision of information and appropriate assistance to migrant workers and members of their families regarding requisite authorisations and formalities and arrangements for departure, travel, arrival, stay, remunerated activities, exit and return, as well as on conditions of work and life in the State of employment and on customs, currency, tax and other relevant laws and regulations.

2. States Parties shall facilitate as appropriate the provision of adequate consular and other services that are necessary to meet

the social, cultural and other needs of migrant workers and members of their families.

Article 66

8–029   1. Subject to paragraph 2 of the present article, the right to undertake operations with a view to the recruitment of workers for employment in another State shall be restricted to:

(a) Public services or bodies of the State in which such operations take place;

(b) Public services or bodies of the State of employment on the basis of agreement between the States concerned;

(c) A body established by virtue of a bilateral or multilateral agreement.

2. Subject to any authorisation, approval and supervision by the public authorities of the States Parties concerned as may be established pursuant to the legislation and practice of those States, agencies, prospective employers or persons acting on their behalf may also be permitted to undertake the said operations.

Article 67

1. States Parties concerned shall co-operate as appropriate in the adoption of measures regarding the orderly return of migrant workers and members of their families to the State of origin when they decide to return or their authorisation of residence or employment expires or when they are in the State of employment in an irregular situation.

2. Concerning migrant workers and members of their families in a regular situation, States Parties concerned shall co-operate as appropriate, on terms agreed upon by those States, with a view to promoting adequate economic conditions for their resettlement and to facilitating their durable social and cultural reintegration in the State of origin.

Article 68

1. States Parties, including States of transit, shall collaborate with a view to preventing and eliminating illegal or clandestine movements and employment of migrant workers in an irregular situation. The measures to be taken to this end within the jurisdiction of each State concerned shall include:

(a) Appropriate measures against the dissemination of misleading information relating to emigration and immigration;

(b) Measures to detect and eradicate illegal or clandestine movements of migrant workers and members of their families and to impose effective sanctions on persons, groups or entities which organise, operate or assist in organising or operating such movements;

(c) Measures to impose effective sanctions on persons, groups or entities which use violence, threats or intimidation against migrant workers or members of their families in an irregular situation.

2. States of employment shall take all adequate and effective measures to eliminate employment in their territory of migrant workers in an irregular situation, including, whenever appropriate, sanctions on employers of such workers. The rights of migrant workers *vis-à-vis* their employer arising from employment shall not be impaired by these measures.

Article 69

1. States Parties shall, when there are migrant workers and 8–030 members of their families within their territory in an irregular situation, take appropriate measures to ensure that such a situation does not persist.

2. Whenever States Parties concerned consider the possibility of regularising the situation of such persons in accordance with applicable national legislation and bilateral or multilateral agreements, appropriate account shall be taken of the circumstances of their entry, the duration of their stay in the States of employment and other relevant considerations, in particular those relating to their family situation.

Article 70

States Parties shall take measures not less favourable than those applied to nationals to ensure that working and living conditions of migrant workers and members of their families in a regular situation are in keeping with the standards of fitness, safety, health and principles of human dignity.

Article 71

1. States Parties shall facilitate, whenever necessary, the repatriation to the State of origin of the bodies of deceased migrant workers or members of their families.

2. As regards compensation matters relating to the death of a migrant worker or a member of his or her family, States Parties shall, as appropriate, provide assistance to the persons concerned with a view to the prompt settlement of such matters. Settlement of these matters shall be carried out on the basis of applicable national law in accordance with the provisions of the present Convention and any relevant bilateral or multilateral agreements.

Note: The Convention consists of 94 Articles: Part VII Articles 72–78 (Application of the Convention) Part VIII Articles 79–84 (General Provisions), Part IX Articles 85–93 (Final Provisions).

In addition to the UN Convention a number of other international instruments focus on the rights of migrant workers and their families. The most notable being the instruments concluded under the auspices of the International Labour Organisation.

INTERNATIONAL LABOUR ORGANISATION[7]

Preamble

8–031 WHEREAS universal and lasting peace can be established only if it is based upon social justice; And whereas conditions of labour exist involving such injustice, hardship, and privation to large numbers of people as to produce unrest so great that the peace and harmony of the world are imperilled; and an improvement of these conditions is urgently required: as, for example, by . . . protection of the interests of workers employed in countries other than their own . . .

INTERNATIONAL LABOUR CONFERENCE CONVENTION (No. 97) CONCERNING MIGRATION FOR EMPLOYMENT (REVISED 1949)[8]

Article 1

Each Member of the International Labour Organisation for which this Convention is in force undertakes to make available on

---

[7] The International Labour Organisation (ILO) was founded in 1919 under the Treaty of Versailles as an autonomous institution associated with the League of Nations. An agreement establishing the relationship between the ILO and the United Nations was approved on December 14, 1946 thus becoming the first specialised agency of the UN. For a recent text of the ILO Constitution see I. Brownlie, *Basic Documents in International Law*, (4th ed.), Oxford University Press, pp. 50–76. There are currently 171 members. One of the functions of the ILO is to produce conventions and recommendations setting norms of labour standards.

[8] Adopted July 1, 1949 by the ILO revising an earlier Convention of the same name adopted in 1939. This was supplemented by Recommendation (No. 86) Concerning Migration for Employment which is likewise a revised version of 1939 Recommendation. Article 19 of the Constitution of the ILO states:

1. . . . it will rest with the Conference to determine whether these proposals should take the form of: (a) an international Convention, or (b) a Recommendation to meet circumstances where the subject, of aspect of it, dealt with is not considered suitable or appropriate at that time for a Convention . . .

5. In the case of a Convention—(a) the Convention will be communicated to all Members for ratification.

6. In the case of a Recommendation—(a) the Recommendation will be communicated to all Members for their consideration with a view to effect being given to it by national

request to the International Labour Office and to other Members—

(a) information on national policies, laws and regulations relating to emigration and immigration;

(b) information on special provisions concerning migration for employment and the conditions of work and livelihood of migrants for employment;

(c) information concerning general agreements and special arrangements on these questions concluded by the Member.

Article 2

Each Member for which this Convention is in force undertakes to 8–032 maintain, or satisfy itself that there is maintained, an adequate and free service to assist migrants for employment, and in particular to provide them with accurate information.

Article 3

1. Each Member for which this Convention is in force undertakes that it will, so far as national laws and regulations permit take all appropriate steps against misleading propaganda relating to emigration and immigration.

2. For this purpose it will where appropriate act in co-operation with other Members concerned.

Article 4

Measures shall be taken as appropriate by each Member, within its jurisdiction, to facilitate the departure, journey and reception of migrants for employment.

Article 5

Each Member for which this Convention is in force undertakes to maintain, within its jurisdiction, appropriate medical services responsible for—

(a) ascertaining, where necessary, both at the time of departure and on arrival, that migrants for employment and the members of their families authorised to accompany or join them are in reasonable health;

legislation or otherwise. There are currently 40 ratifications to the Convention.

(b) ensuring that migrants for employment and members of their families enjoy adequate medical attention and good hygienic conditions at the time of departure, during the journey and on arrival in the territory of destination.

Article 6

8–033   1. Each Member for which this Convention is in force undertakes to apply, without discrimination in respect of nationality, race, religion or sex, to immigrants lawfully within its territory, treatment no less favourable than that which it applies to its own nationals in respect of the following matters:

(a) in so far as such matters are regulated by law or regulations, or as subject to the control of administrative authorities—

   (i) remuneration, including family allowances where these form part of remuneration, hours of work, overtime arrangements, holidays with pay, restrictions on home work, minimum age for employment, apprenticeship and training, women's work and the work of young persons;
   (ii) membership of trade unions and enjoyment of the benefits of collective bargaining;
   (iii) accommodation;

(b) social security (that is to say, legal provision in respect of employment injury, maternity, sickness, invalidity, old age, death, unemployment and family responsibilities, and any other contingency which, according to national laws or regulations, is covered by a social security scheme), subject to the following limitations:

   (i) there may be appropriate arrangements for the maintenance of acquired rights and rights in course of acquisition;
   (ii) national laws or regulations of immigration countries may prescribe special arrangements concerning benefits or portions of benefits which are payable wholly out of public funds, and concerning allowances paid to persons who do not fulfil the contribution conditions prescribed for the award of a normal pension;

(c) employment taxes, dues or contributions payable in respect of the person employed; and

(d) legal proceedings relating to the matters referred to in this Convention.

2. In the case of a federal State the provisions of this Article shall apply in so far as the matters dealt with are regulated by

federal law or regulations or are subject to the control of federal administrative authorities. The extent to which and manner in which these provisions shall be applied in respect of matters regulated by the law or regulations of the constituent States, provinces or cantons, or subject to the control of the administrative authorities thereof, shall be determined by each Member. The Member shall indicate in its annual report upon the application of the Convention the extent to which the matters dealt with in this Article are regulated by federal law or regulations or are subject to the control of federal administrative authorities. In respect of matters which are regulated by the law or regulations of the constituent States, provinces or cantons, or are subject to the control of the administrative authorities thereof, the Member shall take the steps provided for in paragraph 7 (b) of Article 19 of the Constitution of the International Labour Organisation.[9]

Article 7

1. Each Member for which this Convention is in force under-   **8–034** takes that its employment service and other services connected with migration will co-operate in appropriate cases with the corresponding services of other Members.

2. Each Member for which this Convention is in force undertakes to ensure that the services rendered by its public employment service to migrants for employment are rendered free.

Article 8

1. A migrant for employment who has been admitted on a permanent basis and the members of his family who have been authorised to accompany or join him shall not be returned to their territory of origin or the territory from which they emigrated because the migrant is unable to follow his occupation by reason of illness contracted or injury sustained subsequent to entry, unless the person concerned so desires or an international agreement to which the Member is a party so provides.

2. When migrants for employment are admitted on a permanent basis upon arrival in the country of immigration the competent authority of that country may determine that the provisions of paragraph 1 of this Article shall take effect only after a reasonable period which shall in no case exceed five years from the date of admission of such migrants.

Article 9

Each Member for which this Convention is in force undertakes to   **8–035** permit, taking into account the limits allowed by national laws and regulations concerning export and import of currency, the

[9] See above n. 7.

transfer of such part of the earnings and savings of the migrant for employment as the migrant may desire.

Article 10

In cases where the number of migrants going from the territory of one Member to that of another is sufficiently large, the competent authorities of the territories concerned shall, whenever necessary or desirable, enter into agreements for the purpose of regulating matters of common concern arising in connection with the application of the provisions of this Convention.

Article 11

1. For the purpose of this Convention the term "migrant for employment" means a person who migrates from one country to another with a view to being employed otherwise than on his own account and includes any person regularly admitted as a migrant for employment.

2. This Convention does not apply to—

(a) frontier workers;

(b) short-term entry of member of the liberal professions and artistes; and

(c) seamen.

INTERNATIONAL LABOUR CONFERENCE CONVENTION (No. 143) CONCERNING MIGRATIONS IN ABUSIVE CONDITIONS AND THE PROMOTION OF EQUALITY OF OPPORTUNITY AND TREATMENT OF MIGRANT WORKERS[10]

8–036   THE General Conference of the International Labour Organisation, . . . Considering that the Preamble of the Constitution of the International Labour Organisation assigns to it the task of protecting "the interests of workers when employed in countries other than their own", and . . . Considering the right of everyone to leave any country, including his own and to enter his own country, as set forth in the Universal Declaration of Human Rights[11] and the International Covenant on Civil and Political Rights,[12] . . .

---

[10] Adopted June 24, 1975. There are currently 17 ratifications to the Convention.

[11] Article 13(2): everyone has the right to leave any country, including his own, and to return to his own country.

[12] Article 12(2): everyone shall be free to leave any country, including his own. Article 12(4): no one shall be arbitrarily deprived of the right to enter his own country.

Part I. Migrations in abusive conditions

Article 1

Each Member for which this Convention is in force undertakes to respect the basic human rights of all migrant workers.

Article 2

1. Each Member for which this Convention is in force shall 8–037 systematically seek to determine whether there are illegally employed migrant workers on its territory and whether there depart from, pass through or arrive in its territory any movements of migrants for employment in which the migrants are subjected during their journey, on arrival or during their period of residence and employment to conditions contravening relevant international multilateral or bilateral instruments or agreements, or national laws or regulations.

2. The representative organisations of employers and workers shall be fully consulted and enabled to furnish any information in their possession on this subject.

Article 3

Each Member shall adopt all necessary and appropriate measures, both within its jurisdiction and in collaboration with other Members—

(a) to suppress clandestine movements of migrants for employment and illegal employment of migrants, and

(b) against the organisers of illicit or clandestine movements of migrants for employment departing from, passing through or arriving in its territory, and against those who employ workers who have immigrated in illegal conditions,

in order to prevent and to eliminate the abuses referred to in Article 2 of this Convention.

Article 4

In particular, Members shall take such measures as are necessary, 8–038 at the national and the international level, for systematic contact and exchange of information on the subject with other States, in consultation with representative organisations of employers and workers.

Article 5

One of the purposes of the measures taken under Articles 3 and 4 of this Convention shall be that the authors of manpower trafficking can be prosecuted whatever the country from which they exercise their activities.

Article 6

1. Provision shall be made under national laws or regulations for the effective detection of the illegal employment of migrant workers and for the definition and the application of administrative, civil and penal sanctions, which include imprisonment in their range, in respect of the illegal employment of migrant workers, in respect of the organisation of movements of migrants for employment defined as involving the abuses referred to in Article 2 of this Convention, and in respect of knowing assistance to such movements, whether for profit or otherwise.

2. Where an employer is prosecuted by virtue of the provision made in pursuance of this Article, he shall have the right to furnish proof of his good faith.

Article 7

The representative organisations of employers and workers shall be consulted in regard to the laws and regulations and other measures provided for in this Convention and designed to prevent and eliminate the abuses referred to above, and the possibility of their taking initiatives for this purpose shall be recognised.

Article 8

1. On condition that he has resided legally in the territory for the purpose of employment, the migrant worker shall not be regarded as in an illegal or irregular situation by the mere fact of the loss of his employment, which shall not in itself imply the withdrawal of his authorisation of residence or, as the case may be, work permit.

2. Accordingly, he shall enjoy equality of treatment with nationals in respect in particular of guarantees of security of employment, the provision of alternative employment, relief work and retraining.

Article 9

8–039   **1.** Without prejudice to measures designed to control movements of migrants for employment by ensuring that migrant workers enter national territory and are admitted to employment in conformity with the relevant laws and regulations, the migrant worker shall, in cases in which these laws and regulations have not been respected and in which his position cannot be regularised, enjoy equality of treatment for himself and his family in respect of rights arising out of past employment as regards remuneration, social security and other benefits.

2. In case of dispute about the rights referred to in the preceding paragraph, the worker shall have the possibility of presenting his case to a competent body, either himself or through a representative.

3. In case of expulsion of the worker or his family, the cost shall not be borne by them.

4. Nothing in this Convention shall prevent Members from giving persons who are illegally residing or working within the country the right to stay and to take up legal employment.

Part II. Equality of opportunity and treatment

Article 10

Each Member for which the Convention is in force undertakes to declare and pursue a national policy designed to promote and to guarantee, by methods appropriate to national conditions and practice, equality of opportunity and treatment in respect of employment and occupation, of social security, of trade union and cultural rights and of individual and collective freedoms for persons who as migrant workers or as members of their families are lawfully within its territory.

Article 11

1. For the purpose of this Part of this Convention, the term "migrant worker" means a person who migrates or who has migrated from one country to another with a view to being employed otherwise than on his own account and includes any person regularly admitted as a migrant worker.

2. This part of this Convention does not apply to—

(a) frontier workers;

(b) artistes and members of the liberal professions who have entered the country on a short-term basis;

(c) seamen;

(d) persons coming specifically for purposes of training or education;

(e) employees of organisations or undertakings operating within the territory of a country who have been admitted temporarily to that country at the request of their employer to undertake specific duties or assignments, for a limited and defined period of time, and who are required to leave that country on the completion of their duties or assignments.

Article 12

8–040 Each Member shall, by methods appropriate to national conditions and practice—

(a) seek the co-operation of employers' and workers' organisations and other appropriate bodies in promoting the acceptance and observance of the policy provided for in Article 10 of this Convention;

(b) enact such legislation and promote such educational programmes as may be calculated to secure the acceptance and observance of the policy;

(c) take measures, encourage educational programmes and develop other activities aimed at acquainting migrant workers as fully as possible with the policy, with their rights and obligations and with activities designed to give effective assistance to migrant workers in the exercise of their rights and for their protection;

(d) repeal any statutory provisions and modify any administrative instructions or practices which are inconsistent with the policy;

(e) in consultation with representative organisations of employers and workers, formulate and apply a social policy appropriate to national conditions and practice which enables migrant workers and their families to share in advantages enjoyed by its nationals while taking account, without adversely affecting the principle of equality of opportunity and treatment, of such special needs as they may have until they are adapted to the society of the country of employment;

(f) take all steps to assist and encourage the efforts of migrant workers and their families to preserve their national and ethnic identity and their cultural ties with their country of origin, including the possibility for children to be given some knowledge of their mother tongue;

(g) guarantee equality of treatment, with regard to working conditions, for all migrant workers who perform the same activity whatever might be the particular conditions of their employment.

Article 13

1. A Member may take all necessary measures which fall within 8–041 its competence and collaborate with other Members to facilitate the reunification of the families of all migrant workers legally residing in its territory.

2. The members of the family of the migrant worker to which this Article applies are the spouse and dependent children, father and mother.

Article 14

A Member may—

(a) make the free choice of employment, while assuring migrant workers the right to geographical mobility, subject to the conditions that the migrant worker has resided lawfully in its territory for the purpose of employment for a prescribed period not exceeding two years or, if its laws or regulations provide for contracts for a fixed term of less than two years, that the worker has completed his first work contract;

(b) after appropriate consultation with the representative organisations of employers and workers, make regulations concerning recognition of occupational qualifications acquired outside its territory, including certificates and diplomas;

(c) restrict access to limited categories of employment or functions where this is necessary in the interests of the State.[13]

Part III. Final provisions

Article 15

This Convention does not prevent Members from concluding multilateral or bilateral agreements with a view to resolving problems arising from its application. Developing countries were reluctant to ratify the above Convention given that it was designed to combat illegal migration for employment.

---

[13] This Article proved unpopular with the developed nations and led to calls for an instrument to be drawn up under the auspices of the United Nations—see below.

INTERNATIONAL LABOUR CONFERENCE RECOMMENDATION (No. 151) CONCERNING MIGRANT WORKERS[14]

8–042 This Recommendation calls upon Members to apply the provisions of this Recommendation within the framework of a coherent policy on international migration for employment. Such a policy should be based upon the economic and social needs of both countries of origin and countries of employment.[15]

I. Equality of opportunity and treatment

2. Migrant workers and members of their families lawfully within the territory of a Member should enjoy effective equality of opportunity and treatment with nationals of the Member concerned in respect of—

(a) access to vocational guidance and placement services;

(b) access to vocational training and employment of their own choice on the basis of individual suitability for such training or employment, account being taken of qualifications acquired outside the territory of and in the country of employment;

(c) advancement in accordance with their individual character, experience, ability and diligence;

(d) security of employment, the provision of alternative employment, relief work and retraining;

(e) remuneration for work of equal value;

(f) conditions of work, including hours of work, rest periods, annual holidays with pay, occupational safety and occupational health measures, as well as social security measures and welfare facilities and benefits provided in connection with employment;

(g) membership of trade unions, exercise of trade union rights and eligibility for office in trade unions and in labour-management relations bodies, including bodies representing workers in undertakings;

(h) rights of full membership in any form of co-operative;

(i) conditions of life, including housing and the benefits of social service and educational and health facilities.

3. Each Member should ensure the application of the principles set forth in Paragraph 2 of this Recommendation in all activities

---

[14] Adopted June 24, 1975.
[15] Section 1.

under the control of a public authority and promote its observance in all other activities by methods appropriate to national conditions and practice.

4. Appropriate measures should be taken, with the collaboration of employers' and workers' organisations and other bodies concerned, with a view to— 8–043

(a) fostering public understanding and acceptance of the above-mentioned principles;

(b) examining complaints that these principles are not being observed and securing the correction, by conciliation or other appropriate means, of any practices regarded as in conflict therewith.

5. Each Member should ensure that national laws and regulations concerning residence in its territory are so applied that the lawful exercise of rights enjoyed in pursuance of these principles cannot be the reason for non-renewal of a residence permit or for expulsion and is not inhibited by the threat of such measures.

6. A Member may—

(a) make the free choice of employment, while assuring migrant workers the right to geographical mobility, subject to the conditions that the migrant worker has resided lawfully in its territory for the purpose of employment for a prescribed period not exceeding two years or, if its laws or regulations provide for contracts for a fixed term of less than two years, that the worker has completed his first work contract;

(b) after appropriate consultation with the representative organisations of employers and workers, make regulations concerning recognition of occupational qualifications acquired outside its territory, including certificates and diplomas;

(c) restrict access to limited categories of employment or functions where this is necessary in the interests of the State.

7. (1) In order to enable migrant workers and their families to take full advantage of their rights and opportunities in employment and occupation, such measures as may be necessary should be taken, in consultation with the representative organisations of employers and workers—

(a) to inform them, as far as possible in their mother tongue or, if that is not possible, in a language with which they are familiar, of their rights under national law and practice as regards the matters dealt with in Paragraph 2 of this Recommendation;

(b) to advance their knowledge of the language or languages of the country of employment, as far as possible during paid time;

(c) generally, to promote their adaptation to the society of the country of employment and to assist and encourage the efforts of migrant workers and their families to preserve their national and ethnic identity and their cultural ties with their country of origin, including the possibility for children to be given some knowledge of their mother tongue.

(2) Where agreements concerning the collective recruitment of workers have been concluded between Members, they should jointly take the necessary measures before the migrants' departure from their country of origin to introduce them to the language of the country of employment and also to its economic, social and cultural environment.

8–044   **8.** (1) Without prejudice to measures designed to ensure that migrant workers and their families enter national territory and are admitted to employment in conformity with the relevant laws and regulations, a decision should be taken as soon as possible in cases in which these laws and regulations have not been respected so that the migrant worker should know whether his position can be regularised or not.

(2) Migrant workers whose position has been regularised should benefit from all rights which, in accordance with Paragraph 2 of this Recommendation, are provided for migrant workers lawfully within the territory of a Member.

(3) Migrant workers whose position has not been or could not be regularised should enjoy equality of treatment for themselves and their families in respect of rights arising out of present and past employment as regards remuneration, social security and other benefits as well as regards trade union membership and exercise of trade union rights.

(4) In case of dispute about the rights referred to in the preceding sub-paragraphs, the worker should have the possibility of presenting his case to a competent body, either himself or through a representative.

(5) In case of expulsion of the worker or his family, the cost should not be borne by them.

II. Social policy

9. Each Member should, in consultation with representative organisations of employers and workers, formulate and apply a social policy appropriate to national conditions and practice which enables migrant workers and their families to share in advantages enjoyed by its nationals while taking account, without adversely affecting the principle of equality of opportunity and treatment, of such special needs as they may have until they are adapted to the society of the country of employment.

10. With a view to making the policy as responsive as possible to the real needs of migrant workers and their families, it should be based, in particular, on an examination not only of conditions in the territory of the Member but also of those in the countries of origin of the migrants.

11. The policy should take account of the need to spread the social cost of migration as widely and equitably as possible over the entire collectivity of the country of employment, and in particular over those who profit most from the work of migrants.

12. The policy should be periodically reviewed and evaluated and where necessary revised.

A. REUNIFICATION OF FAMILIES

13. (1) All possible measures should be taken both by countries of employment and by countries of origin to facilitate the reunification of families of migrant workers as rapidly as possible. These measures should include, as necessary, national laws or regulations and bilateral and multilateral arrangements.

(2) A prerequisite for the reunification of families should be that the worker has, for his family, appropriate accommodation which meets the standards normally applicable to nationals of the country of employment.

14. Representatives of all concerned, and in particular of employers and workers, should be consulted on the measures to be adopted to facilitate the reunification of families and their co-operation sought in giving effect thereto.

15. For the purpose of the provisions of this Recommendation relating to the reunification of families, the family of the migrant worker should include the spouse and dependent children, father and mother.

16. With a view to facilitating the reunification of families as quickly as possible in accordance with Paragraph 13 of this Recommendation, each Member should take full account of the needs of migrant workers and their families in particular in its policy regarding the construction of family housing, assistance in obtaining this housing and the development of appropriate reception services.

17. Where a migrant worker who has been employed for at **8–045** least one year in a country of employment cannot be joined by his family in that country, he should be entitled—

(a) to visit the country of residence of his family during the paid annual holiday to which he is entitled under the national law and practice of the country of employment without losing during the absence from that country any acquired rights or rights in course of acquisition and, particularly, without having his employment terminated or his right to residence in the country of employment withdrawn during that period; or

(b) to be visited by his family for a period corresponding at least to the annual holiday with pay to which he is entitled.

18. Consideration should be given to the possibility of giving the migrant worker financial assistance towards the cost of the travel envisaged in the preceding Paragraph or a reduction in the normal cost of transport, for instance by the arrangement of group travel.

19. Without prejudice to more favourable provisions which may be applicable to them, persons admitted in pursuance of international arrangements for free movement of labour should have the benefit of the measures provided for in Paragraphs 13 to 18 of this Recommendation.

B. PROTECTION OF THE HEALTH OF MIGRANT WORKERS

20. All appropriate measures should be taken to prevent any special health risks to which migrant workers may be exposed.

21. (1) Every effort should be made to ensure that migrant workers receive training and instruction in occupational safety and occupational hygiene in connection with their practical training or other work preparation and, as far as possible, as part thereof.

(2) In addition, a migrant worker should, during paid working hours and immediately after beginning his employment, be provided with sufficient information in his mother tongue or, if that is not possible, in a language with which he is familiar, on the essential elements of laws and regulations and on provisions of collective agreements concerning the protection of workers and the prevention of accidents as well as on safety regulations and procedures particular to the nature of the work.

22. (1) Employers should take all possible measures so that migrant workers may fully understand instructions, warnings, symbols and other signs relating to safety and health hazards at work.

(2) Where, on account of the migrant worker's lack of familiarity with processes, language difficulties or other reasons, the training or instruction given to other workers is inadequate for

them, special measures which ensure their full understanding should be taken.

(3) Members should have laws or regulations applying the principles set out in this Paragraph and provide that where employers or other persons or organisations having responsibility in this regard fail to observe such laws or regulations, administrative, civil and penal sanctions might be imposed.

C. SOCIAL SERVICES

23. In accordance with the provisions of Paragraph 2 of this 8–046 Recommendation, migrant workers and their families should benefit from the activities of social services and have access thereto under the same conditions as nationals of the country of employment.

24. In addition, social services should be provided which perform, in particular, the following functions in relation to migrant workers and their families—

(a) giving migrant workers and their families every assistance in adapting to the economic, social and cultural environment of the country of employment;

(b) helping migrant workers and their families to obtain information and advice from appropriate bodies, for instance by providing interpretation and translation services; to comply with administrative and other formalities; and to make full use of services and facilities provided in such fields as education, vocational training and language training, health services and social security, housing, transport and recreation: Provided that migrant workers and their families should as far as possible have the right to communicate with public authorities in the country of employment in their own language or in a language with which they are familiar, particularly in the context of legal assistance and court proceedings;

(c) assisting authorities and bodies with responsibilities relating to the conditions of life and work of migrant workers and their families in identifying their needs and in adapting thereto;

(d) giving the competent authorities information and, as appropriate, advice regarding the formulation, implementation and evaluation of social policy with respect to migrant workers;

(e) providing information for fellow workers and foremen and supervisors about the situation and the problems of migrant workers.

8–047   **25.** (1) The social services referred to in Paragraph 24 of this Recommendation may be provided, as appropriate to national conditions and practice, by public authorities, by approved non-profit-making organisations or bodies, or by a combination of both. The public authorities should have the over-all responsibility of ensuring that these social services are at the disposal of migrant workers and their families.

(2) Full use should be made of services which are or can be provided by authorities, organisations and bodies serving the nationals of the country of employment, including employers' and workers' organisations.

26. Each Member should take such measures as may be necessary to ensure that sufficient resources and adequately trained staff are available for the social services referred to in Paragraph 24 of this Recommendation.

27. Each Member should promote co-operation and co-ordination between different social services on its territory and, as appropriate, between these services and corresponding services in other countries, without, however, this co-operation and co-ordination relieving the States of their responsibilities in this field.

28. Each Member should organise and encourage the organisation, at the national, regional or local level, or as appropriate in a branch of economic activity employing substantial numbers of migrant workers, of periodic meetings for the exchange of information and experience. Consideration should also be given to the exchange of information and experience with other countries of employment as well as with the countries of origin of migrant workers.

29. Representatives of all concerned and in particular of employers and workers should be consulted on the organisation of the social services in question and their co-operation sought in achieving the purposes aimed at.

III. Employment and residence

30. In pursuance of the provision of Paragraph 18 of the Migration for Employment Recommendation (Revised) 1949,[16] that Members should, as far as possible, refrain from removing from their territory, on account of lack of means or the state of the employment market, a migrant worker regularly admitted thereto, the loss by such migrant worker of his employment should not in itself imply the withdrawal of his authorisation of residence.

8–048   **31.** A migrant who has lost his employment should be allowed sufficient time to find alternative employment, at least for a

---

[16] See above para. 8–026

period corresponding to that during which he may be entitled to unemployment benefit; the authorisation of residence should be extended accordingly.

32. (1) A migrant worker who has lodged an appeal against the termination of his employment, under such procedures as may be available, should be allowed sufficient time to obtain a final decision thereon.

(2) If it is established that the termination of employment was not justified, the migrant worker should be entitled, on the same terms as national workers, to reinstatement, to compensation for loss of wages or of other payment which results from unjustified termination, or to access to a new job with a right to indemnification. If he is not reinstated, he should be allowed sufficient time to find alternative employment.

33. A migrant worker who is the object of an expulsion order should have a right of appeal before an administrative or judicial instance, according to conditions laid down in national laws or regulations. This appeal should stay the execution of the expulsion order, subject to the duly substantiated requirements of national security or public order. The migrant worker should have the same right to legal assistance as national workers and have the possibility of being assisted by an interpreter.

34. (1) A migrant worker who leaves the country of employment should be entitled, irrespective of the legality of his stay therein—

(a) to any outstanding remuneration for work performed, including severance payments normally due;

(b) to benefits which may be due in respect of any employment injury suffered;

(c) in accordance with national practice—

(i) to compensation in lieu of any holiday entitlement acquired but not used;

(ii) to reimbursement of any social security contributions which have not given and will not give rise to rights under national laws or regulations or international arrangements: Provided that where social security contributions do not permit entitlement to benefits, every effort should be made with a view to the conclusion of bilateral or multilateral agreements to protect the rights of migrants.

(2) Where any claim covered in sub-paragraph (1) of this Paragraph is in dispute, the worker should be able to have his interest represented before the competent body and enjoy equal treatment with national workers as regards legal assistance.

Finally certain provisions of the General Assembly's Resolution on the the Rights of Individuals who are not Nationals of the Country in Which They Live are of relevance for migrant workers.

1985 DECLARATION ON THE HUMAN RIGHTS OF INDIVIDUALS WHO ARE NOT NATIONALS OF THE COUNTRY IN WHICH THEY LIVE[17]

Article 1

8–049 For the purposes of this Declaration, the term "alien" shall apply, with due regard to qualifications made in subsequent articles, to any individual who is not a national of the State in which he or she is present.

Article 2

1. Nothing in this Declaration shall be interpreted as legitimising the illegal entry into and presence in State of any alien, nor shall any provision be interpreted as restricting the right of any State to promulgate laws and regulations concerning the entry of aliens and the terms and conditions of their stay or to establish differences between nationals and aliens. However, such laws and regulations shall not be incompatible with the international legal obligations of that State, including those in the field of human rights.
2. This Declaration shall not prejudice the enjoyment of the rights accorded by domestic law and of the rights which under international law a State is obliged to accord to aliens, even where this Declaration does not recognise such rights or recognises them to a lesser extent.

Article 3

8–050 Every State shall make public its national legislation or regulations affecting aliens.

Article 4

Aliens shall observe the law of the State in which they reside of are present and regard with respect the customs and traditions of the people of that State.

---

[17] G.A.Res. 144 (XL), G.A.O.R., 40th Session, Supp. 53, p. 253 adopted by consensus in 1985. Although not binding on States the Special Rapporteur, Baroness Elles hoped that the Declaration "may become recognised as laying down rules binding upon States" (UN Doc. E/CN, 4/Sub2/393/Rev.1(1982),p. 52.

Articles 5 and 6 relate primarily to rights recognised in other international instruments, *e.g.* the right of life and security of person,[18] the right to choose a spouse, to marry, to found a family[19] and freedom from torture or to cruel, inhuman or degrading treatment or punishment.[20] However, certain provision pertain relate specifically to aliens[21] whilst Article 8 in particular details rights of relevance to migrant workers.

Article 8

1. Aliens lawfully residing in the territory of a State shall also in accordance with the national laws, the following rights, subject to their obligations under Article 4:

(a) The right to safe and healthy working conditions, to fair wages and equal remuneration for work of equal value without distinction of any kind, in particular, women being guaranteed conditions of work not inferior to those enjoyed by men, with equal pay for equal work;

(b) The right to join trade unions and other organisations or associations of their choice and to participate in their activities. No restrictions may be placed on the exercise of this right other than those prescribed by law and which are necessary, in a democratic society, in the interests of national security or public order or for the protection of the rights and freedoms of others;

(c) The right to health, protection, medical care, social security, social services, education, rest and leisure, provided that they fulfil the requirements under relevant regulations for participation and that undue strain is not placed on the resources of the State.

2. With a view to protecting the rights of aliens carrying on lawful paid activities in the country in which they are present, such rights may be specified by the governments concerned in multilateral or bilateral conventions.

---

[18] Art. 5.1(a).
[19] *ibid.* (d).
[20] Art. 6.
[21] Art. 5(f) on the right to retain their own language, culture and tradition; and Art. 5(g) on the right to transfer abroad earnings savings or other personal monetary assets, subject to domestic currency regulations.

RED CROSS AND RED CRESCENT[22] WORK WITH MIGRANTS— DECISION NOVEMBER 12, 1995[23]

8–051 The General Assembly,

Mindful of the importance of migrants among the present global population movements and considering the likely increase in the forthcoming decades,

Noting the restrictive measures taken by host countries and the expressions of racism, xenophobia and discrimination among some of them,

Mindful of the current situation in which humanitarian and social support to migrant workers and their families is becoming more difficult in the host countries, which are themselves facing economic crisis and its consequences,

Convinced that in these circumstances the migratory phenomena present a challenge to the Red Cross and Red Cross Movement which must be faced in the spirit of its Principles, . . .,

Invites National Societies to act against all forms of racism, xenophobia and discrimination, . . .

Requests National Societies to consider action in favour of migrant populations . . .

Invites National Societies to encourage migrants to take part in their activities, either as volunteers or staff, in accordance with the laws in force in each country,

Invites National Societies of countries of origin and host countries to collaborate closely in order to facilitate the settlement of and improve the assistance offered to migrant workers and the protection of their dignity,

Invites National Societies of countries of origin and host countries to collaborate with their respective governments to initiate development projects which would limit the flow of economic migrants,

Requests the Secretary-General to inform National Societies of the measures taken in favour of migrant by the International specialised institutions: . . ., and to act closely with other international organisations especially through the Federations's capacity as observer to the UN General Assembly.

---

[22] For information on the Red Cross and Red Crescent—see Chapter on the Protection of Civilians during hostilities.

[23] Adopted by the General Assembly of the Federation of the Red Cross and Red Crescent (The General Assembly is composed of delegates from all the National Societies, which are members of the Federation). This decision was adopted at the 10th Session held in Geneva, November 27–30, 1995.

CHAPTER 9

PROTECTION OF CIVILIAN POPULATION DURING HOSTILITIES

The protection of civilians during hostilities remains all too 9–001 necessary as engagement in hostilities continues to be a recurring feature of the international scene. The International Tribunals in respect of Rwanda and Yugoslavia were created in response to those particular conflicts, but there persists a need for the protection of those who find themselves unwillingly involved in hostilities. Ratification of the Ottawa Treaty on the Prohibition of Land Mines would go some way towards reducing one particularly dangerous hazard in the lives of those innocently caught up in warfare. Unfortunately the use of force is employed in international relations in spite of efforts to constrain its use. As long as this is the case civilians are likely to be casualties. All the international community can strive to do is to prescribe minimum standards designed to provide civilian protection.

VIENNA DECLARATION AND PROGRAMME OF ACTION (1993)

3. Effective international measures to guarantee and monitor 9–002 the implementation of human rights standards should be taken in respect of people under foreign occupation, and effective legal protection against the violation of their human rights should be provided, in accordance with human rights norms and international law, particularly the Geneva Convention relative to the Protection of Civilian Persons in Time of War, of August 14, 1949, and other applicable norms of humanitarian law.

The following Convention forms part of the international substantive law known as *jus in bello*. Four Geneva Conventions[1] were adopted in 1949. Each Convention deals with the specific protection of a particular category of persons who are not or are no longer involved in hostilities, namely, Conventions for the Protection of War Victims Concerning—Amelioration of the Condition of Wounded and Sick in Armed Forces in the Field (Geneva I); Amelioration of the Condition of Wounded and Sick

---

[1] 75 U.N.T.S. 31; U.K.T.S. 39 (1958), Cmd. 550.

and Shipwrecked Members of Armed Forces at Sea (Geneva II); Treatment of Prisoners of War (Geneva III)[2]; and Protection of Civilian Persons in Time of War (Geneva IV). The Conventions deal with the treatment of persons who have ceased to fight or have fallen into the power of the adversary; essentially they regulate the conduct of hostilities from the humanitarian perspective. They do not relate to the way in which hostilities are conducted.[3] The Geneva Conventions have been supplemented by two Protocols adopted in 1977.[4] Protocol I revises and supplements the protection afforded to the victims of international armed conflict which is defined under the Protocol to include wars of self determination. Protocol II affords protection to the victims of non-international armed conflict. The Geneva Conventions have become part of customary international law.[5] Currently there are 186 Contracting Parties to the Geneva Conventions. The Universal Declaration is silent on respect for human rights in armed conflict and the Four Geneva Conventions are silent on human rights, although drafted in an environment awakening to human rights.[6] Nevertheless each contains an article providing that protected persons may not renounce the rights secured to them by the Conventions[7] and the 1977 Protocols reflect the impact of human rights.[8] The provisions of human rights law and humanitarian law although sharing a common goal, namely the protection of the individual, remain

---

[2] See specifically Chapter on Prisoners.

[3] The conduct of hostilities has been dealt with in multifarious Hague Conventions, such as Convention Relative to the Opening of Hostilities, U.K.T.S. 8 (1910); and Convention Concerning the Laws and Customs of War on Land (Hague IV) U.K.T.S. 9 (1910).

[4] 1977 U.N.J.Y.B. 95; Misc.19 (1977), Cmnd. 6926; 16 I.L.M. 1391.

[5] "The part of conventional international humanitarian law which has beyond doubt become part of international customary law is the law applicable in armed conflict as embodied in the Geneva Conventions of August 12, 1949, for the protection of War Victims. . .; see Article I on the competence of the International Tribunal established for the protection of persons responsible for serious violations of international humanitarian law committed in the territory of former Yugoslavia, since 1991. Article 2 provides that the Tribunal shall have competence to prosecute persons committing or ordering to be committed grave breaches of the Geneva Conventions. . .". See 32 I.L.M. 1159 (1993). See also Article 22 Draft Statute for an International Criminal Court, 33 I.L.M. 253 (1994).

[6] The growing awareness of human rights in the 1950s led to the term "international humanitarian law" being employed.

[7] Article 7, Conventions I, II and IV; and Article 8, Convention III.

[8] Article 75, Protocol I and Article 6, Protocol II concerning fundamental guarantees and penal prosecutions respectively are directly derived from the UN Covenant on Civil and Political Rights. Note too the International Conference on Human Rights in the Teheran Proclamation 1968 made reference to the mass violations of human rights in armed conflicts; "Massive denials of human rights, arising out of aggression or any armed conflict with their tragic consequences, and resulting in untold human misery, engender reactions which could engulf the world in ever growing hostilities. It is the obligation of the international community to co-operate in eradicating such scourges;" para 10.—see Annex.

distinct branches of the law[9] but increasingly the provisions of the Geneva Conventions and human rights instruments may be applied cumulatively. However, while the substantive rules may coincide at least in part, they have a very different enforcement machinery. The Geneva Conventions are implemented by way of the co-operation the Protecting Powers[10] and under the supervision of the International Red Cross.[11]

[9] And must remain so—*e.g.* the protection of the individual during hostilities demands rules which are finely tuned to the specifics of armed conflict and are different to those necessary during peace. Also the rules of armed conflict have an undoubtedly reciprocal advantage for all parties *vis-à-vis* their application.

[10] States have become are increasingly reluctant to appoint a Protecting Power—*i.e.* a third neutral state. Accordingly the role of the International Committee of the Red Cross has assumed greater significance.

[11] The International Committee of the Red Cross (ICRC) was founded in 1863 as a charitable organisation by Henry Dunant. Henry Dunant in June 1859 during a trip through Lombardy was so shocked and moved by what he saw on the battlefield at Solferino that he was prompted to write "*A Memory to Solferino*"(1862). That book and Dunant's proposals contained therein led to the founding of the now universal Red Cross and Red Crescent Movement. Although the cross had been adopted as a tribute to Switzerland and was not intended to have any religious connotation the Red Crescent was used during the Russo-Turkish war in 1876 by the Ottoman Society for Relief to the Wounded. The Red Crescent emblem has now been adopted as being of equal status to the Red Cross. The ICRC is governed by seven fundamental principles: humanity; impartiality; neutrality; independence; voluntary service; unity and universality. Article 5 of the Statute of the International Committee of the Red Cross provides:

1. The International Committee, founded in Geneva in 1863 and formerly recognised in the Geneva Convention and by International Conferences of the Red Cross, is an independent humanitarian organisation having a status of its own. It co-opts its members from among Swiss citizens.
2. The role of the International Committee, in accordance with its Statutes, is in particular:
   (a) to maintain and disseminate the Fundamental Principles of the Movement, namely humanity, impartiality, neutrality, independence, voluntary service, unity and universality;
   (b) to recognise any newly established or reconstituted National Society, which fulfils the conditions set out in Article 4, and to notify other National Societies of such recognition;
   (c) to undertake the tasks incumbent upon it under the Geneva Conventions, to work for the faithful application of international humanitarian law applicable in armed conflicts and to take cognisance of any complaints based on alleged breaches of that law;
   (d) to endeavour at all times—as a neutral institution whose humanitarian work is carried out particularly in time of international and other armed conflicts or internal strife—to ensure the protection of and assistance to military and civilian victims of such events and of their direct results;
   (e) to ensure the operation of the central Tracing Agency as provided in the Geneva Conventions;
   (f) to contribute, in anticipation of armed conflicts, to the training of medical personnel and the preparation of medical equipment , in co-operation with the National Societies, the military and civilian medical services and other competent authorities;
   (g) to work for the understanding and dissemination of knowledge of international humanitarian law applicable in armed conflicts and to prepare any development thereof;
   (h) to carry out mandates entrusted to it by the International Conference.
3. The International Committee may take any humanitarian initiative which comes within its role as a specifically neutral and independent institution and intermediary, and may consider any question requiring examination by such an institution.

GENEVA CONVENTION RELATIVE TO THE PROTECTION OF CIVILIAN PERSONS IN TIME OF WAR (GENEVA CONVENTION IV) AUGUST 12, 1949[12]

PART I. GENERAL PROVISIONS

Article 1

9–003 The High Contracting Parties undertake to respect and to ensure respect for the present Convention in all circumstances.

Article 2

In addition to the provisions which shall be implemented in peace-time, the present Convention shall apply to all cases of declared war or of any other armed conflict which may arise between two or more of the High Contracting Parties, even if the state of war is not recognised by one of them.

The Convention shall also apply to all cases of partial or total occupation of the territory of a High Contracting Party, even if the said occupation meets with no armed resistance.

Although one of the Powers in conflict may not be a party to the present Convention, the Powers who are parties thereto shall remain bound by it in their mutual relations. They shall furthermore be bound by the Convention in relation to the said Power, if the latter accepts and applies the provisions thereof.

Article 3[13]

9–004 In the case of armed conflict not of an international character occurring in the territory of one of the High Contracting Parties, each Party to the conflict shall be bound to apply, as a minimum, the following provisions:

(1) Persons taking no active part in the hostilities, including members of armed forces who have laid down their arms and those placed hors de combat by sickness, wounds, detention, or

---

[12] Geneva Convention relative to the Protection of Civilian Persons in Time of War, August 12, 1949 (Geneva Convention IV). Signed at Geneva, August 12, 1949, 75 U.N.T.S. 31; U.K.T.S. 39 (1958), Cmd. 550; The Fourth Geneva Convention on the Protection of Civilian Persons in time of War broke fresh ground as prior to 1949 only military personnel were afforded protection.

[13] Article 3, which is common to all four Conventions, demands that parties to an international conflict respect certain basic principles. This Article imposes an obligation on *all* parties to an international conflict and *not* only governments. Protocol II (see below) supplements Article 3 with certain specific provisions. However Protocol II is of narrower application than common Article 3 in that it applies only if the insurgent party controls part of the national territory.

any other cause, shall in all circumstances be treated humanely, without any adverse distinction founded on race, colour, religion or faith, sex, birth or wealth, or any other similar criteria.

To this end the following acts are and shall remain prohibited at any time and in any place whatsoever with respect to the above-mentioned persons:

(a) violence to life and person, in particular murder of all kinds, mutilation, cruel treatment and torture;

(b) taking of hostages;

(c) outrages upon personal dignity, in particular humiliating and degrading treatment;

(d) the passing of sentences and the carrying out of executions without previous judgment pronounced by a regularly constituted court, affording all the judicial guarantees which are recognised as indispensable by civilized peoples.[14]

(2) The wounded and sick shall be collected and cared for.

An impartial humanitarian body, such as the International Committee of the Red Cross, may offer its services to the Parties to the conflict.

The Parties to the conflict should further endeavour to bring into force, by means of special agreements, all or part of the other provisions of the present Convention.

The application of the preceding provisions shall not affect the legal status of the Parties to the conflict.

Article 4

Persons protected by the Convention are those who, at a given 9–005 moment and in any manner whatsoever, find themselves, in case of a conflict or occupation, in the hands of a Party to the conflict or Occupying Power of which they are not nationals.

Nationals of a State which is not bound by the Convention are not protected by it. Nationals of a neutral State who find themselves in the territory of a belligerent State, and nationals of a co-belligerent State, shall not be regarded as protected persons while the State of which they are nationals has normal diplomatic representation in the State in whose hands they are.

The provisions of Part II are, however, wider in application, as defined in Article 13. Persons protected by the Geneva Convention for the Amelioration of the Condition of the Wounded and

---

[14] See Chapter on Prisoners.

Sick in Armed Forces in the Field of August 12, 1949, or by the Geneva Convention for the Amelioration of the Condition of Wounded, Sick and Shipwrecked Members of Armed Forces at Sea of August 12, 1949, or by the Geneva Convention relative to the Treatment of Prisoners of War of August 12, 1949, shall not be considered as protected persons within the meaning of the present Convention.

Article 5

Where in the territory of a Party to the conflict, the latter is satisfied that an individual protected person is definitely suspected of or engaged in activities hostile to the security of the State, such individual person shall not be entitled to claim such rights and privileges under the present Convention as would, if exercised in the favour of such individual person, be prejudicial to the security of such State.

Where in occupied territory an individual protected person is detained as a spy or saboteur, or as a person under definite suspicion of activity hostile to the security of the Occupying Power, such person shall, in those cases where absolute military security so requires, be regarded as having forfeited rights of communication under the present Convention.

In each case, such persons shall nevertheless be treated with humanity and, in case of trial, shall not be deprived of the rights of fair and regular trial prescribed by the present Convention. They shall also be granted the full rights and privileges of a protected person under the present Convention at the earliest date consistent with the security of the State or Occupying Power, as the case may be.

Article 6

9–006 The present Convention shall apply from the outset of any conflict or occupation mentioned in Article 2.

In the territory of Parties to the conflict, the application of the present Convention shall cease on the general close of military operations.

In the case of occupied territory, the application of the present Convention shall cease one year after the general close of military operations; however, the Occupying Power shall be bound, for the duration of the occupation, to the extent that such Power exercises the functions of government in such territory, by the provisions of the following Articles of the present Convention: 1 to 12, 27, 29 to 34, 47, 49, 51, 52, 53, 59, 61 to 77, 143.

Protected persons whose release, repatriation or re-establishment may take place after such dates shall meanwhile continue to benefit by the present Convention.

Article 7

In addition to the agreements expressly provided for in Articles 11, 14, 15, 17, 36, 108, 109, 132, 133 and 149,[15] the High Contracting Parties may conclude other special agreements for all matters concerning which they may deem it suitable to make separate provision. No special agreement shall adversely affect the situation of protected persons, as defined by the present Convention, not restrict the rights which it confers upon them.

Protected persons shall continue to have the benefit of such agreements as long as the Convention is applicable to them, except where express provisions to the contrary are contained in the aforesaid or in subsequent agreements, or where more favourable measures have been taken with regard to them by one or other of the Parties to the conflict.

Article 8

Protected persons may in no circumstances renounce in part or in entirety the rights secured to them by the present Convention, and by the special agreements referred to in the foregoing Article, if such there be.[16]

Article 9

The present Convention shall be applied with the co-operation 9–007 and under the scrutiny of the Protecting Powers whose duty it is to safeguard the interests of the Parties to the conflict. For this purpose, the Protecting Powers may appoint, apart from their diplomatic or consular staff, delegates from amongst their own nationals or the nationals of other neutral Powers. The said delegates shall be subject to the approval of the Power with which they are to carry out their duties.

The Parties to the conflict shall facilitate to the greatest extent possible the task of the representatives or delegates of the Protecting Powers.

The representatives or delegates of the Protecting Powers shall not in any case exceed their mission under the present Convention.

They shall, in particular, take account of the imperative necessities of security of the State wherein they carry out their duties.

Article 10

The provisions of the present Convention constitute no obstacle to the humanitarian activities which the International Committee

---

[15] See below.
[16] See introductory note *supra*.

of the Red Cross or any other impartial humanitarian organisation may, subject to the consent of the Parties to the conflict concerned, undertake for the protection of civilian persons and for their relief.

Article 11

The High Contracting Parties may at any time agree to entrust to an international organisation which offers all guarantees of impartiality and efficacy the duties incumbent on the Protecting Powers by virtue of the present Convention.

When persons protected by the present Convention do not benefit or cease to benefit, no matter for what reason, by the activities of a Protecting Power or of an organisation provided for in the first paragraph above, the Detaining Power shall request a neutral State, or such an organisation, to undertake the functions performed under the present Convention by a Protecting Power designated by the Parties to a conflict.

If protection cannot be arranged accordingly, the Detaining Power shall request or shall accept, subject to the provisions of this Article, the offer of the services of a humanitarian organisation, such as the International Committee of the Red Cross, to assume the humanitarian functions performed by Protecting Powers under the present Convention.

Any neutral Power or any organisation invited by the Power concerned or offering itself for these purposes, shall be required to act with a sense of responsibility towards the Party to the conflict on which persons protected by the present Convention depend, and shall be required to furnish sufficient assurances that it is in a position to undertake the appropriate functions and to discharge them impartially.

No derogation from the preceding provisions shall be made by special agreements between Powers one of which is restricted, even temporarily, in its freedom to negotiate with the other Power or its allies by reason of military events, more particularly where the whole, or a substantial part, of the territory of the said Power is occupied.

Whenever in the present Convention mention is made of a Protecting Power, such mention applies to substitute organisations in the sense of the present Article.

The provisions of this Article shall extend and be adapted to cases of nationals of a neutral State who are in occupied territory or who find themselves in the territory of a belligerent State in which the State of which they are nationals has not normal diplomatic representation.

Article 12

In cases where they deem it advisable in the interest of protected 9–008
persons, particularly in cases of disagreement between the Parties
to the conflict as to the application or interpretation of the
provisions of the present Convention, the Protecting Powers shall
lend their good offices with a view to settling the disagreement.

For this purpose, each of the Protecting Powers may, either at
the invitation of one Party or on its own initiative, propose to the
Parties to the conflict a meeting of their representatives, and in
particular of the authorities responsible for protected persons,
possibly on neutral territory suitably chosen. The Parties to the
conflict shall be bound to give effect to the proposals made to
them for this purpose. The Protecting Powers may, if necessary,
propose for approval by the Parties to the conflict a person
belonging to a neutral Power, or delegated by the International
Committee of the Red Cross, who shall be invited to take part in
such a meeting.

PART II. GENERAL PROTECTION OF POPULATIONS AGAINST CERTAIN CONSEQUENCES OF WAR

Article 13

The provisions of Part II cover the whole of the populations of the
countries in conflict, without any adverse distinction based, in
particular, on race, nationality, religion or political opinion, and
are intended to alleviate the sufferings caused by war.

Article 14

In time of peace, the High Contracting Parties and, after the 9–009
outbreak of hostilities, the Parties thereto, may establish in their
own territory and, if the need arises, in occupied areas, hospital
and safety zones and localities so organised as to protect from the
effects of war, wounded, sick and aged persons, children under
15, expectant mothers and mothers of children under seven.

Upon the outbreak and during the course of hostilities, the
Parties concerned may conclude agreements on mutual recognition of the zones and localities they have created. They may for
this purpose implement the provisions of the Draft Agreement
annexed to the present Convention, with such amendments as
they may consider necessary.

The Protecting Powers and the International Committee of the
Red Cross are invited to lend their good offices in order to
facilitate the institution and recognition of these hospital and
safety zones and localities.

Article 15

Any Party to the conflict may, either direct or through a neutral State or some humanitarian organisation, propose to the adverse Party to establish, in the regions where fighting is taking place, neutralised zones intended to shelter from the effects of war the following persons, without distinction:

(a) wounded and sick combatants or non-combatants;

(b) civilian persons who take no part in hostilities, and who, while they reside in the zones, perform no work of a military character.

When the Parties concerned have agreed upon the geographical position, administration, food supply and supervision of the proposed neutralised zone, a written agreement shall be concluded and signed by the representatives of the Parties to the conflict. The agreement shall fix the beginning and the duration of the neutralisation of the zone.

Article 16

The wounded and sick, as well as the infirm, and expectant mothers, shall be the object of particular protection and respect.

As far as military considerations allow, each Party to the conflict shall facilitate the steps taken to search for the killed and wounded, to assist the shipwrecked and other persons exposed to grave danger, and to protect them against pillage and ill-treatment.

Article 17

9–010 The Parties to the conflict shall endeavour to conclude local agreements for the removal from besieged or encircled areas, of wounded, sick, infirm, and aged persons, children and maternity cases, and for the passage of ministers of all religions, medical personnel and medical equipment on their way to such areas.

Article 18

Civilian hospitals organised to give care to the wounded and sick, the infirm and maternity cases, may in no circumstances be the object of attack but shall at all times be respected and protected by the Parties to the conflict.

States which are Parties to a conflict shall provide all civilian hospitals with certificates showing that they are civilian hospitals and that the buildings which they occupy are not used for any purpose which would deprive these hospitals of protection in accordance with Article 19.

In view of the dangers to which hospitals may be exposed by being close to military objectives, it is recommended that such hospitals be situated as far as possible from such objectives.

Article 19

The protection to which civilian hospitals are entitled shall not cease unless they are used to commit, outside their humanitarian duties, acts harmful to the enemy. Protection may, however, cease only after due warning has been given, naming, in all appropriate cases, a reasonable time limit and after such warning has remained unheeded. The fact that sick or wounded members of the armed forces are nursed in these hospitals, or the presence of small arms and ammunition taken from such combatants which have not yet been handed to the proper service, shall not be considered to be acts harmful to the enemy.

Article 20

Persons regularly and solely engaged in the operation and administration of civilian hospitals, including the personnel engaged in the search for, removal and transporting of and caring for wounded and sick civilians, the infirm and maternity cases shall be respected and protected.

In occupied territory and in zones of military operations, the above personnel shall be recognisable by means of an identity card certifying their status,

The management of each hospital shall at all times hold at the disposal of the competent national or occupying authorities an up-to-date list of such personnel.

Article 21

Convoys of vehicles or hospital trains on land or specially 9–011 provided vessels on sea, conveying wounded and sick civilians, the infirm and maternity cases, shall be respected and protected in the same manner as the hospitals provided for in Article 18, and shall be marked, with the consent of the State, by the display of the distinctive emblem. . . .

Article 22

Aircraft exclusively employed for the removal of wounded and sick civilians, the infirm and maternity cases or for the transport of medical personnel and equipment, shall not be attacked, but shall be respected while flying at heights, times and on routes specifically agreed upon between all the Parties to the conflict concerned.

Unless agreed otherwise, flights over enemy or enemy occupied territory are prohibited.

Such aircraft shall obey every summons to land. In the event of a landing thus imposed, the aircraft with its occupants may continue its flight after examination, if any.

Article 23

Each High Contracting Party shall allow the free passage of all consignments of medical and hospital stores and objects necessary for religious worship intended only for civilians of another High Contracting Party, even if the latter is its adversary. It shall likewise permit the free passage of all consignments of essential foodstuffs, clothing and tonics intended for children under 15, expectant mothers and maternity cases.

The obligation of a High Contracting Party to allow the free passage of the consignments indicated in the preceding paragraph is subject to the condition that this Party is satisfied that there are no serious reasons for fearing:

(a) that the consignments may be diverted from their destination,

(b) that the control may not be effective, or

(c) that a definite advantage may accrue to the military efforts or economy of the enemy through the substitution of the above-mentioned consignments for goods which would otherwise be provided or produced by the enemy or through the release of such material, services or facilities as would otherwise be required for the production of such goods.

The Power which allows the passage of the consignments indicated in the first paragraph of this Article may make such permission conditional on the distribution to the persons benefited thereby being made under the local supervision of the Protecting Powers.

Such consignments shall be forwarded as rapidly as possible, and the Power which permits their free passage shall have the right to prescribe the technical arrangements under which such passage is allowed.

Article 24

9–012 The Parties to the conflict shall take the necessary measures to ensure that children under 15, who are orphaned or are separated from their families as a result of the war, are not left to their own resources, and that their maintenance, the exercise of their religion and their education are facilitated in all circumstances. Their education shall, as far as possible, be entrusted to persons of a similar cultural tradition.

The Parties to the conflict shall facilitate the reception of such children in a neutral country for the duration of the conflict with the consent of the Protecting Power, if any, and under due safeguards for the observance of the principles stated in the first paragraph.

They shall, furthermore, endeavour to arrange for all children under 12 to be identified by the wearing of identity discs, or by some other means.

Article 25

All persons in the territory of a Party to the conflict, or in a territory occupied by it, shall be enabled to give news of a strictly personal nature to members of their families, wherever they may be, and to receive news from them. This correspondence shall be forwarded speedily and without undue delay.

If, as a result of circumstances, it becomes difficult or impossible to exchange family correspondence by the ordinary post, the Parties to the conflict concerned shall apply to a neutral intermediary, such as the Central Agency provided for in Article 140, and shall decide in consultation with it how to ensure the fulfilment of their obligations under the best possible conditions, in particular with the co-operation of the National Red Cross (Red Crescent, Red Lion and Sun) Societies.

If the Parties to the conflict deem it necessary to restrict family correspondence, such restrictions shall be confined to the compulsory use of standard forms containing 25 freely chosen words, and to the limitation of the number of these forms despatched to one each month.

Article 26

Each Party to the conflict shall facilitate enquiries made by 9–013 members of families dispersed owing to the war, with the object of renewing contact with one another and of meeting, if possible. It shall encourage, in particular, the work of organisations engaged on this task provided they are acceptable to it and conform to its security regulations.[17]

---

[17] The principle of family unity is enshrined in a number of international instruments— see Chapter on Refugees.

PART III. STATUS AND TREATMENT OF PROTECTED PERSONS

Section I. Provisions common to the territories of the parties to the conflict and to occupied territories

Article 27

Protected persons are entitled, in all circumstances, to respect for their persons, their honour, their family rights, their religious convictions and practices, and their manners and customs. They shall at all times be humanely treated, and shall be protected especially against all acts of violence or threats thereof and against insults and public curiosity.

Women shall be especially protected against any attack on their honour, in particular against rape, enforced prostitution, or any form of indecent assault.[18]

Without prejudice to the provisions relating to their state of health, age and sex, all protected persons shall be treated with the same consideration by the Party to the conflict in whose power they are, without any adverse distinction based, in particular, on race, religion or political opinion.

However, the Parties to the conflict may take such measures of control and security in regard to protected persons as may be necessary as a result of the war.

Article 28

9–014   The presence of a protected person may not be used to render certain points or areas immune from military operations.

Article 29

The Party to the conflict in whose hands protected persons may be, is responsible for the treatment accorded to them by its agents, irrespective of any individual responsibility which may be incurred.

Article 30

Protected persons shall have every facility for making application to the Protecting Powers, the International Committee of the Red Cross, the National Red Cross (Red Crescent, Red Lion and Sun) Society of the country where they may be, as well as to any organisation that might assist them.

---

[18] See Chapter on Women, Section on rape.

These several organisations shall be granted all facilities for that purpose by the authorities, within the bounds set by military or security considerations.

Apart from the visits of the delegates of the Protecting Powers and of the International Committee of the Red Cross, provided for by Article 143, the Detaining or Occupying Powers shall facilitate, as much as possible, visits to protected persons by the representatives of other organisations whose object is to give spiritual aid or material relief to such persons.

Article 31

No physical or moral coercion shall be exercised against protected persons, in particular to obtain information from them or from third parties.

Article 32

The High Contracting Parties specifically agree that each of them is prohibited from taking any measure of such a character as to cause the physical suffering or extermination of protected persons in their hands. This prohibition applies not only to murder, torture, corporal punishments, mutilation and medical or scientific experiments not necessitated by the medical treatment of a protected person, but also to any other measures of brutality whether applied by civilian or military agents.[19]

Article 33

No protected person may be punished for an offence he or she 9–015 has not personally committed. Collective penalties and likewise all measures of intimidation or of terrorism are prohibited.

Pillage is prohibited.

Reprisals against protected persons and their property are prohibited.

Article 34

The taking of hostages is prohibited.

Section II. Aliens in the Territory of a Party to the Conflict

Article 35

All protected persons who may desire to leave the territory at the outset of, or during a conflict, shall be entitled to do so, unless

[19] See also Chapter on Prisoners, Section on torture.

their departure is contrary to the national interests of the State. The applications of such persons to leave shall be decided in accordance with regularly established procedures and the decision shall be taken as rapidly as possible. Those persons permitted to leave may provide themselves with the necessary funds for their journey and take with them a reasonable amount of their effects and articles of personal use.

If any such person is refused permission to leave the territory, he shall be entitled to have refusal reconsidered, as soon as possible by an appropriate court or administrative board designated by the Detaining Power for that purpose.

Upon request, representatives of the Protecting Power shall, unless reasons of security prevent it, or the persons concerned object, be furnished with the reasons for refusal of any request for permission to leave the territory and be given, as expeditiously as possible, the names of all persons who have been denied permission to leave.

Article 36

9–016 Departures permitted under the foregoing Article shall be carried out in satisfactory conditions as regards safety, hygiene, sanitation and food. All costs in connection therewith, from the point of exit in the territory of the Detaining Power, shall be borne by the country of destination, or, in the case of accommodation in a neutral country, by the Power whose nationals are benefited. The practical details of such movements may, if necessary, be settled by special agreements between the Powers concerned.

The foregoing shall not prejudice such special agreements as may be concluded between Parties to the conflict concerning the exchange and repatriation of their nationals in enemy hands.

Article 37

Protected persons who are confined pending proceedings or subject to a sentence involving loss of liberty, shall during their confinement be humanely treated.

As soon as they are released, they may ask to leave the territory in conformity with the foregoing Articles.

Article 38

With the exception of special measures authorised by the present Convention, in particularly by Article 27 and 41 thereof, the situation of protected persons shall continue to be regulated, in principle, by the provisions concerning aliens in time of peace. In any case, the following rights shall be granted to them:

(1) they shall be enabled to receive the individual or collective relief that may be sent to them.

(2) they shall, if their state of health so requires, receive medical attention and hospital treatment to the same extent as the nationals of the State concerned.

(3) they shall be allowed to practise their religion and to receive spiritual assistance from ministers of their faith.

(4) if they reside in an area particularly exposed to the dangers of war, they shall be authorised to move from that area to the same extent as the nationals of the State concerned.

(5) children under 15 years, pregnant women and mothers of children under seven years shall benefit by any preferential treatment to the same extent as the nationals of the State concerned.

Article 39

Protected persons who, as a result of the war, have lost their 9–017
gainful employment, shall be granted the opportunity to find paid
employment. That opportunity shall, subject to security considerations and to the provisions of Article 40, be equal to that
enjoyed by the nationals of the Power in whose territory they are.

Where a Party to the conflict applies to a protected person
methods of control which result in his being unable to support
himself, and especially if such a person is prevented for reasons
of security from finding paid employment on reasonable conditions, the said Party shall ensure his support and that of his
dependents.

Protected persons may in any case receive allowances from
their home country, the Protecting Power, or the relief societies
referred to in Article 30.

Article 40

Protected persons may be compelled to work only to the same
extent as nationals of the Party to the conflict in whose territory
they are.

If protected persons are of enemy nationality, they may only be
compelled to do work which is normally necessary to ensure the
feeding, sheltering, clothing, transport and health of human
beings and which is not directly related to the conduct of military
operations.

In the cases mentioned in the two preceding paragraphs,
protected persons compelled to work shall have the benefit of the
same working conditions and of the same safeguards as national

workers in particular as regards wages, hours of labour, clothing and equipment, previous training and compensation for occupational accidents and diseases.

If the above provisions are infringed, protected persons shall be allowed to exercise their right of complaint in accordance with Article 30.

Article 41

Should the Power, in whose hands protected persons may be, consider the measures of control mentioned in the present Convention to be inadequate, it may not have recourse to any other measure of control more severe than that of assigned residence or internment, in accordance with the provisions of Articles 42 and 43.

In applying the provisions of Article 39, second paragraph, to the cases of persons required to leave their usual places of residence by virtue of a decision placing them in assigned residence elsewhere, the Detaining Power shall be guided as closely as possible by the standards of welfare set forth in Part III, Section IV of this Convention.

Article 42

9–018 The internment or placing in assigned residence of protected persons may be ordered only if the security of the Detaining Power makes it absolutely necessary.

If any person, acting through the representatives of the Protecting Power, voluntarily demands internment, and if his situation renders this step necessary, he shall be interned by the Power in whose hands he may be.

Article 43

Any protected person who has been interned or placed in assigned residence shall be entitled to have such action reconsidered as soon as possible by an appropriate court or administrative board designated by the Detaining Power for that purpose. If the internment or placing in assigned residence is maintained, the court or administrative board shall periodically, and at least twice yearly, give consideration to his or her case, with a view to the favourable amendment of the initial decision, if circumstances permit.

Unless the protected persons concerned object, the Detaining Power shall, as rapidly as possible, give the Protecting Power the names of any protected persons who have been interned or subjected to assigned residence, or who have been released from internment or assigned residence. The decisions of the courts or boards mentioned in the first paragraph of the present Article shall also, subject to the same conditions, be notified as rapidly as possible to the Protecting Power.

Article 44

In applying the measures of control mentioned in the present Convention, the Detaining Power shall not treat as enemy aliens exclusively on the basis of their nationality de jure of an enemy State, refugees who do not, in fact, enjoy the protection of any government.

Article 45

Protected persons shall not be transferred to a Power which is not a party to the Convention.

This provision shall in no way constitute an obstacle to the repatriation of protected persons, or to their return to their country of residence after the cessation of hostilities.

Protected persons may be transferred by the Detaining Power only to a Power which is a party to the present Convention and after the Detaining Power has satisfied itself of the willingness and ability of such transferee Power to apply the present Convention. If protected persons are transferred under such circumstances, responsibility for the application of the present Convention rests on the Power accepting them, while they are in its custody. Nevertheless, if that Power fails to carry out the provisions of the present Convention in any important respect, the Power by which the protected persons were transferred shall, upon being so notified by the Protecting Power, take effective measures to correct the situation or shall request the return of the protected persons. Such request must be complied with.

In no circumstances shall a protected person be transferred to a country where he or she may have reason to fear persecution for his or her political opinions or religious beliefs. The provisions of this Article do not constitute an obstacle to the extradition, in pursuance of extradition treaties concluded before the outbreak of hostilities, of protected persons accused of offences against ordinary criminal law.

Article 46

In so far as they have not been previously withdrawn, restrictive **9–019** measures taken regarding protected persons shall be cancelled as soon as possible after the close of hostilities.

Restrictive measures affecting their property shall be cancelled, in accordance with the law of the Detaining Power, as soon as possible after the close of hostilities.

Section III. Occupied Territories

Article 47

Protected persons who are in occupied territory shall not be deprived, in any case or in any manner whatsoever, of the benefits of the present Convention by any change introduced, as the result of the occupation of a territory, into the institutions or government of the said territory, nor by any agreement con-cluded between the authorities of the occupied territories and the Occupying Power, nor by any annexation by the latter of the whole or part of the occupied territory.

Article 48

9–020 Protected persons who are not nationals of the Power whose territory is occupied, may avail themselves of the right to leave the territory subject to the provisions of Article 35, and decisions therein shall be taken in accordance with the procedure which the Occupying Power shall establish in accordance with the said Article.

Article 49

Individual or mass forcible transfers, as well as deportations of protected persons from occupied territory to the territory of the Occupying Power or to that of any other country, occupied or not, are prohibited, regardless of their motive.

Nevertheless, the Occupying Power may undertake total or partial evacuation of a given area if the security of the population or imperative military reasons so demand. Such evacuations may not involve the displacement of protected persons outside the bounds of the occupied territory except when for material reasons it is impossible to avoid such displacement. Persons thus evacu-ated shall be transferred back to their homes as soon as hostilities in the area in question have ceased.

The Occupying Power undertaking such transfers or evacua-tions shall ensure, to the greatest practicable extent, that proper accommodation is provided to receive the protected persons, that the removals are effected in satisfactory conditions of hygiene, health, safety and nutrition, and that members of the same family are not separated.

The Protecting Power shall be informed of any transfers and evacuations as soon as they have taken place.

The Occupying Power shall not detain protected persons in an area particularly exposed to the dangers of war unless the security of the population or imperative military reasons so demand.

The Occupying Power shall not deport or transfer parts of its own civilian population into the territory it occupies.

Article 50

The Occupying Power shall, with the co-operation of the national and local authorities, facilitate the proper working of all institutions devoted to the care and education of children.

The Occupying Power shall take all necessary steps to facilitate the identification of children and the registration of their parentage. It may not, in any case, change their personal status, nor enlist them in formations or organisations subordinate to it.

Should the local institutions be inadequate for the purpose, the Occupying Power shall make arrangements for the maintenance and education, if possible by persons of their own nationality, language and religion, of children who are orphaned or separated from their parents as a result of the war and who cannot be adequately cared for by a near relative or friend.

A special section of the Bureau set up in accordance with Article 136 shall be responsible for taking all necessary steps to identify children whose identity is in doubt. Particulars of their parents or other near relatives should always be recorded if available.

The Occupying Power shall not hinder the application of any preferential measures in regard to food, medical care and protection against the effects of war which may have been adopted prior to the occupation in favour of children under 15 years, expectant mothers, and mothers of children under seven years.

Article 51

The Occupying Power may not compel protected persons to serve 9–021 in its armed or auxiliary forces. No pressure or propaganda which aims at securing voluntary enlistment is permitted.

The Occupying Power may not compel protected persons to work unless they are over 18 years of age, and then only on work which is necessary either for the needs of the army of occupation, or for the public utility services, or for the feeding, sheltering, clothing, transportation or health of the population of the occupied country. Protected persons may not be compelled to undertake any work which would involve them in the obligation of taking part in military operations. The Occupying Power may not compel protected persons to employ forcible means to ensure the security of the installations where they are performing compulsory labour.

The work shall be carried out only in the occupied territory where the persons whose services have been requisitioned are.

Every such person shall, so far as possible, be kept in his usual place of employment. Workers shall be paid a fair wage and the work shall be proportionate to their physical and intellectual capacities. The legislation in force in the occupied country concerning working conditions, and safeguards as regards, in particular, such matters as wages, hours of work, equipment, preliminary training and compensation for occupational accidents and diseases, shall be applicable to the protected persons assigned to the work referred to in this Article.

In no case shall requisition of labour lead to a mobilisation of workers in an organisation of a military or semi-military character.

Article 52

9–022 No contract, agreement or regulation shall impair the right of any worker, whether voluntary or not and wherever he may be, to apply to the representatives of the Protecting Power in order to request the said Power's intervention.

All measures aiming at creating unemployment or at restricting the opportunities offered to workers in an occupied territory, in order to induce them to work for the Occupying Power, are prohibited.

Article 53

Any destruction by the Occupying Power of real or personal property belonging individually or collectively to private persons, or to the State, or to other public authorities, or to social or co-operative organisations, is prohibited, except where such destruction is rendered absolutely necessary by military operations.

Article 54

The Occupying Power may not alter the status of public officials or judges in the occupied territories, or in any way apply sanctions to or take any measures of coercion or discrimination against them, should they abstain from fulfilling their functions for reasons of conscience.
This prohibition does not prejudice the application of the second paragraph of Article 51. It does not affect the right of the Occupying Power to remove public officials from their posts.

Article 55

To the fullest extent of the means available to it, the Occupying Power has the duty of ensuring the food and medical supplies of the population; it should, in particular, bring in the necessary foodstuffs, medical stores and other articles if the resources of the occupied territory are inadequate.

The Occupying Power may not requisition foodstuffs, articles or medical supplies available in the occupied territory, except for use by the occupation forces and administration personnel, and then only if the requirements of the civilian population have been taken into account. Subject to the provisions of other international Conventions, the Occupying Power shall make arrangements to ensure that fair value is paid for any requisitioned goods.

The Protecting Power shall, at any time, be at liberty to verify the state of the food and medical supplies in occupied territories, except where temporary restrictions are made necessary by imperative military requirements.

Article 56

To the fullest extent of the means available to it, the public 9–023 Occupying Power has the duty of ensuring and maintaining, with the co-operation of national and local authorities, the medical and hospital establishments and services, public health and hygiene in the occupied territory, with particular reference to the adoption and application of the prophylactic and preventive measures necessary to combat the spread of contagious diseases and epidemics. Medical personnel of all categories shall be allowed to carry out their duties.

If new hospitals are set up in occupied territory and if the competent organs of the occupied State are not operating there, the occupying authorities shall, if necessary, grant them the recognition provided for in Article 18. In similar circumstances, the occupying authorities shall also grant recognition to hospital personnel and transport vehicles under the provisions of Articles 20 and 21.

In adopting measures of health and hygiene and in their implementation, the Occupying Power shall take into consideration the moral and ethical susceptibilities of the population of the occupied territory.

Article 57

The Occupying Power may requisition civilian hospitals of hospitals only temporarily and only in cases of urgent necessity for the care of military wounded and sick, and then on condition that suitable arrangements are made in due time for the care and treatment of the patients and for the needs of the civilian population for hospital accommodation.

The material and stores of civilian hospitals cannot be requisitioned so long as they are necessary for the needs of the civilian population.

Article 58

The Occupying Power shall permit ministers of religion to give spiritual assistance to the members of their religious communities.

The Occupying Power shall also accept consignments of books and articles required for religious needs and shall facilitate their distribution in occupied territory.

Article 59

9–024 If the whole or part of the population of an occupied territory is inadequately supplied, the Occupying Power shall agree to relief schemes on behalf of the said population, and shall facilitate them by all the means at its disposal.

Such schemes, which may be undertaken either by States or by impartial humanitarian organisations such as the International Committee of the Red Cross, shall consist, in particular, of the provision of consignments of foodstuffs, medical supplies and clothing.

All Contracting Parties shall permit the free passage of these consignments and shall guarantee their protection.

A Power granting free passage to consignments on their way to territory occupied by an adverse Party to the conflict shall, however, have the right to search the consignments, to regulate their passage according to prescribed times and routes, and to be reasonably satisfied through the Protecting Power that these consignments are to be used for the relief of the needy population and are not to be used for the benefit of the Occupying Power.

Article 60

Relief consignments shall in no way relieve the Occupying Power of any of its responsibilities under Articles 55, 56 and 59. The Occupying Power shall in no way whatsoever divert relief consignments from the purpose for which they are intended, except in cases of urgent necessity, in the interests of the population of the occupied territory and with the consent of the Protecting Power.

Article 61

The distribution of the relief consignments referred to in the foregoing Articles shall be carried out with the co-operation and under the supervision of the Protecting Power. This duty may also be delegated, by agreement between the Occupying Power and the Protecting Power, to a neutral Power, to the International Committee of the Red Cross or to any other impartial humanitarian body.

Such consignments shall be exempt in occupied territory from all charges, taxes or customs duties unless these are necessary in the interests of the economy of the territory. The Occupying Power shall facilitate the rapid distribution of these consignments. All Contracting Parties shall endeavour to permit the transit and transport, free of charge, of such relief consignments on their way to occupied territories.

Article 62

Subject to imperative reasons of security, protected persons in occupied territories shall be permitted to receive the individual relief consignments sent to them.

9–025

Article 63

Subject to temporary and exceptional measures imposed for urgent reasons of security by the Occupying Power:

(a) recognised National Red Cross (Red Crescent, Red Lion and Sun) Societies shall be able to pursue their activities in accordance with Red Cross principles, as defined by the International Red Cross Conferences. Other relief societies shall be permitted to continue their humanitarian activities under similar conditions;

(b) the Occupying Power may not require any changes in the personnel or structure of these societies, which would prejudice the aforesaid activities.

The same principles shall apply to the activities and personnel of special organisations of a non-military character, which already exist or which may be established, for the purpose of ensuring the living conditions of the civilian population by the maintenance of the essential public utility services, by the distribution of relief and by the organisation of rescues.

Article 64[20]

The penal laws of the occupied territory shall remain in force, with the exception that they may be repealed or suspended by the Occupying Power in cases where they constitute a threat to its security or an obstacle to the application of the present Convention.

Subject to the latter consideration and to the necessity for ensuring the effective administration of justice, the tribunals of

[20] For provisions relating to prisoners generally see Chapter on Prisoners.

the occupied territory shall continue to function in respect of all offences covered by the said laws.

The Occupying Power may, however, subject the population of the occupied territory to provisions which are essential to enable the Occupying Power to fulfil its obligations under the present Convention, to maintain the orderly government of the territory, and to ensure the security of the Occupying Power, of the members and property of the occupying forces or administration, and likewise of the establishments and lines of communication used by them.

Article 65

9–026 The penal provisions enacted by the Occupying Power shall not come into force before they have been published and brought to the knowledge of the inhabitants in their own language. The effect of these penal provisions shall not be retroactive.

Article 66

In case of a breach of the penal provisions promulgated by it by virtue of the second paragraph of Article 64 the Occupying Power may hand over the accused to its properly constituted, non-political military courts, on condition that the said courts sit in the occupied country. Courts of appeal shall preferably sit in the occupied country.

Article 67

The courts shall apply only those provisions of law which were applicable prior to the offence, and which are in accordance with general principles of law, in particular the principle that the penalty shall be proportionate to the offence. They shall take into consideration the fact the accused is not a national of the Occupying Power.

Article 68

Protected persons who commit an offence which is solely intended to harm the Occupying Power, but which does not constitute an attempt on the life or limb of members of the occupying forces or administration, nor a grave collective danger, nor seriously damage the property of the occupying forces or administration or the installations used by them, shall be liable to internment or simple imprisonment, provided the duration of such internment or imprisonment is proportionate to the offence committed. Furthermore, internment or imprisonment shall, for such offences, be the only measure adopted for depriving protected persons of liberty. The courts provided for under Article 66 of the present Convention may at their discretion convert a sentence of imprisonment to one of internment for the same period.

The penal provisions promulgated by the Occupying Power in accordance with Articles 64 and 65 may impose the death penalty on a protected person only in cases where the person is guilty of espionage, of serious acts of sabotage against the military installations of the Occupying Power or of intentional offences which have caused the death of one or more persons, provided that such offences were punishable by death under the law of the occupied territory in force before the occupation began.

The death penalty may not be pronounced on a protected person unless the attention of the court has been particularly called to the fact that since the accused is not a national of the Occupying Power, he is not bound to it by any duty of allegiance.

In any case, the death penalty may not be pronounced on a protected person who was under 18 years of age at the time of the offence.

Article 69

In all cases the duration of the period during which a protected **9–027** person accused of an offence is under arrest awaiting trial or punishment shall be deducted from any period of imprisonment of awarded.

Article 70

Protected persons shall not be arrested, prosecuted or convicted by the Occupying Power for acts committed or for opinions expressed before the occupation, or during a temporary interruption thereof, with the exception of breaches of the laws and customs of war.

Nationals of the occupying Power who, before the outbreak of hostilities, have sought refuge in the territory of the occupied State, shall not be arrested, prosecuted, convicted or deported from the occupied territory, except for offences committed after the outbreak of hostilities, or for offences under common law committed before the outbreak of hostilities which, according to the law of the occupied State, would have justified extradition in time of peace.

Article 71

No sentence shall be pronounced by the competent courts of the Occupying Power except after a regular trial.

Accused persons who are prosecuted by the Occupying Power shall be promptly informed, in writing, in a language which they understand, of the particulars of the charges preferred against them, and shall be brought to trial as rapidly as possible. The Protecting Power shall be informed of all proceedings instituted by the Occupying Power against protected persons in respect of charges involving the death penalty or imprisonment for two years or more; it shall be enabled, at any time, to obtain information regarding the state of such proceedings. Furthermore, the Protecting Power shall be entitled, on request, to be furnished with all particulars of these and of any other proceedings instituted by the Occupying Power against protected persons.

The notification to the Protecting Power, as provided for in the second paragraph above, shall be sent immediately, and shall in any case reach the Protecting Power three weeks before the date of the first hearing. Unless, at the opening of the trial, evidence is submitted that the provisions of this Article are fully complied with, the trial shall not proceed. The notification shall include the following particulars:

(a) description of the accused;

(b) place of residence or detention;

(c) specification of the charge or charges (with mention of the penal provisions under which it is brought);

(d) designation of the court which will hear the case;

(e) place and date of the first hearing.

Article 72

9–028 Accused persons shall have the right to present evidence necessary to their defence and may, in particular, call witnesses. They shall have the right to be assisted by a qualified advocate or counsel of their own choice, who shall be able to visit them freely and shall enjoy the necessary facilities for preparing the defence.

Failing a choice by the accused, the Protecting Power may provide him with an advocate or counsel. When an accused person has to meet a serious charge and the Protecting Power is not functioning, the Occupying Power, subject to the consent of the accused, shall provide an advocate or counsel.

Accused persons shall, unless they freely waive such assistance, be aided by an interpreter, both during preliminary investigation and during the hearing in court. They shall have at any time the right to object to the interpreter and to ask for his replacement.

Article 73

A convicted person shall have the right of appeal provided for by the laws applied by the court. He shall be fully informed of his right to appeal or petition and of the time limit within which he may do so.

The penal procedure provided in the present Section shall apply, as far as it is applicable, to appeals. Where the laws applied by the Court make no provision for appeals, the convicted person shall have the right to petition against the finding and sentence to the competent authority of the Occupying Power.

Article 74

Representatives of the Protecting Power shall have the right to attend the trial of any protected person, unless the hearing has, as an exceptional measure, to be held in camera in the interests of the security of the Occupying Power, which shall then notify the Protecting Power. A notification in respect of the date and place of trial shall be sent to the Protecting Power. **9–029**

Any judgment involving a sentence of death, or imprisonment for two years or more, shall be communicated, with the relevant grounds, as rapidly as possible to the Protecting Power. The notification shall contain a reference to the notification made under Article 71 and, in the case of sentences of imprisonment, the name of the place where the sentence is to be served. A record of judgments other than those referred to above shall be kept by the court and shall be open to inspection by representatives of the Protecting Power. Any period allowed for appeal in the case of sentences involving the death penalty, or imprisonment of two years or more, shall not run until notification of judgment has been received by the Protecting Power.

Article 75[21]

In no case shall persons condemned to death be deprived of the right of petition for pardon or reprieve.

No death sentence shall be carried out before the expiration of a period of a least six months from the date of receipt by the Protecting Power of the notification of the final judgment confirming such death sentence, or of an order denying pardon or reprieve.

The six months period of suspension of the death sentence herein prescribed may be reduced in individual cases in circumstances of grave emergency involving an organised threat to the security of the Occupying Power or its forces, provided always that the Protecting Power is notified of such reduction and is given reasonable time and opportunity to make representations to the competent occupying authorities in respect of such death sentences.

---

[21] See also Chapter on Prisoners, Section on capital punishment.

Article 76

Protected persons accused of offences shall be detained in the occupied country, and if convicted they shall serve their sentences therein. They shall, if possible, be separated from other detainees and shall enjoy conditions of food and hygiene which will be sufficient to keep them in good health, and which will be at least equal to those obtaining in prisons in the occupied country.

They shall receive the medical attention required by their state of health. They shall also have the right to receive any spiritual assistance which they may require.

Women shall be confined in separate quarters and shall be under the direct supervision of women.

Proper regard shall be paid to the special treatment due to minors.

Protected persons who are detained shall have the right to be visited by delegates of the Protecting Power and of the International Committee of the Red Cross, in accordance with the provisions of Article 143.

Such persons shall have the right to receive at least one relief parcel monthly.

Article 77

9–030   Protected persons who have been accused of offences or convicted by the courts in occupied territory, shall be handed over at the close of occupation, with the relevant records, to the authorities of the liberated territory.

Article 78

If the Occupying Power considers it necessary, for imperative reasons of security, to take safety measures concerning protected persons, it may, at the most, subject them to assigned residence or to internment.

Decisions regarding such assigned residence or internment shall be made according to a regular procedure to be prescribed by the Occupying Power in accordance with the provisions of the present Convention. This procedure shall include the right of appeal for the parties concerned. Appeals shall be decided with the least possible delay. In the event of the decision being upheld, it shall be subject to periodical review, if possible every six months, by a competent body set up by the said Power.

Protected persons made subject to assigned residence and thus required to leave their homes shall enjoy the full benefit of Article 39 of the present Convention.

Section IV. Regulations for the Treatment of Internees

Article 79

The Parties to the conflict shall not intern protected persons, 9–031 except in accordance with the provisions of Articles 41, 42, 43, 68 and 78.

Article 80

Internees shall retain their full civil capacity and shall exercise such attendant rights as may be compatible with their status.

Article 81

Parties to the conflict who intern protected persons shall be bound to provide free of charge for their maintenance, and to grant them also the medical attention required by their state of health.

No deduction from the allowances, salaries or credits due to the internees shall be made for the repayment of these costs.

The Detaining Power shall provide for the support of those dependent on the internees, if such dependents are without adequate means of support or are unable to earn a living.

Article 82

The Detaining Power shall, as far as possible, accommodate the internees according to their nationality, language and customs. Internees who are nationals of the same country shall not be separated merely because they have different languages.

Throughout the duration of their internment, members of the same family, and in particular parents and children, shall be lodged together in the same place of internment, except when separation of a temporary nature is necessitated for reasons of employment or health or for the purposes of enforcement of the provisions of Chapter IX of the present Section. Internees may request that their children who are left at liberty without parental care shall be interned with them.

Wherever possible, interned members of the same family shall be housed in the same premises and given separate accommodation from other internees, together with facilities for leading a proper family life.

CHAPTER II. PLACES OF INTERNMENT

Article 83

The Detaining Power shall not set up places of internment in 9–032 areas particularly exposed to the dangers of war.

The Detaining Power shall give the enemy Powers, through the intermediary of the Protecting Powers, all useful information regarding the geographical location of places of internment.

Whenever military considerations permit, internment camps shall be indicated by the letters IC, placed so as to be clearly visible in the daytime from the air. The Powers concerned may, however, agree upon any other system of marking. No place other than an internment camp shall be marked as such.

Article 84

Internees shall be accommodated and administered separately from prisoners of war and from persons deprived of liberty for any other reason.

Article 85

The Detaining Power is bound to take all necessary and possible measures to ensure that protected persons shall, from the outset of their internment, be accommodated in buildings or quarters which afford every possible safeguard as regards hygiene and health, and provide efficient protection against the rigours of the climate and the effects of the war. . . .

Article 86

The Detaining Power shall place at the disposal of interned persons, of whatever denomination, premises suitable for the holding of their religious services.

Article 87

Canteens shall be installed in every place of internment, except where other suitable facilities are available. Their purpose shall be to enable internees to make purchases, at prices not higher than local market prices, of foodstuffs and articles of everyday use, including soap and tobacco, such as would increase their personal well-being and comfort.

Profits made by canteens shall be credited to a welfare fund to be set up for each place of internment, and administered for the benefit of the internees attached to such place of internment. The Internee Committee provided for in Article 102 shall have the right to check the management of the canteen and of the said fund.

When a place of internment is closed down, the balance of the welfare fund shall be transferred to the welfare fund of a place of internment for internees of the same nationality, or, if such a place does not exist, to a central welfare fund which shall be administered for the benefit of all internees remaining in the custody of the Detaining Power. In case of a general release, the said profits shall be kept by the Detaining Power, subject to any agreement to the contrary between the Powers concerned.

Article 88

In all places of internment exposed to air raids and other hazards 9–033 of war, shelters adequate in number and structure to ensure the necessary protection shall be installed. In case of alarms, the measures internees shall be free to enter such shelters as quickly as possible, excepting those who remain for the protection of their quarters against the aforesaid hazards. Any protective measures taken in favour of the population shall also apply to them.
All due precautions must be taken in places of internment against the danger of fire.

CHAPTER III. FOOD AND CLOTHING

Article 89

Daily food rations for internees shall be sufficient in quantity, quality and variety to keep internees in a good state of health and prevent the development of nutritional deficiencies. Account shall also be taken of the customary diet of the internees.

Internees shall also be given the means by which they can prepare for themselves any additional food in their possession.

Sufficient drinking water shall be supplied to internees. The use of tobacco shall be permitted.

Internees who work shall receive additional rations in proportion to the kind of labour which they perform.

Expectant and nursing mothers and children under fifteen years of age, shall be given additional food, in proportion to their physiological needs.

Article 90

When taken into custody, internees shall be given all facilities to provide themselves with the necessary clothing, footwear and change of underwear, and later on, to procure further supplies if required. Should any internees not have sufficient clothing, account being taken of the climate, and be unable to procure any, it shall be provided free of charge to them by the Detaining Power.

The clothing supplied by the Detaining Power to internees and the outward markings placed on their own clothes shall not be ignominious nor expose them to ridicule.

Workers shall receive suitable working outfits, including protective clothing, whenever the nature of their work so requires.

CHAPTER IV. HYGIENE AND MEDICAL ATTENTION

Article 91

9–034 Every place of internment shall have an adequate infirmary, under the direction of a qualified doctor, where internees may have the attention they require, as well as appropriate diet. Isolation wards shall be set aside for cases of contagious or mental diseases.

Maternity cases and internees suffering from serious diseases, or whose condition requires special treatment, a surgical operation or hospital care, must be admitted to any institution where adequate treatment can be given and shall receive care not inferior to that provided for the general population.

Internees shall, for preference, have the attention of medical personnel of their own nationality.

Internees may not be prevented from presenting themselves to the medical authorities for examination. The medical authorities of the Detaining Power shall, upon request, issue to every internee who has undergone treatment an official certificate showing the nature of his illness or injury, and the duration and nature of the treatment given. A duplicate of this certificate shall be forwarded to the Central Agency provided for in Article 140.

Treatment, including the provision of any apparatus necessary for the maintenance of internees in good health, particularly dentures and other artificial appliances and spectacles, shall be free of charge to the internee.

Article 92

Medical inspections of internees shall be made at least once a month. Their purpose shall be, in particular, to supervise the general state of health, nutrition and cleanliness of internees, and to detect contagious diseases, especially tuberculosis, malaria, and venereal diseases. Such inspections shall include, in particular, the checking of weight of each internee and, at least once a year, radioscopic examination.

CHAPTER V. RELIGIOUS, INTELLECTUAL AND PHYSICAL ACTIVITIES

Article 93

9–035 Internees shall enjoy complete latitude in the exercise of their religious duties, including attendance at the services of their faith, on condition that they comply with the disciplinary routine prescribed by the detaining authorities.

Ministers of religion who are interned shall be allowed to minister freely to the members of their community. For this purpose the Detaining Power shall ensure their equitable allocation amongst the various places of internment in which there are internees speaking the same language and belonging to the same religion. Should such ministers be too few in number, the Detaining Power shall provide them with the necessary facilities, including means of transport, for moving from one place to another, and they shall be authorised to visit any internees who are in hospital. Ministers of religion shall be at liberty to correspond on matters concerning their ministry with the religious authorities in the country of detention and, as far as possible, with the international religious organisations of their faith. Such correspondence shall not be considered as forming a part of the quota mentioned in Article 107. It shall, however, be subject to the provisions of Article 112.

When internees do not have at their disposal the assistance of ministers of their faith, or should these latter be too few in number, the local religious authorities of the same faith may appoint, in agreement with the Detaining Power, a minister of the internees' faith or, if such a course is feasible from a denominational point of view, a minister of similar religion or a qualified layman. The latter shall enjoy the facilities granted to the ministry he has assumed. Persons so appointed shall comply with all regulations laid down by the Detaining Power in the interests of discipline and security.

Article 94

The Detaining Power shall encourage intellectual, educational and recreational pursuits, sports and games amongst internees, whilst leaving them free to take part in them or not. It shall take all practicable measures to ensure the exercise thereof, in particular by providing suitable premises.

All possible facilities shall be granted to internees to continue their studies or to take up new subjects. The education of children and young people shall be ensured; they shall be allowed to attend schools either within the place of internment or outside.

Internees shall be given opportunities for physical exercise, sports and outdoor games. For this purpose, sufficient open spaces shall be set aside in all places of internment. Special playgrounds shall be reserved for children and young people.

Article 95

The Detaining Power shall not employ internees as workers, **9–036** unless they so desire. Employment which, if undertaken under compulsion by a protected person not in internment, would involve a breach of Articles 40 or 51 of the present Convention, and employment on work which is of a degrading or humiliating character are in any case prohibited.

After a working period of six weeks, internees shall be free to give up work at any moment, subject to eight days' notice.

These provisions constitute no obstacle to the right of the Detaining Power to employ interned doctors, dentists and other medical personnel in their professional capacity on behalf of their fellow internees, or to employ internees for administrative and maintenance work in places of internment and to detail such persons for work in the kitchens or for other domestic tasks, or to require such persons to undertake duties connected with the protection of internees against aerial bombardment or other war risks. No internee may, however, be required to perform tasks for which he is, in the opinion of a medical officer, physically unsuited.

The Detaining Power shall take entire responsibility for all working conditions, for medical attention, for the payment of wages, and for ensuring that all employed internees receive compensation for occupational accidents and diseases. The standards prescribed for the said working conditions and for compensation shall be in accordance with the national laws and regulations, and with the existing practice; they shall in no case be inferior to those obtaining for work of the same nature in the same district. Wages for work done shall be determined on an equitable basis by special agreements between the internees, the Detaining Power, and, if the case arises, employers other than the Detaining Power to provide for free maintenance of internees and for the medical attention which their state of health may require. Internees permanently detailed for categories of work mentioned in the third paragraph of this Article, shall be paid fair wages by the Detaining Power. The working conditions and the scale of compensation for occupational accidents and diseases to internees, thus detailed, shall not be inferior to those applicable to work of the same nature in the same district.

Article 96

All labour detachments shall remain part of and dependent upon a place of internment. The competent authorities of the Detaining Power and the commandant of a place of internment shall be responsible for the observance in a labour detachment of the provisions of the present Convention. The commandant shall keep an up-to-date list of the labour detachments subordinate to him and shall communicate it to the delegates of the Protecting Power, of the International Committee of the Red Cross and of other humanitarian organisations who may visit the places of internment.

CHAPTER VI. PERSONAL PROPERTY AND FINANCIAL RESOURCES

Article 97

Internees shall be permitted to retain articles of personal use. 9–037
Monies, cheques, bonds, etc., and valuables in their possession
may not be taken from them except in accordance with established procedure. Detailed receipts shall be given therefor.

The amounts shall be paid into the account of every internee as
provided for in Article 98. Such amounts may not be converted
into any other currency unless legislation in force in the territory
in which the owner is interned so requires or the internee gives
his consent.

Articles which have above all a personal or sentimental value
may not be taken away.

A woman internee shall not be searched except by a woman.

On release or repatriation, internees shall be given all articles,
monies or other valuables taken from them during internment
and shall receive in currency the balance of any credit to their
accounts kept in accordance with Article 98, with the exception of
any articles or amounts withheld by the Detaining Power by
virtue of its legislation in force. If the property of an internee is so
withheld, the owner shall receive a detailed receipt.

Family or identity documents in the possession of internees
may not be taken away without a receipt being given. At no time
shall internees be left without identity documents. If they have
none, they shall be issued with special documents drawn up by
the detaining authorities, which will serve as their identity papers
until the end of their internment.

Internees may keep on their persons a certain amount of
money, in cash or in the shape of purchase coupons, to enable
them to make purchases.

Article 98

All internees shall receive regular allowances, sufficient to enable 9–038
them to purchase goods and articles, such as tobacco, toilet
requisites, etc. Such allowances may take the form of credits or
purchase coupons.

Furthermore, internees may receive allowances from the Power
to which they owe allegiance, the Protecting Powers, the organisations which may assist them, or their families, as well as the
income on their property in accordance with the law of the
Detaining Power. The amount of allowances granted by the
Power to which they owe allegiance shall be the same for each
category of internees (infirm, sick, pregnant women, etc.) but may
not be allocated by that Power or distributed by the Detaining

Power on the basis of discriminations between internees which are prohibited by Article 27 of the present Convention.

The Detaining Power shall open a regular account for every internee, to which shall be credited the allowances named in the present Article, the wages earned and the remittances received, together with such sums taken from him as may be available under the legislation in force in the territory in which he is interned. Internees shall be granted all facilities consistent with the legislation in force in such territory to make remittances to their families and to other dependants. They may draw from their accounts the amounts necessary for their personal expenses, within the limits fixed by the Detaining Power. They shall at all times be afforded reasonable facilities for consulting and obtaining copies of their accounts. A statement of accounts shall be furnished to the Protecting Power, on request, and shall accompany the internee in case of transfer.

CHAPTER VII. ADMINISTRATION AND DISCIPLINE

Article 99

Every place of internment shall be put under the authority of a responsible officer, chosen from the regular military forces or the regular civil administration of the Detaining Power. The officer in charge of the place of internment must have in his possession a copy of the present Convention in the official language, or one of the official languages, of his country and shall be responsible for its application. The staff in control of internees shall be instructed in the provisions of the present Convention and of the administrative measures adopted to ensure its application.

The text of the present Convention and the texts of special agreements concluded under the said Convention shall be posted inside the place of internment, in a language which the internees understand, or shall be in the possession of the Internee Committee.

Regulations, orders, notices and publications of every kind shall be communicated to the internees and posted inside the places of internment, in a language which they understand.

Every order and command addressed to internees individually must, likewise, be given in a language which they understand.

Article 100

9–039   The disciplinary regime in places of internment shall be consistent with humanitarian principles, and shall in no circumstances include regulations imposing on internees any physical exertion dangerous to their health or involving physical or moral victimisation. Identification by tattooing or imprinting signs or markings on the body, is prohibited. In particular, prolonged standing and roll-calls, punishment drill, military drill and man-oeuvres, or the reduction of food rations, are prohibited.

Article 101

Internees shall have the right to present to the authorities in whose power they are, any petition with regard to the conditions of internment to which they are subjected.

They shall also have the right to apply without restriction through the Internee Committee or, if they consider it necessary, direct to the representatives of the Protecting Power, in order to indicate to them any points on which they may have complaints to make with regard to the conditions of internment.

Such petitions and complaints shall be transmitted forthwith and without alteration, and even if the latter are recognised to be unfounded, they may not occasion any punishment.

Periodic reports on the situation in places of internment and as to the needs of the internees may be sent by the Internee Committees to the representatives of the Protecting Powers.

Article 102

In every place of internment, the internees shall freely elect by secret ballot every six months, the members of a Committee empowered to represent them before the Detaining and the Protecting Powers, the International Committee of the Red Cross and any other organisation which may assist them. The members of the Committee shall be eligible for re-election.

Internees so elected shall enter upon their duties after their election has been approved by the detaining authorities. The reasons for any refusals or dismissals shall be communicated to the Protecting Powers concerned.

Article 103

The Internee Committees shall further the physical, spiritual and **9–040** intellectual well-being of the internees.

In case the internees decide, in particular, to organise a system of mutual assistance amongst themselves, this organisation would be within the competence of the Committees in addition to the special duties entrusted to them under other provisions of the present Convention.

Article 104

Members of Internee Committees shall not be required to perform any other work, if the accomplishment of their duties is rendered more difficult thereby.

Members of Internee Committees may appoint from amongst the internees such assistants as they may require. All material facilities shall be granted to them, particularly a certain freedom of movement necessary for the accomplishment of their duties (visits to labour detachments, receipt of supplies, etc.).

All facilities shall likewise be accorded to members of Internee Committees for communication by post and telegraph with the detaining authorities, the Protecting Powers, the International Committee of the Red Cross and their delegates, and with the organisations which give assistance to internees. Committee members in labour detachments shall enjoy similar facilities for communication with their Internee Committee in the principal place of internment. Such communications shall not be limited, nor considered as forming a part of the quota mentioned in Article 107.

Members of Internee Committees who are transferred shall be allowed a reasonable time to acquaint their successors with current affairs.

Chapter VIII. Relations with the Exterior

Article 105

Immediately upon interning protected persons, the Detaining Powers shall inform them, the Power to which they owe allegiance and their Protecting Power of the measures taken for executing the provisions of the present Chapter. The Detaining Powers shall likewise inform the Parties concerned of any subsequent modifications of such measures.

Article 106

9–041   As soon as he is interned, or at the latest not more than one week after his arrival in a place of internment, and likewise in cases of sickness or transfer to another place of internment or to a hospital, every internee shall be enabled to send direct to his family, on the one hand, and to the Central Agency provided for by Article 140, on the other, an internment card similar, if possible, to the model annexed to the present Convention, informing his relatives of his detention, address and state of health. The said cards shall be forwarded as rapidly as possible and may not be delayed in any way.

Article 107

Internees shall be allowed to send and receive letters and cards. If the Detaining Power deems it necessary to limit the number of letters and cards sent by each internee, the said number shall not be less than two letters and four cards monthly; these shall be drawn up so as to conform as closely as possible to the models annexed to the present Convention. If limitations must be placed on the correspondence addressed to internees, they may be ordered only by the Power to which such internees owe allegiance, possibly at the request of the Detaining Power. Such letters and cards must be conveyed with reasonable despatch; they may not be delayed or retained for disciplinary reasons.

Internees who have been a long time without news, or who find it impossible to receive news from their relatives, or to give them news by the ordinary postal route, as well as those who are at a considerable distance from their homes, shall be allowed to send telegrams, the charges being paid by them in the currency at their disposal. They shall likewise benefit by this provision in cases which are recognised to be urgent.

As a rule, internees' mail shall be written in their own language. The Parties to the conflict may authorise correspondence in other languages.

Article 108

Internees shall be allowed to receive, by post or by any other means, individual parcels or collective shipments containing in particular foodstuffs, clothing, medical supplies, as well as books and objects of a devotional, educational or recreational character which may meet their needs. Such shipments shall in no way free the Detaining Power from the obligations imposed upon it by virtue of the present Convention.

Should military necessity require the quantity of such shipments to be limited, due notice thereof shall be given to the Protecting Power and to the International Committee of the Red Cross, or to any other organisation giving assistance to the internees and responsible for the forwarding of such shipments.

The conditions for the sending of individual parcels and collective shipments shall, if necessary, be the subject of special agreements between the Powers concerned, which may in no case delay the receipt by the internees of relief supplies. Parcels of clothing and foodstuffs may not include books. Medical relief supplies shall, as a rule, be sent in collective parcels.

Article 109

In the absence of special agreements between Parties to the 9–042 conflict regarding the conditions for the receipt and distribution of collective relief shipments, the regulations concerning collective relief which are annexed to the present Convention shall be applied.

The special agreements provided for above shall in no case restrict the right of Internee Committees to take possession of collective relief shipments intended for internees, to undertake their distribution and to dispose of them in the interests of the recipients. Nor shall such agreements restrict the right of representatives of the Protecting Powers, the International Committee of the Red Cross, or any other organisation giving assistance to internees and responsible for the forwarding of collective shipments, to supervise their distribution to the recipients.

Article 110

And relief shipments for internees shall be exempt from import, customs and other dues.

All matter sent by mail, including relief parcels sent by parcel post and remittances of money, addressed from other countries to internees or despatched by them through the post office, either direct or through the Information Bureaux provided for in Article 136 and the Central Information Agency provided for in Article 140, shall be exempt from all postal dues both in the countries of origin and destination and in intermediate countries. To this effect, in particular, the exemption provided by the Universal Postal Convention of 1947[22] and by the agreements of the Universal Postal Union in favour of civilians of enemy nationality detained in camps or civilian prisons, shall be extended to the other interned persons protected by the present Convention. The countries not signatory to the above-mentioned agreements shall be bound to grant freedom from charges in the same circumstances.

The cost of transporting relief shipments which are intended for internees and which, by reason of their weight or any other cause, cannot be sent through the post office, shall be borne by the Detaining Power in all the territories under its control. Other Powers which are Parties to the present Convention shall bear the cost of transport in their respective territories.

Costs connected with the transport of such shipments, which are not covered by the above paragraphs, shall be charged to the senders.

The High Contracting Parties shall endeavour to reduce, so far as possible, the charges for telegrams sent by internees, or addressed to them.

Article 111

9–043 Should military operations prevent the Powers concerned from fulfilling their obligation to ensure the conveyance of the mail and relief shipments provided for in Articles 106, 107, 108 and 113, the

[22] U.K.T.S. 1949 No. 57.

Protecting Powers concerned, the International Committee of the Red Cross or any other organisation duly approved by the Parties to the conflict may undertake to ensure the conveyance of such shipments by suitable means (rail, motor vehicles, vessels or aircraft, etc.). For this purpose, the High Contracting Parties shall endeavour to supply them with such transport, and to allow its circulation, especially by granting the necessary safe-conducts.

Such transport may also be used to convey:

(a) correspondence, lists and reports exchanged between the Central Information Agency referred to in Article 140 and the National Bureaux referred to in Article 136;

(b) correspondence and reports relating to internees which the Protecting Powers, the International Committee of the Red Cross or any other organisation assisting the internees exchange either with their own delegates or with the Parties to the conflict.

These provisions in no way detract from the right of any Party to the conflict to arrange other means of transport if it should so prefer, nor preclude the granting of safe-conducts, under mutually agreed conditions, to such means of transport.

The costs occasioned by the use of such means of transport shall be borne, in proportion to the importance of the shipments, by the Parties to the conflict whose nationals are benefited thereby.

Article 112

The censoring of correspondence addressed to internees or 9–044 despatched by them shall be done as quickly as possible.

The examination of consignments intended for internees shall not be carried out under conditions that will expose the goods contained in them to deterioration. It shall be done in the presence of the addressee, or of a fellow-internee duly delegated by him. The delivery to internees of individual or collective consignments shall not be delayed under the pretext of difficulties of censorship.

Any prohibition of correspondence ordered by the Parties to the conflict either for military or political reasons, shall be only temporary and its duration shall be as short as possible.

Article 113

The Detaining Powers shall provide all reasonable execution facilities for the transmission, through the Protecting Power or the Central Agency provided for in Article 140, or as otherwise required, of wills, powers of attorney, letters of authority, or any other documents intended for internees or despatched by them.

In all cases the Detaining Powers shall facilitate the execution and authentication in due legal form of such documents on behalf of internees, in particular by allowing them to consult a lawyer.

Article 114

The Detaining Power shall afford internees all facilities to enable them to manage their property, provided this is not incompatible with the conditions of internment and the law which is applicable. For this purpose, the said Power may give them permission to leave the place of internment in urgent cases and if circumstances allow.

Article 115

In all cases where an internee is a party to proceedings in any court, the Detaining Power shall, if he so requests, cause the court to be informed of his detention and shall, within legal limits, ensure that all necessary steps are taken to prevent him from being in any way prejudiced, by reason of his internment, as regards the preparation and conduct of his case or as regards the execution of any judgment of the court.

Article 116

Every internee shall be allowed to receive visitors, especially near relatives, at regular intervals and as frequently as possible.

As far as is possible, internees shall be permitted to visit their homes in urgent cases, particularly in cases of death or serious illness of relatives.

CHAPTER IX. PENAL AND DISCIPLINARY SANCTIONS

Article 117

9–045 Subject to the provisions of the present Chapter, the laws in force in the territory in which they are detained will continue to apply to internees who commit offences during internment.

If general laws, regulations or orders declare acts committed by internees to be punishable, whereas the same acts are not punishable when committed by persons who are not internees, such acts shall entail disciplinary punishments only.

No internee may be punished more than once for the same act, or on the same count.

Article 118

The courts or authorities shall in passing sentence take as far as possible into account the fact that the defendant is not a national of the Detaining Power. They shall be free to reduce the penalty prescribed for the offence with which the internee is charged and shall not be obliged, to this end, to apply the minimum sentence prescribed.

Imprisonment in premises without daylight, and, in general, all forms of cruelty without exception are forbidden.

Internees who have served disciplinary or judicial sentences shall not be treated differently from other internees.

The duration of preventive detention undergone by an internee shall be deducted from any disciplinary or judicial penalty involving confinement to which he may be sentenced.

Internee Committees shall be informed of all judicial proceedings instituted against internees whom they represent, and of their result.

Article 119

The disciplinary punishments applicable to internees shall be the following:

(1) a fine which shall not exceed 50 per cent of the wages which the internee would otherwise receive under the provisions of Article 95 during a period of not more than 30 days;

(2) discontinuance of privileges granted over and above the treatment provided for by the present Convention;

(3) fatigue duties, not exceeding two hours daily, in connection with the maintenance of the place of internment;

(4) confinement.

In no case shall disciplinary penalties be inhuman, brutal or dangerous for the health of internees. Account shall be taken of the internee's age, sex and state of health.

The duration of any single punishment shall in no case exceed a maximum of 30 consecutive days, even if the internee is answerable for several breaches of discipline when his case is dealt with, whether such breaches are connected or not.

Article 120

Internees who are recaptured after having escaped or when 9–046 attempting to escape, shall be liable only to disciplinary punishment in respect of this act, even if it is a repeated offence.

Article 118, paragraph 3, notwithstanding, internees punished as a result of escape or attempt to escape, may be subjected to special surveillance, on condition that such surveillance does not affect the state of their health, that it is exercised in a place of internment and that it does not entail the abolition of any of the safeguards granted by the present Convention.

Internees who aid and abet an escape or attempt to escape, shall be liable on this count to disciplinary punishment only.

Article 121

Escape, or attempt to escape, even if it is a repeated offence, shall not be deemed an aggravating circumstance in cases where an internee is prosecuted for offences committed during his escape.

The Parties to the conflict shall ensure that the competent authorities exercise leniency in deciding whether punishment inflicted for an offence shall be of a disciplinary or judicial nature, especially in respect of acts committed in connection with an escape, whether successful or not.

Article 122

Acts which constitute offences against discipline shall be investigated immediately. This rule shall be applied, in particular, in cases of escape or attempt to escape. Recaptured internees shall be handed over to the competent authorities as soon as possible.

In cases of offences against discipline, confinement awaiting trial shall be reduced to an absolute minimum for all internees, and shall not exceed 14 days. Its duration shall in any case be deducted from any sentence of confinement.

The provisions of Articles 124 and 125 shall apply to internees who are in confinement awaiting trial for offences against discipline.

Article 123

9–047 Without prejudice to the competence of courts and higher authorities, disciplinary punishment may be ordered only by the commandant of the place of internment, or by a responsible officer or official who replaces him, or to whom he has delegated his disciplinary powers.

Before any disciplinary punishment is awarded, the accused internee shall be given precise information regarding the offences of which he is accused, and given an opportunity of explaining his conduct and of defending himself. He shall be permitted, in particular, to call witnesses and to have recourse, if necessary, to the services of a qualified interpreter. The decision shall be announced in the presence of the accused and of a member of the Internee Committee.

The period elapsing between the time of award of a disciplinary punishment and its execution shall not exceed one month.

When an internee is awarded a further disciplinary punishment, a period of at least three days shall elapse between the execution of any two of the punishments, if the duration of one of these is 10 days or more.

A record of disciplinary punishments shall be maintained by the commandant of the place of internment and shall be open to inspection by representatives of the Protecting Power.

Article 124

Internees shall not in any case be transferred to penitentiary establishments (prisons, penitentiaries, convict prisons, etc.) to undergo disciplinary punishment therein.

The premises in which disciplinary punishments are undergone shall conform to sanitary requirements: they shall in particular be provided with adequate bedding. Internees undergoing punishment shall be enabled to keep themselves in a state of cleanliness.

Women internees undergoing disciplinary punishment shall be confined in separate quarters from male internees and shall be under the immediate supervision of women.

Article 125

Internees awarded disciplinary punishment shall be allowed to exercise and to stay in the open air at least two hours daily.

They shall be allowed, if they so request, to be present at the daily medical inspections. They shall receive the attention which their state of health requires and, if necessary, shall be removed to the infirmary of the place of internment or to a hospital.

They shall have permission to read and write, likewise to send and receive letters. Parcels and remittances of money, however, may be withheld from them until the completion of their punishment; such consignments shall meanwhile be entrusted to the Internee Committee, who will hand over to the infirmary the perishable goods contained in the parcels.

No internee given a disciplinary punishment may be deprived of the benefit of the provisions of Articles 107 and 143 of the present Convention.

Article 126

The provisions of Articles 71 to 76 inclusive shall apply, by analogy, to proceedings against internees who are in the national territory of the Detaining Power.

CHAPTER X. TRANSFERS OF INTERNEES

Article 127

The transfer of internees shall always be effected humanely. As a 9–048 general rule, it shall be carried out by rail or other means of transport, and under conditions at least equal to those obtaining for the forces of the Detaining Power in their changes of station. If, as an exceptional measure, such removals have to be effected on foot, they may not take place unless the internees are in a fit state of health, and may not in any case expose them to excessive fatigue.

The Detaining Power shall supply internees during transfer with drinking water and food sufficient in quantity, quality and variety to maintain them in good health, and also with the necessary clothing, adequate shelter and the necessary medical attention. The Detaining Power shall take all suitable precautions to ensure their safety during transfer, and shall establish before their departure a complete list of all internees transferred.

Sick, wounded or infirm internees and maternity cases shall not be transferred if the journey would be seriously detrimental to them, unless their safety imperatively so demands.

If the combat zone draws close to a place of internment, the internees in the said place shall not be transferred unless their removal can be carried out in adequate conditions of safety, or unless they are exposed to greater risks by remaining on the spot than by being transferred.

When making decisions regarding the transfer of internees, the Detaining Power shall take their interests into account and, in particular, shall not do anything to increase the difficulties of repatriating them or returning them to their own homes.

Article 128

9–049 In the event of transfer, internees shall be officially advised of their departure and of their new postal address. Such notification shall be given in time for them to pack their luggage and inform their next of kin.

They shall be allowed to take with them their personal effects, and the correspondence and parcels which have arrived for them. The weight of such baggage may be limited if the conditions of transfer so require, but in no case to less than 25 kilograms per internee.

Mail and parcels addressed to their former place of internment shall be forwarded to them without delay.

The commandant of the place of internment shall take, in agreement with the Internee Committee, any measures needed to ensure the transport of the internees' community property and of the luggage the internees are unable to take with them in consequence of restrictions imposed by virtue of the second paragraph.

CHAPTER XI. DEATHS

Article 129

The wills of internees shall be received for safe-keeping by the responsible authorities; and if the event of the death of an internee his will shall be transmitted without delay to a person whom he has previously designated.

Deaths of internees shall be certified in every case by a doctor, and a death certificate shall be made out, showing the causes of death and the conditions under which it occurred.

An official record of the death, duly registered, shall be drawn up in accordance with the procedure relating thereto in force in the territory where the place of internment is situated, and a duly certified copy of such record shall be transmitted without delay to the Protecting Power as well as to the Central Agency referred to in Article 140.

Article 130

The detaining authorities shall ensure that internees who die 9–050 while interned are honourably buried, if possible according to the rites of the religion to which they belonged and that their graves are respected, properly maintained, and marked in such a way that they can always be recognised.

Deceased internees shall be buried in individual graves unless unavoidable circumstances require the use of collective graves. Bodies may be cremated only for imperative reasons of hygiene, on account of the religion of the deceased or in accordance with his expressed wish to this effect. In case of cremation, the fact shall be stated and the reasons given in the death certificate of the deceased. The ashes shall be retained for safe-keeping by the detaining authorities and shall be transferred as soon as possible to the next of kin on their request.

As soon as circumstances permit, and not later than the close of hostilities, the Detaining Power shall forward lists of graves of deceased internees to the Powers on whom deceased internees depended, through the Information Bureaux provided for in Article 136. Such lists shall include all particulars necessary for the identification of the deceased internees, as well as the exact location of their graves.

Article 131

Every death or serious injury of an internee, caused or suspected to have been caused by a sentry, another internee or any other person, as well as any death the cause of which is unknown, shall be immediately followed by an official enquiry by the Detaining Power.

A communication on this subject shall be sent immediately to the Protecting Power. The evidence of any witnesses shall be taken, and a report including such evidence shall be prepared and forwarded to the said Protecting Power.

If the enquiry indicates the guilt of one or more persons, the Detaining Power shall take all necessary steps to ensure the prosecution of the person or persons responsible.

CHAPTER XIII. RELEASE, REPATRIATION AND ACCOMMODATION IN NEUTRAL COUNTRIES

Article 132

Each interned person shall be released by the Detaining Power as soon as the reasons which necessitated his internment no longer exist.

The Parties to the conflict shall, moreover, endeavour during the course of hostilities, to conclude agreements for the release, the repatriation, the return to places of residence or the accommodation in a neutral country of certain classes of internees, in particular children, pregnant women and mothers with infants and young children, wounded and sick, and internees who have been detained for a long time.

Article 133

9–051 Internment shall cease as soon as possible after the close of hostilities.

Internees in the territory of a Party to the conflict against whom penal proceedings are pending for offences not exclusively subject to disciplinary penalties, may be detained until the close of such proceedings and, if circumstances require, until the completion of the penalty. The same shall apply to internees who have been previously sentenced to a punishment depriving them of liberty.

By agreement between the Detaining Power and the Powers concerned, committees may be set up after the close of hostilities, or of the occupation of territories, to search for dispersed internees.

Article 134

The High Contracting Parties shall endeavour, upon the Repatriation close of hostilities or occupation, to ensure the return of all internees to their last place of residence, or to facilitate their residence repatriation.

Article 135

The Detaining Power shall bear the expense of returning released internees to the places where they were residing when interned, or, if it took them into custody while they were in transit or on the high seas, the cost of completing their journey or of their return to their point of departure.

Where a Detaining Power refuses permission to reside in its territory to a released internee who previously had his permanent domicile therein, such Detaining Power shall pay the cost of the said internee's repatriation. If, however, the internee elects to return to his country on his own responsibility or in obedience to the Government of the Power to which he owes allegiance, the Detaining Power need not pay the expenses of his journey beyond the point of his departure from its territory. The Detaining Power need not pay the cost of repatriation of an internee who was interned at his own request.

If internees are transferred in accordance with Article 45, the transferring and receiving Powers shall agree on the portion of the above costs to be borne by each.

The foregoing shall not prejudice such special agreements as may be concluded between Parties to the conflict concerning the exchange and repatriation of their nationals in enemy hands.

Section V. Information Bureaux and Central Agency

Article 136

Upon the outbreak of a conflict and in all cases of occupation, 9–052 each of the Parties to the conflict shall establish an official Information Bureau responsible for receiving and transmitting information in respect of the protected persons who are in its power.

Each of the Parties to the conflict shall, within the shortest possible period, give its Bureau information of any measure taken by it concerning any protected persons who are kept in custody for more than two weeks, who are subjected to assigned residence or who are interned. It shall, furthermore, require its various departments concerned with such matters to provide the aforesaid Bureau promptly with information concerning all changes pertaining to these protected persons, as, for example, transfers, releases, repatriations, escapes, admittances to hospitals, births and deaths.

Article 137

Each national Bureau shall immediately forward information concerning protected persons by the most rapid means to the Powers in whose territory they resided, through the intermediary of the Protecting Powers and likewise through the Central Agency provided for in Article 140. The Bureaux shall also reply to all enquiries which may be received regarding protected persons.

Information Bureaux shall transmit information concerning a protected person unless its transmission might be detrimental to the person concerned or to his or her relatives. Even in such a case, the information may not be withheld from the Central Agency which, upon being notified of the circumstances, will take the necessary precautions indicated in Article 140.

All communications in writing made by any Bureau shall be authenticated by a signature or a seal.

Article 138

9–053 The information received by the national Bureau and transmitted by it shall be of such a character as to make it possible to identify the protected person exactly and to advise his next of kin quickly. The information in respect of each person shall include at least his surname, first names, place and date of birth, nationality last residence and distinguishing characteristics, the first name of the father and the maiden name of the mother, the date, place and nature of the action taken with regard to the individual, the address at which correspondence may be sent to him and the name and address of the person to be informed.

Likewise, information regarding the state of health of internees who are seriously ill or seriously wounded shall be supplied regularly and if possible every week.

Article 139

Each national Information Bureau shall, furthermore, be responsible for collecting all personal valuables left by protected persons mentioned in Article 136, in particular those who have been repatriated or released, or who have escaped or died; it shall forward the said valuables to those concerned, either direct, or, if necessary, through the Central Agency. Such articles shall be sent by the Bureau in sealed packets which shall be accompanied by statements giving clear and full identity particulars of the person to whom the articles belonged, and by a complete list of the contents of the parcel. Detailed records shall be maintained of the receipt and despatch of all such valuables.

Article 140

A Central Information Agency for protected persons, in particular for internees, shall be created in a neutral country. The International Committee of the Red Cross shall, if it deems necessary, propose to the Powers concerned the organisation of such an

Agency, which may be the same as that provided for in Article 123 of the Geneva Convention relative to the Treatment of Prisoners of War of August 12, 1949.[23]

The function of the Agency shall be to collect all information of the type set forth in Article 136 which it may obtain through official or private channels and to transmit it as rapidly as possible to the countries of origin or of residence of the persons concerned, except in cases where such transmissions might be detrimental to the persons whom the said information concerns, or to their relatives. It shall receive from the Parties to the conflict all reasonable facilities for effecting such transmissions.

The High Contracting Parties, and in particular those whose nationals benefit by the services of the Central Agency, are requested to give the said Agency the financial aid it may require.

The foregoing provisions shall in no way be interpreted as restricting the humanitarian activities of the International Committee of the Red Cross and of the relief Societies described in Article 142.

Article 141

The national Information Bureaux and the Central Information Agency shall enjoy free postage for all mail, likewise the exemptions provided for in Article 110, and further, so far as possible, exemption from telegraphic charges or, at least, greatly reduced rates.

PART IV. EXECUTION OF THE CONVENTION

Section I. General Provisions

Article 142

Subject to the measures which the Detaining Powers may con- 9–054 sider essential to ensure their security or to meet any other reasonable need, the representatives of religious organisations, relief societies, or any other organisations assisting the protected persons, shall receive from these Powers, for themselves or their duly accredited agents, all facilities for visiting the protected persons, for distributing relief supplies and material from any source, intended for educational, recreational or religious purposes, or for assisting them in organising their leisure time within the places of internment. Such societies or organisations may be constituted in the territory of the Detaining Power, or in any other country, or they may have an international character.

---

[23] See Chapter on Prisoners.

The Detaining Power may limit the number of societies and organisations whose delegates are allowed to carry out their activities in its territory and under its supervision, on condition, however, that such limitation shall not hinder the supply of effective and adequate relief to all protected persons.

The special position of the International Committee of the Red Cross in this field shall be recognised and respected at all times.

Article 143

9–055   Representatives or delegates of the Protecting Powers shall have permission to go to all places where protected persons are, particularly to places of internment, detention and work.

They shall have access to all premises occupied by protected persons and shall be able to interview the latter without witnesses, personally or through an interpreter.

Such visits may not be prohibited except for reasons of imperative military necessity, and then only as an exceptional and temporary measure. Their duration and frequency shall not be restricted.

Such representatives and delegates shall have full liberty to select the places they wish to visit. The Detaining or Occupying Power, the Protecting Power and when occasion arises the Power of origin of the persons to be visited, may agree that compatriots of the internees shall be permitted to participate in the visits.

The delegates of the International Committee of the Red Cross shall also enjoy the above prerogatives. The appointment of such delegates shall be submitted to the approval of the Power governing the territories where they will carry out their duties.

Article 144

The High Contracting Parties undertake, in time of peace as in time of war, to disseminate the text of the present Convention as widely as possible in their respective countries, and, in particular, to include the study thereof in their programmes of military and, if possible, civil instruction, so that the principles thereof may become known to the entire population.

Any civilian, military, police or other authorities, who in time of war assume responsibilities in respect of protected persons, must possess the text of the Convention and be specially instructed as to its provisions.

Article 145

The High Contracting Parties shall communicate to one another through the Swiss Federal Council and, during hostilities, through the Protecting Powers, the official translations of the present Convention, as well as the laws and regulations which they may adopt to ensure the application thereof.

Article 146

The High Contracting Parties undertake to enact any legislation necessary to provide effective penal sanctions for persons committing, or ordering to be committed, any of the grave breaches of the present Convention defined in the following Article.

Each High Contracting Party shall be under the obligation to search for persons alleged to have committed, or to have ordered to be committed, such grave breaches, and shall bring such persons, regardless of their nationality, before its own courts. It may also, if it prefers, and in accordance with the provisions of its own legislation, hand such persons over for trial to another High Contracting Party concerned, provided such High Contracting Party has made out a prima facie case.

Each High Contracting Party shall take measures necessary for the suppression of all acts contrary to the provisions of the present Convention other than the grave breaches defined in the following Article.

In all circumstances, the accused persons shall benefit by safeguards of proper trial and defence, which shall not be less favourable than those provided by Article 105 and those following of the Geneva Convention relative to the Treatment of Prisoners of War of August 12, 1949. Article 147. Grave breaches to which the preceding Article relates shall be those involving any of the following acts, if committed against persons or property protected by the present Convention: wilful killing, torture or inhuman treatment, including biological experiments, wilfully causing great suffering or serious injury to body or health, unlawful deportation or transfer or unlawful confinement of a protected person, compelling a protected person to serve in the forces of a hostile Power, or wilfully depriving a protected person of the rights of fair and regular trial prescribed in the present Convention, taking of hostages and extensive destruction and appropriation of property, not justified by military necessity and carried out unlawfully and wantonly.[24]

Article 148

No High Contracting Party shall be allowed to absolve itself or any other High Contracting Party of any liability incurred by

---

[24] Article 2 of the International Tribunal established for the protection of persons responsible for serious violations humanitarian law committed in the territory of former Yugoslavia, since 1991. See *supra* n. 5.

itself or by another High Contracting Party in respect of breaches referred to in the preceding Article.

Article 149

At the request of a Party to the conflict, an enquiry shall be instituted, in a manner to be decided between the interested Parties, concerning any alleged violation of the Convention.

If agreement has not been reached concerning the procedure for the enquiry, the Parties should agree on the choice of an umpire who will decide upon the procedure to be followed.

Once the violation has been established, the Parties to the conflict shall put an end to it and shall repress it with the least possible delay.

Section II. Final Provisions

Article 154

9–056 In the relations between the Powers who are bound by the Hague Conventions respecting the Laws and Customs of War on Land, whether that of July 29, 1899, or that of October 18, 1907, and who are parties to the present Convention, this last Convention shall be supplementary to Sections II and III of the Regulations annexed to the above-mentioned Conventions of The Hague.

Article 158

Each of the High Contracting Parties shall be at liberty to denounce the present Convention.

The denunciation shall be notified in writing to the Swiss Federal Council, which shall transmit it to the Governments of all the High Contracting Parties.

The denunciation shall take effect one year after the notification thereof has been made to the Swiss Federal Council. However, a denunciation of which notification has been made at a time when the denouncing Power is involved in a conflict *shall not take effect until peace has been concluded, and until after operations connected with release, repatriation and re-establishment of the persons protected by the present Convention have been terminated.* (emphasis added).

The denunciation shall have effect only in respect of the denouncing Power. It shall in no way impair the obligations which the Parties to the conflict shall remain bound to fulfil by virtue of the principles of the law of nations, as they result from the usages established among civilised peoples, from the laws of humanity and the dictates of the public conscience.

The denunciation of the Convention by one party does not relieve other Contracting parties of the obligations incumbent upon them.

The importance of Article 158 may today be somewhat academic given the customary international status of the Geneva Conventions under contemporary international law.

PROTOCOL ADDITIONAL TO THE GENEVA CONVENTIONS OF AUGUST 12, 1949 AND RELATING TO THE PROTECTION OF VICTIMS OF INTERNATIONAL ARMED CONFLICTS (PROTOCOL I), OF JUNE 8, 1977[25]

PART I. GENERAL PROVISIONS

Article 1. General principles and scope of application

1. The High Contracting Parties undertake to respect and to 9–057 ensure respect for this Protocol in all circumstances.

2. In cases not covered by this Protocol or by other international agreements, civilians and combatants remain under the protection and authority of the principles of international law derived from established custom, from the principles of humanity and from dictates of public conscience.

3. This Protocol, which supplements the Geneva Conventions of August 12, 1949 for the protection of war victims, shall apply in the situations referred to in Article 2 common to those Conventions.

4. The situations referred to in the preceding paragraph include armed conflicts which peoples are fighting against colonial domination and alien occupation and against racist regimes in the exercise of their right of self-determination, as enshrined in the Charter of the United Nations and the Declaration on Principles of International Law concerning Friendly Relations and Co-operation among States in accordance with the Charter of the United Nations.[26]

. . .

Article 14. Limitations on requisition of civilian medical units

1. The Occupying Power has the duty to ensure that the medical needs of the civilian population in occupied territory continue to be satisfied.

2. The Occupying Power shall not, therefore, requisition civilian medical units, their equipment, their material or the services

---

[25] 16 I.L.M. 1391 entered into force June 8, 1977—currently there are 144 Contracting Parties. The 1977 Protocols (Protocol II see below) were adopted in an effort to make good the deficiencies of the Geneva. Protocol 1 extended the definition of "international armed conflict" to include wars of self-determination—see Article 2(4).

[26] G.A. Res. 25/2625, October 24, 1970.

of their personnel, so long as these resources are necessary for the provision of adequate medical services for the civilian population and for the continuing medical care of any wounded and sick already under treatment.

3. Provided that the general rule in paragraph 2 continues to be observed, the Occupying Power may requisition the said resources, subject to the following particular conditions:

(a) that the resources are necessary for the adequate and immediate medical treatment of the wounded and sick members of the armed forces of the Occupying Power or of prisoners of war;

(b) that the requisition continues only while such necessity exists; and

(c) that immediate arrangements are made to ensure that the medical needs of the civilian population, as well as those of any wounded and sick under treatment who are affected by the requisition, continue to be satisfied.

Article 15. Protection of civilian medical and religious personnel[27]

9–058   **1.** Civilian medical personnel shall be respected and protected.

2. If needed, all available help shall be afforded to civilian medical personnel in an area where civilian medical services are disrupted by reason of combat activity.

3. The Occupying Power shall afford civilian medical personnel in occupied territories every assistance to enable them to perform, to the best of their ability, their humanitarian functions. The Occupying Power may not require that, in the performance of those functions, such personnel shall give priority to the treatment of any person except on medical grounds. They shall not be compelled to carry out tasks which are not compatible with their humanitarian mission.

4. Civilian medical personnel shall have access to any place where their services are essential, subject to such supervisory and safety measures as the relevant Party to the conflict may deem necessary.

5. Civilian religious personnel shall be respected and protected. The provisions of the Conventions and of this Protocol concern-

---

[27] The interpretation of medical and religious personnel is extended to mean "those persons assigned by a Party to the conflict, exclusively to the medical purposes or to the administration of medical units to the operation or administration of medical transports". Such assignments may be permanent or temporary and medical personnel may be "military or civilian" (Article 8(3) "Religious personnel" means military or civilian purposes such as chaplains who are exclusively engaged in the work of their ministry—such attachment may be permanent or temporary—Article 8(4).

ing the protection and identification of medical personnel shall apply equally to such persons.

Article 16. General protection of medical duties

1. Under no circumstances shall any person be punished for 9–059 carrying out medical activities compatible with medical ethics, regardless of the person benefiting therefrom.

2. Persons engaged in medical activities shall not be compelled to perform acts or to carry out work contrary to the rules of medical ethics or to other medical rules designed for the benefit of the wounded and sick or to the provisions of the Conventions or of this Protocol, or to refrain from performing acts or from carrying out work required by those rules and provisions.

3. No person engaged in medical activities shall be compelled to give to anyone belonging either to an adverse Party, or to his own Party except as required by the law of the latter Party, any information concerning the wounded and sick who are, or who have been, under his care, if such information would, in his opinion, prove harmful to the patients concerned or to their families. Regulations for the compulsory notification of communicable diseases shall, however, be respected.

Article 17. Role of the civilian population and of aid societies

1. The civilian population shall respect the wounded, sick and shipwrecked, even if they belong to the adverse Party, and shall commit no act of violence against them. The civilian population and aid societies, such as national Red Cross (Red Crescent, Red Lion and Sun) Societies, shall be permitted, even on their own initiative, to collect and care for the wounded, sick and shipwrecked, even in invaded or occupied areas. No one shall be harmed, prosecuted, convicted or punished for such humanitarian acts.

2. The Parties to the conflict may appeal to the civilian population and the aid societies referred to in paragraph 1 to collect and care for the wounded, sick and shipwrecked, and to search for the dead and report their location; they shall grant both protection and the necessary facilities to those who respond to this appeal. If the adverse Party gains or regains control of the area, that Party also shall afford the same protection and facilities for as long as they are needed.

Article 18. Identification

3. In occupied territory and in areas where fighting is taking place or is likely to take place, civilian medical personnel and civilian religious personnel should be recognisable by the distinctive emblem and an identity card certifying their status.

Section II. Medical Transportation

Article 21. Medical vehicles

9–060   Medical vehicles shall be respected and protected in the same way as mobile medical units under the Conventions and this Protocol.

Article 22. Hospital ships and coastal rescue craft

1. The provisions of the Conventions relating to:

(a) vessels described in Articles 22, 24, 25 and 27 of the Second Convention,

(b) their lifeboats and small craft,

(c) their personnel and crews, and

(d) the wounded; sick and shipwrecked on board.

shall also apply where these vessels carry civilian wounded, sick and shipwrecked who do not belong to any of the categories mentioned in Article 13 of the Second Convention. Such civilians shall not, however, be subject to surrender to any Party which is not their own, or to capture at sea. If they find themselves in the power of a Party to the conflict other than their own they shall be covered by the Fourth Convention and by this Protocol.

Article 45

3. Any person who has taken part in hostilities, who is not entitled to prisoner-of-war status and who does not benefit from more favourable treatment in accordance with the Fourth Convention shall have the right at all times to the protection of Article 75 of this Protocol. In occupied territory, any such person, unless he is held as a spy, shall also be entitled, notwithstanding Article 5 of the Fourth Convention, to his rights of communication under that Convention.

PART IV. CIVILIAN POPULATION

Section I. General Protection Against Effects of Hostilities

CHAPTER I. BASIC RULE AND FIELD OF APPLICATION

Article 48.[28] Basic rule

In order to ensure respect for and protection of the civilian 9–061
population and civilian objects, the Parties to the conflict shall at
all times distinguish between the civilian population and combatants and between civilian objects and military objectives and
accordingly shall direct their operations only against military
objectives.

Article 49. Definition of attacks and scope of application

1. Attacks; means acts of violence against the adversary,
whether in offence or in defence.

2. The provisions of this Protocol with respect to attacks apply
to all attacks in whatever territory conducted, including the
national territory belonging to a Party to the conflict but under
the control of an adverse Party.

3. The provisions of this section apply to any land, air or sea
warfare which may affect the civilian population, individual
civilians or civilian objects on land. They further apply to all
attacks from the sea or from the air against objectives on land but
do not otherwise affect the rules of international law applicable in
armed conflict at sea or in the air.

4. The provisions of this section are additional to the rules
concerning humanitarian protection contained in the Fourth Convention, particularly in Part II thereof, and in other international
agreements binding upon the High Contracting Parties, as well as
to other rules of international law relating to the protection of
civilians and civilian objects on land, at sea or in the air against
the effects of hostilities.

CHAPTER II. CIVILIANS AND CIVILIAN POPULATION

Article 50. Definition of civilians and civilian population

1. A civilian is any person who does not belong to one of the 9–062
categories of persons referred to in Article 4 (A) (1), (2), (3) and
(6) of the Third Convention[29] and in Article 43[30] of this Protocol.

---

[28] Article 48 enshrines the kernel principle regarding protection in that it requires that
parties to a conflict "shall at all times distinguish between the civilian population and
combatants". N.B. Article 50 (below) which provides that in the case of doubt as to status
civilian status is to be presumed.

[29] Prisoners of War.

[30] Namely the armed forces.

In case of doubt whether a person is a civilian, that person shall be considered to be a civilian.

2. The civilian population comprises all persons who are civilians.

3. The presence within the civilian population of individuals who do not come within the definition of civilians does not deprive the population of its civilian character.

Article 51. Protection of the civilian population

1. The civilian population and individual civilians shall enjoy general protection against dangers arising from military operations. To give effect to this protection, the following rules, which are additional to other applicable rules of international law, shall be observed in all circumstances.

2. The civilian population as such, as well as individual civilians, shall not be the object of attack. Acts or threats of violence the primary purpose of which is to spread terror among the civilian population are prohibited.

3. Civilians shall enjoy the protection afforded by this section, unless and for such time as they take a direct part in hostilities.

4. Indiscriminate attacks are prohibited. Indiscriminate attacks are:

(a) those which are not directed at a specific military objective;

(b) those which employ a method or means of combat which cannot be directed at a specific military objective; or

(c) those which employ a method or means of combat the effects of which cannot be limited as required by this Protocol;

and consequently, in each such case, are of a nature to strike military objectives and civilians or civilian objects without distinction.

5. Among others, the following types of attacks are to be considered as indiscriminate:

(a) an attack by bombardment by any methods or means which treats as a single military objective a number of clearly separated and distinct military objectives located in a city, town, village or other area containing a similar concentration of civilians or civilian objects; and

(b) an attack which may be expected to cause incidental loss of civilian life, injury to civilians, damage to civilian objects, or a combination thereof, which would be excessive in relation to the concrete and direct military advantage anticipated.

6. Attacks against the civilian population or civilians by way of reprisals are prohibited.

7. The presence or movements of the civilian population or individual civilians shall not be used to render certain points or areas immune from military operations, in particular in attempts to shield military objectives from attacks or to shield, favour or impede military operations. The Parties to the conflict shall not direct the movement of the civilian population or individual civilians in order to attempt to shield military objectives from attacks or to shield military operations.

8. Any violation of these prohibitions shall not release the Parties to the conflict from their legal obligations with respect to the civilian population and civilians, including the obligation to take the precautionary measures provided for in Article 57.

CHAPTER III. CIVILIAN OBJECTS

Article 52. General Protection of civilian objects

1. Civilian objects shall not be the object of attack or of 9–063 reprisals. Civilian objects are all objects which are not military objectives as defined in paragraph 2.

2. Attacks shall be limited strictly to military objectives. In so far as objects are concerned, military objectives are limited to those objects which by their nature, location, purpose or use make an effective contribution to military action and whose total or partial destruction, capture or neutralisation, in the circumstances ruling at the time, offers a definite military advantage.

3. In case of doubt whether an object which is normally dedicated to civilian purposes, such as a place of worship, a house or other dwelling or a school, is being used to make an effective contribution to military action, it shall be presumed not to be so used.

Article 53. Protection of cultural objects and of places of worship

Without prejudice to the provisions of the Hague Convention for 9–064 the Protection of Cultural Property in the Event of Armed Conflict of May 14, 1954,[31] and of other relevant international instruments, it is prohibited:

(a) to commit any acts of hostility directed against the historic monuments, works of art or places of worship which constitute the cultural or spiritual heritage of peoples;

---

[31] 249 U.N.T.S. entered into force August 7, 1956. Essentially the Convention places an obligation on Contracting Parties to protect property of cultural importance in both their own and other States' territory during armed conflict.

(b) to use such objects in support of the military effort;

(c) to make such objects the object of reprisals.

Article 54. Protection of objects indispensable to the survival of the civilian population

1. Starvation of civilians as a method of warfare is prohibited.

2. It is prohibited to attack, destroy, remove or render useless objects indispensable to the survival of the civilian population, such as food-stuffs, agricultural areas for the production of food-stuffs, crops, livestock, drinking water installations and supplies and irrigation works, for the specific purpose of denying them for their sustenance value to the civilian population or to the adverse Party, whatever the motive, whether in order to starve out civilians, to cause them to move away, or for any other motive.

3. The prohibitions in paragraph 2 shall not apply to such of the objects covered by it as are used by an adverse Party:

(a) as sustenance solely for the members of its armed forces; or

(b) if not as sustenance, then in direct support of military action, provided, however, that in no event shall actions against these objects be taken which may be expected to leave the civilian population with such inadequate food or water as to cause its starvation or force its movement.

4. These objects shall not be made the object of reprisals.

5. In recognition of the vital requirements of any Party to the conflict in the defence of its national territory against invasion, derogation from the prohibitions contained in paragraph 2 may be made by a Party to the conflict within such territory under its own control where required by imperative military necessity.

Article 55. Protection of the natural environment

1. Care shall be taken in warfare to protect the natural environment against widespread, long-term and severe damage. This protection includes a prohibition of the use of methods or means of warfare which are intended or may be expected to cause such damage to the natural environment and thereby to prejudice the health or survival of the population.

2. Attacks against the natural environment by way of reprisals are prohibited.

Article 56. Protection of works and installations containing dangerous forces

9–065   **1.** Works or installations containing dangerous forces, namely dams, dykes and nuclear electrical generating stations, shall not be made the object of attack, even where these objects are military objectives, if such attack may cause the release of dangerous forces and consequent severe losses among the civilian population. Other military objectives located at or in the vicinity of these works or installations shall not be made the object of attack if such attack may cause the release of dangerous forces from the works or installations and consequent severe losses among the civilian population.

2. The special protection against attack provided by paragraph 1 shall cease:

(a) for a dam or a dyke only if it is used for other than its normal function and in regular, significant and direct support of military operations and if such attack is the only feasible way to terminate such support;

(b) for a nuclear electrical generating station only if it provides electric power in regular, significant and direct support of military operations and if such attack is the only feasible way to terminate such support;

(c) for other military objectives located at or in the vicinity of these works or installations only if they are used in regular, significant and direct support of military operations and if such attack is the only feasible way to terminate such support.

3. In all cases, the civilian population and individual civilians shall remain entitled to all the protection accorded them by international law, including the protection of the precautionary measures provided for in Article 57. If the protection Ceases and any of the works, installations or military objectives mentioned in paragraph 1 is attacked, all practical precautions shall be taken to avoid the release of the dangerous forces.

4. It is prohibited to make any of the works, installations or military objectives mentioned in paragraph 1 the object of reprisals.

5. The Parties to the conflict shall endeavour to avoid locating any military objectives in the vicinity of the works or installations mentioned in paragraph 1. Nevertheless, installations erected for the sole purpose of defending the protected works or installations from attack are permissible and shall not themselves be made the object of attack, provided that they are not used in hostilities except for defensive actions necessary to respond to attacks against the protected works or installations and that their armament is limited to weapons capable only of repelling hostile action against the protected works or installations.

6. The High Contracting Parties and the Parties to the conflict are urged to conclude further agreements among themselves to provide additional protection for objects containing dangerous forces.

7. In order to facilitate the identification of the objects protected by this article, the Parties to the conflict may mark them with a special sign consisting of a group of three bright orange circles placed on the same axis, . . . The absence of such marking in no way relieves any Party to the conflict of its obligations under this Article.

CHAPTER IV. PRECAUTIONARY MEASURES

Article 57. Precautions in attack

9–066   **1.** In the conduct of military operations, constant care shall be taken to spare the civilian population, civilians and civilian objects.

2. With respect to attacks, the following precautions shall be taken:

(a) those who plan or decide upon an attack shall:

(i) do everything feasible to verify that the objectives to be attacked are neither civilians nor civilian objects and are not subject to special protection but are military objectives within the meaning of paragraph 2 of Article 52 and that it is not prohibited by the provisions of this Protocol to attack them;

(ii) take all feasible precautions in the choice of means and methods of attack with a view to avoiding, and in any event to minimising, incidental loss or civilian life, injury to civilians and damage to civilian objects;

(iii) refrain from deciding to launch any attack which may be expected to cause incidental loss of civilian life, injury to civilians, damage to civilian objects, or a combination thereof, which would be excessive in relation to the concrete and direct military advantage anticipated;

(b) an attack shall be cancelled or suspended if it becomes apparent that the objective is not a military one or is subject to special protection or that the attack may be expected to cause incidental loss of civilian life, injury to civilians, damage to civilian objects, or a combination thereof, which would be excessive in relation to the concrete and direct military advantage anticipated;

(c) effective advance warning shall be given of attacks which may affect the civilian population, unless circumstances do not permit.

3. When a choice is possible between several military objectives for obtaining a similar military advantage, the objective to be selected shall be that the attack on which may be expected to cause the least danger to civilian lives and to civilian objects.

4. In the conduct of military operations at sea or in the air, each Party to the conflict shall, in conformity with its rights and duties under the rules of international law applicable in armed conflict, take all reasonable precautions to avoid losses of civilian lives and damage to civilian objects.

5. No provision of this article may be construed as authorising any attacks against the civilian population, civilians or civilian objects.

Article 58. Precautions against the effects of attacks

The Parties to the conflict shall, to the maximum extent feasible:

(a) without prejudice to Article 49 of the Fourth Convention, **9–067** endeavour to remove the civilian population, individual civilians and civilian objects under their control from the vicinity of military objectives;

(b) avoid locating military objectives within or near densely populated areas;

(c) take the other necessary precautions to protect the civilian population, individual civilians and civilian objects under their control against the dangers resulting from military operations.

CHAPTER VI. CIVIL DEFENCE

Article 61. Definitions and scope

For the purpose of this Protocol:
(1) Civil defence means the performance of some or all of the **9–068** undermentioned humanitarian tasks intended to protect the civilian population against the dangers, and to help it to recover from the immediate effects, of hostilities or disasters and also to provide the conditions necessary for its survival. These tasks are:

(a) warning;

(b) evacuation;

(c) management of shelters;

(d) management of blackout measures;

(e) rescue;

(f) medical services, including first aid, and religious assistance;

(g) fire-fighting;

(h) detection and marking of danger areas;

(i) decontamination and similar protective measures;

(j) provision of emergency accommodation and supplies;

(k) emergency assistance in the restoration and maintenance of order in distressed areas;

(l) emergency repair of indispensable public utilities; (m) emergency disposal of the dead;

(n) assistance in the preservation of objects essential for survival;

(o) complementary activities necessary to carry out any of the tasks mentioned above, including, but not limited to, planning and organisation;

(2) Civil defence organisations; means those establishments and other units which are organised or authorised by the competent authorities of a Party to the conflict to perform any of the tasks mentioned under (1), and which are assigned and devoted exclusively to such tasks;

(3) Personnel; of civil defence organisations means those persons assigned by a Party to the conflict exclusively to the performance of the tasks mentioned under (1), including personnel assigned by the competent authority of that Party exclusively to the administration of these organisations;

(4) Material of civil defence organisations means equipment, supplies and transports used by these organisations for the performance of the tasks mentioned under (1).

Article 62. General protection

9–069   1. Civilian civil defence organisations and their personnel shall be respected and protected, subject to the provisions of this Protocol, particularly the provisions of this section. They shall be entitled to perform their civil defence tasks except in case of imperative military necessity.

2. The provisions of paragraph 1 shall also apply to civilians who, although not members of civilian civil defence organisations, respond to an appeal from the competent authorities and perform civil defence tasks under their control.

3. Buildings and material used for civil defence purposes and shelters provided for the civilian population are covered by Article 52. Objects used for civil defence purposes may not be destroyed or diverted from their proper use except by the Party to which they belong.

Article 63. Civil defence in occupied territories

1. In occupied territories, civilian civil defence organisations shall receive from the authorities the facilities necessary for the performance of their tasks. In no circumstances shall their personnel be compelled to perform activities which would interfere with the proper performance of these tasks. The Occupying Power shall not change the structure or personnel of such organisations in any way which might jeopardise the efficient performance of their mission. These organisations shall not be required to give priority to the nationals or interests of that Power.

2. The Occupying Power shall not compel, coerce or induce civilian civil defence organisations to perform their tasks in any manner prejudicial to the interests of the civilian population.

3. The Occupying Power may disarm civil defence personnel for reasons of security.

4. The Occupying Power shall neither divert from their proper use nor requisition buildings or material belonging to or used by civil defence organisations if such diversion or requisition would be harmful to the civilian population.

5. Provided that the general rule in paragraph 4 continues to be observed, the Occupying Power may requisition or divert these resources, subject to the following particular conditions:

(a) that the buildings or material are necessary for other needs of the civilian population; and

(b) that the requisition or diversion continues only while such necessity exists.

6. The Occupying Power shall neither divert nor requisition shelters provided for the use of the civilian population or needed by such population.

Article 64. Civilian civil defence organisations of neutral or other States not Parties to the conflict and international co-ordinating organisations

1. Articles 62, 63, 65 and 66 shall also apply to the personnel and material of civilian civil defence organisations of neutral or other States not Parties to the conflict which perform civil defence tasks mentioned in Article 61 in the territory of a Party to the conflict, with the consent and under the control of that Party. Notification of such assistance shall be given as soon as possible to any adverse Party concerned. In no circumstances shall this activity be deemed to be an interference in the conflict. This activity should, however, be performed with due regard to the security interests of the Parties to the conflict concerned.

9–070

2. The Parties to the conflict receiving the assistance referred to in paragraph 1 and the High Contracting Parties granting it should facilitate international co-ordination of such civil defence actions when appropriate. In such cases the relevant international organisations are covered by the provisions of this Chapter.

3. In occupied territories, the Occupying Power may only exclude or restrict the activities of civilian civil defence organisations of neutral or other States not Parties to the conflict and of international co-ordinating organisations if it can ensure the adequate performance of civil defence tasks from its own resources or those of the occupied territory.

Article 65. Cessation of protection

9–071   **1.** The protection to which civilian civil defence organisations, their personnel, buildings, shelters and material are entitled shall not cease unless they commit or are used to commit, outside their proper tasks, acts harmful to the enemy. Protection may, however, cease only after a warning has been given setting, whenever appropriate, a reasonable time-limit, and after such warning has remained unheeded.

2. The following shall not be considered as acts harmful to the enemy:

(a) that civil defence tasks are carried out under the direction or control of military authorities;

(b) that civilian civil defence personnel co-operate with military personnel in the performance of civil defence tasks, or that some military personnel are attached to civilian civil defence organisations;

(c) that the performance of civil defence tasks may incidentally benefit military victims, particularly those who are hors de combat.

3. It shall also not be considered as an act harmful to the enemy that civilian civil defence personnel bear light individual weapons for the purpose of maintaining order or for self-defence. However, in areas where land fighting is taking place or is likely to take place, the Parties to the conflict shall undertake the appropriate measures to limit these weapons to handguns, such as pistols or revolvers, in order to assist in distinguishing between civil defence personnel and combatants. Although civil defence personnel bear other light individual weapons in such areas, they shall nevertheless be respected and protected as soon as they have been recognised as such.

4. The formation of civilian civil defence organisations along military lines, and compulsory service in them, shall also not deprive them of the protection conferred by this Chapter.

Article 66. Identification

1. Each Party to the conflict shall endeavour to ensure that its 9–072
civil defence organisations, their personnel, buildings and material, are identifiable while they are exclusively devoted to the
performance of civil defence tasks. Shelters provided for the
civilian population should be similarly identifiable.

2. Each Party to the conflict shall also endeavour to adopt and
implement methods and procedures which will make it possible
to recognise civilian shelters as well as civil defence personnel,
buildings and material on which the international distinctive sign
of civil defence is displayed.

3. In occupied territories and in areas where fighting is taking
place or is likely to take place, civilian civil defence personnel
should be recognisable by the international distinctive sign of
civil defence and by an identity card certifying their status.

4. The international distinctive sign of civil defence is an
equilateral blue triangle on an orange ground when used for the
protection of civil defence organisations, their personnel, buildings and material and for civilian shelters.

5. In addition to the distinctive sign, Parties to the conflict may
agree upon the use of distinctive signals for civil defence identification purposes.

6. . . .

7. In time of peace, the sign described in paragraph 4 may,
with the consent of the competent national authorities, be used
for civil defence identification purposes.

8. The High Contracting Parties and the Parties to the conflict
shall take the measures necessary to supervise the display of the
international distinctive sign of civil defence and to prevent and
repress any misuse thereof.

9. The identification of civil defence medical and religious
personnel, medical units and medical transports is also governed
by Article 18.

**Article 67. Members of the armed forces and military units assigned to
civil defence organisations**

1. Members of the armed forces and military units assigned to 9–073
civil defence organisations shall be respected and protected,
provided that:

    (a) such personnel and such units are permanently assigned
        and exclusively devoted to the performance of any of the
        tasks mentioned in Article 61;

    (b) if so assigned, such personnel do not perform any other
        military duties during the conflict;

(c) such personnel are clearly distinguishable from the other members of the armed forces by prominently displaying the international distinctive sign of civil defence, which shall be as large as appropriate, and such personnel are provided with the identity card . . . certifying their status;

(d) such personnel and such units are equipped only with light individual weapons for the purpose of maintaining order or for self-defence. The provisions of Article 65, paragraph 3 shall also apply in this case;

(e) such personnel do not participate directly in hostilities, and do not commit, or are not used to commit, outside their civil defence tasks, acts harmful to the adverse Party;

(f) such personnel and such units perform their civil defence tasks only within the national territory of their Party.

The non-observance of the conditions stated in (e) above by any member of the armed forces who is bound by the conditions prescribed in (a) and (b) above is prohibited.

2. Military personnel serving within civil defence organisations shall, if they fall into the power of an adverse Party, be prisoners of war. In occupied territory they may, but only in the interest of the civilian population of that territory, be employed on civil defence tasks in so far as the need arises, provided however that, if such work is dangerous, they volunteer for such tasks.

3. The buildings and major items of equipment and transports of military units assigned to civil defence organisations shall be clearly marked with the international distinctive sign of civil defence. This distinctive sign shall be as large as appropriate.

4. The material and buildings of military units permanently assigned to civil defence organisations and exclusively devoted to the performance of civil defence tasks shall, if they fall into the hands of an adverse Party, remain subject to the laws of war. They may not be diverted from their civil defence purpose so long as they are required for the performance of civil defence tasks, except in case of imperative military necessity, unless previous arrangements have been made for adequate provision for the needs of the civilian population.

Section II. Relief in Favour of the Civilian Population

Article 68. Field of application

9–074 The provisions of this Section apply to the civilian population as defined in this Protocol and are supplementary to Articles 23, 55, 59, 60, 61 and 62 and other relevant provisions of the Fourth Convention.

Article 69. Basic needs in occupied territories

1. In addition to the duties specified in Article 55 of the Fourth Convention concerning food and medical supplies, the Occupying Power shall, to the fullest extent of the means available to it and without any adverse distinction, also ensure the provision of clothing, bedding, means of shelter, other supplies essential to the survival of the civilian population of the occupied territory and objects necessary for religious worship.

2. Relief actions for the benefit of the civilian population of occupied territories are governed by Articles 59, 60, 61, 62, 108, 109, 110 and 111 of the Fourth Convention, and by Article 71 of this Protocol, and shall be implemented without delay.

Article 70. Relief actions

1. If the civilian population of any territory under the control of a Party to the conflict, other than occupied territory, is not adequately provided with the supplies mentioned in Article 69, relief actions which are humanitarian and impartial in character and conducted without any adverse distinction shall be undertaken, subject to the agreement of the Parties concerned in such relief actions. Offers of such relief shall not be regarded as interference in the armed conflict or as unfriendly acts. In the distribution of relief consignments, priority shall be given to those persons, such as children, expectant mothers, maternity cases and nursing mothers, who, under the Fourth Convention or under this Protocol, are to be accorded privileged treatment or special protection.

2. The Parties to the conflict and each High Contracting Party shall allow and facilitate rapid and unimpeded passage of all relief consignments, equipment and personnel provided in accordance with this Section, even if such assistance is destined for the civilian population of the adverse Party.

3. The Parties to the conflict and each High Contracting Party which allows the passage of relief consignments, equipment and personnel in accordance with paragraph 2:

(a) shall have the right to prescribe the technical arrangements, including search, under which such passage is permitted;

(b) may make such permission conditional on the distribution of this assistance being made under the local supervision of a Protecting Power;

(c) shall, in no way whatsoever, divert relief consignments from the purpose for which they are intended nor delay their forwarding, except in cases of urgent necessity in the interest of the civilian population concerned.

4. The Parties to the conflict shall protect relief consignments and facilitate their rapid distribution.

5. The Parties to the conflict and each High Contracting Party concerned shall encourage and facilitate effective international co-ordination of the relief actions referred to in paragraph 1.

Article 71. Personnel participating in relief actions

9–075   **1.** Where necessary, relief personnel may form part of the assistance provided in any relief action, in particular for the transportation and distribution of relief consignments; the participation of such personnel shall be subject to the approval of the Party in whose territory they will carry out their duties.

2. Such personnel shall be respected and protected.

3. Each Party in receipt of relief consignments shall, to the fullest extent practicable, assist the relief personnel referred to in paragraph 1 in carrying out their relief mission. Only in case of imperative military necessity may the activities of the relief personnel be limited or their movements temporarily restricted.

4. Under no circumstances may relief personnel exceed the terms of their mission under this Protocol. In particular they shall take account of the security requirements of the Party in whose territory they are carrying out their duties. The mission of any of the personnel who do not respect these conditions may be terminated.

Section III. Treatment of Persons in the Power of a Party to the Conflict

CHAPTER I. FIELD OF APPLICATION AND PROTECTION OF PERSONS AND OBJECTS

Article 72. Field of application

9–076   The provisions of this Section are additional to the rules concerning humanitarian protection of civilians and civilian objects in the power of a Party to the conflict contained in the Fourth Convention, particularly Parts I and III thereof, as well as to other applicable rules of international law relating to the protection of fundamental human rights during international armed conflict.

Article 75. Fundamental guarantees[32]

1. In so far as they are affected by a situation referred to in Article 1 of this Protocol, persons who are in the power of a Party to the conflict and who do not benefit from more favourable

---

[32] Article 75 reflects the impact of the growing awareness of human rights and the protection of the individual.

treatment under the Conventions or under this Protocol shall be treated humanely in all circumstances and shall enjoy, as a minimum, the protection provided by this Article without any adverse distinction based upon race, colour, sex, language, religion or belief, political or other opinion, national or social origin, wealth, birth or other status, or on any other similar criteria. Each Party shall respect the person, honour, convictions and religious practices of all such persons.

2. The following acts are and shall remain prohibited at any time and in any place whatsoever, whether committed by civilian or by military agents:

(a) violence to the life, health, or physical or mental well-being of persons, in particular:

    (i) murder;
    (ii) torture of all kinds, whether physical or mental;
    (iii) corporal punishment; and
    (iv) mutilation;

(b) outrages upon personal dignity, in particular humiliating and degrading treatment, enforced prostitution and any form or indecent assault;

(c) the taking of hostages;

(d) collective punishments; and

(e) threats to commit any of the foregoing acts.

3. Any person arrested, detained or interned for actions related 9–077 to the armed conflict shall be informed promptly, in a language he understands, of the reasons why these measures have been taken. Except in cases of arrest or detention for penal offences, such persons shall be released with the minimum delay possible and in any event as soon as the circumstances justifying the arrest, detention or internment have ceased to exist.

4. No sentence may be passed and no penalty may be executed on a person found guilty of a penal offence related to the armed conflict except pursuant to a conviction pronounced by an impartial and regularly constituted court respecting the generally recognised principles of regular judicial procedure, which include the following:

(a) the procedure shall provide for an accused to be informed without delay of the particulars of the offence alleged against him and shall afford the accused before and during his trial all necessary rights and means of defence;

(b) no one shall be convicted of an offence except on the basis of individual penal responsibility;

(c) no one shall be accused or convicted of a criminal offence on account or any act or omission which did not constitute a criminal offence under the national or international law to which he was subject at the time when it was committed; nor shall a heavier penalty be imposed than that which was applicable at the time when the criminal offence was committed; if, after the commission of the offence, provision is made by law for the imposition of a lighter penalty, the offender shall benefit thereby;

(d) anyone charged with an offence is presumed innocent until proved guilty according to law;

(e) anyone charged with an offence shall have the right to be tried in his presence;

(f) no one shall be compelled to testify against himself or to confess guilt;

(g) anyone charged with an offence shall have the right to examine, or have examined, the witnesses against him and to obtain the attendance and examination of witnesses on his behalf under the same conditions as witnesses against him;

(h) no one shall be prosecuted or punished by the same Party for an offence in respect of which a final judgment acquitting or convicting that person has been previously pronounced under the same law and judicial procedure;

(i) anyone prosecuted for an offence shall have the right to have the judgment pronounced publicly; and

(j) a convicted person shall be advised on conviction or his judicial and other remedies and of the time-limits within which they may be exercised.

9–078   **5.** Women whose liberty has been restricted for reasons related to the armed conflict shall be held in quarters separated from men's quarters. They shall be under the immediate supervision of women. Nevertheless, in cases where families are detained or interned, they shall, whenever possible, be held in the same place and accommodated as family units.

6. Persons who are arrested, detained or interned for reasons related to the armed conflict shall enjoy the protection provided by this Article until their final release, repatriation or re-establishment, even after the end of the armed conflict.

7. In order to avoid any doubt concerning the prosecution and trial of persons accused of war crimes or crimes against humanity, the following principles shall apply:

(a) persons who are accused or such crimes should be submitted for the purpose of prosecution and trial in accordance with the applicable rules of international law; and

(b) any such persons who do not benefit from more favourable treatment under the Conventions or this Protocol shall be accorded the treatment provided by this Article, whether or not the crimes of which they are accused constitute grave breaches of the Conventions or of this Protocol.

8. No provision of this Article may be construed as limiting or infringing any other more favourable provision granting greater protection, under any applicable rules of international law, to persons covered by paragraph 1.

CHAPTER II. MEASURES IN FAVOUR OF WOMEN AND CHILDREN

Article 76. Protection of women[33]

1. Women shall be the object of special respect and shall be protected in particular against rape, forced prostitution and any other form of indecent assault.

2. Pregnant women and mothers having dependent infants who are arrested, detained or interned for reasons related to the armed conflict, shall have their cases considered with the utmost priority.

3. To the maximum extent feasible, the Parties to the conflict shall endeavour to avoid the pronouncement of the death penalty on pregnant women or mothers having dependent infants, for an offence related to the armed conflict. The death penalty for such offences shall not be executed on such women.

Article 77. Protection of children

1. Children shall be the object of special respect and shall be **9–079** protected against any form of indecent assault. The Parties to the conflict shall provide them with the care and aid they require, whether because of their age or for any other reason.

2. The Parties to the conflict shall take all feasible measures in order that children who have not attained the age of 15 years do not take a direct part in hostilities and, in particular, they shall refrain from recruiting them into their armed forces. In recruiting among those persons who have attained the age of 15 years but who have not attained the age of 18 years the Parties to the conflict shall endeavour to give priority to those who are oldest.

3. If, in exceptional cases, despite the provisions of paragraph 2, children who have not attained the age of 15 years take a direct

---

[33] Protocol I spelt out in much clearer terms than before that protection should be afforded to women and children. Note Article 5(g), International Tribunal *supra* n. 5. See also Chapters on Women and Children.

part in hostilities and fall into the power of an adverse Party, they shall continue to benefit from the special protection accorded by this Article, whether or not they are prisoners of war.

4. If arrested, detained or interned for reasons related to the armed conflict, children shall be held in quarters separate from the quarters of adults, except where families are accommodated as family units as provided in Article 75, paragraph 5.

5. The death penalty for an offence related to the armed conflict shall not be executed on persons who had not attained the age of eighteen years at the time the offence was committed.

Article 78. Evacuation of children

9–080　　**1.** No Party to the conflict shall arrange for the evacuation of children, other than its own nationals, to a foreign country except for a temporary evacuation where compelling reasons of the health or medical treatment of the children or, except in occupied territory, their safety, so require. Where the parents or legal guardians can be found, their written consent to such evacuation is required. If these persons cannot be found, the written consent to such evacuation of the persons who by law or custom are primarily responsible for the care of the children is required. Any such evacuation shall be supervised by the Protecting Power in agreement with the Parties concerned, namely, the Party arranging for the evacuation, the Party receiving the children and any Parties whose nationals are being evacuated. In each case, all Parties to the conflict shall take all feasible precautions to avoid endangering the evacuation.

2. Whenever an evacuation occurs pursuant to paragraph 1, each child's education, including his religious and moral education as his parents desire, shall be provided while he is away with the greatest possible continuity.

3. With a view to facilitating the return to their families and country of children evacuated pursuant to this Article, the authorities of the Party arranging for the evacuation and, as appropriate, the authorities of the receiving country shall establish for each child a card with photographs, which they shall send to the Central Tracing Agency of the International Committee of the Red Cross. Each card shall bear, whenever possible, and whenever it involves no risk of harm to the child, the following information:

(a) surname(s) of the child;

(b) the child's first name(s);

(c) the child's sex;

(d) the place and date of birth (or, if that date is not known, the approximate age);

(e) the father's full name;

(f) the mother's full name and her maiden name;

(g) the child's next-of-kin;

(h) the child's nationality;

(i) the child's native language, and any other languages he speaks;

(j) the address of the child's family;

(k) any identification number for the child;

(l) the child's state of health;

(m) the child's blood group;

(n) any distinguishing features;

(o) the date on which and the place where the child was found;

(p) the date on which and the place from which the child left the country;

(q) the child's religion, if any;

(r) the child's present address in the receiving country;

(s) should the child die before his return, the date, place and circumstances of death and place of interment.

CHAPTER III. JOURNALISTS[34]

Article 79. Measures or protection for journalists

1. Journalists engaged in dangerous professional missions in 9–081 areas of armed conflict shall be considered as civilians within the meaning of Article 50, paragraph 1.

2. They shall be protected as such under the Conventions and this Protocol, provided that they take no action adversely affecting their status as civilians, and without prejudice to the right of war correspondents accredited to the armed forces to the status provided for in Article 4 (A)(4) of the Third Convention.

3. They may obtain an identity card . . . This card, which shall be issued by the government of the State of which the Journalist is a national or in whose territory he resides or in which the news medium employing him is located, shall attest to his status as a journalist.

Section II. Repression of Breaches of the Conventions
and of this Protocol

Article 85. Repression of breaches of this Protocol

1. The provisions of the Conventions relating to the repression of breaches and grave breaches, supplemented by this Section,

---

[34] *i.e* Civilians who because of the nature of their activities it was felt necessary to provides special legal protection.

shall apply to the repression of breaches and grave breaches of this Protocol.

3. In addition to the grave breaches defined in Article 11, the following acts shall be regarded as grave breaches of this Protocol, when committed wilfully, in violation of the relevant provisions of this Protocol, and causing death or serious injury to body or health:

(a) making the civilian population or individual civilians the object of attack;

(b) launching an indiscriminate attack affecting the civilian population or civilian objects in the knowledge that such attack will cause excessive loss of life, injury to civilians or damage to civilian objects, as defined in Article 57, paragraph 2 (a)(iii);

(c) launching an attack against works or installations containing dangerous forces in the knowledge that such attack will cause excessive loss of life, injury to civilians or damage to civilian objects, as defined in Article 57, paragraph 2 (a)(iii);

(d) making non-defended localities and demilitarised zones the object of attack;

(e) making a person the object of attack in the knowledge that he is hors de combat;

(f) the perfidious use, in violation of Article 37, of the distinctive emblem of the red cross, red crescent or red lion and sun or of other protective signs recognised by the Conventions or this Protocol.

9–082   **4.** In addition to the grave breaches defined in the preceding paragraphs and in the Conventions, the following shall be regarded as grave breaches of this Protocol, when committed wilfully and in violation of the Conventions or the Protocol:

(a) the transfer by the occupying Power of parts of its own civilian population into the territory it occupies, or the deportation or transfer of all or parts of the population of the occupied territory within or outside this territory, in violation of Article 49 of the Fourth Convention;

(b) unjustifiable delay in the repatriation of prisoners of war or civilians;

(c) practices of apartheid and other inhuman and degrading practices involving outrages upon personal dignity, based on racial discrimination;

(d) making the clearly-recognised historic monuments, works of art or places of worship which constitute the cultural or spiritual heritage of peoples and to which special protection has been given by special arrangement, for example, within the framework of a competent international organisation, the object of attack, causing as a result extensive destruction thereof, where there is no evidence of the violation by the adverse Party of Article 53, subparagraph (b), and when such historic monuments, works of art and places of worship are not located in the immediate proximity of military objectives;

(e) depriving a person protected by the Conventions or referred to in paragraph 2 or this Article of the rights of fair and regular trial.

5. Without prejudice to the application of the Conventions and of this Protocol, grave breaches of these instruments shall be regarded as war crimes.

Article 86. Failure to act

1. The High Contracting Parties and the Parties to the conflict 9–083 shall repress grave breaches, and take measures necessary to suppress all other breaches, of the Conventions or of this Protocol which result from a failure to act when under a duty to do so.

2. The fact that a breach of the Conventions or of this Protocol was committed by a subordinate does not absolve his superiors from penal disciplinary responsibility, as the case may be, if they knew, or had information which should have enabled them to conclude in the circumstances at the time, that he was committing or was going to commit such a breach and if they did not take all feasible measures within their power to prevent or repress the breach.

PROTOCOL ADDITIONAL TO THE GENEVA CONVENTIONS OF AUGUST 12, 1949 AND RELATING TO THE PROTECTION OF VICTIMS ON NON-INTERNATIONAL ARMED CONFLICTS (PROTOCOL II), OF JUNE 8, 1977[35]

Preamble

The High Contracting Parties, Recalling that the humanitarian principles enshrined in Article 3 common to the Geneva Conventions of August 12, 1949, constitute the foundation of respect for the human person in cases of armed conflict not of an international character,

---

[35] 1977 16 I.L.M.1391.

Recalling furthermore that international instruments relating to human rights offer a basic protection to the human person,

Emphasising the need to ensure a better protection for the victims of those armed conflicts,

Recalling that, in cases not covered by the law in force, the human person remains under the protection of the principles of humanity and the dictates or the public conscience,

Have agreed on the following:

PART I. SCOPE OF THIS PROTOCOL

Article 1. Material field of application

9–084   **1.** This Protocol, which develops and supplements Article 3 common to the Geneva Conventions of August 12, 1949 without modifying its existing conditions or application, shall apply to all armed conflicts which are not covered by Article 1 of the Protocol Additional to the Geneva Conventions of August 12, 1949, and relating to the Protection of Victims of International Armed Conflicts (Protocol I) and which take place in the territory of a High Contracting Party between its armed forces and dissident armed forces or other organised armed groups which, under responsible command, exercise such control over a part of its territory as to enable them to carry out sustained and concerted military operations and to implement this Protocol.[36]

2. This Protocol shall not apply to situations of internal disturbances and tensions, such as riots, isolated and sporadic acts of violence and other acts of a similar nature, as not being armed conflicts.

Article 2. Personal field of application

1. This Protocol shall be applied without any adverse distinction founded on race, colour, sex, language, religion or belief, political or other opinion, national or social origin, wealth, birth or other status, (or on any other similar criteria) to all persons affected by an armed conflict as defined in Article 1.

2. At the end of the armed conflict, all the persons who have been deprived of their liberty or whose liberty has been restricted for reasons related to such conflict, as well as those deprived of their liberty or whose liberty is restricted after the conflict for the same reasons, shall enjoy the protection of Articles 5 and 6 until the end of such deprivation or restriction of liberty.

Article 3. Non-intervention

1. Nothing in this Protocol shall be invoked for the purpose of affecting the sovereignty of a State or the responsibility of the

---

[36] The insurgent must be in control of part of the national territory.

government, by all legitimate means, to maintain or re-establish law and order in the State or to defend the national unity and territorial integrity of the State.

2. Nothing in this Protocol shall be invoked as a justification for intervening, directly or indirectly, for any reason whatever, in the armed conflict or in the internal or external affairs of the High Contracting Party in the territory of which that conflict

PART II. HUMANE TREATMENT

Article 4. Fundamental guarantees

1. All persons who do not take a direct part or who have 9–085 ceased to take part in hostilities, whether or not their liberty has been restricted, are entitled to respect for their person, honour and convictions and religious practices. They shall in all circumstances be treated humanely, without any adverse distinction. It is prohibited to order that there shall be no survivors.

2. Without prejudice to the generality of the foregoing, the following acts against the persons referred to in paragraph 1 are and shall remain prohibited at any time and in any place whatsoever:

(a) violence to the life, health and physical or mental well-being of persons, in particular murder as well as cruel treatment such as torture, mutilation or any form of corporal;

(b) collective punishments;

(c) taking of hostages;

(d) acts of terrorism;

(e) outrages upon personal dignity, in particular humiliating and degrading treatment, rape, enforced prostitution and any form or indecent assault;

(f) slavery and the slave trade in all their forms;

(g) pillage;

(h) threats to commit any or the foregoing acts.

3. Children shall be provided with the care and aid they require, and in particular:

(a) they shall receive an education, including religious and moral education, in keeping with the wishes of their parents, or in the absence of parents, of those responsible for their care;

(b) all appropriate steps shall be taken to facilitate the reunion of families temporarily separated;

(c) children who have not attained the age of 15 years shall neither be recruited in the armed forces or groups nor allowed to take part in hostilities;

(d) the special protection provided by this Article to children who have not attained the age of 15 years shall remain applicable to them if they take a direct part in hostilities despite the provisions of subparagraph (c) and are captured;

(e) measures shall be taken, if necessary, and whenever possible with the consent of their parents or persons who by law or custom are primarily responsible for their care, to remove children temporarily from the area in which hostilities are taking place to a safer area within the country and ensure that they are accompanied by persons responsible for their safety and well-being.

Article 5. Persons whose liberty has been restricted

9–086   **1.** In addition to the provisions of Article 4 the following provisions shall be respected as a minimum with regard to persons deprived of their liberty for reasons related to the armed conflict, whether they are interned or detained;

(a) the wounded and the sick shall be treated in accordance with Article 7;

(b) the persons referred to in this paragraph shall, to the same extent as the local civilian population, be provided with food and drinking water and be afforded safeguards as regards health and hygiene and protection against the rigours of the climate and the dangers of the armed conflict;

(c) they shall be allowed to receive individual or collective relief;

(d) they shall be allowed to practise their religion and, if requested and appropriate, to receive spiritual assistance from persons, such as chaplains, performing religious functions;

(e) they shall, if made to work, have the benefit of working conditions and safeguards similar to those enjoyed by the local civilian population.

2. Those who are responsible for the internment or detention of the persons referred to in paragraph 1 shall also, within the limits of their capabilities, respect the following provisions relating to such persons:

(a) except when men and women of a family are accommodated together, women shall be held in quarters separated from those of men and shall be under the immediate supervision of women;

(b) they shall be allowed to send and receive letters and cards, the number of which may be limited by competent authority if it deems necessary;

(c) places of internment and detention shall not be located close to the combat zone. The persons referred to in paragraph 1 shall be evacuated when the places where they are interned or detained become particularly exposed to danger arising out of the armed conflict, if their evacuation can be carried out under adequate conditions of safety;

(d) they shall have the benefit of medical examinations;

(e) their physical or mental health and integrity shall not be endangered by any unjustified act or omission. Accordingly, it is prohibited to subject the persons described in this Article to any medical procedure which is not indicated by the state of health of the person concerned, and which is not consistent with the generally accepted medical standards applied to free persons under similar medical circumstances.

3. Persons who are not covered by paragraph 1 but whose liberty has been restricted in any way whatsoever for reasons related to the armed conflict shall be treated humanely in accordance with Article 4 and with paragraphs 1 (a), (c) and (d), and 2 (b) of this Article.

4. If it is decided to release persons deprived of their liberty, necessary measures to ensure their safety shall be taken by those so deciding.

Article 6. Penal prosecutions

1. This Article applies to the prosecution and punishment of 9–087 criminal offences related to the armed conflict.

2. No sentence shall be passed and no penalty shall be executed on a person found guilty of an offence except pursuant to a conviction pronounced by a court offering the essential guarantees of independence and impartiality.
In particular:

(a) the procedure shall provide for an accused to be informed without delay of the particulars of the offence alleged against him and shall afford the accused before and during his trial all necessary rights and means of defence;

(b) no one shall be convicted of an offence except on the basis of individual penal responsibility;

(c) no one shall be held guilty of any criminal offence on account of any act or omission which did not constitute a criminal offence, under the law, at the time when it was committed; nor shall a heavier penalty be imposed than that which was applicable at the time when the criminal offence was committed; if, after the commission of the offence, provision is made by law for the imposition of a lighter penalty, the offender shall benefit thereby;

(d) anyone charged with an offence is presumed innocent until proved guilty according to law;

(e) anyone charged with an offence shall have the right to be tried in his presence;

(f) no one shall be compelled to testify against himself or to confess guilt.

3. A convicted person shall be advised on conviction of his judicial and other remedies and of the time-limits within which they may be exercised.

4. The death penalty shall not be pronounced on persons who were under the age of 18 years at the time of the offence and shall not be carried out on pregnant women or mothers of young children.

5. At the end of hostilities, the authorities in power shall endeavour to grant the broadest possible amnesty to persons who have participated in the armed conflict, or those deprived of their liberty for reasons related to the armed conflict, whether they are interned or detained.

PART III. WOUNDED, SICK AND SHIPWRECKED

Article 7. Protection and care

9–088 **1.** All the wounded, sick and shipwrecked, whether or not they have taken part in the armed conflict, shall be respected and protected.

2. In all circumstances they shall be treated humanely and shall receive to the fullest extent practicable and with the least possible delay, the medical care and attention required by their condition. There shall be no distinction among them founded on any grounds other than medical ones.

Article 8

Whenever circumstances permit and particularly after an engagement, all possible measures shall be taken, without delay, to search for and collect the wounded, sick and shipwrecked, to protect them against pillage and ill-treatment, to ensure their adequate care, and to search for the dead, prevent their being despoiled, and decently dispose of them.

Article 9. Protection of medical and religious personnel

1. Medical and religious personnel shall be respected and protected and shall be granted all available help for the performance of their duties. They shall not be compelled to carry out tasks which are not compatible with their humanitarian mission.

2. In the performance of their duties medical personnel may not be required to give priority to any person except on medical grounds.

Article 10. General protection of medical duties

1. Under no circumstances shall any person be punished for 9–089 having carried out medical activities compatible with medical ethics, regardless of the person benefiting therefrom.

2. Persons engaged in medical activities shall neither be compelled to perform acts or to carry out work contrary to, nor be compelled to refrain from acts required by, the rules of medical ethics or other rules designed for the benefit of the wounded and sick, or this Protocol.

3. The professional obligations of persons engaged in medical activities regarding information which they may acquire concerning the wounded and sick under their care shall, subject to national law, be respected.

4. Subject to national law, no person engaged in medical activities may be penalised in any way for refusing or failing to give information concerning the wounded and sick who are, or who have been, under his care.

Article 11. Protection of medical units and transports

1. Medical units and transports shall be respected and protected at all times and shall not be the object of attack.

2. The protection to which medical units and transports are entitled shall not cease unless they are used to commit hostile acts, outside their humanitarian function. Protection may, however, cease only after a warning has been given, setting, whenever appropriate, a reasonable time-limit, and after such warning has remained unheeded.

Article 12. The distinctive emblem

Under the direction of the competent authority concerned, the distinctive emblem of the red cross, red crescent or red lion and sun on a white ground shall be displayed by medical and religious personnel and medical units, and on medical transports. It shall be respected in all circumstances. It shall not be used improperly.

PART IV. CIVILIAN POPULATION

Article 13. Protection of the civilian population

9–090   **1.** The civilian population and individual civilians shall enjoy general protection against the dangers arising from military operations. To give effect to this protection, the following rules shall be observed in all circumstances.

2. The civilian population as such, as well as individual civilians, shall not be the object of attack. Acts or threats of violence the primary purpose of which is to spread terror among the civilian population are prohibited.

3. Civilians shall enjoy the protection afforded by this part, unless and for such time as they take a direct part in hostilities.

Article 14. Protection of objects indispensable to the survival of the civilian population

Starvation of civilians as a method of combat is prohibited. It is therefore prohibited to attack, destroy, remove or render useless for that purpose, objects indispensable to the survival of the civilian population such as food-stuffs, agricultural areas for the production of food-stuffs, crops, livestock, drinking water installations and supplies and irrigation works.

Article 15. Protection of works and installations containing dangerous forces

Works or installations containing dangerous forces, namely dams, dykes and nuclear electrical generating stations, shall not be made the object of attack, even where these objects are military objectives, if such attack may cause the release of dangerous forces and consequent severe losses among the civilian population.

Article 16. Protection of cultural objects and of places of worship

Without prejudice to the provisions of the Hague Convention for the Protection of Cultural Property in the Event of Armed Conflict of May 14, 1954,[37] it is prohibited to commit any acts of hostility directed against historic monuments, works of art or places of worship which constitute the cultural or spiritual heritage of peoples, and to use them in support of the military effort.

Article 17. Prohibition of forced movement of civilians

1. The displacement of the civilian population shall not be 9–091 ordered for reasons related to the conflict unless the security of the civilians involved or imperative military reasons so demand. Should such displacements have to be carried out, all possible measures shall be taken in order that the civilian population may be received under satisfactory conditions of shelter, hygiene, health, safety and nutrition.

2. Civilians shall not be compelled to leave their own territory for reasons connected with the conflict.

Article 18. Relief societies and relief actions

1. Relief societies located in the territory of the High Contracting Party, such as Red Cross (Red Crescent, Red Lion and Sun) organisations may offer their services for the performance of their traditional functions in relation to the victims of the armed conflict. The civilian population may, even on its own initiative, offer to collect and care for the wounded, sick and shipwrecked.

2. If the civilian population is suffering undue hardship owing to a lack of the supplies essential for its survival, such as food-stuffs and medical supplies, relief actions for the civilian population which are of an exclusively humanitarian and impartial nature and which are conducted without any adverse distinction shall be undertaken subject to the consent of the High Contracting Party concerned.

Article 25. Denunciation

1. In case a High Contracting Party should denounce this Protocol, the denunciation shall only take effect six months after receipt of the instrument of denunciation. If, however, on the expiry of six months, the denouncing Party is engaged in the situation referred to in Article 1, the denunciation shall not take

---

[37] *Supra* n. 31.

effect before the end of the armed conflict. Persons who have been deprived of liberty, or whose liberty has been restricted, for reasons related to the conflict shall nevertheless continue to benefit from the provisions of this Protocol until their final release.

2. The denunciation shall be notified in writing to the depositary, which shall transmit it to all the High Contracting Parties.

Chapter 10

PRISONERS

INTRODUCTION

The right to liberty is recognised as a fundamental human right   10–001
and the deprivation of liberty should be strictly regulated. Arbitrary detention and torture are tools of repression. Although both
are recognised as contrary to individual dignity they are still
widely practised and the onus is on the international community to
eradicate them. The Optional Protocol to the Convention against
Torture opens the way for preventive visits to places of detention
and the possibility of a "hands on" monitoring of conditions
prevailing in such places. Torture and enforced disappearance are
particularly grave violations of human rights placing a heavy
burden on the international community to provide and enforce
safeguards designed to protect life and liberty. It is equally
important to acknowledge the rights of those detained in less
dramatic circumstances, *i.e.* legitimately in prison, or detained on
medical grounds. Forfeiture of liberty does not remove an individual's right to protection from an abuse of authority, and there is
now a plethora of international norms on medical ethics, the
detention of juveniles and human rights education programmes for
law enforcement officers. The impact of these measures will be
limited unless they are used in and contribute to a culture of
human rights.

WORLD CONFERENCE ON HUMAN RIGHTS, (JUNE 1993) VIENNA DECLARATION

Part II (B) 5. Freedom from torture

54. The World Conference on Human Rights welcomes the 10–002
ratification by many Member States of the Convention against
Torture and Other Cruel, Inhuman or Degrading Treatment or
Punishment and encourages its speedy ratification by all other
Member States.

55. The World Conference on Human Rights emphasises that
one of the most atrocious violations against human dignity is the
act of torture, the result of which destroys the dignity and impairs
the capability of victims to continue their lives and their activities.

56. The World Conference on Human Rights reaffirms that
under human rights law and international humanitarian law,

freedom from torture is a right which must be protected under all circumstances, including in times of internal or international disturbance or armed conflicts.

57. The World Conference on Human Rights therefore urges all States to put an immediate end to the practice of torture and eradicate this evil forever through full implementation of the Universal Declaration of Human Rights as well as the relevant conventions and, where necessary, strengthening of existing mechanisms. The World Conference on Human Rights calls on all States to co-operate fully with the Special Rapporteur on the question of torture in the fulfilment of his mandate.

58. Special attention should be given to ensure universal respect for, and effective implementation of, the Principles of Medical Ethics relevant to the Role of Health Personnel, particularly Physicians, in the Protection of Prisoners and Detainees against Torture and other Cruel, Inhuman or Degrading Treatment or Punishment adopted by the General Assembly of the United Nations.

59. The World Conference on Human Rights stresses the importance of further concrete action within the framework of the United Nations with the view to providing assistance to victims of torture and ensure more effective remedies for their physical, psychological and social rehabilitation. Providing the necessary resources for this purpose should be given high priority, *inter alia*, by additional contributions to the United Nations Voluntary Fund for the Victims of Torture.

60. States should abrogate legislation leading to impunity for those responsible for grave violations of human rights such as torture and prosecute such violations, thereby providing a firm basis for the rule of law.

61. The World Conference on Human Rights reaffirms that efforts to eradicate torture should, first and foremost, be concentrated on prevention and, therefore, calls for the early adoption of an optional protocol to the Convention against Torture and Other Cruel, Inhuman and Degrading Treatment or Punishment, which is intended to establish a preventive system of regular visits to places of detention.

ENFORCED DISAPPEARANCES

10–003   **62.** The World Conference on Human Rights, welcoming the adoption by the General Assembly of the Declaration on the Protection of All Persons from Enforced Disappearance, calls upon all States to take effective legislative, administrative, judicial or other measures to prevent, terminate and punish acts of enforced disappearances. The World Conference on Human Rights reaffirms that it is the duty of all States, under any circumstances, to make investigations whenever there is reason to believe that an enforced disappearance has taken place on a territory under their jurisdiction and, if allegations are confirmed, to prosecute its perpetrators.

UNIVERSAL DECLARATION ON HUMAN RIGHTS 1948

Article 5

No one shall be subjected to torture or to cruel, inhuman or degrading treatment or punishment.

Article 9

No one shall be subjected to arbitrary arrest, detention or exile.

INTERNATIONAL COVENANT ON CIVIL AND POLITICAL RIGHTS, 1966

Article 7

No one shall be subjected to torture or cruel, inhuman or degrading treatment. In particular, no one shall be subjected without his free consent to medical or scientific experimentation.

Human Rights Committee, General Comment No. 20, Article 7[1]

. . .

2. The aim of the provisions of Article 7 of the International **10–004** Covenant on Civil and Political Rights is to protect both the dignity and the physical and mental integrity of the individual. It is the duty of the State party to afford everyone protection through legislative and other measures as may be necessary against the acts prohibited by Article 7, whether inflicted by people acting in their official capacity, outside their official capacity or in a private capacity. The prohibition in Article 7 is complemented by the positive requirements of Article 10, paragraph 1, of the Covenant, which stipulates that "All persons deprived of their liberty shall be treated with humanity and with respect for the inherent dignity of the human person".

---

[1] (44th session, 1992), Compilation of General Comments and General Recommendations Adopted by Human Rights Treaty Bodies, UN Doc. HRI/SGEN/S1/SRev.1 at 30 (1994). General Comment 20 replaces General Comment 7, UN Doc. HRI/GEN/1/Rev.1 at 7 (1994).

3. The text of Article 7 allows of no limitation. The Committee also reaffirms that, even in situations of public emergency such as those referred to in Article 4 of the Covenant, no derogation from the provision of Article 7 is allowed and its provisions must remain in force. The Committee likewise observes that no justification or extenuating circumstances may be invoked to excuse a violation of Article 7 for any reasons, including those based on an order from a superior officer or public authority.

4. The Covenant does not contain any definition of the concepts covered by Article 7, nor does the Committee consider it necessary to draw up a list of prohibited acts or to establish sharp distinctions between the different kinds of punishment or treatment; the distinctions depend on the nature, purpose and severity of the treatment applied.

5. The prohibition in Article 7 relates not only to acts that cause physical pain but also to acts that cause mental suffering to the victim. In the Committee's view, moreover, the prohibition must extend to corporal punishment, including excessive chastisement ordered as punishment for a crime or as an educative or disciplinary measure. It is appropriate to emphasise in this regard that Article 7 protects, in particular, children, pupils and patients in teaching and medical institutions.

6. The Committee notes that prolonged solitary confinement of the detained or imprisoned person may amount to acts prohibited by Article 7. As the Committee has stated in its general comment No. 6 (16), Article 6 of the Covenant refers generally to abolition of the death penalty in terms that strongly suggest that abolition is desirable. Moreover, when the death penalty is applied by a State party for the most serious crimes, it must not only be strictly limited in accordance with Article 6 but it must be carried out in such a way as to cause the least possible physical and mental suffering.

7. Article 7 expressly prohibits medical or scientific experimentation without the free consent of the person concerned. The Committee notes that the reports of States parties generally contain little information on this point. More attention should be given to the need and means to ensure observance of this provision. The Committee also observes that special protection in regard to such experiments is necessary in the case of persons not capable of giving valid consent, and in particular those under any form of detention or imprisonment. Such persons should not be subjected to any medical or scientific experimentation that may be detrimental to their health.

10–005 **8.** The Committee notes that it is not sufficient for the implementation of Article 7 to prohibit such treatment or punishment or to make it a crime. States parties should inform the Committee of the legislative, administrative, judicial and other measures they take to prevent and punish acts of torture and cruel, inhuman and degrading treatment in any territory under their jurisdiction.

9. In the view of the Committee, States parties must not expose individuals to the danger of torture or cruel, inhuman or degrading treatment or punishment upon return to another country by way of their extradition, expulsion or refoulement. States parties should indicate in their reports what measures they have adopted to that end.

10. The Committee should be informed how States parties disseminate, to the population at large, relevant information concerning the ban on torture and the treatment prohibited by Article 7. Enforcement personnel, medical personnel, police officers and any other persons involved in the custody or treatment of any individual subjected to any form of arrest, detention or imprisonment must receive appropriate instruction and training. States parties should inform the Committee of the instruction and training given and the way in which the prohibition of Article 7 forms an integral part of the operational rules and ethical standards to be followed by such persons.

11. In addition to describing steps to provide the general protection against acts prohibited under Article 7 to which anyone is entitled, the State party should provide detailed information on safeguards for the special protection of particularly vulnerable persons. It should be noted that keeping under systematic review interrogation rules, instructions, methods and practices as well as arrangements for the custody and treatment of persons subjected to any form of arrest, detention or imprisonment is an effective means of preventing cases of torture and ill-treatment. To guarantee the effective protection of detained persons, provisions should be made for detainees to be held in places officially recognised as places of detention and for their names and places of detention, as well as for the names of persons responsible for their detention, to be kept in registers readily available and accessible to those concerned, including relatives and friends. To the same effect, the time and place of all interrogations should be recorded, together with the names of all those present and this information should also be available for purposes of judicial or administrative proceedings. Provisions should also be made against incommunicado detention. In that connection, States parties should ensure that any places of detention be free from any equipment liable to be used for inflicting torture or ill-treatment. The protection of the detainee also requires that prompt and regular access be given to doctors and lawyers and, under appropriate supervision when the investigation so requires, to family members.

12. It is important for the discouragement of violations under Article 7 that the law must prohibit the use of admissibility in judicial proceedings of statements or confessions obtained through torture or other prohibited treatment.

10–006   **13.** States parties should indicate when presenting their reports the provisions of their criminal law which penalise torture and cruel, inhuman and degrading treatment or punishment, specifying the penalties applicable to such acts, whether committed by public officials or other persons acting on behalf of the State, or by private persons. Those who violate Article 7, whether by encouraging, ordering, tolerating or perpetrating prohibited acts, must be held responsible. Consequently, those who have refused to obey orders must not be punished or subjected to any adverse treatment.

14. Article 7 should be read in conjunction with Article 2, paragraph 3, of the Covenant. In their reports, States parties should indicate how their legal system effectively guarantees the immediate termination of all the acts prohibited by Article 7 as well as appropriate redress. The right to lodge complaints against maltreatment prohibited by Article 7 must be recognised in the domestic law. Complaints must be investigated promptly and impartially by competent authorities so as to make the remedy effective. The reports of States parties should provide specific information on the remedies available to victims of maltreatment and the procedure that complainants must follow, and statistics on the number of complaints and how they have been dealt with.

15. The Committee has noted that some States have granted amnesty in respect of acts of torture. Amnesties are generally incompatible with the duty of States to investigate such acts; to guarantee freedom from such acts within their jurisdiction; and to ensure that they do not occur in the future. States may not deprive individuals of the right to an effective remedy, including compensation and such full rehabilitation as may be possible.[2]

---

[2] See *Kindler v. Canada infra*, for discussion with respect to the relationship of Article 6 and Article 7 in respect of capital punishment. Torture is regarded as being contrary to customary international law—see U.S. case *Filartiga v. Pena-Irala*, (1980) 630 F.2nd 876, U.S. Court of Appeals, Second Circuit:" . . . although there is no universal agreement as to the precise extent of the "human rights and fundamental freedoms" guaranteed to all by the Charter, there is at present no dissent from the view that the guarantees include, at a bare minimum, the right to be free from torture. This prohibition has become part of international law. . ."
Torture is also characterised as a crime against humanity—see Article 5(f) of the Statute of the International Tribunal for the Prosecution of Persons Responsible for Serious Violations of International Humanitarian Law Committed in the Territory of the Former Yugoslavia, since 1991; the foregoing Tribunal is competent "to prosecute persons committing or ordering to be committed grave breaches of the Geneva Conventions of August 12, 1949, namely . . . (b) torture or inhuman treatment, including biological experiments. . ." see also Statute of the International Tribunal established with respect to Rwanda. Regional organisations have also adopted instruments prohibiting torture—see Article 3 of the European Convention for the Protection of Human Rights and Fundamental Freedoms, 1950, Article 3 "No one shall be subjected to torture, inhuman or degrading treatment or punishment" and the 1987 European Convention for the Prevention of Torture and inhuman or Degrading Treatment or Punishment.

Article 10

1. All persons deprived of their liberty shall be treated with humanity and with respect for the inherent dignity of the human person.[3]

    2. (a)Accused persons shall, save in exceptional circumstances be segregated from convicted persons and shall be subject to separate treatment appropriate to their status as unconvicted persons.

    (b) Accused juvenile persons shall be separated from adults and brought as speedily as possible for adjudication.

    3. The penitentiary system shall comprise treatment of prisoners the essential aim of which shall be their reformation and social rehabilitation. Juvenile offenders shall be segregated from adults and be accorded treatment appropriate to their age and legal status.[4]

CONVENTION AGAINST TORTURE AND OTHER CRUEL, INHUMAN OR DEGRADING TREATMENT OR PUNISHMENT
1984[5]

The States Parties to this Convention, Considering that, in accord- **10–007** ance with the principles proclaimed in the Charter of the United Nations, recognition of the equal and inalienable rights of all members of the human family is the foundation of freedom, justice and peace in the world, Recognising that those rights derive from the inherent dignity of the human person,

    Considering the obligation of States under the Charter, in particular Article 55, to promote universal respect for, and observance of, human rights and fundamental freedoms,

    Having regard to Article 5 of the Universal Declaration of Human Rights and Article 7 of the International Covenant on Civil and Political Rights, both of which provide that no one shall be subjected to torture or to cruel, inhuman or degrading treatment or punishment,

    Having regard also to the Declaration on the Protection of All Persons from Being Subjected to Torture and Other Cruel, Inhuman or Degrading Treatment or Punishment, adopted by the General Assembly on December 9, 1975,[6]

---

[3] The UN Human Rights Committee found a violation of Article 10 in Communication No. 410/1990 *Parkanyi v. Hungary*, 13 H.R.L.J. 345 (1992).

[4] See Chapter on Children, Juvenile Justice.

[5] Misc.12 (1985), Cmnd. 9593. The Convention entered into force in 1987. Currently there are 125 Contracting parties (as of August, 2001).

[6] Res. 3452(XXX) of December 9, 1975.

Desiring to make more effective the struggle against torture and other cruel, inhuman or degrading treatment or punishment throughout the world, Have agreed as follows:

PART I

Article 1

1. For the purposes of this Convention, the term "torture"[7] means any act by which severe pain or suffering, whether physical or mental, is intentionally inflicted on a person for such purposes as obtaining from him or a third person information or a confession, punishing him for an act he or a third person has committed or is suspected of having committed, or intimidating or coercing him or a third person, or for any reason based on discrimination of any kind, when such pain or suffering is inflicted by or at the instigation of or with the consent or acquiescence of a public official or other person acting in an official capacity. It does not include pain or suffering arising only from, inherent in or incidental to lawful sanctions.

2. This article is without prejudice to any international instrument or national legislation which does or may contain provisions of wider application.

Article 2

1. Each State Party shall take effective legislative, administrative, judicial or other measures to prevent acts of torture in any territory under its jurisdiction.

2. No exceptional circumstances whatsoever, whether a state of war or a threat of war, internal political instability or any other public emergency, may be invoked as a justification of torture.

3. An order from a superior officer or a public authority may not be invoked as a justification of torture.

Article 3

1. No State Party shall expel, return ("refouler")[8] or extradite a person to another State where there are substantial grounds for believing that he would be in danger of being subjected to torture.

---

[7] See General Comment XX, *supra* p. 446.

[8] The concept of "refoulement" is discussed fully in Chapter on Refugees at In the context of torture and the obligation on Contracting Parties to the Convention for the Elimination of Torture see Communication No. 3/1993 *Mutombo v. Switzerland*, 15 H.R.L.J. (1994) 164; and Communication No. 15/1994 *Khan v. Canada, ibid* at 426. In both instances the Committee for the Elimination of Torture expressed the view that to return the individuals concerned would consititute a violation of Article 3.

2. For the purpose of determining whether there are such grounds, the competent authorities shall take into account all relevant considerations including, where applicable, the existence in the State concerned of a consistent pattern of gross, flagrant or mass violations of human rights.

Article 4

1. Each State Party shall ensure that all acts of torture are **10–009** offences under its criminal law. The same shall apply to an attempt to commit torture and to an act by any person which constitutes complicity or participation in torture.

2. Each State Party shall make these offences punishable by appropriate penalties which take into account their grave nature.

Article 5

1. Each State Party shall take such measures as may be necessary to establish its jurisdiction over the offences referred to in Article 4 in the following cases:

(a) When the offences are committed in any territory under its jurisdiction or on board a ship or aircraft registered in that State;

(b) When the alleged offender is a national of that State;

(c) When the victim is a national of that State if that State considers it appropriate.

2. Each State Party shall likewise take such measures as may be necessary to establish its jurisdiction over such offences in cases where the alleged offender is present in any territory under its jurisdiction and it does not extradite him pursuant to Article 8 to any of the States mentioned in paragraph 1 of this Article.

3. This Convention does not exclude any criminal jurisdiction exercised in accordance with internal law.

Article 6

1. Upon being satisfied, after an examination of information available to it, that the circumstances so warrant, any State Party in whose territory a person alleged to have committed any offence referred to in Article 4 is present shall take him into custody or take other legal measures to ensure his presence. The custody and other legal measures shall be as provided in the law of that State but may be continued only for such time as is necessary to enable any criminal or extradition proceedings to be instituted.

2. Such State shall immediately make a preliminary inquiry into the facts.

3. Any person in custody pursuant to paragraph 1 of this article shall be assisted in communicating immediately with the nearest appropriate representative of the State of which he is a national, or, if he is a stateless person, with the representative of the State where he usually resides.

4. When a State, pursuant to this article, has taken a person into custody, it shall immediately notify the States referred to in Article 5, paragraph 1, of the fact that such person is in custody and of the circumstances which warrant his detention. The State which makes the preliminary inquiry contemplated in paragraph 2 of this article shall promptly report its findings to the said States and shall indicate whether it intends to exercise jurisdiction.

Article 7

10–010   **1.** The State Party in the territory under whose jurisdiction a person alleged to have committed any offence referred to in Article 4 is found shall in the cases contemplated in Article 5, if it does not extradite him, submit the case to its competent author-ities for the purpose of prosecution.

2. These authorities shall take their decision in the same manner as in the case of any ordinary offence of a serious nature under the law of that State. In the cases referred to in Article 5, paragraph 2, the standards of evidence required for prosecution and conviction shall in no way be less stringent than those which apply in the cases referred to in Article 5, paragraph 1.

3. Any person regarding whom proceedings are brought in connection with any of the offences referred to in Article 4 shall be guaranteed fair treatment at all stages of the proceedings.

Article 8

1. The offences referred to in Article 4 shall be deemed to be included as extraditable offences in any extradition treaty existing between States Parties. States Parties undertake to include such offences as extraditable offences in every extradition treaty to be concluded between them.

2. If a State Party which makes extradition conditional on the existence of a treaty receives a request for extradition from another. State Party with which it has no extradition treaty, it may consider this Convention as the legal basis for extradition in respect of such offences. Extradition shall be subject to the other conditions provided by the law of the requested State.

3. States Parties which do not make extradition conditional on the existence of a treaty shall recognise such offences as extraditable offences between themselves subject to the conditions provided by the law of the requested State.

4. Such offences shall be treated, for the purpose of extradition between States Parties, as if they had been committed not only in the place in which they occurred but also in the territories of the States required to establish their jurisdiction in accordance with Article 5, paragraph 1.

Article 9

1. States Parties shall afford one another the greatest measure 10–011 of assistance in connection with criminal proceedings brought in respect of any of the offences referred to in Article 4, including the supply of all evidence at their disposal necessary for the proceedings.

2. States Parties shall carry out their obligations under paragraph 1 of this article in conformity with any treaties on mutual judicial assistance that may exist between them.

Article 10

1. Each State Party shall ensure that education and information regarding the prohibition against torture are fully included in the training of law enforcement personnel, civil or military, medical personnel, public officials and other persons who may be involved in the custody, interrogation or treatment of any individual subjected to any form of arrest, detention or imprisonment.

2. Each State Party shall include this prohibition in the rules or instructions issued in regard to the duties and functions of any such person.

Article 11

Each State Party shall keep under systematic review interrogation rules, instructions, methods and practices as well as arrangements for the custody and treatment of persons subjected to any form of arrest, detention or imprisonment in any territory under its jurisdiction, with a view to preventing any cases of torture.

Article 12

Each State Party shall ensure that its competent authorities proceed to a prompt and impartial investigation, wherever there is reasonable ground to believe that an act of torture has been committed in any territory under its jurisdiction.

Article 13

Each State Party shall ensure that any individual who alleges he 10–012 has been subjected to torture in any territory under its jurisdiction has the right to complain to, and to have his case promptly and impartially examined by, its competent authorities. Steps shall be taken to ensure that the complainant and witnesses are protected against all ill-treatment or intimidation as a consequence of his complaint or any evidence given.

Article 14

1. Each State Party shall ensure in its legal system that the victim of an act of torture obtains redress and has an enforceable right to fair and adequate compensation, including the means for as full rehabilitation as possible. In the event of the death of the victim as a result of an act of torture, his dependants shall be entitled to compensation.

2. Nothing in this article shall affect any right of the victim or other persons to compensation which may exist under national law.

Article 15

10–013 Each State Party shall ensure that any statement which is established to have been made as a result of torture shall not be invoked as evidence in any proceedings, except against a person accused of torture as evidence that the statement was made.

Article 16

1. Each State Party shall undertake to prevent in any territory under its jurisdiction other acts of cruel, inhuman or degrading treatment or punishment which do not amount to torture as defined in Article 1, when such acts are committed by or at the instigation of or with the consent or acquiescence of a public official or other person acting in an official capacity. In particular, the obligations contained in Articles 10, 11, 12 and 13 shall apply with the substitution for references to torture of references to other forms of cruel, inhuman or degrading treatment or punishment.

2. The provisions of this Convention are without prejudice to the provisions of any other international instrument or national law which prohibits cruel, inhuman or degrading treatment or punishment or which relates to extradition or expulsion.

PART II

Article 17

10–014 **1.** There shall be established a Committee against Torture (hereinafter referred to as the Committee) which shall carry out the functions hereinafter provided. The Committee shall consist of ten experts of high moral standing and recognised competence in the field of human rights, who shall serve in their personal capacity. The experts shall be elected by the States Parties, consideration being given to equitable geographical distribution and to the usefulness of the participation of some persons having legal experience.[9]

2. The members of the Committee shall be elected by secret ballot from a list of persons nominated by States Parties. Each State Party may nominate one person from among its own nationals. States Parties shall bear in mind the usefulness of nominating persons who are also members of the Human Rights Committee established under the International Covenant on Civil and Political Rights and who are willing to serve on the Committee against Torture.

3. Elections of the members of the Committee shall be held at biennial meetings of States Parties convened by the Secretary-General of the United Nations. At those meetings, for which two-thirds of the States Parties shall constitute a quorum, the persons elected to the Committee shall be those who obtain the largest number of votes and an absolute majority of the votes of the representatives of States Parties present and voting.

4. The initial election shall be held no later than six months after the date of the entry into force of this Convention. At least four months before the date of each election, the Secretary-General of the United Nations shall address a letter to the States Parties inviting them to submit their nominations within three months. The Secretary-General shall prepare a list in alphabetical order of all persons thus nominated, indicating the States Parties which have nominated them, and shall submit it to the States Parties.

5. The members of the Committee shall be elected for a term of four years.
They shall be eligible for re-election if renominated. However, the term of five of the members elected at the first election shall expire at the end of two years; immediately after the first election the names of these five members shall be chosen by lot by the chairman of the meeting referred to in paragraph 3 of this article.

6. If a member of the Committee dies or resigns or for any other cause can no longer perform his Committee duties, the State Party which nominated him shall appoint another expert from among its nationals to serve for the remainder of his term, subject to the approval of the majority of the States Parties. The approval shall be considered given unless half or more of the States Parties respond negatively within six weeks after having been informed

---

[9] The initial meeting of the Committee was held in Geneva in 1988. The Committee concluded its 26th session in May 2001.

by the Secretary-General of the United Nations of the proposed appointment.

7. States Parties shall be responsible for the expenses of the members of the Committee while they are in performance of Committee duties.

Article 18

10–015   1. The Committee shall elect its officers for a term of two years. They may be re-elected.

2. The Committee shall establish its own rules of procedure, but these rules shall provide, *inter alia*, that:

(a) Six members shall constitute a quorum;

(b) Decisions of the Committee shall be made by a majority vote of the members present.

3. The Secretary-General of the United Nations shall provide the necessary staff and facilities for the effective performance of the functions of the Committee under this Convention.

4. The Secretary-General of the United Nations shall convene the initial meeting of the Committee. After its initial meeting, the Committee shall meet at such times as shall be provided in its rules of procedure.

5. The States Parties shall be responsible for expenses incurred in connection with the holding of meetings of the States Parties and of the Committee, including reimbursement to the United Nations for any expenses, such as the cost of staff and facilities, incurred by the United Nations pursuant to paragraph 3 of this article.

Article 19

1. The States Parties shall submit to the Committee, through the Secretary-General of the United Nations, reports on the measures they have taken to give effect to their undertakings under this Convention, within one year after the entry into force of the Convention for the State Party concerned. Thereafter the States Parties shall submit supplementary reports every four years on any new measures taken and such other reports as the Committee may request.

2. The Secretary-General of the United Nations shall transmit the reports to all States Parties.

3. Each report shall be considered by the Committee which may make such general comments on the report as it may consider appropriate and shall forward these to the State Party concerned. That State Party may respond with any observations it chooses to the Committee.

4. The Committee may, at its discretion, decide to include any comments made by it in accordance with paragraph 3 of this article, together with the observations thereon received from the State Party concerned, in its annual report made in accordance with Article 24. If so requested by the State Party concerned, the Committee may also include a copy of the report submitted under paragraph 1 of this article.[10]

Article 20

1. If the Committee receives reliable information which **10–016** appears to it to contain well-founded indications that torture is being systematically practised in the territory of a State Party, the Committee shall invite that State Party to co-operate in the examination of the information and to this end to submit observations with regard to the information concerned.

2. Taking into account any observations which may have been submitted by the State Party concerned, as well as any other relevant information available to it, the Committee may, if it decides that this is warranted, designate one or more of its members to make a confidential inquiry and to report to the Committee urgently.

3. If an inquiry is made in accordance with paragraph 2 of this article, the Committee shall seek the co-operation of the State Party concerned. In agreement with that State Party, such an inquiry may include a visit to its territory.

4. After examining the findings of its member or members submitted in accordance with paragraph 2 of this article, the Commission shall transmit these findings to the State Party concerned together with any comments or suggestions which seem appropriate in view of the situation.

5. All the proceedings of the Committee referred to in paragraphs 1 to 4 of this article shall be confidential, and at all stages of the proceedings the co-operation of the State Party shall be sought. After such proceedings have been completed with regard to an inquiry made in accordance with paragraph 2, the Committee may, after consultations with the State Party concerned, decide to include a summary account of the results of the proceedings in its annual report made in accordance with Article 24.

[10] Although there are 125 parties to the Convention, a significant number of States are overdue with the submission of their reports. At the Committee's 16th session it was suggested that the situation in countries which failed to respond to reminders regarding overdue reports should be assessed on the basis of information obtained from other sources, *e.g.* non-governmental organisations.

Article 21

10–017   1. A State Party to this Convention may at any time declare under this article that it recognises the competence of the Committee[11] to receive and consider communications to the effect that a State Party claims that another State Party is not fulfilling its obligations under this Convention. Such communications may be received and considered according to the procedures laid down in this article only if submitted by a State Party which has made a declaration recognising in regard to itself the competence of the Committee. No communication shall be dealt with by the Committee under this article if it concerns a State Party which has not made such a declaration. Communications received under this article shall be dealt with in accordance with the following procedure;

   (a) If a State Party considers that another State Party is not giving effect to the provisions of this Convention, it may, by written communication, bring the matter to the attention of that State Party. Within three months after the receipt of the communication the receiving State shall afford the State which sent the communication an explanation or any other statement in writing clarifying the matter, which should include, to the extent possible and pertinent, reference to domestic procedures and remedies taken, pending or available in the matter;

   (b) If the matter is not adjusted to the satisfaction of both States Parties concerned within six months after the receipt by the receiving State of the initial communication, either State shall have the right to refer the matter to the Committee, by notice given to the Committee and to the other State;

   (c) The Committee shall deal with a matter referred to it under this article only after it has ascertained that all domestic remedies have been invoked and exhausted in the matter, in conformity with the generally recognised principles of international law. This shall not be the rule where the application of the remedies is unreasonably prolonged or is unlikely to bring effective relief to the person who is the victim of the violation of this Convention;

   (d) The Committee shall hold closed meetings when examining communications under this article;

   (e) Subject to the provisions of subparagraph (c), the Committee shall make available its good offices to the States

---

[11] Currently (as of May, 2000) 41 States have recognised the competence of the Committee.

Parties concerned with a view to a friendly solution of the matter on the basis of respect for the obligations provided for in this Convention. For this purpose, the Committee may, when appropriate, set up an ad hoc conciliation commission;

(f) In any matter referred to it under this article, the Committee may call upon the States Parties concerned, referred to in subparagraph (b), to supply any relevant information;

(g) The States Parties concerned, referred to in subparagraph (b), shall have the right to be represented when the matter is being considered by the Committee and to make submissions orally and/or in writing;

(h) The Committee shall, within 12 months after the date of receipt of notice under subparagraph (b), submit a report:

(i) If a solution within the terms of subparagraph (e) is reached, the Committee shall confine its report to a brief statement of the facts and of the solution reached;

(ii) If a solution within the terms of subparagraph (e) is not reached, the Committee shall confine its report to a brief statement of the facts; the written submissions and record of the oral submissions made by the States Parties concerned shall be attached to the report. In every matter, the report shall be communicated to the States Parties concerned.

2. The provisions of this article shall come into force when five **10–018** States Parties to this Convention have made declarations under paragraph 1 of this article. Such declarations shall be deposited by the States Parties with the Secretary-General of the United Nations, who shall transmit copies thereof to the other States Parties. A declaration may be withdrawn at any time by notification to the Secretary-General. Such a withdrawal shall not prejudice the consideration of any matter which is the subject of a communication already transmitted under this article; no further communication by any State Party shall be received under this article after the notification of withdrawal of the declaration has been received by the Secretary-General, unless the State Party concerned has made a new declaration.

Article 22

1. A State Party to this Convention may at any time declare **10–019** under this article that it recognises the competence of the Committee to receive and consider communications from or on behalf

of individuals subject to its jurisdiction who claim to be victims of a violation by a State Party of the provisions of the Convention. No communication shall be received by the Committee if it concerns a State Party which has not made such a declaration.

2. The Committee shall consider inadmissible any communication under this article which is anonymous or which it considers to be an abuse of the right of submission of such communications or to be incompatible with the provisions of this Convention.

3. Subject to the provisions of paragraph 2, the Committee shall bring any communications submitted to it under this article to the attention of the State Party to this Convention which has made a declaration under paragraph 1 and is alleged to be violating any provisions of the Convention. Within six months, the receiving State shall submit to the Committee written explanations or statements clarifying the matter and the remedy, if any, that may have been taken by that State.

4. The Committee shall consider communications received under this article in the light of all information made available to it by or on behalf of the individual and by the State Party concerned.

5. The Committee shall not consider any communications from an individual under this article unless it has ascertained that:

(a) The same matter has not been, and is not being, examined under another procedure of international investigation or settlement;

(b) The individual has exhausted all available domestic remedies; this shall not be the rule where the application of the remedies is unreasonably prolonged or is unlikely to bring effective relief to the person who is the victim of the violation of this Convention.

6. The Committee shall hold closed meetings when examining communications under this article.

7. The Committee shall forward its views to the State Party concerned and to the individual.

8. The provisions of this article shall come into force when five States Parties to this Convention have made declarations under paragraph 1 of this article. Such declarations shall be deposited by the States Parties with the Secretary-General of the United Nations, who shall transmit copies thereof to the other States Parties. A declaration may be withdrawn at any time by notification to the Secretary-General. Such a withdrawal shall not prejudice the consideration of any matter which is the subject of a communication already transmitted under this article; no further communication by or on behalf of an individual shall be received under this article after the notification of withdrawal of the declaration has been received by the Secretary-General, unless the State Party has made a new declaration.[12]

Article 23

The members of the Committee and of the ad hoc conciliation **10–020** commissions which may be appointed under Article 21, paragraph 1(e), shall be entitled to the facilities, privileges and immunities of experts on mission for the United Nations as laid down in the relevant sections of the Convention on the Privileges and Immunities of the United Nations.

Article 24

The Committee shall submit an annual report on its activities under this Convention to the States Parties and to the General Assembly of the United Nations.

Article 30

1. Any dispute between two or more States Parties concerning the interpretation or application of this Convention which cannot be settled through negotiation shall, at the request of one of them, be submitted to arbitration. If within six months from the date of the request for arbitration the Parties are unable to agree on the organisation of the arbitration, any one of those Parties may refer the dispute to the International Court of Justice by request in conformity with the Statute of the Court.

2. Each State may, at the time of signature or ratification of this Convention or accession thereto, declare that it does not consider itself bound by paragraph 1 of this article. The other States Parties shall not be bound by paragraph 1 of this article with respect to any State Party having made such a reservation.

3. Any State Party having made a reservation in accordance with paragraph 2 of this article may at any time withdraw this reservation by notification to the Secretary-General of the United Nations.

Note: An Optional Protocol to the above Convention has been mooted regarding the provision of a system of inspection of places of detention.

Principles of Medical Ethics

The Vienna Declaration in paragraph 58 called for special attention to be given to the following principles of medical ethics and

---

[12] Since the procedure under Article 22 was initiated on June 26, 1987 a total of 48 communications with respect to 12 states have been submitted. Amongst the Contracting Parties against whom the Committee has given an affirmative opinion are Switzerland (Communication No. 3/1993 *supra*), Canada (Communication No /15/1994 *supra*), Austria (Communication No. 8/1991 *Nedizibi v. Austria* (violation of Article 12), and Sweden.

for these principles to be accorded universal respect and effectively implemented.

PRINCIPLES OF MEDICAL ETHICS RELEVANT TO THE ROLE OF HEALTH PERSONNEL, PARTICULARLY PHYSICIANS, IN THE PROTECTION OF PRISONERS AND DETAINEES AGAINST TORTURE AND OTHER CRUEL, INHUMAN OR DEGRADING TREATMENT OR PUNISHMENT, of DECEMBER 18, 1982[13]

Principle 1

10–021 Health personnel, particularly physicians, charged with the medical care of prisoners and detainees have a duty to provide them with protection of their physical and mental health and treatment of disease of the same quality and standard as is afforded to those who are not imprisoned or detained.

Principle 2

It is a gross contravention of medical ethics, as well as an offence under applicable international instruments, for health personnel, particularly physicians, to engage, actively or passively, in acts which constitute participation in, complicity in, incitement to or attempts to commit torture or other cruel, inhuman or degrading treatment or punishment.

Principle 3

It is a contravention of medical ethics for health personnel, particularly physicians, to be involved in any professional relationship with prisoners or detainees the purpose of which is not solely to evaluate, protect or improve their physical and mental health.

Principle 4

10–022 It is a contravention of medical ethics for health personnel, particularly physicians:

(a) To apply their knowledge and skills in order to assist in the interrogation of prisoners and detainees in a manner that may adversely affect the physical or mental health or condition of such prisoners or detainees and which is not in accordance with the relevant international instruments;

---

[13] G.A. Res. 37/194, annex, 37 UN G.A.O.R. Supp. (No. 51) at p. 211, UN Doc. A/37/51 (1982).

(b) To certify, or to participate in the certification of, the fitness of prisoners or detainees for any form of treatment or punishment that may adversely affect their physical or mental health and which is not in accordance with the relevant international instruments, or to participate in any way in the infliction of any such treatment or punishment which is not in accordance with the relevant international instruments.

Principle 5

It is a contravention of medical ethics for health personnel, particularly physicians, to participate in any procedure for restraining a prisoner or detainee unless such a procedure is determined in accordance with purely medical criteria as being necessary for the protection of the physical or mental health or the safety of the prisoner or detainee himself, of his fellow prisoners or detainees, or of his guardians, and presents no hazard to his physical or mental health.

Principle 6

There may be no derogation from the foregoing principles on any ground whatsoever, including public emergency.

UN VOLUNTARY FUND FOR VICTIMS OF TORTURE

Paragraph 59 makes reference to the UN Voluntary Fund for Victims of Torture. This was established by General Assembly Resolution 36/151 of December 16, 1981 and it has the purpose of receiving voluntary contributions for distribution, through established channels of assistance as humanitarian, legal and financial aid to persons who have been tortured and to members of their families. The fund depends entirely on voluntary contributions from governments, private organisations, institutions and individuals and is administered by the Secretary-General of the United Nations along with a Board of Trustees, composed of a Chairman, and four members with wide experience in the field of human rights. The fund has provided practical help to relieve the suffering of victims of torture and their relatives by providing medical and psychological support, opportunities for social and economic reintegration and legal and or financial assistance.In 1995 the fund supported 107 projects implemented by 99 non-governmental organisations and specialised centres. However, financial problems have beset the fund. In May 1996 contributions received amounted to $36,330,000 whereas the amount requested for assistance was $365.9 million.

CAPITAL PUNISHMENT

10–023 Although not specifically mentioned in the Vienna Declaration the international community's efforts to abolish the death penalty warrants some consideration.

The principal provisions at the international level are Article 6 of the International Covenant on Civil and Political Rights and Article 1 of the Second Optional Protocol on Civil and Political Rights Aiming at the Abolition of the Death Penalty.

INTERNATIONAL COVENANT ON CIVIL AND POLITICAL RIGHTS, 1966

Article 6

1. Every human being has the inherent right to life. This right shall be protected by law. No one shall be arbitrarily deprived of his life.

2. In countries which have not abolished the death penalty, sentence of death may be imposed only for the most serious crimes in accordance with the law in force at the time of the commission of the crime and not contrary to the provisions of the present Covenant and to the Convention on the Prevention and Punishment on the Crime of Genocide. This penalty can only be carried out pursuant to a final judgment rendered by a competent court.

3. . . . .

4. Anyone sentenced to death shall have the right to seek pardon or commutation of the sentence. Amnesty, pardon or commutation of the sentence of death may be granted in all cases.

5. Sentence of death shall not be imposed for crimes committed by persons below 18 years of age and shall not be carried out on pregnant women.

6. Nothing in this article shall be invoked to delay or to prevent the abolition of capital punishment by any State party to the present Covenant.

Note: Economic and Social Council resolution 1984/50, adopted May 25, 1984, concerning Safeguards Guaranteeing Protection of the Rights of Those Facing the Death Penalty which in essence reflects the provisions of Article 6 of the ICCPR:

In countries which have not abolished the death penalty, capital punishment may be imposed only for the most serious crimes, intentionally committed with lethal or extremely grave consequences.

Capital punishment may be imposed only for a crime for which the death penalty is prescribed by law at the time of its commission.

Persons below 18 years of age, pregnant women, new mothers or persons who have become insane shall not be sentenced to death.

Capital punishment may be imposed only when guilt is determined by clear and convincing evidence leaving no room for an alternative explanation of the facts.

Capital punishment may be carried out only after a final judgement rendered by a competent court allowing all possible safeguards to the defendant, including adequate legal assistance.

Anyone sentenced to death shall have the right of appeal to a court of higher jurisdiction.

Anyone sentenced to death shall have the right to seek pardon or commutation of sentence.

Capital punishment shall not be carried out pending any appeal, recourse procedure or proceeding relating to pardon or commutation of the sentence.

Where capital punishment occurs, it shall be carried out so as to inflict the minimum possible suffering.

Human Rights Committee, General Comment No. 6, Article 6[14]

1. The right to life enunciated in Article 6 of the Covenant has **10–024** been dealt with in all State reports. It is the supreme right from which no derogation is permitted even in time of public emergency which threatens the life of the nation (Article 4). However, the Committee has noted that quite often the information given concerning Article 6 was limited to only one or other aspect of this right. It is a right which should not be interpreted narrowly.

2. The Committee observes that war and other acts of mass violence continue to be a scourge of humanity and take the lives of thousands of innocent human beings every year. Under the Charter of the United Nations the threat or use of force by any State against another State, except in exercise of the inherent right of self-defence, is already prohibited. The Committee considers that States have the supreme duty to prevent wars, acts of genocide and other acts of mass violence causing arbitrary loss of life. Every effort they make to avert the danger of war, especially thermonuclear war, and to strengthen international peace and security would constitute the most important condition and guarantee for the safeguarding of the right to life. In this respect, the Committee notes, in particular, a connection between Article 6

---

[14] (16th session, 1982), UN Doc. HRI\GEN\1\Rev.1 at 6 (1994).

and Article 20, which states that the law shall prohibit any propaganda for war (paragraph 1) or incitement to violence (paragraph 2) as therein described.

10–025 **3.** The protection against arbitrary deprivation of life which is explicitly required by the third sentence of Article 6 (1) is of paramount importance. The Committee considers that States parties should take measures not only to prevent and punish deprivation of life by criminal acts, but also to prevent arbitrary killing by their own security forces. The deprivation of life by the authorities of the State is a matter of the utmost gravity. Therefore, the law must strictly control and limit the circumstances in which a person may be deprived of his life by such authorities.

4. States parties should also take specific and effective measures to prevent the disappearance of individuals, something which unfortunately has become all too frequent and leads too often to arbitrary deprivation of life. Furthermore, States should establish effective facilities and procedures to investigate thoroughly cases of missing and disappeared persons in circumstances which may involve a violation of the right to life.

5. Moreover, the Committee has noted that the right to life has been too often narrowly interpreted. The expression "inherent right to life" cannot properly be understood in a restrictive manner, and the protection of this right requires that States adopt positive measures. In this connection, the Committee considers that it would be desirable for States parties to take all possible measures to reduce infant mortality and to increase life expectancy, especially in adopting measures to eliminate malnutrition and epidemics.

6. While it follows from Article 6 (2) to (6) that States parties are not obliged to abolish the death penalty totally they are obliged to limit its use and, in particular, to abolish it for other than the "most serious crimes". Accordingly, they ought to consider reviewing their criminal laws in this light and, in any event, are obliged to restrict the application of the death penalty to the "most serious crimes". The article also refers generally to abolition in terms which strongly suggest (paragraphs 2 (2) and (6)) that abolition is desirable. The Committee concludes that all measures of abolition should be considered as progress in the enjoyment of the right to life within the meaning of Article 40, and should as such be reported to the Committee. The Committee notes that a number of States have already abolished the death penalty or suspended its application. Nevertheless, States' reports show that progress made towards abolishing or limiting the application of the death penalty is quite inadequate.

7. The Committee is of the opinion that the expression "most serious crimes" must be read restrictively to mean that the death penalty should be a quite exceptional measure. It also follows from the express terms of Article 6 that it can only be imposed in accordance with the law in force at the time of the commission of the crime and not contrary to the Covenant. The procedural guarantees therein prescribed must be observed, including the right to a fair hearing by an independent tribunal, the presumption of innocence, the minimum guarantees for the defence, and the right to review by a higher tribunal. These rights are applicable in addition to the particular right to seek pardon or commutation of the sentence.

SECOND OPTIONAL PROTOCOL ON CIVIL AND POLITICAL RIGHTS AIMING AT THE ABOLITION OF THE DEATH PENALTY[15]

Article 1

1. No one within the jurisdiction of a State party to the present **10–026** Protocol shall be executed.

2. Each State party shall take all necessary measures to abolish the death penalty within its jurisdiction.

Note: Article 2.1. which provides "No reservation is admissible to the present Protocol, except for a reservation at the time of ratification or accession that provides for the application of the death penalty in time of war pursuant to a conviction for a most serious crime of a military nature committed during war time".

In addition to the Second Optional Protocol regional organisation have promulgated instruments designed to eliminate the death penalty—see, *e.g.* Protocol to the European Convention on the Protection of Human Rights and Fundamental Freedoms, Concerning the Abolition of the Death Penalty, 1983;[16] and the Protocol to the American Convention on Human Rights to Abolish the Death Penalty, 1990.[17] For a discussion by the United Nations Humans Rights Committee as to whether the death row phenomenon associated with capital punishment constitutes a violation of I.C.P.P.R. and in particular Article 7 see Communication No. 470/1991, *Kindler v. Canada* 14 H.R.L.J. (1993) 307; *cf Soering v. United Kingdom*, E.C.H.R. judgment of July 7, 1989 Series A, No 161; 11 H.R.L.J. (1990) 335.

---

[15] Adopted by the General Assembly on December 15, 1989 (59 votes in favour; 26 against; and 48 abstentions). The Protocol entered into force in 1991. Currently 45 States have adopted the Optional Protocol.

[16] Protocol No. 6 E.T.S. No. 114.

[17] 29 I.L.M. (1990) P1447.

Enforced Disappearances

The Resolution referred to in paragraph 62 is that adopted by the General Assembly in December, 1992, namely The Declaration on the Protection of all Persons From Enforced Disappearances.[18]

THE DECLARATION ON PROTECTION OF PERSONS FROM ENFORCED DISAPPEARANCES

The General Assembly,

Considering that, in accordance with the principles proclaimed in ments, recognition of the inherent dignity and of the equal and inalienable rights of all members of the human family is the foundation of freedom, justice and peace in the world,

Bearing in mind the obligation of States under the Charter, in vance of, human rights and fundamental freedoms,

Deeply concerned that in many countries, often in a persistent manner, enforced disappearances occur, in the sense that persons are arrested, detained or abducted against their will or otherwise deprived of their liberty by officials of different branches or levels of Government, or by organised groups or private individuals acting on behalf of, or with the support, direct or indirect, consent or acquiescence of the Government, followed by a refusal to disclose the fate or whereabouts of the persons concerned or a refusal to acknowledge the deprivation of their liberty, which places such persons outside the protection of the law,

Considering that enforced disappearance undermines the deepest values of any society committed to respect for the rule of law, human rights and fundamental freedoms, and that the systematic practice of such acts is of the nature of a crime against humanity,

Bearing in mind that, while the acts which comprise enforced disappearance constitute a violation of the prohibition. . . , it is none the less important to devise an instrument which characterises all acts of enforced disappearance of persons as very serious offences and sets forth standards designed to punish and prevent their commission,

1. Proclaims the present Declaration on the Protection of all Persons from Enforced Disappearance, as a body of principles for all States;

2. Urges that all efforts be made so that the Declaration becomes generally known and respected;

Article 1

10–027   1. Any act of enforced disappearance is an offence to human dignity. It is condemned as a denial of the purposes of the Charter of the United Nations and as a grave and flagrant

---

[18] G.A. Res. 47/133, 47 U.N. GAOR Supp. (No. 49) at 207, U.N. Doc. A/47/49 (1992). Adopted by General Assembly resolution 47/133 of December 18, 1992.

violation of the human rights and fundamental freedoms pro-claimed in the Universal Declaration of Human Rights and reaffirmed and developed in international instruments in this field.

2. Any act of enforced disappearance places the persons sub-jected thereto outside the protection of the law and inflicts severe suffering on them and their families. It constitutes a violation of the rules of international law guaranteeing, *inter alia*, the right to recognition as a person before the law, the right to liberty and security of the person and the right not to be subjected to torture and other cruel, inhuman or degrading treatment or punishment. It also violates or constitutes a grave threat to the right to life.

Article 2

1. No State shall practise, permit or tolerate enforced **10–028** disappearances.

2. States shall act at the national and regional levels and in cooperation with the United Nations to contribute by all means to the prevention and eradication of enforced disappearance.

Article 3

Each State shall take effective legislative, administrative, judicial or other measures to prevent and terminate acts of enforced disappearance in any territory under its jurisdiction.

Article 4

1. All acts of enforced disappearance shall be offences under criminal law punishable by appropriate penalties which shall take into account their extreme seriousness.

2. Mitigating circumstances may be established in national legislation for persons who, having participated in enforced disappearances, are instrumental in bringing the victims forward alive or in providing voluntarily information which would con-tribute to clarifying cases of enforced disappearance.

Article 5

In addition to such criminal penalties as are applicable, enforced disappearances render their perpetrators and the State or State authorities which organise, acquiesce in or tolerate such disap-pearances liable under civil law, without prejudice to the inter-national responsibility of the State concerned in accordance with the principles of international law.

Article 6

1. No order or instruction of any public authority, civilian, military or other, may be invoked to justify an enforced disap-

pearance. Any person receiving such an order or instruction shall
have the right and duty not to obey it.

2. Each State shall ensure that orders or instructions directing,
authorising or encouraging any enforced disappearance are
prohibited.

3. Training of law enforcement officials shall emphasise the
provisions in paragraphs 1 and 2 of the present article.

Article 7

10–029 No circumstances whatsoever, whether a threat of war, a state of
war, internal political instability or any other public emergency,
may be invoked to justify enforced disappearances.

Article 8

1. No State shall expel, return (refouler) or extradite a person
to another State where there are substantial grounds to believe
that he would be in danger of enforced disappearance.

2. For the purpose of determining whether there are such
grounds, the competent authorities shall take into account all
relevant considerations including, where applicable, the existence
in the State concerned of a consistent pattern of gross, flagrant or
mass violations of human rights.

Article 9

1. The right to a prompt and effective judicial remedy as a
means of determining the whereabouts or state of health of
persons deprived of their liberty and/or identifying the authority
ordering or carrying out the deprivation of liberty is required to
prevent enforced disappearances under all circumstances, including those referred to in Article 7 above.

2. In such proceedings, competent national authorities shall
have access to all places where persons deprived of their liberty
are being held and to each part of those places, as well as to any
place in which there are grounds to believe that such persons
may be found.

3. Any other competent authority entitled under the law of the
State or by any international legal instrument to which the State is
a party may also have access to such places.

Article 10

1. Any person deprived of liberty shall be held in an officially
recognised place of detention and, in conformity with national
law, be brought before a judicial authority promptly after
detention.

2. Accurate information on the detention of such persons and their place or places of detention, including transfers. shall be made promptly available to their family members, their counsel or to any other persons having a legitimate interest in the information unless a wish to the contrary has been manifested by the persons concerned.

3. An official up-to-date register of all persons deprived of their liberty shall be maintained in every place of detention. Additionally, each State shall take steps to maintain similar centralised registers. The information contained in these registers shall be made available to the persons mentioned in the preceding paragraph, to any judicial or other competent and independent national authority and to any other competent authority entitled under the law of the State concerned or any international legal instrument to which a State concerned is a party, seeking to trace the whereabouts of a detained person.

Article 11

All persons deprived of liberty must be released in a manner **10–030** permitting reliable verification that they have actually been released and, further, have been released in conditions in which their physical integrity and ability fully to exercise their rights are assured.

Article 12

1. Each State shall establish rules under its national law indicating those officials authorised to order deprivation of liberty, establishing the conditions under which such orders may be given, and stipulating penalties for officials who, without legal justification, refuse to provide information on any detention.

2. Each State shall likewise ensure strict supervision, including a clear chain of command, of all law enforcement officials responsible for apprehensions, arrests, detentions, custody, transfers and imprisonment, and of other officials authorised by law to use force and firearms.

Article 13

1. Each State shall ensure that any person having knowledge or a legitimate interest who alleges that a person has been subjected to enforced disappearance has the right to complain to a competent and independent State authority and to have that complaint promptly, thoroughly and impartially investigated by that authority. Whenever there are reasonable grounds to believe that an enforced disappearance has been committed, the State shall promptly refer the matter to that authority for such an investigation, even if there has been no formal complaint. No measure shall be taken to curtail or impede the investigation.

2. Each State shall ensure that the competent authority shall have the necessary powers and resources to conduct the investigation effectively, including powers to compel attendance of witnesses and production of relevant documents and to make immediate on-site visits.

3. Steps shall be taken to ensure that all involved in the investigation, including the complainant, counsel, witnesses and those conducting the investigation, are protected against ill-treatment, intimidation or reprisal.

4. The findings of such an investigation shall be made available upon request to all persons concerned, unless doing so would jeopardize an ongoing criminal investigation.

5. Steps shall be taken to ensure that any ill-treatment, intimidation or reprisal or any other form of interference on the occasion of the lodging of a complaint or during the investigation procedure is appropriately punished.

6. An investigation, in accordance with the procedures described above, should be able to be conducted for as long as the fate of the victim of enforced disappearance remains unclarified.

Article 14

10–031 Any person alleged to have perpetrated an act of enforced disappearance in a particular State shall, when the facts disclosed by an official investigation so warrant, be brought before the competent civil authorities of that State for the purpose of prosecution and trial unless he has been extradited to another State wishing to exercise jurisdiction in accordance with the relevant international agreements in force. All States should take any lawful and appropriate action available to them to bring to justice all persons presumed responsible for an act of enforced disappearance, who are found to be within their jurisdiction or under their control.

Article 15

The fact that there are grounds to believe that a person has participated in acts of an extremely serious nature such as those referred to in Article 4, paragraph 1, above, regardless of the motives, shall be taken into account when the competent authorities of the State decide whether or not to grant asylum.

Article 16

1. Persons alleged to have committed any of the acts referred to in Article 4, paragraph 1, above, shall be suspended from any

official duties during the investigation referred to in Article 13 above.

2. They shall be tried only by the competent ordinary courts in each State, and not by any other special tribunal, in particular military courts.

3. No privileges, immunities or special exemptions shall be admitted in such trials, without prejudice to the provisions contained in the Vienna Convention on Diplomatic Relations.

4. The persons presumed responsible for such acts shall be guaranteed fair treatment in accordance with the relevant provisions of the Universal Declaration of Human Rights and other relevant international agreements in force at all stages of the investigation and eventual prosecution and trial.

Article 17

1. Acts constituting enforced disappearance shall be considered   10–032 a continuing offence as long as the perpetrators continue to conceal the fate and the whereabouts of persons who have disappeared and these facts remain unclarified.

2. When the remedies provided for in Article 2 of the International Covenant on Civil and Political Rights are no longer effective, the statute of limitations relating to acts of enforced disappearance shall be suspended until these remedies are re-established.

3. Statutes of limitations, where they exist, relating to acts of enforced disappearance shall be substantial and commensurate with the extreme seriousness of the offence.

Article 18

1. Persons who have or are alleged to have committed offences referred to in Article 4, paragraph 1, above, shall not benefit from any special amnesty law or similar measures that might have the effect of exempting them from any criminal proceedings or sanction.

2. In the exercise of the right of pardon, the extreme seriousness of acts of enforced disappearance shall be taken into account.

Article 19

The victims of acts of enforced disappearance and their family shall obtain redress and shall have the right to adequate compensation, including the means for as complete a rehabilitation as possible. In the event of the death of the victim as a result of an act of enforced disappearance, their dependants shall also be entitled to compensation.

Article 20

10–033   **1.** States shall prevent and suppress the abduction of children of parents subjected to enforced disappearance and of children born during their mother's enforced disappearance, and shall devote their efforts to the search for and identification of such children and to the restitution of the children to their families of origin.

2. Considering the need to protect the best interests of children referred to in the preceding paragraph, there shall be an opportunity, in States which recognise a system of adoption, for a review of the adoption of such children and, in particular, for annulment of any adoption which originated in enforced disappearance. Such adoption should, however, continue to be in force if consent is given, at the time of the review, by the child's closest relatives.

3. The abduction of children of parents subjected to enforced disappearance or of children born during their mother's enforced disappearance, and the act of altering or suppressing documents attesting to their true identity, shall constitute an extremely serious offence, which shall be punished as such.

4. For these purposes, States shall, where appropriate, conclude bilateral and multilateral agreements.

Article 21

The provisions of the present Declaration are without prejudice to the provisions enunciated in the Universal Declaration of Human Rights or in any other international instrument, and shall not be construed as restricting or derogating from any of those provisions.

PRISONERS OF WAR

GENEVA CONVENTION RELATIVE TO THE TREATMENT OF PRISONERS OF WAR, OF AUGUST 12, 1949 (GENEVA CONVENTION III) AUGUST 12, 1949[19]

PART I. GENERAL PROVISIONS

Article 1

The High Contracting Parties undertake to respect and to ensure respect for the present Convention in all circumstances.

---

[19] Entered into force: October 21, 1950. Currently there are 187 Contracting Parties. See Introduction to Chapter on The Protection of Civilians During Hostilities.

Article 2

In addition to the provisions which shall be implemented in peace **10–034** time, the present Convention shall apply to all cases of declared war or of any other armed conflict which may arise between two or more of the High Contracting Parties, even if the state of war is not recognised by one of them.

The Convention shall also apply to all cases of partial or total occupation of the territory of a High Contracting Party, even if the said occupation meets with no armed resistance. Although one of the Powers in conflict may not be a party to the present Convention, the Powers who are parties thereto shall remain bound by it in their mutual relations. They shall furthermore be bound by the Convention in relation to the said Power, if the latter accepts and applies the provisions thereof.

Article 3

In the case of armed conflict not of an international character occurring in the territory of one of the High Contracting Parties, each Party to the conflict shall be bound to apply, as a minimum, the following provisions:

(1) Persons taking no active part in the hostilities, including members of armed forces who have laid down their arms and those placed hors de combat by sickness, wounds, detention, or any other cause, shall in all circumstances be treated humanely, without any adverse distinction founded on race, colour, religion or faith, sex, birth or wealth, or any other similar criteria. To this end the following acts are and shall remain prohibited at any time and in any place whatsoever with respect to the above-mentioned persons:

  (a) violence to life and person, in particular murder of all kinds, mutilation, cruel treatment and torture;
  (b) taking of hostages;
  (c) outrages upon personal dignity, in particular, humiliating and degrading treatment;
  (d) the passing of sentences and the carrying out of executions without previous judgment pronounced by a regularly constituted court affording all the judicial guarantees which are recognised as indispensable by civilised peoples.

(2) The wounded and sick shall be collected and cared for.

An impartial humanitarian body, such as the International Committee of the Red Cross, may offer its services to the Parties to the conflict.

The Parties to the conflict should further endeavour to bring into force, by means of special agreements, all or part of the other provisions of the present Convention.

The application of the preceding provisions shall not affect the legal status of the Parties to the conflict.

Article 4

10–035 A. Prisoners of war in the sense of the present Convention, are persons belonging to one of the following categories, who have fallen into the power of the enemy:

(1) Members of the armed forces of a Party to the conflict, as well as members of militias or volunteer corps forming part of such armed forces.

(2) Members of other militias and members of other volunteer corps, including those of organised resistance movements, belonging to a Party to the conflict and operating in or outside their own territory, even if this territory is occupied, provided that such militias or volunteer corps, including such organised resistance movements, fulfil the following conditions:

(a) that of being commanded by a person responsible for his subordinates;

(b) that of having a fixed distinctive sign recognisable at a distance;

(c) that of carrying arms openly;

(d) that of conducting their operations in accordance with the laws and customs of war.

(3) Members of regular armed forces who profess allegiance to a government or an authority not recognised by the Detaining Power.

(4) Persons who accompany the armed forces without actually being members thereof, such as civilian members of military aircraft crews, war correspondents, supply contractors, members of labour units or of services responsible for the welfare of the armed forces, provided that they have received authorisation, from the armed forces which they accompany, who shall provide them for that purpose with an identity card similar to the annexed model.

(5) Members of crews, including masters, pilots and apprentices, of the merchant marine and the crews of civil aircraft of the Parties to the conflict, who do not benefit by more favourable treatment under any other provisions of international law.

(6) Inhabitants of a non-occupied territory, who on the approach of the enemy spontaneously take up arms to resist the invading forces, without having had time to form themselves into regular armed units, provided they carry arms openly and respect the laws and customs of war.

B. The following shall likewise be treated as prisoners of war under the present Convention:

(1) Persons belonging, or having belonged, to the armed forces of the occupied country, if the occupying Power considers it necessary by reason of such allegiance to intern them, even though it has originally liberated them while hostilities were going on outside the territory it occupies, in particular where such persons have made an unsuccessful attempt to rejoin the armed forces to which they belong and which are engaged in combat, or where they fail to comply with a summons made to them with a view to internment.

(2) The persons belonging to one of the categories enumerated in the present Article, who have been received by neutral or non-belligerent Powers on their territory and whom these Powers are required to intern under international law, without prejudice to any more favourable treatment which these Powers may choose to give and with the exception of Articles 8, 10, 15, 30, fifth paragraph, 58–67, 92, 126 and, where diplomatic relations exist between the Parties to the conflict and the neutral or non-belligerent Power concerned, those Articles concerning the Protecting Power. Where such diplomatic relations exist, the Parties to a conflict on whom these persons depend shall be allowed to perform towards them the functions of a Protecting Power as provided in the present Convention, without prejudice to the functions which these Parties normally exercise in conformity with diplomatic and consular usage and treaties.

C. This Article shall in no way affect the status of medical personnel and chaplains as provided for in Article 33 of the present Convention.

Article 5

The present Convention shall apply to the persons referred to in **10–036** Article 4 from the time they fall into the power of the enemy and until their final release and repatriation.

Should any doubt arise as to whether persons, having committed a belligerent act and having fallen into the hands of the enemy, belong to any of the categories enumerated in Article 4, such persons shall enjoy the protection of the present Convention until such time as their status has been determined by a competent tribunal.

Article 6

In addition to the agreements expressly provided for in Articles 10, 23, 28, 33, 60, 65, 66, 67, 72, 73, 75, 109, 110, 118, 119, 122 and 132, the High Contracting Parties may conclude other special agreements for all matters concerning which they may deem it suitable to make separate provision. No special agreement shall adversely affect the situation of prisoners of war, as defined by the present Convention, nor restrict the rights which it confers upon them. Prisoners of war shall continue to have the benefit of such agreements as long as the Convention is applicable to them, except where express provisions to the contrary are contained in the aforesaid or in subsequent agreements, or where more favourable measures have been taken with regard to them by one or other of the Parties to the conflict.

Article 7

Prisoners of war may in no circumstances renounce in part or in entirety the rights secured to them by the present Convention, and by the special agreements referred to in the foregoing Article, if such there be.

Article 8

The present Convention shall be applied with the co-operation and under the scrutiny of the Protecting Powers whose duty it is to safeguard the interests of the Parties to the conflict. For this purpose, the Protecting Powers may appoint, apart from their diplomatic or consular staff, delegates from amongst their own nationals or the nationals of other neutral Powers. The said delegates shall be subject to the approval of the Power with which they are to carry out their duties.

The Parties to the conflict shall facilitate to the greatest extent possible the task of the representatives or delegates of the Protecting Powers.

The representatives or delegates of the Protecting Powers shall not in any case exceed their mission under the present Convention. They shall, in particular, take account of the imperative necessities of security of the State wherein they carry out their duties.

Article 9

The provisions of the present Convention constitute no obstacle **10–037** to the humanitarian activities which the International Committee of the Red Cross[20] or any other impartial humanitarian organisation may, subject to the consent of the Parties to the conflict concerned, undertake for the protection of prisoners of war and for their relief.

Article 10

The High Contracting Parties may at any time agree to entrust to an organisation which offers all guarantees of impartiality and efficacy the duties incumbent on the Protecting Powers by virtue of the present Convention.

When prisoners of war do not benefit or cease to benefit, no matter for what reason, by the activities of a Protecting Power or of an organisation provided for in the first paragraph above, the Detaining Power shall request a neutral State, or such an organisation, to undertake the functions performed under the present Convention by a Protecting Power designated by the Parties to a conflict.

If protection cannot be arranged accordingly, the Detaining Power shall request or shall accept, subject to the provisions of this Article, the offer of the services of a humanitarian organisation, such as the International Committee of the Red Cross to assume the humanitarian functions performed by Protecting Powers under the present Convention.

Any neutral Power or any organisation invited by the Power concerned or offering itself for these purposes, shall be required to act with a sense of responsibility towards the Party to the conflict on which persons protected by the present Convention depend, and shall be required to furnish sufficient assurances that it is in a position to undertake the appropriate functions and to discharge them impartially.

No derogation from the preceding provisions shall be made by special agreements between Powers one of which is restricted, even temporarily, in its freedom to negotiate with the other Power or its allies by reason of military events, more particularly where the whole, or a substantial part, of the territory of the said Power is occupied.

Whenever in the present Convention mention is made of a Protecting Power, such mention applies to substitute organisations in the sense of the present Article.

---

[20] For information re the International Committee of the Red Cross see chapter on the Protection of Civilians During Hostilities.

Article 11

10–038 In cases where they deem it advisable in the interest of protected persons, particularly in cases of disagreement between the Parties to the conflict as to the application or interpretation of the provisions of the present Convention, the Protecting Powers shall lend their good offices with a view to settling the disagreement.

For this purpose, each of the Protecting Powers may, either at the invitation of one Party or on its own initiative, propose to the Parties to the conflict a meeting of their representatives, and in particular of the authorities responsible for prisoners of war, possibly on neutral territory suitably chosen. The Parties to the conflict shall be bound to give effect to the proposals made to them for this purpose. The Protecting Powers may, if necessary, propose for approval by the Parties to the conflict a person belonging to a neutral Power, or delegated by the International Committee of the Red Cross, who shall be invited to take part in such a meeting.

PART II. GENERAL PROTECTION OF PRISONERS OF WAR

Article 12

Prisoners of war are in the hands of the enemy Power, but not of the individuals or military units who have captured them. Irrespective of the individual responsibilities that may exist, the Detaining Power is responsible for the treatment given them.

Prisoners of war may only be transferred by the Detaining Power to a Power which is a party to the Convention and after the Detaining Power has satisfied itself of the willingness and ability of such transferee Power to apply the Convention. When prisoners of war are transferred under such circumstances, responsibility for the application of the Convention rests on the Power accepting them while they are in its custody.

Nevertheless, if that Power fails to carry out the provisions of the Convention in any important respect, the Power by whom the prisoners of war were transferred shall, upon being notified by the Protecting Power, take effective measures to correct the situation or shall request the return of the prisoners of war. Such requests must be complied with.

Article 13

10–039 Prisoners of war must at all times be humanely treated. Any unlawful act or omission by the Detaining Power causing death or seriously endangering the health of a prisoner of war in its custody is prohibited, and will be regarded as a serious breach of the present Convention. In particular, no prisoner of war may be subjected to physical mutilation or to medical or scientific experiments of any kind which are not justified by the medical, dental or hospital treatment of the prisoner concerned and carried out in his interest.

Likewise, prisoners of war must at all times be protected, particularly against acts of violence or intimidation and against insults and public curiosity.

Measures of reprisal against prisoners of war are prohibited.

Article 14

Prisoners of war are entitled in all circumstances to respect for their persons and their honour.

Women shall be treated with all the regard due to their sex and shall in all cases benefit by treatment as favourable as that granted to men.

Prisoners of war shall retain the full civil capacity which they enjoyed at the time of their capture. The Detaining Power may not restrict the exercise, either within or without its own territory, of the rights such capacity confers except in so far as the captivity requires.

Article 15

The Power detaining prisoners of war shall be bound to provide free of charge for their maintenance and for the medical attention required by their state of health.

Article 16

Taking into consideration the provisions of the present Convention relating to rank and sex, and subject to any privileged treatment which may be accorded to them by reason of their state of health, age or professional qualifications, all prisoners of war shall be treated alike by the Detaining Power, without any adverse distinction based on race, nationality, religious belief or political opinions, or any other distinction founded on similar criteria.

PART III. CAPTIVITY

Section 1. Beginning of Captivity

Article 17

Every prisoner of war, when questioned on the subject, is bound 10–040 to give only his surname, first names and rank, date of birth, and army, regimental, personal or serial number, or failing this, equivalent information.

If he wilfully infringes this rule, he may render himself liable to a restriction of the privileges accorded to his rank or status.

Each Party to a conflict is required to furnish the persons under its jurisdiction who are liable to become prisoners of war, with an identity card showing the owner's surname, first names, rank, army, regimental, personal or serial number or equivalent information, and date of birth. The identity card may, furthermore, bear the signature or the fingerprints, or both, of the owner, and may bear, as well, any other information the Party to the conflict may wish to add concerning persons belonging to its armed forces. As far as possible the card shall measure 6.5 x 10 cm and shall be issued in duplicate. The identity card shall be shown by the prisoner of war upon demand, but may in no case be taken away from him.

No physical or mental torture, nor any other form of coercion, may be inflicted on prisoners of war to secure from them information of any kind whatever. Prisoners of war who refuse to answer may not be threatened, insulted, or exposed to unpleasant or disadvantageous treatment of any kind. Prisoners of war who, owing to their physical or mental condition, are unable to state their identity, shall be handed over to the medical service. The identity of such prisoners shall be established by all possible means, subject to the provisions of the preceding paragraph.

The questioning of prisoners of war shall be carried out in a language which they understand.

Article 18

All effects and articles of personal use, except arms, horses, military equipment and military documents, shall remain in the possession of prisoners of war, likewise their metal helmets and gas masks and like articles issued for personal protection. Effects and articles used for their clothing or feeding shall likewise remain in their possession, even if such effects and articles belong to their regulation military equipment.

At no time should prisoners of war be without identity documents. The Detaining Power shall supply such documents to prisoners of war who possess none.

Badges of rank and nationality, decorations and articles having above all a personal or sentimental value may not be taken from prisoners of war.

Sums of money carried by prisoners of war may not be taken away from them except by order of an officer, and after the amount and particulars of the owner have been recorded in a special register and an itemised receipt has been given, legibly inscribed with the name, rank and unit of the person issuing the said receipt. Sums in the currency of the Detaining Power, or which are changed into such currency at the prisoner's request, shall be placed to the credit of the prisoner's account as provided in Article 64.

The Detaining Power may withdraw articles of value from prisoners of war only for reasons of security; when such articles are withdrawn, the procedure laid down for sums of money impounded shall apply.

Such objects, likewise sums taken away in any currency other than that of the Detaining Power and the conversion of which has not been asked for by the owners, shall be kept in the custody of the Detaining Power and shall be returned in their initial shape to prisoners of war at the end of their captivity.

Article 19

Prisoners of war shall be evacuated, as soon as possible after their 10–041
capture, to camps situated in an area far enough from the combat zone for them to be out of danger.

Only those prisoners of war who, owing to wounds or sickness, would run greater risks by being evacuated than by remaining where they are, may be temporarily kept back in a danger zone.

Prisoners of war shall not be unnecessarily exposed to danger while awaiting evacuation from a fighting zone.

Article 20

The evacuation of prisoners of war shall always be effected humanely and in conditions similar to those for the forces of the Detaining Power in their changes of station.

The Detaining Power shall supply prisoners of war who are being evacuated with sufficient food and potable water, and with the necessary clothing and medical attention. The Detaining Power shall take all suitable precautions to ensure their safety during evacuation, and shall establish as soon as possible a list of the prisoners of war who are evacuated.

If prisoners of war must, during evacuation, pass through transit camps, their stay in such camps shall be as brief as possible.

Section II. Internment of Prisoners of War

Chapter I. General Observations

Article 21

The Detaining Power may subject prisoners of war to internment. 10–042
It may impose on them the obligation of not leaving, beyond certain limits, the camp where they are interned, or if the said

camp is fenced in, of not going outside its perimeter. Subject to the provisions of the present Convention relative to penal and disciplinary sanctions, prisoners of war may not be held in close confinement except where necessary to safeguard their health and then only during the continuation of the circumstances which make such confinement necessary.

Prisoners of war may be partially or wholly released on parole or promise, in so far as is allowed by the laws of the Power on which they depend. Such measures shall be taken particularly in cases where this may contribute to the improvement of their state of health. No prisoner of war shall be compelled to accept liberty on parole or promise.

Upon the outbreak of hostilities, each Party to the conflict shall notify the adverse Party of the laws and regulations allowing or forbidding its own nationals to accept liberty on parole or promise. Prisoners of war who are paroled or who have given their promise in conformity with the laws and regulations so notified, are bound on their personal honour scrupulously to fulfil, both towards the Power on which they depend and towards the Power which has captured them, the engagements of their paroles or promises. In such cases, the Power on which they depend is bound neither to require nor to accept from them any service incompatible with the parole or promise given.

Article 22

Prisoners of war may be interned only in premises located on land and affording every guarantee of hygiene and healthfulness. Except in particular cases which are justified by the interest of the prisoners themselves, they shall not be interned in penitentiaries.

Prisoners of war interned in unhealthy areas, or where the climate is injurious for them, shall be removed as soon as possible to a more favourable climate.

The Detaining Power shall assemble prisoners of war in camps or camp compounds according to their nationality, language and customs, provided that such prisoners shall not be separated from prisoners of war belonging to the armed forces with which they were serving at the time of their capture, except with their consent.

Article 23

10–043 No prisoner of war may at any time be sent to, or detained in areas where he may be exposed to the fire of the combat zone, nor may his presence be used to render certain points or areas immune from military operations.

Prisoners of war shall have shelters against air bombardment and other hazards of war, to the same extent as the local civilian population. With the exception of those engaged in the protection of their quarters against the aforesaid hazards, they may enter such shelters as soon as possible after the giving of the alarm. Any other protective measure taken in favour of the population shall also apply to them.

Detaining Powers shall give the Powers concerned, through the intermediary of the Protecting Powers, all useful information regarding the geographical location of prisoner of war camps. Whenever military considerations permit, prisoner of war camps shall be indicated in the day-time by the letters PW or PG, placed so as to be clearly visible from the air. The Powers concerned may, however, agree upon any other system of marking. Only prisoner of war camps shall be marked as such.

Article 24

Transit or screening camps of a permanent kind shall be fitted out under conditions similar to those described in the present Section, and the prisoners therein shall have the same treatment as in other camps.

Chapter II. Quarters, Food and Clothing of Prisoners of War

Article 25

Prisoners of war shall be quartered under conditions as favourable as those for the forces of the Detaining Power who are billeted in the same area. The said conditions shall make allowance for the habits and customs of the prisoners and shall in no case be prejudicial to their health.

The foregoing provisions shall apply in particular to the dormitories of prisoners of war as regards both total surface and minimum cubic space, and the general installations, bedding and blankets.

The premises provided for the use of prisoners of war individually or collectively, shall be entirely protected from dampness and adequately heated and lighted, in particular between dusk and lights out. All precautions must be taken against the danger of fire.

In any camps in which women prisoners of war, as well as men, are accommodated, separate dormitories shall be provided for them.

Article 26

The basic daily food rations shall be sufficient in quantity, quality 10–044 and variety to keep prisoners of war in good health and to prevent loss of weight or the development of nutritional deficiencies. Account shall also be taken of the habitual diet of the prisoners.

The Detaining Power shall supply prisoners of war who work with such additional rations as are necessary for the labour on which they are employed.

Sufficient drinking water shall be supplied to prisoners of war. The use of tobacco shall be permitted.

Prisoners of war shall, as far as possible, be associated with the preparation of their meals; they may be employed for that purpose in the kitchens. Furthermore, they shall be given the means of preparing, themselves, the additional food in their possession.

Adequate premises shall be provided for messing.

Collective disciplinary measures affecting food are prohibited.

Article 27

Clothing, underwear and footwear shall be supplied to prisoners of war in sufficient quantities by the Detaining Power, which shall make allowance for the climate of the region where the prisoners are detained. Uniforms of enemy armed forces captured by the Detaining Power should, if suitable for the climate, be made available to clothe prisoners of war.

The regular replacement and repair of the above articles shall be assured by the Detaining Power. In addition, prisoners of war who work shall receive appropriate clothing, wherever the nature of the work demands.

Article 28

Canteens shall be installed in all camps, where prisoners of war may procure foodstuffs, soap and tobacco and ordinary articles in daily use. The tariff shall never be in excess of local market prices.

The profits made by camp canteens shall be used for the benefit of the prisoners; a special fund shall be created for this purpose. The prisoners' representative shall have the right to collaborate in the management of the canteen and of this fund.

When a camp is closed down, the credit balance of the special fund shall be handed to an international welfare organisation, to be employed for the benefit of prisoners of war of the same nationality as those who have contributed to the fund. In case of a general repatriation, such profits shall be kept by the Detaining Power, subject to any agreement to the contrary between the Powers concerned.

CHAPTER III. HYGIENE AND MEDICAL ATTENTION

Article 29

10–045 The Detaining Power shall be bound to take all sanitary measures necessary to ensure the cleanliness and healthfulness of camps and to prevent epidemics.

Prisoners of war shall have for their use, day and night, conveniences which conform to the rules of hygiene and are maintained in a constant state of cleanliness. In any camps in which women prisoners of war are accommodated, separate conveniences shall be provided for them.

Also, apart from the baths and showers with which the camps shall be furnished prisoners of war shall be provided with sufficient water and soap for their personal toilet and for washing their personal laundry; the necessary installations, facilities and time shall be granted them for that purpose.

Article 30

Every camp shall have an adequate infirmary where prisoners of war may have the attention they require, as well as appropriate diet. Isolation wards shall, if necessary, be set aside for cases of contagious or mental disease.

Prisoners of war suffering from serious disease, or whose condition necessitates special treatment, a surgical operation or hospital care, must be admitted to any military or civilian medical unit where such treatment can be given, even if their repatriation is contemplated in the near future. Special facilities shall be afforded for the care to be given to the disabled, in particular to the blind, and for their rehabilitation, pending repatriation.

Prisoners of war shall have the attention, preferably, of medical personnel of the Power on which they depend and, if possible, of their nationality.

Prisoners of war may not be prevented from presenting themselves to the medical authorities for examination. The detaining authorities shall, upon request, issue to every prisoner who has undergone treatment, an official certificate indicating the nature of his illness or injury, and the duration and kind of treatment received. A duplicate of this certificate shall be forwarded to the Central Prisoners of War Agency.

The costs of treatment, including those of any apparatus necessary for the maintenance of prisoners of war in good health, particularly dentures and other artificial appliances, and spectacles, shall be borne by the Detaining Power.

Article 31

Medical inspections of prisoners of war shall be held at least once **10–046** a month. They shall include the checking and the recording of the weight of each prisoner of war.

Their purpose shall be, in particular, to supervise the general state of health, nutrition and cleanliness of prisoners and to detect contagious diseases, especially tuberculosis, malaria and venereal disease. For this purpose the most efficient methods available shall be employed, *e.g.* periodic mass miniature radiography for the early detection of tuberculosis.

Article 32

Prisoners of war who, though not attached to the medical service of their armed forces, are physicians, surgeons, dentists, nurses or medical orderlies, may be required by the Detaining Power to exercise their medical functions in the interests of prisoners of war dependent on the same Power. In that case they shall continue to be prisoners of war, but shall receive the same treatment as corresponding medical personnel retained by the Detaining Power. They shall be exempted from any other work under Article 49.

CHAPTER IV. MEDICAL PERSONNEL AND CHAPLAINS RETAINED
TO ASSIST PRISONERS OF WAR

Article 33

Members of the medical personnel and chaplains while retained by the Detaining Power with a view to assisting prisoners of war, shall not be considered as prisoners of war. They shall, however, receive as a minimum the benefits and protection of the present Convention, and shall also be granted all facilities necessary to provide for the medical care of, and religious ministration to prisoners of war.

They shall continue to exercise their medical and spiritual functions for the benefit of prisoners of war, preferably those belonging to the armed forces upon which they depend, within the scope of the military laws and regulations of the Detaining Power and under the control of its competent services, in accordance with their professional etiquette. They shall also benefit by the following facilities in the exercise of their medical or spiritual functions:

(a) They shall be authorised to visit periodically prisoners of war situated in working detachments or in hospitals outside the camp. For this purpose, the Detaining Power shall place at their disposal the necessary means of transport.

(b) The senior medical officer in each camp shall be responsible to the camp military authorities for everything connected with the activities of retained medical personnel. For this purpose, Parties to the conflict shall agree at the outbreak of hostilities on the subject of the corresponding ranks of the medical personnel, including that of societies mentioned in

Article 26 of the Geneva Convention for the Amelioration of the Condition of the Wounded and Sick in Armed Forces in the Field of August 12, 1949.[21] This senior medical officer, as well as chaplains, shall have the right to deal with the competent authorities of the camp on all questions relating to their duties. Such authorities shall afford them all necessary facilities for correspondence relating to these questions.

(c) Although they shall be subject to the internal discipline of the camp in which they are retained, such personnel may not be compelled to carry out any work other than that concerned with their medical or religious duties.

During hostilities, the Parties to the conflict shall agree concerning the possible relief of retained personnel and shall settle the procedure to be followed.

None of the preceding provisions shall relieve the Detaining Power of its obligations with regard to prisoners of war from the medical or spiritual point of view.

CHAPTER V. RELIGIOUS, INTELLECTUAL AND PHYSICAL ACTIVITIES

Article 34

Prisoners of war shall enjoy complete latitude in the exercise of their religious duties, including attendance at the service of their faith, on condition that they comply with the disciplinary routine prescribed by the military authorities.

Adequate premises shall be provided where religious services may be held.

Article 35

Chaplains who fall into the hands of the enemy Power and who 10–047 remain or are retained with a view to assisting prisoners of war, shall be allowed to minister to them and to exercise freely their ministry amongst prisoners of war of the same religion, in accordance with their religious conscience. They shall be allocated among the various camps and labour detachments containing prisoners of war belonging to the same forces, speaking the same language or practising the same religion. They shall enjoy the necessary facilities, including the means of transport provided for in Article 33, for visiting the prisoners of war outside their camp. They shall be free to correspond, subject to censorship, on matters

---

[21] Geneva Convention (I) U.N.T.S. No. 970.

concerning their religious duties with the ecclesiastical authorities in the country of detention and with international religious organisations. Letters and cards which they may send for this purpose shall be in addition to the quota provided for in Article 71.

Article 36

Prisoners of war who are ministers of religion, without having officiated as chaplains to their own forces, shall be at liberty, whatever their denomination, to minister freely to the members of their community. For this purpose, they shall receive the same treatment as the chaplains retained by the Detaining Power. They shall not be obliged to do any other work.

Article 37

When prisoners of war have not the assistance of a retained chaplain or of a prisoner of war minister of their faith, a minister belonging to the prisoners' or a similar denomination, or in his absence a qualified layman, if such a course is feasible from a confessional point of view, shall be appointed, at the request of the prisoners concerned, to fill this office. This appointment, subject to the approval of the Detaining Power, shall take place with the agreement of the community of prisoners concerned and, wherever necessary, with the approval of the local religious authorities of the same faith. The person thus appointed shall comply with all regulations established by the Detaining Power in the interests of discipline and military security.

Article 38

While respecting the individual preferences of every prisoner, the Detaining Power shall encourage the practice of intellectual, educational, and recreational pursuits, sports and games amongst prisoners, and shall take the measures necessary to ensure the exercise thereof by providing them with adequate premises and necessary equipment.

Prisoners shall have opportunities for taking physical exercise, including sports and games, and for being out of doors. Sufficient open spaces shall be provided for this purpose in all camps.

CHAPTER VI. DISCIPLINE

Article 39

10–048 Every prisoner of war camp shall be put under the immediate authority of a responsible commissioned officer belonging to the regular armed forces of the Detaining Power. Such officer shall have in his possession a copy of the present Convention; he shall ensure that its provisions are known to the camp staff and the guard and shall be responsible, under the direction of his government, for its application.

Prisoners of war, with the exception of officers, must salute and show to all officers of the Detaining Power the external marks of respect provided for by the regulations applying in their own forces.

Officer prisoners of war are bound to salute only officers of a higher rank of the Detaining Power; they must, however, salute the camp commander regardless of his rank.

Article 40

The wearing of badges of rank and nationality, as well as of decorations, shall be permitted.

Article 41

In every camp the text of the present Convention and its Annexes and the contents of any special agreement provided for in Article 6, shall be posted, in the prisoners' own language, in places where all may read them. Copies shall be supplied, on request, to the prisoners who cannot have access to the copy which has been posted.

Regulations, orders, notices and publications of every kind relating to the conduct of prisoners of war shall be issued to them in a language which they understand. Such regulations, orders and publications shall be posted in the manner described above and copies shall be handed to the prisoners' representative. Every order and command addressed to prisoners of war individually must likewise be given in a language which they understand.

Article 42

The use of weapons against prisoners of war, especially against those who are escaping or attempting to escape, shall constitute an extreme measure, which shall always be preceded by warnings appropriate to the circumstances.

CHAPTER VII. RANK OF PRISONERS OF WAR

Article 43

Upon the outbreak of hostilities, the Parties to the conflict shall **10–049** communicate to one another the titles and ranks of all the persons mentioned in Article 4 of the present Convention, in order to ensure equality of treatment between prisoners of equivalent rank. Titles and ranks which are subsequently created shall form the subject of similar communications.

The Detaining Power shall recognise promotions in rank which have been accorded to prisoners of war and which have been duly notified by the Power on which these prisoners depend.

Article 44

Officers and prisoners of equivalent status shall be treated with the regard due to their rank and age.

In order to ensure service in officers' camps, other ranks of the same armed forces who, as far as possible, speak the same language, shall be assigned in sufficient numbers, account being taken of the rank of officers and prisoners of equivalent status. Such orderlies shall not be required to perform any other work.

Supervision of the mess by the officers themselves shall be facilitated in every way.

Article 45

Prisoners of war other than officers and prisoners of equivalent status shall be treated with the regard due to their rank and age.

Supervision of the mess by the prisoners themselves shall be facilitated in every way.

CHAPTER VIII. TRANSFER OF PRISONERS OF WAR AFTER THEIR ARRIVAL IN CAMP

Article 46

10–050 The Detaining Power, when deciding upon the transfer of prisoners of war, shall take into account the interests of the prisoners themselves, more especially so as not to increase the difficulty of their repatriation.

The transfer of prisoners of war shall always be effected humanely and in conditions not less favourable than those under which the forces of the Detaining Power are transferred. Account shall always be taken of the climatic conditions to which the prisoners of war are accustomed and the conditions of transfer shall in no case be prejudicial to their health.

The Detaining Power shall supply prisoners of war during transfer with sufficient food and drinking water to keep them in good health, likewise with the necessary clothing, shelter and medical attention. The Detaining Power shall take adequate precautions especially in case of transport by sea or by air, to ensure their safety during transfer, and shall draw up a complete list of all transferred prisoners before their departure.

Article 47

Sick or wounded prisoners of war shall not be transferred as long as their recovery may be endangered by the journey, unless their safety imperatively demands it.

If the combat zone draws closer to a camp, the prisoners of war in the said camp shall not be transferred unless their transfer can be carried out in adequate conditions of safety, or unless they are exposed to greater risks by remaining on the spot than by being transferred.

Article 48

In the event of transfer, prisoners of war shall be officially advised of their departure and of their new postal address. Such notifications shall be given in time for them to pack their luggage and inform their next of kin.

They shall be allowed to take with them their personal effects, and the correspondence and parcels which have arrived for them. The weight of such baggage may be limited, if the conditions of transfer so require, to what each prisoner can reasonably carry, which shall in no case be more than 25kg per head.

Mail and parcels addressed to their former camp shall be forwarded to them without delay. The camp commander shall take, in agreement with the prisoners' representative, any measures needed to ensure the transport of the prisoners' community property and of the luggage they are unable to take with them in consequence of restrictions imposed by virtue of the second paragraph of this Article.

The costs of transfers shall be borne by the Detaining Power.

Section III. Labour of Prisoners of War

Article 49

The Detaining Power may utilise the labour of prisoners of war 10–051 who are physically fit, taking into account their age, sex, rank and physical aptitude, and with a view particularly to maintaining them in a good state of physical and mental health.

Non-commissioned officers who are prisoners of war shall only be required to do supervisory work. Those not so required may ask for other suitable work which shall, so far as possible, be found for them.

If officers or persons of equivalent status ask for suitable work, it shall be found for them, so far as possible, but they may in no circumstances be compelled to work.

Article 50

Besides work connected with camp administration, installation or maintenance, prisoners of war may be compelled to do only such work as is included in the following classes:

(a) agriculture;

(b) industries connected with the production or the extraction of raw materials, and manufacturing industries, with the exception of metallurgical, machinery and chemical industries; public works and building operations which have no military character or purpose;

(c) transport and handling of stores which are not military in character or purpose;

(d) commercial business, and arts and crafts;

(e) domestic service;

(f) public utility services having no military character or purpose.

Should the above provisions be infringed, prisoners of war shall be allowed to exercise their right of complaint, in conformity with Article 78.

Article 51

10–052 Prisoners of war must be granted suitable working conditions, especially as regards accommodation, food, clothing and equipment; such conditions shall not be inferior to those enjoyed by nationals of the Detaining Power employed in similar work; account shall also be taken of climatic conditions.

The Detaining Power, in utilising the labour of prisoners of war, shall ensure that in areas in which such prisoners are employed, the national legislation concerning the protection of labour, and, more particularly, the regulations for the safety of workers, are duly applied.

Prisoners of war shall receive training and be provided with the means of protection suitable to the work they will have to do and similar to those accorded to the nationals of the Detaining Power. Subject to the provisions of Article 52, prisoners may be submitted to the normal risks run by these civilian workers.

Conditions of labour shall in no case be rendered more arduous by disciplinary measures.

Article 52

Unless he be a volunteer, no prisoner of war may be employed on labour which is of an unhealthy or dangerous nature.

No prisoner of war shall be assigned to labour which would be looked upon as humiliating for a member of the Detaining Power's own forces.

The removal of mines or similar devices shall be considered as dangerous labour.

Article 53

The duration of the daily labour of prisoners of war, including the time of the journey to and fro, shall not be excessive, and must in no case exceed that permitted for civilian workers in the district, who are nationals of the Detaining Power and employed on the same work.

Prisoners of war must be allowed, in the middle of the day's work, a rest of not less than one hour. This rest will be the same as that to which workers of the Detaining Power are entitled, if the latter is of longer duration. They shall be allowed in addition a rest of 24 consecutive hours every week, preferably on Sunday or the day of rest in their country of origin. Furthermore, every prisoner who has worked for one year shall be granted a rest of eight consecutive days, during which his working pay shall be paid him.

If methods of labour such as piece work are employed, the length of the working period shall not be rendered excessive thereby.

Article 54

The working pay due to prisoners of war shall be fixed in **10–053** accordance with the provisions of Article 62 of the present Convention.

Prisoners of war who sustain accidents in connection with work, or who contract a disease in the course, or in consequence of their work, shall receive all the care their condition may require. The Detaining Power shall furthermore deliver to such prisoners of war a medical certificate enabling them to submit their claims to the Power on which they depend, and shall send a duplicate to the Central Prisoners of War Agency provided for in Article 123.

Article 55

The fitness of prisoners of war for work shall be periodically verified by medical examinations at least once a month. The examinations shall have particular regard to the nature of the work which prisoners of war are required to do.

If any prisoner of war considers himself incapable of working, he shall be permitted to appear before the medical authorities of his camp. Physicians or surgeons may recommend that the prisoners who are, in their opinion, unfit for work, be exempted therefrom.

Article 56

The organisation and administration of labour detachments shall be similar to those of prisoner of war camps.

Every labour detachment shall remain under the control of and administratively part of a prisoner of war camp. The military authorities and the commander of the said camp shall be responsible, under the direction of their government, for the observance of the provisions of the present Convention in labour detachments.

The camp commander shall keep an up-to-date record of the labour detachments dependent on his camp, and shall communicate it to the delegates of the Protecting Power, of the International Committee of the Red Cross, or of other agencies giving relief to prisoners of war, who may visit the camp.

Article 57

The treatment of prisoners of war who work for private persons, even if the latter are responsible for guarding and protecting them, shall not be inferior to that which is provided for by the present Convention. The Detaining Power, the military authorities and the commander of the camp to which such prisoners belong shall be entirely responsible for the maintenance, care, treatment, and payment of the working pay of such prisoners of war.

Such prisoners of war shall have the right to remain in communication with the prisoners' representatives in the camps on which they depend.

Section IV. Financial Resources of Prisoners of War

Article 58

10–054 Upon the outbreak of hostilities, and pending an arrangement on this matter with the Protecting Power, the Detaining Power may determine the maximum amount of money in cash or in any similar form, that prisoners may have in their possession. Any amount in excess, which was properly in their possession and which has been taken or withheld from them, shall be placed to their account, together with any monies deposited by them, and shall not be converted into any other currency without their consent.

If prisoners of war are permitted to purchase services or commodities outside the camp against payment in cash, such payments shall be made by the prisoner himself or by the camp administration who will charge them to the accounts of the prisoners concerned. The Detaining Power will establish the necessary rules in this respect.

Article 59

Cash which was taken from prisoners of war, in accordance with Article 18, at the time of their capture, and which is in the currency of the Detaining Power, shall be placed to their separate accounts, in accordance with the provisions of Article 64 of the present Section.

The amounts, in the currency of the Detaining Power, due to the conversion of sums in other currencies that are taken from the prisoners of war at the same time, shall also be credited to their separate accounts.

Article 60

The Detaining Power shall grant all prisoners of war a monthly advance of pay, the amount of which shall be fixed by conversion, into the currency of the said Power, . . .

Article 61

The Detaining Power shall accept for distribution as supplemen- 10–055 tary pay to prisoners of war sums which the Power on which the prisoners depend may forward to them, on condition that the sums to be paid shall be the same for each prisoner of the same category, shall be payable to all prisoners of that category depending on that Power, and shall be placed in their separate accounts, at the earliest opportunity, in accordance with the provisions of Article 64. Such supplementary pay shall not relieve the Detaining Power of any obligation under this Convention.

Article 62

Prisoners of war shall be paid a fair working rate of pay by the detaining authorities direct. The rate shall be fixed by the said authorities, . . .

Article 63

Prisoners of war shall be permitted to receive remittances of money addressed to them individually or collectively. . . .

Article 64

The Detaining Power shall hold an account for each prisoner of war, . . .

Article 65

Every item entered in the account of a prisoner of war shall be countersigned or initialled by him, or by the prisoners' representative acting on his behalf.

Prisoners of war shall at all times be afforded reasonable facilities for consulting and obtaining copies of their accounts, which may likewise be inspected by the representatives of the Protecting Powers at the time of visits to the camp.

When prisoners of war are transferred from one camp to another, their personal accounts will follow them. In case of transfer from one Detaining Power to another, the monies which are their property and are not in the currency of the Detaining Power will follow them. They shall be given certificates for any other monies standing to the credit of their accounts.

The Parties to the conflict concerned may agree to notify to each other at specific intervals through the Protecting Power, the amount of the accounts of the prisoners of war.

Article 66

10–056 On the termination of captivity, through the release of a prisoner of war or his repatriation, the Detaining Power shall give him a statement, signed by an authorised officer of that Power, showing the credit balance then due to him. The Detaining Power shall also send through the Protecting Power to the government upon which the prisoner of war depends, lists giving all appropriate particulars of all prisoners of war whose captivity has been terminated by repatriation, release, escape, death or any other means, and showing the amount of their credit balances. Such lists shall be certified on each sheet by an authorised representative of the Detaining Power.

Any of the above provisions of this Article may be varied by mutual agreement between any two Parties to the conflict.

The Power on which the prisoner of war depends shall be responsible for settling with him any credit balance due to him from the Detaining Power on the termination of his captivity.

Article 67

Advances of pay, issued to prisoners of war in conformity with Article 60, shall be considered as made on behalf of the Power on which they depend. Such advances of pay, as well as all payments made by the said Power under Article 63, . . ., and Article 68, shall form the subject of arrangements between the Powers concerned, at the close of hostilities.

Article 68

Any claim by a prisoner of war for compensation in respect of any injury or other disability arising out of work shall be referred to the Power on which he depends, through the Protecting Power.

In accordance with Article 54, the Detaining Power will, in all cases, provide the prisoner of war concerned with a statement showing the nature of the injury or disability, the circumstances in which it arose and particulars of medical or hospital treatment given for it. This statement will be signed by a responsible officer of the Detaining Power and the medical particulars certified by a medical officer.

Any claim by a prisoner of war for compensation in respect of personal effects monies or valuables impounded by the Detaining Power under Article 18 and not forthcoming on his repatriation, or in respect of loss alleged to be due to the fault of the Detaining Power or any of its servants, shall likewise be referred to the Power on which he depends. Nevertheless, any such personal effects required for use by the prisoners of war whilst in captivity shall be replaced at the expense of the Detaining Power. The Detaining Power will, in all cases, provide the prisoner of war with a statement, signed by a responsible officer, showing all available information regarding the reasons why such effects, monies or valuables have not been restored to him. A copy of this statement will be forwarded to the Power on which he depends through the Central Prisoners of War Agency provided for in Article 123.

Section V. Relations of Prisoners of War With the Exterior

Article 69

Immediately upon prisoners of war falling into its power, the 10–057 Detaining Power shall inform them and the Powers on which they depend, through the Protecting Power, of the measures taken to carry out the provisions of the present Section. They shall likewise inform the parties concerned of any subsequent modifications of such measures.

Article 70

Immediately upon capture, or not more than one week after arrival at a camp, even if it is a transit camp, likewise in case of sickness or transfer to hospital or to another camp, every prisoner of war shall be enabled to write direct to his family, on the one hand, and to the Central Prisoners of War Agency provided for in Article 123, on the other hand, a card similar, if possible, to the model annexed to the present Convention, informing his relatives of his capture, address and state of health. The said cards shall be forwarded as rapidly as possible and may not be delayed in any manner.

Article 71

Prisoners of war shall be allowed to send and receive letters and cards. If the Detaining Power deems it necessary to limit the number of letters and cards sent by each prisoner of war, the said number shall not be less than two letters and four cards monthly, exclusive of the capture cards provided for in Article 70, and conforming as closely as possible to the models annexed to the present Convention. Further limitations may be imposed only if the Protecting Power is satisfied that it would be in the interests of the prisoners of war concerned to do so owing to difficulties of translation caused by the Detaining Power's inability to find sufficient qualified linguists to carry out the necessary censorship. If limitations must be placed on the correspondence addressed to prisoners of war, they may be ordered only by the Power on which the prisoners depend, possibly at the request of the Detaining Power. Such letters and cards must be conveyed by the most rapid method at the disposal of the Detaining Power; they may not be delayed or retained for disciplinary reasons.

Prisoners of war who have been without news for a long period, or who are unable to receive news from their next of kin or to give them news by the ordinary postal route, as well as those who are at a great distance from their homes, shall be permitted to send telegrams, the fees being charged against the prisoners of war's accounts with the Detaining Power or paid in the currency at their disposal. They shall likewise benefit by this measure in cases of urgency.

As a general rule, the correspondence of prisoners of war shall be written in their native language. The Parties to the conflict may allow correspondence in other languages. Sacks containing prisoner of war mail must be securely sealed and labelled so as clearly to indicate their contents, and must be addressed to offices of destination.

Article 72

10–058   Prisoners of war shall be allowed to receive by post or by any other means individual parcels or collective shipments containing, in particular, foodstuffs, clothing, medical supplies and articles of a religious, educational or recreational character which may meet their needs, including books, devotional articles, scientific equipment, examination papers, musical instruments, sports outfits and materials allowing prisoners of war to pursue their studies or their cultural activities.

Such shipments shall in no way free the Detaining Power from the obligations imposed upon it by virtue of the present Convention.

The only limits which may be placed on these shipments shall be those proposed by the Protecting Power in the interest of the prisoners themselves, or by the International Committee of the Red Cross or any other organisation giving assistance to the prisoners, in respect of their own shipments only, on account of exceptional strain on transport or communications.

The conditions for the sending of individual parcels and collective relief shall, if necessary, be the subject of special agreements between the Powers concerned, which may in no case delay the receipt by the prisoners of relief supplies. Books may not be included in parcels of clothing and foodstuffs. Medical supplies shall, as a rule, be sent in collective parcels.

Article 73

In the absence of special agreements between the Powers concerned on the conditions for the receipt and distribution of collective relief shipments, the rules and regulations concerning collective shipments, which are annexed to the present Convention, shall be applied.

The special agreements referred to above shall in no case restrict the right of prisoners' representatives to take possession of collective relief shipments intended for prisoners of war, to proceed to their distribution or to dispose of them in the interest of the prisoners.

Nor shall such agreements restrict the right of representatives of the Protecting Power, the International Committee of the Red Cross or any other organisation giving assistance to prisoners of war and responsible for the forwarding of collective shipments, to supervise their distribution to the recipients.

Article 74

All relief shipments for prisoners of war shall be exempt from import, customs and other dues. Correspondence, relief shipments and authorised remittances of money addressed to prisoners of war or despatched by them through the post office, either direct or through the Information Bureaux provided for in Article 122 and the Central Prisoners of War Agency provided for in Article 123, shall be exempt from any postal dues, both in the countries of origin and destination, and in intermediate countries.

If relief shipments intended for prisoners of war cannot be sent through the post office by reason of weight or for any other cause, the cost of transportation shall be borne by the Detaining Power in all the territories under its control. The other Powers party to the Convention shall bear the cost of transport in their respective territories. In the absence of special agreements between the Parties concerned, the costs connected with transport of such shipments, other than costs covered by the above exemption, shall be charged to the senders. The High Contracting Parties shall endeavour to reduce, so far as possible, the rates charged for telegrams sent by prisoners of war, or addressed to them.

Article 75

Should military operations prevent the Powers concerned from fulfilling their obligation to assure the transport of the shipments referred to in Articles 70, 71, 72 and 77, the Protecting Powers concerned, the International Committee of the Red Cross or any other organisation duly approved by the Parties to the conflict may undertake to ensure the conveyance of such shipments by suitable means (railway wagons, motor vehicles, vessels or aircraft, etc.). For this purpose, the High Contracting Parties shall endeavour to supply them with such transport and to allow its circulation, especially by granting the necessary safe-conducts.

Such transport may also be used to convey:

(a) correspondence, lists and reports exchanged between the Central Information Agency referred to in Article 123 and the National Bureaux referred to in Article 122;

(b) correspondence and reports relating to prisoners of war which the Protecting Powers, the International Committee of the Red Cross or any other body assisting the prisoners, exchange either with their own delegates or with the Parties to the conflict.

These provisions in no way detract from the right of any Party to the conflict to arrange other means of transport, if it should so prefer, nor preclude the granting of safe-conducts, under mutually agreed conditions, to such means of transport.

In the absence of special agreements, the costs occasioned by the use of such means of transport shall be borne proportionally by the Parties to the conflict whose nationals are benefited thereby.

Article 76

10–059 The censoring of correspondence addressed to prisoners of war or despatched by them shall be done as quickly as possible. Mail shall be censored only by the despatching State and the receiving State, and once only by each.

The examination of consignments intended for prisoners of war shall not be carried out under conditions that will expose the goods contained in them to deterioration; except in the case of written or printed matter, it shall be done in the presence of the addressee, or of a fellow-prisoner duly delegated by him. The delivery to prisoners of individual or collective consignments shall not be delayed under the pretext of difficulties of censorship.

Any prohibition of correspondence ordered by Parties to the conflict, either for military or political reasons, shall be only temporary and its duration shall be as short as possible.

Article 77

The Detaining Powers shall provide all facilities for the transmission, through the Protecting Power or the Central Prisoners of War Agency provided for in Article 123 of instruments, papers or documents intended for prisoners of war or despatched by them, especially powers of attorney and wills.

In all cases they shall facilitate the preparation and execution of such documents on behalf of prisoners of war; in particular, they shall allow them to consult a lawyer and shall take what measures are necessary for the authentication of their signatures.

Section VI. Relations Between Prisoners of War and the Authorities

CHAPTER I. COMPLAINTS OF PRISONERS OF WAR RESPECTING THE CONDITIONS OF CAPTIVITY

Article 78

Prisoners of war shall have the right to make known to the military authorities in whose power they are, their requests regarding the conditions of captivity to which they are subjected. **10–060**

They shall also have the unrestricted right to apply to the representatives of the Protecting Powers either through their prisoners' representative or, if they consider it necessary, direct, in order to draw their attention to any points on which they may have complaints to make regarding their conditions of captivity.

These requests and complaints shall not be limited nor considered to be a part of the correspondence quota referred to in Article 71. They must be transmitted immediately. Even if they are recognised to be unfounded, they may not give rise to any punishment.

Prisoners' representatives may send periodic reports on the situation in the camps and the needs of the prisoners of war to the representatives of the Protecting Powers.

CHAPTER II. PRISONER OF WAR REPRESENTATIVES

Article 79

In all places where there are prisoners of war, except in those where there are officers, the prisoners shall freely elect by secret ballot, every six months, and also in case of vacancies, prisoners' representatives entrusted with representing them before the military authorities, the Protecting Powers, the International Committee of the Red Cross and any other organisation which may assist them. These prisoners' representatives shall be eligible for re-election.

In camps for officers and persons of equivalent status or in mixed camps, the senior officer among the prisoners of war shall be recognised as the camp prisoners' representative. In camps for officers, he shall be assisted by one or more advisers chosen by the officers; in mixed camps, his assistants shall be chosen from among the prisoners of war who are not officers and shall be elected by them.

Officer prisoners of war of the same nationality shall be stationed in labour camps for prisoners of war, for the purpose of carrying out the camp administration duties for which the prisoners of war are responsible. These officers may be elected as prisoners' representatives under the first paragraph of this Article. In such a case the assistants to the prisoners' representatives shall be chosen from among those prisoners of war who are not officers.

Every representative elected must be approved by the Detaining Power before he has the right to commence his duties. Where the Detaining Power refuses to approve a prisoner of war elected by his fellow prisoners of war, it must inform the Protecting Power of the reason for such refusal.

In all cases the prisoners' representative must have the same nationality, language and customs as the prisoners of war whom he represents. Thus, prisoners of war distributed in different sections of a camp, according to their nationality, language or customs, shall have for each section their own prisoners' representative, in accordance with the foregoing paragraphs.

Article 80

10–061 Prisoners' representatives shall further the physical, spiritual and intellectual well-being of prisoners of war.

In particular, where the prisoners decide to organise amongst themselves a system of mutual assistance, this organisation will be within the province of the prisoners' representative, in addition to the special duties entrusted to him by other provisions of the present Convention. Prisoners' representatives shall not be held responsible, simply by reason of their duties, for any offences committed by prisoners of war.

Article 81

Prisoners' representatives shall not be required to perform any other work, if the accomplishment of their duties is thereby made more difficult.

Prisoners' representatives may appoint from amongst the prisoners such assistants as they may require. All material facilities shall be granted them, particularly a certain freedom of movement necessary for the accomplishment of their duties (inspection of labour detachments, receipt of supplies, etc.).

Prisoners' representatives shall be permitted to visit premises where prisoners of war are detained, and every prisoner of war shall have the right to consult freely his prisoners' representative.

All facilities shall likewise be accorded to the prisoners' representatives for communication by post and telegraph with the detaining authorities, the Protecting Powers, the International Committee of the Red Cross and their delegates, the Mixed Medical Commissions and the bodies which give assistance to prisoners of war. Prisoners' representatives of labour detachments shall enjoy the same facilities for communication with the prisoners' representatives of the principal camp. Such communications shall not be restricted, nor considered as forming a part of the quota mentioned in Article 71.

Prisoners' representatives who are transferred shall be allowed a reasonable time to acquaint their successors with current affairs.

In case of dismissal, the reasons therefor shall be communicated to the Protecting Power.

CHAPTER III. PENAL AND DISCIPLINARY SANCTIONS

I. General Provisions

Article 82

A prisoner of war shall be subject to the laws, regulations and **10–062** orders in force in the armed forces of the Detaining Power; the Detaining Power shall be justified in taking judicial or disciplinary measures in respect of any offence committed by a prisoner of war against such laws, regulations or orders. However, no proceedings or punishments contrary to the provisions of this Chapter shall be allowed.

If any law, regulation or order of the Detaining Power shall declare acts committed by a prisoner of war to be punishable, whereas the same acts would not be punishable if committed by a member of the forces of the Detaining Power, such acts shall entail disciplinary punishments only.

Article 83

In deciding whether proceedings in respect of an offence alleged to have been committed by a prisoner of war shall be judicial or disciplinary, the Detaining Power shall ensure that the competent authorities exercise the greatest leniency and adopt, wherever possible, disciplinary rather than judicial measures.

Article 84

A prisoner of war shall be tried only by a military court, unless the existing laws of the Detaining Power expressly permit the civil courts to try a member of the armed forces of the Detaining Power in respect of the particular offence alleged to have been committed by the prisoner of war.

In no circumstances whatever shall a prisoner of war be tried by a court of any kind which does not offer the essential guarantees of independence and impartiality as generally recognised, and, in particular, the procedure of which does not afford the accused the rights and means of defence provided for in Article 105.

Article 85

10–063 Prisoners of war prosecuted under the laws of the Detaining Power for acts committed prior to capture shall retain, even if convicted, the benefits of the present Convention.

Article 86

No prisoner of war may be punished more than once for the same act or on the same charge.

Article 87

Prisoners of war may not be sentenced by the military authorities and courts of the Detaining Power to any penalties except those provided for in respect of members of the armed forces of the said Power who have committed the same acts.

When fixing the penalty, the courts or authorities of the Detaining Power shall take into consideration, to the widest extent possible, the fact that the accused, not being a national of the Detaining Power, is not bound to it by any duty of allegiance, and that he is in its power as the result of circumstances independent of his own will. The said courts or authorities shall be at liberty to reduce the penalty provided for the violation of which the prisoner of war is accused, and shall therefore not be bound to apply the minimum penalty prescribed.

Collective punishment for individual acts, corporal punishment, imprisonment in premises without daylight and, in general, any form of torture or cruelty, are forbidden.

No prisoner of war may be deprived of his rank by the Detaining Power, or prevented from wearing his badges.

Article 88

Officers, non-commissioned officers and men who are prisoners of war undergoing a disciplinary or judicial punishment, shall not be subjected to more severe treatment than that applied in respect of the same punishment to members of the armed forces of the Detaining Power of equivalent rank.

A woman prisoner of war shall not be awarded or sentenced to a punishment more severe, or treated whilst undergoing punishment more severely, than a woman member of the armed forces of the Detaining Power dealt with for a similar offence.

In no case may a woman prisoner of war be awarded or sentenced to a punishment more severe, or treated whilst undergoing punishment more severely, than a male member of the armed forces of the Detaining Power dealt with for a similar offence.

Prisoners of war who have served disciplinary or judicial sentences may not be treated differently from other prisoners of war.

II. Disciplinary Sanctions

Article 89

The disciplinary punishments applicable to prisoners of war are **10–064** the following:

(1) A fine which shall not exceed 50 per cent of the advances of pay and working pay which the prisoner of war would otherwise receive under the provisions of Articles 60 and 62 during a period of not more than 30 days.

(2) Discontinuance of privileges granted over and above the treatment provided for by the present Convention.

(3) Fatigue duties not exceeding two hours daily.

(4) Confinement.

The punishment referred to under (3) shall not be applied to officers. In no case shall disciplinary punishments be inhuman, brutal or dangerous to the health of prisoners of war.

Article 90

The duration of any single punishment shall in no case exceed 30 days. Any period of confinement awaiting the hearing of a disciplinary offence or the award of disciplinary punishment shall be deducted from an award pronounced against a prisoner of war.

The maximum of 30 days provided above may not be exceeded, even if the prisoner of war is answerable for several acts at the same time when he is awarded punishment, whether such acts are related or not.

The period between the pronouncing of an award of disciplinary punishment and its execution shall not exceed one month.

When a prisoner of war is awarded a further disciplinary punishment, a period of at least three days shall elapse between the execution of any two of the punishments, if the duration of one of these is 10 days or more.

Article 91

10–065 The escape of a prisoner of war shall be deemed to have succeeded when:

(1) he has joined the armed forces of the Power on which he depends, or those of an allied Power;

(2) he has left the territory under the control of the Detaining Power, or of an ally of the said Power;

(3) he has joined a ship flying the flag of the Power on which he depends, or of an allied Power, in the territorial waters of the Detaining Power, the said ship not being under the control of the last named Power.

Prisoners of war who have made good their escape in the sense of this Article and who are recaptured, shall not be liable to any punishment in respect of their previous escape.

Article 92

A prisoner of war who attempts to escape and is recaptured before having made good his escape in the sense of Article 91 shall be liable only to a disciplinary punishment in respect of this act, even if it is a repeated offence.

A prisoner of war who is recaptured shall be handed over without delay to the competent military authority.

Article 88, fourth paragraph, notwithstanding, prisoners of war punished as a result of an unsuccessful escape may be subjected to special surveillance. Such surveillance must not affect the state of their health, must be undergone in a prisoner of war camp, and must not entail the suppression of any of the safeguards granted them by the present Convention.

Article 93

Escape or attempt to escape, even if it is a repeated offence, shall not be deemed an aggravating circumstance if the prisoner of war is subjected to trial by judicial proceedings in respect of an offence committed during his escape or attempt to escape.

In conformity with the principle stated in Article 83, offences committed by prisoners of war with the sole intention of facilitating their escape and which do not entail any violence against life or limb, such as offences against public property, theft without intention of self-enrichment, the drawing up or use of false papers, or the wearing of civilian clothing, shall occasion disciplinary punishment only.

Prisoners of war who aid or abet an escape or an attempt to escape shall be liable on this count to disciplinary punishment only.

Article 94

If an escaped prisoner of war is recaptured, the Power on which he depends shall be notified thereof in the manner defined in Article 122, provided notification of his escape has been made.   **10–066**

Article 95

A prisoner of war accused of an offence against discipline shall not be kept in confinement pending the hearing unless a member of the armed forces of the Detaining Power would be so kept if he were accused of a similar offence, or if it is essential in the interests of camp order and discipline.

Any period spent by a prisoner of war in confinement awaiting the disposal of an offence against discipline shall be reduced to an absolute minimum and shall not exceed 14 days.

The provisions of Articles 97 and 98 of this Chapter shall apply to prisoners of war who are in confinement awaiting the disposal of offences against discipline.

Article 96

Acts which constitute offences against discipline shall be investigated immediately. Without prejudice to the competence of courts and superior military authorities, disciplinary punishment may be ordered only by an officer having disciplinary powers in his capacity as camp commander, or by a responsible officer who replaces him or to whom he has delegated his disciplinary powers.   **10–067**

In no case may such powers be delegated to a prisoner of war or be exercised by a prisoner of war.

Before any disciplinary award is pronounced, the accused shall be given precise information regarding the offences of which he is accused, and given an opportunity of explaining his conduct and of defending himself. He shall be permitted, in particular, to call witnesses and to have recourse, if necessary, to the services of a qualified interpreter. The decision shall be announced to the accused prisoner of war and to the prisoners' representative.

A record of disciplinary punishments shall be maintained by the camp commander and shall be open to inspection by representatives of the Protecting Power.

Article 97

Prisoners of war shall not in any case be transferred to penitentiary establishments (prisons, penitentiaries, convict prisons, etc.) to undergo disciplinary punishment therein.

All premises in which disciplinary punishments are undergone shall conform to the sanitary requirements set forth in Article 25. A prisoner of war undergoing punishment shall be enabled to keep himself in a state of cleanliness, in conformity with Article 29.

Officers and persons of equivalent status shall not be lodged in the same quarters as non-commissioned officers or men.

Women prisoners of war undergoing disciplinary punishment shall be confined in separate quarters from male prisoners of war and shall be under the immediate supervision of women.

Article 98

A prisoner of war undergoing confinement as a disciplinary punishment, shall continue to enjoy the benefits of the provisions of this Convention except in so far as these are necessarily rendered inapplicable by the mere fact that he is confined. In no case may he be deprived of the benefits of the provisions of Articles 78 and 126.

A prisoner of war awarded disciplinary punishment may not be deprived of the prerogatives attached to his rank.

Prisoners of war awarded disciplinary punishment shall be allowed to exercise and to stay in the open air at least two hours daily.

They shall be allowed, on their request, to be present at the daily medical inspections. They shall receive the attention which their state of health requires and, if necessary, shall be removed to the camp infirmary or to a hospital.

They shall have permission to read and write, likewise to send and receive letters. Parcels and remittances of money however, may be withheld from them until the completion of the punishment; they shall meanwhile be entrusted to the prisoners' representative, who-will hand over to the infirmary the perishable goods contained in such parcels.

III. Judicial Proceedings

Article 99

No prisoner of war may be tried or sentenced for an act which is not forbidden by the law of the Detaining Power or by international law, in force at the time the said act was committed.

No moral or physical coercion may be exerted on a prisoner of war in order to induce him to admit himself guilty of the act of which he is accused.

No prisoner of war may be convicted without having had an opportunity to present his defence and the assistance of a qualified advocate or counsel.

Article 100

Prisoners of war and the Protecting Powers shall be informed as 10–068 soon as possible of the offences which are punishable by the death sentence under the laws of the Detaining Power. Other offences shall not thereafter be made punishable by the death penalty without the concurrence of the Power on which the prisoners of war depend.

The death sentence cannot be pronounced on a prisoner of war unless the attention of the court has, in accordance with Article 87, second paragraph, been particularly called to the fact that since the accused is not a national of the Detaining Power, he is not bound to it by any duty of allegiance, and that he is in its power as the result of circumstances independent of his own will.

Article 101

If the death penalty is pronounced on a prisoner of war, the sentence shall not be executed before the expiration of a period of at least six months from the date when the Protecting Power receives, at an indicated address, the detailed communication provided for in Article 107.

Article 102

A prisoner of war can be validly sentenced only if the sentence has been pronounced by the same courts according to the same procedure as in the case of members of the armed forces of the Detaining Power, and if, furthermore, the provisions of the present Chapter have been observed.

Article 103

Judicial investigations relating to a prisoner of war shall be conducted as rapidly as circumstances permit and so that his trial shall take place as soon as possible. A prisoner of war shall not be confined while awaiting trial unless a member of the armed forces of the Detaining Power would be so confined if he were accused of a similar offence, or if it is essential to do so in the interests of national security. In no circumstances shall this confinement exceed three months.

Any period spent by a prisoner of war in confinement awaiting trial shall be deducted from any sentence of imprisonment passed upon him and taken into account in fixing any penalty. The provisions of Articles 97 and 98 of this Chapter shall apply to a prisoner of war whilst in confinement awaiting trial.

Article 104

10–069 In any case in which the Detaining Power has decided to institute judicial proceedings against a prisoner of war, it shall notify the Protecting Power as soon as possible and at least three weeks before the opening of the trial. This period of three weeks shall run as from the day on which such notification reaches the Protecting Power at the address previously indicated by the latter to the Detaining Power.

The said notification shall contain the following information:

(1) Surname and first names of the prisoner of war, his rank, his army, regimental, personal or serial number, his date of birth, and his profession or trade, if any;

(2) Place of internment or confinement;

(3) Specification of the charge or charges on which the prisoner of war is to be arraigned, giving the legal provisions applicable;

(4) Designation of the court which will try the case, likewise the date and place fixed for the opening of the trial.

The same communication shall be made by the Detaining Power to the prisoners' representative.

If no evidence is submitted, at the opening of a trial, that the notification referred to above was received by the Protecting Power, by the prisoner of war and by the prisoners' representative concerned, at least three weeks before the opening of the trial, then the latter cannot take place and must be adjourned.

Article 105

The prisoner of war shall be entitled to assistance by one of his prisoner comrades, to defence by a qualified advocate or counsel of his own choice, to the calling of witnesses and, if he deems necessary, to the services of a competent interpreter. He shall be advised of these rights by the Detaining Power in due time before the trial.

Failing a choice by the prisoner of war, the Protecting Power shall find him an advocate or counsel, and shall have at least one week at its disposal for the purpose. The Detaining Power shall deliver to the said Power, on request, a list of persons qualified to present the defence. Failing a choice of an advocate or counsel by the prisoner of war or the Protecting Power, the Detaining Power shall appoint a competent advocate or counsel to conduct the defence.

The advocate or counsel conducting the defence on behalf of the prisoner of war shall have at his disposal a period of two weeks at least before the opening of the trial, as well as the necessary facilities to prepare the defence of the accused. He may, in particular, freely visit the accused and interview him in private. He may also confer with any witnesses for the defence, including prisoners of war. He shall have the benefit of these facilities until the term of appeal or petition has expired.

Particulars of the charge or charges on which the prisoner of war is to be arraigned, as well as the documents which are generally communicated to the accused by virtue of the laws in force in the armed forces of the Detaining Power, shall be communicated to the accused prisoner of war in a language which he understands, and in good time before the opening of the trial. The same communication in the same circumstances shall be made to the advocate or counsel conducting the defence on behalf of the prisoner of war.

The representatives of the Protecting Power shall be entitled to attend the trial of the case, unless, exceptionally, this is held in camera in the interest of State security. In such a case the Detaining Power shall advise the Protecting Power accordingly.

Article 106

Every prisoner of war shall have, in the same manner as the members of the armed forces of the Detaining Power, the right of appeal or petition from any sentence pronounced upon him, with a view to the quashing or revising of the sentence or the reopening of the trial. He shall be fully informed of his right to appeal or petition and of the time limit within which he may do so. **10–070**

Article 107

Any judgment and sentence pronounced upon a prisoner of war shall be immediately reported to the Protecting Power in the form of a summary communication, which shall also indicate whether he has the right of appeal with a view to the quashing of the sentence or the reopening of the trial. This communication shall likewise be sent to the prisoners' representative concerned. It shall also be sent to the accused prisoner of war in a language he understands, if the sentence was not pronounced in his presence. The Detaining Power shall also immediately communicate to the Protecting Power the decision of the prisoner of war to use or to waive his right of appeal.

Furthermore, if a prisoner of war is finally convicted or if a sentence pronounced on a prisoner of war in the first instance is a death sentence, the Detaining Power shall as soon as possible address to the Protecting Power a detailed communication containing:

(1) the precise wording of the finding and sentence;

(2) a summarised report of any preliminary investigation and of the trial, emphasising in particular the elements of the prosecution and the defence;

(3) notification, where applicable, of the establishment where the sentence will be served.

The communications provided for in the foregoing sub-paragraphs shall be sent to the Protecting Power at the address previously made known to the Detaining Power.

Article 108

10–071 Sentences pronounced on prisoners of war after a conviction has become duly enforceable, shall be served in the same establishments and under the same conditions as in the case of members of the armed forces of the Detaining Power. These conditions shall in all cases conform to the requirements of health and humanity.

A woman prisoner of war on whom such a sentence has been pronounced shall be confined in separate quarters and shall be under the supervision of women.

In any case, prisoners of war sentenced to a penalty depriving them of their liberty shall retain the benefit of the provisions of Articles 78 and 126 of the present Convention. Furthermore, they shall be entitled to receive and despatch correspondence, to receive at least one relief parcel monthly, to take regular exercise in the open air, to have the medical care required by their state of health, and the spiritual assistance they may desire. Penalties to which they may be subjected shall be in accordance with the provisions of Article 87, third paragraph.

PART IV. TERMINATION OF CAPTIVITY

Section I. Direct Repatriation and Accommodation in Neutral Countries

Article 109

Subject to the provisions of the third paragraph of this Article, Parties to the conflict are bound to send back to their own country, regardless of number or rank, seriously wounded and seriously sick prisoners of war, after having cared for them until they are fit to travel, in accordance with the first paragraph of the following Article.

Throughout the duration of hostilities, Parties to the conflict shall endeavour, with the co-operation of the neutral Powers concerned, to make arrangements for the accommodation in neutral countries of the sick and wounded prisoners of war referred to in the second paragraph of the following Article. They may, in addition, conclude agreements with a view to the direct repatriation or internment in a neutral country of able-bodied prisoners of war who have undergone a long period of captivity.

No sick or injured prisoner of war who is eligible for repatriation under the first paragraph of this Article, may be repatriated against his will during hostilities.

Article 110

The following shall be repatriated direct:

(1) Incurably wounded and sick whose mental or physical fitness seems to have been gravely diminished.

(2) Wounded and sick who, according to medical opinion, are not likely to recover within one year, whose condition requires treatment and whose mental or physical fitness seems to have been gravely diminished.

(3) Wounded and sick who have recovered, but whose mental or physical fitness seems to have been gravely and permanently diminished.

The following may be accommodated in a neutral country:

(1) Wounded and sick whose recovery may be expected within one year of the date of the wound or the beginning of the illness, if treatment in a neutral country might increase the prospects of a more certain and speedy recovery.

(2) Prisoners of war whose mental or physical health, according to medical opinion, is seriously threatened by continued

captivity, but whose accommodation in a neutral country might remove such a threat.

The conditions which prisoners of war accommodated in a neutral country must fulfil in order to permit their repatriation shall be fixed, as shall likewise their status, by agreement between the Powers concerned. In general, prisoners of war who have been accommodated in a neutral country, and who belong to the following categories, should be repatriated:

(1) Those whose state of health has deteriorated so as to fulfil the condition laid down for direct repatriation;

(2) Those whose mental or physical powers remain, even after treatment, considerably impaired.

If no special agreements are concluded between the Parties to the conflict concerned, to determine the cases of disablement or sickness entailing direct repatriation or accommodation in a neutral country, such cases shall be settled in accordance with the principles laid down in the Model Agreement concerning direct repatriation and accommodation in neutral countries of wounded and sick prisoners of war and in the Regulations concerning Mixed Medical Commissions annexed to the present Convention.

Article 111

10–072 The Detaining Power, the Power on which the prisoners of war depend, and a neutral Power agreed upon by these two Powers, shall endeavour to conclude agreements which will enable prisoners of war to be interned in the territory of the said neutral Power until the close of hostilities.

Article 112

Upon the outbreak of hostilities, Mixed Medical Commissions shall be appointed to examine sick and wounded prisoners of war, and to make all appropriate decisions regarding them. The appointment, duties and functioning of these Commissions shall be in conformity with the provisions of the Regulations annexed to the present Convention.

However, prisoners of war who, in the opinion of the medical authorities of the Detaining Power, are manifestly seriously injured or seriously sick, may be repatriated without having to be examined by a Mixed Medical Commission.

Article 113

Besides those who are designated by the medical authorities of the Detaining Power, wounded or sick prisoners of war belonging to the categories listed below shall be entitled to present themselves for examination by the Mixed Medical Commissions provided for in the foregoing Article:

(1) Wounded and sick proposed by a physician or surgeon who is of the same nationality, or a national of a Party to the conflict allied with the Power on which the said prisoners depend, and who exercises his functions in the camp.

(2) Wounded and sick proposed by their prisoners' representative.

(3) Wounded and sick proposed by the Power on which they depend, or by an organisation duly recognised by the said Power and giving assistance to the prisoners.

Prisoners of war who do not belong to one of the three foregoing categories may nevertheless present themselves for examination by Mixed Medical Commissions, but shall be examined only after those belonging to the said categories.

The physician or surgeon of the same nationality as the prisoners who present themselves for examination by the Mixed Medical Commission, likewise the prisoners' representative of the said prisoners, shall have permission to be present at the examination.

Article 114

Prisoners of war who meet with accidents shall, unless the injury is self-inflicted, have the benefit of the provisions of this Convention as regards repatriation or accommodation in a neutral country. 10–073

Article 115

No prisoner of war on whom a disciplinary punishment has been imposed and who is eligible for repatriation or for accommodation in a neutral country, may be kept back on the plea that he has not undergone his punishment.

Prisoners of war detained in connection with a judicial prosecution or conviction, and who are designated for repatriation or accommodation in a neutral country, may benefit by such measures before the end of the proceedings or the completion of the punishment, if the Detaining Power consents.

Parties to the conflict shall communicate to each other the names of those who will be detained until the end of the proceedings or the completion of the punishment.

Article 116

The cost of repatriating prisoners of war or of transporting them to a neutral country shall be borne, from the frontiers of the Detaining Power, by the Power on which the said prisoners depend.

Article 117

No repatriated person may be employed on active military service.

Section II. Release and Repatriation of Prisoners of War
at the Close of Hostilities

Article 118

10–074 Prisoners of war shall be released and repatriated without delay after the cessation of active hostilities.

In the absence of stipulations to the above effect in any agreement concluded between the Parties to the conflict with a view to the cessation of hostilities, or failing any such agreement, each of the Detaining Powers shall itself establish and execute without delay a plan of repatriation in conformity with the principle laid down in the foregoing paragraph.

In either case, the measures adopted shall be brought to the knowledge of the prisoners of war.

The costs of repatriation of prisoners of war shall in all cases be equitably apportioned between the Detaining Power and the Power on which the prisoners depend. This apportionment shall be carried out on the following basis:

(a) If the two Powers are contiguous, the Power on which the prisoners of war depend shall bear the costs of repatriation from the frontiers of the Detaining Power.

(b) If the two Powers are not contiguous, the Detaining Power shall bear the costs of transport of prisoners of war over its own territory as far as its frontier or its port of embarkation nearest to the territory of the Power on which the prisoners of war depend. The Parties concerned shall agree between themselves as to the equitable apportionment of the remaining costs of the repatriation. The conclusion of this agreement shall in no circumstances justify any delay in the repatriation of the prisoners of war.

Article 119

Repatriation shall be effected in conditions similar to those laid down in Articles 46 to 48 inclusive of the present Convention for the transfer of prisoners of war, having regard to the provisions of Article 118 and to those of the following paragraphs.

On repatriation, any articles of value impounded from prisoners of war under Article 18, and any foreign currency which has not been converted into the currency of the Detaining Power, shall be restored to them. Articles of value and foreign currency which, for any reason whatever, are not restored to prisoners of war on repatriation, shall be despatched to the Information Bureau set up under Article 122.

Prisoners of war shall be allowed to take with them their personal effects, and any correspondence and parcels which have arrived for them. The weight of such baggage may be limited, if the conditions of repatriation so require, to what each prisoner can reasonably carry. Each prisoner shall in all cases be authorised to carry at least 25kg. The other personal effects of the repatriated prisoner shall be left in the charge of the Detaining Power which shall have them forwarded to him as soon as it has concluded an agreement to this effect, regulating the conditions of transport and the payment of the costs involved, with the Power on which the prisoner depends.

Prisoners of war against whom criminal proceedings for an indictable offence are pending may be detained until the end of such proceedings, and, if necessary, until the completion of the punishment. The same shall apply to prisoners of war already convicted for an indictable offence.

Parties to the conflict shall communicate to each other the names of any prisoners of war who are detained until the end of the proceedings or until punishment has been completed. By agreement between the Parties to the conflict, commissions shall be established for the purpose of searching for dispersed prisoners of war and of assuring their repatriation with the least possible delay.

Section III. Death of Prisoners of War

Article 120

Wills of prisoners of war shall be drawn up so as to satisfy the **10–075** conditions of validity required by the legislation of their country of origin, which will take steps to inform the Detaining Power of its requirements in this respect. At the request of the prisoner of war and, in all cases, after death, the will shall be transmitted without delay to the Protecting Power; a certified copy shall be sent to the Central Agency.

Death certificates, in the form annexed to the present Convention, or lists certified by a responsible officer, of all persons who die as prisoners of war shall be forwarded as rapidly as possible to the Prisoner of War Information Bureau established in accordance with Article 122. The death certificates or certified lists shall show particulars of identity as set out in the third paragraph of Article 17, and also the date and place of death, the cause of death, the date and place of burial and all particulars necessary to identify the graves.

The burial or cremation of a prisoner of war shall be preceded by a medical examination of the body with a view to confirming death and enabling a report to be made and, where necessary, establishing identity.

The detaining authorities shall ensure that prisoners of war who have died in captivity are honourably buried, if possible according to the rites of the religion to which they belonged, and that their graves are respected, suitably maintained and marked so as to be found at any time. Wherever possible, deceased prisoners of war who depended on the same Power shall be interred in the same place.

Deceased prisoners of war shall be buried in individual graves unless unavoidable circumstances require the use of collective graves. Bodies may be cremated only for imperative reasons of hygiene, on account of the religion of the deceased or in accordance with his express wish to this effect. In case of cremation, the fact shall be stated and the reasons given in the death certificate of the deceased.

In order that graves may always be found, all particulars of burials and graves shall be recorded with a Graves Registration Service established by the Detaining Power. Lists of graves and particulars of the prisoners of war interred in cemeteries and elsewhere shall be transmitted to the Power on which such prisoners of war depended. Responsibility for the care of these graves and for records of any subsequent moves of the bodies shall rest on the Power controlling the territory, if a Party to the present Convention. These provisions shall also apply to the ashes, which shall be kept by the Graves Registration Service until proper disposal thereof in accordance with the wishes of the home country.

Article 121

10–076 Every death or serious injury of a prisoner of war caused or suspected to have been caused by a sentry, another prisoner of war, or any other person, as well as any death the cause of which is unknown, shall be immediately followed by an official enquiry by the Detaining Power.

A communication on this subject shall be sent immediately to the Protecting Power. Statements shall be taken from witnesses, especially from those who are prisoners of war, and a report including such statements shall be forwarded to the Protecting Power.

If the enquiry indicates the guilt of one or more persons, the Detaining Power shall take all measures for the prosecution of the person or persons responsible.

PART V. INFORMATION BUREAUX AND RELIEF SOCIETIES FOR PRISONERS OF WAR

Article 122

Upon the outbreak of a conflict and in all cases of occupation, 10–077 each of the Parties to the conflict shall institute an official Information Bureau for prisoners of war who are in its power. Neutral or non-belligerent Powers who may have received within their territory persons belonging to one of the categories referred to in Article 4, shall take the same action with respect to such persons. The Power concerned shall ensure that the Prisoners of War Information Bureau is provided with the necessary accommodation, equipment and staff to ensure its efficient working. It shall be at liberty to employ prisoners of war in such a Bureau under the conditions laid down in the Section of the present Convention dealing with work by prisoners of war.

Within the shortest possible period, each of the Parties to the conflict shall give its Bureau the information referred to in the fourth, fifth and sixth paragraphs of this Article regarding any enemy person belonging to one of the categories referred to in Article 4, who has fallen into its power. Neutral or non-belligerent Powers shall take the same action with regard to persons belonging to such categories whom they have received within their territory. The Bureau shall immediately forward such information by the most rapid means to the Powers concerned, through the intermediary of the Protecting Powers and likewise of the Central Agency provided for in Article 123.

This information shall make it possible quickly to advise the next of kin concerned. Subject to the provisions of Article 17, the information shall include, in so far as available to the Information Bureau, in respect of each prisoner of war, his surname, first names, rank, army, regimental, personal or serial number, place and full date of birth, indication of the Power on which he depends, first name of the father and maiden name of the mother, name and address of the person to be informed and the address to which correspondence for the prisoner may be sent.

The Information Bureau shall receive from the various departments concerned information regarding transfers, releases, repatriations, escapes, admissions to hospital, and deaths, and shall transmit such information in the manner described in the third paragraph above. Likewise, information regarding the state of health of prisoners of war who are seriously ill or seriously wounded shall be supplied regularly, every week if possible.

The Information Bureau shall also be responsible for replying to all enquiries sent to it concerning prisoners of war, including those who have died in captivity; it will make any enquiries necessary to obtain the information which is asked for if this is not in its possession.

All written communications made by the Bureau shall be authenticated by a signature or a seal.

The Information Bureau shall furthermore be charged with collecting all personal valuables, including sums in currencies other than that of the Detaining Power and documents of importance to the next of kin, left by prisoners of war who have been repatriated or released, or who have escaped or died, and shall forward the said valuables to the Powers concerned. Such articles shall be sent by the Bureau in sealed packets which shall be accompanied by statements giving clear and full particulars of the identity of the person to whom the articles belonged, and by a complete list of the contents of the parcel. Other personal effects of such prisoners of war shall be transmitted under arrangements agreed upon between the Parties to the conflict concerned.

Article 123

10–078 A Central Prisoners of War Information Agency shall be created in a neutral country. The International Committee of the Red Cross shall, if it deems necessary, propose to the Powers concerned the organisation of such an Agency.

The function of the Agency shall be to collect all the information it may obtain through official or private channels respecting prisoners of war, and to transmit it as rapidly as possible to the country of origin of the prisoners of war or to the Power on which they depend. It shall receive from the Parties to the conflict all facilities for effecting such transmissions.

The High Contracting Parties, and in particular those whose nationals benefit by the services of the Central Agency, are requested to give the said Agency the financial aid it may require. The foregoing provisions shall in no way be interpreted as restricting the humanitarian activities of the International Committee of the Red Cross, or of the relief societies provided for in Article 125.

Article 124

The national Information Bureaux and the Central Information Agency shall enjoy free postage for mail, likewise all the exemptions provided for in Article 74, and further, so far as possible, exemption from telegraphic charges or, at least, greatly reduced rates.

Article 125

Subject to the measures which the Detaining Powers may con- **10–079** sider essential to ensure their security or to meet any other reasonable need, the representatives of religious organisations, relief societies, or any other organisation assisting prisoners of war, shall receive from the said Powers, for themselves and their duly accredited agents, all necessary facilities for visiting the prisoners, for distributing relief supplies and material, from any source, intended for religious, educational or recreative purposes, and for assisting them in organising their leisure time within the camps. Such societies or organisations may be constituted in the territory of the Detaining Power or in any other country, or they may have an international character.

The Detaining Power may limit the number of societies and organisations whose delegates are allowed to carry out their activities in its territory and under its supervision, on condition, however, that such limitation shall not hinder the effective operation of adequate relief to all prisoners of war.

The special position of the International Committee of the Red Cross in this field shall be recognised and respected at all times.

As soon as relief supplies or material intended for the above-mentioned purposes are handed over to prisoners of war, or very shortly afterwards, receipts for each consignment, signed by the prisoners' representative, shall be forwarded to the relief society or organisation making the shipment. At the same time, receipts for these consignments shall be supplied by the administrative authorities responsible for guarding the prisoners.

PART VI. EXECUTION OF THE CONVENTION

Section I. General Provisions

Article 126

Representatives or delegates of the Protecting Powers shall have permission to go to all places where prisoners of war may be, particularly to places of internment, imprisonment and labour, and shall have access to all premises occupied by prisoners of war; they shall also be allowed to go to the places of departure, passage and arrival of prisoners who are being transferred. They shall be able to interview the prisoners, and in particular the prisoners' representatives, without witnesses, either personally or through an interpreter.

Representatives and delegates of the Protecting Powers shall have full liberty to select the places they wish to visit. The duration and frequency of these visits shall not be restricted. Visits may not be prohibited except for reasons of imperative military necessity, and then only as an exceptional and temporary measure.

The Detaining Power and the Power on which the said prisoners of war depend may agree, if necessary, that compatriots of these prisoners of war be permitted to participate in the visits.

The delegates of the International Committee of the Red Cross shall enjoy the same prerogatives. The appointment of such delegates shall be submitted to the approval of the Power detaining the prisoners of war to be visited.

Article 127

10–080 The High Contracting Parties undertake, in time of peace as in time of war, to disseminate the text of the present Convention as widely as possible in their respective countries, and, in particular, to include the study thereof in their programmes of military and, if possible, civil instruction, so that the principles thereof may become known to all their armed forces and to the entire population.

Any military or other authorities, who in time of war assume responsibilities in respect of prisoners of war, must possess the text of the Convention and be specially instructed as to its provisions.

Article 128

The High Contracting Parties shall communicate to one another through the Swiss Federal Council and, during hostilities, through the Protecting Powers, the official translations of the present Convention, as well as the laws and regulations which they may adopt to ensure the application thereof.

Article 129

The High Contracting Parties undertake to enact any legislation necessary to provide effective penal sanctions for persons committing, or ordering to be committed, any of the grave breaches of the present Convention defined in the following Article.

Each High Contracting Party shall be under the obligation to search for persons alleged to have committed or to have ordered to be committed, such grave breaches, and shall bring such persons, regardless of their nationality, before its own courts. It may also, if it prefers, and in accordance with the provisions of its own legislation, hand such persons over for trial to another High Contracting Party concerned, provided such High Contracting Party has made out a prima facie case.

Each High Contracting Party shall take measures necessary for the suppression of all acts contrary to the provisions of the present Convention other than the grave breaches defined in the following Article.

In all circumstances, the accused persons shall benefit by safeguards of proper trial and defence, which shall not be less favourable than those provided by Article 105 and those following of the present Convention.

Article 130

Grave breaches to which the preceding Article relates shall be those involving any of the following acts, if committed against persons or property protected by the Convention: wilful killing, torture or inhuman treatment, including biological experiments, wilfully causing great suffering or serious injury to body or health, compelling a prisoner of war to serve in the forces of the hostile Power, or wilfully depriving a prisoner of war of the rights of fair and regular trial prescribed in this Convention. **10–081**

Article 131

No High Contracting Party shall be allowed to absolve itself or any other High Contracting Party of any liability incurred by itself or by another High Contracting Party in respect of breaches referred to in the preceding Article.

Article 132

At the request of a Party to the conflict, an enquiry shall be instituted, in a manner to be decided between the interested Parties, concerning any alleged violation of the Convention.

If agreement has not been reached concerning the procedure for the enquiry, the Parties should agree on the choice of an umpire who will decide upon the procedure to be followed. Once the violation has been established, the Parties to the conflict shall put an end to it and shall repress it with the least possible delay.

PROTOCOL ADDITIONAL TO THE GENEVA CONVENTIONS OF AUGUST 12, 1949 AND RELATING TO THE PROTECTION OF VICTIMS OF INTERNATIONAL ARMED CONFLICTS (PROTOCOL I), OF JUNE 8, 1977[22]

PART I. GENERAL PROVISIONS

Article 1. General principles and scope of application

10–082　　**3.** This Protocol, which supplements the Geneva Conventions of August 12, 1949 for the protection of war victims, shall apply in the situations referred to in Article 2 common to those Conventions.

4. The situations referred to in the preceding paragraph include armed conflicts which peoples are fighting against colonial domination and alien occupation and against racist regimes in the exercise of their right of self-determination, as enshrined in the Charter of the United Nations and the Declaration on Principles of International Law concerning Friendly Relations and Co-operation among States in accordance with the Charter of the United Nations.

Article 11. Protection of persons

1. The physical or mental health and integrity of persons who are in the power of the adverse Party or who are interned, detained or otherwise deprived of liberty as a result of a situation referred to in Article 1 shall not be endangered by any unjustified act or omission. Accordingly, it is prohibited to subject the persons described in this Article to any medical procedure which is not indicated by the state of health of the person concerned and which is not consistent with generally accepted medical standards which would be applied under similar medical circumstances to persons who are nationals of the Party conducting the procedure and who are in no way deprived of liberty.

2. It is, in particular, prohibited to carry out on such persons, even with their consent:

(a) physical mutilations;

(b) medical or scientific experiments;

(c) removal of tissue or organs for transplantation, except where these acts are justified in conformity with the conditions provided for in paragraph 1.

---

[22] 16 ILM 1391. Entered into force December 7, 1978. As of April 30, 1996 the number of States parties to the Protocol was 144.

PART III. METHODS AND MEANS OF WARFARE COMBATANT AND PRISONERS OF WAR

Article 41. Safeguard of an enemy hors de combat

1. A person who is recognised or who, in the circumstances **10–083** should be recognised to be hors de combat shall not be made the object of attack.

2. A person is hors de combat if:

(a) he is in the power of an adverse Party;

(b) he clearly expresses an intention to surrender; or

(c) he has been rendered unconscious or is otherwise incapacitated by wounds or sickness, and therefore is incapable of defending himself;

provided that in any of these cases he abstains from any hostile act and does not attempt to escape.

3. When persons entitled to protection as prisoners of war have fallen into the power or an adverse Party under unusual conditions of combat which prevent their evacuation as provided for in Part III, Section I, of the Third Convention, they shall be released and all feasible precautions shall be taken to ensure their safety.

Article 45. Protection of persons who have taken part in hostilities

1. A person who takes part in hostilities and falls into the **10–084** power of an adverse Party shall be presumed to be a prisoner of war, and therefore shall be protected by the Third Convention, if he claims the status of prisoner of war, or if he appears to be entitled to such status, or if the Party on which he depends claims such status on his behalf by notification to the detaining Power or to the Protecting Power. Should any doubt arise as to whether any such person is entitled to the status of prisoner of war, he shall continue to have such status and, therefore, to be protected by the Third Convention and this Protocol until such time as his status has been determined by a competent tribunal.

2. If a person who has fallen into the power of an adverse Party is not held as a prisoner of war and is to be tried by that Party for an offence arising out of the hostilities, he shall have the right to assert his entitlement to prisoner-of-war status before a judicial tribunal and to have that question adjudicated. Whenever possible under the applicable procedure, this adjudication shall occur before the trial for the offence. The representatives of the Protecting Power shall be entitled to attend the proceedings in which that question is adjudicated, unless, exceptionally, the proceedings are held in camera in the interest of State security. In such a case the detaining Power shall advise the Protecting Power accordingly.

3. Any person who has taken part in hostilities, who is not entitled to prisoner-of-war status and who does not benefit from more favourable treatment in accordance with the Fourth Convention shall have the right at all times to the protection of Article 75 of this Protocol. In occupied territory, any such person, unless he is held as a spy, shall also be entitled, notwithstanding Article 5 of the Fourth Convention, to his rights of communication under that Convention.

Article 46. Spies

10–085   **1.** Notwithstanding any other provision of the Conventions or of this Protocol, any member of the armed forces of a Party to the conflict who falls into the power of an adverse Party while engaging in espionage shall not have the right to the status of prisoner of war and may be treated as a spy.

2. A member of the armed forces of a Party to the conflict who, on behalf of that Party and in territory controlled by an adverse Party, gathers or attempts to gather information shall not be considered as engaging in espionage if, while so acting, he is in the uniform of his armed forces.

3. A member of the armed forces of a Party to the conflict who is a resident of territory occupied by an adverse Party and who, on behalf of the Party on which he depends, gathers or attempts to gather information of military value within that territory shall not be considered as engaging in espionage unless he does so through an act of false pretences or deliberately in a clandestine manner. Moreover, such a resident shall not lose his right to the status of prisoner of war and may not be treated as a spy unless he is captured while engaging in espionage.

4. A member of the armed forces of a Party to the conflict who is not a resident of territory occupied by an adverse Party and who has engaged in espionage in that territory shall not lose his right to the status of prisoner of war and may not be treated as a spy unless he is captured before he has rejoined the armed forces to which he belongs.

Article 47. Mercenaries

1. A mercenary shall not have the right to be a combatant or a prisoner of war.

2. A mercenary is any person who:

(a) is specially recruited locally or abroad in order to fight in an armed conflict;

(b) does, in fact, take a direct part in the hostilities;

(c) is motivated to take part in the hostilities essentially by the desire for private gain and, in fact, is promised, by or on behalf of a Party to the conflict, material compensation substantially in excess of that promised or paid to combatants of similar ranks and functions in the armed forces of that Party;

(d) is neither a national of a Party to the conflict nor a resident of territory controlled by a Party to the conflict;

(e) is not a member of the armed forces of a Party to the conflict; and

(f) has not been sent by a State which is not a Party to the conflict on official duty as a member of its armed forces.

PROTOCOL ADDITIONAL TO THE GENEVA CONVENTIONS OF AUGUST 12, 1949 AND RELATING TO THE PROTECTION OF VICTIMS ON NON-INTERNATIONAL ARMED CONFLICTS (PROTOCOL II) OF JUNE 8, 1977[23]

Article 2. Personal field of application

1. This Protocol shall be applied without any adverse distinc- 10–086 tion founded on race, colour, sex, language, religion or belief, political or other opinion, national or social origin, wealth, birth or other status, or on any other similar criteria to all persons affected by an armed conflict as defined in Article 1.

2. At the end of the armed conflict, all the persons who have been deprived of their liberty or whose liberty has been restricted for reasons related to such conflict, as well as those deprived of their liberty or whose liberty is restricted after the conflict for the same reasons, shall enjoy the protection of Articles 5 and 6 until the end of such deprivation or restriction of liberty.

---

[23] This Protocol, which develops and supplements Article 3 common to the Geneva Conventions of August 12, 1949 without modifying its existing conditions or application, shall apply to all armed conflicts which are not covered by Article 1 of the Protocol Additional to the Geneva Conventions of August 12, 1949, and relating to the Protection of Victims of International Armed Conflicts (Protocol I) and which take place in the territory of a High Contracting Party between its armed forces and dissident armed forces or other organized armed groups which, under responsible command, exercise such control over a part of its territory as to enable them to carry out sustained and concerted military operations and to implement this Protocol (Article 1(1)).

This Protocol shall not apply to situations of internal disturbances and tensions, such as riots, isolated and sporadic acts of violence and other acts of a similar nature, as not being armed conflicts (Article 2(1)).

PART II. HUMANE TREATMENT

Article 4. Fundamental guarantees

10–087   **1.** All persons who do not take a direct part or who have ceased to take part in hostilities, whether or not their liberty has been restricted, are entitled to respect for their person, honour and convictions and religious practices. They shall in all circumstances be treated humanely, without any adverse distinction. It is prohibited to order that there shall be no survivors.

2. Without prejudice to the generality of the foregoing, the following acts against the persons referred to in paragraph 1 are and shall remain prohibited at any time and in any place:

(a) violence to the life, health and physical or mental well-being of persons, in particular murder as well as cruel treatment such as torture, mutilation or any form of corporal punishment;

(b) collective punishments;

(c) taking of hostages;

(d) acts of terrorism;

(e) outrages upon personal dignity, in particular humiliating and degrading treatment, rape, enforced prostitution and any form or indecent assault;

(f) slavery and the slave trade in all their forms;

(g) pillage;

(h) threats to commit any or the foregoing acts.

Article 5. Persons whose liberty has been restricted

1. In addition to the provisions of Article 4 the following provisions shall be respected as a minimum with regard to persons deprived of their liberty for reasons related to the armed conflict, whether they are interned or detained;

(a) the wounded and the sick shall be treated in accordance with Article 7;

(b) the persons referred to in this paragraph shall, to the same extent as the local civilian population, be provided with food and drinking water and be afforded safeguards as regards health and hygiene and protection against the rigours of the climate and the dangers of the armed conflict;

(c) they shall be allowed to receive individual or collective;

(d) they shall be allowed to practise their religion and, if requested and appropriate, to receive spiritual assistance from persons, such as chaplains, performing religious functions;

(e) they shall, if made to work, have the benefit of working conditions and safeguards similar to those enjoyed by the local civilian population.

2. Those who are responsible for the internment or detention of the persons referred to in paragraph 1 shall also, within the limits of their capabilities, respect the following provisions relating to such persons:

(a) except when men and women of a family are accommodated together, women shall be held in quarters separated from those of men and shall be under the immediate supervision of women;

(b) they shall be allowed to send and receive letters and cards, the number of which may be limited by competent authority if it deems necessary;

(c) places of internment and detention shall not be located close to the combat zone. The persons referred to in paragraph 1 shall be evacuated when the places where they are interned or detained become particularly exposed to danger arising out of the armed conflict, if their evacuation can be carried out under adequate conditions of safety;

(d) they shall have the benefit of medical examinations;

(e) their physical or mental health and integrity shall not be endangered by any unjustified act or omission. Accordingly, it is prohibited to subject the persons described in this Article to any medical procedure which is not indicated by the state of health of the person concerned, and which is not consistent with the generally accepted medical standards applied to free persons under similar medical circumstances.

3. Persons who are not covered by paragraph 1 but whose liberty has been restricted in any way whatsoever for reasons related to the armed conflict shall be treated humanely in accordance with Article 4 and with paragraphs 1 (a), (c) and (d), and 2 (b) of this Article.

4. If it is decided to release persons deprived of their liberty, necessary measures to ensure their safety shall be taken by those so deciding.

ARTICLE 6. Penal prosecutions

1. This Article applies to the prosecution and punishment of **10–088** criminal offences related to the armed conflict.

2. No sentence shall be passed and no penalty shall be executed on a person found guilty of an offence except pursuant to a conviction pronounced by a court offering the essential guarantees of independence and impartiality.

In particular:

(a) the procedure shall provide for an accused to be informed without delay of the particulars of the offence alleged against him and shall afford the accused before and during his trial all necessary rights and means of defence;

(b) no one shall be convicted of an offence except on the basis of individual penal responsibility;

(c) no one shall be held guilty of any criminal offence on account of any act or omission which did not constitute a criminal offence, under the law, at the time when it was committed; nor shall a heavier penalty be imposed than that which was applicable at the time when the criminal offence was committed; if, after the commission of the offence, provision is made by law for the imposition of a lighter penalty, the offender shall benefit thereby;

(d) anyone charged with an offence is presumed innocent until proved guilty according to law;

(e) anyone charged with an offence shall have the right to be tried in his presence;

(f) no one shall be compelled to testify against himself or to confess guilt.

3. A convicted person shall be advised on conviction of his judicial and other remedies and of the time-limits within which they may be exercised.

4. The death penalty shall not be pronounced on persons who were under the age of 18 years at the time of the offence and shall not be carried out on pregnant women or mothers of young children.

5. At the end of hostilities, the authorities in power shall endeavour to grant the broadest possible amnesty to persons who have participated in the armed conflict, or those deprived of their liberty for reasons related to the armed conflict, whether they are interned or detained.

RIGHTS OF PRISONERS AND DETAINEES

Although not specifically identified in the Vienna Declaration, the international community has focused on certain other issues relevant to the treatment of prisoners in particular with respect to the adminstration of justice. What has been promulgated is essentially "soft law".[24]

What follows below is not an in depth consideration of these rules but rather an identification of the principal documents and their contents.

BASIC PRINCIPLES FOR THE TREATMENT OF PRISONERS[25]

1. All prisoners shall be treated with the respect due to their **10–089** inherent dignity and value as human beings.

2. There shall be no discrimination on the grounds of race, colour, sex, language, religion, political or other opinion, national or social origin, property, birth or other status.

3. It is, however, desirable to respect the religious beliefs and cultural precepts of the group to which prisoners belong, whenever local conditions so require.

4. The responsibility of prisons for the custody of prisoners and for the protection of society against crime shall be discharged in keeping with a State's other social objectives and its fundamental responsibilities for promoting the well-being and development of all members of society.

5. Except for those limitations that are demonstrably necessitated by the fact of incarceration, all prisoners shall retain the human rights and fundamental freedoms set out in the Universal Declaration of Human Rights, and, where the State concerned is a party, the International Covenant on Economic, Social and Cultural Rights, and the International Covenant on Civil and Political Rights and the Optional Protocol thereto, as well as such other rights as are set out in other United Nations covenants.

6. All prisoners shall have the right to take part in cultural activities and education aimed at the full development of the human personality.

7. Efforts addressed to the abolition of solitary confinement as a punishment, or to the restriction of its use, should be undertaken and encouraged.

8. Conditions shall be created enabling prisoners to undertake meaningful remunerated employment which will facilitate their reintegration into the country's labour market and permit them to contribute to their own financial support and to that of their families.

9. Prisoners shall have access to the health services available in the country without discrimination on the grounds of their legal situation.

---

[24] See consideration of Article 10 ICCPR *supra*, para. 10–006.
[25] G.A. Res. 45/111, annex, 45 UN G.A.O.R. Supp. (No. 49A) at p. 200, UN Doc. A/45/49 (1990).

10. With the participation and help of the community and social institutions, and with due regard to the interests of victims, favourable conditions shall be created for the reintegration of the ex-prisoner into society under the best possible conditions.

11. The above Principles shall be applied impartially.

BODY OF PRINCIPLES FOR THE PROTECTION OF ALL PERSONS UNDER ANY FORM OF DETENTION OR IMPRISONMENT[26]

SCOPE OF THE BODY OF PRINCIPLES

10–090 These principles apply for the protection of all persons under any form of detention or imprisonment.

Principle 1

All persons under any form of detention or imprisonment shall be treated in a humane manner and with respect for the inherent dignity of the human person.

Principle 2

Arrest, detention or imprisonment shall only be carried out strictly in accordance with the provisions of the law and by competent officials or persons authorised for that purpose.

Principle 3

There shall be no restriction upon or derogation from any of the human rights of persons under any form of detention or imprisonment recognised or existing in any State pursuant to law, conventions, regulations or custom on the pretext that this Body of Principles does not recognise such rights or that it recognises them to a lesser extent.

Principle 4

Any form of detention or imprisonment and all measures affecting the human rights of a person under any form of detention or imprisonment shall be ordered by, or be subject to the effective control of, a judicial or other authority.

Principle 5

1. These principles shall be applied to all persons within the territory of any given State, without distinction of any kind, such

---

[26] G.A. Res. 43/173, annex, 43 UN G.A.O.R. Supp. (No. 49) at p. 298, UN Doc. A/43/49 (1988).

as race, colour, sex, language, religion or religious belief, political or other opinion, national, ethnic or social origin, property, birth or other status.

2. Measures applied under the law and designed solely to protect the rights and special status of women, especially pregnant women and nursing mothers, children and juveniles, aged, sick or handicapped persons shall not be deemed to be discriminatory. The need for, and the application of, such measures shall always be subject to review by a judicial or other authority.

Principle 6

No person under any form of detention or imprisonment shall be **10–091** subjected to torture or to cruel, inhuman or degrading treatment or punishment.[27]

No circumstance whatever may be invoked as a justification for torture or other cruel, inhuman or degrading treatment or punishment.

Principle 7

1. States should prohibit by law any act contrary to the rights and duties contained in these principles, make any such act subject to appropriate sanctions and conduct impartial investigations upon complaints.

2. Officials who have reason to believe that a violation of this Body of Principles has occurred or is about to occur shall report the matter to their superior authorities and, where necessary, to other appropriate authorities or organs vested with reviewing or remedial powers.

3. Any other person who has ground to believe that a violation of this Body of Principles has occurred or is about to occur shall have the right to report the matter to the superiors of the officials involved as well as to other appropriate authorities or organs vested with reviewing or remedial powers.

Principle 8

Persons in detention shall be subject to treatment appropriate to their unconvicted status. Accordingly, they shall, whenever possible, be kept separate from imprisoned persons.

---

[27] The term "cruel, inhuman or degrading treatment or punishment" should be interpreted so as to extend the widest possible protection against abuses, whether physical or mental, including the holding of a detained or imprisoned person in conditions which deprive him, temporarily or permanently of the use of any of his natural senses, such as sight or hearing, or of his awareness of place and the passing of time.

Principle 9

10–092 The authorities which arrest a person, keep him under detention or investigate the case shall exercise only the powers granted to them under the law and the exercise of these powers shall be subject to recourse to a judicial or other authority.

Principle 10

Anyone who is arrested shall be informed at the time of his arrest of the reason for his arrest and shall be promptly informed of any charges against him.

Principle 11

1. A person shall not be kept in detention without being given an effective opportunity to be heard promptly by a judicial or other authority. A detained person shall have the right to defend himself or to be assisted by counsel as prescribed by law.
2. A detained person and his counsel, if any, shall receive prompt and full communication of any order of detention, together with the reasons therefor.
3. A judicial or other authority shall be empowered to review as appropriate the continuance of detention.

Principle 12

1. There shall be duly recorded:

(a) The reasons for the arrest;

(b) The time of the arrest and the taking of the arrested person to a place of custody as well as that of his first appearance before a judicial or other authority;

(c) The identity of the law enforcement officials concerned;

(d) Precise information concerning the place of custody.

2. Such records shall be communicated to the detained person, or his counsel, if any, in the form prescribed by law.

Principle 13

Any person shall, at the moment of arrest and at the commencement of detention or imprisonment, or promptly thereafter, be provided by the authority responsible for his arrest, detention or imprisonment, respectively with information on and an explanation of his rights and how to avail himself of such rights.

Principle 14

A person who does not adequately understand or speak the 10–093 language used by the authorities responsible for his arrest, detention or imprisonment is entitled to receive promptly in a language which he understands the information referred to in principle 10, principle 11, paragraph 2, principle 12, paragraph 1, and principle 13 and to have the assistance, free of charge, if necessary, of an interpreter in connection with legal proceedings subsequent to his arrest.

Principle 15

Notwithstanding the exceptions contained in principle 16, paragraph 4, and principle 18, paragraph 3, communication of the detained or imprisoned person with the outside world, and in particular his family or counsel, shall not be denied for more than a matter of days.

Principle 16

1. Promptly after arrest and after each transfer from one place of detention or imprisonment to another, a detained or imprisoned person shall be entitled to notify or to require the competent authority to notify members of his family or other appropriate persons of his choice of his arrest, detention or imprisonment or of the transfer and of the place where he is kept in custody.

2. If a detained or imprisoned person is a foreigner, he shall also be promptly informed of his right to communicate by appropriate means with a consular post or the diplomatic mission of the State of which he is a national or which is otherwise entitled to receive such communication in accordance with international law or with the representative of the competent international organisation, if he is a refugee or is otherwise under the protection of an intergovernmental organisation.

3. If a detained or imprisoned person is a juvenile or is incapable of understanding his entitlement, the competent authority shall on its own initiative undertake the notification referred to in the present principle. Special attention shall be given to notifying parents or guardians.

4. Any notification referred to in the present principle shall be made or permitted to be made without delay. The competent authority may however delay a notification for a reasonable period where exceptional needs of the investigation so require.

Principle 17

1. A detained person shall be entitled to have the assistance of 10–094 a legal counsel. He shall be informed of his right by the competent authority promptly after arrest and shall be provided with reasonable facilities for exercising it.

2. If a detained person does not have a legal counsel of his own choice, he shall be entitled to have a legal counsel assigned to him by a judicial or other authority in all cases where the interests of justice so require and without payment by him if he does not have sufficient means to pay.

Principle 18

1. A detained or imprisoned person shall be entitled to communicate and consult with his legal counsel.

2. A detained or imprisoned person shall be allowed adequate time and facilities for consultation with his legal counsel.

3. The right of a detained or imprisoned person to be visited by and to consult and communicate, without delay or censorship and in full confidentiality, with his legal counsel may not be suspended or restricted save in exceptional circumstances, to be specified by law or lawful regulations, when it is considered indispensable by a judicial or other authority in order to maintain security and good order.

4. Interviews between a detained or imprisoned person and his legal counsel may be within sight, but not within the hearing, of a law enforcement official.

5. Communications between a detained or imprisoned person and his legal counsel mentioned in the present principle shall be inadmissible as evidence against the detained or imprisoned person unless they are connected with a continuing or contemplated crime.

Principle 19

A detained or imprisoned person shall have the right to be visited by and to correspond with, in particular, members of his family and shall be given adequate opportunity to communicate with the outside world, subject to reasonable conditions and restrictions as specified by law or lawful regulations.

Principle 20

If a detained or imprisoned person so requests, he shall, if possible, be kept in a place of detention or imprisonment reasonably near his usual place of residence.

Principle 21

10–095 **1.** It shall be prohibited to take undue advantage of the situation of a detained or imprisoned person for the purpose of compelling him to confess, to incriminate himself otherwise or to testify against any other person.

2. No detained person while being interrogated shall be subject to violence, threats or methods of interrogation which impair his capacity of decision or his judgment.

Principle 22

No detained or imprisoned person shall, even with his consent, be subjected to any medical or scientific experimentation which may be detrimental to his health.

Principle 23

1. The duration of any interrogation of a detained or imprisoned person and of the intervals between interrogations as well as the identity of the officials who conducted the interrogations and other persons present shall be recorded and certified in such form as may be prescribed by law.

2. A detained or imprisoned person, or his counsel when provided by law, shall have access to the information described in paragraph 1 of the present principle.

Principle 24

A proper medical examination shall be offered to a detained or imprisoned person as promptly as possible after his admission to the place of detention or imprisonment, and thereafter medical care and treatment shall be provided whenever necessary. This care and treatment shall be provided free of charge.

Principle 25

A detained or imprisoned person or his counsel shall, subject only to reasonable conditions to ensure security and good order in the place of detention or imprisonment, have the right to request or petition a judicial or other authority for a second medical examination or opinion.

Principle 26

The fact that a detained or imprisoned person underwent a **10–096** medical examination, the name of the physician and the results of such an examination shall be duly recorded. Access to such records shall be ensured. Modalities therefore shall be in accordance with relevant rules of domestic law.

Principle 27

Non-compliance with these principles in obtaining evidence shall be taken into account in determining the admissibility of such evidence against a detained or imprisoned person.

Principle 28

A detained or imprisoned person shall have the right to obtain within the limits of available resources, if from public sources, reasonable quantities of educational, cultural and informational material, subject to reasonable conditions to ensure security and good order in the place of detention or imprisonment.

Principle 29

1. In order to supervise the strict observance of relevant laws and regulations, places of detention shall be visited regularly by qualified and experienced persons appointed by, and responsible to, a competent authority distinct from the authority directly in charge of the administration of the place of detention or imprisonment.

2. A detained or imprisoned person shall have the right to communicate freely and in full confidentiality with the persons who visit the places of detention or imprisonment in accordance with paragraph 1 of the present principle, subject to reasonable conditions to ensure security and good order in such places.

Principle 30

1. The types of conduct of the detained or imprisoned person that constitute disciplinary offences during detention or imprisonment, the description and duration of disciplinary punishment that may be inflicted and the authorities competent to impose such punishment shall be specified by law or lawful regulations and duly published.

2. A detained or imprisoned person shall have the right to be heard before disciplinary action is taken. He shall have the right to bring such action to higher authorities for review.

Principle 31

10–097 The appropriate authorities shall endeavour to ensure, according to domestic law, assistance when needed to dependent and, in particular, minor members of the families of detained or imprisoned persons and shall devote a particular measure of care to the appropriate custody of children left with out supervision.

Principle 32

1. A detained person or his counsel shall be entitled at any time to take proceedings according to domestic law before a judicial or other authority to challenge the lawfulness of his

detention in order to obtain his release without delay, if it is unlawful.

2. The proceedings referred to in paragraph 1 of the present principle shall be simple and expeditious and at no cost for detained persons without adequate means. The detaining authority shall produce without unreasonable delay the detained person before the reviewing authority.

Principle 33

1. A detained or imprisoned person or his counsel shall have the right to make a request or complaint regarding his treatment, in particular in case of torture or other cruel, inhuman or degrading treatment, to the authorities responsible for the administration of the place of detention and to higher authorities and, when necessary, to appropriate authorities vested with reviewing or remedial powers.

2. In those cases where neither the detained or imprisoned person nor his counsel has the possibility to exercise his rights under paragraph 1 of the present principle, a member of the family of the detained or imprisoned person or any other person who has knowledge of the case may exercise such rights.

3. Confidentiality concerning the request or complaint shall be maintained if so requested by the complainant.

4. Every request or complaint shall be promptly dealt with and replied to without undue delay. If the request or complaint is rejected or, in case of inordinate delay, the complainant shall be entitled to bring it before a judicial or other authority.

Neither the detained or imprisoned person nor any complainant under paragraph 1 of the present principle shall suffer prejudice for making a request or complaint.

Principle 34

Whenever the death or disappearance of a detained or **10–098** imprisoned person occurs during his detention or imprisonment, an inquiry into the cause of death or disappearance shall be held by a judicial or other authority, either on its own motion or at the instance of a member of the family of such a person or any person who has knowledge of the case. When circumstances so warrant, such an inquiry shall be held on the same procedural basis whenever the death or disappearance occurs shortly after the termination of the detention or imprisonment. The findings of such inquiry or a report thereon shall be made available upon request, unless doing so would jeopardise an ongoing criminal investigation.

Principle 35

1. Damage incurred because of acts or omissions by a public official contrary to the rights contained in these principles shall be compensated according to the applicable rules or liability provided by domestic law.

2. Information required to be recorded under these principles shall be available in accordance with procedures provided by domestic law for use in claiming compensation under the present principle.

Principle 36

1. A detained person suspected of or charged with a criminal offence shall be presumed innocent and shall be treated as such until proved guilty according to law in a public trial at which he has had all the guarantees necessary for his defence.

2. The arrest or detention of such a person pending investigation and trial shall be carried out only for the purposes of the administration of justice on grounds and under conditions and procedures specified by law. The imposition of restrictions upon such a person which are not strictly required for the purpose of the detention or to prevent hindrance to the process of investigation or the administration of justice, or for the maintenance of security and good order in the place of detention shall be forbidden.

Principle 37

A person detained on a criminal charge shall be brought before a judicial or other authority provided by law promptly after his arrest. Such authority shall decide without delay upon the lawfulness and necessity of detention. No person may be kept under detention pending investigation or trial except upon the written order of such an authority. A detained person shall, when brought before such an authority, have the right to make a statement on the treatment received by him while in custody.

Principle 38

10–099 A person detained on a criminal charge shall be entitled to trial within a reasonable time or to release pending trial.

Principle 39

Except in special cases provided for by law, a person detained on a criminal charge shall be entitled, unless a judicial or other authority decides otherwise in the interest of the administration of justice, to release pending trial subject to the conditions that may be imposed in accordance with the law. Such authority shall keep the necessity of detention under review.

General clause

Nothing in this Body of Principles shall be construed as restricting or derogating from any right defined in the International Covenant on Civil and Political Rights. Mention may also be made of the Standard Minimum Rules for the Treatment of Prisoners.[28] These rules are not intended to describe in detail a model system of penal institutions. They seek only, on the basis of the general consensus of contemporary thought and the essential elements of the most adequate systems of today, to set out what is generally accepted as being good principle and practice in the treatment of prisoners and the management of institutions.[29] It is further stated that not all of the rules are capable of application in all places and at all times but that they should serve to stimulate a constant endeavour to overcome practical difficulties in the way of their application, in the knowledge that they represent, as a whole, the minimum conditions which are accepted as suitable by the United Nations.The Rules are not intended to preclude experiment and practices, provided these are in harmony with the principles and seek to further the purposes which derive from the text of the rules as a whole. It will always be justifiable for the central prison administration to authorise departures from the rules in this spirit. Part I of the rules covers the general management of institutions, and is applicable to all categories of prisoners, criminal or civil, untried or convicted, including prisoners subject to "security measures" or corrective measures ordered by the judge. Part II contains rules applicable only to the special categories dealt with in each section. Nevertheless, the rules under section A, applicable to prisoners under sentence, shall be equally applicable to categories of prisoners dealt with in sections B[30], C[31] and D[32], provided they do not conflict with the rules governing those categories and are for

---

[28] Adopted August 30, 1955 by the First United Nations Congress on the Prevention of Crime and the Treatment of Offenders, UN Doc. A/CONF/611, annex I, E.S.C. res. 663C, 24 UN ESCOR Supp. (No. 1) at 11, UN Doc. E/3048 (1957), amended E.S.C. res. 2076, 62 UN ESCOR Supp. (No. 1) at p. 35, UN Doc. E/5988 (1977).

[29] Preamble; The rules are to be applied impartially without discrimination on grounds of race, colour, sex, language, religion, political or other opinion, national or social origin, property, birth or other status. Although it is recognised that it is necessary to respect the religious beliefs and moral precepts of the group to which a prisoner belongs.

[30] *i.e.* Insane and mentally abnormal prisoners.

[31] Prisoners under arrest or awaiting trial.

[32] Civil Prisoners.

their benefit. The rules do not seek to regulate the management of institutions set aside for young persons such as Borstal institutions or correctional schools, but in general part I would be equally applicable in such institutions. The category of young prisoners should include at least all young persons who come within the jurisdiction of juvenile courts. As a rule, such young persons should not be sentenced to imprisonment.[33]

JUVENILES[34]

UNITED NATIONS STANDARD MINIMUM RULES FOR THE ADMINISTRATION OF JUVENILE JUSTICE ("THE BEIJING RULES")[35]

PART ONE

GENERAL PRINCIPLES[36]

1. Fundamental perspectives

10–100   1.1 Member States shall seek, in conformity with their respective general interests, to further the well-being of the juvenile and her or his family.

1.2 Member States shall endeavour to develop conditions that will ensure for the juvenile a meaningful life in the community, which, during that period in life when she or he is most susceptible to deviant behaviour, will foster a process of personal development and education that is as free from crime and delinquency as possible.

1.3 Sufficient attention shall be given to positive measures that involve the full mobilisation of all possible resources, including the family, volunteers and other community groups, as well as schools and other community institutions, for the purpose of promoting the well-being of the juvenile, with a view to reducing the need for intervention under the law, and of effectively, fairly and humanely dealing with the juvenile in conflict with the law.

1.4 Juvenile justice shall be conceived as an integral part of the national development process of each country, within a com-

---

[33] For measures specifically relating to juveniles, see below.

[34] See Arts 6(5); 10(3) and 14 1966 UN Covenant on Civil and Political Rights; and Arts 37 and 40, UN Convention on the Rights of the Child, see Chapter on Children: Juvenile Justice.

[35] G.A. Res. 40/33, annex, 40 UN G.A.O.R. Supp. (No. 53) at 207, UN Doc. A/40/53 (1985).

[36] The Standard Minimum Rules are to be applied to juvenile offenders impartially, without distinction of any kind, for example as to race, colour, sex, language, religion, political or other opinions, national or social origin, property, birth or other status.

prehensive framework of social justice for all juveniles, thus, at the same time, contributing to the protection of the young and the maintenance of a peaceful order in society.

1.5 These Rules shall be implemented in the context of economic, social and cultural conditions prevailing in each Member State.

1.6 Juvenile justice services shall be systematically developed and co-ordinated with a view to improving and sustaining the competence of personnel involved in the services, including their methods, approaches and attitudes.

Commentary

These broad fundamental perspectives refer to comprehensive social policy in general and aim at promoting juvenile welfare to the greatest possible extent, which will minimise the necessity of intervention by the juvenile justice system, and in turn, will reduce the harm that may be caused by any intervention. Such care measures for the young, before the onset of delinquency, are basic policy requisites designed to obviate the need for the application of the Rules.

Rules 1.1 to 1.3 point to the important role that a constructive social policy for juveniles will play, *inter alia*, in the prevention of juvenile crime and delinquency. Rule 1.4 defines juvenile justice as an integral part of social justice for juveniles, while rule 1.6 refers to the necessity of constantly improving juvenile justice, without falling behind the development of progressive social policy for juveniles in general and bearing in mind the need for consistent improvement of staff services.

Rule 1.5 seeks to take account of existing conditions in Member States which would cause the manner of implementation of particular rules necessarily to be different from the manner adopted in other States.

. . .

2.3 Efforts shall be made to establish, in each national jurisdic- **10–101** tion, a set of laws, rules and provisions specifically applicable to juvenile offenders and institutions and bodies entrusted with the functions of the administration of juvenile justice and designed:

(a) To meet the varying needs of juvenile offenders, while protecting their basic rights;

(b) To meet the needs of society;

(c) To implement the following rules thoroughly and fairly.

Commentary

The Standard Minimum Rules are deliberately formulated so as to be applicable within different legal systems and, at the same time, to set some minimum standards for the handling of juvenile offenders under any definition of a juvenile and under any system of dealing with juvenile offenders. The Rules are always to be applied impartially and without distinction of any kind.

Rule 2.1 therefore stresses the importance of the Rules always being applied impartially and without distinction of any kind.

The rule follows the formulation of principle 2 of the Declaration of the Rights of the Child.

Rule 2.2 defines "juvenile" and "offence" as the components of the notion of the "juvenile offender", who is the main subject of these Standard Minimum Rules (see, however, also rules 3 and 4).

It should be noted that age limits will depend on, and are explicitly made dependent on, each respective legal system, thus fully respecting the economic, social, political, cultural and legal systems of Member States. This makes for a wide variety of ages coming under the definition of "juvenile", ranging from 7 years to 18 years or above. Such a variety seems inevitable in view of the different national legal systems and does not diminish the impact of these Standard Minimum Rules.

Rule 2.3 is addressed to the necessity of specific national legislation for the optimal implementation of these Standard Minimum Rules, both legally and practically.

3. Extension of the Rules

10–102 3.1 The relevant provisions of the Rules shall be applied not only to juvenile offenders but also to juveniles who may be proceeded against for any specific behaviour that would not be punishable if committed by an adult.

3.2 Efforts shall be made to extend the principles embodied in the Rules to all juveniles who are dealt with in welfare and care proceedings.

3.3 Efforts shall also be made to extend the principles embodied in the Rules to young adult offenders.

Commentary

Rule 3 extends the protection afforded by the Standard Minimum Rules for the Administration of Juvenile Justice to cover:

(a) The so-called "status offences" prescribed in various national legal systems where the range of behaviour considered to be an offence is wider for juveniles than it is for adults (for example, truancy, school and family disobedience, public drunkenness, etc.) (rule 3.1);

(b) Juvenile welfare and care proceedings (rule 3.2);

(c) Proceedings dealing with young adult offenders, depending of course on each given age limit (rule 3.3).

The extension of the Rules to cover these three areas seems to be justified. Rule 3.1 provides minimum guarantees in those fields, and rule 3.2 is considered a desirable step in the direction of more fair, equitable and humane justice for all juveniles in conflict with the law.

4. Age of criminal responsibility

4.1 In those legal systems recognising the concept of the age of **10–103** criminal responsibility for juveniles, the beginning of that age shall not be fixed at too low an age level, bearing in mind the facts of emotional, mental and intellectual maturity.

Commentary

The minimum age of criminal responsibility differs widely owing to history and culture. The modern approach would be to consider whether a child can live up to the moral and psychological components of criminal responsibility; that is, whether a child, by virtue of her or his individual discernment and understanding, can be held responsible for essentially antisocial behaviour.

If the age of criminal responsibility is fixed too low or if there is no lower age limit at all, the notion of responsibility would become meaningless. In general, there is a close relationship between the notion of responsibility for delinquent or criminal behaviour and other social rights and responsibilities (such as marital status, civil majority, etc.).

Efforts should therefore be made to agree on a reasonable lowest age limit that is applicable internationally.

5. Aims of juvenile justice

5.1 The juvenile justice system shall emphasise the well-being **10–104** of the juvenile and shall ensure that any reaction to juvenile offenders shall always be in proportion to the circumstances of both the offenders and the offence.

Commentary

Rule 5 refers to two of the most important objectives of juvenile justice. The first objective is the promotion of the well-being of the juvenile. This is the main focus of those legal systems in which juvenile offenders are dealt with by family courts or administrative authorities, but the well-being of the juvenile should also be emphasised in legal systems that follow the criminal court model, thus contributing to the avoidance of merely punitive sanctions (see also rule 14). The second objective is "the principle of proportionality". This principle is well-known as an instrument for curbing punitive sanctions, mostly expressed in terms of just deserts in relation to the gravity of the offence. The response to young offenders should be based on the consideration not only of the gravity of the offence but also of personal circumstances. The individual circumstances of the offender (for example, social status, family situation, the harm caused by the offence or other factors affecting personal circumstances) should influence the proportionality of the reactions (for example by having regard to the offender's endeavour to indemnify the victim or to her or his willingness to turn to wholesome and useful life).

By the same token, reactions aiming to ensure the welfare of the young offender may go beyond necessity and therefore infringe upon the fundamental rights of the young individual, as has been observed in some juvenile justice systems. Here, too, the proportionality of the reaction to the circumstances of both the offender and the offence, including the victim, should be safeguarded.

In essence, rule 5 calls for no less and no more than a fair reaction in any given cases of juvenile delinquency and crime.

The issues combined in the rule may help to stimulate development in both regards: new and innovative types of reactions are as desirable as precautions against any undue widening of the net of formal social control over juveniles.

6. Scope of discretion

10–105 6.1 In view of the varying special needs of juveniles as well as the variety of measures available, appropriate scope for discretion shall be allowed at all stages of proceedings and at the different levels of juvenile justice administration, including investigation, prosecution, adjudication and the follow-up of dispositions.

6.2 Efforts shall be made, however, to ensure sufficient accountability at all stages and levels in the exercise of any such discretion.

6.3 Those who exercise discretion shall be specially qualified or trained to exercise it judiciously and in accordance with their functions and mandates.

Commentary

Rules 6.1, 6.2 and 6.3 combine several important features of effective, fair and humane juvenile justice administration: the need to permit the exercise of discretionary power at all significant levels of processing so that those who make determinations can take the actions deemed to be most appropriate in each individual case; and the need to provide checks and balances in order to curb any abuses of discretionary power and to safeguard the rights of the young offender. Accountability and professionalism are instruments best apt to curb broad discretion. Thus, professional qualifications and expert training are emphasised here as a valuable means of ensuring the judicious exercise of discretion in matters of juvenile offenders (see also rules 1.6 and 2.2). The formulation of specific guidelines on the exercise of discretion and the provision of systems of review, appeal and the like in order to permit scrutiny of decisions and accountability are emphasised in this context. Such mechanisms are not specified here, as they do not easily lend themselves to incorporation into international standard minimum rules, which cannot possibly cover all differences in justice systems.

7. Rights of juveniles

7.1 Basic procedural safeguards such as the presumption of **10–106** innocence, the right to be notified of the charges, the right to remain silent, the right to counsel, the right to the presence of a parent or guardian, the right to confront and cross-examine witnesses and the right to appeal to a higher authority shall be guaranteed at all stages of proceedings.

Commentary

Rule 7.1 emphasises some important points that represent essential elements for a fair and just trial and that are internationally recognised in existing human rights instruments (see also rule 14). The presumption of innocence, for instance, is also to be found in Article 11 of the Universal Declaration of Human rights and in Article 14, paragraph 2, of the International Covenant on Civil and Political Rights.

Rules 14 *et seq* of these Standard Minimum Rules specify issues that are important for proceedings in juvenile cases, in particular, while rule 7.1 affirms the most basic procedural safeguards in a general way.

8. Protection of privacy

8.1 The juvenile's right to privacy shall be respected at all **10–107** stages in order to avoid harm being caused to her or him by undue publicity or by the process of labelling.

8.2 In principle, no information that may lead to the identification of a juvenile offender shall be published.

Commentary

Rule 8 stresses the importance of the protection of the juvenile's right to privacy. Young persons are particularly susceptible to stigmatisation. Criminological research into labelling processes has provided evidence of the detrimental effects (of different kinds) resulting from the permanent identification of young persons as "delinquent" or "criminal".

Rule 8 stresses the importance of protecting the juvenile from the adverse effects that may result from the publication in the mass media of information about the case (for example, the names of young offenders, alleged or convicted). The interest of the individual should be protected and upheld, at least in principle. (The general contents of rule 8 are further specified in rule 21)

9. Saving clause

9.1 Nothing in these Rules shall be interpreted as precluding the application of the Standard Minimum Rules for the Treatment of Prisoners adopted by the United Nations and other human rights instruments and standards recognised by the international community that relate to the care and protection of the young.

Commentary

Rule 9 is meant to avoid any misunderstanding in interpreting and implementing the present Rules in conformity with principles contained in relevant existing or emerging international human rights instruments and standards—such as the Universal Declaration of Human Rights, the International Covenant on Economic, Social and Cultural Rights and the International Covenant on Civil and Political Rights, and the Declaration of the Rights of the Child and the draft convention on the rights of the child. It should be understood that the application of the present Rules is without prejudice to any such international instruments which may contain provisions of wider application (see also rule 27).

Part Two deals with Investigation and Prosecution; Part Three—Adjudication and Disposition; Part Four—Non-institutional treatment; Part Five—Institutional treatment and Part Six—Research, Planning, Policy Formulation and Evaluation.

UNITED NATIONS RULES FOR THE PROTECTION OF JUVENILES DEPRIVED OF THEIR LIBERTY[37]

I. FUNDAMENTAL PERSPECTIVES

10–108   1. The juvenile justice system should uphold the rights and safety and promote the physical and mental well-being of juveniles. Imprisonment should be used as a last resort.

---

[37] G.A. Res. 45/113, annex, 45 UN G.A.O.R. Supp. (No. 49A) at 205, UN Doc. A/45/49 (1990).

2. Juveniles should only be deprived of their liberty in accordance with the principles and procedures set forth in these Rules and in the United Nations Standard Minimum Rules for the Administration of Juvenile Justice (The Beijing Rules).

Deprivation of the liberty of a juvenile should be a disposition of last resort and for the minimum necessary period and should be limited to exceptional cases. The length of the sanction should be determined by the judicial authority, without precluding the possibility of his or her early release.

3. The Rules are intended to establish minimum standards accepted by the United Nations for the protection of juveniles deprived of their liberty in all forms, consistent with human rights and fundamental freedoms, and with a view to counteracting the detrimental effects of all types of detention and to fostering integration in society.

4. The Rules should be applied impartially, without discrimination of any kind as to race, colour, sex, age, language, religion, nationality, political or other opinion, cultural beliefs or practices, property, birth or family status, ethnic or social origin, and disability. The religious and cultural beliefs, practices and moral concepts of the juvenile should be respected.

5. The Rules are designed to serve as convenient standards of reference and to provide encouragement and guidance to professionals involved in the management of the juvenile justice system.

6. The Rules should be made readily available to juvenile justice personnel in their national languages. Juveniles who are not fluent in the language spoken by the personnel of the detention facility should have the right to the services of an interpreter free of charge whenever necessary, in particular during medical examinations and disciplinary proceedings.

7. Where appropriate, States should incorporate the Rules into their legislation or amend it accordingly and provide effective remedies for their breach, including compensation when injuries are inflicted on juveniles. States should also monitor the application of the Rules.

8. The competent authorities should constantly seek to increase the awareness of the public that the care of detained juveniles and preparation for their return to society is a social service of great importance, and to this end active steps should be taken to foster open contacts between the juveniles and the local community.

9. Nothing in the Rules should be interpreted as precluding the application of the relevant United Nations and human rights instruments and standards, recognised by the international community, that are more conducive to ensuring the rights, care and protection of juveniles, children and all young persons.

10. In the event that the practical application of particular Rules contained in sections II to V, inclusive, presents any conflict with the Rules contained in the present section, compliance with the latter shall be regarded as the predominant requirement.

II. Scope and Application of the Rules

10–109   **11.** For the purposes of the Rules, . . .

(a) A juvenile is every person under the age of 18. The age limit below which it should not be permitted to deprive a child of his or her liberty should be determined by law;

(b) The deprivation of liberty means any form of detention or imprisonment or the placement of a person in a public or private custodial setting, from which this person is not permitted to leave at will, by order of any judicial, administrative or other public authority.

12. The deprivation of liberty should be effected in conditions and circumstances which ensure respect for the human rights of juveniles. Juveniles detained in facilities should be guaranteed the benefit of meaningful activities and programmes which would serve to promote and sustain their health and self-respect, to foster their sense of responsibility and encourage those attitudes and skills that will assist them in developing their potential as members of society.

13. Juveniles deprived of their liberty shall not for any reason related to their status be denied the civil, economic, political, social or cultural rights to which they are entitled under national or international law, and which are compatible with the deprivation of liberty.

14. The protection of the individual rights of juveniles with special regard to the legality of the execution of the detention measures shall be ensured by the competent authority, while the objectives of social integration should be secured by regular inspections and other means of control carried out, according to international standards, national laws and regulations, by a duly constituted body authorised to visit the juveniles and not belonging to the detention facility.

15. The Rules apply to all types and forms of detention facilities in which juveniles are deprived of their liberty.

Sections I, II, IV and V of the Rules apply to all detention facilities and institutional settings in which juveniles are detained, and section III applies specifically to juveniles under arrest or awaiting trial.

16. The Rules shall be implemented in the context of the economic, social and cultural conditions prevailing in each Member State.

III. Juveniles Under Arrest or Awaiting Trial

17. Juveniles who are detained under arrest or awaiting trial **10–110** ("untried") are presumed innocent and shall be treated as such. Detention before trial shall be avoided to the extent possible and limited to exceptional circumstances. Therefore, all efforts shall be made to apply alternative measures. When preventive detention is nevertheless used, juvenile courts and investigative bodies shall give the highest priority to the most expeditious processing of such cases to ensure the shortest possible duration of detention. Untried detainees should be separated from convicted juveniles.

18. The conditions under which an untried juvenile is detained should be consistent with the rules set out below, with additional specific provisions as are necessary and appropriate, given the requirements of the presumption of innocence, the duration of the detention and the legal status and circumstances of the juvenile. These provisions would include, but not necessarily be restricted to, the following:

(a) Juveniles should have the right of legal counsel and be enabled to apply for free legal aid, where such aid is available, and to communicate regularly with their legal advisers. Privacy and confidentiality shall be ensured for such communications;

(b) Juveniles should be provided, where possible, with opportunities to pursue work, with remuneration, and continue education or training, but should not be required to do so. Work, education or training should not cause the continuation of the detention;

(c) Juveniles should receive and retain materials for their leisure and recreation as are compatible with the interests of the administration of justice.

IV. The Management of Juvenile Facilities

A. Records

19. All reports, including legal records, medical records and **10–111** records of disciplinary proceedings, and all other documents relating to the form, content and details of treatment, should be placed in a confidential individual file, which should be kept up to date, accessible only to authorised persons and classified in such a way as to be easily understood. Where possible, every juvenile should have the right to contest any fact or opinion contained in his or her file so as to permit rectification of inaccurate, unfounded or unfair statements. In order to exercise this right, there should be procedures that allow an appropriate third party to have access to and to consult the file on request. Upon release, the records of juveniles shall be sealed, and, at an appropriate time, expunged.

20. No juvenile should be received in any detention facility without a valid commitment order of a judicial, administrative or other public authority. The details of this order should be immediately entered in the register. No juvenile should be detained in any facility where there is no such register.

B. *Admission, registration, movement and transfer*

21. In every place where juveniles are detained, a complete and secure record of the following information should be kept concerning each juvenile received:

(a) Information on the identity of the juvenile;

(b) The fact of and reasons for commitment and the authority therefor;

(c) The day and hour of admission, transfer and release;

(d) Details of the notifications to parents and guardians on every admission, transfer or release of the juvenile in their care at the time of commitment;

(e) Details of known physical and mental health problems, including drug and alcohol abuse.

22. The information on admission, place, transfer and release should be provided without delay to the parents and guardians or closest relative of the juvenile concerned.

23. As soon as possible after reception, full reports and relevant information on the personal situation and circumstances of each juvenile should be drawn up and submitted to the administration.

24. On admission, all juveniles shall be given a copy of the rules governing the detention facility and a written description of their rights and obligations in a language they can understand, together with the address of the authorities competent to receive complaints, as well as the address of public or private agencies and organisations which provide legal assistance. For those juveniles who are illiterate or who cannot understand the language in the written form, the information should be conveyed in a manner enabling full comprehension.

25. All juveniles should be helped to understand the regulations governing the internal organisation of the facility, the goals and methodology of the care provided, the disciplinary requirements and procedures, other authorised methods of seeking information and of making complaints and all such other matters as are necessary to enable them to understand fully their rights and obligations during detention.

26. The transport of juveniles should be carried out at the expense of the administration in conveyances with adequate ventilation and light, in conditions that should in no way subject them to hardship or indignity. Juveniles should not be transferred from one facility to another arbitrarily.

C. Classification and placement

27. As soon as possible after the moment of admission, each **10–112** juvenile should be interviewed, and a psychological and social report identifying any factors relevant to the specific type and level of care and programme required by the juvenile should be prepared. This report, together with the report prepared by a medical officer who has examined the juvenile upon admission, should be forwarded to the director for purposes of determining the most appropriate placement for the juvenile within the facility and the specific type and level of care and programme required and to be pursued. When special rehabilitative treatment is required, and the length of stay in the facility permits, trained personnel of the facility should prepare a written, individualised treatment plan specifying treatment objectives and time-frame and the means, stages and delays with which the objectives should be approached.

28. The detention of juveniles should only take place under conditions that take full account of their particular needs, status and special requirements according to their age, personality, sex and type of offence, as well as mental and physical health, and which ensure their protection from harmful influences and risk situations. The principal criterion for the separation of different categories of juveniles deprived of their liberty should be the provision of the type of care best suited to the particular needs of the individuals concerned and the protection of their physical, mental and moral integrity and well-being.

29. In all detention facilities juveniles should be separated from adults, unless they are members of the same family. Under controlled conditions, juveniles may be brought together with carefully selected adults as part of a special programme that has been shown to be beneficial for the juveniles concerned.

30. Open detention facilities for juveniles should be established. Open detention facilities are those with no or minimal security measures. The population in such detention facilities should be as small as possible. The number of juveniles detained in closed facilities should be small enough to enable individualised treatment. Detention facilities for juveniles should be decentralised and of such size as to facilitate access and contact between the juveniles and their families. Small-scale detention facilities should be established and integrated into the social, economic and cultural environment of the community.

D. Physical environment and accommodation

10–113   **31.** Juveniles deprived of their liberty have the right to facilities and services that meet all the requirements of health and human dignity.

32. The design of detention facilities for juveniles and the physical environment should be in keeping with the rehabilitative aim of residential treatment, with due regard to the need of the juvenile for privacy, sensory stimuli, opportunities for association with peers and participation in sports, physical exercise and leisure-time activities. The design and structure of juvenile detention facilities should be such as to minimise the risk of fire and to ensure safe evacuation from the premises.

There should be an effective alarm system in case of fire, as well as formal and drilled procedures to ensure the safety of the juveniles. Detention facilities should not be located in areas where there are known health or other hazards or risks.

33. Sleeping accommodation should normally consist of small group dormitories or individual bedrooms, while bearing in mind local standards. During sleeping hours there should be regular, unobtrusive supervision of all sleeping areas, including individual rooms and group dormitories, in order to ensure the protection of each juvenile. Every juvenile should, in accordance with local or national standards, be provided with separate and sufficient bedding, which should be clean when issued, kept in good order and changed often enough to ensure cleanliness.

34. Sanitary installations should be so located and of a sufficient standard to enable every juvenile to comply, as required, with their physical needs in privacy and in a clean and decent manner.

35. The possession of personal effects is a basic element of the right to privacy and essential to the psychological well-being of the juvenile. The right of every juvenile to possess personal effects and to have adequate storage facilities for them should be fully recognised and respected. Personal effects that the juvenile does not choose to retain or that are confiscated should be placed in safe custody. An inventory thereof should be signed by the juvenile. Steps should be taken to keep them in good condition. All such articles and money should be returned to the juvenile on release, except in so far as he or she has been authorised to spend money or send such property out of the facility. If a juvenile receives or is found in possession of any medicine, the medical officer should decide what use should be made of it.

36. To the extent possible juveniles should have the right to use their own clothing. Detention facilities should ensure that each juvenile has personal clothing suitable for the climate and adequate to ensure good health, and which should in no manner be degrading or humiliating. Juveniles removed from or leaving a facility for any purpose should be allowed to wear their own clothing.

37. Every detention facility shall ensure that every juvenile receives food that is suitably prepared and presented at normal meal times and of a quality and quantity to satisfy the standards of dietetics, hygiene and health and, as far as possible, religious and cultural requirements. Clean drinking water should be available to every juvenile at any time.

E. Education, vocational training and work

38. Every juvenile of compulsory school age has the right to education suited to his or her needs and abilities and designed to prepare him or her for return to society. Such education should be provided outside the detention facility in community schools wherever possible and, in any case, by qualified teachers through programmes integrated with the education system of the country so that, after release, juveniles may continue their education without difficulty. Special attention should be given by the administration of the detention facilities to the education of juveniles of foreign origin or with particular cultural or ethnic needs. Juveniles who are illiterate or have cognitive or learning difficulties should have the right to special education.

39. Juveniles above compulsory school age who wish to continue their education should be permitted and encouraged to do so, and every effort should be made to provide them with access to appropriate educational programmes.

40. Diplomas or educational certificates awarded to juveniles while in detention should not indicate in any way that the juvenile has been institutionalised.

41. Every detention facility should provide access to a library that is adequately stocked with both instructional and recreational books and periodicals suitable for the juveniles, who should be encouraged and enabled to make full use of it.

42. Every juvenile should have the right to receive vocational training in occupations likely to prepare him or her for future employment.

43. With due regard to proper vocational selection and to the requirements of institutional administration, juveniles should be able to choose the type of work they wish to perform.

44. All protective national and international standards applicable to child labour and young workers should apply to juveniles deprived of their liberty.

45. Wherever possible, juveniles should be provided with the opportunity to perform remunerated labour, if possible within the local community, as a complement to the vocational training provided in order to enhance the possibility of finding suitable employment when they return to their communities. The type of work should be such as to provide appropriate training that will be of benefit to the juveniles following release. The organisation and methods of work offered in detention facilities should resemble as closely as possible those of similar work in the community, so as to prepare juveniles for the conditions of normal occupational life.

46. Every juvenile who performs work should have the right to an equitable remuneration. The interests of the juveniles and of their vocational training should not be subordinated to the purpose of making a profit for the detention facility or a third party. Part of the earnings of a juvenile should normally be set aside to constitute a savings fund to be handed over to the juvenile on release. The juvenile should have the right to use the remainder of those earnings to purchase articles for his or her own use or to indemnify the victim injured by his or her offence or to send it to his or her family or other persons outside the detention facility.

F. Recreation

10–114   **47.** Every juvenile should have the right to a suitable amount of time for daily free exercise, in the open air whenever weather permits, during which time appropriate recreational and physical training should normally be provided. Adequate space, installations and equipment should be provided for these activities. Every juvenile should have additional time for daily leisure activities, part of which should be devoted, if the juvenile so wishes, to arts and crafts skill development. The detention facility should ensure that each juvenile is physically able to participate in the available programmes of physical education. Remedial physical education and therapy should be offered, under medical supervision, to juveniles needing it.

G. Religion

10–115   **48.** Every juvenile should be allowed to satisfy the needs of his or her religious and spiritual life, in particular by attending the services or meetings provided in the detention facility or by conducting his or her own services and having possession of the necessary books or items of religious observance and instruction of his or her denomination. If a detention facility contains a sufficient number of juveniles of a given religion, one or more qualified representatives of that religion should be appointed or approved and allowed to hold regular services and to pay pastoral visits in private to juveniles at their request. Every juvenile should have the right to receive visits from a qualified representative of any religion of his or her choice, as well as the right not to participate in religious services and freely to decline religious education, counselling or indoctrination.

H. Medical care

49. Every juvenile shall receive adequate medical care, both preventive and remedial, including dental, ophthalmological and mental health care, as well as pharmaceutical products and special diets as medically indicated. All such medical care should, where possible, be provided to detained juveniles through the appropriate health facilities and services of the community in which the detention facility is located, in order to prevent stigmatisation of the juvenile and promote self-respect and integration into the community.

50. Every juvenile has a right to be examined by a physician immediately upon admission to a detention facility, for the purpose of recording any evidence of prior ill-treatment and identifying any physical or mental condition requiring medical attention.

51. The medical services provided to juveniles should seek to detect and should treat any physical or mental illness, substance abuse or other condition that may hinder the integration of the juvenile into society. Every detention facility for juveniles should have immediate access to adequate medical facilities and equipment appropriate to the number and requirements of its residents and staff trained in preventive health care and the handling of medical emergencies. Every juvenile who is ill, who complains of illness or who demonstrates symptoms of physical or mental difficulties, should be examined promptly by a medical officer.

52. Any medical officer who has reason to believe that the physical or mental health of a juvenile has been or will be injuriously affected by continued detention, a hunger strike or any condition of detention should report this fact immediately to the director of the detention facility in question and to the independent authority responsible for safeguarding the well-being of the juvenile.

53. A juvenile who is suffering from mental illness should be treated in a specialised institution under independent medical management. Steps should be taken, by arrangement with appropriate agencies, to ensure any necessary continuation of mental health care after release.

54. Juvenile detention facilities should adopt specialised drug abuse prevention and rehabilitation programmes administered by qualified personnel. These programmes should be adapted to the age, sex and other requirements of the juveniles concerned, and detoxification facilities and services staffed by trained personnel should be available to drug- or alcohol-dependent juveniles.

55. Medicines should be administered only for necessary treatment on medical grounds and, when possible, after having obtained the informed consent of the juvenile concerned. In particular, they must not be administered with a view to eliciting information or a confession, as a punishment or as a means of restraint.

Juveniles shall never be testers in the experimental use of drugs and treatment. The administration of any drug should always be authorised and carried out by qualified medical personnel.

I. Notification of illness, injury and death

10–116   **56.** The family or guardian of a juvenile and any other person designated by the juvenile have the right to be informed of the state of health of the juvenile on request and in the event of any important changes in the health of the juvenile. The director of the detention facility should notify immediately the family or guardian of the juvenile concerned, or other designated person, in case of death, illness requiring transfer of the juvenile to an outside medical facility, or a condition requiring clinical care within the detention facility for more than 48 hours.

Notification should also be given to the consular authorities of the State of which a foreign juvenile is a citizen.

57. Upon the death of a juvenile during the period of deprivation of liberty, the nearest relative should have the right to inspect the death certificate, see the body and determine the method of disposal of the body. Upon the death of a juvenile in detention, there should be an independent inquiry into the causes of death, the report of which should be made accessible to the nearest relative. This inquiry should also be made when the death of a juvenile occurs within six months from the date of his or her release from the detention facility and there is reason to believe that the death is related to the period of detention.

58. A juvenile should be informed at the earliest possible time of the death, serious illness or injury of any immediate family member and should be provided with the opportunity to attend the funeral of the deceased or go to the bedside of a critically ill relative.

J. Contacts with the wider community

59. Every means should be provided to ensure that juveniles have adequate communication with the outside world, which is an integral part of the right to fair and humane treatment and is essential to the preparation of juveniles for their return to society. Juveniles should be allowed to communicate with their families, friends and other persons or representatives of reputable outside organisations, to leave detention facilities for a visit to their home and family and to receive special permission to leave the detention facility for educational, vocational or other important reasons. Should the juvenile be serving a sentence, the time spent outside a detention facility should be counted as part of the period of sentence.

60. Every juvenile should have the right to receive regular and frequent visits, in principle once a week and not less than once a month, in circumstances that respect the need of the juvenile for privacy, contact and unrestricted communication with the family and the defence counsel.

61. Every juvenile should have the right to communicate in writing or by telephone at least twice a week with the person of his or her choice, unless legally restricted, and should be assisted as necessary in order effectively to enjoy this right.

Every juvenile should have the right to receive correspondence.

62. Juveniles should have the opportunity to keep themselves informed regularly of the news by reading newspapers, periodicals and other publications, through access to radio and television programmes and motion pictures, and through the visits of the representatives of any lawful club or organisation in which the juvenile is interested.

K. Limitations of physical restraint and the use of force

63. Recourse to instruments of restraint and to force for any **10–117** purpose should be prohibited, except as set forth in rule 64 below.

64. Instruments of restraint and force can only be used in exceptional cases, where all other control methods have been exhausted and failed, and only as explicitly authorised and specified by law and regulation. They should not cause humiliation or degradation, and should be used restrictively and only for the shortest possible period of time. By order of the director of the administration, such instruments might be resorted to in order to prevent the juvenile from inflicting self-injury, injuries to others or serious destruction of property. In such instances, the director should at once consult medical and other relevant personnel and report to the higher administrative authority.

65. The carrying and use of weapons by personnel should be prohibited in any facility where juveniles are detained.

L. Disciplinary procedures

10–118 **66.** Any disciplinary measures and procedures should maintain the interest of safety and an ordered community life and should be consistent with the upholding of the inherent dignity of the juvenile and the fundamental objective of institutional care, namely, instilling a sense of justice, self-respect and respect for the basic rights of every person.

67. All disciplinary measures constituting cruel, inhuman or degrading treatment shall be strictly prohibited, including corporal punishment, placement in a dark cell, closed or solitary confinement or any other punishment that may compromise the physical or mental health of the juvenile concerned. The reduction of diet and the restriction or denial of contact with family members should be prohibited for any purpose. Labour should always be viewed as an educational tool and a means of promoting the self-respect of the juvenile in preparing him or her for return to the community and should not be imposed as a disciplinary sanction. No juvenile should be sanctioned more than once for the same disciplinary infraction. Collective sanctions should be prohibited.

68. Legislation or regulations adopted by the competent administrative authority should establish norms concerning the following, taking full account of the fundamental characteristics, needs and rights of juveniles:

(a) Conduct constituting a disciplinary offence;

(b) Type and duration of disciplinary sanctions that may be inflicted;

(c) The authority competent to impose such sanctions;

(d) The authority competent to consider appeals.

69. A report of misconduct should be presented promptly to the competent authority, which should decide on it without undue delay. The competent authority should conduct a thorough examination of the case.

70. No juvenile should be disciplinarily sanctioned except in strict accordance with the terms of the law and regulations in force. No juvenile should be sanctioned unless he or she has been informed of the alleged infraction in a manner appropriate to the full understanding of the juvenile, and given a proper opportunity of presenting his or her defence, including the right of appeal to a competent impartial authority. Complete records should be kept of all disciplinary proceedings.

71. No juveniles should be responsible for disciplinary functions except in the supervision of specified social, educational or sports activities or in self-government programmes.

M. Inspection and complaints

72. Qualified inspectors or an equivalent duly constituted **10–119** authority not belonging to the administration of the facility should be empowered to conduct inspections on a regular basis and to undertake unannounced inspections on their own initiative, and should enjoy full guarantees of independence in the exercise of this function. Inspectors should have unrestricted access to all persons employed by or working in any facility where juveniles are or may be deprived of their liberty, to all juveniles and to all records of such facilities.

73. Qualified medical officers attached to the inspecting authority or the public health service should participate in the inspections, evaluating compliance with the rules concerning the physical environment, hygiene, accommodation, food, exercise and medical services, as well as any other aspect or conditions of institutional life that affect the physical and mental health of juveniles. Every juvenile should have the right to talk in confidence to any inspecting officer.

74. After completing the inspection, the inspector should be required to submit a report on the findings. The report should include an evaluation of the compliance of the detention facilities with the present rules and relevant provisions of national law, and recommendations regarding any steps considered necessary to ensure compliance with them. Any facts discovered by an inspector that appear to indicate that a violation of legal provisions concerning the rights of juveniles or the operation of a juvenile detention facility has occurred should be communicated to the competent authorities for investigation and prosecution.

75. Every juvenile should have the opportunity of making requests or complaints to the director of the detention facility and to his or her authorised representative.

76. Every juvenile should have the right to make a request or complaint, without censorship as to substance, to the central administration, the judicial authority or other proper authorities through approved channels, and to be informed of the response without delay.

77. Efforts should be made to establish an independent office (ombudsman) to receive and investigate complaints made by juveniles deprived of their liberty and to assist in the achievement of equitable settlements.

78. Every juvenile should have the right to request assistance from family members, legal counsellors, humanitarian groups or others where possible, in order to make a complaint. Illiterate juveniles should be provided with assistance should they need to use the services of public or private agencies and organisations which provide legal counsel or which are competent to receive complaints.

N. Return to the community

10–120   **79.** All juveniles should benefit from arrangements designed to assist them in returning to society, family life, education or employment after release. Procedures, including early release, and special courses should be devised to this end.

80. Competent authorities should provide or ensure services to assist juveniles in re-establishing themselves in society and to lessen prejudice against such juveniles. These services should ensure, to the extent possible, that the juvenile is provided with suitable residence, employment, clothing, and sufficient means to maintain himself or herself upon release in order to facilitate successful reintegration. The representatives of agencies providing such services should be consulted and should have access to juveniles while detained, with a view to assisting them in their return to the community.

V. PERSONNEL

81. Personnel should be qualified and include a sufficient number of specialists such as educators, vocational instructors, counsellors, social workers, psychiatrists and psychologists.

These and other specialist staff should normally be employed on a permanent basis. This should not preclude part-time or volunteer workers when the level of support and training they can provide is appropriate and beneficial. Detention facilities should make use of all remedial, educational, moral, spiritual, and other resources and forms of assistance that are appropriate and available in the community, according to the individual needs and problems of detained juveniles.

82. The administration should provide for the careful selection and recruitment of every grade and type of personnel, since the proper management of detention facilities depends on their integrity, humanity, ability and professional capacity to deal with juveniles, as well as personal suitability for the work.

83. To secure the foregoing ends, personnel should be appointed as professional officers with adequate remuneration to attract and retain suitable women and men. The personnel of juvenile detention facilities should be continually encouraged to fulfil their duties and obligations in a humane, committed, professional, fair and efficient manner, to conduct themselves at all times in such a way as to deserve and gain the respect of the juveniles, and to provide juveniles with a positive role model and perspective.

10–121   **84.** The administration should introduce forms of organisation and management that facilitate communications between different categories of staff in each detention facility so as to enhance co-operation between the various services engaged in the care of juveniles, as well as between staff and the administration, with a view to ensuring that staff directly in contact with juveniles are able to function in conditions favourable to the efficient fulfilment of their duties.

85. The personnel should receive such training as will enable them to carry out their responsibilities effectively, in particular training in child psychology, child welfare and international standards and norms of human rights and the rights of the child, including the present Rules. The personnel should maintain and improve their knowledge and professional capacity by attending courses of in-service training, to be organised at suitable intervals throughout their career.

86. The director of a facility should be adequately qualified for his or her task, with administrative ability and suitable training and experience, and should carry out his or her duties on a full-time basis.

87. In the performance of their duties, personnel of detention facilities should respect and protect the human dignity and fundamental human rights of all juveniles, in particular, as follows:

(a) No member of the detention facility or institutional personnel may inflict, instigate or tolerate any act of torture or any form of harsh, cruel, inhuman or degrading treatment, punishment, correction or discipline under any pretext or circumstance whatsoever;

(b) All personnel should rigorously oppose and combat any act of corruption, reporting it without delay to the competent authorities;

(c) All personnel should respect the present Rules. Personnel who have reason to believe that a serious violation of the present Rules has occurred or is about to occur should report the matter to their superior authorities or organs vested with reviewing or remedial power;

(d) All personnel should ensure the full protection of the physical and mental health of juveniles, including protection from physical, sexual and emotional abuse and exploitation, and should take immediate action to secure medical attention whenever required;

(e) All personnel should respect the right of the juvenile to privacy, and, in particular, should safeguard all confidential matters concerning juveniles or their families learned as a result of their professional capacity;

(f) All personnel should seek to minimise any differences between life inside and outside the detention facility which tend to lessen due respect for the dignity of juveniles as human beings.

UNITED NATIONS GUIDELINES FOR THE PREVENTION OF JUVENILE DELINQUENCY (THE RIYADH GUIDELINES)[38]

I. FUNDAMENTAL PRINCIPLES

10–122   **1.** The prevention of juvenile delinquency is an essential part of crime prevention in society. By engaging in lawful, socially useful activities and adopting a humanistic orientation towards society and outlook on life, young persons can develop non-criminogenic attitudes.

2. The successful prevention of juvenile delinquency requires efforts on the part of the entire society to ensure the harmonious development of adolescents, with respect for and promotion of their personality from early childhood.

3. For the purposes of the interpretation of the present Guidelines, a child-centred orientation should be pursued. Young persons should have an active role and partnership within society and should not be considered as mere objects of socialisation or control.

4. In the implementation of the present Guidelines, in accordance with national legal systems, the well-being of young persons from their early childhood should be the focus of any preventive programme.

5. The need for and importance of progressive delinquency prevention policies and the systematic study and the elaboration of measures should be recognised. These should avoid criminalising and penalising a child for behaviour that does not cause serious damage to the development of the child or harm to others. Such policies and measures should involve:

(a) The provision of opportunities, in particular educational opportunities, to meet the varying needs of young persons and to serve as a supportive framework for safeguarding the personal development of all young persons, particularly those who are demonstrably endangered or at social risk and are in need of special care and protection;

(b) Specialised philosophies and approaches for delinquency prevention, on the basis of laws, processes, institutions,

---

[38] G.A. Res. 45/112, annex, 45 UN G.A.O.R. Supp. (No. 49A) p. 201, UN Doc. A/45/49 (1990).

facilities and a service delivery network aimed at reducing the motivation, need and opportunity for, or conditions giving rise to, the commission of infractions;

(c) Official intervention to be pursued primarily in the overall interest of the young person and guided by fairness and equity;

(d) Safeguarding the well-being, development, rights and interests of all young persons;

(e) Consideration that youthful behaviour or conduct that does not conform to overall social norms and values is often part of the maturation and growth process and tends to disappear spontaneously in most individuals with the transition to adulthood;

(f) Awareness that, in the predominant opinion of experts, labelling a young person as "deviant", "delinquent" or "pre-delinquent" often contributes to the development of a consistent pattern of undesirable behaviour by young persons.

6. Community-based services and programmes should be developed for the prevention of juvenile delinquency, particularly where no agencies have yet been established. Formal agencies of social control should only be utilised as a means of last resort.

II. SCOPE OF THE GUIDELINES

7. The present Guidelines should be interpreted and implemented within the broad framework of the Universal Declaration of Human Rights, the International Covenant on Economic, Social and Cultural Rights, the International Covenant on Civil and Political Rights, the Declaration of the Rights of the Child and the Convention on the Rights of the Child, and in the context of the United Nations Standard Minimum Rules for the Administration of Juvenile Justice (The Beijing Rules), as well as other instruments and norms relating to the rights, interests and well-being of all children and young persons. **10–123**

8. The present Guidelines should also be implemented in the context of the economic, social and cultural conditions prevailing in each Member State.

III. GENERAL PREVENTION

9. Comprehensive prevention plans should be instituted at every level of Government and include the following: **10–124**

(a) In-depth analyses of the problem and inventories of programmes, services, facilities and resources available;

(b) Well-defined responsibilities for the qualified agencies, institutions and personnel involved in preventive efforts;

(c) Mechanisms for the appropriate co-ordination of prevention efforts between governmental and non-governmental agencies;

(d) Policies, programmes and strategies based on prognostic studies to be continuously monitored and carefully evaluated in the course of implementation;

(e) Methods for effectively reducing the opportunity to commit delinquent acts;

(f) Community involvement through a wide range of services and programmes;

(g) Close interdisciplinary co-operation between national, State, provincial and local governments, with the involvement of the private sector representative citizens of the community to be served, and labour, child-care, health education, social, law enforcement and judicial agencies in taking concerted action to prevent juvenile delinquency and youth crime;

(h) Youth participation in delinquency prevention policies and processes, including recourse to community resources, youth self-help, and victim compensation and assistance programmes;

(i) Specialised personnel at all levels.

IV. SOCIALISATION PROCESSES

10. Emphasis should be placed on preventive policies facilitating the successful socialisation and integration of all children and young persons, in particular through the family, the community, peer groups, schools, vocational training and the world of work, as well as through voluntary organisations. Due respect should be given to the proper personal development of children and young persons, and they should be accepted as full and equal partners in socialisation and integration processes.

A. Family

10–125 **11.** Every society should place a high priority on the needs and well-being of the family and of all its members.

12. Since the family is the central unit responsible for the primary socialisation of children, governmental and social efforts to preserve the integrity of the family, including the extended family, should be pursued. The society has a responsibility to assist the family in providing care and protection and in ensuring the physical and mental well-being of children. Adequate arrangements including day-care should be provided.

13. Governments should establish policies that are conducive to the bringing up of children in stable and settled family environments. Families in need of assistance in the resolution of conditions of instability or conflict should be provided with requisite services.

14. Where a stable and settled family environment is lacking and when community efforts to assist parents in this regard have failed and the extended family cannot fulfil this role, alternative placements, including foster care and adoption, should be considered. Such placements should replicate, to the extent possible, a stable and settled family environment, while, at the same time, establishing a sense of permanency for children, thus avoiding problems associated with "foster drift".

15. Special attention should be given to children of families affected by problems brought about by rapid and uneven economic, social and cultural change, in particular the children of indigenous, migrant and refugee families. As such changes may disrupt the social capacity of the family to secure the traditional rearing and nurturing of children, often as a result of role and culture conflict, innovative and socially constructive modalities for the socialisation of children have to be designed.

16. Measures should be taken and programmes developed to provide families with the opportunity to learn about parental roles and obligations as regards child development and child care, promoting positive parent-child relationships, sensitising parents to the problems of children and young persons and encouraging their involvement in family and community-based activities.

17. Governments should take measures to promote family cohesion and harmony and to discourage the separation of children from their parents, unless circumstances affecting the welfare and future of the child leave no viable alternative.

18. It is important to emphasise the socialisation function of the family and extended family; it is also equally important to recognise the future role, responsibilities, participation and partnership of young persons in society.

19. In ensuring the right of the child to proper socialisation, Governments and other agencies should rely on existing social and legal agencies, but, whenever traditional institutions and customs are no longer effective, they should also provide and allow for innovative measures.

B. Education

20. Governments are under an obligation to make public education accessible to all young persons. **10–126**

21. Education systems should, in addition to their academic and vocational training activities, devote particular attention to the following:

(a) Teaching of basic values and developing respect for the child's own cultural identity and patterns, for the social values of the country in which the child is living, for civilisations different from the child's own and for human rights and fundamental freedoms;

(b) Promotion and development of the personality, talents and mental and physical abilities of young people to their fullest potential;

(c) Involvement of young persons as active and effective participants in, rather than mere objects of, the educational process;

(d) Undertaking activities that foster a sense of identity with and of belonging to the school and the community;

(e) Encouragement of young persons to understand and respect diverse views and opinions, as well as cultural and other differences;

(f) Provision of information and guidance regarding vocational training, employment opportunities and career development;

(g) Provision of positive emotional support to young persons and the avoidance of psychological maltreatment;

(h) Avoidance of harsh disciplinary measures, particularly corporal punishment.

22. Educational systems should seek to work together with parents, community organisations and agencies concerned with the activities of young persons.

23. Young persons and their families should be informed about the law and their rights and responsibilities under the law, as well as the universal value system, including United Nations instruments.

24. Educational systems should extend particular care and attention to young persons who are at social risk. Specialised prevention programmes and educational materials, curricula, approaches and tools should be developed and fully utilised.

25. Special attention should be given to comprehensive policies and strategies for the prevention of alcohol, drug and other substance abuse by young persons. Teachers and other professionals should be equipped and trained to prevent and deal with these problems. Information on the use and abuse of drugs, including alcohol, should be made available to the student body.

26. Schools should serve as resource and referral centres for the provision of medical, counselling and other services to young persons, particularly those with special needs and suffering from abuse, neglect, victimisation and exploitation.

27. Through a variety of educational programmes, teachers and other adults and the student body should be sensitised to the problems, needs and perceptions of young persons, particularly those belonging to underprivileged, disadvantaged, ethnic or other minority and low-income groups.

28. School systems should attempt to meet and promote the highest professional and educational standards with respect to curricula, teaching and learning methods and approaches, and the recruitment and training of qualified teachers. Regular monitoring and assessment of performance by the appropriate professional organisations and authorities should be ensured.

29. School systems should plan, develop and implement extra-curricular activities of interest to young persons, in co-operation with community groups.

30. Special assistance should be given to children and young persons who find it difficult to comply with attendance codes, and to "drop-outs".

31. Schools should promote policies and rules that are fair and just; students should be represented in bodies formulating school policy, including policy on discipline, and decision-making.

C. Community

32. Community-based services and programmes which 10–127 respond to the special needs, problems, interests and concerns of young persons and which offer appropriate counselling and guidance to young persons and their families should be developed, or strengthened where they exist.

33. Communities should provide, or strengthen where they exist, a wide range of community-based support measures for young persons, including community development centres, recreational facilities and services to respond to the special problems of children who are at social risk. In providing these helping measures, respect for individual rights should be ensured.

34. Special facilities should be set up to provide adequate shelter for young persons who are no longer able to live at home or who do not have homes to live in.

35. A range of services and helping measures should be provided to deal with the difficulties experienced by young persons in the transition to adulthood. Such services should include special programmes for young drug abusers which emphasise care, counselling, assistance and therapy-oriented interventions.

36. Voluntary organisations providing services for young persons should be given financial and other support by Governments and other institutions.

37. Youth organisations should be created or strengthened at the local level and given full participatory status in the management of community affairs. These organisations should encourage youth to organise collective and voluntary projects, particularly projects aimed at helping young persons in need of assistance.

38. Government agencies should take special responsibility and provide necessary services for homeless or street children; information about local facilities, accommodation, employment and other forms and sources of help should be made readily available to young persons.

39. A wide range of recreational facilities and services of particular interest to young persons should be established and made easily accessible to them.

D. Mass media

10–128   **40.** The mass media should be encouraged to ensure that young persons have access to information and material from a diversity of national and international sources.

41. The mass media should be encouraged to portray the positive contribution of young persons to society.

42. The mass media should be encouraged to disseminate information on the existence of services, facilities and opportunities for young persons in society.

43. The mass media generally, and the television and film media in particular, should be encouraged to minimise the level of pornography, drugs and violence portrayed and to display violence and exploitation disfavourably, as well as to avoid demeaning and degrading presentations, especially of children, women and interpersonal relations, and to promote egalitarian principles and roles.

44. The mass media should be aware of its extensive social role and responsibility, as well as its influence, in communications relating to youthful drug and alcohol abuse. It should use its power for drug abuse prevention by relaying consistent messages through a balanced approach. Effective drug awareness campaigns at all levels should be promoted.

V. SOCIAL POLICY

10–129   **45.** Government agencies should give high priority to plans and programmes for young persons and should provide sufficient funds and other resources for the effective delivery of services, facilities and staff for adequate medical and mental health care, nutrition, housing and other relevant services, including drug and alcohol abuse prevention and treatment, ensuring that such resources reach and actually benefit young persons.

46. The institutionalisation of young persons should be a measure of last resort and for the minimum necessary period, and the best interests of the young person should be of paramount importance. Criteria authorising formal intervention of this type should be strictly defined and limited to the following situations:

(a) where the child or young person has suffered harm that has been inflicted by the parents or guardians;

(b) where the child or young person has been sexually, physically or emotionally abused by the parents or guardians;

(c) where the child or young person has been neglected, abandoned or exploited by the parents or guardians;

(d) where the child or young person is threatened by physical or moral danger due to the behaviour of the parents or guardians; and

(e) where a serious physical or psychological danger to the child or young person has manifested itself in his or her own behaviour and neither the parents, the guardians, the juvenile himself or herself nor non-residential community services can meet the danger by means other than institutionalisation.

47. Government agencies should provide young persons with the opportunity of continuing in full-time education, funded by the State where parents or guardians are unable to support the young persons, and of receiving work experience.

48. Programmes to prevent delinquency should be planned and developed on the basis of reliable, scientific research findings, and periodically monitored, evaluated and adjusted accordingly.

49. Scientific information should be disseminated to the professional community and to the public at large about the sort of behaviour or situation which indicates or may result in physical and psychological victimisation, harm and abuse, as well as exploitation, of young persons.

50. Generally, participation in plans and programmes should be voluntary. Young persons themselves should be involved in their formulation, development and implementation.

51. Government should begin or continue to explore, develop and implement policies, measures and strategies within and outside the criminal justice system to prevent domestic violence against and affecting young persons and to ensure fair treatment to these victims of domestic violence.

VI. LEGISLATION AND JUVENILE JUSTICE ADMINISTRATION

10–130   **52.** Governments should enact and enforce specific laws and procedures to promote and protect the rights and well-being of all young persons.

53. Legislation preventing the victimisation, abuse, exploitation and the use for criminal activities of children and young persons should be enacted and enforced.

54. No child or young person should be subjected to harsh or degrading correction or punishment measures at home, in schools or in any other institutions.

55. Legislation and enforcement aimed at restricting and controlling accessibility of weapons of any sort to children and young persons should be pursued.

56. In order to prevent further stigmatisation, victimisation and criminalisation of young persons, legislation should be enacted to ensure that any conduct not considered an offence or not penalised if committed by an adult is not considered an offence and not penalised if committed by a young person.

57. Consideration should be given to the establishment of an office of ombudsman or similar independent organ, which would ensure that the status, rights and interests of young persons are upheld and that proper referral to available services is made.

The ombudsman or other organ designated would also supervise the implementation of the Riyadh Guidelines, the Beijing Rules and the Rules for the Protection of Juveniles Deprived of their Liberty. The ombudsman or other organ would, at regular intervals, publish a report on the progress made and on the difficulties encountered in the implementation of the instrument.

Child advocacy services should also be established.

58. Law enforcement and other relevant personnel, of both sexes, should be trained to respond to the special needs of young persons and should be familiar with and use, to the maximum extent possible, programmes and referral possibilities for the diversion of young persons from the justice system.

59. Legislation should be enacted and strictly enforced to protect children and young persons from drug abuse and drug traffickers.

VII. RESEARCH, POLICY DEVELOPMENT AND CO-ORDINATION

10–131   **60.** Efforts should be made and appropriate mechanisms established to promote, on both a multidisciplinary and an intra-disciplinary basis, interaction and co-ordination between economic, social, education and health agencies and services, the justice system, youth, community and development agencies and other relevant institutions.

61. The exchange of information, experience and expertise gained through projects, programmes, practices and initiatives relating to youth crime, delinquency prevention and juvenile justice should be intensified at the national, regional and international levels.

62. Regional and international co-operation on matters of youth crime, delinquency prevention and juvenile justice involving practitioners, experts and decision makers should be further developed and strengthened.

63. Technical and scientific co-operation on practical and policy-related matters, particularly in training, pilot and demonstration projects, and on specific issues concerning the prevention of youth crime and juvenile delinquency should be strongly supported by all Governments, the United Nations system and other concerned organisations.

64. Collaboration should be encouraged in undertaking scientific research with respect to effective modalities for youth crime and juvenile delinquency prevention and the findings of such research should be widely disseminated and evaluated.

65. Appropriate United Nations bodies, institutes, agencies and offices should pursue close collaboration and co-ordination on various questions related to children juvenile justice and youth crime and juvenile delinquency prevention.

66. On the basis of the present Guidelines, the United Nations Secretariat, in co-operation with interested institutions, should play an active role in the conduct of research, scientific collaboration, the formulation of policy options and the review and monitoring of their implementation, and should serve as a source of reliable information on effective modalities for delinquency prevention.

CHAPTER 11

AFTER VIENNA

WORLD CONFERENCE ON HUMAN RIGHTS (JUNE 1993)
VIENNA DECLARATION

PART II(F). FOLLOW-UP TO THE WORLD CONFERENCE ON HUMAN RIGHTS

11–001   **99.** The World Conference on Human Rights recommends that the General Assembly, the Commission on Human Rights and other organs and agencies of the United Nations system related to human rights consider ways and means for the full implementation, without delay, of the recommendations contained in the present Declaration, including the possibility of proclaiming a United Nations decade for human rights. The World Conference on Human Rights further recommends that the Commission on Human Rights annually review the progress towards this end.

100. The World Conference on Human Rights requests the Secretary-General of the United Nations to invite on the occasion of the 50th anniversary of the Universal Declaration of Human Rights all States, all organs and agencies of the United Nations system related to human rights, to report to him on the progress made in the implementation of the present Declaration and to submit a report to the General Assembly at its 53rd session, through the Commission on Human Rights and the Economic and Social Council. Likewise, regional and, as appropriate, national human rights institutions, as well as non-governmental organisations, may present their views to the Secretary-General on the progress made in the implementation of the present Declaration. Special attention should be paid to assessing the progress towards the goal of universal ratification of international human rights treaties and protocols adopted within the framework of the United Nations system.

PART II(A). INCREASED CO-ORDINATION ON HUMAN RIGHTS WITHIN THE UNITED NATIONS SYSTEM

18. The World Conference on Human Rights recommends to the General Assembly that when examining the report of the Conference at its 48th session, it begins, as a matter of priority, consideration of the question of the establishment of a High Commissioner for Human Rights for the promotion and protection of all human rights.

HIGH COMMISSIONER FOR THE PROMOTION AND PROTECTION OF ALL HUMAN RIGHTS[1]

The General Assembly,

11–002

Reaffirming its commitment to the purposes and principles of the Charter of the United Nations,

Emphasising the responsibilities of all States, in conformity with the Charter, to promote and encourage respect for all human rights and fundamental freedoms for all, without distinction as to race, sex, language or religion,

Emphasising the need to observe the Universal Declaration of Human Rights and for the full implementation of the human rights instruments, including the International Covenant on Civil and Political Rights, the International Covenant on Economic, Social and Cultural Rights, as well as the Declaration on the Right to Development,

Reaffirming that the right to development is a universal and inalienable right which is a fundamental part of the rights of the human person,

Considering that the promotion and the protection of all human rights is one of the priorities of the international community,

Recalling that one of the purposes of the United Nations enshrined in the Charter is to achieve international co-operation in promoting and encouraging respect for human rights,

Reaffirming the commitment made under Article 56 of the Charter to take joint and separate action in co-operation with the United Nations for the achievement of the purposes set forth in Article 55 of the Charter,

Emphasising the need for the promotion and protection of all human rights to be guided by the principles of impartiality, objectivity and non-selectivity, in the spirit of constructive international dialogue and co-operation,

Aware that all human rights are universal, indivisible, interdependent and interrelated and that as such they should be given the same emphasis,

Affirming its commitment to the Vienna Declaration and Programme of Action, adopted by the World Conference on Human Rights, held at Vienna from June 14 to 25, 1993,

Convinced that the World Conference on Human Rights made an important contribution to the cause of human rights and that its recommendations should be implemented through effective action by all States, the competent organs of the United Nations and the specialised agencies, in co-operation with non-governmental organisations,

Acknowledging the importance of strengthening the provision of advisory services and technical assistance by the Centre for

---

[1] A/RES/48/141 adopted December 20, 1993.

Human Rights of the Secretariat and other relevant programmes and bodies of the United Nations system for the purpose of the promotion and protection of all human rights,

Determined to adapt, strengthen and streamline the existing mechanisms to promote and protect all human rights and fundamental freedoms while avoiding unnecessary duplication,

Recognising that the activities of the United Nations in the field of human rights should be rationalised and enhanced in order to strengthen the United Nations machinery in this field and to further the objectives of universal respect for observance of international human rights standards,

Reaffirming that the General Assembly, the Economic and Social Council and the Commission on Human Rights are the responsible organs for decision-and policy-making for the promotion and protection of all human rights,

Reaffirming the necessity for a continued adaptation of the United Nations human rights machinery to the current and future needs in the promotion and protection of human rights and the need to improve its co-ordination, efficiency and effectiveness, as reflected in the Vienna Declaration and Programme of Action and within the framework of a balanced and sustainable development for all people,

Having considered the recommendation contained in paragraph 18 of section II of the Vienna Declaration and Programme of Action,

11–003 **1.** Decides to create the post of the High Commissioner for Human Rights;

2. Decides that the High Commissioner for Human Rights shall: (1)

(a) Be a person of high moral standing and personal integrity and shall possess expertise, including in the field of human rights, and the general knowledge and understanding of diverse cultures necessary for impartial, objective, non-selective and effective performance of the duties of the High Commissioner;

(b) Be appointed by the Secretary-General of the United Nations and approved by the General Assembly, with due regard to geographical rotation, and have a fixed term of four years with a possibility of one renewal for another fixed term of four years;

(c) Be of the rank of Under-Secretary-General;

3. Decides that the High Commissioner for Human Rights shall:

(a) Function within the framework of the Charter of the United Nations, the Universal Declaration of Human Rights, other international instruments of human rights and international law, including the obligations, within this framework, to respect the sovereignty, territorial integrity and domestic jurisdiction of States and to promote the universal respect for and observance of all human rights, in the recognition that, in the framework of the purposes and principles of the Charter, the promotion and protection of all human rights is a legitimate concern of the international community;

(b) Be guided by the recognition that all human rights—civil, cultural, economic, political and social—are universal, indivisible, interdependent and interrelated and that, while the significance of national and regional particularities and various historical, cultural and religious backgrounds must be borne in mind, it is the duty of States, regardless of their political, economic and cultural systems, to promote and protect all human rights and fundamental freedoms;

(c) Recognise the importance of promoting a balanced and sustainable development for all people and of ensuring realisation of the right to development, as established in the Declaration on the Right to Development;

4. Decides that the High Commissioner for Human Rights shall **11–004** be the United Nations official with principal responsibility for United Nations human rights activities under the direction and authority of the Secretary-General; within the framework of the overall competence, authority and decisions of the General Assembly, the Economic and Social Council and the Commission on Human Rights, the High Commissioner's responsibilities shall be:

(a) To promote and protect the effective enjoyment by all of all civil, cultural, economic, political and social rights;

(b) To carry out the tasks assigned to him/her by the competent bodies of the United Nations system in the field of human rights and to make recommendations to them with a view to improving the promotion and protection of all human rights;

(c) To promote and protect the realisation of the right to development and to enhance support from relevant bodies of the United Nations system for this purpose;

(d) To provide, through the Centre for Human Rights of the Secretariat and other appropriate institutions, advisory services and technical and financial assistance, at the request of the State concerned and, where appropriate, the regional human rights organisations, with a view to supporting actions and programmes in the field of human rights;

(e) To co-ordinate relevant United Nations education and public information programmes in the field of human rights;

(f) To play an active role in removing the current obstacles and in meeting the challenges to the full realisation of all human rights and in preventing the continuation of human rights violations throughout the world, as reflected in the Vienna Declaration and Programme of Action;

(g) To engage in a dialogue with all Governments in the implementation of his/her mandate with a view to securing respect for all human rights;

(h) To enhance international co-operation for the promotion and protection of all human rights;

(i) To co-ordinate the human rights promotion and protection activities throughout the United Nations system;

(j) To rationalise, adapt, strengthen and streamline the United Nations machinery in the field of human rights with a view to improving its efficiency and effectiveness;

(k) To carry out overall supervision of the Centre for Human Rights;

11–005   5. Requests the High Commissioner for Human Rights to report annually on his/her activities, in accordance with his/her mandate, to the Commission on Human Rights and, through the Economic and Social Council, to the General Assembly;

6. Decides that the Office of the High Commissioner for Human Rights shall be located at Geneva and shall have a liaison office in New York;

7. Requests the Secretary-General to provide appropriate staff and resources, within the existing and future regular budgets of the United Nations, to enable the High Commissioner to fulfil his/her mandate, without diverting resources from the development programmes and activities of the United Nations;

8. Also requests the Secretary-General to report to the General Assembly at its 49th session on the implementation of the present resolution.

On February 14, 1994 Mr Jose Ayala-Lasso was nominated as the first UN High Commissioner for Human Rights and on April 5, 1994 he took up his position at Geneva. Mr Jose Ayala-Lasso issued a statement on April 9, 1996 to the 52nd Commission on Human Rights in which he made the following observations.

. . . in keeping with the 1998 five year review of the implementation of the Vienna Declaration and Programme of Action I

will invite all the relevant United Nations agencies and programmes to carry out a thorough evaluation of that document.
1998 coincides with the 50th anniversary of the Universal
Declaration of Human Rights: it will be an important opportunity to widen support for human rights promotion and
protection world wide and to constructively engage the broader
human rights community both nationally and internationally.

. . . to fulfil the vision of the General Assembly, which in
December 1994 proclaimed the United Nations Decade for
Human Rights Education,[2] a plan of action has been put in place
focusing on stimulating and supporting local and national
activities. The plan encourages the establishment of national
committees for human rights education composed of human
rights representatives of both the public and private sectors. I
welcome the goals set by the Decade . . .

In keeping with the spirit and accepted principle of the universality of human rights, it is incumbent and evermore necessary
for States, collectively or individually to assert a greater financial
commitment to this cause. The challenges and dynamic nature of
human rights promotion and protection, further accelerated by
the adoption of the Vienna Declaration and Programme of Action
and the establishment of the office of the High Commissioner for
Human Rights necessitate commensurate political will and financial support . . .

As High Commissioner for Human Rights I would like to forge
a new alliance based on the spirit of co-operation and dialogue
among all the actors involved in the promotion and protection of
human rights, all working with one main objective in mind:
making human rights a reality.

My work is and remains focused on rendering international
human rights norms more operative and the action of the United
Nations Secretariat more responsive to meeting this objective.

A formidable challenge still lies ahead which must be
addressed in partnership with all those concerned with human
rights: we need a more substantive commitment to human rights
and perhaps less formalism. We need better dialogue among the
various relevant parts of the international system both within and
outside the United Nations to back up our intentions and aspirations in the fields of human rights and make them real.

To succeed in the implementation of the United Nations
programme will not only require that the necessary resources be
placed at the disposal of the High Commissioner but also that
greater co-ordination is achieved with the operational agencies
and programmes of the United Nations in order to bring human

---

[2] G.A. Res. 48/127, December 20, 1993. See below, para. 11–007.

rights and their enjoyment every day closer to the millions of women, children and men that still today are victims of violations.

In all my efforts I am guided by the spirit that made possible the Vienna Declaration and Programme of Action.

. . . The Commission on Human Rights . . . today more than ever before must not only be concerned with the identification of human rights problems but also with the realisation of the international standards it has set and the contribution the United Nations system must make towards their enjoyment.

HUMAN RIGHTS EDUCATION DECADE

**WORLD CONFERENCE ON HUMAN RIGHTS (JUNE 1993)
VIENNA DECLARATION**

PART II(D). HUMAN RIGHTS EDUCATION

11–006 **78.** The World Conference on Human Rights considers human rights education, training and public information essential for the promotion and achievement of stable and harmonious relations among communities and for fostering mutual understanding, tolerance and peace.

79. States should strive to eradicate illiteracy and should direct education towards the full development of the human personality and to the strengthening of respect for human rights and fundamental freedoms. The World Conference on Human Rights calls on all States and institutions to include human rights, humanitarian law, democracy and rule of law as subjects in the curricula of all learning institutions in formal and non-formal settings.

80. Human rights education should include peace, democracy, development and social justice, as set forth in international and regional human rights instruments, in order to achieve common understanding and awareness with a view to strengthening universal commitment to human rights.

81. Taking into account the World Plan of Action on Education for Human Rights and Democracy, adopted in March 1993 by the International Congress on Education for Human Rights and Democracy of the United Nations Educational, Scientific and Cultural Organisation, and other human rights instruments, the World Conference on Human Rights recommends that States develop specific programmes and strategies for ensuring the widest human rights education and the dissemination of public information, taking particular account of the human rights needs of women.

82. Governments, with the assistance of intergovernmental organisations, national institutions and non-governmental organisations, should promote an increased awareness of human rights and mutual tolerance. The World Conference on Human Rights underlines the importance of strengthening the World Public Information Campaign for Human Rights carried out by the United Nations. They should initiate and support education in human rights and undertake effective dissemination of public information in this field. The advisory services and technical assistance programmes of the United Nations system should be able to respond immediately to requests from States for educational and training activities in the field of human rights as well as for special education concerning standards as contained in international human rights instruments and in humanitarian law and their application to special groups such as military forces, law enforcement personnel, police and the health profession. The proclamation of a United Nations decade for human rights education in order to promote, encourage and focus these educational activities should be considered.

HUMAN RIGHTS EDUCATION DECADE[3]

The General Assembly, 11–007

Guided by the fundamental and universal principles enshrined in the Charter of the United Nations and the Universal Declaration of Human Rights,

Reaffirming Article 26 of the Universal Declaration of Human Rights, . . .

Recalling the provisions of other international human rights instruments, . . .

Convinced that human rights education is a universal priority in that it contributes to a concept of development consistent with the dignity of the human person, which must include consideration of the diversity of groups such as children, women, youths, persons with disabilities, the ageing, indigenous people, minorities and other groups,

Aware that human rights education involves more than providing information but rather is a comprehensive life-long process by which people at all levels of development and in all strata of society learn respect for the dignity of others and the means and methods of ensuring that respect within a democratic society,

Taking into account the efforts made by educators and non-governmental organisations in all parts of the world, as well as by intergovernmental organisations, . . .

Considering the World Plan of Action on Education for Human Rights and Democracy, adopted by the International Congress on Education for Human Rights and Democracy, convened by the

[3] See *supra* n. 2.

United Nations Educational, Scientific and Cultural Organisation at Montreal from March 8 to 11, 1993, and the statement by the Congress that education for human rights and democracy is itself a human right, and a prerequisite for the realisation of human rights, democracy and social justice,

Aware of the experience in human rights education of United Nations peace-building operations, . . .

Bearing in mind the Vienna Declaration and Programme of Action, adopted by the World Conference on Human Rights at Vienna on June 25, 1993, in particular section II, paragraphs 78 to 82,

1. Appeals to all Governments to step up their efforts to eradicate illiteracy and to direct education towards the full development of the human personality and to the strengthening of respect for human rights and fundamental freedoms;

2. Urges governmental and non-governmental educational agencies to intensify their efforts to establish and implement programmes of human rights education, as recommended in the Vienna Declaration and Programme of Action;

3. Takes note of the World Plan of Action on Education for Human Rights and Democracy adopted by the International Congress on Education for Human Rights and Democracy, and recommends that Governments and non-governmental organisations consider it in preparing national plans for human rights education;

4. . . .

5. Requests the Secretary-General to consider the establishment of a voluntary fund for human rights education, with special provision for the support of the human rights education activities of non-governmental organisations, to be administered by the Centre for Human Rights of the Secretariat;

6. Invites the specialised agencies and United Nations programmes to develop suitable activities in their respective fields of competence to further the objectives of human rights education;

7. Requests the Secretary-General to bring the present resolution to the attention of all members of the international community and to intergovernmental and non-governmental organisations concerned with human rights and education;

8. Calls upon international, regional and national non-governmental organisations, in particular those concerned with women, labour, development and the environment, as well as all other social justice groups, human rights advocates, educators, religious organisations and the media, to increase their involvement in formal and non-formal education in human rights and to co-operate with the Centre for Human Rights in preparing for a United Nations decade for human rights education;

9. Urges the existing human rights monitoring bodies to place particular emphasis on the implementation by Member States of their international obligation to promote human rights education;

10. . . .

CONCLUSION

POST VIENNA

A review of the progress made towards implementation of the Vienna Declaration took place in 1998. The conclusion was then and still holds true that implementation of human rights throughout the world has been inconsistent. On a positive note the end of apartheid in South Africa and the emergence of democratic government in Central and Eastern Europe symbolise advances made towards "making human rights a reality".[4] Conversely national laws remain in force and new legislation is adopted which discriminates against women, fails to recognise economic, social and cultural rights and does not adequately protect individuals in penal proceedings. Additionally grave human rights violations affecting large numbers of people frequently occur worldwide.

It is apparent that there is a growing recognition that what is required is not more substantive human rights but rather more effective implementation of the existing instruments. This is evidenced by the absence of any such new instruments, the developments being focused on refining existing rights and better means of enforcing them. The need for effective monitoring of human rights has brought the efficacy of the existing United Nations human rights treaty system into the spot light. It is recognised that the current system of monitoring by the bodies created to oversee the implementation of the treaties is cumbersome and protracted and that a streamlining of the various mechanism is demanded. The format of such a streamlining has yet to be decided.[5]

Improvements to the treaty system will only be effective if they are made in the context of a developing culture of human rights. Such a culture will only evolve and be sustained if current and future generations receive an education informed by human rights. This is characterised by the UN High Commissioner as "an ultimate break through in the global promotion and protection of

11–008

---

[4] Note by the United Nations Secretary-General, September 11, 1998 on presenting the Report of the United Nations High Commissioner for Human Rights, to the General Assembly.

[5] See The UN Human Rights System. Universality at the Crossroads, Professor Anne Bayefsky. Report carried out in collaboration with UNHCR. Available from Transnational Publishers (June 2001). The Report makes a number of recommendations designed to improve the existing Treaty system.

human rights, which should be the overall goal of the United Nations human rights programme in the twenty-first century"

In the conclusion to the first edition of this text it was observed that the "historic potentials" of the Vienna Declaration demanded the political will and co-ordinated efforts of governments, international organisations and human rights bodies, national human rights institutions and non governmental organisations. That same political will requires to be as evident today as at any time previously in order to make realisation of the goals of the Vienna Declaration a reality. In the words of the High Commissioner the Vienna Declaration "should continue to chart the course of human rights activities throughout the world in the years to come."

CHARTER OF THE UNITED NATIONS 1945[1]

The purposes of the United Nations are:

3. . . . promoting and encouraging respect for human rights and A1–001 for fundamental freedoms for all without distinction to race, sex, language or religion;

Article 55

With a view to the creation of conditions of stability and well being which are necessary for peaceful and friendly relations among nations based on respect for principle of equal rights and self-determination of peoples, the United Nations shall promote:

. . .

    (c) universal respect for, and observance of, human rights and fundamental freedoms for all without distinction as to race, sex, language, or religion.

Article 56

All members pledge themselves to take joint and separate action in co-operation with the Organisation for the achievement of the purposes set forth in Article 55.

UNIVERSAL DECLARATION OF HUMAN RIGHTS[2]

Preamble

Whereas recognition of the inherent dignity and of the equal and A1–002 inalienable rights of all members of the human family is the foundation of freedom, justice and peace in the world,

Whereas disregard and contempt for human rights have resulted in barbarous acts which have outraged the conscience of mankind, and the advent of a world in which human beings shall enjoy freedom of speech and belief and freedom from fear and want has been proclaimed as the highest aspiration of the common people,

---

[1] U.N.T.S. xvi; U.K.T.S. 67 (1946), Cmd. 7015.
[2] G.A. Res. 217A(III), UN Doc. A/810 at 71 (1948).

Whereas it is essential, if man is not to be compelled to have recourse, as a last resort, to rebellion against tyranny and oppression, that human rights should be protected by the rule of law,

Whereas it is essential to promote the development of friendly relations between nations,

Whereas the peoples of the United Nations have in the Charter reaffirmed their faith in fundamental human rights, in the dignity and worth of the human person and in the equal rights of men and women and have determined to promote social progress and better standards of life in larger freedom,

Whereas Member States have pledged themselves to achieve, in co-operation with the United Nations, the promotion of universal respect for and observance of human rights and fundamental freedoms,

Whereas a common understanding of these rights and freedoms is of the greatest importance for the full realisation of this pledge,

Now, therefore,

The General Assembly,

Proclaims this Universal Declaration of Human Rights as a common standard of achievement for all peoples and all nations, to the end that every individual and every organ of society, keeping this Declaration constantly in mind, shall strive by teaching and education to promote respect for these rights and freedoms and by progressive measures, national and international, to secure their universal and effective recognition and observance, both among the peoples of Member States themselves and among the peoples of territories under their jurisdiction.

Article 1

A1–003   All human beings are born free and equal in dignity and rights. They are endowed with reason and conscience and should act towards one another in a spirit of brotherhood.

Article 2

Everyone is entitled to all the rights and freedoms set forth in this Declaration, without distinction of any kind, such as race, colour, sex, language, religion, political or other opinion, national or social origin, property, birth or other status.

Furthermore, no distinction shall be made on the basis of the political, jurisdictional or international status of the country or territory to which a person belongs, whether it be independent, trust, non-self-governing or under any other limitation of sovereignty.

Article 3

Everyone has the right to life, liberty and security of person.

Article 4

No one shall be held in slavery or servitude; slavery and the slave trade shall be prohibited in all their forms.

Article 5

No one shall be subjected to torture or to cruel, inhuman or **A1–004** degrading treatment or punishment.

Article 6

Everyone has the right to recognition everywhere as a person before the law.

Article 7

All are equal before the law and are entitled without any discrimination to equal protection of the law. All are entitled to equal protection against any discrimination in violation of this Declaration and against any incitement to such discrimination.

Article 8

Everyone has the right to an effective remedy by the competent national tribunals for acts violating the fundamental rights granted him by the constitution or by law.

Article 9

No one shall be subjected to arbitrary arrest, detention or exile. **A1–005**

Article 10

Everyone is entitled in full equality to a fair and public hearing by an independent and impartial tribunal, in the determination of his rights and obligations and of any criminal charge against him.

Article 11

1. Everyone charged with a penal offence has the right to be presumed innocent until proved guilty according to law in a public trial at which he has had all the guarantees necessary for his defence.

2. No one shall be held guilty of any penal offence on account of any act or omission which did not constitute a penal offence, under national or international law, at the time when it was

committed. Nor shall a heavier penalty be imposed than the one
that was applicable at the time the penal offence was committed.

Article 12

A1–006 No one shall be subjected to arbitrary interference with his
privacy, family, home or correspondence, nor to attacks upon his
honour and reputation. Everyone has the right to the protection
of the law against such interference or attacks.

Article 13

1. Everyone has the right to freedom of movement and residence within the borders of each State.
2. Everyone has the right to leave any country, including his
own, and to return to his country. . . .

Article 20

1. Everyone has the right to freedom of peaceful assembly and
association.
2. No one may be compelled to belong to an association.

Article 21

1. Everyone has the right to take part in the government of his
country, directly or through freely chosen representatives.
2. Everyone has the right to equal access to public service in his
country.
3. The will of the people shall be the basis of the authority of
government; this will shall be expressed in periodic and genuine
elections which shall be by universal and equal suffrage and shall
be held by secret vote or by equivalent free voting procedures.

Article 22

A1–007 Everyone, as a member of society, has the right to social security
and is entitled to realisation, through national effort and international co-operation and in accordance with the organisation
and resources of each State, of the economic, social and cultural
rights indispensable for his dignity and the free development of
his personality.

Article 23

1. Everyone has the right to work, to free choice of employment, to just and favourable conditions of work and to protection
against unemployment.

2. Everyone, without any discrimination, has the right to equal pay for equal work.

3. Everyone who works has the right to just and favourable remuneration ensuring for himself and his family an existence worthy of human dignity, and supplemented, if necessary, by other means of social protection.

4. Everyone has the right to form and to join trade unions for the protection of his interests.

Article 24

Everyone has the right to rest and leisure, including reasonable **A1–008** limitation of working hours and periodic holidays with pay.

Article 25

1. Everyone has the right to a standard of living adequate for the health and well-being of himself and of his family, including food, clothing, housing and medical care and necessary social services, and the right to security in the event of unemployment, sickness, disability, widowhood, old age or other lack of livelihood in circumstances beyond his control.

2. Motherhood and childhood are entitled to special care and assistance. All children, whether born in or out of wedlock, shall enjoy the same social protection.

Article 26

1. Everyone has the right to education. Education shall be free, at least in the elementary and fundamental stages. Elementary education shall be compulsory. Technical and professional education shall be made generally available and higher education shall be equally accessible to all on the basis of merit.

2. Education shall be directed to the full development of the human personality and to the strengthening of respect for human rights and fundamental freedoms. It shall promote understanding, tolerance and friendship among all nations, racial or religious groups, and shall further the activities of the United Nations for the maintenance of peace.

3. Parents have a prior right to choose the kind of education that shall be given to their children.

Article 27

1. Everyone has the right freely to participate in the cultural life **A1–009** of the community, to enjoy the arts and to share in scientific advancement and its benefits.

2. Everyone has the right to the protection of the moral and material interests resulting from any scientific, literary or artistic production of which he is the author.

Article 28

Everyone is entitled to a social and international order in which the rights and freedoms set forth in this Declaration can be fully realised.

Article 29

1. Everyone has duties to the community in which alone the free and full development of his personality is possible.

2. In the exercise of his rights and freedoms, everyone shall be subject only to such limitations as are determined by law solely for the purpose of securing due recognition and respect for the rights and freedoms of others and of meeting the just requirements of morality, public order and the general welfare in a democratic society.

3. These rights and freedoms may in no case be exercised contrary to the purposes and principles of the United Nations.

Article 30

Nothing in this Declaration may be interpreted as implying for any State, group or person any right to engage in any activity or to perform any act aimed at the destruction of any of the rights and freedoms set forth herein.

INTERNATIONAL COVENANT ON CIVIL AND POLITICAL RIGHTS[3]

Preamble

A1–010   The States Parties to the present Covenant,

Considering that, in accordance with the principles proclaimed in the Charter of the United Nations, recognition of the inherent dignity and of the equal and inalienable rights of all members of the human family is the foundation of freedom, justice and peace in the world,

Recognising that these rights derive from the inherent dignity of the human person,

---

[3] G.A. Res. 21/2200A, G.A.O.R., 21st Session, Supp., p. 52, UN Doc. A/6316 (1966), 999 U.N.T.S. 171, entered into force March 23, 1976. Currently there are 147 Contracting Parties.

Recognising that, in accordance with the Universal Declaration of Human Rights, the ideal of free human beings enjoying civil and political freedom and freedom from fear and want can only be achieved if conditions are created whereby everyone may enjoy his civil and political rights, as well as his economic, social and cultural rights,

Considering the obligation of States under the Charter of the United Nations to promote universal respect for, and observance of, human rights and freedoms,

Realising that the individual, having duties to other individuals and to the community to which he belongs, is under a responsibility to strive for the promotion and observance of the rights recognised in the present Covenant,

Agree upon the following articles:

Part I

Article 1

1. All peoples have the right of self-determination. By virtue of **A1–011** that right they freely determine their political status and freely pursue their economic, social and cultural development.

2. All peoples may, for their own ends, freely dispose of their natural wealth and resources without prejudice to any obligations arising out of international economic co-operation, based upon the principle of mutual benefit, and international law. In no case may a people be deprived of its own means of subsistence.

3. The States Parties to the present Covenant, including those having responsibility for the administration of Non-Self-Governing and Trust Territories, shall promote the realisation of the right of self-determination, and shall respect that right, in conformity with the provisions of the Charter of the United Nations.

Part II

Article 2

1. Each State Party to the present Covenant undertakes to **A1–012** respect and to ensure to all individuals within its territory and subject to its jurisdiction the rights recognised in the present Covenant, without distinction of any kind, such as race, colour, sex, language, religion, political or other opinion, national or social origin, property, birth or other status.

2. Where not already provided for by existing legislative or other measures, each State Party to the present Covenant undertakes to take the necessary steps, in accordance with its constitutional processes and with the provisions of the present Covenant, to adopt such legislative or other measures as may be necessary to give effect to the rights recognised in the present Covenant.

3. Each State Party to the present Covenant undertakes:

(a) To ensure that any person whose rights or freedoms as herein recognised are violated shall have an effective remedy, notwithstanding that the violation has been committed by persons acting in an official capacity;

(b) To ensure that any person claiming such a remedy shall have his right thereto determined by competent judicial, administrative or legislative authorities, or by any other competent authority provided for by the legal system of the State, and to develop the possibilities of judicial remedy;

(c) To ensure that the competent authorities shall enforce such remedies when granted.

Article 3

A1–013 The States Parties to the present Covenant undertake to ensure the equal right of men and women to the enjoyment of all civil and political right set forth in the present Covenant.

Article 4

1. In time of public emergency which threatens the life of the nation and the existence of which is officially proclaimed, the States Parties to the present Covenant may take measures derogating from their obligations under the present Covenant to the extent strictly required by the exigencies of the situation, provided that such measures are not inconsistent with their other obligations under international law and do not involve discrimination solely on the ground of race, colour, sex, language, religion or social origin.

2. No derogation from articles 6, 7, 8 (paragraphs 1 and 2), 11, 15, 16 and 18 may be made under this provision.

3. Any State Party to the present Covenant availing itself of the right of derogation shall immediately inform the other States Parties to the present Covenant, through the intermediary of the Secretary-General of the United Nations, of the provisions from which it has derogated and of the reasons by which it was actuated. A further communication shall be made, through the same intermediary, on the date on which it terminates such derogation.

Article 5

1. Nothing in the present Covenant may be interpreted as implying for any State, group or person any right to engage in

any activity or perform any act aimed at the destruction of any of the rights and freedoms recognised herein or at their limitation to a greater extent than is provided for in the present Covenant.

2. There shall be no restriction upon or derogation from any of the fundamental human rights recognised or existing in any State Party to the present Covenant pursuant to law, conventions, regulations or custom on the pretext that the present Covenant does not recognise such rights or that it recognises them to a lesser extent.

Part III

Article 6

1. Every human being has the inherent right to life. This right A1–014 shall be protected by law. No one shall be arbitrarily deprived of his life.

2. In countries which have not abolished the death penalty, sentence of death may be imposed only for the most serious crimes in accordance with the law in force at the time of the commission of the crime and not contrary to the provisions of the present Covenant and to the Convention on the Prevention and Punishment of the Crime of Genocide. This penalty can only be carried out pursuant to a final judgement rendered by a competent court.

3. When deprivation of life constitutes the crime of genocide, it is understood that nothing in this article shall authorise any State Party to the present Covenant to derogate in any way from any obligation assumed under the provisions of the Convention on the Prevention and Punishment of the Crime of Genocide.

4. Anyone sentenced to death shall have the right to seek pardon or commutation of the sentence. Amnesty, pardon or commutation of the sentence of death may be granted in all cases.

5. Sentence of death shall not be imposed for crimes committed by persons below 18 years of age and shall not be carried out on pregnant women.

6. Nothing in this article shall be invoked to delay or to prevent the abolition of capital punishment by any State Party to the present Covenant.

Article 7

No one shall be subjected to torture or to cruel, inhuman or A1–015 degrading treatment or punishment. In particular, no one shall be subjected without his free consent to medical or scientific experimentation.

Article 8

1. No one shall be held in slavery; slavery and the slave-trade in all their forms shall be prohibited.

2. No one shall be held in servitude.

3. (a) No one shall be required to perform forced or compulsory labour;

(b) Paragraph 3(a) shall not be held to preclude, in countries where imprisonment with hard labour may be imposed as a punishment for a crime, the performance of hard labour in pursuance of a sentence to such punishment by a competent court;

(c) For the purpose of this paragraph the term "forced or compulsory labour" shall not include:

(i) Any work or service, not referred to in subparagraph (b), normally required of a person who is under detention in consequence of a lawful order of a court, or of a person during conditional release from such detention;

(ii) Any service of a military character and, in countries where conscientious objection is recognised, any national service required by law of conscientious objectors;

(iii) Any service exacted in cases of emergency or calamity threatening the life or well-being of the community;

(iv) Any work or service which forms part of normal civil obligations.

Article 9

A1–016   **1.** Everyone has the right to liberty and security of person. No one shall be subjected to arbitrary arrest or detention. No one shall be deprived of his liberty except on such grounds and in accordance with such procedure as are established by law.

2. Anyone who is arrested shall be informed, at the time of arrest, of the reasons for his arrest and shall be promptly informed of any charges against him.

3. Anyone arrested or detained on a criminal charge shall be brought promptly before a judge or other officer authorised by law to exercise judicial power and shall be entitled to trial within a reasonable time or to release. It shall not be the general rule that persons awaiting trial shall be detained in custody, but release may be subject to guarantees to appear for trial, at any other stage of the judicial proceedings, and, should occasion arise, for execution of the judgment.

4. Anyone who is deprived of his liberty by arrest or detention shall be entitled to take proceedings before a court, in order that court may decide without delay on the lawfulness of his detention and order his release if the detention is not lawful.

5. Anyone who has been the victim of unlawful arrest or detention shall have an enforceable right to compensation.

Article 10

1. All persons deprived of their liberty shall be treated with humanity and with respect for the inherent dignity of the human person.

2. (a) Accused persons shall, save in exceptional circumstances, be segregated from convicted persons and shall be subject to separate treatment appropriate to their status as unconvicted persons;

(b) Accused juvenile persons shall be separated from adults and brought as speedily as possible for adjudication.

3. The penitentiary system shall comprise treatment of prisoners the essential aim of which shall be their reformation and social rehabilitation. Juvenile offenders shall be segregated from adults and be accorded treatment appropriate to their age and legal status.

Article 11

No one shall be imprisoned merely on the ground of inability to **A1–017** fulfil a contractual obligation.

Article 12

1. Everyone lawfully within the territory of a State shall, within that territory, have the right to liberty of movement and freedom to choose his residence.

2. Everyone shall be free to leave any country, including his own.

3. The above-mentioned rights shall not be subject to any restrictions except those which are provided by law, are necessary to protect national security, public order (ordre public), public health or morals or the rights and freedoms of others, and are consistent with the other rights recognised in the present Covenant.

4. No one shall be arbitrarily deprived of the right to enter his own country.

Article 13

An alien lawfully in the territory of a State Party to the present **A1–018** Covenant may be expelled therefrom only in pursuance of a decision reached in accordance with law and shall, except where compelling reasons of national security otherwise require, be allowed to submit the reasons against his expulsion and to have his case reviewed by, and be represented for the purpose before, the competent authority or a person or persons especially designated by the competent authority.

Article 14

1. All persons shall be equal before the courts and tribunals. In the determination of any criminal charge against him, or of his rights and obligations in a suit at law, everyone shall be entitled to a fair and public hearing by a competent, independent and impartial tribunal established by law. The press and the public may be excluded from all or part of a trial for reasons of morals, public order (ordre public) or national security in a democratic society, or when the interest of the private lives of the parties so requires, or to the extent strictly necessary in the opinion of the court in special circumstances where publicity would prejudice the interests of justice; but any judgement rendered in a criminal case or in a suit at law shall be made public except where the interest of juvenile persons otherwise requires or the proceedings concern matrimonial disputes or the guardianship of children.

2. Everyone charged with a criminal offence shall have the right to be presumed innocent until proved guilty according to law.

3. In the determination of any criminal charge against him, everyone shall be entitled to the following minimum guarantees, in full equality:

(a) To be informed promptly and in detail in a language which he understands of the nature and cause of the charge against him;

(b) To have adequate time and facilities for the preparation of his defence and to communicate with counsel of his own choosing;

(c) To be tried without undue delay;

(d) To be tried in his presence, and to defend himself in person or through legal assistance of his own choosing; to be informed, if he does not have legal assistance, of this right; and to have legal assistance assigned to him, in any case where the interests of justice so require, and without payment by him in any such case if he does not have sufficient means to pay for it;

(e) To examine, or have examined, the witnesses against him and to obtain the attendance and examination of witnesses on his behalf under the same conditions as witnesses against him;

(f) To have the free assistance of an interpreter if he cannot understand or speak the language used in court;

(g) Not to be compelled to testify against himself or to confess guilt.

4. In the case of juvenile persons, the procedure shall be such as will take account of their age and the desirability of promoting their rehabilitation.

5. Everyone convicted of a crime shall have the right to his conviction and sentence being reviewed by a higher tribunal according to law.

6. When a person has by a final decision been convicted of a criminal offence and when subsequently his conviction has been reversed or he has been pardoned on the ground that a new or newly discovered fact shows conclusively that there has been a miscarriage of justice, the person who has suffered punishment as a result of such conviction shall be compensated according to law, unless it is proved that the non-disclosure of the unknown fact in time is wholly or partly attributable to him.

7. No one shall be liable to be tried or punished again for an offence for which he has already been finally convicted or acquitted in accordance with the law and penal procedure of each country.

Article 15

1. No one shall be held guilty of any criminal offence on **A1–019** account of any act or omission which did not constitute a criminal offence, under national or international law, at the time when it was committed. Nor shall a heavier penalty be imposed than the one that was applicable at the time when the criminal offence was committed. If, subsequent to the commission of the offence, provision is made by law for the imposition of the lighter penalty, the offender shall benefit thereby.

2. Nothing in this article shall prejudice the trial and punishment of any person for any act or omission which, at the time when it was committed, was criminal according to the general principles of law recognised by the community of nations.

Article 16

Everyone shall have the right to recognition everywhere as a person before the law.

Article 17

1. No one shall be subjected to arbitrary or unlawful interference with his privacy, family, home or correspondence, nor to unlawful attacks on his honour and reputation.

2. Everyone has the right to the protection of the law against such interference or attacks.

Article 18

A1–020   **1.** Everyone shall have the right to freedom of thought, conscience and religion. This right shall include freedom to have or to adopt a religion or belief of his choice, and freedom, either individually or in community with others and in public or private, to manifest his religion or belief in worship, observance, practice and teaching.

2. No one shall be subject to coercion which would impair his freedom to have or to adopt a religion or belief of his choice.

3. Freedom to manifest one's religion or beliefs may be subject only to such limitations as are prescribed by law and are necessary to protect public safety, order, health, or morals or the fundamental rights and freedoms of others.

4. The States Parties to the present Covenant undertake to have respect for the liberty of parents and, when applicable, legal guardians to ensure the religious and moral education of their children in conformity with their own convictions.

Article 19

1. Everyone shall have the right to hold opinions without interference.

2. Everyone shall have the right to freedom of expression; this right shall include freedom to seek, receive and impart information and ideas of all kinds, regardless of frontiers, either orally, in writing or in print, in the form of art, or through any other media of his choice.

3. The exercise of the rights provided for in paragraph 2 of this article carries with it special duties and responsibilities. It may therefore be subject to certain restrictions, but these shall only be such as are provided by law and are necessary:

(a) For respect of the rights or reputations of others;
(b) For the protection of national security or of public order (ordre public), or of public health or morals.

Article 20

A1–021   **1.** Any propaganda for war shall be prohibited by law.

2. Any advocacy of national, racial or religious hatred that constitutes incitement to discrimination, hostility or violence shall be prohibited by law.

Article 21

The right of peaceful assembly shall be recognised. No restrictions may be placed on the exercise of this right other than those imposed in conformity with the law and which are necessary in a democratic society in the interests of national security or public safety, public order (ordre public), the protection of public health or morals or the protection of the rights and freedoms of others.

Article 22

1. Everyone shall have the right to freedom of association with others, including the right to form and join trade unions for the protection of his interests.

2. No restrictions may be placed on the exercise of this right other than those which are prescribed by law and which are necessary in a democratic society in the interests of national security or public safety, public order (ordre public), the protection of public health or morals or the protection of the rights and freedoms of others. This article shall not prevent the imposition of lawful restrictions on members of the armed forces and of the police in their exercise of this right.

3. Nothing in this article shall authorise States Parties to the International Labour Organisation Convention of 1948 concerning Freedom of Association and Protection of the Right to Organise to take legislative measures which would prejudice, or to apply the law in such a manner as to prejudice, the guarantees provided for in that Convention.

Article 23

1. The family is the natural and fundamental group unit of **A1–022** society and is entitled to protection by society and the State.

2. The right of men and women of marriageable age to marry and to found a family shall be recognised.

3. No marriage shall be entered into without the free and full consent of the intending spouses.

4. States Parties to the present Covenant shall take appropriate steps to ensure equality of rights and responsibilities of spouses as to marriage, during marriage and at its dissolution. In the case of dissolution, provision shall be made for the necessary protection of any children.

Article 24

1. Every child shall have, without any discrimination as to race, colour, sex, language, religion, national or social origin, property or birth, the right to such measures of protection as are required by his status as a minor, on the part of his family, society and the State.

2. Every child shall be registered immediately after birth and shall have a name.

3. Every child has the right to acquire a nationality.

Article 25

Every citizen shall have the right and the opportunity, without any of the distinctions mentioned in article 2 and without unreasonable restrictions:

(a) To take part in the conduct of public affairs, directly or through freely chosen representatives;

(b) To vote and to be elected at genuine periodic elections which shall be by universal and equal suffrage and shall be held by secret ballot, guaranteeing the free expression of the will of the electors;

(c) To have access, on general terms of equality, to public service in his country.

Article 26

A1–023 All persons are equal before the law and are entitled without any discrimination to the equal protection of the law. In this respect, the law shall prohibit any discrimination and guarantee to all persons equal and effective protection against discrimination on any ground such as race, colour, sex, language, religion, political or other opinion, national or social origin, property, birth or other status.

Article 27

In those States in which ethnic, religious or linguistic minorities exist, persons belonging to such minorities shall not be denied the right, in community with the other members of their group, to enjoy their own culture, to profess and practise their own religion, or to use their own language.

Part IV

Article 28

A1–024   **1.** There shall be established a Human Rights Committee (hereafter referred to in the present Covenant as the Committee). It shall consist of eighteen members and shall carry out the functions hereinafter provided.

2. The Committee shall be composed of nationals of the States Parties to the present Covenant who shall be persons of high moral character and recognised competence in the field of human rights, consideration being given to the usefulness of the participation of some persons having legal experience.

3. The members of the Committee shall be elected and shall serve in their personal capacity.

Article 29

1. The members of the Committee shall be elected by secret ballot from a list of persons possessing the qualifications prescribed in article 28 and nominated for the purpose by the States Parties to the present Covenant.

2. Each State Party to the present Covenant may nominate not more than two persons. These persons shall be nationals of the nominating State.

3. A person shall be eligible for renomination.

Article 30

1. The initial election shall be held no later than six months **A1–025** after the date of the entry into force of the present Covenant.

2. At least four months before the date of each election to the Committee, other than an election to fill a vacancy declared in accordance with article 34, the Secretary-General of the United Nations shall address a written invitation to the States Parties to the present Covenant to submit their nominations for membership of the Committee within three months.

3. The Secretary-General of the United Nations shall prepare a list in alphabetical order of all the persons thus nominated, with an indication of the States Parties which have nominated them, and shall submit it to the States Parties to the present Covenant no later than one month before the date of each election.

4. Elections of the members of the Committee shall be held at a meeting of the States Parties to the present Covenant convened by the Secretary General of the United Nations at the Headquarters of the United Nations. At that meeting, for which two thirds of the States Parties to the present Covenant shall constitute a quorum, the persons elected to the Committee shall be those nominees who obtain the largest number of votes and an absolute majority of the votes of the representatives of States Parties present and voting.

Article 31

1. The Committee may not include more than one national of the same State.

2. In the election of the Committee, consideration shall be given to equitable geographical distribution of membership and to the

representation of the different forms of civilisation and of the principal legal systems.

Article 32

A1–026   1. The members of the Committee shall be elected for a term of four years. They shall be eligible for re-election if renominated. However, the terms of nine of the members elected at the first election shall expire at the end of two years; immediately after the first election, the names of these nine members shall be chosen by lot by the Chairman of the meeting referred to in article 30, paragraph 4.

2. Elections at the expiry of office shall be held in accordance with the preceding articles of this part of the present Covenant.

Article 33

1. If, in the unanimous opinion of the other members, a member of the Committee has ceased to carry out his functions for any cause other than absence of a temporary character, the Chairman of the Committee shall notify the Secretary-General of the United Nations, who shall then declare the seat of that member to be vacant.

2. In the event of the death or the resignation of a member of the Committee, the Chairman shall immediately notify the Secretary-General of the United Nations, who shall declare the seat vacant from the date of death or the date on which the resignation takes effect.

Article 34

A1–027   1. When a vacancy is declared in accordance with Article 33 and if the term of office of the member to be replaced does not expire within six months of the declaration of the vacancy, the Secretary-General of the United Nations shall notify each of the States Parties to the present Covenant, which may within two months submit nominations in accordance with Article 29 for the purpose of filling the vacancy.

2. The Secretary-General of the United Nations shall prepare a list in alphabetical order of the persons thus nominated and shall submit it to the States Parties to the present Covenant. The election to fill the vacancy shall then take place in accordance with the relevant provisions of this part of the present Covenant.

3. A member of the Committee elected to fill a vacancy declared in accordance with Article 33 shall hold office for the remainder of the term of the member who vacated the seat on the Committee under the provisions of that article.

Article 35

The members of the Committee shall, with the approval of the General Assembly of the United Nations, receive emoluments from United Nations resources on such terms and conditions as the General Assembly may decide, having regard to the importance of the Committee's responsibilities.

Article 36

The Secretary-General of the United Nations shall provide the necessary staff and facilities for the effective performance of the functions of the Committee under the present Covenant.

Article 37

1. The Secretary-General of the United Nations shall convene the initial meeting of the Committee at the Headquarters of the United Nations.

2. After its initial meeting, the Committee shall meet at such times as shall be provided in its rules of procedure.

3. The Committee shall normally meet at the Headquarters of the United Nations or at the United Nations Office at Geneva.

Article 38

Every member of the Committee shall, before taking up his **A1–028** duties, make a solemn declaration in open committee that he will perform his functions impartially and conscientiously.

Article 39

1. The Committee shall elect its officers for a term of two years. They may be re-elected.

2. The Committee shall establish its own rules of procedure, but these rules shall provide, *inter alia*, that:

   (a) Twelve members shall constitute a quorum;

   (b) Decisions of the Committee shall be made by a majority vote of the members present.

Article 40

1. The States Parties to the present Covenant undertake to submit reports on the measures they have adopted which give effect to the rights recognised herein and on the progress made in the enjoyment of those rights:

(a) Within one year of the entry into force of the present Covenant for the States Parties concerned;

(b) Thereafter whenever the Committee so requests.

2. All reports shall be submitted to the Secretary-General of the United Nations, who shall transmit them to the Committee for consideration. Reports shall indicate the factors and difficulties, if any, affecting the implementation of the present Covenant.

3. The Secretary-General of the United Nations may, after consultation with the Committee, transmit to the specialised agencies concerned copies of such parts of the reports as may fall within their field of competence.

4. The Committee shall study the reports submitted by the States Parties to the present Covenant. It shall transmit its reports, and such general comments as it may consider appropriate, to the States Parties. The Committee may also transmit to the Economic and Social Council these comments along with the copies of the reports it has received from States Parties to the present Covenant.

5. The States Parties to the present Covenant may submit to the Committee observations on any comments that may be made in accordance with paragraph 4 of this article.

Article 41

A1–029   1. A State Party to the present Covenant may at any time declare under this article that it recognises the competence of the Committee to receive and consider communications to the effect that a State Party claims that another State Party is not fulfilling its obligations under the present Covenant.

A1–030   Communications under this article may be received and considered only if submitted by a State Party which has made a declaration recognising in regard to itself the competence of the Committee.

No communication shall be received by the Committee if it concerns a State Party which has not made such a declaration. Communications received under this article shall be dealt with in accordance with the following procedure:

(a) If a State Party to the present Covenant considers that another State Party is not giving effect to the provisions of the present Covenant, it may, by written communication, bring the matter to the attention of that State Party. Within three months after the receipt of the communication the receiving State shall afford the State which sent the communication an explanation, or any other statement in writing clarifying the matter which should include, to the extent possible and pertinent, reference to domestic procedures and remedies taken, pending, or available in the matter;

(b) If the matter is not adjusted to the satisfaction of both States Parties concerned within six months after the receipt by the receiving State of the initial communication, either State shall have the right to refer the matter to the Committee, by notice given to the Committee and to the other State;

(c) The Committee shall deal with a matter referred to it only after it has ascertained that all available domestic remedies have been invoked and exhausted in the matter, in conformity with the generally recognised principles of international law. This shall not be the rule where the application of the remedies is unreasonably prolonged;

(d) The Committee shall hold closed meetings when examining communications under this article;

(e) Subject to the provisions of sub-paragraph (c), the Committee shall make available its good offices to the States Parties concerned with a view to a friendly solution of the matter on the basis of respect for human rights and fundamental freedoms as recognised in the present Covenant;

(f) In any matter referred to it, the Committee may call upon the States Parties concerned, referred to in sub-paragraph (b), to supply any relevant information;

(g) The States Parties concerned, referred to in sub-paragraph (b), shall have the right to be represented when the matter is being considered in the Committee and to make submissions orally and/or in writing;

(h) The Committee shall, within twelve months after the date of receipt of notice under sub-paragraph (b), submit a report:

(i) If a solution within the terms of sub-paragraph (e) is reached, the Committee shall confine its report to a brief statement of the facts and of the solution reached;

(ii) If a solution within the terms of sub-paragraph (e) is not reached, the Committee shall confine its report to a brief statement of the facts; the written submissions and record of the oral submissions made by the States Parties concerned shall be attached to the report.

In every matter, the report shall be communicated to the States Parties concerned.

2. The provisions of this article shall come into force when ten States Parties to the present Covenant have made declarations under paragraph I of this article. Such declarations shall be deposited by the States Parties with the Secretary-General of the United Nations, who shall transmit copies thereof to the other States Parties. A declaration may be withdrawn at any time by notification to the Secretary-General. Such a withdrawal shall not prejudice the consideration of any matter which is the subject of a communication already transmitted under this article; no further communication by any State Party shall be received after the notification of withdrawal of the declaration has been received by the Secretary-General, unless the State Party concerned has made a new declaration.

Article 42

A1–031   **1.** (a) If a matter referred to the Committee in accordance with article 41 is not resolved to the satisfaction of the States Parties concerned, the Committee may, with the prior consent of the States Parties concerned, appoint an ad hoc Conciliation Commission (hereinafter referred to as the Commission). The good offices of the Commission shall be made available to the States Parties concerned with a view to an amicable solution of the matter on the basis of respect for the present Covenant;

   (b) The Commission shall consist of five persons acceptable to the States Parties concerned. If the States Parties concerned fail to reach agreement within three months on all or part of the composition of the Commission, the members of the Commission concerning whom no agreement has been reached shall be elected by secret ballot by a two-thirds majority vote of the Committee from among its members.

2. The members of the Commission shall serve in their personal capacity. They shall not be nationals of the States Parties concerned, or of a State not Party to the present Covenant, or of a State Party which has not made a declaration under Article 41.

3. The Commission shall elect its own Chairman and adopt its own rules of procedure.

4. The meetings of the Commission shall normally be held at the Headquarters of the United Nations or at the United Nations Office at Geneva. However, they may be held at such other convenient places as the Commission may determine in consultation with the Secretary-General of the United Nations and the States Parties concerned.

5. The secretariat provided in accordance with Article 36 shall also service the commissions appointed under this article.

6. The information received and collated by the Committee shall be made available to the Commission and the Commission may call upon the States Parties concerned to supply any other relevant information.

7. When the Commission has fully considered the matter, but in any event not later than twelve months after having been seized of the matter, it shall submit to the Chairman of the Committee a report for communication to the States Parties concerned:

(a) If the Commission is unable to complete its consideration of the matter within twelve months, it shall confine its report to a brief statement of the status of its consideration of the matter;

(b) If an amicable solution to the matter on the basis of respect for human rights as recognised in the present Covenant is reached, the Commission shall confine its report to a brief statement of the facts and of the solution reached;

(c) If a solution within the terms of sub-paragraph (b) is not reached, the Commission's report shall embody its findings on all questions of fact relevant to the issues between the States Parties concerned, and its views on the possibilities of an amicable solution of the matter. This report shall also contain the written submissions and a record of the oral submissions made by the States Parties concerned;

(d) If the Commission's report is submitted under sub-paragraph (c), the States Parties concerned shall, within three months of the receipt of the report, notify the Chairman of the Committee whether or not they accept the contents of the report of the Commission.

8. The provisions of this article are without prejudice to the responsibilities of the Committee under Article 41.

9. The States Parties concerned shall share equally all the expenses of the members of the Commission in accordance with estimates to be provided by the Secretary-General of the United Nations.

10. The Secretary-General of the United Nations shall be empowered to pay the expenses of the members of the Commission, if necessary, before reimbursement by the States Parties concerned, in accordance with paragraph 9 of this article.

Article 43

The members of the Committee, and of the ad hoc conciliation **A1–032** commissions which may be appointed under Article 42, shall be entitled to the facilities, privileges and immunities of experts on mission for the United Nations as laid down in the relevant sections of the Convention on the Privileges and Immunities of the United Nations.

Article 44

A1–033 The provisions for the implementation of the present Covenant shall apply without prejudice to the procedures prescribed in the field of human rights by or under the constituent instruments and the conventions of the United Nations and of the specialised agencies and shall not prevent the States Parties to the present Covenant from having recourse to other procedures for settling a dispute in accordance with general or special international agreements in force between them.

Article 45

The Committee shall submit to the General Assembly of the United Nations, through the Economic and Social Council, an annual report on its activities.

Part V

Article 46

Nothing in the present Covenant shall be interpreted as impairing the provisions of the Charter of the United Nations and of the constitutions of the specialised agencies which define the respective responsibilities of the various organs of the United Nations and of the specialised agencies in regard to the matters dealt with in the present Covenant.

Article 47

Nothing in the present Covenant shall be interpreted as impairing the inherent right of all peoples to enjoy and utilise fully and freely their natural wealth and resources.

Part VI

Article 48

A1–034   1. The present Covenant is open for signature by any State Member of the United Nations or member of any of its specialised agencies, by any State Party to the Statute of the International Court of Justice, and by any other State which has been invited by the General Assembly of the United Nations to become a Party to the present Covenant.

2. The present Covenant is subject to ratification.

Instruments of ratification shall be deposited with the Secretary-General of the United Nations.

3. The present Covenant shall be open to accession by any State referred to in paragraph 1 of this article.

4. Accession shall be effected by the deposit of an instrument of accession with the Secretary-General of the United Nations.

5. The Secretary-General of the United Nations shall inform all States which have signed this Covenant or acceded to it of the deposit of each instrument of ratification or accession.

Article 49

1. The present Covenant shall enter into force three months **A1–035** after the date of the deposit with the Secretary-General of the United Nations of the 35th instrument of ratification or instrument of accession.

2. For each State ratifying the present Covenant or acceding to it after the deposit of the 35th instrument of ratification or instrument of accession, the present Covenant shall enter into force three months after the date of the deposit of its own instrument of ratification or instrument of accession.

Article 50

The provisions of the present Covenant shall extend to all parts of federal States without any limitations or exceptions.

Article 51

1. Any State Party to the present Covenant may propose an amendment and file it with the Secretary-General of the United Nations. The Secretary-General of the United Nations shall thereupon communicate any proposed amendments to the States Parties to the present Covenant with a request that they notify him whether they favour a conference of States Parties for the purpose of considering and voting upon the proposals. In the event that at least one third of the States Parties favours such a conference, the Secretary-General shall convene the conference under the auspices of the United Nations. Any amendment adopted by a majority of the States Parties present and voting at the conference shall be submitted to the General Assembly of the United Nations for approval.

2. Amendments shall come into force when they have been approved by the General Assembly of the United Nations and accepted by a two-thirds majority of the States Parties to the present Covenant in accordance with their respective constitutional processes.

3. When amendments come into force, they shall be binding on those States Parties which have accepted them, other States Parties still being bound by the provisions of the present Covenant and any earlier amendment which they have accepted.

Article 52

A1–036 Irrespective of the notifications made under Article 48, paragraph 5, the Secretary-General of the United Nations shall inform all States referred to in paragraph I of the same article of the following particulars:

(a) Signatures, ratifications and accessions under Article 48;

(b) The date of the entry into force of the present Covenant under Article 49 and the date of the entry into force of any amendments under Article 51.

Article 53

1. The present Covenant, of which the Chinese, English, French, Russian and Spanish texts are equally authentic, shall be deposited in the archives of the United Nations.

2. The Secretary-General of the United Nations shall transmit certified copies of the present Covenant to all States referred to in Article 48.

OPTIONAL PROTOCOL TO THE INTERNATIONAL COVENANT ON CIVIL AND POLITICAL RIGHTS[4]

A1–037 *The* STATES PARTIES TO THE PRESENT PROTOCOL,

Considering that in order further to achieve the purposes of the International Covenant on Civil and Political Rights (hereinafter referred to as the Covenant) and the implementation of its provisions it would be appropriate to enable the Human Rights Committee set up in part IV of the Covenant (hereinafter referred to as the Committee) to receive and consider, as provided in the present Protocol, communications from individuals claiming to be victims of violations of any of the rights set forth in the Covenant.

Have agreed as follows:

Article 1

A State Party to the Covenant that becomes a Party to the present Protocol recognises the competence of the Committee to receive

---

[4] G.A. Res. 21/2200A G.A.O.R., 21st Session, Supp., p. 59, UN Doc. A/6316 (1966), 999 U.N.T.S. 302, entered into force March 23, 1976. Currently there are 89 Contracting Parties to the Optional Protocol.

and consider communications from individuals subject to its jurisdiction who claim to be victims of a violation by that State Party of any of the rights set forth in the Covenant. No communication shall be received by the Committee if it concerns a State Party to the Covenant which is not a Party to the present Protocol.

Article 2

Subject to the provisions of Article 1, individuals who claim that any of their rights enumerated in the Covenant have been violated and who have exhausted all available domestic remedies may submit a written communication to the Committee for consideration.

Article 3

The Committee shall consider inadmissible any communication **A1–038** under the present Protocol which is anonymous, or which it considers to be an abuse of the right of submission of such communications or to be incompatible with the provisions of the Covenant.

Article 4

1. Subject to the provisions of Article 3, the Committee shall bring any communications submitted to it under the present Protocol to the attention of the State Party to the present Protocol alleged to be violating any provision of the Covenant.

2. Within six months, the receiving State shall submit to the Committee written explanations or statements clarifying the matter and the remedy, if any, that may have been taken by that State.

Article 5

1. The Committee shall consider communications received under the present Protocol in the light of all written information made available to it by the individual and by the State Party concerned.

2. The Committee shall not consider any communication from an individual unless it has ascertained that:

(a) The same matter is not being examined under another procedure of international investigation or settlement;

(b) The individual has exhausted all available domestic remedies. This shall not be the rule where the application of the remedies is unreasonably prolonged.

3. The Committee shall hold closed meetings when examining communications under the present Protocol.

4. The Committee shall forward its views to the State Party concerned and to the individual.

Article 6

The Committee shall include in its annual report under Article 45 of the Covenant a summary of its activities under the present Protocol.

Article 7

Pending the achievement of the objectives of resolution 1514(XV) adopted by the General Assembly of the United Nations on December 14, 1960 concerning the Declaration on the Granting of Independence to Colonial Countries and Peoples, the provisions of the present Protocol shall in no way limit the right of petition granted to these peoples by the Charter of the United Nations and other international conventions and instruments under the United Nations and its specialised agencies.

Article 8

A1–039   **1.** The present Protocol is open for signature by any State which has signed the Covenant.

2. The present Protocol is subject to ratification by any State which has ratified or acceded to the Covenant. Instruments of ratification shall be deposited with the Secretary-General of the United Nations.

3. The present Protocol shall be open to accession by any State which has ratified or acceded to the Covenant.

4. Accession shall be effected by the deposit of an instrument of accession with the Secretary-General of the United Nations.

5. The Secretary-General of the United Nations shall inform all States which have signed the present Protocol or acceded to it of the deposit of each instrument of ratification or accession.

Article 9

1. Subject to the entry into force of the Covenant, the present Protocol shall enter into force three months after the date of the deposit with the Secretary-General of the United Nations of the tenth instrument of ratification or instrument of accession.

2. For each State ratifying the present Protocol or acceding to it after the deposit of the tenth instrument of ratification or instrument of accession, the present Protocol shall enter into force three months after the date of the deposit of its own instrument of ratification or instrument of accession.

Article 10

The provisions of the present Protocol shall extend to all parts of federal States without any limitations or exceptions.

Article 11

1. Any State Party to the present Protocol may propose an amendment and file it with the Secretary-General of the United Nations. The Secretary-General shall thereupon communicate any proposed amendments to the States Parties to the present Protocol with a request that they notify him whether they favour a conference of States Parties for the purpose of considering and voting upon the proposal. In the event that at least one third of the States Parties favours such a conference, the Secretary-General shall convene the conference under the auspices of the United Nations. Any amendment adopted by a majority of the States Parties present and voting at the conference shall be submitted to the General Assembly of the United Nations for approval.

2. Amendments shall come into force when they have been approved by the General Assembly of the United Nations and accepted by a two-thirds majority of the States Parties to the present Protocol in accordance with their respective constitutional processes.

3. When amendments come into force, they shall be binding on those States Parties which have accepted them, other States Parties still being bound by the provisions of the present Protocol and any earlier amendment which they have accepted.

Article 12

1. Any State Party may denounce the present Protocol at any **A1–040** time by written notification addressed to the Secretary-General of the United Nations. Denunciation shall take effect three months after the date of receipt of the notification by the Secretary-General.

2. Denunciation shall be without prejudice to the continued application of the provisions of the present Protocol to any communication submitted under Article 2 before the effective date of denunciation.

Article 13

Irrespective of the notifications made under Article 8, paragraph 5, of the present Protocol, the Secretary-General of the United

Nations shall inform all States referred to in Article 48, paragraph I, of the Covenant of the following particulars:

(a) Signatures, ratifications and accessions under Article 8;

(b) The date of the entry into force of the present Protocol under Article 9 and the date of the entry into force of any amendments under Article 11;

(c) Denunciations under Article 12.

Article 14

1. The present Protocol, of which the Chinese, English, French, Russian and Spanish texts are equally authentic, shall be deposited in the archives of the United Nations.

2. The Secretary-General of the United Nations shall transmit certified copies of the present Protocol to all States referred to in Article 48 of the Covenant.

SECOND OPTIONAL PROTOCOL TO THE INTERNATIONAL COVENANT ON CIVIL AND POLITICAL RIGHTS, AIMING AT THE ABOLITION OF THE DEATH PENALTY (1990)[5]

A1–041 *The States Parties to the present Protocol,*

Believing that abolition of the death penalty contributes to enhancement of human dignity and progressive development of human rights,

Recalling Article 3 of the Universal Declaration of Human Rights, adopted on December 10, 1948, and Article 6 of the International Covenant on Civil and Political Rights, adopted on December 16, 1966,

Noting that Article 6 of the International Covenant on Civil and Political Rights refers to abolition of the death penalty in terms that strongly suggest that abolition is desirable,

Convinced that all measures of abolition of the death penalty should be considered as progress in the enjoyment of the right to life,

Desirous to undertake hereby an international commitment to abolish the death penalty,

Have agreed as follows:

Article 1

1. No one within the jurisdiction of a State Party to the present Protocol shall be executed.

---

[5] G.A. Res. 44/128, annex, G.A.O.R., 44th Session, Supp., p. 207, UN Doc. A/44/49 (1989), entered into force July 11, 1991. There are currently 45 Contracting Parties.

2. Each State Party shall take all necessary measures to abolish the death penalty within its jurisdiction.

Article 2

1. No reservation is admissible to the present Protocol, except A1–042 for a reservation made at the time of ratification or accession that provides for the application of the death penalty in time of war pursuant to a conviction for a most serious crime of a military nature committed during wartime.

2. The State Party making such a reservation shall at the time of ratification or accession communicate to the Secretary-General of the United Nations the relevant provisions of its national legislation applicable during wartime.

3. The State Party having made such a reservation shall notify the Secretary-General of the United Nations of any beginning or ending of a state of war applicable to its territory.

Article 3

The States Parties to the present Protocol shall include in the reports they submit to the Human Rights Committee, in accordance with Article 40 of the Covenant, information on the measures that they have adopted to give effect to the present Protocol.

Article 4

With respect to the States Parties to the Covenant that have made a declaration under Article 41, the competence of the Human Rights Committee to receive and consider communications when a State Party claims that another State Party is not fulfilling its obligations shall extend to the provisions of the present Protocol, unless the State Party concerned has made a statement to the contrary at the moment of ratification or accession.

Article 5

With respect to the States Parties to the first Optional Protocol to A1–043 the International Covenant on Civil and Political Rights adopted on December 16, 1966, the competence of the Human Rights Committee to receive and consider communications from individuals subject to its jurisdiction shall extend to the provisions of the present Protocol, unless the State Party concerned has made a statement to the contrary at the moment of ratification or accession.

Article 6

1. The provisions of the present Protocol shall apply as additional provisions to the Covenant.

2. Without prejudice to the possibility of a reservation under Article 2 of the present Protocol, the right guaranteed in Article 1, paragraph 1, of the present Protocol shall not be subject to any derogation under Article 4 of the Covenant.

Article 7

1. The present Protocol is open for signature by any State that has signed the Covenant.

2. The present Protocol is subject to ratification by any State that has ratified the Covenant or acceded to it. Instruments of ratification shall be deposited with the Secretary-General of the United Nations.

3. The present Protocol shall be open to accession by any State that has ratified the Covenant or acceded to it.

4. Accession shall be effected by the deposit of an instrument of accession with the Secretary-General of the United Nations.

5. The Secretary-General of the United Nations shall inform all States that have signed the present Protocol or acceded to it of the deposit of each instrument of ratification or accession.

Article 8

1. The present Protocol shall enter into force three months after the date of the deposit with the Secretary-General of the United Nations of the tenth instrument of ratification or accession.

2. For each State ratifying the present Protocol or acceding to it after the deposit of the tenth instrument of ratification or accession, the present Protocol shall enter into force three months after the date of the deposit of its own instrument of ratification or accession.

Article 9

The provisions of the present Protocol shall extend to all parts of federal States without any limitations or exceptions.

Article 10

A1–044 The Secretary-General of the United Nations shall inform all States referred to in Article 48, paragraph 1, of the Covenant of the following particulars:

(a) Reservations, communications and notifications under Article 2 of the present Protocol;

(b) Statements made under Articles 4 or 5 of the present Protocol;

(c) Signatures, ratifications and accessions under Article 7 of the present Protocol:

(d) The date of the entry into force of the present Protocol under Article 8 thereof.

Article 11

1. The present Protocol, of which the Arabic, Chinese, English, French, Russian and Spanish texts are equally authentic, shall be deposited in the archives of the United Nations.

2. The Secretary-General of the United Nations shall transmit certified copies of the present Protocol to all States referred to in Article 48 of the Covenant.

INTERNATIONAL COVENANT ON ECONOMIC, SOCIAL AND CULTURAL RIGHTS[6]

Preamble

The States Parties to the present Covenant,   A1–045

Considering that, in accordance with the principles proclaimed in the Charter of the United Nations, recognition of the inherent dignity and of the equal and inalienable rights of all members of the human family is the foundation of freedom, justice and peace in the world,

Recognising that these rights derive from the inherent dignity of the human person,

Recognising that, in accordance with the Universal Declaration of Human Rights, the ideal of free human beings enjoying freedom from fear and want can only be achieved if conditions are created whereby everyone may enjoy his economic, social and cultural rights, as well as his civil and political rights,

Considering the obligation of States under the Charter of the United Nations to promote universal respect for, and observance of, human rights and freedoms,

Realising that the individual, having duties to other individuals and to the community to which he belongs, is under a responsibility to strive for the promotion and observance of the rights recognised in the present Covenant,

Agree upon the following articles:

Part I

Article 1

1. All peoples have the right of self-determination. By virtue of A1–046 that right they freely determine their political status and freely pursue their economic, social and cultural development.

[6] G.A. Res. 21/2200A, G.A.O.R., 21st Session, Supp., p. 49, UN Doc. A/6316 (1966), 993 U.N.T.S. 3, entered into force January 3, 1976. Currently there are 145 Contracting Parties.

2. All peoples may, for their own ends, freely dispose of their natural wealth and resources without prejudice to any obligations arising out of international economic co-operation, based upon the principle of mutual benefit, and international law. In no case may a people be deprived of its own means of subsistence.

3. The States Parties to the present Covenant, including those having responsibility for the administration of Non-Self-Governing and Trust Territories, shall promote the realisation of the right of self-determination, and shall respect that right, in conformity with the provisions of the Charter of the United Nations.

Part II

Article 2

1. Each State Party to the present Covenant undertakes to take steps, individually and through international assistance and co-operation, especially economic and technical, to the maximum of its available resources, with a view to achieving progressively the full realisation of the rights recognised in the present Covenant by all appropriate means, including particularly the adoption of legislative measures.

2. The States Parties to the present Covenant undertake to guarantee that the rights enunciated in the present Covenant will be exercised without discrimination of any kind as to race, colour, sex, language, religion, political or other opinion, national or social origin, property, birth or other status.

3. Developing countries, with due regard to human rights and their national economy, may determine to what extent they would guarantee the economic rights recognised in the present Covenant to non-nationals.

Article 3

The States Parties to the present Covenant undertake to ensure the equal right of men and women to the enjoyment of all economic, social and cultural rights set forth in the present Covenant.

Article 4

The States Parties to the present Covenant recognise that, in the enjoyment of those rights provided by the State in conformity with the present Covenant, the State may subject such rights only to such limitations as are determined by law only in so far as this may be compatible with the nature of these rights and solely for the purpose of promoting the general welfare in a democratic society.

Article 5

1. Nothing in the present Covenant may be interpreted as implying for any State, group or person any right to engage in any activity or to perform any act aimed at the destruction of any of the rights or freedoms recognised herein, or at their limitation to a greater extent than is provided for in the present Covenant.

2. No restriction upon or derogation from any of the fundamental human rights recognised or existing in any country in virtue of law, conventions, regulations or custom shall be admitted on the pretext that the present Covenant does not recognise such rights or that it recognises them to a lesser extent.

Part III

Article 6

1. The States Parties to the present Covenant recognise the right **A1–047** to work, which includes the right of everyone to the opportunity to gain his living by work which he freely chooses or accepts, and will take appropriate steps to safeguard this right.

2. The steps to be taken by a State Party to the present Covenant to achieve the full realisation of this right shall include technical and vocational guidance and training programmes, policies and techniques to achieve steady economic, social and cultural development and full and productive employment under conditions safeguarding fundamental political and economic freedoms to the individual.

Article 7

The States Parties to the present Covenant recognise the right of everyone to the enjoyment of just and favourable conditions of work which ensure, in particular:

    (a) Remuneration which provides all workers, as a minimum, with:

        (i) Fair wages and equal remuneration for work of equal value without distinction of any kind, in particular women being guaranteed conditions of work not inferior to those enjoyed by men, with equal pay for equal work;

        (ii) A decent living for themselves and their families in accordance with the provisions of the present Covenant;

(b) Safe and healthy working conditions;

(c) Equal opportunity for everyone to be promoted in his employment to an appropriate higher level, subject to no considerations other than those of seniority and competence;

(d) Rest, leisure and reasonable limitation of working hours and periodic holidays with pay, as well as remuneration for public holidays.

Article 8

A1–048   **1.** The States Parties to the present Covenant undertake to ensure:

(a) The right of everyone to form trade unions and join the trade union of his choice, subject only to the rules of the organisation concerned, for the promotion and protection of his economic and social interests. No restrictions may be placed on the exercise of this right other than those prescribed by law and which are necessary in a democratic society in the interests of national security or public order or for the protection of the rights and freedoms of others;

(b) The right of trade unions to establish national federations or confederations and the right of the latter to form or join international trade-union organisations;

(c) The right of trade unions to function freely subject to no limitations other than those prescribed by law and which are necessary in a democratic society in the interests of national security or public order or for the protection of the rights and freedoms of others;

(d) The right to strike, provided that it is exercised in conformity with the laws of the particular country.

2. This article shall not prevent the imposition of lawful restrictions on the exercise of these rights by members of the armed forces or of the police or of the administration of the State.
3. Nothing in this article shall authorise States Parties to the International Labour Organisation Convention of 1948 concerning Freedom of Association and Protection of the Right to Organise to take legislative measures which would prejudice, or apply the law in such a manner as would prejudice, the guarantees provided for in that Convention.

Article 9

The States Parties to the present Covenant recognise the right of everyone to social security, including social insurance.

Article 10

The States Parties to the present Covenant recognise that: A1–049
   1. The widest possible protection and assistance should be accorded to the family, which is the natural and fundamental group unit of society, particularly for its establishment and while it is responsible for the care and education of dependent children. Marriage must be entered into with the free consent of the intending spouses.
   2. Special protection should be accorded to mothers during a reasonable period before and after childbirth. During such period working mothers should be accorded paid leave or leave with adequate social security benefits.
   3. Special measures of protection and assistance should be taken on behalf of all children and young persons without any discrimination for reasons of parentage or other conditions. Children and young persons should be protected from economic and social exploitation. Their employment in work harmful to their morals or health or dangerous to life or likely to hamper their normal development should be punishable by law. States should also set age limits below which the paid employment of child labour should be prohibited and punishable by law.

Article 11

   1. The States Parties to the present Covenant recognise the right of everyone to an adequate standard of living for himself and his family, including adequate food, clothing and housing, and to the continuous improvement of living conditions. The States Parties will take appropriate steps to ensure the realisation of this right, recognising to this effect the essential importance of international co-operation based on free consent.
   2. The States Parties to the present Covenant, recognising the fundamental right of everyone to be free from hunger, shall take, individually and through international co-operation, the measures, including specific programmes, which are needed:

   (a) To improve methods of production, conservation and distribution of food by making full use of technical and scientific knowledge, by disseminating knowledge of the principles of nutrition and by developing or reforming agrarian systems in such a way as to achieve the most efficient development and utilisation of natural resources;

   (b) Taking into account the problems of both food-importing and food-exporting countries, to ensure an equitable distribution of world food supplies in relation to need.

Article 12

1. The States Parties to the present Covenant recognise the right of everyone to the enjoyment of the highest attainable standard of physical and mental health.

2. The steps to be taken by the States Parties to the present Covenant to achieve the full realisation of this right shall include those necessary for:

(a) The provision for the reduction of the stillbirth-rate and of infant mortality and for the healthy development of the child;

(b) The improvement of all aspects of environmental and industrial hygiene;

(c) The prevention, treatment and control of epidemic, endemic, occupational and other diseases;

(d) The creation of conditions which would assure to all medical service and medical attention in the event of sickness.

Article 13

A1–050   1. The States Parties to the present Covenant recognise the right of everyone to education. They agree that education shall be directed to the full development of the human personality and the sense of its dignity, and shall strengthen the respect for human rights and fundamental freedoms. They further agree that education shall enable all persons to participate effectively in a free society, promote understanding, tolerance and friendship among all nations and all racial, ethnic or religious groups, and further the activities of the United Nations for the maintenance of peace.

2. The States Parties to the present Covenant recognise that, with a view to achieving the full realisation of this right:

(a) Primary education shall be compulsory and available free to all;

(b) Secondary education in its different forms, including technical and vocational secondary education, shall be made generally available and accessible to all by every appropriate means, and in particular by the progressive introduction of free education;

(c) Higher education shall be made equally accessible to all, on the basis of capacity, by every appropriate means, and in particular by the progressive introduction of free education;

(d) Fundamental education shall be encouraged or intensified as far as possible for those persons who have not received or completed the whole period of their primary education;

(e) The development of a system of schools at all levels shall be actively pursued, an adequate fellowship system shall be established, and the material conditions of teaching staff shall be continuously improved.

3. The States Parties to the present Covenant undertake to have respect for the liberty of parents and, when applicable, legal guardians to choose for their children schools, other than those established by the public authorities, which conform to such minimum educational standards as may be laid down or approved by the State and to ensure the religious and moral education of their children in conformity with their own convictions.

4. No part of this article shall be construed so as to interfere with the liberty of individuals and bodies to establish and direct educational institutions, subject always to the observance of the principles set forth paragraph I of this article and to the requirement that the education give in such institutions shall conform to such minimum standards as may laid down by the State.

Article 14

Each State Party to the present Covenant which, at the time of **A1–051** becoming. Party, has not been able to secure in its metropolitan territory or other territories under its jurisdiction compulsory primary education, free of charge, undertakes, within two years, to work out and adopt a detailed plan of action for the progressive implementation, within a reasonable number of years, to be fixed in the plan, of the principle of compulsory education free of charge for all.

Article 15

1. The States Parties to the present Covenant recognise the right of everyone:

(a) To take part in cultural life;

(b) To enjoy the benefits of scientific progress and its applications;

(c) To benefit from the protection of the moral and material interests resulting from any scientific, literary or artistic production of which he is the author.

2. The steps to be taken by the States Parties to the present Covenant to achieve the full realisation of this right shall include those necessary for the conservation, the development and the diffusion of science and culture.

3. The States Parties to the present Covenant undertake to respect the freedom indispensable for scientific research and creative activity.

4. The States Parties to the present Covenant recognise the benefits to be derived from the encouragement and development of international contacts and co-operation in the scientific and cultural fields.

Part IV

Article 16

A1–052 **1.** The States Parties to the present Covenant undertake to submit in conformity with this part of the Covenant reports on the measures which they have adopted and the progress made in achieving the observance of the rights recognised herein.

2. (a) All reports shall be submitted to the Secretary-General of the United Nations, who shall transmit copies to the Economic and Social Council for consideration in accordance with the provisions of the present Covenant;

(b) The Secretary-General of the United Nations shall also transmit to the specialised agencies copies of the reports, or any relevant parts therefrom, from States Parties to the present Covenant which are also members of these specialised agencies in so far as these reports, or parts therefrom, relate to any matters which fall within the responsibilities of the said agencies in accordance with their constitutional instruments.

Article 17

A1–053 **1.** The States Parties to the present Covenant shall furnish their reports in stages, in accordance with a programme to be established by the Economic and Social Council within one year of the entry into force of the present Covenant after consultation with the States Parties and the specialised agencies concerned.

2. Reports may indicate factors and difficulties affecting the degree of fulfilment of obligations under the present Covenant.

3. Where relevant information has previously been furnished to the United Nations or to any specialised agency by any State Party to the present Covenant, it will not be necessary to reproduce that information, but a precise reference to the information so furnished will suffice.

Article 18

Pursuant to its responsibilities under the Charter of the United Nations in the field of human rights and fundamental freedoms, the Economic and Social Council may make arrangements with the specialised agencies in respect of their reporting to it on the progress made in achieving the observance of the provisions of the present Covenant falling within the scope of their activities. These reports may include particulars of decisions and recommendations on such implementation adopted by their competent organs.

Article 19

The Economic and Social Council may transmit to the Commission on Human Rights for study and general recommendation or, as appropriate, for information the reports concerning human rights submitted by States in accordance with articles 16 and 17, and those concerning human rights submitted by the specialised agencies in accordance with article 18.

Article 20

The States Parties to the present Covenant and the specialised agencies concerned may submit comments to the Economic and Social Council on any general recommendation under article 19 or reference to such general recommendation in any report of the Commission on Human Rights or any documentation referred to therein.

Article 21

The Economic and Social Council may submit from time to time **A1–054** to the General Assembly reports with recommendations of a general nature and a summary of the information received from the States Parties to the present Covenant and the specialised agencies on the measures taken and the progress made in achieving general observance of the rights recognised in the present Covenant.

Article 22

The Economic and Social Council may bring to the attention of other organs of the United Nations, their subsidiary organs and specialised agencies concerned with furnishing technical assistance any matters arising out of the reports referred to in this part of the present Covenant which may assist such bodies in deciding, each within its field of competence, on the advisability of international measures likely to contribute to the effective progressive implementation of the present Covenant.

Article 23

The States Parties to the present Covenant agree that international action for the achievement of the rights recognised in the present

Covenant includes such methods as the conclusion of conventions, the adoption of recommendations, the furnishing of technical assistance and the holding of regional meetings and technical meetings for the purpose of consultation and study organised in conjunction with the Governments concerned.

Article 24

Nothing in the present Covenant shall be interpreted as impairing the provisions of the Charter of the United Nations and of the constitutions of the specialised agencies which define the respective responsibilities of the various organs of the United Nations and of the specialised agencies in regard to the matters dealt with in the present Covenant.

Article 25

Nothing in the present Covenant shall be interpreted as impairing the inherent right of all peoples to enjoy and utilise fully and freely their natural wealth and resources.

Part IV

Article 26

A1–055   1. The present Covenant is open for signature by any State Member of the United Nations or member of any of its specialised agencies, by any State Party to the Statute of the International Court of Justice, and by any other State which has been invited by the General Assembly of the United Nations to become a party to the present Covenant.

2. The present Covenant is subject to ratification. Instruments of ratification shall be deposited with the Secretary-General of the United Nations.

3. The present Covenant shall be open to accession by any State referred to in paragraph 1 of this article.

4. Accession shall be effected by the deposit of an instrument of accession with the Secretary-General of the United Nations.

5. The Secretary-General of the United Nations shall inform all States which have signed the present Covenant or acceded to it of the deposit of each instrument of ratification or accession.

Article 27

A1–056 1. The present Covenant shall enter into force three months after the date of the deposit with the Secretary-General of the United Nations of the 35th instrument of ratification or instrument of accession.

2. For each State ratifying the present Covenant or acceding to it after the deposit of the 35th instrument of ratification or instrument of accession, the present Covenant shall enter into force three months after the date of the deposit of its own instrument of ratification or instrument of accession.

Article 28

The provisions of the present Covenant shall extend to all parts of federal States without any limitations or exceptions.

Article 29

1. Any State Party to the present Covenant may propose an amendment and file it with the Secretary-General of the United Nations. The Secretary-General shall thereupon communicate any proposed amendments to the States Parties to the present Covenant with a request that they notify him whether they favour a conference of States Parties for the purpose of considering and voting upon the proposals. In the event that at least one third of the States Parties favours such a conference, the Secretary-General shall convene the conference under the auspices of the United Nations. Any amendment adopted by a majority of the States Parties present and voting at the conference shall be submitted to the General Assembly of the United Nations for approval.

2. Amendments shall come into force when they have been approved by the General Assembly of the United Nations and accepted by a two-thirds majority of the States Parties to the present Covenant in accordance with their respective constitutional processes.

3. When amendments come into force they shall be binding on those States Parties which have accepted them, other States Parties still being bound by the provisions of the present Covenant and any earlier amendment which they have accepted.

Article 30

Irrespective of the notifications made under Article 26, paragraph 5, the Secretary-General of the United Nations shall inform all States referred to in paragraph I of the same article of the following particulars:

(a) Signatures, ratifications and accessions under Article 26;

(b) The date of the entry into force of the present Covenant under Article 27 and the date of the entry into force of any amendments under Article 29.

Article 31

1. The present Covenant, of which the Chinese, English, French, Russian and Spanish texts are equally authentic, shall be deposited in the archives of the United Nations.

2. The Secretary-General of the United Nations shall transmit certified copies of the present Covenant to all States referred to in Article 26.

PROCLAMATION OF TEHERAN, FINAL ACT OF THE INTERNATIONAL CONFERENCE ON HUMAN RIGHTS[7]

A1–057 The International Conference on Human Rights,

Having met at Teheran from April 22 to May 13, 1968 to review the progress made in the twenty years since the adoption of the Universal Declaration of Human Rights and to formulate a programme for the future,

Having considered the problems relating to the activities of the United Nations for the promotion and encouragement of respect for human rights and fundamental freedoms,

Bearing in mind the resolutions adopted by the Conference,

Noting that the observance of the International Year for Human Rights takes place at a time when the world is undergoing a process of unprecedented change,

Having regard to the new opportunities made available by the rapid progress of science and technology,

Believing that, in an age when conflict and violence prevail in many parts of the world, the fact of human interdependence and the need for human solidarity are more evident than ever before,

Recognising that peace is the universal aspiration of mankind and that peace and justice are indispensable to the full realisation of human rights and fundamental freedoms,

Solemnly proclaims that:

1. It is imperative that the members of the international community fulfil their solemn obligations to promote and encourage respect for human rights and fundamental freedoms for all without distinctions of any kind such as race, colour, sex, language, religion, political or other opinions;

A1–058   **2.** The Universal Declaration of Human Rights states a common understanding of the peoples of the world concerning the inalienable and inviolable rights of all members of the human family and constitutes an obligation for the members of the international community;

3. The International Covenant on Civil and Political Rights, the International Covenant on Economic, Social and Cultural Rights, the Declaration on the Granting of Independence to Colonial Countries and Peoples, the International Convention on the Elimination of All Forms of Racial Discrimination as well as other conventions and declarations in the field of human rights adopted

---

[7] Teheran, April 22 to May 13, 1968, UN Doc. A/CONF. 32/41 at 3 (1968).

under the auspices of the United Nations, the specialised agencies and the regional intergovernmental organisations, have created new standards and obligations to which States should conform;

4. Since the adoption of the Universal Declaration of Human Rights the United Nations has made substantial progress in defining standards for the enjoyment and protection of human rights and fundamental freedoms. During this period many important international instruments were adopted but much remains to be done in regard to the implementation of those rights and freedoms;

5. The primary aim of the United Nations in the sphere of human rights is the achievement by each individual of the maximum freedom and dignity. For the realisation of this objective, the laws of every country should grant each individual, irrespective of race, language, religion or political belief, freedom of expression, of information, of conscience and of religion, as well as the right to participate in the political, economic, cultural and social life of his country;

6. States should reaffirm their determination effectively to enforce the principles enshrined in the Charter of the United Nations and in other international instruments that concern human rights and fundamental freedoms;

7. Gross denials of human rights under the repugnant policy of apartheid is a matter of the gravest concern to the international community. This policy of apartheid, condemned as a crime against humanity, continues seriously to disturb international peace and security. It is therefore imperative for the international community to use every possible means to eradicate this evil. The struggle against apartheid is recognised as legitimate;

8. The peoples of the world must be made fully aware of the evils of racial discrimination and must join in combating them. The implementation of this principle of non-discrimination, embodied in the Charter of the United Nations, the Universal Declaration of Human Rights, and other international instruments in the field of human rights, constitutes a most urgent task of mankind at the international as well as at the national level. All ideologies based on racial superiority and intolerance must be condemned and resisted;

9. Eight years after the General Assembly's Declaration on the Granting of Independence to Colonial Countries and Peoples the problems of colonialism continue to preoccupy the international community. It is a matter of urgency that all Member States should co-operate with the appropriate organs of the United Nations so that effective measures can be taken to ensure that the Declaration is fully implemented;

10. Massive denials of human rights, arising out of aggression **A1–059** or any armed conflict with their tragic consequences, and resulting in untold human misery, engender reactions which could engulf the world in ever growing hostilities. It is the obligation of the international community to co-operate in eradicating such scourges;

11. Gross denials of human rights arising from discrimination on grounds of race, religion, belief or expressions of opinion outrage the conscience of mankind and endanger the foundations of freedom, justice and peace in the world;

12. The widening gap between the economically developed and developing countries impedes the realisation of human rights in the international community. The failure of the Development Decade to reach its modest objectives makes it all the more imperative for every nation, according to its capacities, to make the maximum possible effort to close this gap;

13. Since human rights and fundamental freedoms are indivisible, the full realisation of civil and political rights without the enjoyment of economic, social and cultural rights is impossible. The achievement of lasting progress in the implementation of human rights is dependent upon sound and effective national and international policies of economic and social development;

14. The existence of over seven hundred million illiterates throughout the world is an enormous obstacle to all efforts at realising the aims and purposes of the Charter of the United Nations and the provisions of the Universal Declaration of Human Rights. International action aimed at eradicating illiteracy from the face of the earth and promoting education at all levels requires urgent attention;

15. The discrimination of which women are still victims in various regions of the world must be eliminated. An inferior status for women is contrary to the Charter of the United Nations as well as the provisions of the Universal Declaration of Human Rights. The full implementation of the Declaration on the Elimination of Discrimination against Women is a necessity for the progress of mankind;

16. The protection of the family and of the child remains the concern of the international community. Parents have a basic human right to determine freely and responsibly the number and the spacing of their children;

17. The aspirations of the younger generation for a better world, in which human rights and fundamental freedoms are fully implemented, must be given the highest encouragement. It is imperative that youth participate in shaping the future of mankind;

18. While recent scientific discoveries and technological advances have opened vast prospects for economic, social and cultural progress, such developments may nevertheless endanger the rights and freedoms of individuals and will require continuing attention;

19. Disarmament would release immense human and material resources now devoted to military purposes. These resources should be used for the promotion of human rights and fundamental freedoms. General and complete disarmament is one of the highest aspirations of all peoples;

Therefore,

The International Conference on Human Rights,

1. Affirming its faith in the principles of the Universal Declaration of Human Rights and other international instruments in this field,

2. Urges all peoples and governments to dedicate themselves to the principles enshrined in the Universal Declaration of Human Rights and to redouble their efforts to provide for all human beings a life consonant with freedom and dignity and conducive to physical, mental, social and spiritual welfare.

VIENNA DECLARATION AND PROGRAMME OF ACTION (1993)[8]

The World Conference on Human Rights,   A1–060

Considering that the promotion and protection of human rights is a matter of priority for the international community, and that the Conference affords a unique opportunity to carry out a comprehensive analysis of the international human rights system and of the machinery for the protection of human rights, in order to enhance and thus promote a fuller observance of those rights, in a just and balanced manner,

Recognising and affirming that all human rights derive from the dignity and worth inherent in the human person, and that the human person is the central subject of human rights and fundamental freedoms, and consequently should be the principal beneficiary and should participate actively in the realisation of these rights and freedoms,

Reaffirming their commitment to the purposes and principles contained in the Charter of the United Nations and the Universal Declaration of Human Rights,

Reaffirming the commitment contained in Article 56 of the Charter of the United Nations to take joint and separate action, placing proper emphasis on developing effective international co-operation for the realisation of the purposes set out in Article 55, including universal respect for, and observance of, human rights and fundamental freedoms for all,

Emphasising the responsibilities of all States, in conformity with the Charter of the United Nations, to develop and encourage

---

[8] UN Doc. A/49/668 adopted June 25, 1993; see also 14 H.R.L.J. 352 (1993); and 32 I.L.M. 1661 (1993). The Declaration and Programme of Action was endorsed by the General Assembly in Resolution 48/121 on December 20, 1993.

respect for human rights and fundamental freedoms for all, without distinction as to race, sex, language or religion,

Recalling the Preamble to the Charter of the United Nations, in particular the determination to reaffirm faith in fundamental human rights, in the dignity and worth of the human person, and in the equal rights of men and women and of nations large and small,

Recalling also the determination expressed in the Preamble of the Charter of the United Nations to save succeeding generations from the scourge of war, to establish conditions under which justice and respect for obligations arising from treaties and other sources of international law can be maintained, to promote social progress and better standards of life in larger freedom, to practise tolerance and good neighbourliness, and to employ international machinery for the promotion of the economic and social advancement of all peoples,

A1–061 *Emphasising* that the Universal Declaration of Human Rights, which constitutes a common standard of achievement for all peoples and all nations, is the source of inspiration and has been the basis for the United Nations in making advances in standard setting as contained in the existing international human rights instruments, in particular the International Covenant on Civil and Political Rights and the International Covenant on Economic, Social and Cultural Rights.

Considering the major changes taking place on the international scene and the aspirations of all the peoples for an international order based on the principles enshrined in the Charter of the United Nations, including promoting and encouraging respect for human rights and fundamental freedoms for all and respect for the principle of equal rights and self-determination of peoples, peace, democracy, justice, equality, rule of law, pluralism, development, better standards of living and solidarity,

Deeply concerned by various forms of discrimination and violence, to which women continue to be exposed all over the world,

Recognising that the activities of the United Nations in the field of human rights should be rationalised and enhanced in order to strengthen the United Nations machinery in this field and to further the objectives of universal respect for observance of international human rights standards,

Having taken into account the Declarations adopted by the three regional meetings at Tunis, San Josi and Bangkok and the contributions made by Governments, and bearing in mind the suggestions made by intergovernmental and non-governmental organisations, as well as the studies prepared by independent experts during the preparatory process leading to the World Conference on Human Rights,

Welcoming the International Year of the World's Indigenous People 1993 as a reaffirmation of the commitment of the international community to ensure their enjoyment of all human rights and fundamental freedoms and to respect the value and diversity of their cultures and identities,

Recognising also that the international community should devise ways and means to remove the current obstacles and meet challenges to the full realisation of all human rights and to prevent the continuation of human rights violations resulting thereof throughout the world,

Invoking the spirit of our age and the realities of our time which call upon the peoples of the world and all States Members of the United Nations to rededicate themselves to the global task of promoting and protecting all human rights and fundamental freedoms so as to secure full and universal enjoyment of these rights,

Determined to take new steps forward in the commitment of the international community with a view to achieving substantial progress in human rights endeavours by an increased and sustained effort of international co-operation and solidarity,

Solemnly adopts the Vienna Declaration and Programme of Action.

I

1. The World Conference on Human Rights reaffirms the **A1-062** solemn commitment of all States to fulfil their obligations to promote universal respect for, and observance and protection of, all human rights and fundamental freedoms for all in accordance with the Charter of the United Nations, other instruments relating to human rights, and international law. The universal nature of these rights and freedoms is beyond question.

In this framework, enhancement of international co-operation in the field of human rights is essential for the full achievement of the purposes of the United Nations.

Human rights and fundamental freedoms are the birthright of all human beings; their protection and promotion is the first responsibility of Governments.

2. All peoples have the right of self-determination. By virtue of that right they freely determine their political status, and freely pursue their economic, social and cultural development.

Taking into account the particular situation of peoples under colonial or other forms of alien domination or foreign occupation, the World Conference on Human Rights recognises the right of peoples to take any legitimate action, in accordance with the Charter of the United Nations, to realise their inalienable right of self-determination. The World Conference on Human Rights considers the denial of the right of self-determination as a violation of human rights and underlines the importance of the effective realisation of this right.

In accordance with the Declaration on Principles of International Law concerning Friendly Relations and Co-operation Among States in accordance with the Charter of the United Nations, this shall not be construed as authorising or encouraging any action which would dismember or impair, totally or in part, the territorial integrity or political unity of sovereign and independent States conducting themselves in compliance with the principle of equal rights and self-determination of peoples and thus possessed of a Government representing the whole people belonging to the territory without distinction of any kind.

3. Effective international measures to guarantee and monitor the implementation of human rights standards should be taken in respect of people under foreign occupation, and effective legal protection against the violation of their human rights should be provided, in accordance with human rights norms and international law, particularly the Geneva Convention relative to the Protection of Civilian Persons in Time of War, of August 14, 1949, and other applicable norms of humanitarian law.

4. The promotion and protection of all human rights and fundamental freedoms must be considered as a priority objective of the United Nations in accordance with its purposes and principles, in particular the purpose of international co-operation. In the framework of these purposes and principles, the promotion and protection of all human rights is a legitimate concern of the international community. The organs and specialised agencies related to human rights should therefore further enhance the co-ordination of their activities based on the consistent and objective application of international human rights instruments.

A1–063   5. All human rights are universal, indivisible and interdependent and interrelated. The international community must treat human rights globally in a fair and equal manner, on the same footing, and with the same emphasis. While the significance of national and regional particularities and various historical, cultural and religious backgrounds must be borne in mind, it is the duty of States, regardless of their political, economic and cultural systems, to promote and protect all human rights and fundamental freedoms.

6. The efforts of the United Nations system towards the universal respect for, and observance of, human rights and fundamental freedoms for all, contribute to the stability and well-being necessary for peaceful and friendly relations among nations, and to improved conditions for peace and security as well as social and economic development, in conformity with the Charter of the United Nations.

7. The processes of promoting and protecting human rights should be conducted in conformity with the purposes and

principles of the Charter of the United Nations, and international law.

8. Democracy, development and respect for human rights and fundamental freedoms are interdependent and mutually reinforcing. Democracy is based on the freely expressed will of the people to determine their own political, economic, social and cultural systems and their full participation in all aspects of their lives. In the context of the above, the promotion and protection of human rights and fundamental freedoms at the national and international levels should be universal and conducted without conditions attached. The international community should support the strengthening and promoting of democracy, development and respect for human rights and fundamental freedoms in the entire world.

9. The World Conference on Human Rights reaffirms that least developed countries committed to the process of democratisation and economic reforms, many of which are in Africa, should be supported by the international community in order to succeed in their transition to democracy and economic development.

10. The World Conference on Human Rights reaffirms the right to development, as established in the Declaration on the Rights to Development, as a universal and inalienable right and an integral part of fundamental human rights.

As stated in the Declaration on the Right to Development, the human person is the central subject of development.

While development facilitates the enjoyment of all human rights, the lack of development may not be invoked to justify the abridgement of internationally recognised human rights.

States should co-operate with each other in ensuring development and eliminating obstacles to development. The international community should promote an effective international co-operation for the realisation of the right to development and the elimination of obstacles to development.

Lasting progress towards the implementation of the right to development requires effective development policies at the national level, as well as equitable economic relations and a favourable economic environment at the international level.

11. The right to development should be fulfilled so as to meet equitably the developmental and environmental needs of present and future generations. The World Conference on Human Rights recognises that illicit dumping of toxic and dangerous substances and waste potentially constitutes a serious threat to the human rights to life and health of everyone.

Consequently, the World Conference on Human Rights calls on all States to adopt and vigorously implement existing conventions relating to the dumping of toxic and dangerous products and waste and to co-operate in the prevention of illicit dumping.

Everyone has the right to enjoy the benefits of scientific progress and its applications. The World Conference on Human Rights notes that certain advances, notably in the biomedical and life sciences as well as in information technology, may have potentially adverse consequences for the integrity, dignity and human rights of the individual, and calls for international co-operation to ensure that human rights and dignity are fully respected in this area of universal concern.

A1–064   **12.** The World Conference on Human Rights calls upon the international community to make all efforts to help alleviate the external debt burden of developing countries, in order to supplement the efforts of the Governments of such countries to attain the full realisation of the economic, social and cultural rights of their people.

13. There is a need for States and international organisations, in co-operation with non-governmental organisations, to create favourable conditions at the national, regional and international levels to ensure the full and effective enjoyment of human rights. States should eliminate all violations of human rights and their causes, as well as obstacles to the enjoyment of these rights.

14. The existence of widespread extreme poverty inhibits the full and effective enjoyment of human rights; its immediate alleviation and eventual elimination must remain a high priority for the international community.

15. Respect for human rights and for fundamental freedoms without distinction of any kind is a fundamental rule of international human rights law. The speedy and comprehensive elimination of all forms of racism and racial discrimination, xenophobia and related intolerance is a priority task for the international community. Governments should take effective measures to prevent and combat them. Groups, institutions, inter-governmental and non-governmental organisations and individuals are urged to intensify their efforts in co-operating and co-ordinating their activities against these evils.

16. The World Conference on Human Rights welcomes the progress made in dismantling apartheid and calls upon the international community and the United Nations system to assist in this process.

The World Conference on Human Rights also deplores the continuing acts of violence aimed at undermining the quest for a peaceful dismantling of apartheid.

17. The acts, methods and practices of terrorism in all its forms and manifestations as well as linkage in some countries to drug trafficking are activities aimed at the destruction of human rights, fundamental freedoms and democracy, threatening territorial integrity, security of States and destabilising legitimately constituted Governments. The international community should take the necessary steps to enhance co-operation to prevent and combat terrorism.

18. The human rights of women and of the girl-child are an **A1–065** inalienable, integral and indivisible part of universal human rights. The full and equal participation of women in political, civil, economic, social and cultural life, at the national, regional and international levels, and the eradication of all forms of discrimination on grounds of sex are priority objectives of the international community.

Gender-based violence and all forms of sexual harassment and exploitation, including those resulting from cultural prejudice and international trafficking, are incompatible with the dignity and worth of the human person, and must be eliminated. This can be achieved by legal measures and through national action and international co-operation in such fields as economic and social development, education, safe maternity and health care, and social support.

The human rights of women should form an integral part of the United Nations human rights activities, including the promotion of all human rights instruments relating to women.

The World Conference on Human Rights urges Governments, institutions, intergovernmental and non-governmental organisations to intensify their efforts for the protection and promotion of human rights of women and the girl-child.

19. Considering the importance of the promotion and protection of the rights of persons belonging to minorities and the contribution of such promotion and protection to the political and social stability of the States in which such persons live,

The World Conference on Human Rights reaffirms the obligation of States to ensure that persons belonging to minorities may exercise fully and effectively all human rights and fundamental freedoms without any discrimination and in full equality before the law in accordance with the Declaration on the Rights of Persons Belonging to National or Ethnic, Religious and Linguistic Minorities.

The persons belonging to minorities have the right to enjoy their own culture, to profess and practise their own religion and to use their own language in private and in public, freely and without interference or any form of discrimination.

20. The World Conference on Human Rights recognises the **A1–066** inherent dignity and the unique contribution of indigenous people to the development and plurality of society and strongly reaffirms the commitment of the international community to their economic, social and cultural well-being and their enjoyment of the fruits of sustainable development. States should ensure the full and free participation of indigenous people in all aspects of society, in particular in matters of concern to them. Considering the importance of the promotion and protection of the rights of indigenous people, and the contribution of such promotion and protection to the political and social stability of the States in which such people live, States should, in accordance with international law, take concerted positive steps to ensure respect for all human rights and fundamental freedoms of indigenous people, on the basis of equality and non-discrimination, and recognise the value and diversity of their distinct identities, cultures and social organisation.

A1–067   **21.** The World Conference on Human Rights, welcoming the early ratification of the Convention on the Rights of the Child by a large number of States and noting the recognition of the human rights of children in the World Declaration on the Survival, Protection and Development of Children and Plan of Action adopted by the World Summit for Children, urges universal ratification of the Convention by 1995 and its effective implementation by States parties through the adoption of all the necessary legislative, administrative and other measures and the allocation to the maximum extent of the available resources. In all actions concerning children, non-discrimination and the best interest of the child should be primary considerations and the views of the child given due weight. National and international mechanisms and programmes should be strengthened for the defence and protection of children, in particular, the girl-child, abandoned children, street children, economically and sexually exploited children, including through child pornography, child prostitution or sale of organs, children victims of diseases including acquired immunodeficiency syndrome, refugee and displaced children, children in detention, children in armed conflict, as well as children victims of famine and drought and other emergencies. International co-operation and solidarity should be promoted to support the implementation of the Convention and the rights of the child should be a priority in the United Nations system-wide action on human rights.

The World Conference on Human Rights also stresses that the child for the full and harmonious development of his or her personality should grow up in a family environment which accordingly merits broader protection.

22. Special attention needs to be paid to ensuring non-discrimination, and the equal enjoyment of all human rights and fundamental freedoms by disabled persons, including their active participation in all aspects of society.

A1–068   **23.** The World Conference on Human Rights reaffirms that everyone, without distinction of any kind, is entitled to the right to seek and to enjoy in other countries asylum from persecution, as well as the right to return to one's own country. In this respect it stresses the importance of the Universal Declaration of Human

Rights, the 1951 Convention relating to the Status of Refugees, its 1967 Protocol and regional instruments. It expresses its appreciation to States that continue to admit and host large numbers of refugees in their territories, and to the Office of the United Nations High Commissioner for Refugees for its dedication to its task. It also expresses its appreciation to the United Nations Relief and Works Agency for Palestine Refugees in the Near East.

The World Conference on Human Rights recognises that gross violations of human rights, including in armed conflicts, are among the multiple and complex factors leading to displacement of people.

The World Conference on Human Rights recognises that, in view of the complexities of the global refugee crisis and in accordance with the Charter of the United Nations, relevant international instruments and international solidarity and in the spirit of burden-sharing, a comprehensive approach by the international community is needed in co-ordination and co-operation with the countries concerned and relevant organisations, bearing in mind the mandate of the United Nations High Commissioner for Refugees. This should include the development of strategies to address the root causes and effects of movements of refugees and other displaced persons, the strengthening of emergency preparedness and response mechanisms, the provision of effective protection and assistance, bearing in mind the special needs of women and children, as well as the achievement of durable solutions, primarily through the preferred solution of dignified and safe voluntary repatriation, including solutions such as those adopted by the international refugee conferences. The World Conference on Human Rights underlines the responsibilities of States, particularly as they relate to the countries of origin.

In the light of the comprehensive approach, the World Conference on Human Rights emphasises the importance of giving special attention including through intergovernmental and humanitarian organisations and finding lasting solutions to questions related to internally displaced persons including their voluntary and safe return and rehabilitation.

In accordance with the Charter of the United Nations and the principles of humanitarian law, the World Conference on Human Rights further emphasises the importance of and the need for humanitarian assistance to victims of all natural and man-made disasters.

24. Great importance must be given to the promotion and **A1–069** protection of the human rights of persons belonging to groups which have been rendered vulnerable, including migrant workers, the elimination of all forms of discrimination against them, and the strengthening and more effective implementation of existing human rights instruments. States have an obligation to create and maintain adequate measures at the national level, in particular in the fields of education, health and social support, for the promotion and protection of the rights of persons in vulnerable sectors of their populations and to ensure the participation of those among them who are interested in finding a solution to their own problems.

25. The World Conference on Human Rights affirms that extreme poverty and social exclusion constitute a violation of human dignity and that urgent steps are necessary to achieve better knowledge of extreme poverty and its causes, including those related to the problem of development, in order to promote the human rights of the poorest, and to put an end to extreme poverty and social exclusion and to promote the enjoyment of the fruits of social progress. It is essential for States to foster participation by the poorest people in the decision-making process by the community in which they live, the promotion of human rights and efforts to combat extreme poverty.

26. The World Conference on Human Rights welcomes the progress made in the codification of human rights instruments, which is a dynamic and evolving process, and urges the universal ratification of human rights treaties. All States are encouraged to accede to these international instruments; all States are encouraged to avoid, as far as possible, the resort to reservations.

27. Every State should provide an effective framework of remedies to redress human rights grievances or violations. The administration of justice, including law enforcement and prosecutorial agencies and, especially, an independent judiciary and legal profession in full conformity with applicable standards contained in international human rights instruments, are essential to the full and non-discriminatory realisation of human rights and indispensable to the processes of democracy and sustainable development. In this context, institutions concerned with the administration of justice should be properly funded, and an increased level of both technical and financial assistance should be provided by the international community. It is incumbent upon the United Nations to make use of special programmes of advisory services on a priority basis for the achievement of a strong and independent administration of justice.

A1–070 **28.** The World Conference on Human Rights expresses its dismay at massive violations of human rights especially in the form of genocide, "ethnic cleansing" and systematic rape of women in war situations, creating mass exodus of refugees and displaced and persons. While strongly condemning such abhorrent practices it reiterates the call that perpetrators of such crimes be punished and such practices immediately stopped.

29. The World Conference on Human Rights expresses grave concern about continuing human rights violations in all parts of the world in disregard of standards as contained in international human rights instruments and international humanitarian law and about the lack of sufficient and effective remedies for the victims.

The World Conference on Human Rights is deeply concerned about violations of human rights during armed conflicts, affecting the civilian population, especially women, children, the elderly and the disabled. The Conference therefore calls upon States and all parties to armed conflicts strictly to observe international humanitarian law, as set forth in the Geneva Conventions of 1949 and other rules and principles of international law, as well as minimum standards for protection of human rights, as laid down in international conventions.

The World Conference on Human Rights reaffirms the right of the victims to be assisted by humanitarian organisations, as set forth in the Geneva Conventions of 1949 and other relevant instruments of international humanitarian law, and calls for the safe and timely access for such assistance.

30. The World Conference on Human Rights also expresses its dismay and condemnation that gross and systematic violations and situations that constitute serious obstacles to the full enjoyment of all human rights continue to occur in different parts of the world. Such violations and obstacles include, as well as torture and cruel, inhuman and degrading treatment or punishment, summary and arbitrary executions, disappearances, arbitrary detentions, all forms of racism, racial discrimination and apartheid, foreign occupation and alien domination, xenophobia, poverty, hunger and other denials of economic, social and cultural rights, religious intolerance, terrorism, discrimination against women and lack of the rule of law.

31. The World Conference on Human Rights calls upon States to refrain from any unilateral measure not in accordance with international law and the Charter of the United Nations that creates obstacles to trade relations among States and impedes the full realisation of the human rights set forth in the Universal Declaration of Human Rights and international human rights instruments, in particular the rights of everyone to a standard of living adequate for their health and well-being, including food and medical care, housing and the necessary social services. The World Conference on Human Rights affirms that food should not be used as a tool for political pressure.

32. The World Conference on Human Rights reaffirms the **A1–071** importance of ensuring the universality, objectivity and non-selectivity of the consideration of human rights issues.

33. The World Conference on Human Rights reaffirms that States are duty-bound, as stipulated in the Universal Declaration of Human Rights and the International Covenant on Economic,

Social and Cultural Rights and in other international human rights instruments, to ensure that education is aimed at strengthening the respect of human rights and fundamental freedoms. The World Conference on Human Rights emphasises the importance of incorporating the subject of human rights education programmes and calls upon States to do so. Education should promote understanding, tolerance, peace and friendly relations between the nations and all racial or religious groups and encourage the development of United Nations activities in pursuance of these objectives. Therefore, education on human rights and the dissemination of proper information, both theoretical and practical, play an important role in the promotion and respect of human rights with regard to all individuals without distinction of any kind such as race, sex, language or religion, and this should be integrated in the education policies at the national as well as international levels. The World Conference on Human Rights notes that resource constraints and institutional inadequacies may impede the immediate realisation of these objectives.

34. Increased efforts should be made to assist countries which so request to create the conditions whereby each individual can enjoy universal human rights and fundamental freedoms. Governments, the United Nations system as well as other multilateral organisations are urged to increase considerably the resources allocated to programmes aiming at the establishment and strengthening of national legislation, national institutions and related infrastructures which uphold the rule of law and democracy, electoral assistance, human rights awareness through training, teaching and education, popular participation and civil society.

The programmes of advisory services and technical co-operation under the Centre for Human Rights should be strengthened as well as made more efficient and transparent and thus become a major contribution to improving respect for human rights. States are called upon to increase their contributions to these programmes, both through promoting a larger allocation from the United Nations regular budget, and through voluntary contributions.

35. The full and effective implementation of United Nations activities to promote and protect human rights must reflect the high importance accorded to human rights by the Charter of the United Nations and the demands of the United Nations human rights activities, as mandated by Member States. To this end, United Nations human rights activities should be provided with increased resources.

36. The World Conference on Human Rights reaffirms the important and constructive role played by national institutions for the promotion and protection of human rights, in particular in their advisory capacity to the competent authorities, their role in remedying human rights violations, in the dissemination of human rights information, and education in human rights.

The World Conference on Human Rights encourages the establishment and strengthening of national institutions, having regard to the "Principles relating to the status of national institutions" and recognising that it is the right of each State to choose the framework which is best suited to its particular needs at the national level.

37. Regional arrangements play a fundamental role in promot- **A1–072** ing and protecting human rights. They should reinforce universal human rights standards, as contained in international human rights instruments, and their protection. The World Conference on Human Rights endorses efforts under way to strengthen these arrangements and to increase their effectiveness, while at the same time stressing the importance of co-operation with the United Nations human rights activities.

The World Conference on Human Rights reiterates the need to consider the possibility of establishing regional and subregional arrangements for the promotion and protection of human rights where they do not already exist.

38. The World Conference on Human Rights recognises the important role of non-governmental organisations in the promotion of all human rights and in humanitarian activities at national, regional and international levels. The World Conference on Human Rights appreciates their contribution to increasing public awareness of human rights issues, to the conduct of education, training and research in this field, and to the promotion and protection of all human rights and fundamental freedoms. While recognising that the primary responsibility for standard-setting lies with States, the conference also appreciates the contribution of non-governmental organisations to this process. In this respect, the World Conference on Human Rights emphasises the importance of continued dialogue and co-operation between Governments and non-governmental organisations. Non-governmental organisations and their members genuinely involved in the field of human rights should enjoy the rights and freedoms recognised in the Universal Declaration of Human Rights, and the protection of the national law. These rights and freedoms may not be exercised contrary to the purposes and principles of the United Nations. Non-governmental organisations should be free to carry out their human rights activities, without interference, within the framework of national law and the Universal Declaration of Human Rights.

39. Underlining the importance of objective, responsible and impartial information about human rights and humanitarian issues, the World Conference on Human Rights encourages the

increased involvement of the media, for whom freedom and protection should be guaranteed within the framework of national law.

II

A. INCREASED CO-ORDINATION ON HUMAN RIGHTS WITHIN THE UNITED NATIONS SYSTEM

A1–073 **1.** The World Conference on Human Rights recommends increased co-ordination in support of human rights and fundamental freedoms within the United Nations system. To this end, the World Conference on Human Rights urges all United Nations organs, bodies and the specialised agencies whose activities deal with human rights to co-operate in order to strengthen, rationalise and streamline their activities, taking into account the need to avoid unnecessary duplication. The World Conference on Human Rights also recommends to the Secretary-General that high-level officials of relevant United Nations bodies and specialised agencies at their annual meeting, besides co-ordinating their activities, also assess the impact of their strategies and policies on the enjoyment of all human rights.

2. Furthermore, the World Conference on Human Rights calls on regional organisations and prominent international and regional finance and development institutions to assess also the impact of their policies and programmes on the enjoyment of human rights.

3. The World Conference on Human Rights recognises that relevant specialised agencies and bodies and institutions of the United Nations system as well as other relevant intergovernmental organisations whose activities deal with human rights play a vital role in the formulation, promotion and implementation of human rights standards, within their respective mandates, and should take into account the outcome of the World Conference on Human Rights within their fields of competence.

4. The World Conference on Human Rights strongly recommends that a concerted effort be made to encourage and facilitate the ratification of and accession or succession to international human rights treaties and protocols adopted within the framework of the United Nations system with the aim of universal acceptance. The Secretary-General, in consultation with treaty bodies, should consider opening a dialogue with States not having acceded to these human rights treaties, in order to identify obstacles and to seek ways of overcoming them.

5. The World Conference on Human Rights encourages States to consider limiting the extent of any reservations they lodge to international human rights instruments, formulate any reservations as precisely and narrowly as possible, ensure that none is incompatible with the object and purpose of the relevant treaty and regularly review any reservations with a view to withdrawing them.

6. The World Conference on Human Rights, recognising the need to maintain consistency with the high quality of existing international standards and to avoid proliferation of human rights instruments, reaffirms the guidelines relating to the elaboration of new international instruments contained in General Assembly resolution 41/120 of December 4, 1986 and calls on the United Nations human rights bodies, when considering the elaboration of new international standards, to keep those guidelines in mind, to consult with human rights treaty bodies on the necessity for drafting new standards and to request the Secretariat to carry out technical reviews of proposed new instruments.

7. The World Conference on Human Rights recommends that human rights officers be assigned if and when necessary to regional offices of the United Nations Organisation with the purpose of disseminating information and offering training and other technical assistance in the field of human rights upon the request of concerned Member States. Human rights training for international civil servants who are assigned to work relating to human rights should be organised.

8. The World Conference on Human Rights welcomes the convening of emergency sessions of the Commission on Human Rights as a positive initiative and that other ways of responding to acute violations of human rights be considered by the relevant organs of the United Nations system.

Resources

9. The World Conference on Human Rights, concerned by the A1–074 growing disparity between the activities of the Centre for Human Rights and the human, financial and other resources available to carry them out, and bearing in mind the resources needed for other important United Nations programmes, requests the Secretary-General and the General Assembly to take immediate steps to increase substantially the resources for the human rights programme from within the existing and future regular budgets of the United Nations, and to take urgent steps to seek increased extra-budgetary resources.

10. Within this framework, an increased proportion of the regular budget should be allocated directly to the Centre for Human Rights to cover its costs and all other costs borne by the Centre for Human Rights, including those related to the United

Nations human rights bodies. Voluntary funding of the Centre's technical co-operation activities should reinforce this enhanced budget; the World Conference on Human Rights calls for generous contributions to the existing trust funds.

11. The World Conference on Human Rights requests the Secretary-General and the General Assembly to provide sufficient human, financial and other resources to the Centre for Human Rights to enable it effectively, efficiently and expeditiously to carry out its activities.

12. The World Conference on Human Rights, noting the need to ensure that human and financial resources are available to carry out the human rights activities, as mandated by intergovernmental bodies, urges the Secretary-General, in accordance with Article 101 of the Charter of the United Nations, and Member States to adopt a coherent approach aimed at securing that resources commensurate to the increased mandates are allocated to the Secretariat. The World Conference on Human Rights invites the Secretary-General to consider whether adjustments to procedures in the programme budget cycle would be necessary or helpful to ensure the timely and effective implementation of human rights activities as mandated by Member States.

Centre for Human Rights

13. The World Conference on Human Rights stresses the importance of strengthening the United Nations Centre for Human Rights.

14. The Centre for Human Rights should play an important role in co-ordinating system-wide attention for human rights. The focal role of the Centre can best be realised if it is enabled to co-operate fully with other United Nations bodies and organs. The co-ordinating role of the Centre for Human Rights also implies that the office of the Centre for Human Rights in New York is strengthened.

15. The Centre for Human Rights should be assured adequate means for the system of thematic and country rapporteurs, experts, working groups and treaty bodies. Follow-up on recommendations should become a priority matter for consideration by the Commission on Human Rights.

16. The Centre for Human Rights should assume a larger role in the promotion of human rights. This role could be given shape through co-operation with Member States and by an enhanced programme of advisory services and technical assistance. The existing voluntary funds will have to be expanded substantially for these purposes and should be managed in a more efficient and co-ordinated way. All activities should follow strict and transparent project management rules and regular programme and project evaluations should be held periodically. To this end, the results of such evaluation exercises and other relevant information should be made available regularly. The Centre should, in particular, organise at least once a year information meetings open to all Member States and organisations directly involved in these projects and programmes.

Adaptation and strengthening of the United Nations machinery for human rights, including the question of the establishment of a United Nations High Commissioner for Human Rights.

17. The World Conference on Human Rights recognises the necessity for a continuing adaptation of the United Nations human rights machinery to the current and future needs in the promotion and protection of human rights, as reflected in the present Declaration and within the framework of a balanced and sustainable development for all people. In particular, the United Nations human rights organs should improve their co-ordination, efficiency and effectiveness.

18. The World Conference on Human Rights recommends to the General Assembly that when examining the report of the Conference at its 48th session, it begin, as a matter of priority, consideration of the question of the establishment of a High Commissioner for Human Rights for the promotion and protection of all human rights.

B. EQUALITY, DIGNITY AND TOLERANCE

1. Racism, racial discrimination, xenophobia and other forms of intolerance

19. The World Conference on Human Rights considers the A1–075 elimination of racism and racial discrimination, in particular in their institutionalised forms such as apartheid or resulting from doctrines of racial superiority or exclusivity or contemporary forms and manifestations of racism, as a primary objective for the international community and a worldwide promotion programme in the field of human rights. United Nations organs and agencies should strengthen their efforts to implement such a programme of action related to the third decade to combat racism and racial discrimination as well as subsequent mandates to the same end. The World Conference on Human Rights strongly appeals to the international community to contribute generously to the Trust Fund for the Programme for the Decade for Action to Combat Racism and Racial Discrimination.

20. The World Conference on Human Rights urges all Governments to take immediate measures and to develop strong policies to prevent and combat all forms and manifestations of racism, xenophobia or related intolerance, where necessary by enactment of appropriate legislation, including penal measures, and by the establishment of national institutions to combat such phenomena.

21. The World Conference on Human Rights welcomes the decision of the Commission on Human Rights to appoint a Special Rapporteur on contemporary forms of racism, racial discrimination, xenophobia and related intolerance. The World Conference on Human Rights also appeals to all States parties to the International Convention on the Elimination of All Forms of Racial Discrimination to consider making the declaration under article 14 of the Convention.

22. The World Conference on Human Rights calls upon all Governments to take all appropriate measures in compliance with their international obligations and with due regard to their respective legal systems to counter intolerance and related violence based on religion or belief, including practices of discrimination against women and including the desecration of religious sites, recognising that every individual has the right to freedom of thought, conscience, expression and religion. The Conference also invites all States to put into practice the provisions of the Declaration on the Elimination of All Forms of Intolerance and of Discrimination Based on Religion or Belief.

23. The World Conference on Human Rights stresses that all persons who perpetrate or authorise criminal acts associated with ethnic cleansing are individually responsible and accountable for such human rights violations, and that the international community should exert every effort to bring those legally responsible for such violations to justice.

24. The World Conference on Human Rights calls on all States to take immediate measures, individually and collectively, to combat the practice of ethnic cleansing to bring it quickly to an end. Victims of the abhorrent practice of ethnic cleansing are entitled to appropriate and effective remedies.

2. Persons belonging to national or ethnic, religious and linguistic minorities

A1–076   **25.** The World Conference on Human Rights calls on the Commission on Human Rights to examine ways and means to promote and protect effectively the rights of persons belonging to minorities as set out in the Declaration on the Rights of Persons belonging to National or Ethnic, Religious and Linguistic Minorities. In this context, the World Conference on Human Rights calls upon the Centre for Human Rights to provide, at the request of Governments concerned and as part of its programme of advisory services and technical assistance, qualified expertise on minority issues and human rights, as well as on the prevention and resolution of disputes, to assist in existing or potential situations involving minorities.

26. The World Conference on Human Rights urges States and the international community to promote and protect the rights of persons belonging to national or ethnic, religious and linguistic minorities in accordance with the Declaration on the Rights of Persons belonging to National or Ethnic, Religious and Linguistic Minorities.

27. Measures to be taken, where appropriate, should include facilitation of their full participation in all aspects of the political, economic, social, religious and cultural life of society and in the economic progress and development in their country.

Indigenous people

28. The World Conference on Human Rights calls on the **A1–077** Working Group on Indigenous Populations of the Sub-Commission on Prevention of Discrimination and Protection of Minorities to complete the drafting of a declaration on the rights of indigenous people at its 11th session.

29. The World Conference on Human Rights recommends that the Commission on Human Rights consider the renewal and updating of the mandate of the Working Group on Indigenous Populations upon completion of the drafting of a declaration on the rights of indigenous people.

30. The World Conference on Human Rights also recommends that advisory services and technical assistance programmes within the United Nations system respond positively to requests by States for assistance which would be of direct benefit to indigenous people. The World Conference on Human Rights further recommends that adequate human and financial resources be made available to the Centre for Human Rights within the overall framework of strengthening the Centre's activities as envisaged by this document.

31. The World Conference on Human Rights urges States to ensure the full and free participation of indigenous people in all aspects of society, in particular in matters of concern to them.

32. The World Conference on Human Rights recommends that the General Assembly proclaim an international decade of the world's indigenous people, to begin from January 1994, including action-orientated programmes, to be decided upon in partnership with indigenous people. An appropriate voluntary trust fund should be set up for this purpose. In the framework of such a decade, the establishment of a permanent forum for indigenous people in the United Nations system should be considered.

Migrant workers

33. The World Conference on Human Rights urges all States to guarantee the protection of the human rights of all migrant workers and their families.

34. The World Conference on Human Rights considers that the creation of conditions to foster greater harmony and tolerance between migrant workers and the rest of the society of the State in which they reside is of particular importance.

35. The World Conference on Human Rights invites States to consider the possibility of signing and ratifying, at the earliest possible time, the International Convention on the Rights of All Migrant Workers and Members of Their Families.

3. The equal status and human rights of women

A1–078 **36.** The World Conference on Human Rights urges the full and equal enjoyment by women of all human rights and that this be a priority for Governments and for the United Nations. The World Conference on Human Rights also underlines the importance of the integration and full participation of women as both agents and beneficiaries in the development process, and reiterates the objectives established on global action for women towards sustainable and equitable development set forth in the Rio Declaration on Environment and Development and chapter 24 of Agenda 21, adopted by the United Nations Conference on Environment and Development (Rio de Janeiro, Brazil, June 3–14, 1992).

37. The equal status of women and the human rights of women should be integrated into the mainstream of United Nations system-wide activity. These issues should be regularly and systematically addressed throughout relevant United Nations bodies and mechanisms. In particular, steps should be taken to increase co-operation and promote further integration of objectives and goals between the Commission on the Status of Women, the Commission on Human Rights, the Committee for the Elimination of Discrimination against Women, the United Nations Development Fund for Women, the United Nations Development Programme and other United Nations agencies. In this context, co-operation and co-ordination should be strengthened between the Centre for Human Rights and the Division for the Advancement of Women.

38. In particular, the World Conference on Human Rights stresses the importance of working towards the elimination of violence against women in public and private life, the elimination of all forms of sexual harassment, exploitation and trafficking in women, the elimination of gender bias in the administration of justice and the eradication of any conflicts which may arise between the rights of women and the harmful effects of certain traditional or customary practices, cultural prejudices and religious extremism. The World Conference on Human Rights calls upon the General Assembly to adopt the draft declaration on violence against women and urges States to combat violence against women in accordance with its provisions. Violations of the human rights of women in situations of armed conflict are violations of the fundamental principles of international human rights and humanitarian law. All violations of this kind, including in particular murder, systematic rape, sexual slavery, and forced pregnancy, require a particularly effective response.

39. The World Conference on Human Rights urges the eradica- A1–079 tion of all forms of discrimination against women, both hidden and overt. The United Nations should encourage the goal of universal ratification by all States of the Convention on the Elimination of All Forms of Discrimination against Women by the year 2000. Ways and means of addressing the particularly large number of reservations to the Convention should be encouraged. *Inter alia*, the Committee on the Elimination of Discrimination against Women should continue its review of reservations to the Convention. States are urged to withdraw reservations that are contrary to the object and purpose of the Convention or which are otherwise incompatible with international treaty law.

40. Treaty monitoring bodies should disseminate necessary information to enable women to make more effective use of existing implementation procedures in their pursuits of full and equal enjoyment of human rights and non-discrimination. New procedures should also be adopted to strengthen implementation of the commitment to women's equality and the human rights of women. The Commission on the Status of Women and the Committee on the Elimination of Discrimination against Women should quickly examine the possibility of introducing the right of petition through the preparation of an optional protocol to the Convention on the Elimination of All Forms of Discrimination against Women. The World Conference on Human Rights welcomes the decision of the Commission on Human Rights to consider the appointment of a special rapporteur on violence against women at its 50th session.

41. The World Conference on Human Rights recognises the importance of the enjoyment by women of the highest standard of physical and mental health throughout their life span. In the context of the World Conference on Women and the Convention on the Elimination of All Forms of Discrimination against Women, as well as the Proclamation of Tehran of 1968, the World Conference on Human Rights reaffirms, on the basis of equality between women and men, a woman's right to accessible and adequate health care and the widest range of family planning services, as well as equal access to education at all levels.

42. Treaty monitoring bodies should include the status of women and the human rights of women in their deliberations and findings, making use of gender-specific data. States should be encouraged to supply information on the situation of women de jure and de facto in their reports to treaty monitoring bodies. The World Conference on Human Rights notes with satisfaction that the Commission on Human Rights adopted at its 49th session resolution 1993/46 of March 8, 1993 stating that rapporteurs and working groups in the field of human rights should also be encouraged to do so. Steps should also be taken by the Division for the Advancement of Women in co-operation with other United Nations bodies, specifically the Centre for Human Rights, to ensure that the human rights activities of the United Nations regularly address violations of women's human rights, including gender-specific abuses. Training for United Nations human rights and humanitarian relief personnel to assist them to recognise and deal with human rights abuses particular to women and to carry out their work without gender bias should be encouraged.

43. The World Conference on Human Rights urges Governments and regional and international organisations to facilitate the access of women to decision-making posts and their greater participation in the decision-making process. It encourages further steps within the United Nations Secretariat to appoint and promote women staff members in accordance with the Charter of the United Nations, and encourages other principal and subsidiary organs of the United Nations to guarantee the participation of women under conditions of equality.

44. The World Conference on Human Rights welcomes the World Conference on Women to be held in Beijing in 1995 and urges that human rights of women should play an important role in its deliberations, in accordance with the priority themes of the World Conference on Women of equality, development and peace.

4. The rights of the child

A1–080   **45.** The World Conference on Human Rights reiterates the principle of "First Call for Children" and, in this respect, underlines the importance of major national and international efforts, especially those of the United Nations Children's Fund, for promoting respect for the rights of the child to survival, protection, development and participation.

46. Measures should be taken to achieve universal ratification of the Convention on the Rights of the Child by 1995 and the universal signing of the World Declaration on the Survival, Protection and Development of Children and Plan of Action adopted by the World Summit for Children, as well as their effective implementation. The World Conference on Human Rights urges States to withdraw reservations to the Convention on the Rights of the Child contrary to the object and purpose of the Convention or otherwise contrary to international treaty law.

47. The World Conference on Human Rights urges all nations to undertake measures to the maximum extent of their available resources, with the support of international co-operation, to achieve the goals in the World Summit Plan of Action. The Conference calls on States to integrate the Convention on the Rights of the Child into their national action plans. By means of these national action plans and through international efforts, particular priority should be placed on reducing infant and maternal mortality rates, reducing malnutrition and illiteracy rates and providing access to safe drinking water and to basic education. Whenever so called for, national plans of action should be devised to combat devastating emergencies resulting from natural disasters and armed conflicts and the equally grave problem of children in extreme poverty.

48. The World Conference on Human Rights urges all States, with the support of international co-operation, to address the acute problem of children under especially difficult circumstances. Exploitation and abuse of children should be actively combated, including by addressing their root causes. Effective measures are required against female infanticide, harmful child labour, sale of children and organs, child prostitution, child pornography; as well as other forms of sexual abuse.

49. The World Conference on Human Rights supports all measures by the United Nations and its specialised agencies to ensure the effective protection and promotion of human rights of the girl-child. The World Conference on Human Rights urges States to repeal existing laws and regulations and remove customs and practices which discriminate against and cause harm to the girl-child.

50. The World Conference on Human Rights strongly supports the proposal that the Secretary-General initiate a study into means of improving the protection of children in armed conflicts. Humanitarian norms should be implemented and measures taken in order to protect and facilitate assistance to children in war zones. Measures should include protection for children against indiscriminate use of all weapons of war, especially anti-personnel mines. The need for aftercare and rehabilitation of children traumatised by war must be addressed urgently. The Conference calls on the Committee on the Rights of the Child to study the question of raising the minimum age of recruitment into armed forces.

51. The World Conference on Human Rights recommends that matters relating to human rights and the situation of children be regularly reviewed and monitored by all relevant organs and mechanisms of the United Nations system and by the supervisory bodies of the specialised agencies in accordance with their mandates.

52. The World Conference on Human Rights recognises the important role played by non-governmental organisations in the effective implementation of all human rights instruments and, in particular, the Convention on the Rights of the Child.

53. The World Conference on Human Rights recommends that the Committee on the Rights of the Child, with the assistance of the Centre for Human Rights, be enabled expeditiously and effectively to meet its mandate, especially in view of the unprecedented extent of ratification and subsequent submission of country reports.

5. Freedom from torture

A1–081 **54.** The World Conference on Human Rights welcomes the ratification by many Member States of the Convention against Torture and Other Cruel, Inhuman or Degrading Treatment or Punishment and encourages its speedy ratification by all other Member States.

55. The World Conference on Human Rights emphasises that one of the most atrocious violations against human dignity is the act of torture, the result of which destroys the dignity and impairs the capability of victims to continue their lives and their activities.

56. The World Conference on Human Rights reaffirms that under human rights law and international humanitarian law, freedom from torture is a right which must be protected under all circumstances, including in times of internal or international disturbance or armed conflicts.

57. The World Conference on Human Rights therefore urges all States to put an immediate end to the practice of torture and eradicate this evil forever through full implementation of the Universal Declaration of Human Rights as well as the relevant conventions and, where necessary, strengthening of existing mechanisms. The World Conference on Human Rights calls on all States to co-operate fully with the Special Rapporteur on the question of torture in the fulfilment of his mandate.

58. Special attention should be given to ensure universal respect for, and effective implementation of, the Principles of Medical Ethics relevant to the Role of Health Personnel, particularly Physicians, in the Protection of Prisoners and Detainees against Torture and other Cruel, Inhuman or Degrading Treatment or Punishment adopted by the General Assembly of the United Nations.

59. The World Conference on Human Rights stresses the importance of further concrete action within the framework of the United Nations with the view to providing assistance to victims of torture and ensure more effective remedies for their physical, psychological and social rehabilitation. Providing the necessary resources for this purpose should be given high priority, *inter alia*, by additional contributions to the United Nations Voluntary Fund for the Victims of Torture.

60. States should abrogate legislation leading to impunity for those responsible for grave violations of human rights such as torture and prosecute such violations, thereby providing a firm basis for the rule of law.

61. The World Conference on Human Rights reaffirms that efforts to eradicate torture should, first and foremost, be concentrated on prevention and, therefore, calls for the early adoption of an optional protocol to the Convention against Torture and Other Cruel, In human and Degrading Treatment or Punishment, which is intended to establish a preventive system of regular visits to places of detention.

Enforced disappearances

62. The World Conference on Human Rights, welcoming the A1–082 adoption by the General Assembly of the Declaration on the Protection of All Persons from Enforced Disappearance, calls upon all States to take effective legislative, administrative, judicial or other measures to prevent, terminate and punish acts of enforced disappearances. The World Conference on Human Rights reaffirms that it is the duty of all States, under any circumstances, to make investigations whenever there is reason to believe that an enforced disappearance has taken place on a territory under their jurisdiction and, if allegations are confirmed, to prosecute its perpetrators.

6. The rights of the disabled person

63. The World Conference on Human Rights reaffirms that all human rights and fundamental freedoms are universal and thus unreservedly include persons with disabilities. Every person is born equal and has the same rights to life and welfare, education and work, living independently and active participation in all aspects of society. Any direct discrimination or other negative discriminatory treatment of a disabled person is therefore a violation of his or her rights. The World Conference on Human Rights calls on Governments, where necessary, to adopt or adjust legislation to assure access to these and other rights for disabled persons.

64. The place of disabled persons is everywhere. Persons with disabilities should be guaranteed equal opportunity through the elimination of all socially determined barriers, be they physical, financial, social or psychological, which exclude or restrict full participation in society.

65. Recalling the World Programme of Action concerning Disabled Persons, adopted by the General Assembly at its 37th session, the World Conference on Human Rights calls upon the General Assembly and the Economic and Social Council to adopt the draft standard rules on the equalisation of opportunities for persons with disabilities, at their meetings in 1993.

C. CO-OPERATION, DEVELOPMENT AND STRENGTHENING OF HUMAN RIGHTS

A1–083   **66.** The World Conference on Human Rights recommends that priority be given to national and international action to promote democracy, development and human rights.

67. Special emphasis should be given to measures to assist in the strengthening and building of institutions relating to human rights, strengthening of a pluralistic civil society and the protection of groups which have been rendered vulnerable. In this context, assistance provided upon the request of Governments for the conduct of free and fair elections, including assistance in the human rights aspects of elections and public information about elections, is of particular importance. Equally important is the assistance to be given to the strengthening of the rule of law, the promotion of freedom of expression and the administration of justice, and to the real and effective participation of the people in the decision-making processes.

68. The World Conference on Human Rights stresses the need for the implementation of strengthened advisory services and technical assistance activities by the Centre for Human Rights. The Centre should make available to States upon request assistance on specific human rights issues, including the preparation of reports under human rights treaties as well as for the implementation of coherent and comprehensive plans of action for the promotion and protection of human rights. Strengthening the institutions of human rights and democracy, the legal protection of human rights, training of officials and others, broad-based education and public information aimed at promoting respect for human rights should all be available as components of these programmes.

69. The World Conference on Human Rights strongly recommends that a comprehensive programme be established within the United Nations in order to help States in the task of building and strengthening adequate national structures which have a direct impact on the overall observance of human rights and the maintenance of the rule of law. Such a programme, to be co-ordinated by the Centre for Human Rights, should be able to provide, upon the request of the interested Government, technical and financial assistance to national projects in reforming penal

and correctional establishments, education and training of lawyers, judges and security forces in human rights, and any other
sphere of activity relevant to the good functioning of the rule of
law. That programme should make available to States assistance
for the implementation of plans of action for the promotion and
protection of human rights.

70. The World Conference on Human Rights requests the **A1–084**
Secretary-General of the United Nations to submit proposals to
the United Nations General Assembly, containing alternatives for
the establishment, structure, operational modalities and funding
of the proposed programme.

71. The World Conference on Human Rights recommends that
each State consider the desirability of drawing up a national
action plan identifying steps whereby that State would improve
the promotion and protection of human rights.

72. The World Conference on Human Rights on Human Rights
reaffirms that the universal and inalienable right to development,
as established in the Declaration on the Right to Development,
must be implemented and realised. In this context, the World
Conference on Human Rights welcomes the appointment by the
Commission on Human Rights of a thematic working group on
the right to development and urges that the Working Group, in
consultation and co-operation with other organs and agencies of
the United Nations system, promptly formulate, for early consideration by the United Nations General Assembly, comprehensive
and effective measures to eliminate obstacles to the implementation and realisation of the Declaration on the Right to Development and recommending ways and means towards the realisation
of the right to development by all States.

73. The World Conference on Human Rights recommends that
non-governmental and other grass-roots organisations active in
development and/or human rights should be enabled to play a
major role on the national and international levels in the debate,
activities and implementation relating to the right to development
and, in co-operation with Governments, in all relevant aspects of
development co-operation.

74. The World Conference on Human Rights appeals to Governments, competent agencies and institutions to increase considerably the resources devoted to building well-functioning legal
systems able to protect human rights, and to national institutions
working in this area. Actors in the field of development co-
operation should bear in mind the mutually reinforcing interrela-
tionship between development, democracy and human rights.
Co-operation should be based on dialogue and transparency. The
World Conference on Human Rights also calls for the establishment of comprehensive programmes, including resource banks of
information and personnel with expertise relating to the strengthening of the rule of law and of democratic institutions.

75. The World Conference on Human Rights encourages the Commission on Human Rights, in co-operation with the Committee on Economic, Social and Cultural Rights, to continue the examination of optional protocols to the International Covenant on Economic, Social and Cultural Rights.

76. The World Conference on Human Rights recommends that more resources be made available for the strengthening or the establishment of regional arrangements for the promotion and protection of human rights under the programmes of advisory services and technical assistance of the Centre for Human Rights. States are encouraged to request assistance for such purposes as regional and subregional workshops, seminars and information exchanges designed to strengthen regional arrangements for the promotion and protection of human rights in accord with universal human rights standards as contained in international human rights instruments.

77. The World Conference on Human Rights supports all measures by the United Nations and its relevant specialised agencies to ensure the effective promotion and protection of trade union rights, as stipulated in the International Covenant on Economic, Social and Cultural Rights and other relevant international instruments. It calls on all States to abide fully by their obligations in this regard contained in international instruments.

D. HUMAN RIGHTS EDUCATION

A1–085   **78.** The World Conference on Human Rights considers human rights education, training and public information essential for the promotion and achievement of stable and harmonious relations among communities and for fostering mutual understanding, tolerance and peace.

79. States should strive to eradicate illiteracy and should direct education towards the full development of the human personality and to the strengthening of respect for human rights and fundamental freedoms. The World Conference on Human Rights calls on all States and institutions to include human rights, humanitarian law, democracy and rule of law as subjects in the curricula of all learning institutions in formal and non-formal settings.

80. Human rights education should include peace, democracy, development and social justice, as set forth in international and regional human rights instruments, in order to achieve common understanding and awareness with a view to strengthening universal commitment to human rights.

81. Taking into account the World Plan of Action on Education for Human Rights and Democracy, adopted in March 1993 by the International Congress on Education for Human Rights and Democracy of the United Nations Educational, Scientific and

Cultural Organisation, and other human rights instruments, the World Conference on Human Rights recommends that States develop specific programmes and strategies for ensuring the widest human rights education and the dissemination of public information, taking particular account of the human rights needs of women.

82. Governments, with the assistance of intergovernmental organisations, national institutions and non-governmental organisations, should promote an increased awareness of human rights and mutual tolerance. The World Conference on Human Rights underlines the importance of strengthening the World Public Information Campaign for Human Rights carried out by the United Nations. They should initiate and support education in human rights and undertake effective dissemination of public information in this field. The advisory services and technical assistance programmes of the United Nations system should be able to respond immediately to requests from States for educational and training activities in the field of human rights as well as for special education concerning standards as contained in international human rights instruments and in humanitarian law and their application to special groups such as military forces, law enforcement personnel, police and the health profession. The proclamation of a United Nations decade for human rights education in order to promote, encourage and focus these educational activities should be considered.

E. IMPLEMENTATION AND MONITORING METHODS

83. The World Conference on Human Rights urges Governments to incorporate standards as contained in international human rights instruments in domestic legislation and to strengthen national structures, institutions and organs of society which play a role in promoting and safeguarding human rights. **A1–086**

84. The World Conference on Human Rights recommends the strengthening of United Nations activities and programmes to meet requests for assistance by States which want to establish or strengthen their own national institutions for the promotion and protection of human rights.

85. The World Conference on Human Rights also encourages the strengthening of co-operation between national institutions for the promotion and protection of human rights, particularly through exchanges of information and experience, as well as co-operation with regional organisations and the United Nations.

86. The World Conference on Human Rights strongly recommends in this regard that representatives of national institutions for the promotion and protection of human rights convene periodic meetings under the auspices of the Centre for Human

Rights to examine ways and means of improving their mechanisms and sharing experiences.

87. The World Conference on Human Rights recommends to the human rights treaty bodies, to the meetings of chairpersons of the treaty bodies and to the meetings of States parties that they continue to take steps aimed at co-ordinating the multiple reporting requirements and guidelines for preparing State reports under the respective human rights conventions and study the suggestion that the submission of one overall report on treaty obligations undertaken by each State would make these procedures more effective and increase their impact.

88. The World Conference on Human Rights recommends that the States parties to international human rights instruments, the General Assembly and the Economic and Social Council should consider studying the existing human rights treaty bodies and the various thematic mechanisms and procedures with a view to promoting greater efficiency and effectiveness through better co-ordination of the various bodies, mechanisms and procedures, taking into account the need to avoid unnecessary duplication and overlapping of their mandates and tasks.

89. The World Conference on Human Rights recommends continued work on the improvement of the functioning, including the monitoring tasks, of the treaty bodies, taking into account multiple proposals made in this respect, in particular those made by the treaty bodies themselves and by the meetings of the chairpersons of the treaty bodies. The comprehensive national approach taken by the Committee on the Rights of the Child should also be encouraged.

A1–087   **90.** The World Conference on Human Rights recommends that States parties to human rights treaties consider accepting all the available optional communication procedures.

91. The World Conference on Human Rights views with concern the issue of impunity of perpetrators of human rights violations, and supports the efforts of the Commission on Human Rights and the Sub-Commission on Prevention of Discrimination and Protection of Minorities to examine all aspects of the issue.

92. The World Conference on Human Rights recommends that the Commission on Human Rights examine the possibility for better implementation of existing human rights instruments at the international and regional levels and encourages the International Law Commission to continue its work on an international criminal court.

93. The World Conference on Human Rights appeals to States which have not yet done so to accede to the Geneva Conventions of August 12, 1949 and the Protocols thereto, and to take all appropriate national measures, including legislative ones, for their full implementation.

94. The World Conference on Human Rights recommends the speedy completion and adoption of the draft declaration on the right and responsibility of individuals, groups and organs of society to promote and protect universally recognised human rights and fundamental freedoms.

95. The World Conference on Human Rights underlines the importance of preserving and strengthening the system of special procedures, rapporteurs, representatives, experts and working groups of the Commission on Human Rights and the Sub-Commission on the Prevention of Discrimination and Protection of Minorities, in order to enable them to carry out their mandates in all countries throughout the world, providing them with the necessary human and financial resources. The procedures and mechanisms should be enabled to harmonise and rationalise their work through periodic meetings. All States are asked to co-operate fully with these procedures and mechanisms.

96. The World Conference on Human Rights recommends that the United Nations assume a more active role in the promotion and protection of human rights in ensuring full respect for international humanitarian law in all situations of armed conflict, in accordance with the purposes and principles of the Charter of the United Nations.

97. The World Conference on Human Rights, recognising the important role of human rights components in specific arrangements concerning some peace-keeping operations by the United Nations, recommends that the Secretary-General take into account the reporting, experience and capabilities of the Centre for Human Rights and human rights mechanisms, in conformity with the Charter of the United Nations.

98. To strengthen the enjoyment of economic, social and cultural rights, additional approaches should be examined, such as a system of indicators to measure progress in the realisation of the rights set forth in the International Covenant on Economic, Social and Cultural Rights. There must be a concerted effort to ensure recognition of economic, social and cultural rights at the national, regional and international levels.

F. FOLLOW-UP TO THE WORLD CONFERENCE ON HUMAN RIGHTS

99. The World Conference on Human Rights recommends that **A1–088** the General Assembly, the Commission on Human Rights and other organs and agencies of the United Nations system related to human rights consider ways and means for the full implementation, without delay, of the recommendations contained in the present Declaration, including the possibility of proclaiming a United Nations decade for human rights. The World Conference on Human Rights further recommends that the Commission on Human Rights annually review the progress towards this end.

100. The World Conference on Human Rights requests the Secretary-General of the United Nations to invite on the occasion of the 50th anniversary of the Universal Declaration of Human Rights all States, all organs and agencies of the United Nations system related to human rights, to report to him on the progress made in the implementation of the present Declaration and to submit a report to the General Assembly at its 53rd session, through the Commission on Human Rights and the Economic and Social Council. Likewise, regional and, as appropriate, national human rights institutions, as well as non-governmental organisations, may present their views to the Secretary-General on the progress made in the implementation of the present Declaration. Special attention should be paid to assessing the progress towards the goal of universal ratification of international human rights treaties and protocols adopted within the framework of the United Nations system.

UN FOURTH WORLD CONFERENCE ON WOMEN (SEPTEMBER 1995) BEIJING DECLARATION— PLATFORM FOR ACTION[1]

A. WOMEN AND POVERTY

47. More than 1 billion people in the world today, the great **B1–001** majority of whom are women, live in unacceptable conditions of poverty, mostly in the developing countries. Poverty has various causes, including structural ones. Poverty is a complex, multi-dimensional problem, with origins in both the national and international domains. The globalisation of the world's economy and the deepening interdependence among nations present challenges and opportunities for sustained economic growth and development, as well as risks and uncertainties for the future of the world economy. The uncertain global economic climate has been accompanied by economic restructuring as well as, in a certain number of countries, persistent, unmanageable levels of external debt and structural adjustment programmes. In addition, all types of conflict, displacement of people and environmental degradation have undermined the capacity of Governments to meet the basic needs of their populations. Transformations in the world economy are profoundly changing the parameters of social development in all countries. One significant trend has been the increased poverty of women, the extent of which varies from region to region. The gender disparities in economic power-sharing are also an important contributing factor to the poverty of women. Migration and consequent changes in family structures have placed additional burdens on women, especially those who provide for several dependants. Macroeconomic policies need rethinking and reformulation to address such trends. These policies focus almost exclusively on the formal sector. They also tend to impede the initiatives of women and fail to consider the differential impact on women and men. The application of gender analysis to a wide range of policies and programmes is therefore critical to poverty reduction strategies. In order to eradicate poverty and achieve sustainable development, women and men must participate fully and equally in the formulation of macroeconomic and social policies and strategies for the eradication of

[1] A CONF. 177/20 October 17, 1995; 35 ILM (1996); See also Chapter Two.

poverty. The eradication of poverty cannot be accomplished through anti-poverty programmes alone but will require democratic participation and changes in economic structures in order to ensure access for all women to resources, opportunities and public services. Poverty has various manifestations, including lack of income and productive resources sufficient to ensure a sustainable livelihood; hunger and malnutrition; ill health; limited or lack of access to education and other basic services; increasing morbidity and mortality from illness; homelessness and inadequate housing; unsafe environments; and social discrimination and exclusion. It is also characterised by lack of participation in decision-making and in civil, social and cultural life. It occurs in all countries—as mass poverty in many developing countries and as pockets of poverty amidst wealth in developed countries. Poverty may be caused by an economic recession that results in loss of livelihood or by disaster or conflict. There is also the poverty of low-wage workers and the utter destitution of people who fall outside family support systems, social institutions and safety nets.

48. In the past decade the number of women living in poverty has increased disproportionately to the number of men, particularly in the developing countries. The feminisation of poverty has also recently become a significant problem in the countries with economies in transition as a short-term consequence of the process of political, economic and social transformation. In addition to economic factors, the rigidity of socially ascribed gender roles and women's limited access to power, education, training and productive resources as well as other emerging factors that may lead to insecurity for families are also responsible. The failure to adequately mainstream a gender perspective in all economic analysis and planning and to address the structural causes of poverty is also a contributing factor.

B1–002   **49.** Women contribute to the economy and to combating poverty through both remunerated and unremunerated work at home, in the community and in the workplace. The empowerment of women is a critical factor in the eradication of poverty.

50. While poverty affects households as a whole, because of the gender division of labour and responsibilities for household welfare, women bear a disproportionate burden, attempting to manage household consumption and production under conditions of increasing scarcity. Poverty is particularly acute for women living in rural households.

51. Women's poverty is directly related to the absence of economic opportunities and autonomy, lack of access to economic resources, including credit, land ownership and inheritance, lack of access to education and support services and their minimal participation in the decision-making process. Poverty can also force women into situations in which they are vulnerable to sexual exploitation.

52. In too many countries, social welfare systems do not take sufficient account of the specific conditions of women living in poverty, and there is a tendency to scale back the services provided by such systems. The risk of falling into poverty is greater for women than for men, particularly in old age, where social security systems are based on the principle of continuous remunerated employment. In some cases, women do not fulfil this requirement because of interruptions in their work, due to the unbalanced distribution of remunerated and unremunerated work. Moreover, older women also face greater obstacles to labour-market reentry.

53. In many developed countries, where the level of general education and professional training of women and men are similar and where systems of protection against discrimination are available, in some sectors the economic transformations of the past decade have strongly increased either the unemployment of women or the precarious nature of their employment. The proportion of women among the poor has consequently increased. In countries with a high level of school enrolment of girls, those who leave the educational system the earliest, without any qualification, are among the most vulnerable in the labour market.

54. In countries with economies in transition and in other countries undergoing fundamental political, economic and social transformations, these transformations have often led to a reduction in women's income or to women being deprived of income.

55. Particularly in developing countries, the productive capacity of women should be increased through access to capital, resources, credit, land, technology, information, technical assistance and training so as to raise their income and improve nutrition, education, health care and status within the household. The release of women's productive potential is pivotal to breaking the cycle of poverty so that women can share fully in the benefits of development and in the products of their own labour.

56. Sustainable development and economic growth that is both sustained and sustainable are possible only through improving the economic, social, political, legal and cultural status of women. Equitable social development that recognises empowering the poor, particularly women, to utilise environmental resources sustainably is a necessary foundation for sustainable development.

57. The success of policies and measures aimed at supporting or strengthening the promotion of gender equality and the improvement of the status of women should be based on the integration of the gender perspective in general policies relating to all spheres of society as well as the implementation of positive measures with adequate institutional and financial support at all levels.

B1–003 *Strategic objective A.1. Review, adopt and maintain macroeconomic policies and development strategies that address the needs and efforts of women in poverty*

Actions to be taken

58. By Governments:

(a) Review and modify, with the full and equal participation of women, macroeconomic and social policies with a view to achieving the objectives of the Platform for Action;

(b) Analyse, from a gender perspective, policies and programmes—including those related to macroeconomic stability, structural adjustment, external debt problems, taxation, investments, employment, markets and all relevant sectors of the economy—with respect to their impact on poverty, on inequality and particularly on women; assess their impact on family well-being and conditions and adjust them, as appropriate, to promote more equitable distribution of productive assets, wealth, opportunities, income and services;

(c) Pursue and implement sound and stable macroeconomic and sectoral policies that are designed and monitored with the full and equal participation of women, encourage broad-based sustained economic growth, address the structural causes of poverty and are geared towards eradicating poverty and reducing gender-based inequality within the overall framework of achieving people-centred sustainable development;

B1–004 (d) Restructure and target the allocation of public expenditures to promote women's economic opportunities and equal access to productive resources and to address the basic social, educational and health needs of women, particularly those living in poverty;

(e) Develop agricultural and fishing sectors, where and as necessary, in order to ensure, as appropriate, household and national food security and food self-sufficiency, by allocating the necessary financial, technical and human resources;

(f) Develop policies and programmes to promote equitable distribution of food within the household;

(g) Provide adequate safety nets and strengthen State-based and community-based support systems, as an integral part of social policy, in order to enable women living in poverty to withstand adverse economic environments and preserve their livelihood, assets and revenues in times of crisis;

(h) Generate economic policies that have a positive impact on the employment and income of women workers in both the formal and informal sectors and adopt specific measures to address women's unemployment, in particular their long-term unemployment;

(i) Formulate and implement, when necessary, specific economic, social, agricultural and related policies in support of female-headed households;

(j) Develop and implement anti-poverty programmes, including employment schemes, that improve access to food for women living in poverty, including through the use of appropriate pricing and distribution mechanisms;

(k) Ensure the full realisation of the human rights of all women migrants, including women migrant workers, and their protection against violence and exploitation; introduce measures for the empowerment of documented women migrants, including women migrant workers; facilitate the productive employment of documented migrant women through greater recognition of their skills, foreign education and credentials, and facilitate their full integration into the labour force;

(l) Introduce measures to integrate or reintegrate women living in poverty and socially marginalised women into productive employment and the economic mainstream; ensure that internally displaced women have full access to economic opportunities and that the qualifications and skills of immigrant and refugee women are recognised;

(m) Enable women to obtain affordable housing and access to land by, among other things, removing all obstacles to access, with special emphasis on meeting the needs of women, especially those living in poverty and female heads of household;

(n) Formulate and implement policies and programmes that enhance the access of women agricultural and fisheries producers (including subsistence farmers and producers, especially in rural areas) to financial, technical, extension and marketing services; provide access to and control of land, appropriate infrastructure and technology in order to increase women's incomes and promote household food security, especially in rural areas and, where appropriate, encourage the development of producer-owned, market-based co-operatives;

(o) Create social security systems wherever they do not exist, or review them with a view to placing individual women and men on an equal footing, at every stage of their lives;

(p) Ensure access to free or low-cost legal services, including legal literacy, especially designed to reach women living in poverty;

(q) Take particular measures to promote and strengthen policies and programmes for indigenous women with their full participation and respect for their cultural diversity, so that they have opportunities and the possibility of choice in the development process in order to eradicate the poverty that affects them.

B1–005   **59.** By multilateral financial and development institutions, including the World Bank, the International Monetary Fund and regional development institutions, and through bilateral development co-operation:

(a) In accordance with the commitments made at the World Summit for Social Development, seek to mobilise new and additional financial resources that are both adequate and predictable and mobilised in a way that maximises the availability of such resources and uses all available funding sources and mechanisms with a view to contributing towards the goal of poverty eradication and targeting women living in poverty;

(b) Strengthen analytical capacity in order to more systematically strengthen gender perspectives and integrate them into the design and implementation of lending programmes, including structural adjustment and economic recovery programmes;

(c) Find effective development-oriented and durable solutions to external debt problems in order to help them to finance programmes and projects targeted at development, including the advancement of women, *inter alia*, through the immediate implementation of the terms of debt forgiveness agreed upon in the Paris Club in December 1994, which encompassed debt reduction, including cancellation or other debt relief measures and develop techniques of debt conversion applied to social development programmes and projects in conformity with the priorities of the Platform for Action;

(d) Invite the international financial institutions to examine innovative approaches to assisting low-income countries with a high proportion of multilateral debt, with a view to alleviating their debt burden;

(e) Ensure that structural adjustment programmes are designed to minimise their negative effects on vulnerable and disadvantaged groups and communities and to assure their positive effects on such groups and communities by preventing their marginalisation in economic and social activities and devising measures to ensure that they gain access to and control over economic resources and economic and social activities; take actions to reduce inequality and economic disparity;

(f) Review the impact of structural adjustment programmes on social development by means of gender-sensitive social impact assessments and other relevant methods, in order to develop policies to reduce their negative effects and improve their positive impact, ensuring that women do not bear a disproportionate burden of transition costs; complement adjustment lending with enhanced, targeted social development lending;

(g) Create an enabling environment that allows women to build and maintain sustainable livelihoods.

60. By national and international non-governmental organisa- **B1–006** tions and women's groups:

(a) Mobilise all parties involved in the development process, including academic institutions, non-governmental organisations and grass-roots and women's groups, to improve the effectiveness of anti-poverty programmes directed towards the poorest and most disadvantaged groups of women, such as rural and indigenous women, female heads of household, young women and older women, refugees and migrant women and women with disabilities, recognising that social development is primarily the responsibility of Governments;

(b) Engage in lobbying and establish monitoring mechanisms, as appropriate, and other relevant activities to ensure implementation of the recommendations on poverty eradication outlined in the Platform for Action and aimed at ensuring accountability and transparency from the State and private sectors;

(c) Include in their activities women with diverse needs and recognise that youth organisations are increasingly becoming effective partners in development programmes;

(d) In co-operation with the government and private sectors, participate in the development of a comprehensive national strategy for improving health, education and social services so that girls and women of all ages living in poverty have full access to such services; seek funding to secure access to services with a gender perspective and to extend those services in order to reach the rural and remote areas that are not covered by government institutions;

(e) In co-operation with Governments, employers, other social partners and relevant parties, contribute to the development of education and training and retraining policies to ensure that women can acquire a wide range of skills to meet new demands;

(f) Mobilise to protect women's right to full and equal access to economic resources, including the right to inheritance and to ownership of land and other property, credit, natural resources and appropriate technologies.

Strategic objective A.2. Revise laws and administrative practices to ensure women's equal rights and access to economic resources

Actions to be taken

B1–007 61. By Governments:

(a) Ensure access to free or low-cost legal services, including legal literacy, especially designed to reach women living in poverty;

(b) Undertake legislative and administrative reforms to give women full and equal access to economic resources, including the right to inheritance and to ownership of land and other property, credit, natural resources and appropriate technologies;

(c) Consider ratification of Convention No. 169 of the International Labour Organisation (ILO) as part of their efforts to promote and protect the rights of indigenous people.

Strategic objective A.3. Provide women with access to savings and credit mechanisms and institutions

Actions to be taken

62. By Governments:

(a) Enhance the access of disadvantaged women, including women entrepreneurs, in rural, remote and urban areas to financial services through strengthening links between the formal banks and intermediary lending organisations, including legislative support, training for women and institutional strengthening for intermediary institutions with a view to mobilising capital for those institutions and increasing the availability of credit;

(b) Encourage links between financial institutions and non-governmental organisations and support innovative lending practices, including those that integrate credit with women's services and training and provide credit facilities to rural women.

63. By commercial banks, specialised financial institutions and **B1–008** the private sector in examining their policies:

(a) Use credit and savings methodologies that are effective in reaching women in poverty and innovative in reducing transaction costs and redefining risk;

(b) Open special windows for lending to women, including young women, who lack access to traditional sources of collateral;

(c) Simplify banking practices, for example by reducing the minimum deposit and other requirements for opening bank accounts;

(d) Ensure the participation and joint ownership, where possible, of women clients in the decision-making of institutions providing credit and financial services.

64. By multilateral and bilateral development co-operation organisations: Support, through the provision of capital and/or resources, financial institutions that serve low-income, small-scale and micro-scale women entrepreneurs and producers, in both the formal and informal sectors.

65. By Governments and multilateral financial institutions, as appropriate:
Support institutions that meet performance standards in reaching large numbers of low-income women and men through capitalisation, refinancing and institutional development support in forms that foster self-sufficiency.

66. By international organisations:
Increase funding for programmes and projects designed to promote sustainable and productive entrepreneurial activities for income-generation among disadvantaged women and women living in poverty.

Strategic objective A.4. Develop gender-based methodologies and conduct research to address the feminisation of poverty
Actions to be taken

67. By Governments, intergovernmental organisations, aca- **B1–009** demic and research institutions and the private sector:

(a) Develop conceptual and practical methodologies for incorporating gender perspectives into all aspects of economic policy-making, including structural adjustment planning and programmes;

(b) Apply these methodologies in conducting gender-impact analyses of all policies and programmes, including structural adjustment programmes, and disseminate the research findings.

68. By national and international statistical organisations:

(a) Collect gender and age-disaggregated data on poverty and all aspects of economic activity and develop qualitative and quantitative statistical indicators to facilitate the assessment of economic performance from a gender perspective

(b) Devise suitable statistical means to recognise and make visible the full extent of the work of women and all their contributions to the national economy, including their contribution in the unremunerated and domestic sectors, and examine the relationship of women's unremunerated work to the incidence of and their vulnerability to poverty.

F. WOMEN AND THE ECONOMY

B1–010 There are considerable differences in women's and men's access to and opportunities to exert power over economic structures in their societies. In most parts of the world, women are virtually absent from or are poorly represented in economic decision-making, including the formulation of financial, monetary, commercial and other economic policies, as well as tax systems and rules governing pay. Since it is often within the framework of such policies that individual men and women make their decisions, *inter alia*, on how to divide their time between remunerated and unremunerated work, the actual development of these economic structures and policies has a direct impact on women's and men's access to economic resources, their economic power and consequently the extent of equality between them at the individual and family levels as well as in society as a whole.

151. In many regions, women's participation in remunerated work in the formal and non-formal labour market has increased significantly and has changed during the past decade. While women continue to work in agriculture and fisheries, they have also become increasingly involved in micro, small and medium-sized enterprises and, in some cases, have become more dominant in the expanding informal sector. Due to, *inter alia*, difficult economic situations and a lack of bargaining power resulting from gender inequality, many women have been forced to accept low pay and poor working conditions and thus have often become preferred workers. On the other hand, women have entered the workforce increasingly by choice when they have become aware of and demanded their rights. Some have succeeded in entering and advancing in the workplace and improving their pay and working conditions. However, women have been particularly affected by the economic situation and restructuring processes, which have changed the nature of employment and, in some cases, have led to a loss of jobs, even for professional and skilled women. In addition, many women have entered the informal sector owing to the lack of other opportunities. Women's participation and gender concerns are still largely absent from and should be integrated in the policy formulation process of the multilateral institutions that define the terms and, in co-operation with Governments, set the goals of structural adjustment programmes, loans and grants.

152. Discrimination in education and training, hiring and remuneration, promotion and horizontal mobility practices, as well as inflexible working conditions, lack of access to productive resources and inadequate sharing of family responsibilities, combined with a lack of or insufficient services such as child care, continue to restrict employment, economic, professional and other opportunities and mobility for women and make their involvement stressful. Moreover, attitudinal obstacles inhibit women's participation in developing economic policy and in some regions restrict the access of women and girls to education and training for economic management.

153. Women's share in the labour force continues to rise and almost everywhere women are working more outside the household, although there has not been a parallel lightening of responsibility for unremunerated work in the household and community. Women's income is becoming increasingly necessary to households of all types. In some regions, there has been a growth in women's entrepreneurship and other self-reliant activities, particularly in the informal sector. In many countries, women are the majority of workers in non-standard work, such as temporary, casual, multiple part-time, contract and home-based employment.

154. Women migrant workers, including domestic workers, **B1–011** contribute to the economy of the sending country through their remittances and also to the economy of the receiving country through their participation in the labour force. However, in many receiving countries, migrant women experience higher levels of unemployment compared with both nonmigrant workers and male migrant workers.

155. Insufficient attention to gender analysis has meant that women's contributions and concerns remain too often ignored in economic structures, such as financial markets and institutions, labour markets, economics as an academic discipline, economic and social infrastructure, taxation and social security systems, as well as in families and households. As a result, many policies and programmes may continue to contribute to inequalities between women and men. Where progress has been made in integrating gender perspectives, programme and policy effectiveness has also been enhanced.

156. Although many women have advanced in economic structures, for the majority of women, particularly those who face additional barriers, continuing obstacles have hindered their ability to achieve economic autonomy and to ensure sustainable livelihoods for themselves and their dependants. Women are active in a variety of economic areas, which they often combine, ranging from wage labour and subsistence farming and fishing to the informal sector. However, legal and customary barriers to ownership of or access to land, natural resources, capital, credit, technology and other means of production, as well as wage differentials, contribute to impeding the economic progress of women. Women contribute to development not only through remunerated work but also through a great deal of unremunerated work. On the one hand, women participate in the production of goods and services for the market and household consumption, in agriculture, food production or family enterprises. Though included in the United Nations System of National Accounts and therefore in international standards for labour statistics, this unremunerated work—particularly that related to agriculture—is often undervalued and under-recorded. On the other hand, women still also perform the great majority of unremunerated domestic work and community work, such as caring for children and older persons, preparing food for the family, protecting the environment and providing voluntary assistance to vulnerable and disadvantaged individuals and groups. This work is often not measured in quantitative terms and is not valued in national accounts. Women's contribution to development is seriously underestimated, and thus its social recognition is limited. The full visibility of the type, extent and distribution of this unremunerated work will also contribute to a better sharing of responsibilities.

157. Although some new employment opportunities have been created for women as a result of the globalisation of the economy, there are also trends that have exacerbated inequalities between women and men. At the same time, globalisation, including economic integration, can create pressures on the employment situation of women to adjust to new circumstances and to find new sources of employment as patterns of trade change. More analysis needs to be done of the impact of globalisation on women's economic status.

158. These trends have been characterised by low wages, little **B1–012** or no labour standards protection, poor working conditions, particularly with regard to women's occupational health and safety, low skill levels, and a lack of job security and social security, in both the formal and informal sectors. Women's unemployment is a serious and increasing problem in many countries and sectors. Young workers in the informal and rural sectors and migrant female workers remain the least protected by labour and immigration laws. Women, particularly those who are heads of households with young children, are limited in their employment opportunities for reasons that include inflexible working conditions and inadequate sharing, by men and by society, of family responsibilities.

159. In countries that are undergoing fundamental political, economic and social transformation, the skills of women, if better utilised, could constitute a major contribution to the economic life of their respective countries. Their input should continue to be developed and supported and their potential further realised.

160. Lack of employment in the private sector and reductions in public services and public service jobs have affected women disproportionately. In some countries, women take on more unpaid work, such as the care of children and those who are ill or elderly, compensating for lost household income, particularly when public services are not available. In many cases, employment creation strategies have not paid sufficient attention to occupations and sectors where women predominate; nor have they adequately promoted the access of women to those occupations and sectors that are traditionally male.

161. For those women in paid work, many experience obstacles that prevent them from achieving their potential. While some are increasingly found in lower levels of management, attitudinal discrimination often prevents them from being promoted further. The experience of sexual harassment is an affront to a worker's dignity and prevents women from making a contribution commensurate with their abilities. The lack of a family-friendly work environment, including a lack of appropriate and affordable child care, and inflexible working hours further prevent women from achieving their full potential.

162. In the private sector, including transnational and national enterprises, women are largely absent from management and policy levels, denoting discriminatory hiring and promotion policies and practices. The unfavourable work environment as well as the limited number of employment opportunities available have led many women to seek alternatives. Women have increasingly become self-employed and owners and managers of micro, small and medium-scale enterprises. The expansion of the informal sector, in many countries, and of self-organised and independent enterprises is in large part due to women, whose collaborative, self-help and traditional practices and initiatives in production and trade represent a vital economic resource. When they gain access to and control over capital, credit and other resources, technology and training, women can increase production, marketing and income for sustainable development.

163. Taking into account the fact that continuing inequalities and noticeable progress co-exist, rethinking employment policies is necessary in order to integrate the gender perspective and to draw attention to a wider range of opportunities as well as to address any negative gender implications of current patterns of work and employment. To realise fully equality between women and men in their contribution to the economy, active efforts are required for equal recognition and appreciation of the influence that the work, experience, knowledge and values of both women and men have in society.

164. In addressing the economic potential and independence of women, Governments and other actors should promote an active and visible policy of mainstreaming a gender perspective in all policies and programmes so that before decisions are taken, an analysis is made of the effects on women and men, respectively.

B1–013 *Strategic objective F.1. Promote women's economic rights and independence, including access to employment, appropriate working conditions and control over economic resources*

Actions to be taken

165. By Governments:

(a) Enact and enforce legislation to guarantee the rights of women and men to equal pay for equal work or work of equal value;

(b) Adopt and implement laws against discrimination based on sex in the labour market, especially considering older women workers, hiring and promotion, the extension of employment benefits and social security, and working conditions;

(c) Eliminate discriminatory practices by employers and take appropriate measures in consideration of women's reproductive role and functions, such as the denial of employment and dismissal due to pregnancy or breast-feeding, or requiring proof of contraceptive use, and take effective measures to ensure that pregnant women, women on maternity leave or women re-entering the labour market after childbearing are not discriminated against;

(d) Devise mechanisms and take positive action to enable women to gain access to full and equal participation in the formulation of policies and definition of structures through such bodies as ministries of finance and trade, national economic commissions, economic research institutes and other key agencies, as well as through their participation in appropriate international bodies;

(e) Undertake legislation and administrative reforms to give women equal rights with men to economic resources, including access to ownership and control over land and other forms of property, credit, inheritance, natural resources and appropriate new technology;

(f) Conduct reviews of national income and inheritance tax **B1–014** and social security systems to eliminate any existing bias against women;

(g) Seek to develop a more comprehensive knowledge of work and employment through, *inter alia*, efforts to measure and better understand the type, extent and distribution of unremunerated work, particularly work in caring for dependants and unremunerated work done for family farms or businesses, and encourage the sharing and dissemination of information on studies and experience in this field, including the development of methods for assessing its value in quantitative terms, for possible reflection in accounts that may be produced separately from, but consistent with, core national accounts;

(h) Review and amend laws governing the operation of financial institutions to ensure that they provide services to women and men on an equal basis;

(i) Facilitate, at appropriate levels, more open and transparent budget processes;

(j) Revise and implement national policies that support the traditional savings, credit and lending mechanisms for women;

(k) Seek to ensure that national policies related to international and regional trade agreements do not have an adverse impact on women's new and traditional economic activities;

(l) Ensure that all corporations, including transnational corporations, comply with national laws and codes, social security regulations, applicable international agreements, instruments and conventions, including those related to the environment, and other relevant laws;

(m) Adjust employment policies to facilitate the restructuring of work patterns in order to promote the sharing of family responsibilities;

(n) Establish mechanisms and other forums to enable women entrepreneurs and women workers to contribute to the formulation of policies and programmes being developed by economic ministries and financial institutions;

(o) Enact and enforce equal opportunity laws, take positive action and ensure compliance by the public and private sectors through various means;

(p) Use gender-impact analyses in the development of macro and micro-economic and social policies in order to monitor such impact and restructure policies in cases where harmful impact occurs;

(q) Promote gender-sensitive policies and measures to empower women as equal partners with men in technical, managerial and entrepreneurial fields;

(r) Reform laws or enact national policies that support the establishment of labour laws to ensure the protection of all women workers, including safe work practices, the right to organise and access to justice.

B1–015 *Strategic objective F.2. Facilitate women's equal access to resources, employment, markets and trade*

Actions to be taken

166. By Governments:

(a) Promote and support women's self-employment and the development of small enterprises, and strengthen women's access to credit and capital on appropriate terms equal to those of men through the scaling-up of institutions dedicated to promoting women's entrepreneurship, including, as appropriate, non-traditional and mutual credit schemes, as well as innovative linkages with financial institutions;

(b) Strengthen the incentive role of the State as employer to develop a policy of equal opportunities for women and men;

(c) Enhance, at the national and local levels, rural women's income-generating potential by facilitating their equal access to and control over productive resources, land, credit, capital, property rights, development programmes and co-operative structures;

(d) Promote and strengthen micro-enterprises, new small businesses, co-operative enterprises, expanded markets and other employment opportunities and, where appropriate, facilitate the transition from the informal to the formal sector, especially in rural areas;

(e) Create and modify programmes and policies that recognise and strengthen women's vital role in food security and provide paid and unpaid women producers, especially those involved in food production, such as farming, fishing and aquaculture, as well as urban enterprises, with equal access to appropriate technologies, transportation, extension services, marketing and credit facilities at the local and community levels;

(f) Establish appropriate mechanisms and encourage intersectoral institutions that enable women's co-operatives to optimise access to necessary services;

(g) Increase the proportion of women extension workers and other government personnel who provide technical assistance or administer economic programmes;

(h) Review, reformulate, if necessary, and implement policies, including business, commercial and contract law and government regulations, to ensure that they do not discriminate against micro, small and medium-scale enterprises owned by women in rural and urban areas;

(i) Analyse, advise on, co-ordinate and implement policies that integrate the needs and interests of employed, self-employed and entrepreneurial women into sectoral and inter-ministerial policies, programmes and budgets;

(j) Ensure equal access for women to effective job training, retraining, counselling and placement services that are not limited to traditional employment areas;

(k) Remove policy and regulatory obstacles faced by women in social and development programmes that discourage private and individual initiative;

(l) Safeguard and promote respect for basic workers' rights, including the prohibition of forced labour and child labour, freedom of association and the right to organise and bargain collectively, equal remuneration for men and women for work of equal value and non-discrimination in employment, fully implementing the conventions of the

International Labour Organisation in the case of States Parties to those conventions and, taking into account the principles embodied in the case of those countries that are not parties to those conventions in order to achieve truly sustained economic growth and sustainable development.

B1–016   **167.** By Governments, central banks and national development banks, and private banking institutions, as appropriate:

(a) Increase the participation of women, including women entrepreneurs, in advisory boards and other forums to enable women entrepreneurs from all sectors and their organisations to contribute to the formulation and review of policies and programmes being developed by economic ministries and banking institutions;

(b) Mobilise the banking sector to increase lending and refinancing through incentives and the development of intermediaries that serve the needs of women entrepreneurs and producers in both rural and urban areas, and include women in their leadership, planning and decision-making;

(c) Structure services to reach rural and urban women involved in micro, small and medium-scale enterprises, with special attention to young women, low-income women, those belonging to ethnic and racial minorities, and indigenous women who lack access to capital and assets; and expand women's access to financial markets by identifying and encouraging financial supervisory and regulatory reforms that support financial institutions' direct and indirect efforts to better meet the credit and other financial needs of the micro, small and medium-scale enterprises of women;

(d) Ensure that women's priorities are included in public investment programmes for economic infrastructure, such as water and sanitation, electrification and energy conservation, transport and road construction; promote greater involvement of women beneficiaries at the project planning and implementation stages to ensure access to jobs and contracts.

168. By Governments and non-governmental organisations:

(a) Pay special attention to women's needs when disseminating market, trade and resource information and provide appropriate training in these fields;

(b) Encourage community economic development strategies that build on partnerships among Governments, and encourage members of civil society to create jobs and address the social circumstances of individuals, families and communities.

169. By multilateral funders and regional development banks, **B1–017** as well as bilateral and private funding agencies, at the international, regional and subregional levels:

(a) Review, where necessary reformulate, and implement policies, programmes and projects, to ensure that a higher proportion of resources reach women in rural and remote areas;

(b) Develop flexible funding arrangements to finance intermediary institutions that target women's economic activities, and promote self-sufficiency and increased capacity in and profitability of women's economic enterprises;

(c) Develop strategies to consolidate and strengthen their assistance to the micro, small and medium-scale enterprise sector, in order to enhance the opportunities for women to participate fully and equally and work together to co-ordinate and enhance the effectiveness of this sector, drawing upon expertise and financial resources from within their own organizations as well as from bilateral agencies, Governments and non-governmental organisations.

170. By international, multilateral and bilateral development co-operation organisations:
Support, through the provision of capital and/or resources, financial institutions that serve low-income, small and micro-scale women entrepreneurs and producers in both the formal and informal sectors.

171. By Governments and/or multilateral financial institutions:
Review rules and procedures of formal national and international financial institutions that obstruct replication of the Grameen Bank prototype, which provides credit facilities to rural women.

172. By international organisations:
Provide adequate support for programmes and projects designed to promote sustainable and productive entrepreneurial activities among women, in particular the disadvantaged.

Strategic objective F.3. Provide business services, training and access to **B1–018**
markets, information and technology, particularly to low-income women

Actions to be taken

173. By Governments in co-operation with non-governmental organisations and the private sector:

(a) Provide public infrastructure to ensure equal market access for women and men entrepreneurs;

(b) Develop programmes that provide training and retraining, particularly in new technologies, and affordable services to women in business management, product development, financing, production and quality control, marketing and the legal aspects of business;

(c) Provide outreach programmes to inform low-income and poor women, particularly in rural and remote areas, of opportunities for market and technology access, and provide assistance in taking advantage of such opportunities;

(d) Create non-discriminatory support services, including investment funds for women's businesses, and target women, particularly low-income women, in trade promotion programmes;

(e) Disseminate information about successful women entrepreneurs in both traditional and non-traditional economic activities and the skills necessary to achieve success, and facilitate networking and the exchange of information;

(f) Take measures to ensure equal access of women to ongoing training in the workplace, including unemployed women, single parents, women re-entering the labour market after an extended temporary exit from employment owing to family responsibilities and other causes, and women displaced by new forms of production or by retrenchment, and increase incentives to enterprises to expand the number of vocational and training centres that provide training for women in non-traditional areas;

(g) Provide affordable support services, such as high-quality, flexible and affordable child-care services, that take into account the needs of working men and women.

174. By local, national, regional and international business organisations and non-governmental organisations concerned with women's issues:

Advocate, at all levels, for the promotion and support of women's businesses and enterprises, including those in the informal sector, and the equal access of women to productive resources.

B1–019 *Strategic objective F.4. Strengthen women's economic capacity and commercial networks*

Actions to be taken

175. By Governments:

(a) Adopt policies that support business organisations, non-governmental organisations, co-operatives, revolving loan funds, credit unions, grass-roots organisations, women's self-help groups and other groups in order to provide services to women entrepreneurs in rural and urban areas;

(b) Integrate a gender perspective into all economic restructuring and structural adjustment policies and design programmes for women who are affected by economic restructuring, including structural adjustment programmes, and for women who work in the informal sector;

(c) Adopt policies that create an enabling environment for women's self-help groups, workers' organisations and co-operatives through non-conventional forms of support and by recognising the right to freedom of association and the right to organise;

(d) Support programmes that enhance the self-reliance of special groups of women, such as young women, women with disabilities, elderly women and women belonging to racial and ethnic minorities;

(e) Promote gender equality through the promotion of women's studies and through the use of the results of studies and gender research in all fields, including the economic, scientific and technological fields;

(f) Support the economic activities of indigenous women, taking into account their traditional knowledge, so as to improve their situation and development;

(g) Adopt policies to extend or maintain the protection of labour laws and social security provisions for those who do paid work in the home;

(h) Recognise and encourage the contribution of research by women scientists and technologists;

(i) Ensure that policies and regulations do not discriminate against micro, small and medium-scale enterprises run by women.

176. By financial intermediaries national training institutes, **B1–020** credit unions, non-governmental organisations, women's associations, professional organisations and the private sector, as appropriate:

(a) Provide, at the national, regional and international levels, training in a variety of business-related and financial management and technical skills to enable women, especially

young women, to participate in economic policy-making at
those levels;

(b) Provide business services, including marketing and trade
information, product design and innovation, technology
transfer and quality, to women's business enterprises,
including those in export sectors of the economy;

(c) Promote technical and commercial links and establish joint
ventures among women entrepreneurs at the national,
regional and international levels to support community-
based initiatives;

(d) Strengthen the participation of women, including marginalised women, in production and marketing co-
operatives by providing marketing and financial support,
especially in rural and remote areas;

(e) Promote and strengthen women's micro-enterprises, new
small businesses, co-operative enterprises, expanded markets and other employment opportunities and, where
appropriate, facilitate the transition from the informal to the
formal sector, in rural and urban areas;

(f) Invest capital and develop investment portfolios to finance
women's business enterprises;

(g) Give adequate attention to providing technical assistance,
advisory services, training and retraining for women connected with the entry to the market economy;

(h) Support credit networks and innovative ventures, including
traditional savings schemes;

(i) Provide networking arrangements for entrepreneurial
women, including opportunities for the mentoring of inex-
perienced women by the more experienced;

(j) Encourage community organisations and public authorities
to establish loan pools for women entrepreneurs, drawing
on successful small-scale co-operative models.

177. By the private sector, including transnational and national
corporations:

(a) Adopt policies and establish mechanisms to grant contracts
on a non-discriminatory basis;

(b) Recruit women for leadership, decision-making and management and provide training programmes, all on an equal
basis with men;

(c) Observe national labour, environment, consumer, health
and safety laws, particularly those that affect women.

Strategic objective F.5. Eliminate occupational segregation and all forms of employment discrimination

Actions to be taken

178. By Governments, employers, employees, trade unions and **B1–021** women's organisations:

(a) Implement and enforce laws and regulations and encourage voluntary codes of conduct that ensure that international labour standards, such as International Labour Organisation Convention No. 100 on equal pay and workers' rights, apply equally to female and male workers;

(b) Enact and enforce laws and introduce implementing measures, including means of redress and access to justice in cases of non-compliance, to prohibit direct and indirect discrimination on grounds of sex, including by reference to marital or family status, in relation to access to employment, conditions of employment, including training, promotion, health and safety, as well as termination of employment and social security of workers, including legal protection against sexual and racial harassment;

(c) Enact and enforce laws and develop workplace policies against gender discrimination in the labour market, especially considering older women workers, in hiring and promotion, and in the extension of employment benefits and social security, as well as regarding discriminatory working conditions and sexual harassment; mechanisms should be developed for the regular review and monitoring of such laws;

(d) Eliminate discriminatory practices by employers on the **B1–022** basis of women's reproductive roles and functions, including refusal of employment and dismissal of women due to pregnancy and breast-feeding responsibilities;

(e) Develop and promote employment programmes and services for women entering and/or re-entering the labour market, especially poor urban, rural and young women, the self-employed and those negatively affected by structural adjustment;

(f) Implement and monitor positive public-and private-sector employment, equity and positive action programmes to address systemic discrimination against women in the labour force, in particular women with disabilities and women belonging to other disadvantaged groups, with respect to hiring, retention and promotion, and vocational training of women in all sectors;

(g) Eliminate occupational segregation, especially by promoting the equal participation of women in highly skilled jobs and senior management positions, and through other measures, such as counselling and placement, that stimulate their on-the-job career development and upward mobility in the labour market, and by stimulating the diversification of occupational choices by both women and men; encourage women to take up non-traditional jobs, especially in science and technology, and encourage men to seek employment in the social sector;

(h) Recognise collective bargaining as a right and as an important mechanism for eliminating wage inequality for women and to improve working conditions;

(i) Promote the election of women trade union officials and ensure that trade union officials elected to represent women are given job protection and physical security in connection with the discharge of their functions;

(j) Ensure access to and develop special programmes to enable women with disabilities to obtain and retain employment, and ensure access to education and training at all proper levels, in accordance with the Standard Rules on the Equalisation of Opportunities for Persons with Disabilities; adjust working conditions, to the extent possible, in order to suit the needs of women with disabilities, who should be assured legal protection against unfounded job loss on account of their disabilities;

(k) Increase efforts to close the gap between women's and men's pay, take steps to implement the principle of equal remuneration for equal work of equal value by strengthening legislation, including compliance with international labour laws and standards, and encourage job evaluation schemes with gender-neutral criteria;

(l) Establish and/or strengthen mechanisms to adjudicate matters relating to wage discrimination;

(m) Set specific target dates for eliminating all forms of child labour that are contrary to accepted international standards and ensure the full enforcement of relevant existing laws and, where appropriate, enact the legislation necessary to implement the Convention on the Rights of the Child and International Labour Organisation standards, ensuring the protection of working children, in particular, street children, through the provision of appropriate health, education and other social services;

(n) Ensure that strategies to eliminate child labour also address the excessive demands made on some girls for unpaid work in their household and other households, where applicable;

(o) Review, analyse and, where appropriate, reformulate the wage structures in female-dominated professions, such as teaching, nursing and child care, with a view to raising their low status and earnings;

(p) Facilitate the productive employment of documented migrant women (including women who have been determined refugees according to the 1951 Convention relating to the Status of Refugees) through greater recognition of foreign education and credentials and by adopting an integrated approach to labour market training that incorporates language training.

Strategic objective F.6. Promote harmonization of work and family responsibilities for women and men **B1–023**

Actions to be taken

179. By Governments:

(a) Adopt policies to ensure the appropriate protection of labour laws and social security benefits for part-time, temporary, seasonal and home-based workers; promote career development based on work conditions that harmonise work and family responsibilities;

(b) Ensure that full and part-time work can be freely chosen by women and men on an equal basis, and consider appropriate protection for atypical workers in terms of access to employment, working conditions and social security;

(c) Ensure, through legislation, incentives and/or encouragement, opportunities for women and men to take job-protected parental leave and to have parental benefits; promote the equal sharing of responsibilities for the family by men and women, including through appropriate legislation, incentives and/or encouragement, and also promote the facilitation of breast-feeding for working mothers;

(d) Develop policies, *inter alia*, in education to change attitudes that reinforce the division of labour based on gender in order to promote the concept of shared family responsibility for work in the home, particularly in relation to children and elder care;

(e) Improve the development of, and access to, technologies that facilitate occupational as well as domestic work, encourage self-support, generate income, transform gender-prescribed roles within the productive process and enable women to move out of low-paying jobs;

(f) Examine a range of policies and programmes, including social security legislation and taxation systems, in accordance with national priorities and policies, to determine how to promote gender equality and flexibility in the way people divide their time between and derive benefits from education and training, paid employment, family responsibilities, volunteer activity and other socially useful forms of work, rest and leisure.

180. By Governments, the private sector and non-governmental organisations, trade unions and the United Nations, as appropriate:

(a) Adopt appropriate measures involving relevant governmental bodies and employers' and employees' associations so that women and men are able to take temporary leave from employment, have transferable employment and retirement benefits and make arrangements to modify work hours without sacrificing their prospects for development and advancement at work and in their careers;

(b) Design and provide educational programmes through innovative media campaigns and school and community education programmes to raise awareness on gender equality and non-stereotyped gender roles of women and men within the family; provide support services and facilities, such as on-site child care at workplaces and flexible working arrangements;

(c) Enact and enforce laws against sexual and other forms of harassment in all workplaces.

H. INSTITUTIONAL MECHANISMS FOR THE ADVANCEMENT OF WOMEN

B1–024   **196.** National machineries for the advancement of women have been established in almost every Member State to, *inter alia*, design, promote the implementation of, execute, monitor, evaluate, advocate and mobilise support for policies that promote the advancement of women. National machineries are diverse in form and uneven in their effectiveness, and in some cases have declined. Often marginalised in national government structures, these mechanisms are frequently hampered by unclear mandates, lack of adequate staff, training, data and sufficient resources, and insufficient support from national political leadership.

197. At the regional and international levels, mechanisms and institutions to promote the advancement of women as an integral part of mainstream political, economic, social and cultural development, and of initiatives on development and human rights, encounter similar problems emanating from a lack of commitment at the highest levels.

198. Successive international conferences have underscored the need to take gender factors into account in policy and programme planning. However, in many instances this has not been done.

199. Regional bodies concerned with the advancement of women have been strengthened, together with international machinery, such as the Commission on the Status of Women and the Committee on the Elimination of Discrimination against Women. However, the limited resources available continue to impede full implementation of their mandates.

200. Methodologies for conducting gender-based analysis in policies and programmes and for dealing with the differential effects of policies on women and men have been developed in many organisations and are available for application but are often not being applied or are not being applied consistently.

201. A national machinery for the advancement of women is the central policy-co-ordinating unit inside government. Its main task is to support government-wide mainstreaming of a gender-equality perspective in all policy areas. The necessary conditions for an effective functioning of such national machineries include:

(a) Location at the highest possible level in the Government, falling under the responsibility of a Cabinet minister;

(b) Institutional mechanisms or processes that facilitate, as appropriate, decentralised planning, implementation and monitoring with a view to involving non-governmental organisations and community organisations from the grass-roots upwards;

(c) Sufficient resources in terms of budget and professional capacity;

(d) Opportunity to influence development of all government policies.

202. In addressing the issue of mechanisms for promoting the advancement of women, Governments and other actors should promote an active and visible policy of mainstreaming a gender perspective in all policies and programmes so that, before decisions are taken, an analysis is made of the effects on women and men, respectively.

B1–025 *Strategic objective H.1. Create or strengthen national machineries and other governmental bodies*

Actions to be taken

203. By Governments:

(a) Ensure that responsibility for the advancement of women is vested in the highest possible level of government; in many cases, this could be at the level of a Cabinet minister;

(b) Based on a strong political commitment, create a national machinery, where it does not exist, and strengthen, as appropriate, existing national machineries, for the advancement of women at the highest possible level of government; it should have clearly defined mandates and authority; critical elements would be adequate resources and the ability and competence to influence policy and formulate and review legislation; among other things, it should perform policy analysis, undertake advocacy, communication, co-ordination and monitoring of implementation;

(c) Provide staff training in designing and analysing data from a gender perspective;

(d) Establish procedures to allow the machinery to gather information on government-wide policy issues at an early stage and continuously use it in the policy development and review process within the Government;

(e) Report, on a regular basis, to legislative bodies on the progress of efforts, as appropriate, to mainstream gender concerns, taking into account the implementation of the Platform for Action;

(f) Encourage and promote the active involvement of the broad and diverse range of institutional actors in the public, private and voluntary sectors to work for equality between women and men.

B1–026 *Strategic objective H.2. Integrate gender perspectives in legislation, public policies, programmes and projects*

Actions to be taken

204. By Governments:

(a) Seek to ensure that before policy decisions are taken, an analysis of their impact on women and men, respectively, is carried out;

(b) Regularly review national policies, programmes and projects, as well as their implementation, evaluating the impact of employment and income policies in order to guarantee that women are direct beneficiaries of development and that their full contribution to development, both remunerated and unremunerated, is considered in economic policy and planning;

(c) Promote national strategies and aims on equality between women and men in order to eliminate obstacles to the exercise of women's rights and eradicate all forms of discrimination against women;

(d) Work with members of legislative bodies, as appropriate, to promote a gender perspective in all legislation and policies;

(e) Give all ministries the mandate to review policies and programmes from a gender perspective and in the light of the Platform for Action; locate the responsibility for the implementation of that mandate at the highest possible level; establish and/or strengthen an inter-ministerial co-ordination structure to carry out this mandate, to monitor progress and to network with relevant machineries.

205. By national machinery:

(a) Facilitate the formulation and implementation of government policies on equality between women and men, develop appropriate strategies and methodologies, and promote co-ordination and co-operation within the central Government in order to ensure mainstreaming of a gender perspective in all policy-making processes;

(b) Promote and establish co-operative relationships with relevant branches of government, centres for women's studies and research, academic and educational institutions, the private sector, the media, non-governmental organisations, especially women's organisations, and all other actors of civil society;

(c) Undertake activities focusing on legal reform with regard, inter alia, to the family, conditions of employment, social security, income tax, equal opportunity in education, positive measures to promote the advancement of women, and the perception of attitudes and a culture favourable to equality, as well as promote a gender perspective in legal policy and programming reforms;

(d) Promote the increased participation of women as both active agents and beneficiaries of the development process, which would result in an improvement in the quality of life for all;

(e) Establish direct links with national, regional and international bodies dealing with the advancement of women;

(f) Provide training and advisory assistance to government agencies in order to integrate a gender perspective in their policies and programmes.

B1–027 *Strategic objective H.3. Generate and disseminate gender-disaggregated data and information for planning and evaluation*

Actions to be taken

206. By national, regional and international statistical services and relevant governmental and United Nations agencies, in co-operation with research and documentation organisations, in their respective areas of responsibility:

(a) Ensure that statistics related to individuals are collected, compiled, analysed and presented by sex and age and reflect problems, issues and questions related to women and men in society;

(b) Collect, compile, analyse and present on a regular basis data disaggregated by age, sex, socio-economic and other relevant indicators, including number of dependants, for utilisation in policy and programme planning and implementation;

(c) Involve centres for women's studies and research organisations in developing and testing appropriate indicators and research methodologies to strengthen gender analysis, as well as in monitoring and evaluating the implementation of the goals of the Platform for Action;

(d) Designate or appoint staff to strengthen gender-statistics programmes and ensure co-ordination, monitoring and linkage to all fields of statistical work, and prepare output that integrates statistics from the various subject areas;

(e) Improve data collection on the full contribution of women and men to the economy, including their participation in the informal sector(s);

B1–028   (f) Develop a more comprehensive knowledge of all forms of work and employment by:

(i) Improving data collection on the unremunerated work which is already included in the United

Nations System of National Accounts, such as in agriculture, particularly subsistence agriculture, and other types of non-market production activities;

(ii) Improving measurements that at present underestimate women's unemployment and underemployment in the labour market;

(iii) Developing methods, in the appropriate forums, for assessing the value, in quantitative terms, of unremunerated work that is outside national accounts, such as caring for dependants and preparing food, for possible reflection in satellite or other official accounts that may be produced separately from but are consistent with core national accounts, with a view to recognising the economic contribution of women and making visible the unequal distribution of remunerated and unremunerated work between women and men;

(g) Develop an international classification of activities for time-use statistics that is sensitive to the differences between women and men in remunerated and unremunerated work, and collect data disaggregated by sex. At the national level, subject to national constraints:

(i) Conduct regular time-use studies to measure, in quantitative terms, unremunerated work, including recording those activities that are performed simultaneously with remunerated or other unremunerated activities;

(ii) Measure, in quantitative terms, unremunerated work that is outside national accounts and work to improve methods to assess and accurately reflect its value in satellite or other official accounts that are separate from but consistent with core national accounts;

(h) Improve concepts and methods of data collection on the measurement of poverty among women and men, including their access to resources;

(i) Strengthen vital statistical systems and incorporate gender analysis into publications and research; give priority to gender differences in research design and in data collection and analysis in order to improve data on morbidity; and improve data collection on access to health services, including access to comprehensive sexual and reproductive health services, maternal care and family planning, with special priority for adolescent mothers and for elder care;

(j) Develop improved gender-disaggregated and age-specific data on the victims and perpetrators of all forms of violence

against women, such as domestic violence, sexual harassment, rape, incest and sexual abuse, and trafficking in
women and girls, as well as on violence by agents of the
State;

(k) Improve concepts and methods of data collection on the
participation of women and men with disabilities, including
their access to resources.

B1–029 207. By Governments:

(a) Ensure the regular production of a statistical publication on
gender that presents and interprets topical data on women
and men in a form suitable for a wide range of non-
technical users;

(b) Ensure that producers and users of statistics in each country regularly review the adequacy of the official statistical
system and its coverage of gender issues, and prepare a
plan for needed improvements, where necessary;

(c) Develop and encourage the development of quantitative
and qualitative studies by research organisations, trade
unions, employers, the private sector and non-
governmental organisations on the sharing of power and
influence in society, including the number of women and
men in senior decision-making positions in both the public
and private sectors;

(d) Use more gender-sensitive data in the formulation of policy
and implementation of programmes and projects.

208. By the United Nations:

(a) Promote the development of methods to find better ways to
collect, collate and analyse data that may relate to the
human rights of women, including violence against
women, for use by all relevant United Nations bodies;

(b) Promote the further development of statistical methods to
improve data that relate to women in economic, social,
cultural and political development;

(c) Prepare a new issue of The World's Women at regular five-
year intervals and distribute it widely;

(d) Assist countries, upon request, in the development of
gender policies and programmes;

(e) Ensure that the relevant reports, data and publications of
the Statistical Division of the United Nations Secretariat

and the International Research and Training Institute for the Advancement of Women on progress at the national and international levels are transmitted to the Commission on the Status of Women in a regular and co-ordinated fashion.

209. By multilateral development institutions and bilateral donors:

Encourage and support the development of national capacity in developing countries and in countries with economies in transition by providing resources and technical assistance so that countries can fully measure the work done by women and men, including both remunerated and unremunerated work, and, where appropriate, use satellite or other official accounts for unremunerated work.

GLOBAL COMPACT

C1–001 At the World Economic Forum, Davos, on January 31, 1999, UN Secretary-General Kofi A. Annan challenged world business leaders to "embrace and enact" the Global Compact, both in their individual corporate practices and by supporting appropriate public policies. These principles cover topics in human rights, labour and environment.

Human Rights

The Secretary-General asked world business to:

Principle 1: support and respect the protection of international human rights within their sphere of influence; and

Principle 2: make sure their own corporations are not complicit in human rights abuses.

Labour

The Secretary-General asked world business to uphold:

Principle 3: freedom of association and the effective recognition of the right to collective bargaining;

Principle 4: the elimination of all forms of forced and compulsory labour;

Principle 5: the effective abolition of child labour; and

Principle 6: the elimination of discrimination in respect of employment and occupation.

Environment

The Secretary-General asked world business to:

Principle 7: support a precautionary approach to environmental challenges;

Principle 8: undertake initiatives to promote greater environmental responsibility; and

Principle 9: encourage the development and diffusion of environmentally friendly technologies.

BIBLIOGRAPHY

General Texts

Henry Steiner and Philip Alston, *International Human Rights in Context*, (2nd ed., 2000) (Oxford University Press)

Amnesty International, *The International Report*, (Annual) (Amnesty International)

Ralph Beddard, *Human Rights and Europe*, (3rd ed., 1993) (Grotius Publications)

Elizabeth Beterly, *Public International Law: A Guide to Information Sources*, (1991) (Mansell Publishing)

Ian Brownlie, *Basic Documents in Human Rights*, (4th ed., 1995) (Oxford University Press)

P.R. Ghandi *Blackstone's International Law Documents*, (2nd ed., 2000) (Blackstone Press)

Hurst Hannum and Dana D. Fischer (eds) *U.S. Ratification of the International Covenants on Human Rights*, (1993) (American Society of International Law)

D.J. Harris, *Cases and Materials on International Law*, (5th ed., 1998) (Sweet and Maxwell)

Louis Henkin and John Lawrence Hargrove (eds) *Human Rights: An Agenda For The Next Century*, (1994) (American Society of International Law)

Human Rights Watch, *Human Rights Watch World Report*, (Annual) (Human Rights Watch)

Edward Lawson, (ed.) *Encyclopaedia of Human Rights*, (2nd ed., 1996) (Taylor and Francis)

Liesbeth Lijnzaad, *Reservations to U.N. Human Rights Treaties— Ratify and Ruin?* (1994) (Martinus Nijhoff Publishers)

United Nations, *Status of International Instruments: Chart of Ratifications as at 31st December 1997*, (1997) (United Nations Publications)

United Nations, *Human Rights on CD-Rom*, (1998) (United Nations Publications)

Children

The International Journal of Children's Rights, (Kluwer Law International)

Philip Alston, (ed.) *The Best Interests of the Child: Reconciling Culture and Human Rights*, (1994) (Clarendon Press)

Childhood Stolen: Grave Human Rights Violations Against Children, (1995) (Amnesty International)

David Balton, "The Convention on the Rights of the Child: Prospects for International Enforcement", [1990] H.R.Q. 12

Jaap Doek (ed.) *Children on the Move—How to Implement Their Right to Family Life,* (1995) (Martinus Nijhoff Publishers)

Thomas Hammarberg, *"The U.N. Convention on the Rights of the Child—and How to Make it Work",* [1990] H.R.Q. 12

James R. Himes (ed.) *Implementing the Convention on the Rights of the Child—Resource Mobilisation in Low Income Countries,* (1995) (Martinus Nijhoff Publishers/UNICEF)

Mary John (ed.) *A Charge Against Society: The Child's Right to Protection,* (1996) (Jessica Kingsley Publishers)

Michael Jupp, *"The U.N. Convention on the Rights of the Child: An Opportunity for Advocates",* [1990] H.R.Q. 12

Howard Mann, *"International Law and the Child Soldier",* 36 I.C.L.Q. 32

Per Miljeteig Olssen, *"Advocacy of Childrens' Rights—The Convention as More than a Legal Document",* H.R.Q. 12

Maria Rita Saulle, *The Rights of the Child: International Instruments* (1995), (Transnational Publishers Inc.)

United Nations, *Convention on the Rights of The Child: World Campaign for Human Rights,* (1992) (United Nations Publications)

Geraldine Van Bueren *The International Law on the Rights of the Child,* (1995), (Martinus Nijhoff Publishers)

Geraldine Van Bueren, *International documents on children,* (2nd ed., 1998), (Martinus Nijhoff Publishers)

Eugeen Verhellen (ed.) *Monitoring Children's Rights* (1996) (Martinus Nijhoff Publishers)

Women

Belinda Clark, *"The Vienna Convention Reservations Regime and the Convention on Discrimination Against Women",* A.J.I.L. Vol. 85

Gudmundur Alfredsson & Katarina Tomasevski (eds) *A Thematic Guide to Documents on the Human Rights of Women,* (1995) (Martinus Nijhoff Publishers/Raoul Wallenberg Institute)

Amnesty International, *Human Rights are Women's Right,* (1995) (Amnesty International)

Morago Atoki, *"Should Female Circumcision Continue To Be Banned?"* (1995) Fem. Legal Studies, Vol. III No. 2

Noreen Burrows, *"The 1979 Convention on the Elimination of All Forms of Discrimination Against Women",* (1985) N.I.L.R.

Andrew C. Byrnes, *"The 'Other' Human Rights Treaty Body: The Work of the Committee on the Elimination of Discrimination Against Women",* (1989) Yale Journal of International Law Vol. 14, No. 1

Rebecca J. Cook, (1993) *"Women's International Human Rights Law: The Way Forward",* H.R.Q. Vol. 15, 230

D.G. Dallmeyer (ed.) *Reconceiving Reality: Women and International Law,* (1993) (American Society of International Law

Rebecca Grant and Kathleen Newland, (eds), *Gender and International Relations* (1991), (Open University Press)

Hilkka Pietila and Jeanne Vickers, *"Making Women Matter—The Role of the United Nations"* (1994), (Zed Books Ltd.)

Catherine N. Niarchos, *"Women, War and Rape: Challenges Facing the International Tribunal for the Former Yugoslavia"*, (1995) H.R.Q. Vol. 15

The World's Women 2000: Trends and Statistics, (United Nations Publications)

Strategies for Confronting Domestic Violence: A Resource Manual, (United Nations Publications).

Women: New Challenges for the 21st Century, (1995), (United Nations Publications)

Rebecca M.M. Wallace, *"Ward v. Canada: A Glimmer of Hope for Victims of Domestic Violence?"*, (1995) Jur. Rev. 390

Refugees

Playing Human Pinball: Home Office Practice in "Safe Third Country" Asylum Cases, (1995), (Amnesty International)

Jacqueline R. Castell, *"Rape, Sexual Assault and the Meaning of Persecution"*, International Journal of Refugee Law, Vol. 4, No. 1

Vera Gowlland-Debbas, *The Problem of Refugees in the Light of Contemporary International Law Issues*, (1995), (Martinus Nijhoff Publishers)

Michael Haran, *" 'Social Group' for the purposes of asylum claims"*, 1995 I.N.L.P. Vol. 9, No. 2

James C. Hathaway, *"Reconceiving Refugee Law as Human Rights Protection"*, (1991) Journal of Refugee Studies, Vol. 4, No. 2

Nancy Kelly, *"Gender Related Persecution: Assessing the Asylum Claims of Women"*, (1993) Cornell International Law Journal, Vol. 26

Harold Hongju Koh, *"Reflections on Refoulment and Haitian Centers Council"*, Harvard International Law Journal, Vol. 35

Koichi Koizumi, *"Refugee Policy Formation in Japan: Developments and Implications"*, (1992) Journal of Refugee Studies, Vol. 5, No. 2

Concise Report on the World Population Situation in 1993 with Special Emphasis on Refugees, Population Studies No. 138, (1993) (United Nations Publications)

Minorities

International Journal on Minority and Group Rights, (Kluwer Law International)

Gudmunder Alfredsson and Alfred de Zayas, *"Protection by the U.N."*, (1993) H.R.L.J., Vol. 14

Yoram Dinstein, *"Collective Human Rights of Peoples and Minorities"*, 25 I.C.L.Q. 102

Jerome B. Elkind and Anthony Shaw, *"The Municipal Enforcement of the Prohibition against Racial Discrimination: A Case Study on New Zealand and the 1981 Springbok Tour"*, (1984) B.Y.I.L. 189

Theodor Meron, *"The Meaning and Reach of the International Convention on the Elimination of All Forms of Racial Discrimination"*, (1985) A.J.I.L. Vol. 79

Karl Josef Partsch, *"Elimination of Racial Discrimination in the Enjoyment of Civil and Political Rights"*, (1979) Texas International Law Journal, Vol. 14: 19

Patrick Thornberry, *"Self Determination, Minorities, Human Rights: A Review of International Instruments"*, 38 I.C.L.Q. 867

Egon Schwelb, *"The International Convention on the Elimination of All Forms of Racial Discrimination"*, Human Rights Study Series No. 5 (United Nations Publications)

Persons With Disabilities

Access Denied: Disability and Human Rights, (1994) (Liberty)

Human Rights and Disabled Persons, Human Rights Study Series No. 6, (United Nations Publications)

Indigenous Peoples

Russel Lawrence Barsh, *"Indigenous Peoples: An Emerging Object of International Law"*, 80 A.J.I.L. 369

The Americans: Human Rights Violations Against Indigenous Peoples, (1992), (Amnesty International)

Cynthia Price Cohen (ed.) *Human Rights of Indigenous Peoples*, (1996), (Transnational Publishers Inc.)

INDEX